MW00357130

THE CIVIL WAR ERA AND RECONSTRUCTION

VOLUME 1

THE CIVIL WAR ERA AND RECONSTRUCTION

An Encyclopedia of Social, Political, Cultural, and Economic History

VOLUME 1

MARY ELLEN SNODGRASS

SHARPE REFERENCE
an imprint of M.E. Sharpe, Inc.

SHARPE REFERENCE

Sharpe Reference is an imprint of M.E. Sharpe, Inc.

M.E. Sharpe, Inc.
80 Business Park Drive
Armonk, NY 10504

Cover images (clockwise from top left) were provided by: The Granger Collection, New York; The Granger Collection, New York; Transcendental Graphics/Getty Images; Buyenlarge/Getty Images; MPI/Stringer/Getty Images; Fotosearch/Stringer/Getty Images.

Library of Congress Cataloging-in-Publication Data

Mary Ellen Snodgrass.
The Civil War era and Reconstruction: an encyclopedia of social, political, cultural, and economic history / Mary Ellen Snodgrass.
2 v.; cm.
Includes bibliographical references and index.
ISBN 978-0-7656-8257-4 (hardcover: alk. paper)
1. United States—History—Civil War, 1861–1865—Encyclopedias. 2. Reconstruction (U.S. history, 1865–1877)—Encyclopedias. I. Title.

E468.S65 2011
973.703—dc22 2010050253

Printed and bound in the United States

The paper used in this publication meets the minimum requirements of American National Standard for Information Sciences—Permanence of Paper for Printed Library Materials, ANSI Z 39.48.1984.

CW (c) 10 9 8 7 6 5 4 3 2 1

Publisher: Myron E. Sharpe
Vice President and Director of New Product Development: Donna Sanzone
Vice President and Production Director: Carmen Chetti
Executive Development Editor: Jeff Hacker
Project Manager: Laura Brengelman
Program Coordinator: Cathleen Prisco
Editorial Assistant: Lauren LoPinto
Text Design and Cover Design: Jesse Sanchez

Contents

Volume 2

Topic Finder

Cities, States, Regions, Features

Economy, Industry, Commerce, Finance

Education

Family, Community, Society

Historical Events, Periods, Holidays

Law, Legislation, and the Judiciary

Military Affairs

Movements and Ideologies

Native Americans

Organizations and Institutions (Non-Governmental)

Politics and Government

Religion and Religious Groups

Science, Technology, Medicine

Transportation, Communication, and the Press

Western Settlement

Women and Gender

Acknowledgments

I could not have completed this text without advice from researchers, theologians, archivists, genealogists, historians, and researchers. Historical and genealogical societies, college libraries, church and synagogue authorities, the Library of Congress, and specialists in Quaker, Mennonite, and black church history elucidated details and suggested variant points of view on Indian genocide and on the rescue operations of missionaries and philanthropists. I found particularly helpful the electronic version of *Harper's Weekly,* the Latter Day Saints online Family History and Genealogy Records, and the databases of Alexandria Street Press. I relied on a long list of reference librarians, the backbone of scholarship:

Wanda K. Adams, reference, Leavenworth Public Library, Leavenworth, Kansas

Beverly Adler, reference, Central Oregon Community College, Bend, Oregon

Stan Bankert, community relations, and Laurie Yourist, reference, York Public Library, York, Pennsylvania

Jeff Beck and Beth Swift, archivists, Wabash College Library, Crawfordsville, Indiana

Mary Bowler, archivist, Idaho State Historical Society, Boise, Idaho

Bridget Bradley, reference, District of Columbia Public Library, Washington, D.C.

Judy Brown, Western historian, Denver Public Library, Denver, Colorado

Paige Brunner, reference, Detroit Public Library, Detroit, Michigan

Tom Carey, librarian, San Francisco History Center, San Francisco, California

Janice H. Chadbourne, reference, Boston Public Library, Boston, Massachusetts

Peggy Chambliss, manager, Georgia Public Library Service, Augusta, Georgia

Genevieve Dazet, reference, Missouri State Library, Jefferson City, Missouri

Allison DePrey, reference, Indiana Historical Society, Indianapolis, Indiana

Terri Dood, Bozeman Public Library, Bozeman, Montana

Katie Ehrlich, researcher, and Rabbi Gideo Shloush, Adereth El, New York City, New York

David J. Ellison, reference, Manitowoc Public Library, Manitowoc, Wisconsin

Gwen Gosney Erickson, archivist, Guilford College, Greensboro, North Carolina

Laurie Finlayson, reference, Renton Public Library, Renton, Washington

Carmen Anne Cosner Forsee, reference, Pickens County Library, Jasper, Georgia

Ira Galtman, archivist, American Express Company, New York City, New York

Fred Gervasi, National Park Seminary, Washington, D.C.

Michael Gillman, reference, Sacramento Public Library, Sacramento, California

Joyce Girvin, reference, Temple of Israel, Wilmington, North Carolina

Cheri Goldner, reference, Akron–Summit County Public Library, Akron, Ohio

Mike Good, reference, Henry County Public Library, Clinton, Missouri

Joan Green, reference, Stark County District Library, Canton, Ohio

Doris Hansen, volunteer reference, Manitowoc Public Library, Manitowoc, Wisconsin

Catherine Hanson, reference, California State Library, Sacramento, California

Donna Harrington, manager, Pickens County Library, Jasper, Georgia

Jon Harwood, director, Rock Springs Library, Green River, Wyoming

Carol Hauck, reference, Deadwood Public Library, Deadwood, South Dakota

Adele Heagney, reference, St. Louis Public Library, St. Louis, Missouri

Merinda Hensley and Suzanne Im, reference, University of Illinois, Urbana

Caitlin Hoag, reference, Kalamazoo Public Library, Kalamazoo, Michigan

Amy Hopkins, reference, Centralia Public Library, Centralia, Missouri

Beth M. Howse, special collections, Fisk University Library, Nashville, Tennessee

Sarah Huggins, reference, Library of Virginia, Richmond, Virginia

Kay Jabusch, librarian, Wrangell Public Library, Wrangell, Alaska

James K. Jeffrey, genealogist, Denver Public Library, Denver, Colorado
Rodney Katz, reference, Library of Congress, Washington, D.C.
Jewel Kimbler, reference, Adair County Public Library, Columbia, Kentucky
Marc Kloszewski, reference, Indiana Free Library, Indiana, Pennsylvania
Lisa Kulyk-Bourque, reference, Lynn Public Library, Lynn, Massachusetts
Rebecca Lafferty, reference, Clarksburg–Harrison Public Library, Clarksburg, West Virginia
Alice LaViolette, government research, Oregon State Library, Salem, Oregon
Sharen Lee, reference, Live Oak Public Libraries, Savannah, Georgia
Suzanne K. Loder, reference, Portsmouth Public Library, Portsmouth, New Hampshire
Virginia Lopez, reference, New Mexico State Library, Santa Fe, New Mexico.
Kathy Madison, reference, Virginia City Public Library, Virginia City, Montana
Kathy Marquis and Susan M. Simpson, reference, Albany County Public Library, Laramie, Wyoming
Jerry McCoy, archivist, Martin Luther King, Jr., Memorial Library, Washington, D.C.
Dylan McDonald, archivist, Center for Sacramento History, Sacramento, California
Judy McGeath, reference, Indianapolis–Marion County Public Library, Indianapolis, Indiana
Katherine McSharry, duty librarian, Dublin Public Library, Dublin, Ireland
Crystal Mensch-Nelson, director, Dakota Territorial Museum, Yankton, South Dakota
Romie Minor, archivist, Detroit Public Library, Detroit, Michigan
Cindy Moore, reference, Sweetwater County Library, Green River, Wyoming.
Susan Nawrocki, reference, Columbus–Lowndes County Library, Columbus, Mississippi
Glen Neumann, reference, Chicago Public Library, Chicago, Illinois
Virginia L. Norman, reference, Public Library of Cincinnati and Hamilton County, Cincinnati, Ohio
Karen Paige, reference, California State Library, Sacramento, California
Julie Pinnell, Nebraska Library Commission, Lincoln, Nebraska
Mark Plew, anthropologist, Boise State University, Boise, Idaho
Jackie Polsgrove-Roberts, genealogist, Cass County Public Library, Harrisonville, Missouri
Gerlinda Riojas, reference, Corpus Christi Public Library, Corpus Christi, Texas
Brian Rogers, reference, Missouri State Archives, Jefferson City, Missouri
James Scott, reference, Sacramento Public Library, Sacramento, California
Tracy Carr Seabold, reference director, Mississippi Library Commission, Jackson, Mississippi
Jeff Sheets, director, Abilene Historical Center, Abilene, Kansas
Vonnie Shelton, reference, McCracken County Public Library, Paducah, Kentucky
Sam Shipley, reference, Dodge City Public Library, Dodge City, Kansas
Rebecca Shives, reference, York County Library System, York, Pennsylvania
Lynn Shurden, reference, Bolivar County Public Library, Cleveland, Mississippi
Trent Sindelar, reference, St. Louis Public Library, St. Louis, Missouri
Rose Speirs and Carolyn Weber, reference; Carolyn Weber, assistant director, Adams Museum and House, Deadwood, South Dakota
Darlene Staffeldt, state librarian, and Jim Kammerer, reference, Montana State Library, Helena, Montana
Ken S. Stewart, administrator, South Dakota State Archives, Pierre, South Dakota
Zoe Ann Stoltz, reference historian, Montana Historical Society, Helena, Montana
Linda Sueyoshi, reference, Hawaii State Library, Honolulu, Hawaii
Vicki L. Thornton, reference, St. Joseph Public Library, St. Joseph, Missouri
Abby Turner, marketing, Bozeman Chamber of Commerce, Bozeman, Montana
Kathleen S. Turner, reference, Daniel Library, The Citadel, Charleston, South Carolina
Ann W. Upton, Quaker bibliographer, Haverford College, Haverford, Pennsylvania
Irene Wainwright, archivist, New Orleans Public Library, New Orleans, Louisiana
Priscilla Wegars, curator of anthropology, University of Idaho, Moscow, Idaho
Andy Wenberg, reference librarian, Sheridan County Public Library, Sheridan, Wyoming
Faith Yoman, reference, New Mexico State Library, Santa Fe, New Mexico

For Louis Nunnery, a gentleman of the Old South.

Preface

The Civil War Era and Reconstruction: An Encyclopedia of Social, Political, Cultural, and Economic History surveys the emergence of a nation from an upheaval that threatened the authority of the U.S. Constitution and dissolution of the republic. The text covers nonmilitary events, legal issues, philosophies, technology, agriculture, and expansion during a 17-year period (1861–1877) filled with anticipation of greatness.

Prefatory essays preview basic issues of civilization: Politics and Government; Economy, Business, and Industry; Foreign Affairs; and Family, Community, and Society. Alphabetized entries order information under name, theme, location, and economic and political significance, from abolitionism and the reading of the Emancipation Proclamation to the abasement of Jim Crow laws, from gold rushes to coinage and taxation, and from exploration of the West and law enforcement to statehood, changes to the American flag, and the celebration of the first national centennial. Events picture Americans absorbed in the fight to free slaves and the challenge of carving out new lives and careers on the Plains. A heavy irony of racial acculturation sets the teaching of slaves by the Freedmen's Bureau and the Americanization of European immigrants simultaneous with the massacres of Indians at Sand Creek and Washita, two unconscionable chapters in U.S. military history.

Commentary summarizes the moral and religious tenets of individuals whose struggles with conscience shaped a national ethic, notably slave autobiographer Harriet Jacobs, Rabbi Isaac Mayer Wise, nurse Clara Barton, poet Walt Whitman, Asian coolie laborers, and the volunteer medics of the U.S. Sanitary Commission. Enhancing historical data are citations from the personal writings of expeditioner William Healey Dall, literacy advocate Sarah Stickney Ellis, reformer Elizabeth Cady Stanton, Secretary of War Edwin M. Stanton, and Asa Mercer, transporter of mail-order brides to bachelor communities in the Pacific Northwest.

Research materials derive from period sources—personal diaries and pioneer journals of Union General Ulysses S. Grant and actor Fanny Kemble, short stories by Mark Twain and Bret Harte, letters of editor Lydia Maria Child and President Rutherford B. Hayes, wartime coverage and cartoons from *Harper's Weekly* and the *New York Tribune,* memoirs of writer Louisa May Alcott and cowboy Charles Siringo, wartime reflections of Union General William Tecumseh Sherman and Secretary of the Navy Gideon Welles, speeches of suffragist Susan B. Anthony and orator Sojourner Truth, histories and commentaries on the Oregon Trail and Texas Rangers, and overviews of technological progress of the Transcontinental Railroad, shipping, mining, gas and electricity, department store merchandising, boards of health, and telecommunications by telephone and transoceanic cables. Rounding out the text, additional study aids particularize people, places, dates, concepts, and events, including a list of Indian reservations and the tribes who occupied them.

A glossary of more than 100 terms provides definitions for significant concepts in the text—the Southern demand for states' rights, the consortium of penologists who humanized the incarceration of felons, the blockade of ports that limited free trade in the Confederate States of America, President Andrew Johnson's amnesty for secessionists, congressional protective tariffs on imported steel, the rise of the Ku Klux Klan paramilitary, ad hominem attacks on President Abraham Lincoln, the labeling of Plains Indian renegades as hostiles, the offer of governmental easements for rail and telegraph lines, the caste system that targeted freedmen for trespass and vagrancy in Southern courts and chain gangs, and the adulteration of such products as bread, milk, and cough syrup, an issue raised by the woman suffrage movement.

A chronology presents an 18-year timeline of events from 1860 to 1877 that honors the civil rights of former slaves, a state banking system, stagecoach lines, and early labor organizers. The timeline notes the rise of wealth from the Comstock Lode and Standard Oil as well as the passage of anticruelty laws, the formation of baseball leagues and American Reform Judaism, and the publication of the *Washington Post.* Also included are the achievements of memorable people: plant hybridizer Luther Burbank, poet Julia Ward Howe, educator Charlotte Forten, peacemaker Cheyenne Chief Black Kettle, and battlefield photographer and portraitist Mathew Brady.

A bibliography presents primary sources written by eyewitnesses to Quaker dissent, relay teams of the Underground Railroad, anti-Chinese rabble-rouser Dennis Kearney, biographer Elizabeth Cabot Agassiz, federal census takers, merchandiser Montgomery Ward, marksman George W. Wingate, home economist Juliet Corson, historian Jefferson Davis, polemicist Matilda Joslyn Gage, publisher Horace Greeley, editor Sarah Joseph Hale, and Ward Hill Lamon, bodyguard of President Abraham Lincoln.

An exhaustive index covers major topics, such as the Treaty of Washington (1871), Nez Percé Chief Joseph, cotton, buffalo, Jay Gould, polygamy, Yosemite Valley, literacy, and urbanization and city life.

The United States in 1860**

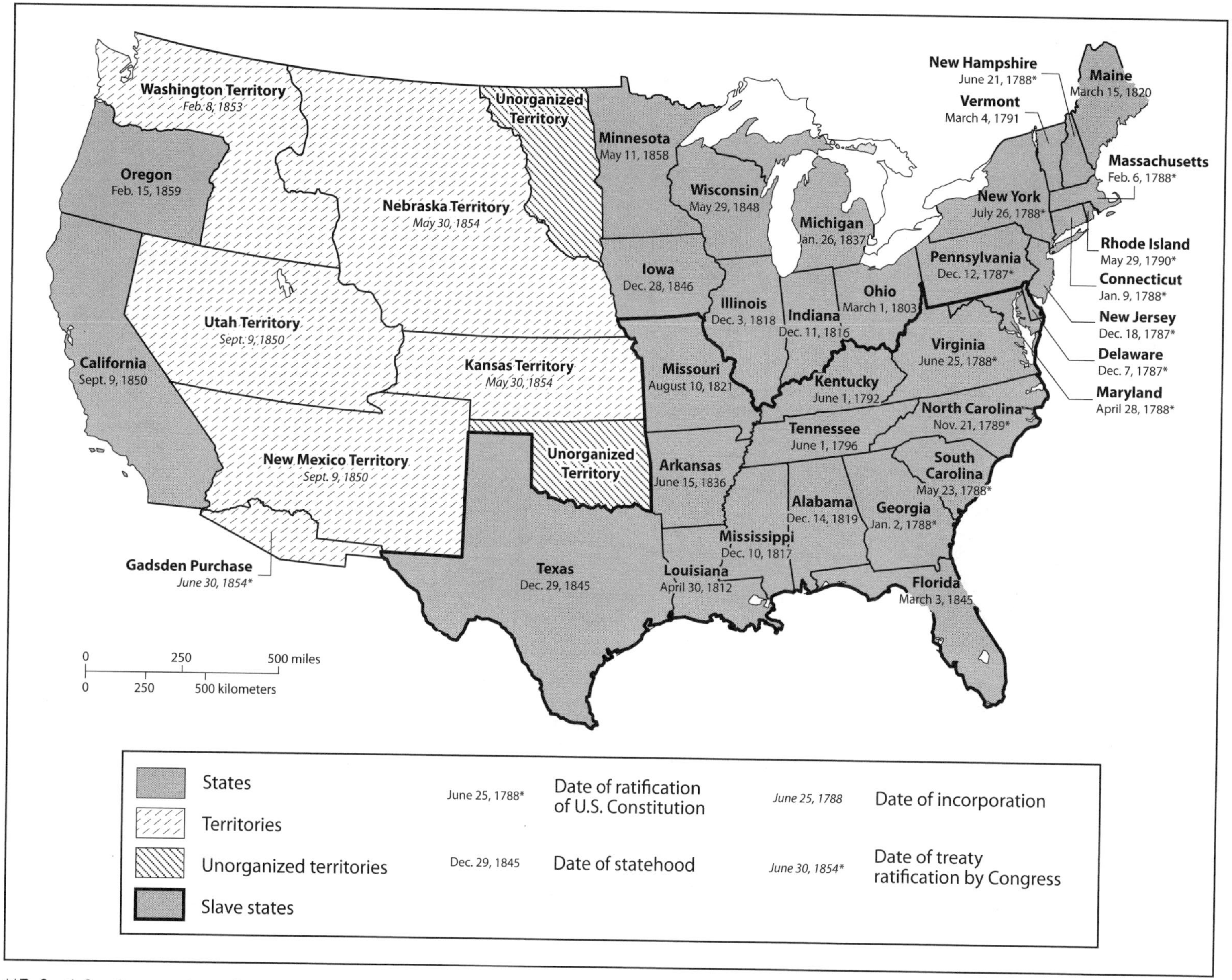

**To South Carolina secession on December 20, 1860.

Reconstruction, 1865–1877

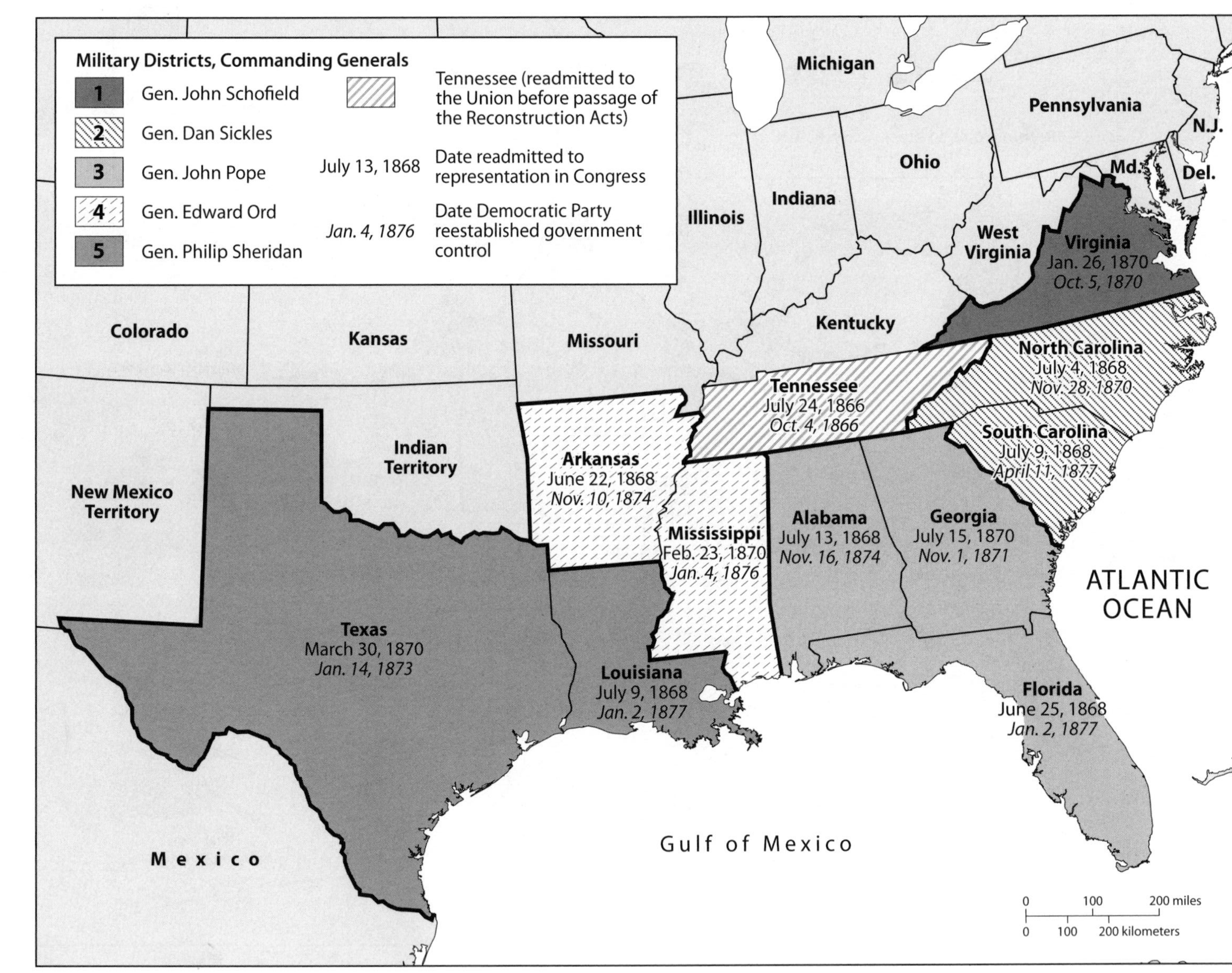

Essays

Politics and Government

The 1860s and 1870s brought sweeping changes to politics in the United States that required flexibility and ingenuity in governance. Despite ongoing negotiations and compromises to maintain sectional balance, the mounting tension over slavery in the 1850s pushed the North and South toward fracture. Contemporaneous with the formation of a new third party, the pro-North Republicans, attorney Abraham Lincoln, a former Whig from Illinois, exhibited his grasp of the issues in debates with his Democratic opponent for U.S. senator in 1858, Stephen A. Douglas. Lincoln believed that enmity among citizens would lead to war and cautioned that the nation would founder under the unresolved issue of slavery. His denunciation of the U.S. Supreme Court's ruling in the incendiary case of *Dred Scott v. Sandford* (1857)—in which the justices held that a black man could not become a U.S. citizen under the Constitution—established the candidate's dedication to human rights and national sovereignty.

Compelling and straightforward, "Honest Abe" convinced voters and the press of his respect for law and democracy. In a pivotal speech on February 27, 1860, at the Cooper Union in New York City, Lincoln—now seeking the Republic nomination for president—voiced his intent to halt the spread of bondage into the American West. At the time, black Americans consisted of 488,000 free blacks and 3.95 million, or 89 percent, slaves. In his speech, Lincoln refuted the legitimacy of states' rights, the issue over which Southern states threatened to secede from the Union. On election day in November, New Englanders and Midwesterners allied behind an antislavery, antiwar platform. The loss of Democratic strongholds to Southern Democratic and Constitutional Union candidates in Alabama, Arkansas, the Carolinas, Florida, Georgia, Louisiana, Mississippi, Tennessee, Texas, and Virginia catapulted Congress toward solid Republican control.

The success of Lincoln and his running mate Hannibal Hamlin of Maine further polarized members of political constituencies, who anticipated Lincoln's threat to the entrenched Southern plantation system. On December 20, states' rights advocates in South Carolina seceded from the Union, setting off a domino effect across the agrarian South. Democratic Senator Jefferson Davis of Mississippi resigned from Congress on January 21, 1861, and, out of loyalty to the South and to the principles of states' rights, on February 9 accepted the provisional presidency of the Confederate States of America. By the end of January, the withdrawal of Mississippi, Florida, Alabama, Georgia, and Louisiana cleft the 33-state union into two political entities; Texas followed on February 1.

The political unease over Lincoln's election precipitated assassination plots. On February 22, 1861, Allan Pinkerton, chief of the U.S. Intelligence Service, learned from Kate Warne, the nation's first female detective, and her partner, investigator Hattie Lawton, of a cabal against President-Elect Lincoln during his travel from Springfield, Illinois, through Baltimore, Maryland, to Washington, D.C. Swift action kept the Lincoln family safe as their train sped to the capital for his March 4 swearing in.

The Sixteenth President

Lincoln's first 100 days in office demanded skilled coordination. The ineluctable conflict introduced to Americans the notion of freedom for blacks and the possibility of full citizenship for former slaves. To isolate seditious, polygamous Utah Mormons from mainstream Christian pioneers, Lincoln shrank Utah by carving out Nevada Territory, thereby defeating utopist Brigham Young's plan to create a religious mega-state called Deseret. On March 7, 1861, the Union confiscation of plantations around Beaufort, South Carolina, initiated the Port Royal Experiment, a receiving and literacy center for former slaves. It prefigured the Bureau of Refugees, Freedmen, and Abandoned Lands, a resettlement initiative under the purview of the War Department.

When President Lincoln refused to grant an audience to Southern emissaries, Davis plotted the bombardment of Fort Sumter, South Carolina, on April 12, 1861, the first engagement of the Civil War. To their credit, U.S. lawmakers managed to gear up for combat while continuing to expand national interests west of the Mississippi River Valley. The promise of gold and silver in the San Juan Mountains of Colorado Territory ensured the growth

To preserve the Union, President Lincoln and his cabinet—which included four former rivals for the 1860 Republican nomination—expanded the powers of the executive branch to an unprecedented degree. *(Archive Photos/Stringer/Getty Images)*

of the U.S. Treasury to cover the cost of equipping and fielding the Army of the Potomac and of unleashing the Anaconda Plan, by which 90 Union ships blockaded ports along a 3,500-mile (5,600-kilometer) stretch of coastline from Virginia to Texas.

The commander in chief, the focus of Southern hatred, formulated an emergency plan to protect the nation's capital. In April 1861, after Confederate sympathizers attacked a Massachusetts militia on its way to Washington, Lincoln took Baltimore by surprise by placing the city under martial law; Pinkerton cut telegraph wires to and from the city. The rapid deployment of Union General Benjamin Franklin Butler prevented Maryland secessionists from closing a stranglehold on the federal government. After suspending the right of habeas corpus in Baltimore on May 13, Lincoln sequestered pro-Southern state legislators, Mayor George William Brown, city councilmen, Police Commissioner Charles Howard, and Police Chief Marshall Kane at Fort McHenry, Maryland, a federal prison for political dissidents and prisoners of war.

Because Union soldiers stopped enforcing the Fugitive Slave Law of 1850, which required Northern states to return escaped slaves to the South, more runaways proceeded north over the Mason-Dixon Line. The bleed-out of bondsmen spelled the end of Southern slavery.

The Price of War

Politicians predicting a rapid end to combat changed their opinion after the harrowing First Battle of Bull Run at Manassas, Virginia, on July 21, 1861. To tend the wounded, Lincoln had already foreseen the need for a head nurse. He named Dorothea Dix to an unpaid job as supervisor of wartime nurse care for the U.S. Sanitary Commission, making her the first female to receive a presidential appointment.

Congressional consternation followed rebel officer John Robert Baylor's claim of southern Arizona and New Mexico for the Confederacy on August 1. Federal legislators acted four days later by passing the Revenue Act of 1861, which levied a flat-rate tax, the country's first income tax, to finance the military.

To shake the confidence of secessionists, Congress freed blacks whom Union troops captured from Confederate forces. Another assault on slavery came from General John Charles Frémont, who on August 30, 1861, unilaterally issued a proclamation—subsequently revoked by Lincoln—that liberated the slaves of Missouri. On September 22, Lincoln struck a blow for emancipation by abolishing slavery in any Confederate state that remained outside the Union. Confederate President Davis made a feeble counterthreat to enslave any black Union trooper seized by rebels.

U.S. government officials devised wartime strategies to defend the nation and its soldiers. Early in 1862, Secretary of War Edwin M. Stanton sought relief for prisoners of war held at Libby Prison in Richmond, Virginia, and back pay for their families. Congress bolstered the economy by declaring greenback fiat money legal tender for requiting debts. The closure of trade on the Lower Mississippi River on February 23 began limiting the flow of goods and munitions to rebels through the New Orleans Delta.

In May, looking to normality for the nation's farmland, Lincoln created the U.S. Bureau of Agriculture and fostered frontier settlement by signing the Homestead Act, which distributed free land in the trans-Mississippi West. Congress also anticipated a Western peace policy by passing the Indian Property Protection Act of 1862, which shielded nonhostile Indians from land usurpation by whites.

Throughout the first summer of war, Lincoln envisioned a nation spread from the Atlantic to the Pacific, where the Transcontinental Railroad would provide transportation and mail service. The Morrill Land-Grant Act would distribute 17.4 million acres (7 million hectares) of public land for the construction of agricultural and vocational colleges. To underwrite national development, Congress passed the Revenue Act of 1862, which created the Office of Internal Revenue and imposed a progressive 3 percent tax. To further thwart the Mormon utopist dream of Deseret, an amorphous enclave of Latter Day Saints across the Southwest, legislators passed the Morrill Anti-Bigamy Act to criminalize polygamy.

Aggression on Multiple Fronts

The federal government continued to flex its authority over the unruly South and the unregulated West. The Federal Militia Act of 1862 sought 300,000 volunteers for the Union army, a number that doubled two weeks later. To spread news of congressional action and the war, the Union military celebrated the transcontinental telegraph, which met in Salt Lake City on October 24. On January 1, 1863, Lincoln's Emancipation Proclamation ended slavery in America and transformed the Southern economy and caste system.

Even as abolitionists rejoiced at the liberation of black Americans, the Indian situation worsened, starting with the nation's largest mass execution—the hanging of 38 Sioux in Mankato, Minnesota. The military took a free hand in murdering Chiricahua Apache Chief Mangas Coloradas at Fort McLane, New Mexico, and massacring more than 300 Shoshone on the Idaho–Utah border. In March, General James Henry Carleton exiled 500 Mescalero Apache to Bosque Redondo, New Mexico, an incarceration camp where natives died from epidemic smallpox and other illnesses triggered by starvation and unsanitary conditions. Lincoln continued to map out future states by separating Arizona from New Mexico on February 24, 1863. However, the quelling of guerrilla warfare by tribes in the prairie states remained out of reach so long as federal armed forces concentrated their strength and resources on winning the Civil War.

While war consumed energies and armaments, the U.S. government faced additional pressures from across the nation. In March 1863, Southern Cheyenne Chief Black Kettle parlayed with Lincoln over the sufferings of Plains Indians. The president also found time that month to foster American technology by establishing the National Academy of Sciences and to ponder conscientious objection to the war from pacifist Mennonites, Quakers, and Shakers. At the same time, he commissioned Colonel Robert Gould Shaw as commander of the Fifty-fourth Massachusetts Volunteer Infantry, the nation's first regiment of freedmen.

After the Battle of Vicksburg, Mississippi, on May 22, 1863, Lincoln instituted a day of thanks to promote national order, propriety, and unity. The remembrance prefaced his declaration of a national Thanksgiving at the urging of Sarah Josepha Hale, editor of *Godey's Ladies' Book*. In the background, the stirrings of the Women's National Loyal League, the first national women's political organization, and the International Union of Machinists and Blacksmiths' demand for an eight-hour workday foreshadowed domestic conflicts to come.

A Political Turning Point

The national contretemps reached a climax on July 3, 1863, at the Battle of Gettysburg, Pennsylvania, a height of aggression by American against American. With little monetary support, Jefferson Davis struggled on against the devaluation of Confederate currency, the collapse of the slave economy, worsening starvation in Southern states, and the disastrous turn of the war to Union favor.

Unrest required the suppression of John Hunt Morgan's rogue Confederate cavalry outside Cincinnati, Ohio, and the crushing of draft riots, which ravaged New York City on July 13–16. On August 21, another outburst of lawlessness by raiders William Clarke Quantrill, Jesse James, and Thomas Coleman "Cole" Younger resulted in the sack of Lawrence, Kansas, and the slaughter of abolitionists. At the same time, the laying of tracks for the Central Pacific Railroad boded well for the Union.

These crucial events preceded an unforeseen presidential gesture on November 19 at the dedication of a Union burial ground at the Gettysburg battle site. Lincoln's Gettysburg Address, an earnest encomium to patriotism and self-sacrifice, honored battle-torn Pennsylvania farmland. In the two-minute speech, he summarized the essence of a governing system empowered by the will of common citizens rather than aristocracy or royalty.

The election of 1864 became the first for any nation embroiled in a major war. Because of lagging support in Indiana, New York, and Pennsylvania, Lincoln's campaign required overtures toward inclusion and the creation of a new title for Republicans—the National Union Party. The war continued to grind away at governance, requiring additional call-ups of 200,000 and 500,000 Union volunteers and a congressional increase of tax rates based on citizens' ability to pay. Lincoln's Democratic opponent, General George Brinton McClellan, hammered Republicans for misdirecting military leadership, for levying excise taxes on luxury goods, and for issuing the Emancipation Proclamation. At the heart of divergence between the two candidates lay McClellan's proposal for a negotiated peace and Lincoln's intent to force secessionists to surrender. To ease the fractured nation into wholeness, the president controlled radical plans to punish rebels. Instead, he crafted the "Ten Percent Plan," which restored to the Union all Southern states in which at least 10 percent of the citizens declared themselves loyal.

Reelection confirmed citizen support for Lincoln's aims—for a unified nation and for technological progress and the settlement of the West. The simultaneous actions of combat in the East and the creation of Montana Territory in the West attested to the Republicans' ability to look beyond cataclysm to a prosperous future. A second high point in combat on September 2, 1864, handed Unionists a war prize: the capture of Atlanta, Georgia, by Union General William Tecumseh Sherman. On the Union army's march east to the Atlantic Coast, the burning of Columbia, South Carolina, and the devastation of homes, towns, and fields quelled the South's vision of victory and put out of service its rail and telegraph lines. Despite doubts about Lincoln's lenient Reconstruction plan and his ability to rein in inflation and pay war debts, the North, swept by pride in its army and leadership, acclaimed him for a second term in the White House. He retained executive power as well as 78 percent of Republican votes in the U.S. House of Representatives and 81 percent in the Senate.

Genocide or Peace

Before President Lincoln's second swearing in, an atrocity in the West forced the U.S. government to rethink its strategies for suppressing the Indian Wars. On November 29, 1864, after Colonel John M. Chivington and his military in Colorado murdered more than 150 Cheyenne—many of them women and children—at the Sand Creek Massacre, rumblings in the press aroused national concern for the Western states and for the future of first peoples. A simultaneous backlash against emancipation and citizen rights arose in Pulaski, Tennessee, on December 24, with the formation of the Ku Klux Klan, a paramilitary hate group mobilized to punish blacks for the unavoidable end to slavery.

Some nine weeks later, Congress authorized the Freedmen's Bureau to foster racial equality and relief for freedmen. Two days after that, on March 4, 1864, Lincoln delivered a second inaugural, a vision of conciliation between North and South in which he called for a binding up of the nation's wounds—a metaphor implying a single body battered by political differences.

On April 9, 1865, a week after the burning of Richmond, Virginia, and the ouster of Jefferson Davis and his cabinet from power, General Robert E. Lee surrendered the Confederate army to Union General Ulysses S. Grant at Appomattox, Virginia. The capitulation not only settled the civil uprising, but also launched Grant on one of the nation's most promising political careers.

The assassination of President Lincoln on April 14, 1865, and the stabbing of Secretary of State William Henry Seward staggered Washington and the nation with the loss of a congenial leader and a great-hearted peacemaker. The rapid changeover to leadership by President Andrew Johnson, a Southern sympathizer and a former slave owner, stymied Grant's attempt to guide the new president toward settling the nation's chaos without vengeance or recrimination.

As the presidential entourage bore Lincoln's remains to burial in Springfield, Illinois, U.S. military burial details turned Arlington, the Virginia home of Robert E. Lee and Mary Custis Lee—into a national cemetery. The confiscation enabled the Union to punish a West Point graduate who had chosen loyalty to Virginia over allegiance to the nation.

On May 23 and 24, 1865, a two-day, 7-mile (11-kilometer) Grand Review of the Armies paraded through the streets of Washington in a statement of restored sovereignty. The growing power of the executive branch of government required commissioning of the Secret Service to assist U.S. marshals in preventing and investigating federal crime. On July 7, the hanging of five presidential assassins at Fort McNair in Washington attested to Confederates that they had lost all hope of elongating the Civil War through guerrilla tactics.

Remaking a Nation

Success in the West actualized Lincoln's vision of prosperity through expansion and technological advancement. On September 20, 1865, the Missouri, Kansas, & Texas Railroad accessed cattle ranches and carried longhorns to abattoirs (slaughterhouses) farther north. Congress restored mail service to the South. On December 6, the adoption of the Thirteenth Amendment to the Constitution formalized the abolition of slavery, a dark blot on the national conscience since the seventeenth century.

The service of women to the Underground Railroad and to political pressure groups preceded legislator Thaddeus Stevens's presentation to Congress of the "Petition for Universal Suffrage" on January 29, 1866. The advance of women toward full citizenship split politicians over the demand for black enfranchisement and for extending the vote to females. Congress chose black civil rights over women's equality by backing the Civil Rights Act of 1866, which outlawed job and housing discrimination by prejudicial state laws. The choice proved prophetic of the need for a government crackdown on residual racism, which precipitated a riot in Memphis, Tennessee, pitting white police and firefighters against returning black veterans.

The amelioration of state animosities began on July 24, 1866, with congressional acceptance of Tennessee into the Union. In the same week, General Grant, a short-term secretary of war under President Johnson, guided through political channels the establishment of black regiments trained to fight Indians. On March 2, 1867, a day after Congress added Nebraska to the Union, the first Reconstruction Act divided the rebel states into five districts under the supervision of government occupation forces. Three weeks later, the second Reconstruction Act launched voter registration and delegate selection for state constitutional conventions, an essential clarification of state powers and objectives. On March 30, 1867, Secretary of State Seward's purchase of Alaska from imperial Russia raised political speculation that the nation had gone too far in investing in the Pacific Coast while war debt still undermined the U.S. Treasury.

After Congress reinforced the Freedmen's Bureau with more funding and the offer of forfeited lands for sale to former slaves, the third Reconstruction Act—passed by Congress over President Johnson's veto on July 19, 1867—expanded military authority over voter registration. The flexing of legislative muscle attested to an ongoing sectional suppression of such underground reactionaries as Colonel Alcibiades DeBlanc and the Knights of the White Camellia of St. Mary's Parish, Louisiana. Politicians

A House committee reported articles of impeachment against President Andrew Johnson in February 1868. In the culmination of what historians regard as a political dispute over his lenient Reconstruction policies, the president won acquittal by a single vote. *(Mathew Brady/Stringer/Getty Images)*

created Wyoming Territory and annexed a coaling station in the Midway Islands, the gateway to trade with Pacific Rim nations and East Asia. New antagonisms colored press headlines following the "Erie Wars," a bitter rivalry over control of Erie Railroad stock, and the three-stage Treaty of Medicine Lodge (1867), which aimed to ensure peace along the Arkansas River. Washington officials bolstered the legislative branch over executive powers by lobbing impeachment charges against President Johnson for contempt of Congress.

The Grant Administration

In the midst of capital wrangling, the presidential campaign of 1868 attested to the firm hold of Republicans on the nation's business and to the popularity of General Grant. Some 500,000 free black males favored him for championing the enfranchisement of former slaves. Grant's Democratic opponent, Horatio Seymour, a fiscal conservative, proposed limiting presidential powers, retiring the war debt with greenbacks rather than gold, and speeding up the Reconstruction process. Rather than debate the issues, Democratic campaigners chose to launch an ad hominem attack on Grant, a handsome Union military hero, by depicting him as a drunkard. To the detriment of Republican campaigners, New York's William Magear "Boss" Tweed hustled thousands of Irish immigrants through corrupt naturalization procedures and into citizenship to bolster the Democratic vote.

Grant's claim of 52.7 percent of the popular vote and 214 of 294 electoral votes assured the nation a strong eighteenth president. Contributing to Republican confidence, the party held 71 percent of seats in the U.S. House of Representatives and 84 percent in the Senate.

In a lame-duck slap at former abolitionists, President Johnson extended unconditional amnesty to Confederates on Christmas Day 1868. His eagerness to ingratiate the Republican Party with former secessionists matched the tenor of Congress, which passed the fourth Reconstruction Act on July 9, 1868, accepting state constitutions passed by a simple state majority. As Arkansas, Florida, the Carolinas, and Louisiana rejoined the Union, the Fourteenth Amendment to the Constitution, giving equal protection of the law to former slaves, won ratification—also on July 9.

Indians and Aliens

The press put before the national readership disturbing news of the deterioration of peace in the West. On November 27, 1868, the U.S. Cavalry massacre of 103 peaceful Arapaho and Cheyenne at Washita, Oklahoma, demoralized natives. The unprovoked slaughter brought shame on General George Armstrong Custer and the U.S. military for savagery; congressional investigations produced evidence of genocidal intent among military leaders.

Indians gained and lost in subsequent events. On March 1, the advance of the Atchison, Topeka, & Santa Fe Railroad from Kansas to Pueblo, Colorado, threatened migratory game and the subsistence of tribes. President Grant's appointment of General Ely Samuel Parker made the Seneca tribesman the first native commissioner of Indian affairs, a hopeful gesture to natives who were leery of the collusion of soldiers, Indian agents, and missionaries.

While Congress shepherded Virginia, Mississippi, Texas, and Georgia into the Union, the Union Pacific Railroad and mining companies gathered political and economic clout in the West. Congress continued to favor racial equality by nullifying California taxes on aliens and banning violations of the civil rights of Chinese immigrants. To extend the reach of the office of the U.S. attorney general, President Grant on June 22, 1870, established the federal Department of Justice. Significantly, justice wavered in the West, as railroad agents and hunters destroyed buffalo herds, the agent of cohesion that fed and unified Plains Indians. While game animals disappeared from the prairies and stockmen enclosed grazing land for their cattle, Congress on March 1, 1872, established an artificial nature preserve at Yellowstone, the world's first national park.

As though creating similar reserves for Indians, Indian agents in August 1873 forced the Arapaho, Sioux, and Cheyenne to settle at Fort Robinson, Nebraska. Two years later, the U.S. Army coerced the Comanche to a reservation at Comanche County, Oklahoma, and the Sioux to the Great Sioux Reservation in South Dakota. Incarceration annihilated the political strength of native leaders and disheartened their followers. Only the Apache guerrilla commander Geronimo remained at large as a symbol of Indian resolve to remain free.

Broadening Electorate

Grant's easy reelection defeated hopes of the Liberal Republican Party, a splinter group that the press dubbed the "Cincinnati soreheads." Led by Missouri Senator Carl Schurz, liberals agitated for more honest government, for the demobilization of occupation forces in the South, and for a conclusion to Reconstruction. In a gesture to women's rights, Victoria Claflin Woodhull's leadership of the Equal Rights Party with running mate Frederick Douglass in May 1872 condemned political leaders for

A cartoon from the 1880s portrays two phases of Reconstruction: "The Strong Government, 1869–1877," with President Ulysses S. Grant in a sack labeled "carpet bag and bayonet," and "The Weak Government, 1877–1881," with President Rutherford B. Hayes pushing a plow labeled "Let 'em alone policy." *(Library of Congress)*

the absence of women and blacks from the governing process. For the first time in history, male and female reporters and telegraph operators kept Americans informed immediately of party convention proceedings, including the candidacy of eccentric newspaper editor Horace Greeley. Within 12 weeks of his reinstatement by the election of 1872, Grant and the Republican Congress passed the General Mining Act, empowering government control of claims on public land, and the Amnesty Act, which restored citizenship to all but 500 secessionists.

During the nation's centennial year, the presidential election of 1876 put to the test the strictures of the Constitution regarding the authority of the Electoral College. Following an era of governmental corruption and vote buying, Republicans chose as their candidate Rutherford B. Hayes, an abolitionist attorney and a soldier of impeccable character. Democrats, hungry for congressional power, nominated Samuel J. Tilden, who, in 1871, had prosecuted corrupt New York politicians and convicted Boss Tweed of bribery, conspiracy, and embezzlement of $6 million from the New York City treasury. The Democratic platform called for the ousting of carpetbaggers from the South, tariff reform, limited immigration of Asian aliens, and an end to government land deals with railroad moguls.

During the campaign, additional issues arose from the Greenback Party in Indianapolis, which lobbied for the flooding of the economy with paper currency and for the enfranchisement of women. Simultaneously, the Prohibition Party demanded the criminalization of the production and sale of whiskey, wine, and beer. Contributing uncertainty to the outcome was the admission of Colorado to the Union three months before the election; because there was no time to organize voting districts, the state legislature cast ballots for the citizenry.

The election awarded the popular vote to Tilden, but left in doubt contested counts in Florida, Louisiana, Oregon, and South Carolina. To validate a winner, on January 29, 1877, a new federal law enacted by the lame-duck Congress authorized five congressmen, five senators, and five Supreme Court justices to form a supervisory board called the Electoral Commission. The panel voted to inaugurate Hayes, making Tilden the first winner of the popular vote to lose by electoral vote. President-Elect Hayes agreed to the Compromise of 1877, by which he would appoint one cabinet member from the South and would relieve the former Confederacy of occupation forces and end Reconstruction.

Further Reading

Blue, Frederick J. *No Taint of Compromise: Crusaders in Antislavery Politics.* Baton Rouge: Louisiana State University Press, 2005.

Calloway, Colin G., ed. *Our Hearts Fell to the Ground: Plains Indian Views of How the West Was Lost.* Boston: Bedford/St. Martin's, 1996.

Cozzens, Peter, ed. *Eyewitnesses to the Indian Wars, 1865–1890.* 5 vols. Mechanicsburg, PA: Stackpole, 2001–2005.

Etulain, Richard W. *Beyond the Missouri: The Story of the American West.* Albuquerque: University of New Mexico Press, 2006.

Foner, Eric. *Politics and Ideology in the Age of the Civil War.* New York: Oxford University Press, 1980.

———. *Reconstruction: America's Unfinished Revolution, 1863–1877.* New York: HarperCollins, 2002.

Foner, Eric, and Olivia Mahoney. *America's Reconstruction: People and Politics After the Civil War.* New York: HarperPerennial, 1995.

Goodwin, Doris Kearns. *Team of Rivals: The Political Genius of Abraham Lincoln.* New York: Simon & Schuster, 2005.

Green, Michael S. *Politics and America in Crisis: The Coming of the Civil War.* Santa Barbara, CA: Praeger, 2010.

Lamar, Howard R., ed. *New Encyclopedia of the American West.* New Haven, CT: Yale University Press, 1998.

McPherson, James M. *Battle Cry of Freedom: The Civil War Era.* New York: Oxford University Press, 1988.

Oakes, James. *The Radical and the Republican: Frederick Douglass, Abraham Lincoln, and the Triumph of Antislavery Politics.* New York: W.W. Norton, 2007.

Simon, James F. *Lincoln and Chief Justice Taney: Slavery, Secession, and the President's War Powers.* New York: Simon & Schuster, 2006.

Stephenson, Nathaniel W. *Abraham Lincoln and the Union: A Chronicle of the Embattled North.* New York: BiblioBazaar, 2008.

Economy, Business, and Industry

The antebellum and postwar U.S. economy directed the nation toward global dominance of trade, shipping, finance, and technology. Surges of immigration undergirded America's rise to leadership in agriculture, industry, mining, transportation, and telecommunications. In 1861, after Congress incorporated the territories of Colorado and Dakota and added Kansas as the thirty-fourth state, President Abraham Lincoln's administration conducted an aggressive campaign to control the mineral resources of the West.

Over the next three years, Lincoln oversaw the creation of the Montana and Nevada territories and admitted coal-rich West Virginia to the Union. With the Civil War winding down, Lincoln indicated his intent to add more states to the restored nation by dispatching a three-year engineering survey, the Western Union Telegraph Expedition, to map the Pacific coastline from California, Oregon, and Washington Territory north and west along the border with British Columbia. To salvage and preserve plants and seeds, purchase plant stock from foreign countries, and compile statistics concerning the soil and climatic conditions in which crops grew best, his administration formed an independent U.S. Bureau of Agriculture within the Department of the Interior.

Meanwhile, on March 2, 1861, Congress passed and outgoing president James Buchanan signed the Morrill Tariff to raise duties 70 percent on imported iron, textiles, and manufactured goods, protecting American industry from cheap foreign wares. On May 20, 1862, legislators authorized a revolutionary concept—the Homestead Act, a supervised distribution of free land to extend property ownership to all except secessionists. As Lincoln envisioned, the pioneering of the West prefaced a period of national productivity unprecedented in world history.

Republican legislators foresaw a viable national economy through abolitionism. Beginning with the banning of slavery in Nebraska, Congress engineered the collapse of the plantation system, a New World feudal order based on human bondage. Southern land ownership concentrated wealth in the hands of a shrinking plutocracy, the members of which prided themselves on keeping acreage in the family by passing on a generations-old tradition to their sons. The agrarian economy, dependent on a racially stratified hierarchy, set the South apart from the rest of the nation in terms of culture, productivity, and philosophy. By 1860, while Northern factories, mines, lumber mills, and shipyards thrived on the labor of immigrants from Germany, Ireland, Italy, Scandinavia, and Slavic countries, some 100 Southern and Southwestern plantations goaded more than 100 slaves each into brutal, dawn-to-dusk toil.

The two economies—North and South—bore little resemblance to each other. While labor dilemmas in the North produced boom and bust cycles and conflicts between workers and managers, the totalitarian nature of slavery exhausted field workers and prompted runaways to escape before they died in harness. When black families produced surplus children, the slave master could liquidate his stock by separating parent from child and selling extra slaves at auction.

War and Change

Economic competition preceded the outbreak of war and generated an era of barter, theft, blockade running, and black marketing. On March 23, 1861, New Orleans importers cut into the New York market by selling goods duty free. Because of the embargo of the Mississippi River Valley and the blockading of the Lower Mississippi Delta as part of the Union's Anaconda Plan, the fiscal, human, and political costs of strife tested the nation's resilience.

For the Southern smallholder, such as the indentured and free tobacco farmers of Maryland and Tennessee, working the land with family members and occasional hired hands cost relatively little in contrast to the daily overhead of a plantation. For the Western pioneer, a short-term homestead, ranch, or mining operation required little capitalization. In the South in the mid-1860s, however, the size of slave-run estates made them physically unwieldy, impractical, and politically troubling to legislators. Market fluctuations depleted the plantation system, beginning with declines in agriculture in Delaware and Maryland and with underselling by growers of the short-staple cotton that flourished farther north; west into the loess soil of Natchez, Mississippi; and as far onto the frontier as Arkansas, Missouri, and Texas.

To head off financial collapse during the looming war, the Union began stabilizing federal funds by taxing incomes and luxuries and by circulating national paper notes and coinage to replace state specie and token money. Previously, a lack of standardized currency had caused problems in commerce and government. During gold strikes, companies secured raw ore with private coinage in denominations appropriate to commercial needs. The convenience of shaping metal blanks and stamping them in steam presses into legal tender eased trade during the California Gold Rush of 1849, when buyers and sellers weighed and sacked gold dust in bags or issued scrip or paper notes.

The demand for specie grew in March 1862 after the Holladay Overland Mail & Express linked Atchison, Kansas, and Walla Walla, Washington, increasing freight, mail, and passenger service to the Pacific Northwest. Within six weeks, a silver strike enticed 10,000 settlers to Austin, Nevada, an influx that placed more demands on national currency and finance.

Banking and Currency Regulation

The war economy strapped the Confederacy and the Union of cash and endangered reserves of precious metals. Confederate treasurer Christopher Memminger circulated printed notes redeemable for hard currency at war's end. By April 1862, a treasury shortfall of bullion in Richmond, Virginia, suspended the operation, but Alabama and Georgia continued printing paper bills. Further reduction of Confederate liquidity resulted from the Lyons-Seward Treaty of July 7, 1862, by which the United States and Great Britain curtailed the Atlantic slave trade by seizing slave ships.

On August 29, Secretary of the Treasury Salmon P. Chase began issuing $1 and $2 greenbacks, the nation's first fiat money based on symbolism rather than precious metal. The outlook for the Union treasury stock of precious metals improved from a gold strike north of the Cache Valley in Montana and a gold and silver strike on the Owyhee River in Idaho. Advancing commerce and governmental oversight of frontier resources, the transcontinental telegraph came together in Salt Lake City on October 24, providing a valuable communications network to buyers, sellers, investors, and speculators.

To establish fiscal control, President Lincoln revolutionized the U.S. financial system by promoting the National Bank Act. At its signing on February 26, 1863, the law chartered banks, furthered the sale of federal bonds, and standardized a national currency system based on federal bank notes. By October 1866, while state banks declined in number, 1,644 national banks dominated the

The Union blockade of Southern ports and embargo of the Mississippi Valley—the "Anaconda Plan" of General Winfield Scott—pressed the economic advantage of the North and partially succeeded in cutting off supplies to Confederate forces. *(Buyenlarge/Getty Images)*

U.S. economy and forced a confusing array of state currencies out of use. As the federal banking network spread to Colorado, New Mexico, and Wyoming, Comptroller Hugh McCulloch wielded the power to approve charters for new banks, issue lending and investment regulations, promote efficiency and innovative financial services, and penalize financial institutions that failed to comply with banking statutes.

With the first run of $450 million in notes, the newly formed U.S. Bureau of Engraving and Printing backed paper fiat money on citizen trust rather than convertibility to gold or silver. The U.S. Treasury anticipated that the paper bills would stem inflation and curtail reckless gold speculation.

Agrarian Revolution

The demise of slavery and the Southern plantation system, the expansion of greenhouse propagation, and the birth of Western farms, orchards, and cattle and sheep ranches marked a turning point for the national agricultural system. Following the collapse of the Southern economy after President Lincoln issued the Emancipation Proclamation of January 1, 1863, plantations shed their colonial legacy of a privileged class and survived on bartered or hired labor. Combat left the South depleted of cash, stock, seed, and implements and, because of malnutrition, deaths, and amputations, lacking in vigorous farmers and farmhands.

The sharecropping system that replaced press gangs reduced black workers to debt bondage and made them responsible for crop failures and undersized harvests. Large tenant farms and sugarcane businesses, such as Euphemie Fuselier's Albania Plantation in Bayou Teche, Louisiana, adopted the tactics of industrialized agriculture by employing spare hands on a cash basis.

In a regressive move, Mississippi re-created a microcosm of slavery by leasing black criminals as a source of cheap labor. A brutal system of punishment and forced toil mimicked the plantation system by coercing shackled work gangs to cultivate cotton, tap pines for turpentine, build roads and railways, drain bogs, and dig ditches and irrigation lines. Ironically, convicts rebuilt a state that had incurred severe loss to the infrastructure during battles to set slaves free.

Because employees ensured their own prosperity, they required less management and threat to make them productive. The shift in responsibility encouraged black farm families to enroll in land-grant colleges to seek more education and more scientific methods of food growth and preservation and household and land management. Farmers increased yields by intercropping barley, buckwheat, oats, and rye and increased profits by growing the three major money crops: corn, cotton, and rice. Some freedmen profited from General William Tecumseh Sherman's offer of 40-acre (16-hectare) plots and the loan of U.S. Army mules to farm abandoned plantations in South Carolina.

On the prairie, wheat became the moneymaker in North Dakota's Red River Valley and Idaho's northern counties and among German, Norwegian, and Swedish immigrants in Minnesota. In 1866, Coloradans devised the "Colorado system," a New World approach to water sharing for pasture, plant, and orchard irrigation. The produce farms of Dayton, Nevada, earned top dollar for fresh vegetables sold in mining communities. The building of rail lines and reservoirs, John Deere's invention of the steel plow, aerating soil with the straddle-row cultivator and the spring-tooth harrow, cultivating with the steam tractor, deep-well drilling, pumping water with windmills, and fencing with Joseph Glidden's barbed wire increased efficiency and convenience to settlers homesteading in remote areas.

Coal and Steel

Contributing more markets and more opportunities for advancement, the formation of the Atchison, Topeka, & Santa Fe Railroad expanded the reach of rail trade from Chicago to Pueblo, Colorado. As tracks crisscrossed North America, steel rails, bridges, and trusses offered better and safer service than iron structures. The building of the Missouri, Kansas, & Texas Railroad, the nation's longest rails-to-trails project, boosted ranch efficiency and profitability. The growth of the Kansas Pacific Railway moved in a northwesterly direction from Salina, Kansas, to stockmen in Laramie, Wyoming.

Demand for rail transport increased the prosperity of Bethlehem Steel, the second-largest mass steel producer in the United States. To meet the wartime orders for gun mounts, caissons, projectiles, and armor plating for U.S. naval vessels, German and Irish immigrants worked 12-hour days shaping 20,000 tons (18,000 metric tons) of rails annually. They produced peacetime parts for engines, switches, ships, and bridges and symbolized to a competitive world the rise of American industry. Zenas King patented the bowstring arch truss bridge and started the nation's largest highway bridge works. Using a prefabricated tubular arch, his company, King Iron Bridge and Manufacturing, built 5,000 rural

Barbed wire, patented (1874) and manufactured by Joseph Glidden, enabled frontier farmers to keep grazing cattle off their land. Violently resisted by many cattlemen, barbed wire hastened the end of open-range ranching in the West. *(The Granger Collection, New York)*

spans east of the Rocky Mountains at the rate of 250–300 per year.

Industrial growth through dam, prison, and skyscraper construction and shipbuilding put demands on coal. The most abundant fossil fuel in the United States, it replaced wood as the primary fuel for homes and industry. Lump or steamboat coal for blast furnaces brought higher prices than chestnut, pea, or bag coal, which was used for stoking kitchen and parlor stoves, puddling furnaces, and blacksmith forges. The wealth of the Lehigh mines at the Mammoth coalfields of southwestern Pennsylvania extended 30 acres (12 hectares) in a stratum 70 feet (21 meters) deep. In subterranean shafts, miners accepted danger, compromised health, and shortened life span as the costs of earning a living.

Through union negotiation and the agitation of Irish labor leader Mary Harris "Mother" Jones, colliery employees collaborated with management to secure steady employment and wages. Their synergy rid the workplace of child labor and reduced hazards from cave-ins, flooding, collapsing gob (waste) piles, runaway trams, and methane gas explosions. In the Southeast, as leaders of the New South replaced agrarianism with an industrial base, coal and coke mining replaced plantations as a major employer of unskilled labor. On the frontier, mining attracted farmers away from seasonal agriculture to year-round work that guaranteed a steady cash income. With a fleet of steel-hulled merchant vessels and cheap fuel, global shipping became an attainable goal for U.S. merchants.

Postwar Finance

To create a sound postwar fiscal foundation, Congress put innovative ideas into action. The U.S. Secret Service, organized by Treasury Secretary Hugh McCulloch and headed by William P. Wood, assisted the U.S. Marshals Service in suppressing monetary felonies, especially counterfeiting. To simplify global commerce, the Metric Act of 1866 legalized the use of metric weights and measures in commercial calculations. On July 28, 1866, the Anglo-American Telegraph Company's completion of an Atlantic cable, which transmitted eight words per minute, enhanced bank-to-bank transactions between U.S. financial institutions and London. The British North America Act of July 1, 1867, enhanced finance, commerce, and trade between the United States and Canada. An English firm, the Cook Travel Agency, incorporated North America into British and European excursion routes, introducing potential investors to the United States.

Frontier resources and the burgeoning cattle business along the Chisholm Trail continued to spread venture capitalism across the Plains to the West Coast. Vast changes in the Midwest, particularly the formation of the National

Grange of the Order of Patrons of Husbandry in 1867, accompanied the arrival of the railroad and attendant greed and corruption by such railroad tycoons as James "Diamond Jim" Fisk, Jr., and Jason "Jay" Gould. After a copper and gold strike in October 1866, prospectors overran Elizabethtown, New Mexico, with demands for housing, supplies, and food service. The clamor for coins increased following new strikes at the Consolidated Virginia Mine and at the Comstock Lode in Virginia City, Nevada.

According to British traveler William Fraser Rae's report in *Westward by Rail* (1870), Western merchants rejected greenbacks and accepted only gold or silver coins. To the demands of financiers, the San Francisco Mint increased the amount of silver specie in circulation, a boost to U.S. trade with East Asia and Pacific Rim nations. The purchase of Alaska from imperial Russia on March 30, 1867, and the telegraph connection between Key West, Florida, and Havana, Cuba, expanded regulated banking and the use of standard currency up the Pacific Coast and southeast into the Gulf of Mexico and the Caribbean. On August 28, to ensure coaling stations for Pacific steamers, the United States annexed the Midway Islands and reengineered harbors to accommodate deep-hulled vessels.

In 1872, Congress voided the income tax at the demand of Northeastern capitalists and politicians. President Ulysses S. Grant further boosted the dollar's buying power by signing the Tariff of 1872, which lowered import duties on foreign luxuries, including wines, silks, and spices.

Emerging Enterprise

As postwar prosperity boomed, new businesses sprang up, from Alexander Turney Stewart's and Marshall Field's urban department stores to municipal hospitals and medical clinics and rail depots, trading posts, restaurants, and inns along the Transcontinental Railroad. Pharmaceutical researcher Eli Lilly created one of the world's most respected drug laboratories and the first prescription drug manufacturing firm. Land-grant colleges introduced careers for women in home economics research, innkeeping, hygiene and sanitation, restaurant management, and hospital dietetics. Seamstresses empowered the growing sweatshop industry by cutting and stitching cheap garments and housewares.

In 1870, the United Fruit Company, one of the first multinational corporations in the Americas, began monopolizing the transport of bananas from Costa Rica, Guatemala, and Honduras to the United States. Asian immigrants and freedmen crowded into cities seeking menial jobs gardening, peddling produce, laundering, waiting tables, cooking, housekeeping, and tending children. Gold rushes generated instant towns in South Dakota and Wyoming that required trading posts, cafés, and express and telegraph offices. The Great Atlantic and Pacific Tea Company, the nation's prototype of the cross-country cut-rate supermarket chain, introduced store brands, economy, and self-service shopping coast to coast.

Great Lakes freight lines invigorated shipbuilding and commercial fishing. Barges sped timber, coal, iron ore, and limestone to Pittsburgh steel mills and Ohio railheads. Night traffic required the outfitting of lighthouses and reef lights, the staffing of lifeboat stations, and the dredging of shoals, wrecks, and snags from harbors, all sources of jobs for laborers and engineers. After the Great Chicago Fire of 1871, boatyards demasted tall ships and revamped propeller lakers and schooners to produce more lumber and steam barges, package freighters, and screw tugs. An energized shore renewed hopes of a business resurgence. Larger replacement vessels lowered freight rates and increased competition among investors.

The flurry of lumbering along the Great Lakes rapidly denuded timberland of usable stands. As wood harvesting moved west, timber barons gripped workers in a financial stranglehold. In Newport, Michigan, a lumberjack's pay fell to 15 cents per 100 board feet (0.24 cubic meters). Wages took the form of scrip exchanged only at company stores. Timber companies monopolized retail trade and produced debt peonage by lending cash at high interest. Owners created an agro-forest economy by buying up local produce, thus creating a symbiotic relationship with farmers. Frederick Weyerhaeuser, the reputed "Timber King," harvested millions of board feet of hardwoods and soft yellow pine in Arkansas, Louisiana, Washington, and Wisconsin. In 1872, he established the Mississippi River Boom and Logging Company, which employed some 20,000 laborers. He showed his respect for the land by protecting the undergrowth that replenished clear-cut woodlands.

Other entrepreneurs excelled at innovation. In Hawaii, King Kamehameha IV and Queen Emma Naea Rooke built up waterfronts at Lahaina and Honolulu, experimented with new hybrid rice seed, imported honeybees, and added a waterworks, an interisland steam line, and gas lines. Gas marketers began replacing whale and vegetable oils with invisible butane, carbon monoxide, ethylene, hydrogen, methane, or propane gas for lighting American cities. Pioneering utilities soon monopolized the gas distribution in each company's region. In 1870, John D. Rockefeller exploited petroleum, an alternative fuel to coal and gas, by incorporating Standard Oil.

Transportation magnates replaced the endless jolting of stagecoaches with the gas-lighted Pullman car, a luxurious accommodation for transcontinental journeys. Tourism found new outlets with the creation of Yellowstone National Park, America's Cup yachting regattas, P.T. Barnum's traveling circus, William Frederick "Buffalo Bill" Cody's Wild West show in Chicago, Colorado rodeos, Washington, D.C.'s Corcoran Gallery and the Freedom Memorial, horse racing at Baltimore and Saratoga Springs in upstate New York, and sport fishing off Fort Myers, Florida.

Boom and Bust

A stock market crash in New York City on September 18, 1873, triggered the Panic of 1873 and initiated the Long Depression, a five-year economic decline. Manufacturers and steelmakers lost contracts and laid off workers, forcing the United States into a slowdown and generating an unemployment rate of 14 percent. Some 5,000 business failures slashed buying power, especially among jobless workers. The panic downsized unions by 73 percent, a setback that lasted five years. The fourth Coinage Act of February 12, 1873, dropped silver from federal currency standards and replaced the bimetal system with a gold standard. The shift reduced livelihoods in Colorado, Idaho, and Nevada, the primary silver-producing states.

The depressed money supply jeopardized farms, mining operations, and small businesses and destabilized Jay Cooke & Company, which had overtaxed its credit to finance the Northern Pacific Railway through Minnesota to the Great Lakes. The collapse of the Jay Cooke bank toppled other banks, 18,000 businesses, and 89 railroads, while deflating prices and real estate values. Contemporaneous with the financial downturn, Nebraska farmers suffered bankruptcy from the destruction of crops and trees by an invasion of grasshoppers, which also gnawed greenery in Colorado, Kansas, and Oklahoma.

The huge profits of venture capitalism generated discontent among the working class. During the lengthy economic decline, capitalists Andrew Carnegie, Cyrus McCormick, and John D. Rockefeller financed their individual projects and enriched themselves at the expense of competitors.

In Arkansas and Texas, prominent voices in the Greenback Party arose from former slaves and members of the Knights of Labor and the Grange, an agrarian society bent on economic and political self-betterment. Liberal economists identified the gold standard and usury as the root causes of monetary deflation and the five-year depression. While Greenbackers demanded repeal of the specie act, the federal offer of "hard money" eased suspicions of paper money. The return to national banks of U.S. Treasury Department power over currency silenced protests of government control of finances. Because citizens declined the opportunity to demand gold for paperbacks, the Greenbackers gradually faded from the political scene.

World Financial Giant

The rise of U.S. plutocrats attested to the world that American banks had replaced European money markets as global financial command posts. The insurance industry initiated additional forms of speculation. Instead of buying bonds and stocks, entrepreneurs invested in risk management in the lives and welfare of ordinary citizens. While protecting orphans and widows from penury, insurance firms, such as the Prudential Insurance Company of Newark, New Jersey, amassed capital to underwrite farm and factory expansion.

As the United States became industrialized, the rise of the moneyed few attested to the control of banking, oil and coal, railroads, telegraph, and steel mills by monopolies. Capitalists maintained a stranglehold on jobs by firing and blacklisting dissatisfied workers, replacing laborers with non-English-speaking immigrants, reducing wages while increasing production rates, and breaking unions and strikes.

The middle class denounced unfair competition against small businesses. Newspapers sanctioned advertising that blamed high consumer costs and tight credit on financiers, land speculators, importers, and wholesalers. Economic downturns empowered labor leaders to pursue a strategy of giving more people jobs and a larger share of company earnings. The attempt to solve complex issues—inflation, monetary and land reform, contract prison labor, public works, racism against blacks and Asians, and women's rights—sapped the efforts of individual reformers.

A nationwide union, the Order of the Knights of St. Crispin, organized in Massachusetts by skilled shoemakers, grew into the country's largest labor group and a vocal outlet for workers by 1870. The association alerted workers to the aggregation of wealth, the connivance of land grabbers, and the tangle of technicalities, delays, and bias that created a class of underpaid and overworked laborers. The Knights developed a collective mentality that excluded capitalists, doctors, financiers, investors, lawyers, and liquor manufacturers, whom they rejected as social parasites. Lobbyists hammered at Congress to boost the economy and enhance the buying power of the laboring class. In 1872, to win the votes of labor, Republicans made the unsettled issue of shorter workdays a party objective.

An Era of Reform

Signaling impatience with the extremes of big money, reformers put into publication 120 journals to vocalize worker discontent. In Colorado in 1876, Plains nesters resorted to Grange lobbying to protect smallholders from the domination of beef barons and rail and storage middlemen. In addition to demanding the regulation of railroad hauling rates and the protection of waterways, Greenback Party members promoted the circulation of more currency as a boost to low-interest farm loans. Politicians anticipated that inflated farm prices would ease agricultural debts and break the fiscal tyranny that financiers and rail barons wielded over stockmen and cotton and grain dealers.

With the *Munn v. Illinois* decision of 1877, the U.S. Supreme Court sided with farmers against price fixing at rail depots and grain elevators. Subsequently, the price war initiated by the Pennsylvania Railroad and Standard Oil over shipping rates increased profitability for American farms and timber operations.

That same year, the Workingmen's Party of California denounced wealthy speculators and charged the Central Pacific Railroad with profiteering on cheap Asian labor. Unfortunately for Chinese Americans, in November, reckless labor rhetoric in San Francisco by populist orator Dennis Kearney turned ethnic differences into scapegoating of Asians.

The end of the 1870s promised expansion and opportunity through such scientific and technological advancement as Luther Burbank's hybridizing of flowers and fruits and the web printer, which folded and precision-cut a continuous flow of sheets at a considerable reduction in cost to publishers and advertisers. Some 1,500 Volga Russian Mennonites experimented with "Turkey Red" wheat, turning Kansas into a Midwestern breadbasket. Telephone networks raised telecommunication to new levels of efficiency, another plus for high-speed business transactions.

Further Reading

Appleby, Joyce. *The Relentless Revolution: A History of Capitalism.* New York: W.W. Norton, 2010.

Beatty, Jack. *Age of Betrayal: The Triumph of Money in America, 1865–1900.* New York: Alfred A. Knopf, 2008.

Borsella, Cristogianni. *On Persecution, Identity and Activism.* Wellesley, MA: Dante University Press, 2005.

Roland, Alex, W. Jeffrey Bolster, and Alexander Keyssar. *The Way of the Ship: America's Maritime History Reenvisioned, 1600–2000.* Hoboken, NJ: Wiley, 2008.

Snodgrass, Mary Ellen. *Coins and Currency: An Historical Encyclopedia.* Jefferson, NC: McFarland, 2003.

Walton, Gary M., and Hugh Rockoff. *History of the American Economy.* 10th ed. Mason, OH: Thomas/South-Western, 2005.

Whitten, David O., and Bessie E. Whitten. *The Birth of Big Business in the United States, 1860–1914: Commercial, Extractive, and Industrial Enterprise.* Westport, CT: Greenwood, 2006.

Foreign Affairs

Throughout the Civil War and Reconstruction, U.S. politicians struggled to balance domestic concerns with international relations. Alarming developments in trade heightened tensions between the United States and its allies in Europe, the Caribbean, and Latin America. As early as 1859, according to Confederate spy and procurement officer Caleb Huse, the Southern states negotiated the sale of 100,000 Austrian Lorenz .54-caliber rifles from Vienna, an accurate musket for sharpshooters to be delivered at the port of Hamburg, Germany. During the secession crisis, increased shipments of anthracite coal from Pennsylvania to Canada and the Caribbean suggested the buildup of British refueling stations in preparation for war.

U.S. harbor surveillance of cargos and obligatory bonds of trust annoyed Lord Richard Lyons, the British envoy to Washington, D.C., who issued lame threats against the bluster of Secretary of State William Henry Seward. In private, Lyons feared that the United States might invade Canada. To Lord John Russell, the British secretary of state for foreign affairs, Lyons predicted that no European nation would side with the South because of the "taint of slavery," which most European nations had abolished by 1818.

Arbitration increased between the United States and European allies, particularly the British, whose goodwill President Abraham Lincoln courted. Britain's status as a global power and possessor of the world's most efficient navy and merchant fleet made its neutrality essential to the Union cause. Meanwhile, the South grasped at frail hopes that both France and Great Britain might side with and finance secessionists by recognizing the sovereignty of the Confederacy.

Economic concerns conflicted with global treaties and accords. In 1860, 80 percent of England's fiber imports came from the American cotton states. British textile mills, run by 5 million workers, thrived on a surplus of cotton bales that fed the industry until late 1863. The Confederate treasury depended on cash from the cotton factories of Fraser, Trenholm, & Company of Liverpool, England; Charleston, South Carolina; Savannah, Georgia; Wilmington, North Carolina; and New York.

George Trenholm, a Charleston native, operated a packet route from Liverpool to Charleston and served as the Confederacy's British banker and financier to Huse and his spy ring. After the Union imposed a blockade of Southern ports in April 1861, Fraser Trenholm resolved to exploit the rising price of plantation goods. The firm offered to purchase all loads of cotton, tobacco, and turpentine that its fleet of blockade runners could slip through Southern ports to the British in Bermuda and Nassau and to the Spanish in Havana.

The Cotton Conundrum

The sale and transport of cotton consumed U.S., Canadian, and European diplomats. Because there were no factories in Confederate states, cotton was worthless in warehouses, where secessionists stockpiled all they could buy to convert plantation wealth into cash. With hard currency, Southern suppliers could purchase uniforms, tents, ordnance, and ammunition from European manufacturers.

Because of the growing demand for cotton, the Union studied the possibility that planters might expand slavery into Mexico and, under the aegis of the British, establish a new cotton-growing region. Simultaneously, as some 55,000 Canadian volunteers joined the Union army, the British feared that Canada might take up the abolitionist cause and devote favored trade to its North American neighbor. However, new sources of cotton in Egypt and India eased British dependence on Southern supplies and reduced the Crown's willingness to build warships to equip the militaries of slave-owning states.

In France, Napoleon III revived hopes of continued trade in cotton under the Declaration of Paris of 1856, an international pledge to halt privateering. Signatories included the United Kingdom, France, Austria, Hungary, the Ottoman Empire, Prussia, Russia, and Sardinia. In 1857, the United States, lacking a large navy, refused to support the French measure, because the nation might have to rely on privateers. President Lincoln quashed French commercial aims by dispatching Archbishop John Joseph Hughes of New York to appeal to the Empress Eugénie.

Hughes, a subtle diplomat popularly known as "Dagger John," implied to the Spanish-born empress that the Confederacy might invade Cuba and proposed that France free itself of dependence on Southern cotton by promoting plantations in Algeria. Hughes continued his European tour by visiting Ireland and conferring with Spanish bishops at the Vatican. Upon his return, he reassured President Lincoln that the British would not raise an army in Ireland because of the people's close ties with Irish immigrants in North America. As a result of Hughes's skillful negotiations, he became America's first Roman Catholic cardinal.

War Disguised as Commerce

Immediately after the Confederate attack on Fort Sumter, South Carolina, on April 12, 1861, retired British naval officers ventured into blockade running as a source of 1,000 percent profits, ranging to $5,000 per month. Along with spies, profiteers, and journalists, blockade runners lived the high life in Nassau, the capital of Caribbean privateering. During this same period, Huse passed through Maine on his way to London to purchase 70,000 more rifles and 7,000 pistols, making the London Armoury Company the Confederacy's main arms supplier.

President Lincoln wisely appointed abolitionist Charles Francis Adams as U.S. ambassador to the Court of St. James. Despite the pro-Confederate stance of Chancellor of the Exchequer William Gladstone, Adams's diplomatic skill with Lord Russell discouraged the British from allying with the Confederacy and dissuaded them from receiving a Confederate deputation of Ambrose Dudley Mann, Pierre Adolphe Rost, and William Lowndes Yancey for official talks. On June 1, under the Prize Proclamation, the British outlawed the importation of privateer plunder into English harbors. Lincoln raised the budget for spying and instructed Adams in London to thwart English trade deals with the Confederacy. Without undue alarm, Adams alerted Russell to the construction of two ironclad ships for the Confederate navy. Russell impeded the sale and purchased the vessels for the British navy to keep warship technology from aiding secessionists.

Although Queen Victoria's Proclamation of Neutrality under international law on May 14, 1861, declared the secessionist South a rogue power, British ships ferried contraband goods to the Confederacy through the Gulf of Mexico and the Caribbean. On May 21, Secretary of State William Henry Seward demanded that Great Britain stop all trade with the United States' "domestic enemies."

On January 29, 1862, the Union scored an early victory when Captain George Colvocoresses, the Greek American commander of the USS *Supply,* belayed the *Stephen Hart,* an American-built Confederate schooner, in the Marquesas Keys south of Sarasota, Florida. Captained by Charles Norton Dyett, a Yorkshire sailor, the schooner carried no registry title or bill of lading, but it bore Confederate correspondence and flew the British ensign on its route from Deal, England, to the rebel agent Charles John Helm at Cardenas, Cuba. Owned by New Orleans shippers, the *Stephen Hart* bore a cargo of Enfield rifles, cartridge belts, powder flasks, blankets, socks, and shoes. Because of the "flagrant criminality" in transporting contraband, Colvocoresses conveyed the *Stephen Hart* to the U.S. Navy in New York. The first officer, Benjamin H. Chadwick, admitted that the previous June 14, the ship had transported lard and turpentine from New Orleans to Havana in violation of the blockade.

Freelancing Gunboats

Confederate President Jefferson Davis continued to circumvent British and French neutrality by pursuing nonmilitary deals. To introduce the Confederacy as a new nation, he appointed Mann as commissioner to Belgium and the Vatican and Rost as commissioner to Spain. Special agent Yancey met with Lord Russell to assure the British that the Confederacy had no wish to reopen the slave trade. Stephen Mallory, secretary of the Confederate navy, dispatched a secret agent, naval veteran James Dunwoody Bulloch, to contract privately for sloops-of-war from the shipyards of John Laird, Sons & Company of Birkenhead, Merseyside, and to hire English mariners. President Lincoln instructed Ambassador Adams to oppose the breach of international accords and to protest the sale of arms to the South as a violation of neutrality.

Protesting the Union's interference in what they claimed to be legitimate trade, pro-South members of Parliament rationalized Laird's private sale as justifiable shipyard construction of commercial vessels. In all, Laird supplied the Confederacy with the raiders *Alabama, Florida, Georgia,* and *Shenandoah*; the tenders *Archer, Clarence, Tacony,* and *Tuscaloosa*; and the independent vessels *Chickamauga, Nashville, Retribution, Sumter,* and *Tallahassee.* Under questioning by the British government, Laird lied, saying that he had made the warships for the Spanish government and that the crew of the *Alabama* had purloined her from Liverpool.

To evade the strictures of Britain's Foreign Enlistments Act, which outlawed aid to the armed forces of any state

Despite British neutrality, the *Alabama* and other ships built in England for the Confederacy often attacked Union vessels. The USS *Kearsarge (left)* finally sank the British-built Confederate sloop of war *Alabama* in the English Channel on June 19, 1864. *(MPI/Stringer/Getty Images)*

warring with another state at peace with Great Britain, rebel captains launched their destroyers unarmed. Bulloch also equipped the iron-hulled screw steamer CSS *Fingal* with an arsenal of 14,000 Enfield rifles, four cannon, 3,000 sabers, 1,000 short rifles with bayonets, 400 barrels of powder, 2 million percussion caps, and 7 tons (6 metric tons) of shells, as well as medicine, blankets, leather goods, textiles, and naval uniforms. Flying the Union Jack and commanded by an English captain, the steamer left harbor at Greenock, Scotland; loaded crew and passengers at Holyhead, Wales; stocked coal in Bermuda; and docked safely at Savannah, Georgia. To ready the CSS *Alabama,* in late July 1862, agents hired English crewmen and sailed upcoast to Portballintrae, Ireland. After the crew rendezvoused with the CSS *Agrippa* at Terceira in the Spanish Azores, the captain, Raphael Semmes, outfitted the fleet with eight cannon. The destroyers from Liverpool began wreaking havoc on the Union's merchant marine by boarding ships, offloading usable cargo, and burning the pirated remains in the Atlantic, Caribbean, and Gulf of Mexico.

Lincoln continued to maneuver against an Anglo-Confederate alliance. On September 22, 1862, his phrasing of the Emancipation Proclamation aimed in part to deter foreign powers from recognizing Confederate sovereignty. Its formal issuance on January 1, 1863, won the support of libertarians in England and France. Union agents infiltrated English gun running by offering competitive contracts for munitions.

Despite their efforts, U.S. spies were unable to halt the career of the *Alabama* and its captain. The crew plundered or scuttled 69 Union vessels and sailed undeterred until the USS *Kearsarge* sank the war-weary *Alabama* on June 19, 1864, off Cherbourg, France. Before the Union could arrest Semmes, Evan Parry Jones, master of the British steamer yacht *Deerhound,* rescued him and transported him to Southampton. While President Lincoln lionized the crew of the *Kearsarge,* representatives of the Royal Navy gave Semmes a hero's reception and a gold sword honoring his seamanship.

Spying and Lying

U.S. Consul Thomas Haines Dudley, a New Jersey–born spy for President Lincoln, gathered evidence in Liverpool shipyards that the British had flouted their neutrality by building a total of 324 blockade runners and commerce raiders. He presented details of espionage revealing Confederate recruitment of British seamen to Queen's Advocate Sir John Harding, whose nervous breakdown prevented him from interceding. Meanwhile, Confederate looting raised shippers' insurance rates to 4 percent of the value of vessel and cargo and forced Union merchants to transport 75 percent of their loads via British carriers.

In 1862, Union warships stopped the British trading barks *Bermuda* and *Springbok* outside harbors at Bermuda and Nassau. Under false manifests issued from London merchants, the ships were delivering to Southern rebels "warlike" cargo—medicines, army blankets, Confederate uniform buttons, and nitrates for making gunpowder. The Yankee navy also seized drugs, boots, other leather goods, shirts, blankets, and powder from the steamer *Gertrude* before it could reach Charleston, South Carolina. Union patrols deflected a disguised cargo of artillery harnesses, munitions, boots, blankets, and hops from the British sidewheeler *Peterhoff* in the Danish West Indies before it could anchor at the neutral wharves of Matamoros, Texas, and transport the goods over the international waters of the Rio Grande to Brownsville. Danish officials and the London *Times* disputed a court for condemning the ship, which bore British mail through Danish waters.

Despite Union surveillance, in the first weeks of 1863, cotton worth $4.5 million slipped through the Union net to England. As of March 3, the Privateering Bill conferred on Lincoln the power to issue letters of marque and reprisal to halt Confederate destruction of the U.S. Merchant Marine. As a direct threat of possible war with England, Seward, with Lincoln's approval, warned Lord Russell that the launching of more war sloops from Liverpool was "a thing to be deprecated above all things."

President Lincoln's relationship with the British government exhibited the uncertainties of civil war and disclosed the possibility of new global alliances with Confederate President Davis and his 11 Southern states. On November 8, 1861, an impolitic decision by Captain Charles Wilkes of the USS *San Jacinto* allowed the seizure of Confederate legates James Murray Mason and John Slidell from the British mail steamer RMS *Trent.* Mason represented the Confederacy as envoy to Great Britain and France; Slidell had accepted a diplomatic commission to France to negotiate a Franco-Confederate alliance. Under international law, the matter of jurisdiction over the high seas would have devolved to an admiralty court, but Wilkes, with the approval of Secretary of the Navy Gideon Welles, chose to transport his prisoners to Fort Warren, Boston.

On November 30, British Prime Minister Lord Palmerston (John Henry Temple) demanded Mason's and Slidell's release and sent 14,000 combat forces to Canada to bolster the colonial militia. Both Britain and the United States avoided overt confrontations that might force Britain to declare war on the Union. Through the behind-the-scenes efforts, Ambassador Adams convinced Lord Russell that Wilkes had acted precipitately. On December 26, Seward released the two ministers and made a show of denouncing Wilkes's bad judgment for jailing "personal contraband." News of the freeing of Mason and Slidell improved the British attitude toward the Union and assuaged French outrage at American high-handedness on the open seas.

A series of events cinched an Anglo-American entente. On July 22, 1862, the signing of the Lyons-Seward Treaty by the United States and Britain to curtail the Atlantic slave trade established goodwill through shared humanitarianism. In late 1863, English actor Fanny Kemble, the ex-wife of Georgia slave owner Pierce Butler, exposed her husband's greed and brutality in her *Journal of a Residence of a Georgian Plantation, 1838–1839,* a best-seller in England. Her insights into human bondage, along with the Union victory at Antietam, Maryland, on September 30, 1862, helped to dissuade the British from sympathizing with the South, which seemed doomed to defeat.

A subsequent breach of the neutral U.S.–Canadian border on October 19, 1864, preceded a Confederate raid launched from Montreal on St. Albans, Vermont. The invaders robbed three banks of $208,000. The press depicted the attack as a desperate attempt to finance a demoralized secessionist military.

Peace and Commerce

The postwar economy ruined London arms dealers and turned U.S. weapons manufacturers into freelance suppliers of rifles and pistols for foreign armies. In the lull that followed the steady procurement of Union arms, Colt, Remington, and Winchester aimed their marketing at France and Prussia. To entice business, they introduced innovative gun design—the Hotchkiss machine gun, Sharps 1874 carbine, .44 Henry rifle models, Winchester Model 1873 rifle, Colt .45 Peacemaker revolver, and Remington Rolling Block rifle—and lower prices through mass production. Samuel Remington's Paris sales office dispatched rifles and bullets to surrounding nations. During the Franco-Prussian War (1870–1871), the French military contracted for 100,000 rifles and

18 million paper shot shells and smokeless cartridges, manufactured by Union Metallic Cartridge Company in Bridgeport, Connecticut.

An unforeseen emergence of monarchy in North America stirred U.S.–European animosities. While briefly serving President Andrew Johnson as secretary of war, Union hero Ulysses S. Grant, the nation's first four-star general, mustered 50,000 Civil War veterans along the Texas–Mexico border as a show of force against the French occupation of Mexico. The invasion began at Veracruz on December 17, 1861, with French-allied Spanish forces from Cuba. On January 6, 1862, support arrived at Puebla north of Veracruz from some 8,000 French insurgents of Archduke Ferdinand Maximilian Joseph of Austria, a relative of Napoleon III. The interlopers, aided by the Belgian Brigade and the Austrian Corps, supported the Confederacy, proclaimed a Catholic empire, and set up a monarchy on June 7, 1863, under Emperor Maximilian I.

President Lincoln favored a republican Mexico, but he had no troops to spare from the Civil War. In May 1865, Austrian appeasement of President Andrew Johnson failed, as did the Empress Charlotte's appeals for more troops from Napoleon and from Pope Pius IX. In violation of the Monroe Doctrine, Maximilian's soldiers remained a military presence in Mexico until their withdrawal on March 12, 1867. The end of the Franco-Mexican War followed official U.S. protests to Austria and, on June 19, the execution of Maximilian at Querétaro before a firing squad.

Ghost Issues

The predations of the Civil War returned to haunt Anglo-American negotiations on April 13, 1869. Without consulting the U.S. Senate, President Ulysses S. Grant, or Secretary of State Hamilton Fish, Republican Senator Charles Sumner of Massachusetts, chairman of the Committee on Foreign Relations, pressed for settlement of the "*Alabama* claims." Backed by angry Unionists, Sumner rallied the Senate to reject the Clarendon-Johnson Treaty of 1868. A clandestine entente negotiated by cable, that agreement between former President Johnson and Lord Clarendon, the British minister of foreign affairs, glossed over outstanding discord related to Britain's assistance to secessionists during the Civil War.

Basing his claims on evidence gathered by Ambassador Adams, Sumner charged Great Britain with supplying funds, heavy artillery, mariners, and ships to the Confederacy, thereby lengthening the war by two years. For restitution of itemized claims, Sumner demanded $2.125 billion in reparations and the removal of the British flag from North American soil. The British, speaking through Sir Edward Thornton, the ambassador to Washington, D.C., requested arbitration.

On January 9, 1871, the Treaty of Washington settled the dispute by obligating Britain to reimburse the United States for wartime damages. The *Alabama* alone had scuttled 450 ships and amassed combat prizes worth $6 million. Former ambassador Adams came out of retirement to join Secretary of State Fish and an intermediary, Canadian ambassador Sir John Rose, along with international mediators from Brazil, England, Italy, Switzerland, and the United States in resolving U.S. claims against Britain. Muddling issues, London raised counterclaims concerning imprecise boundaries in the San Juan passage between Vancouver Island and Washington Territory and monetary claims for fish taken by U.S. vessels trolling the waters off Canada and Newfoundland.

After Adams broke the stalemate, on September 21, 1872, at Geneva, Fish accepted compensation of $15.5 million in gold for the U.S. Treasury and an apology from Queen Victoria for the predations caused by the Confederate war vessels *Alabama, Florida,* and *Shenandoah,* which British shipyards had sold to the rebel government. In addition, American trawlers gained access to fishing grounds off Newfoundland, New Brunswick, Nova Scotia, Prince Edward Island, and Quebec, as well as navigation rights along the Canadian side of Lake Michigan and the St. Lawrence Seaway. The Canadians received fishing reparations of $5.5 million and free commercial access to fish oil and saltwater fish markets in the United States. The treaty set a precedent for international law.

Diplomacy and Future Wars

Subsequent foreign affairs generated fewer headlines but foreshadowed later international predicaments. U.S. expansionists secured the purchase of Alaska and the Midway Islands and considered annexing the Dominican Republic; however, they steered clear of Cuba, a Spanish possession then in the throes of a fledgling peasant revolt. Washington recognized the inadvisability of war with Spain, which would pit the depleted U.S. military against a modern navy.

During Cuba's Ten Years' War (1868–1878) for independence from Spain, American collaborators with Cuban rebels violated neutrality laws by transporting supplies to General Manuel Quesada on the sidewheeler *Virginius,* a Scots-built Confederate blockade runner. The steamer, sailed by Louisiana-born Captain Joseph Fry, succeeded in a two-year mission to rebels under either the American or Cuban flag. Spain considered the *Virginius* a pirate vessel.

The ship survived a close call in June 1873 in Aspinwall, Colombia, when the USS *Kansas* rescued the mission from the Spanish man-of-war *Bazan* by declaring the *Virginius* an American vessel. An eight-hour chase, initiated on October 30, 1873, by the Spanish corvette *Tornado,* taxed the aging boilers of the *Virginius.* Mariners dumped equipment and armaments to lighten the sidewheeler. The passengers and crew proposed detonating the ship rather than relinquishing it to the Spanish, but Captain Fry chose to surrender. A subsequent squabble resulted from Fry's claims that he had anchored off Morante Bay, Jamaica, in British territorial waters.

After the capture of the freebooting *Virginius* on October 31, 1873, by Captain Dionisio Costilla, Spanish loyalist troops lowered the American flag and trampled it and jailed 52 American and English crewmen and 103 Cuban passengers for piracy. Among the expeditionary forces onboard were two Cuban generals, three colonels, and a captain. Predictable military tribunals at Fort Dolores under General Juan Nepomuceno Burriel found the captives guilty. On November 4 and 7, Spanish officials shot 53 kneeling crewmen and passengers in the back at Santiago. They martyred Fry, whom the Spanish charged with attempting to deliver to Cuban insurrectionists 300 Remington rifles, 300,000 cartridges, 800 daggers, 800 machetes, gunpowder, and boots. The American press reported that cavalrymen directed their horses to trample the remains, which burial crews dumped in a swampy ditch. A mob severed the captives' heads and elevated them on pikes for a city procession. Burriel censored telegraph lines to keep the news from reaching foreign consuls. The arrival of a British man-of-war, the HMS *Niobe,* on November 8 and the threat of a British bombardment by Captain Sir Lambton Loraine ended the firing squads and spared the remaining captives.

Because of the ineptitude of U.S. envoy Daniel Sickles in demanding compensation and punishment for the atrocities, the United States edged closer to war with Spain. Nevadans awarded Loraine a silver brick; both Confederate and Union veterans volunteered to launch a strike force on Cuba. The *New York Tribune* urged prompt retaliation. General Burriel ignored the diplomatic efforts of Great Britain and the United States, which the *New York Herald* ridiculed as formulaic and gutless.

Finally, on December 8, through the diplomacy of U.S. Secretary of State Fish and José Polo de Bernabé, Spain's minister to Washington, D.C., Spain surrendered the *Virginius* and 103 surviving mariners and passengers to the U.S. corvette *Juniata.* As a sop to Spain, Attorney General George Henry Williams judged that Captain Fry had traveled illegally under the American flag. On November 29, 1873, the Spanish agreed to reparations for the *Virginius* incident. On March 5, 1875, Spain remunerated the United States $80,000 for the executed Americans and a lesser amount to indemnify Great Britain. Protest of the incident loomed once more during the hostilities preceding the Spanish-American War.

Less contentious negotiations in the Pacific produced positive results for the United States and the Kingdom of Hawaii. In March 1874, King David Kalakaua's election caused riots among islanders, who preferred the Dowager Queen Emma Naea Rooke. The U.S. Navy responded by landing men from the USS *Portsmouth* and *Tuscarora,* and the British dispatched a squadron from the HMS *Tenedos.* Seeking to end an economic downturn in Hawaii, King Kalakaua visited President Grant in Washington. The king negotiated with Secretary of State Fish on the colonization of the Hawaiian Islands to provide a U.S. naval base at Pu'u Loa, later known as Pearl Harbor.

On January 1, 1875, the Reciprocity Treaty between Hawaii and the United States granted mutual duty-free trading rights in the islands and at Portland and San Francisco of Hawaiian produce—arrowroot, bananas, castor oil, hides, nuts, rice, and sugar—in exchange for military protection of the island cluster. The accord encouraged American investors to establish sugar plantations on the islands.

Further Reading

DeConde, Alexander, Richard Dean Burns, and Fredrik Logevall, eds. *Encyclopedia of American Foreign Policy.* 2nd ed. New York: Scribner's, 2002.

Jones, Howard. *Abraham Lincoln and a New Birth of Freedom: The Union and Slavery in the Diplomacy of the Civil War.* Lincoln: University of Nebraska Press, 1999.

———. *Blue and Gray Diplomacy: A History of Union and Confederate Foreign Relations.* Chapel Hill: University of North Carolina Press, 2010.

LaFeber, Walter. *The New Empire: An Interpretation of American Expansion, 1860–1898.* Ithaca, NY: Cornell University Press, 1998.

Merli, Frank J. *Great Britain and the Confederate Navy, 1861–1865.* Bloomington: Indiana University Press, 1970.

Monaghan, Jay. *Abraham Lincoln Deals with Foreign Affairs: A Diplomat in Carpet Slippers.* Lincoln: University of Nebraska Press, 1997.

Sexton, Jay. *Debtor Diplomacy: Finance and American Foreign Relations in the Civil War Era, 1837–1873.* Oxford, UK: Clarendon, 2005.

Family, Community, and Society

The conflicts and achievements of the Civil War and Reconstruction illustrate the human extremes of a dynamic era in American history. Individuals from coast to coast debated social and religious issues that tested their personal tenets, notably, abortion, anti-Semitism, miscegenation, nativism, pacifism, polygamy, Sabbatarianism, temperance, white supremacy, and women's rights. The closed societies of Indians, Hawaiians, mestizos, coolie laborers, Orthodox Jews, Mormons, and slaves protected insiders from the undermining of their culture through assimilation with majority whites of Catholic and Protestant European backgrounds.

In a sermon delivered in 1861, third Mormon president John Taylor claimed his sacred priesthood in a government that he described as a "theodemocracy," which placed the tenets of Latter Day Saints above constitutional law. One dissident wife, former Mormon Fanny Stenhouse, composed an exposé of female distaste for male dominance, *Tell It All: The Tyranny of Mormonism* (1872), to witness growing philosophical division among Mormons, particularly girls and women subjugated under polygamy.

To preserve ethnic enclaves, such insulated cultures focused on the young. To instill vigilance, verbal cultures taught cautionary tales, as with the kahuna (priest) recitations of *'olelo no'eau* (Hawaiian proverbs), gendered talk-story between Chinese American mothers and daughters, Hispanic warnings of the wandering wraith La Llorona (the "Weeping Woman"), and Caribbean-dialect dilemma tales and trickster stories of Anansi the Spider at brush arbor schools in Southern slave quarters.

Children attended monocultural worship services and schools, such as the sectarian Mormon academies in Salt Lake City, Utah. They memorized prayers and lessons in their native language, notably, Hebrew literature taught at yeshivas in such cities as Detroit and Philadelphia and Southern Cheyenne teachings shared by firesides in Colorado.

Threats to the Status Quo

Visitors to adobe dwellings outside Fort Buchanan, Arizona, and to the insular native villages of the Apache, Blackfeet, Pawnee, and Seminole observed foodways, dance lodges, chanting, clan ritual, costume, and oral myth based on centuries of communal living. Unfortunately for multicultural relations, even the brief interaction among racial groups at Missouri River wharves and Great Basin outposts spread influenza, scarlet fever, whooping cough, and other European diseases among virgin-soil populations. Waves of sickness wiped out whole villages within weeks and threatened the viability of native peoples. Such was the plight of the Mandan of the Dakotas. To survive, in 1862, the remaining 125 Mandan syncretized a tribe by affiliating with the Arikara and Hidatsa at Fort Berthold Indian Reservation in North Dakota.

As a result of susceptibility in the Pacific, measles reduced the population of native Hawaiians at Lahaina and Honolulu by 20 percent and left some survivors blind, deaf, and crippled. At a military Indian camp at Bosque Redondo, New Mexico, soldiers infected hundreds of Navajo girls and women with gonorrhea and syphilis. Cholera sapped the Wichita of Kansas and beset the Sioux of Nebraska and the Caddo of Colorado. Smallpox threatened with annihilation the Menominee of Wisconsin, the Paiute of Nevada, the Assiniboine of Montana, and the Bella Bella, Skallam, and Tsimshian of Washington Territory and Alaska. In 1862, the combined effects of famine and smallpox devastated the Comancheros, depopulating members through protracted suffering and death and lowered fertility.

The judgmental white world tended to patronize or heap scorn on outsiders, particularly native peoples. Anthropocentrism imposed white standards and behaviors on schoolchildren, especially native orphans whose parents had died in the Indian Wars or succumbed to pestilence. Indian school staff stripped native waifs of their language and dignity. Regimentation drove a wedge between adult Cherokee, Choctaw, Iroquois, and Muscogee and their families over such issues as amulets, haircuts, and going barefoot. Racially superior ministers and Indian agents denigrated nomadic hunter-gatherers for their skin garments, proofs of manhood, ear and lip piercings with bone earrings and labrets (lip studs), nature-based healing, and meat- and fish-centered nutritional systems, factors affecting the assimilation of the Aleut, Haida, Shoshone, and Ute. Instead of valuing tribes as preliterate aborigines, social activists labeled them ignorant savages, a pejorative that the Mission Indians and Yahi of California shared with the Southwestern Comancheros and native Hawaiians under the scrutiny of puritanical New England preachers.

White society teetered on the edge of total usurpation of native lands and the annihilation of the native peoples. Racists exhibited their own style of barbarity by prostituting Hawaiian, Chinese, and mestizo women and by trafficking in Apache and Navajo child bondage. Genocidal American soldiers beheaded Mangas Coloradas, bayoneted Crazy Horse, and slaughtered the Arapaho and Cheyenne elderly, women, and children at the massacres of Sand Creek and Washita. Ironically, some of the most notorious Indian fighters—Edward Canby, Christopher "Kit" Carson, John M. Chivington, George Armstrong Custer, Philip Sheridan, and William Tecumseh Sherman—had earned their military renown in combat during the Civil War to emancipate slaves.

In 1865, Brigham Young led the Mormon militia against Ute renegades attacking communities of Latter Day Saints on the Arizona–Utah border. Soldiers murdered adults and posted skulls on poles but spared infants and toddlers, whom Mormons adopted. After ratification of the Fourteenth Amendment to the Constitution on July 9, 1868, subsequent U.S. Supreme Court tests of the definition of "citizenship" gave rights to Chinese Americans, Hispanics, and the offspring of illegal aliens, but not to Indians.

Community and Cohesion

Among nonwhites, ethnic continuity nurtured a spiritual wholeness. For the Hispanic mixed-race peoples of the Southwest—Californios, Comancheros, and mestizos—Roman Catholicism, the Spanish language, Tex-Mex *corridos* (popular ballads and protests), commerce, and ranchos provided anchorage. Tradition fortified native integrity for the Hispanic settlers of El Paso, Texas; Santa Fe, New Mexico; Tucson, Arizona; and Monterey, Santa Ana, San Diego, and San Fernando, California. Like the Gypsies of Europe, mixed-blood peoples became expert at enduring harsh social censure by adapting to the outskirts of white respectability.

Asian Americans found similar shelter from persecution in the close confines of Chinatown, the generic name for Asian communities in Baltimore, Boston, Chicago, Denver, Detroit, Honolulu, New York, Philadelphia, San Francisco, and Washington, D.C. Unlike Hispanics, male coolie laborers arrived on the Pacific Coast for a single purpose—to work at building railroads and mining gold and silver. Enslaved Asian females obliged the mining camps of Oregon and Idaho as "comfort girls" and barmaids. When employment for Asians ended in the mines and dance halls and on railroad crews, white enclaves ousted those who did not fit the stereotype of cook, launderer, or household do-all. Restrictive immigration laws prevented Chinese males from importing their families. As a result, bachelor societies in California and Oregon languished without the warmth and stability of wives and children. Language barriers exacerbated by alphabetic differences reduced Asians to the "exotics" of America, known for Buddhism, acupuncture, herbal healing, tearooms, opium smoking, and leprosy.

The presence of nonwhites posed a perplexing social contretemps for majority Americans. Blacks in bondage in the South preserved their West African lifestyle in animistic worship, work songs, Congo-style shared meals, Mandingan good luck rites, and Dahomean field cultivation. While nomadic Native Americans sought dominion over such ancestral hunting grounds as the Black Hills of the Dakotas and the Great Basin of the Utes and allied to protect migratory buffalo, the basis of life for Plains Indians, African slaves struggled to escape from overwork, torture, and the breeding of black children as a farm commodity.

In Colorado, Indian Territory (Oklahoma), Kansas, and Texas—areas where white and black society abutted Indian borders—Indians, mulattos, and Métis (those of mixed Indian and European heritage) found ways to thrive amid the cultural overlaps as healers, domestics, guides, herders, stage drivers, and loggers. The mongrelized culture of cowboys and soldiers accommodated such racial anomalies as Anglo-Comanche woodcutter Quanah Parker, black bronco buster Nat Love, black stagecoach driver Mary Fields, black nurse Biddy Mason, Afro-Seminole army scout John Horse, and mustang trainer George Bent, an Anglo-Cheyenne.

Slave Assimilation

Overt civil disobedience of the Fugitive Slave Law of 1850 set neighbor against neighbor, parishioner against pastor, and individual against a statute that required citizens to assist U.S. marshals in recovering slaves in flight from their masters, even when fleeing slaves traversed free states north and west of the Mason-Dixon Line. Setting an example of outspoken libertarianism, editors

Frederick Douglass and William Lloyd Garrison and orators Anna Elizabeth Dickinson, Abby Kelley Foster, Lucretia Mott, and Sojourner Truth pressed white fence-sitters into action to rescue runaway slaves from recapture, torture, and lives shortened by bondage. At Pittsburgh, Pennsylvania, memoirist and journalist Jane Swisshelm not only directed fugitives to safety, but provoked a racist mob with editorials in her abolitionist newspaper, the *St. Cloud Visitor.*

Humanitarian values compelled female abolitionists to intercede for black mothers and their children who awaited family dissolution in the slave pens at auction houses in Charleston, South Carolina; Annapolis, Maryland; and Richmond, Virginia. In a milieu stymied by Victorian prudery, white women campaigned for laws to shield young black girls from the groping hands of white sexual predators at the notorious concubine markets of New Orleans.

In New England and the Northeast, especially along the Atlantic Coast, white, black, and Indian abolitionist families opened their homes, farms, churches, and businesses to runaway slaves. One notable Underground Railroad conductor, tailor William Lambert of Detroit, conspired with a vast network of secret agents along the Detroit River who reputedly rescued 30,000 runaways from as far south as Florida and Louisiana.

Homeschooling of blacks generated heroic defiance of unjust laws. Against local laws in the South, victims such as Alabama slave Jenny Proctor feared to touch books or show curiosity about letters and numbers, lest they incur the lash. Out of sight of vigilant patrollers, daring teachers assembled covert reading classes for illiterate slaves in remote barn lofts, canebreaks, and swamps. In a hovel in Natchez, Mississippi, slave cook Milla Granson taught midnight lessons while lookouts watched for intruders. In Hampton, Virginia, in 1861, mulatto instructor Mary Smith Kelsey Peake defied unjust statutes by assembling day and night classes, which formed the basis of Hampton University. At Hopewell Plantation in Alabama, seamstress and nurse Lucy Skipworth operated a clandestine school in the absence of her owner; around August 15, 1863, threats from whites ended her literacy lessons.

In Augusta, Georgia, Methodist minister Ned Purdy, teacher of a backyard slave academy, endured the conse-

Assimilating the former slave population—such as these freedmen in Richmond, Virginia, in 1865—was the great social challenge in the aftermath of the Civil War. The government founded the Freedmen's Bureau in 1865 to help ease the transition. *(Buyenlarge/ Getty Images)*

quences of civil disobedience after a court sentenced him to 60 lashes, a fine of $50, and an active prison sentence. Until the end of the Civil War, three black Georgians—Mary Beasley, Catherine Deveaux, and her daughter, Jane Deveaux—staffed a learning center at Savannah's Second African Baptist Church, where students cowered in a garret to avoid detection by Confederate patrollers. Actor Fanny Kemble's second diary, *Journal of a Residence of a Georgian Plantation, 1838–1839* (1863), disclosed a mother's efforts to aid black parents with education, sanitation, hospital care, and flight via the Underground Railroad. Historians lionize the diary for helping to convince the British not to aid the Confederacy during the American Civil War.

On the tramp north, refugees found welcome, rest, and healing, especially along the Pilgrim's Pathway, a network of interrelated Quaker families through southeastern Pennsylvania farmland. By acting on conscience and instructing their children and extended family to respect biblical adjuncts to help the oppressed, slave harborers faced ridicule, harassment, arson, and legal prosecution. Prominent among them, Graceanna Lewis and her parents and sisters operated a rehabilitation center at Kimberton, Pennsylvania. In an era daunted by the dehumanization of blacks after the U.S. Supreme Court's *Dred Scott* (1857) decision, stopovers at white homes such as that of Rowland Thomas Robinson in Ferrisburg, Vermont, introduced repressed blacks to acceptance and benevolence as well as jobs and learning.

Humanitarians as far west as Texas, Kansas, Ohio, and Illinois relayed fugitive slaves along Underground Railroad routes through the Dakotas and over the Great Lakes to a chain of reception centers formed on the north shores of the Great Lakes in Ontario, Quebec, and the Canadian Maritime Provinces. Major black communities at Amherstburg, Boylston, Buxton, Chatham, Colchester, Dresden, Sandwich, St. Catharines, and Windsor became havens where former slave families could rebuild their lives.

The Trek West

On the frontier, families encountered unfamiliar quandaries as they crossed prairies through the lands of hostile Plains Indians. Along the Oregon Trail, a 2,000-mile (3,200-kilometer) overland route from Independence, Missouri, to the Pacific Coast, parents modeled courage by bartering with Indians for fresh fish and meat, greens, and healing herbs and by facing rain, snowstorms, and rugged terrain a day at a time. From falls, snakebites, and wagon breakdowns to cholera, dysentery, malaria, and Indian attack and kidnap, travelers persevered despite suffering and loss, leaving their stillborn and dead at lonely gravesites along the way. Diaries such as *Mollie: The Journal of Mollie Dorsey Sanford in Nebraska and Colorado Territories, 1857–1866* (1959) and the letters of Alice Kirk Grierson and Elinore Pruitt Stewart preserved women's private thoughts about westering.

Over the Mormon Emigrant Trail, which turned southwest from Independence Rock, Wyoming, toward Utah, more than 68,000 Latter Day Saints built foot and wagon bridges and log ferries as aids to the pioneers who followed. Where the dense traffic over rutted lanes filled prime campsites, mobbed ferry landings, and limited forage, hunting, water sources, and combustibles for campfires, newcomers spread horizontally and widened the route to Salt Lake City.

Technology and tourism rapidly reduced the isolation of pioneers. Overland stages, telegraph stations, and telephones enabled travelers to communicate with Eastern relatives and businesses. With the completion of the transcontinental telegraph, the California State Telegraph Company passed through Omaha, Nebraska, to Carson City, Nevada, and met the Pacific Telegraph Company at Salt Lake City, Utah, on October 24, 1861. The expanding communications network and the Transcontinental Railroad produced a sense of union in a nation that was still recovering from Civil War. By 1878, a sophisticated telephone system allowed communication in one-fifteenth of a second through Omaha, Nebraska, and Cheyenne, Wyoming, to Salt Lake City, Utah; Reno, Nevada; and Sacramento, California.

A tribute to the valor of transient adults and children, the *Little House on the Prairie* series, published in the early twentieth century, captured the memories of Laura Ingalls Wilder, who grew up with her older sister Mary and younger sisters Carrie and Grace in a series of residences—covered wagon, cabin, sod hut, and town cottage—in Iowa, Kansas, Minnesota, Missouri, South Dakota, and Wisconsin. Beginning with her post–Civil War childhood, Laura pictured her belabored father, Charles Philip Ingalls, working in forest and field and as storekeeper, bookkeeper, and timekeeper for the Chicago & North Western Railroad at De Smet in Dakota Territory. Meanwhile, his wife, Caroline Quiner Ingalls, lived the daily responsibility of a single parent and instilled cunning and caution in her four girls.

A parallel to Louisa May Alcott's citified memories in *Little Women* (1868–1869), the *Little House* books honored matriarchy, a family order that placed Caroline and Laura's

French Canadian grandmother and other female settlers in scenes of shared meals, fiddling, square dancing, and storytelling. In the background, the wilderness offered face-to-face confrontations with bears and wolves, as well as the freedom that enticed pioneer families to abandon urbanization for an unfettered life on the Plains.

The Urban Challenge

The growth of cities produced an urban wilderness fraught with unique dangers and temptations. For the middle and upper classes, technology introduced permanent change to the concepts of family, community, and society. Streetcars, elevated trains, and bicycles augmented casual commutes to parks, baseball fields, beaches, and museums, as well as to markets and department stores, such as Levi Strauss & Company, I. Magnin, Montgomery Ward, and Macy's. In immigrant sections, tenement dwellings tended to fill with people of the same language and culture groups—Chinatown in San Francisco, the French Quarter in New Orleans, Germantown in Philadelphia, Greektown in Detroit, Harlem and Little Italy in New York, black Summerhill and Shermantown in Atlanta, and the diverse immigrant subsections of Roxbury in Boston.

Schooling varied by cultural background and ability to pay. For Catholic, Jewish, Lutheran, and Quaker families, parochial schools built scholarship and character and guided youth toward service in such outreaches as the Sisters of Charity, freedmen's schools, Lutheran catechism, and B'nai B'rith. Higher education at Atlanta College, female seminaries, Oberlin College, and Smith College balanced the expectations for excellence among privileged males with that of blacks and females.

Population density heightened the dangers of cities. Dependence on dray animals left streets littered with dung, which drew flies and vermin. Unsanitary drinking water hosted contagious disease—enteritis, diphtheria, smallpox, trachoma, tuberculosis, and yellow fever. Without extended family or state welfare, destitute adults turned to alcohol, went insane, committed suicide, and disappeared from their homes, leaving homeless children without protection and guidance.

City crime forced children to cope on the streets with varied hazards, particularly bullies and gangs, pickpockets, shoplifters, prostitutes, bootleggers, gamblers, and grifters. Like Laura Ingalls Wilder in the wilderness and young armed riders and hostlers for the Pony Express, city children tempered trust with prudence and self-defense. To prevent juvenile delinquency, municipal leaders formed boards of health, built almshouses and reformatories, and hired truancy officers and fire and police departments. Charles Loring Brace of New York City, founder of the Children's Aid Society, formed orphan trains to dispatch homeless youth to potential adoption in the Dakotas, Illinois, Indiana, Kansas, Michigan, Nebraska, New Mexico, Oklahoma, and Oregon.

Safety and Security

The 1860s and 1870s worked miracles on the everyday welfare of individuals. Contributing to public safety, freedmen mustered black militias—the Groton, Connecticut, Home Guard; Brooklyn's Hannibal Guards; the United States League of Gileadites in Springfield, Massachusetts; Boston's Massasoit Guards and Sons of Liberty; and the Independent Company in Poughkeepsie, New York—to ward off slave kidnappers and bounty hunters. In the style of ad hoc paramilitary groups, black patrols manned a collective self-defense and peacekeeping mission in the absence of police protection for ghetto dwellers.

In the South, the sight of ex-slaves in Montgomery, Alabama, and Columbia, South Carolina, jolted former enslavers. To ease civic concerns, local lawmakers threatened the newly freed with Black Codes and immediate jailing for trespass and vagrancy. Unfortunately for former slaves, heightened security for white neighborhoods precipitated convict leasing, a reversion to enslavement in punishment of trivial offenses.

To upgrade home life, suffragists and teachers at the Boston Normal School of Cooking, the New York Cooking School, and land-grant colleges urged mothers to rally communities against adulterated food and over-the-counter nostrums, particularly milk whitened with chalk dust, preserved fruit and vegetables colored with copper sulfate, bread permeated with sawdust and other fillers, and cough syrup and fever reducers laced with alcohol and opium. Civic pride promoted community solidarity, often expressed for favorite home sports teams, especially the Chicago White Stockings, Louisville Grays, Philadelphia Athletics, and St. Louis Browns baseball squads.

Overall, the nation profited from improved health care and nutrition. Refrigerated railcars carried a broader variety of meats, citrus fruit, and vegetables to grocers. Engineers drained swamps and piped clean water to homes. In the mid-1860s, Catholic, Episcopal, and Quaker groups, charities, and municipalities absorbed the orphans of the streets and those bereft of parents during the Civil War. American cities began building more hospitals to cope with the sick, injured, and handicapped poor and mentally incompetent, including alcoholics, drugs addicts, epileptics, and the mentally ill.

Bellevue Hospital operated a city emergency ward and ambulance service for Manhattan and promoted the opening of the New York City Department of Health as a defense against outbreaks of plague, yellow fever, and other epidemic contagion. To boost the survival rate for parturient women and newborns, Maria Zakrzewska opened the New England Hospital for Women and Children in Boston as a treatment center and medical college for nurses and midwives. At Battle Creek, Michigan, Ellen Gould White evolved hydrotherapeutic protocols for patients at the Western Health Reform Institute. In Sacramento, California, the Central Pacific Railroad provided a company hospital to treat rail workers and their families. Nationwide, a hospital network founded in 1870 to tend sick and injured merchant seamen developed into a service to control contagion. In 1912, the name of the Public Health and Marine Hospital Service was shortened to the Public Health Service.

Further Reading

Burlingame, Dwight F., ed. *Philanthropy in America: A Comprehensive Historical Encyclopedia.* Santa Barbara, CA: ABC-CLIO, 2004.

Butchart, Ronald E. *Northern Schools, Southern Blacks, and Reconstruction: Freedmen's Education, 1862–1875.* Westport, CT: Greenwood, 1980.

Crenson, Matthew A. *Building the Invisible Orphanage: A Prehistory of the American Welfare System.* Cambridge, MA: Harvard University Press, 1998.

Hollis, Margaret Belser, and Allen H. Stokes, eds. *Twilight on the South Carolina Rice Fields: Letters of the Heyward Family, 1862–1871.* Columbia: University of South Carolina Press, 2010.

Samito, Christian G., ed. *Changes in Law and Society During the Civil War and Reconstruction: A Legal History Documentary Reader.* Carbondale: Southern Illinois University Press, 2009.

Woodward, C. Vann, ed. *Mary Chesnut's Civil War.* New Haven, CT: Yale University Press, 1981.

Woodworth, Steven E. *The Human Tradition in the Civil War and Reconstruction.* Wilmington, DE: Scholarly Resources, 2000.

Zinn, Howard. *A People's History of the United States: 1492–Present.* New York: HarperCollins, 2003.

A–Z Entries

A

Abolitionism

By the beginning of the Civil War, abolitionism in the United States commandeered a wide array of pacifists, libertarians, and religious supporters in the crusade to end human bondage. Protests among Congregationalists, Mennonites, Methodist Episcopalians, Presbyterians, Quakers, Shakers, Unitarians, and evangelicals focused on the wrongs of profiteering from the flesh trade, propagating slaves as a human crop, buying women for concubines, and trading in slave-made, slave-harvested goods, particularly cane sugar, cotton, indigo, molasses, pharmaceuticals, rice, rum, tea, and tobacco.

Passage of the Fugitive Slave Law of 1850 fomented a decade of hot tempers, but did not halt the self-freeing of runaways. Free blacks—notably Frederick Douglass, John Mercer Langston, Susie King Taylor, Charles Lenox Remond, Martin Robinson Delany, Henry Highland Garnet, Sojourner Truth, Harriet Tubman, and William Wells Brown—challenged the law for violating the most sacred of democratic principles, the rights to habeas corpus and jury trial. In a speech to the U.S. Senate on March 11, 1850, Whig William Henry Seward of New York predicted that the violence of enslavement would give place to the humanity and economy of emancipation, a prophecy he helped make a reality during his service as secretary of state under presidents Abraham Lincoln and Andrew Johnson.

At risk of fortunes and lives, the abolitionist press, an unprecedented development in North American journalism, spawned antislavery newspapers espousing humanitarianism and libertarian principles. By giving voice to black and white journalists and to eyewitness accounts by kidnap victims and former slaves rescued by the Underground Railroad, editors fostered abolitionist sentiment across the nation and beyond its boundaries. Spokespersons for the antislavery movement educated themselves on Underground Railroad philosophy and strategies by reading potent periodicals from different parts of the country, including William Lloyd Garrison's *The Liberator*, an uncompromising voice for liberation that remained in print in Boston for 35 years. A number of other antislavery papers flourished from the 1780s through the Civil War years and beyond.

The libertarian media aired bad news as well as good, including violence in "Bleeding Kansas" during the 1850s and the terrorism of William Clarke Quantrill, a renegade Confederate soldier who sacked Lawrence, Kansas, on August 21, 1863. The adversarial give-and-take between editor and letter writer raised readers' consciousness and built consensus. Readers valued descriptions of opportunities for free blacks in Canada, where some 40,000 runaway slaves made new lives.

The most vocal abolitionists proposed civil disobedience—sabotage, law breaking, riot, murder, race war, and anarchy—to quell the states' rights faction and their prolonging of the Southern plantation system. They denounced President-Elect Abraham Lincoln for his pledge to leave slavery intact. The Massachusetts Anti-Slavery Society published 100,000 emancipation pamphlets annually to appeal to the sensibilities of those undecided on the issue.

The outbreak of the Civil War on April 12, 1861, initiated the collapse of the American bondage system and prompted an outcry for recruiting free blacks to aid the Union's war effort. During the four-year conflict, a half million freed slaves served as blacksmiths, child rescuers, cooks, day laborers, educators, guides, launderers, navigators, nurses, provisioners, scouts, spies, and wagoneers. Bold libertarians demanded the enfranchisement of blacks as citizens. Federal law enforcers halted the slave trade, freed slaves in the District of Columbia, and recognized ambassadors from the black republics of Haiti and Liberia.

On January 1, 1863, President Abraham Lincoln began dismantling the system of purchasing, breeding, and selling slaves by issuing the Emancipation Proclamation. The document declared the freedom of all slaves residing in the ten states still in rebellion against the Union—Alabama, Arkansas, Florida, Georgia, Louisiana, Mississippi, North Carolina, South Carolina, Texas, and Virginia. (The proclamation exempted Tennessee, because its citizens had restored loyalty to the Union.) Abolitionists honored

The Abolitionist Press

Periodical	Founder/Editor	Dates of Publication	Place of Publication
American Freeman	Sherman Miller Booth, Ichabod Codding, William M. Sullivan	1854–1861	Waukesha, Wis.
Anti-Slavery Bugle	Abby Kelley Foster, James Barnaby, Oliver Johnson, Marius Robinson, Benjamin S. Jones	1845–1861	Salem, Ohio
Brooklyn Eagle	Henry C. Murphy, Walt Whitman	1841–1955	Brooklyn, N.Y.
Christian Examiner	Orestes Augustus Brownson	1824–1869	New York City
Christian Recorder	Mother Bethel African Methodist Episcopal Church	1861–1902	Philadelphia
Fredonia Censor	Willard McKinstry	1821–1865	Fredonia, N.Y.
Freedman's Record	John A. Andrew	1865–1866	Boston
Green Mountain Freeman	Daniel P. Thompson, Joseph Poland	1844–1878	Montpelier, Vt.
Harper's Weekly	James Harper	1857–1916	New York City
Hartford Evening Press	Joseph Hawley	1837–1861	Hartford, Conn.
The Independent	Henry Chandler Bowen, Henry Ward Beecher, Theodore Tilton	1848–1861	New York City
Kansas Post	Moritz Pinner	1859–1861	Kansas City, Kans.
The Liberator	William Lloyd Garrison, Isaac Knapp	1831–1865	Boston
Lorain County News	J.F. Harmon, V.A. Shankland	1860–1865	Lorain County, Ohio
Markesan Journal	James Burton Pond, John Parker	1859–1862	Markesan, Wis.
Mercer County Whig	Thomas Jeff Nickum	1851–1866	Mercer, Pa.
Morning Star	Oren Burbank Cheney, William Burr	1826–1865	Limerick, Maine, Dover, N.H.
National Anti-Slavery Standard	David Child, Lydia Maria Francis Child, Sydney Howard Gay, Aaron Powell, Nathaniel P. Rogers	1840–1871	Boston
New York Daily Tribune	Horace Greeley, Sydney Howard Gay	1841–1924	New York City
Northern Independent	William Hosmer	1856–1867	Syracuse, N.Y.
Principia	William Goodell, Lavinia Goodell, George B. Cheever	1852–1864	New York City
True American	James Catlin, Henry Catlin, Martha Van Rensselaer Catlin	1853–1861	Erie, Pa.

Source: Adapted from Mary Ellen Snodgrass, *The Underground Railroad: An Encyclopedia of People, Places, and Operations,* Armonk, NY: M.E. Sharpe, 2008, p. 6–9.

Lincoln as the "Great Emancipator" for his humanity and compassion.

Subsequent measures chipped away at prejudice. Legislation in 1862 allowed blacks to deliver mail, to observe congressional sessions, and, more important, to be sworn in as witnesses in court trials. Several state courts accepted the testimony of black victims. The integration of lectures and public gatherings began quelling myths of black disinterest in civic affairs. In February 1863, H. Ford Douglas composed a letter to *Douglass' Monthly* proposing more self-help opportunities for free blacks to improve their education, practical training, and spirituality.

In 1864, educator Satirra Douglas, an emissary of the Women's Loyal League of Chicago, taught at a freedmen's school in Kansas; Charlotte Forten, who held classes in Sea Island, Georgia, reported in the May and June 1864 issues of the *Atlantic Monthly* that children were progressing with the aid of eager parents. Successful pupils began entering colleges to become the first generation of professionals from plantation slavery.

The Thirteenth Amendment to the U.S. Constitution, adopted in December 1865, acknowledged decades of struggle to eradicate enslavement within the republic, declaring, "neither slavery nor involuntary servitude . . . shall exist within the United States or any place subject to their jurisdiction." Abolitionists, still working toward equality between the races, rechanneled their zeal toward achieving workers' and women's rights, equalizing municipal laws, overcoming poverty and homelessness, promoting temperance, and ending child labor.

See also: Child, Lydia Maria; Douglass, Frederick; Everett, Edward; Quantrill, William; Sojourner Truth; Temperance Movement; Thirteenth Amendment (1865).

Further Reading

Blue, Frederick J. *No Taint of Compromise: Crusaders in Antislavery Politics.* Baton Rouge: Louisiana State University Press, 2005.

Danky, James P., ed. *African-American Newspapers and Periodicals: A National Bibliography.* Cambridge, MA: Harvard University Press, 1998.

Lowance, Mason, ed. *Against Slavery: An Abolitionist Reader.* New York: Penguin, 2000.

Snodgrass, Mary Ellen. *Civil Disobedience: An Encyclopedic History of Dissidence in the United States.* Armonk, NY: M.E. Sharpe, 2009.

———. *The Underground Railroad: An Encyclopedia of People, Places, and Operations.* Armonk, NY: M.E. Sharpe, 2007.

Agassiz, Louis (1807–1873)

Earth scientist and lecturer Jean Louis Rodolphe Agassiz advanced the study of nature through field research. A native of Môtier in Fribourg, Switzerland, he was born on May 28, 1807, and studied at home under his parents, the Reverend Louis Rodolphe Agassiz, a Protestant pastor, and Rose Mayor Agassiz, the daughter of a physician.

After attending high school in Bienne, Agassiz completed his preliminary education at a Lausanne academy before studying biology, botany, and medicine at the universities of Heidelberg, Munich, and Zurich. At age 22, he completed a doctorate at Erlangen, and the next year received his medical degree at Munich.

Agassiz focused on the glaciers and other natural phenomena of the Swiss Alps and the effects of the Ice Age on visible parts of the terrain. He declared that a great convulsion had "modified the surface of our globe, [and] found its surface covered with ice, at least from the North Pole to the Mediterranean and Caspian seas." His mentors, Baron Georges Cuvier and Alexander von Humboldt, directed him toward geology and zoology and a specialty in fresh water fish from the Amazon River in Brazil and from Lake Neuchâtel in Switzerland. Because Agassiz lacked the funds for self-directed research, Humboldt underwrote the Amazon project with a gift of £50.

Agassiz gained renown both as an empiricist and as a teacher. In 1832, he taught natural history at the University of Neuchâtel, where he developed an interest in fossil fish. Using field specimens from Great Britain and Scotland, he published a five-volume illustrated treatise on 1,000 specimens, *Recherches sur les poissons fossiles* (Research on Fossil Fish, 1833–1843).

At age 30, Agassiz delivered an innovative paper on glaciation to the Helvetic Society of Natural History. In 1838, a year after he presented his description of the Ice Age, the Royal Society of London made him a member and awarded him the Copley Medal for scientific achievement.

He subsequently published *Etudes critiques sur les mollusques fossiles* (Critical Studies on Fossil Mollusks, 1840–1845), *Etudes sur les glaciers* (Study on Glaciers, 1840), and *Monographie des poissons fossiles du vieux grès rouge, ou système dévonien* (Monograph on Fossil Fish of the Old Red Sandstone, or Devonian System of the British Isles and of Russia, 1844–1845). Because of his scholarship, the University of Neuchâtel gained a reputation for meticulous research.

American Educator

On a grant from King Frederick William IV of Prussia, Agassiz went to Boston, Massachusetts, in fall 1846 to lecture on zoology at the Lowell Institute and to teach geology and zoology at the Lawrence Scientific School, which opened in 1847 with an emphasis on engineering and applied science. Using vessels of the U.S. Coast Survey, he examined the formation of the Florida reefs. He published *Lake Superior: Its Physical Character, Vegetation, and Animals* (1850), which included a comparison of the region's flora and fauna to that of the Jura Mountains of Switzerland. For the *Christian Examiner,* he issued an origination theory that was consistent with the book of Genesis and its description of a supreme being. A divine intelligence, Agassiz contended, had ordered and harmonized plant and animal species with the physical planet.

In 1852, four forays to Charleston, South Carolina, compromised Agassiz's health with the onset of malaria. Over an eight-year span, cyclical fevers altered his plans to build a permanent marine observation station on the Atlantic Coast.

Agassiz promoted scientific exchanges based on respect for the individual intellect, a perspective that later influenced agronomist Luther Burbank, among others. At Harvard and Cornell universities, Agassiz taught his concept of the uniqueness of nature on the North American continent, which he based on his research into the gar pike, a species limited to the waters of Lake Michigan as far east as Lake Erie, Lake Ontario, and the St. Lawrence Seaway. In 1855, he settled squabbles within the American Association for the Advancement of Science.

Under the mentorship of Harvard University President Edward Everett, Agassiz established research programs leading to graduate degrees and challenged the thinking of naturalist Charles Darwin's landmark text *On the Origin of Species* (1859). Agassiz published four volumes of his *Natural History of the United States* (1857–1862) and the *Essay on Classification* (1857). In 1859, he founded at Cambridge, Massachusetts, the Museum of Comparative Zoology, which featured "Contributions to the Natural History of the United States."

As Agassiz's eyesight began to fail in 1862, he sought a balance between office work and field survey. He preferred studying the Western Hemisphere because few previous studies impinged on the formation of new theory. Upon returning to fieldwork in Brazil in April 1865, which he described in *A Journey in Brazil* (1868), he examined more than 80,000 fish specimens, but found little evidence to support his theory of glaciation in South America. On a tour of Colorado, Iowa, Kansas, Minnesota, Nebraska, Utah, and Wyoming, he exulted in the slabs lining the Platte River Basin. Returning in 1868, Agassiz determined that glacial meltwater had formed the Mississippi, Missouri, and Ohio rivers.

He delivered lectures on geology at the Smithsonian Institution, which he served as regent. To ease his expenses, his second wife, Elizabeth Cabot Cary Agassiz, opened a girl's school for 80 pupils on the upper floor of their home. Both Agassiz and his son, Alexander Agassiz, taught classes there.

Scientist and Organizer

Agassiz enlisted sea captains and woodsmen to provide local specimens for his museum. He explored the Strait of Magellan and joined the U.S. Coast Survey of 1869 and a Coast Guard oceanographic voyage in 1872, two projects involving seafloor dredging around the Western Hemisphere. He catalogued life-forms on Penikese, an island in Buzzards Bay, Massachusetts, that New York merchant John Anderson donated to him along with $50,000 for equipment. Agassiz turned the property and its house and barn into the Anderson School of Natural History, a living laboratory of marine zoology where 50 students engaged with specimens rather than theory.

Agassiz's career left serious questions about his concepts and beliefs, some of which he published in a series for the *Atlantic Monthly.* After his death on December 14, 1873, his theories of racial evolution from separate origins earned criticism for their denigration of black Africans as naturally inferior to whites. With self-assurance, he declared in the form of a rhetorical question, "Have we not . . . the distinct assertion that the Ethiopian can not change his skin nor the leopard his spots?" The biography *Louis Agassiz: His Life and Correspondence,* compiled by Elizabeth Cabot Cary Agassiz, preserves the notable friendships and collaborative traditions that the scientist maintained with the global intellectual community.

See also: Burbank, Luther; Everett, Edward; Yosemite Valley.

Further Reading

Conn, Steven. *Museums and American Intellectual Life, 1876–1926.* Chicago: University of Chicago Press, 2000.

Elliott, Clark A., and Margaret W. Rossiter, eds. *Science at Harvard University: Historical Perspectives.* Bethlehem, PA: Lehigh University Press, 1992.

Irmscher, Christoph. *The Poetics of Natural History from John Bartram to William James.* New Brunswick, NJ: Rutgers University Press, 1999.

Rozwadowski, Helen M. *Fathoming the Ocean: The Discovery and Exploration of the Deep Sea.* Cambridge, MA: Harvard University Press, 2005.

Agriculture

During the agrarian phase of North American development that colonists began in the mid-1600s, farmers broke more virgin land than ever in the course of history. Their efforts on 400 million acres (160 million hectares) fed the country as well as client nations that bought American cotton, grain, meat, tobacco, and such processed foods as Borden's condensed milk, Fleischmann's yeast, and German-style ales. Before the Industrial Revolution, more than half of the U.S. population worked on farms. In Ocala in north-central Florida, the loss of 90 percent of eligible males to military service after April 1861 forced women and children to herd livestock and to superintend the planting, tending, and harvesting of cotton, rice, sugarcane, and tobacco.

To ensure prosperity for some 33 million citizens, President Abraham Lincoln on May 15, 1862, created within the Department of the Interior an independent U.S. Bureau of Agriculture. He appointed experts to salvage and preserve plants and seeds, test seeds from foreign countries, and compile statistics concerning the soil and climatic conditions in which specific crops grew best. The new department took shape at a turning point in national agricultural systems, as the death of slavery and the Southern plantation system made way for the expansion of greenhouse propagation, as well as the proliferation of Western farms, orchards, and cattle and sheep ranches. The bureau's 30 scientists introduced new varieties of plants and livestock, tested farm implements, analyzed soil, answered citizens' agricultural questions, and forecast farm needs.

Land-Grant Colleges

On July 2, 1862, congressional ratification of the Morrill Land-Grant Act authorized federal distribution of 17.4 million acres (7 million hectares) of public land at the prorated acreage of 30,000 (12,150 hectares) per legislator. States lacking public land received parcels on the frontier.

Under the legislation, educators began constructing the original 59 public agricultural and vocational colleges, called land-grant colleges. The first, Iowa State Agricultural College, opened on September 11, 1862. Kansas State University and Massachusetts Agricultural College began construction in 1863. In 1867, educator Samuel Chapman Armstrong, president of Hampton Normal and Agricultural Institute in Norfolk, Virginia, aimed at fostering rudimentary skills in graduates with a two-year program. In 1868, the College of California merged with the Agricultural, Mining and Mechanical Arts College to form the University of California, Berkeley, a leader in higher education in the American West. In 1873, Kansas State Agricultural College opened a department of domestic economy, where department head Nellie Kedzie Jones focused on critical thinking skills for farm wives and other rural women.

Reconstruction Farming

War left the South depleted of cash, stock, seed, and implements and lacking in vigorous farmers and farmhands because of deaths and amputations resulting from combat. In the midlands of South Carolina, following Union General William Tecumseh Sherman's scorched-earth policy of 1864–1865, devastated plantations gave place to 2,246 smallholdings of 10–50 acres (4–20 hectares) each for sharecropping or tenant farming.

Restrictive Black Codes returned freedmen to farm labor and destroyed dreams of a redistribution of wealth. Those seeking property under the Homestead Act of 1862 despaired at the unfit acreage of the West, which bore no resemblance to the lush South. Some freedmen returned to their former masters and accepted tenancy or work for hire. Landlords provided dray animals, implements, and seeds in exchange for toil. Others chose raw land along the Mississippi Valley in Arkansas, Illinois, Iowa, Minnesota, Missouri, and Wisconsin.

To invigorate self-sustaining farms such as those struggling in the South, reformer Oliver Hudson Kelley, a staff member of the Bureau of Agriculture, founded the Grange Movement. In January 1866, at the urging of President Andrew Johnson, Kelley made a postwar fact-finding mission below the Mason-Dixon Line, where tobacco barns, cotton gins, granaries, and sugarhouses lay in ruins and weeds choked the tobacco, corn, rice, and sugarcane fields of a defeated people. As an antidote to a moribund regional agriculture, especially in Alabama and Mississippi, in 1867, Kelley established the Grange cooperative (formally known as the National Grange of the Order of Patrons of Husbandry) in Washington, D.C.

Overall, 89 percent of black farmers maintained Southern residency and continued to work in rural agriculture in a climate and terrain that they understood. In Georgia and the Carolinas, those who could manage a winter operation bolstered profits from cotton and tobacco in the summer with woodlot management and sawmilling in winter. Among Quakers in Guilford County, North Carolina, experimental projects directed by William A. Sampson of Maine received the financial backing of the Baltimore Association of Friends to Advise and Assist Friends in the Southern States. The association sought to halt the outflow of threadbare farmers from the South.

At Swarthmore, a 240-acre (97-hectare) farm, in 1866, Sampson modeled fertilizer mills that pulverized cattle bones, seed barns provided with running water, sanitary poultry houses, and vermin-proof corncribs and granaries. He explained the need for drainage and the use of artificial manure—composed of alfalfa, buckwheat, clover, cowpeas, and vetch—as cover crops to prevent winter soil erosion, suppress weeds, and build up nitrogen in the soil. Within a year, he educated 1,000 visitors to his experimental fields.

Following the Civil War, national production of corn, cotton, and rice rose by 65 percent; grain farmers also profited from intercropping barley, buckwheat, oats, and rye. Wheat became the moneymaker in North Dakota's Red River Valley and Idaho's northern counties and among German, Norwegian, and Swedish immigrants in Eden Prairie, Enfield, and Spring Grove, Minnesota.

Modernizing Techniques

Science and technology assisted the postwar agrarians with cyclical obstacles, particularly drought. In Hawaii in 1861,

King Kamehameha IV experimented with new hybrid rice seed, imported honeybees, and added a waterworks to ensure even distribution of fresh water. Contributing to recruitment efforts on California farms, promoter John W. North distributed leaflets in 1870 enticing farmers to colonize the southern end of the state and to irrigate the plain with canals from the Santa Ana River.

In 1866, Coloradans devised the "Colorado system," a New World approach to water sharing that replaced the English common law concept of riparian (shore) rights, which banned the redirection of streams from their original banks to fields and pastures. In the western part of the state, experiments in alfalfa, bean, beet, and potato fields and pasturage required significant irrigation of dry land. The diversion of natural water flows won the backing of Moses Hallett, chief justice of the Colorado Supreme Court. In 1872, Hallett legitimized the rights of those practicing dry farming without regard to previous ownership of land. The law influenced the adoption of irrigation rights in Arizona, Idaho, Montana, Nevada, New Mexico, Utah, and Wyoming. Litigation over priorities affirmed the states' rights to supervise water distribution, as occurred on the truck farms of Dayton, Nevada, where horticulturists stored water at the surface and underground and earned top dollar for fresh vegetables sold in mining communities.

In Utah, Mormon pioneers diverted mountain streams south along the Wasatch Mountains and founded 400 farm towns in the belief that they could make the desert grow to supply hay and vegetable markets. In October 1873, a convention of nonmineral investors from Kansas, Nebraska, New Mexico, Utah, and Wyoming met with Colorado Governor Samuel Hitt Elbert at Denver to promote congressional aid to Western lands requiring canals and reservoirs for irrigation, the first interstate cooperative seeking drought relief. In New Mexico, the construction of log flumes channeled irrigation water to settlers' fields, turning the San Juan Valley into a prosperous area for grain and stock.

The building of rail lines and reservoirs, John Deere's invention of the steel plow, aerating soil with the straddle-row cultivator and the spring-tooth harrow, plowing with the steam tractor, deep-well drilling, irrigating with windmills, and fencing with Joseph Glidden's barbed wire all increased efficiency and convenience to settlers homesteading in remote areas. As former slaves from the Carolinas and Georgia migrated to the rich soil of the Mississippi Delta, agronomists debated the use of powdered and liquid fertilizers to revitalize depleted soil, a concept still new to farmers. Along the Mississippi Valley, Congress spent vast outlays to prevent unpredictable floodwaters from swamping levees and suppressing agriculture.

In Georgia, acceptance of geological and soil analysis and soil enrichment enabled an all-time cotton bonanza of 726,406 bales in 1870. When Texans joined the cotton-growing South, Maine industrialist William Deering promoted the importation of bales into New England for processing in the region's looms.

As agriculture flourished in the Elkhorn, Platte, and Republican river valleys in Nebraska, farm families weathered disasters, including drought, low crop yields, and prairie fires. William Healey Dall's overview *Alaska and Its Resources* (1870) stressed the value of recognizing and propagating healing plants even on the Alaskan tundra.

In the Great Plains states, insect control demanded immediate attention. An infestation of Rocky Mountain locusts from the Niobrara River to the Republican River Valley on July 13, 1874, fattened chickens, turkeys, and hogs, but destroyed alfalfa, beans, and corn, and apple and peach trees. States issued relief funds after the gnawing insects invaded Colorado, Kansas, and Oklahoma; they chewed cloth and harnesses and devoured carrots, onions, potatoes, and turnips underground. The following spring, Plains farmers set fire to fields to burn out insect eggs. Nature repaid the diligent. In 1875, Midwestern farm ledgers recorded an abundant grain crop.

Cooperative Farming

Farmers learned from industrial laborers the value of collective bargaining and group lobbying. In Sterling, Michigan, the influx of Belgian, British, and German farmers introduced distinct group methods, ranging from cooperative dairying to market farming at Detroit markets. For the citrus and vegetable growers of Orange County, California, railways boosted profits from the rapid distribution of perishable lemons and oranges, apricots, beets, celery, grapes, lima beans, and walnuts. In addition to demanding the regulation of railroad hauling rates and the protection of waterways, Greenback Party members sought more currency in circulation as a boost to low-interest farm loans. Politicians anticipated that inflated farm prices would ease agricultural debts and break the stranglehold that banks and rail barons held over stockmen and cotton and grain dealers.

In 1874, some 1,200 Hutterites began emigrating from Radichev, Russia, to North American farms and ranches that resembled the agrarian landscape of the Steppes. German Russians contributed the dual-purpose dairy and beef cow and the lightweight draft horse. The Dakota

Territory Bureau of Immigration welcomed the original 450 communal immigrants as stabilizers of towns and agriculture. In September 1874, some 1,500 Volga Russian Mennonites purchased 100,000 acres (40,000 hectares) around Topeka, Kansas, and initiated the planting of "Turkey Red" wheat, the hardy winter variety that made Kansas into the nation's breadbasket.

Collective efforts spread success from farm to farm, in part through the reportage of such specialized journals as *American Agriculturist, Chemical Farming, The Country, Farmer's Magazine, Popular Science,* and *Poultry World,* and through monthly and annual reports from the Bureau of Agriculture. In Walla Walla, Washington, the institution of an annual fair in 1870 displayed local success at growing pome fruit and wool and making butter. In 1875, Grangers in Alabama, California, Louisiana, Michigan, Mississippi, and the Carolinas pressed for free agricultural academies to teach technologically advanced farming and livestock breeding methods. Farm members of the American Club in Litchfield, Connecticut, adopted a 24-point standard for purchasing Jersey calves, beginning with a small, lean head and progressing to a serene and malleable nature.

The Illinois and Iowa Grange, a cooperative of 800,000 farmers, chose Montgomery Ward as its purchasing agent and general supply house. The co-op saved members one-third to one-half of the cost of dealing with local merchants. In exchange for Grange patronage, Ward allowed the members a ten-day grace period on cash purchases. In Colorado in 1876, nesters resorted to Grange lobbying to protect smallholders from the domination of beef barons and rail and storage middlemen.

See also: Bureau of Agriculture, U.S.; Cereals and Grains; Home Economics.

Further Reading

Barron, Hal S. *Mixed Harvest: The Second Great Transformation in the Rural North, 1870–1930.* Chapel Hill: University of North Carolina Press, 1997.

Blake, Tupper Ansel, Madeleine Graham Blake, and William Kittredge. *Balancing Water: Restoring the Klamath Basin.* Berkeley: University of California Press, 2000.

Brown, Gary. *Texas Gulag: The Chain Gang Years, 1875–1925.* Austin: Republic of Texas, 2002.

Conlin, Joseph R. *The American Past: A Survey of American History.* 9th ed. Boston: Wadsworth/Cengage Learning, 2009.

Nolen, Claude H. *African American Southerners in Slavery, Civil War, and Reconstruction.* Jefferson, NC: McFarland, 2001.

Sherow, James E. *The Grasslands of the United States: An Environmental History.* Santa Barbara, CA: ABC-CLIO, 2007.

Alaska

In 1861, Alaska consisted of unexplored lands and island clusters under the waning watch of czarist Russia. Up to that time, the country had been largely uninvestigated and unmapped by whites.

In May 1861, Alexandre "Buck" Choquette, a French Canadian prospector from Quebec, tramped north from Victoria, British Columbia, and chartered Tlingit guides to take him north to Wrangell Island, a waterbird habitat rich in forests, peatlands, and muskegs (bogs). Choquette met a Tlingit woman, Georgiana Shakes, and married her in July. Traveling by canoe, his party discovered placer gold (gold found in a flood plain) on September 12 in the Stikine River bed on the Alaska Panhandle north of Ketchikan.

The news of gold increased outside interest in the region. Fortune hunters flocked to the Pacific Northwest in spring 1862, arriving in Stikine Village in British Columbia northeast of the Alaskan border. Miners leaving by water raced prospectors sledding up frozen rivers and streams across the Alaskan frontier to Glenora or to Telegraph Creek, British Columbia.

To prevent lawlessness and to suppress commercial control by the Hudson's Bay Company, British Columbian authorities put the area under the stricter watch of two warships and three gunboats. The brief creation of Stikine Territory extended British jurisdiction over the collection of taxes and duties.

Sir James Douglas, the lieutenant governor of British Columbia, warned travelers from Puget Sound north to the Stikine River of heightened animosity between prospectors and Tsimshian Indians, which the liquor trade worsened. On September 12, 1862, U.S., British, and Russian prospectors boarded the warship HMS *Devastation* to avoid open clashes with Indians. The ship's departure to Sitka on September 14 helped to stabilize the area, but the Alaska Panhandle continued to require policing for the next two years.

Western Union Expedition

By 1865, a single telegraph cable linked Alaska 178 miles (286 kilometers) across the Bering Strait to Siberia. On a grant from President Abraham Lincoln, the Western Union Telegraph Expedition, a three-year engineering survey led by Smithsonian Institution naturalist Major Robert Kennicott, began mapping the coastline from California, Oregon, and Washington Territory north and west along the U.S. border with British Columbia. In early March of that year, the party traveled in an armed flotilla led by the steamers USS *Saginaw* and *George S. Wright* and the flagship *Nightingale,* which previously had transported slaves.

In addition to mapping and other scientific research, the scientists planned to rendezvous that month with a Russian expedition, led by diplomat and engineer Major Serge Abasa, aboard the *Olga.* Their goal was to string telegraph wires 2,800 miles (4,500 kilometers) and connect them with two undersea cables, thereby joining the eastern Pacific Coast with the Amur River in Siberia. To assist the project, Abasa hired 800 aboriginal Yakut laborers, bought 300 packhorses, and bargained with the Lamut of Shelikov Bay to buy reindeer for mounts.

During their meticulous exploration, Major Kennicott's team sent 1,700 biological specimens to the Smithsonian, including one of a new species of owl. At Russian Alaska, he portaged from Norton Sound up the Yukon River to Fort Nulato.

After Kennicott's sudden death on May 3, 1866, at age 31 of congestive heart failure, or possibly strychnine poisoning, the Western Union expedition became the charge of naturalist William Healey Dall, an expert on invertebrates and fish and the party's acting surgeon. Dall identified geological landmarks and provided scientific data on the region and its resources, including mummies and fossils of prehistoric native Alaskans and details on mollusks, the titmouse, and gray and spiked whales.

The corps continued to coastal Siberia aboard the schooner *Nightingale,* captained by Charles Melville Scammon, for whom Scammon Bay, Alaska, is named. Work crews stringing telegraph wire by dogsled crept 400 miles (640 miles) from Quesnel, British Columbia, to the Bulkley River, hampered by frozen ground and late supplies.

U.S. Acquisition

On March 30, 1867, the status of Alaska altered significantly with the signing of a treaty with Russia that extended U.S. jurisdiction to within 500 miles (800 kilometers) of Asia. Days later, Congress and President Andrew Johnson backed the accord and the purchase of Alaska, which enriched the treasury of Czar Alexander II by $7.2 million, a means of covering the cost of the disastrous Crimean War (1853–1856). Brokered by Baron Eduard Andreevich Stoeckl, the Russian ambassador, and U.S. Secretary of State William Henry Seward, the deal prevented future clashes over U.S. expansion across North America.

The negotiators relied on information from Kennicott's associate, Lieutenant Henry Martyn Bannister, who reported to the Smithsonian details of Alaska's weather extremes and natural resources, particularly Eskimo dogs and possible deposits of coal, gold, graphite, and iron. The purchase required the liquidation of seal fur trading and timber cutting by the Russian-American Company, which had dominated commerce from 1821 until the depletion of the sea otter.

At a cost of 2.5 cents per acre, the Alaska Purchase encompassed approximately 586,000 square miles (1.52 million square kilometers), a landmass twice that of Texas, and required political fence-mending between Congress and President Andrew Johnson. Although Alaskans celebrated March 30 as Seward's Day, the media, led by Horace Greeley, editor of the *New York Tribune,* ridiculed the deal as "Polaria," "Seward's Folly," "Seward's Icebox," and "Walrussia."

During the final weeks of debate, Thaddeus Stevens, a Republican congressman from Pennsylvania, argued that the territory offered forests, mines, fishing, and open land for settlement; others proposed that Alaska was a platform from which to cripple the Hudson's Bay Company and to launch anti-British strikes into Canada. Benjamin Franklin Butler, a Democratic congressman from Massachusetts, suggested an alternate plan—that the United States buy Crete instead and free the Mediterranean from incursions by the Turks at half the cost of Alaska. Despite completion of negotiations on April 9, 1867, President Johnson held off payment to Russia for his "Polar Bear Garden" until July 4, 1868.

On October 18, 1867, the day Russian-American Company Governor Dmitri Petrovich Maksutov left office, the U.S. flag replaced the standard of Alexander II on the flagpole on Castle Hill at Fort Sitka, in view of 250 American soldiers. That date, marked by the firing of guns on the U.S. warship *Ossipee* and the withdrawal of 80 Russian troops, became a regional holiday called Alaska Day. The acquisition placed the territory on the Gregorian calendar (replacing the Julian calendar followed by the Russians) and required a westward shift of the International Date Line.

The valuable sealing grounds in the Pribilof Islands came under the control of U.S. Secretary of the Treasury Hugh McCulloch. The harbor at New Archangel (now Sitka) on the Alaska Panhandle broadened American trading opportunities and supported the salmon canning industry. To honor Seward's investment, Charles Ranhofer, master chef at Delmonico's Restaurant in New York City, invented baked Alaska, a dessert of sponge cake topped with ice cream and meringue and broiled to create a hard shell.

U.S. Secretary of State William Henry Seward *(seated at left)* signs the Alaska Purchase treaty with Russia on March 30, 1867. Standing in front of the globe is the Russian minister to the United States, Baron Eduard Stoeckl, who also signed the agreement. *(The Granger Collection, New York)*

The territory passed to governance by the Twenty-third Infantry under Commander Jefferson Columbus Davis. He maintained firm control of native chiefs, whom he treated as naughty children. He ignored complaints from the Tlingit that the land was not for sale to the "Boston men," their term for Americans. When federal supply ships were late, Davis's soldiers bought from Indian vendors berries, birds, fish, and venison, which sold for 50 cents per hindquarter.

On New Year's Eve 1869, Commander Davis stemmed a minor uprising led by Chief Cholckeka and Sitka Jack, who attacked and disarmed a sentry. The crew of the USS *Saginaw* retaliated on January 14–15 by firing on a Kake village on Kuiu Island and torching canoes, houses, and winter food caches. Davis walked to the chief's village, seized Cholckeka by the ear, and yanked him into the guardhouse.

Investigating Opportunities

When funding for the Western Union expedition ended with the collapse of the Russian American telegraph in 1867, William Dall continued independent research until fall 1868. Upon returning to the Smithsonian Institution in Washington, D.C., he began identifying and cataloguing specimens of plants and animals. In addition to lecturing, he issued *Alaska and Its Resources* (1870), which included line drawings of dogsleds, kayaks, and forts and eyewitness accounts of Inuit homes, deer and bear hunting, Yukon fishing, commercially valuable furs, local diseases, and healing plants.

Dall accepted an assignment to the U.S. Coast Survey and until 1874 continued missions on the schooner *Yukon* to the Aleutian Islands to investigate the remains of prehistoric settlements. His collection of echinoderms, fossils, and mollusks passed to Louis Agassiz at the Museum of Comparative Zoology at Harvard University; botanist Asa Gray catalogued plant specimens.

Additional events encouraged a more favorable impression of the Department of Alaska among Americans, including the scaling of the Makushin volcano by George Davidson. Education of native Alaskans began in schools opened in 1867 by Catholic, Congregationalist, Episcopalian, Moravian, Presbyterian, and Swedish Evangelical missions. On September 19, 1868, Thomas G. Murphy, an Irish tailor, launched the first territorial newspaper, the *Sitka Times,* which he issued handwritten for two months before initiating the *Alaska Times.*

In 1870, barter, which included the exchange of gold, fish, and pelts, by the Alaska Commercial Company quickly depleted the fur seal population. Gold discoveries in 1872 lured another wave of fortune hunters to the Alaska Panhandle. In 1874, prospector George Halt pushed across the Chilkoot Pass in search of ore.

General Oliver Otis Howard, commissioner of the Department of the Columbia, visited in early summer 1875 to inspect Puget Sound reservation life of the Neah Bay, Skokomish, Swinomish, and Tulalip and attendant missionaries. At a potlatch, or native giveaway ritual, the general distributed a hundred blankets and returned the body of Chief Fernandeste, a Stickeen leader who had killed himself rather than be imprisoned by whites. Meanwhile, meteorologist Edward William Nelson amassed objects belonging to the Native Americans, which he collected for the Smithsonian and described in *The Eskimo About Bering Strait* (1881).

A strike at Juneau on Windham Bay in 1876 redirected gold hunters farther north. The U.S. Signal Service opened weather stations at Barrow, Sitka, St. Michael, and Unalaska. Amanda Reed McFarland, a widowed Presbyterian educator from Fairmont, West Virginia, opened an academy for 28 native girls in the dance hall at Fort Wrangell.

Because the posting of soldiers to Alaska proved burdensome, pointless, and costly, in March 1877, President Rutherford B. Hayes passed jurisdiction to revenue agents of the Department of the Treasury. The *New York Tribune* reported a savings of $50,000 per year. On the command of Secretary of War George McCrary, the U.S. military began withdrawing from the territory to fight Indians in the West. As the last company departed Sitka in June 1877, cartoonist Thomas Nast pictured the coast lined with laughing polar bears.

See also: Diseases and Epidemics; Howard, Oliver Otis; Seward, William Henry.

Further Reading

Berton, Pierre. *The Klondike Fever: The Life and Death of the Last Great Gold Rush.* New York: Carroll & Graf, 2004.

Black, Lydia T. *Russians in Alaska, 1732–1867.* Fairbanks: University of Alaska Press, 2004.

Conlin, Joseph. *The American Past: A Survey of American History.* 9th ed. Boston: Wadsworth/Cengage Learning, 2009.

Russell, Dick. *Eye of the Whale: Epic Passage from Baja to Siberia.* New York: Simon & Schuster, 2001.

Taylor, John M. *William Henry Seward: Lincoln's Right Hand.* New York: HarperCollins, 1991.

Alcott, Louisa May (1832–1888)

Louisa May "Lu" Alcott, an author who thrived in a literary market dominated by Nathaniel Hawthorne and Herman Melville, was a soft-spoken advocate of abolitionism and woman suffrage. A native of Germantown, Pennsylvania, she was born on November 29, 1832, to social worker Abigail "Abba" May and educator Amos Bronson Alcott.

She spent her childhood at the Wayside, an Underground Railroad safehouse in Sudbury, Massachusetts, where a tunnel connected the main dwelling to a hiding place in a wine house. From her parents and uncle, the Reverend Samuel Joseph May, co-founder of the American Anti-Slavery Society, she learned the concepts of child-centered schools, libertarianism, and civil rights. She later flourished in Boston under the influence of the intellectuals of her day—Ralph Waldo Emerson, Margaret Fuller, Julia Ward Howe, James Russell Lowell, Elizabeth Peabody, and Henry David Thoreau, who was her private tutor.

Alcott remained unmarried and devoted to writing and activism. With her older sister Anna, she worked as a caregiver for the elderly, laundress and housekeeper, seamstress, tutor, memoirist, fiction writer and playwright, and editor of a children's magazine, *Merry's Museum.* Under "L.M. Alcott" and other gender-neutral pen names, she freelanced for the *American Union, Atlantic Monthly, Flag of Our Union, Frank Leslie's Chimney Corner, Peterson's Magazine,* and *The Woman's Journal,* a suffragist publication edited by Lucy Stone. To ensure income for the Alcott family at Orchard House in Concord, Massachusetts, she published a collection of stories titled *Flower Fables* (1854) and a succession of Gothic melodrama and mysteries—*The Marble Woman* (1865), *Moods* (completed in 1865 and published in 1882), *The Abbot's Ghost* (1867), *Behind a Mask* (1875), and *A Modern Mephistopheles* (1877). In addition, she wrote essays on slavery, the boycott of slave-raised or slave-made goods, women's rights, and temperance. In 1878, she became the first Concord woman to register to vote.

Eyewitness Accounts

In August 1863, editor Frank B. Sanborn published in *The Commonwealth* Alcott's popular letters from Union

Hospital, a converted hotel and tavern on Thirtieth Street in Georgetown, D.C., where she volunteered as a ward nurse for the U.S. Sanitary Commission. Alcott found the job a "rough school" for the demands on her strength and for the ague, loneliness, and demise of combat victims arriving on Christmas Day 1862 in 40 ambulances from the Battle of Fredericksburg. Duties in the damp, gangrene-smelling hospital required Alcott to bathe and dose patients, moisten and rebandage wounds, and write notes dictated by soldiers. She admitted, "I indulged in a most unpatriotic wish that I was safe at home again," but she accepted a promotion to night duty and earned a total of $10. With altruistic fervor, Alcott, like poet Walt Whitman, toured Armory Square Hospital at B and Sixteenth streets in Washington, D.C. She questioned the lack of religious services and inquired about an infirmary for black regiments.

After two months of service, early in February 1863, Alcott fell ill with typhoid. Fever reduced her to delirium for three weeks and required the shaving of her brown hair, which she described as a yard and a half long. Treatment of her fever, aching limbs, and ulcerated throat with mercury-laced calomel caused hallucinations and flashbacks, which pursued her on the train ride home through New York. When her strength returned, she wrote the Gothic novel *Pauline's Passion and Punishment* (1862), published under the pseudonym A.M. Barnard. She serialized her wartime letters in *Commonwealth,* and compiled them in *Hospital Sketches* (1863), a first-person report of combat wounds and disease.

In the proto-feminist treatise *Moods* (1882), she urged women to take charge of their destiny: "The duty we owe ourselves is greater than that we owe [others]," she wrote. In "Transcendental Wild Oats" (1873), issued in *The Independent,* Alcott denounced the diminution of female labor at the utopian commune at Fruitlands near Harvard, where the Alcotts struggled against penury for six months and women served as beasts of burden. Alcott ridiculed the failed haven by turning "Fruitlands" into the pun "apple slump."

Author and activist Louisa May Alcott is best known for her classic children's novel *Little Women* (1868–1869), a warm depiction of middle-class life in New England. Alcott also campaigned for abolition, women's rights, temperance, and aid to the poor. *(Hulton Archive/Stringer/Getty Images)*

Proto-Feminist

Alcott attained stature as a classic writer of domestic literature with the autobiographical novels *Little Women* (1868–1869) and *Good Wives* (1869), which glimpsed female empowerment. Her works appealed to philanthropist Sophia Smith, the founder of Smith College, one of the nation's largest colleges for women.

By age 37, Alcott found herself enriched by royalties but weakened by arthritis and exhaustion. Through the characterization of Margaret "Marmee" March, a pacifist and head of household while her husband served as a chaplain to Union forces, *Little Women* valorized mothers as advocates of volunteerism and physical exercise for girls and as conduits of culture, character, and spirituality. Protagonist Jo March, Alcott's alter ego, and her siblings Amy, Beth, and Meg prefigure a stout feminism tempered with sisterhood, self-sacrifice, and compassion. Alcott continued her woman-centered bent with *An Old-Fashioned Girl* (1870), *Little Men* (1871), and *Eight Cousins,* which was issued serially from February 1874 to November 1875 in *Good Things* and from January to October 1875 in *St. Nicholas.* The latter provided insight into New England family life, morality, and the home training and education of girls during and after the Civil War.

In the antebellum era, Alcott acknowledged the similarity between misogyny and racism. She foresaw equality and social justice in women's lives through female cooperation and mutual respect. In *Work: A Story of Experience* (1873), she noted the degrees of idealism in "eager women just beginning their protest against the wrongs that had wrecked their peace; subdued women who had been worsted in the unequal conflict and given it up; resolute women with 'No surrender' written all over their strong-minded countenances." In the sequel, *Beginning Again* (1875), female characters grow and prosper in careers that offer financial independence and in relationships with men that precede satisfying lives as wives and mothers.

In 1877, Alcott actualized her principles by joining physician Harriet Winifred Clisby, Unitarian teacher Abby Morton Diaz, reformer Mary Thorn Lewis Gannett, and writer Julia Ward Howe in founding the Women's Educational and Industrial Union. The outreach organization offered employment, medical care, and legal aid to poor female laborers.

Alcott died in Boston on March 6, 1888, from mercury poisoning and overwork. More than a century later, in 1995, her long novel *A Long Fatal Love Chase* was published for the first time. Film versions of *Little Women, Little Men, Jo's Boys, The Inheritance,* and *An Old-Fashioned Thanksgiving* continue to entertain audiences.

See also: Abolitionism; Smith, Sophia; Stone, Lucy.

Further Reading

Clark, Beverly Lyon, ed. *Louisa May Alcott: The Contemporary Reviews.* Cambridge, UK: Cambridge University Press, 2004.

Keyser, Elizabeth Lennox. *Whispers in the Dark: The Fiction of Louisa May Alcott.* Knoxville: University of Tennessee Press, 1993.

McMillen, Sally. *Seneca Falls and the Origins of the Women's Rights Movement.* New York: Oxford University Press, 2008.

Snodgrass, Mary Ellen. *Encyclopedia of Feminist Literature.* New York: Facts on File, 2006.

American Flag

The flag of the United States first flew as the Continental Colors on January 1, 1776, at the order of General George Washington, leader of the Continental army. A symbol of unity for all patriots, the national banner replaced a variety of regimental colors. A contrast of alternating red and white horizontal stripes and an inset copy of the rectangular British Union Jack in the upper-left corner, it fluttered from a staff at Prospect Hill during the colonists' siege on the British at Boston, Massachusetts. Navy Captain John Paul Jones flew the colors, also known as the Grand Union Flag, on December 2, 1775, from the staff of the man-of-war *Alfred* while it rode at anchor in Philadelphia Harbor. The needlework was that of Margaret Manny, a milliner and professional flag maker in Philadelphia, who stitched the banner for the Continental navy. General Washington continued brandishing the colors throughout the American Revolution.

On May 5, 1861, four weeks after the onset of the Civil War, antislavery propagandist Lydia Maria Child celebrated Union enthusiasm for the flag in a letter to a friend. Because the nation continued to support slavery, she doubted the reality of universal democracy for women and nonwhite citizens. Of the Stars and Stripes, she noted, "I should so delight in having it thoroughly worthy of being honored." But the return of runaways to the overseer's lash under the Fugitive Slave Law of 1850 robbed her of reverence for Old Glory: "When such things are done under the U.S. flag, I cannot and I will not say, 'God bless it!'" In anguish at the injustice of human bondage, she cursed the banner and wished, "May it be trampled in the dust, kicked by rebels, and spit upon by tyrants!"

The addition of a circle of stars in place of the Union Jack honored the 13 colonies. The new design featured alternating red and white stripes—seven red and six white—and centered a constellation of 13 five-pointed stars on a field of royal blue, the standard artistic symbol of loyalty.

Legend recognizes 24-year-old Elizabeth Griscom "Betsy" Ross, a widowed flag maker and upholsterer, as the seamstress chosen to actualize a design sketched by General Washington and two signers of the Declaration of Independence, merchant Robert Morris, Jr., and Colonel George Ross, both of Pennsylvania. An alternate legend declares Congressman Francis Hopkinson of New Jersey as the designer of the first "Stars and Stripes," which flew on naval staffs and in front of federal buildings. Whichever story predominates, the American flag became a beacon of unity and pride and an embodiment of a nation's self-image.

In proof of the banner's historic use, artists John Singleton Copley, Emanuel Gottlieb Leutze, Charles Willson Peale, John Trumbull, and Charles H. Weisberger pictured the "Betsy Ross flag" fluttering on ships' ensigns and flagstaffs and carried by Washington's color guard. The Second Continental Congress legitimized the design with a resolution passed on June 14, 1777, the nation's first Flag Day. The first official display marked the siege of Fort Schuyler, New York, the following August 3, when American soldiers sewed strips of sheets and red cloth to a blue rectangle cut from Captain Abraham Swarthout's cloak. On September 11, 1777, marching soldiers again unfurled the national flag during the Battle of the Brandywine to halt British General William Howe's advance up the Chesapeake Bay toward Philadelphia.

During the Civil War, the Stars and Stripes became an icon of hope to Unionists and a bitter reminder to Southerners of the country they had deserted in the name of slavery and states' rights. Although the U.S. flag remained unchanged by the illegal secession of Southern states from the Union, beginning on March 4, 1861, a month before the rebel attack on Fort Sumter, South Carolina, Southern leaders demanded a unique banner for the Confederate States of America. Ironically, secessionists maintained the spirit, colors, and basic design of the U.S. flag. For 11 weeks, the first rebel colors, known as the "Stars and Bars," featured a horizontal field divided into thirds, with two red stripes separated by a white stripe. Centering a blue field in the upper left was a circle of seven stars, denoting the states that led the defection from the Union.

In the coming weeks, the withdrawal of additional Southern states from the Union increased the number of stars on the Confederate flag to 9, 11, and finally 13. (The 13-star flag reflected the Confederacy's claim that the border states of Kentucky and Missouri had joined their union.) On May 1, 1863, the shift to a white banner with a red field in the upper-left corner featured an X of blue lined with white and dotted with 13 regularly spaced white stars. With more imaginative variants, individual states saluted states' autonomy, a central issue of the Civil War.

In Nashville, Tennessee, master mariner William Driver, captain of the ship *Old Glory,* concealed a large American flag by sewing it into a comforter. The banner remained out of sight of Confederate confiscators until the seizure of Nashville by the Sixth Ohio Regiment on February 25, 1862, when Old Glory flew from the spire of the state capitol.

As the nation reunited and granted statehood to more Western territories, the flag's blue field exhibited an increasing number of stars. By July 4, 1861, the addition of Kansas to the Union produced a five-row star display featuring 34 stars distributed in the pattern 7–7–6–7–7:

Two years later on the Fourth of July, the separation of West Virginia as a state apart from Virginia evened the rows to five horizontals, comprised of seven stars each:

Later flag alterations required more mathematical variance of the rows. When Nevada, the thirty-sixth state, joined the Union, the 1865 flag changed the row distribution to 8–6–8–6–8:

A Boston-based weekly, *The Youth's Companion,* launched the American Flag Movement of 1888. The high-minded staff elevated banner display to a gesture of reverence and loyalty to country. The magazine staff sold American flags to 26,000 public schools with the aim of promoting patriotism in the younger generation. On September 8, 1892, in an article on Columbus Day, Francis Julius Bellamy, a Baptist minister and freelance writer, proposed the first draft of the Pledge of Allegiance.

With the addition of Nebraska in 1867, the pattern changed to 8–7–7–7–8, for a total of 37 stars:

For the American centennial in 1876, presentations of the flag on buildings and monuments reinvigorated patriotic ideals and respect for U.S. history. After ten years as the official emblem, the admission of Colorado as the thirty-eighth state on July 4, 1877, resulted in an asymmetric spread of 8–7–8–7–8:

The pattern remained the same for the next 13 years, until 1890, when the addition of Idaho, Montana, North Dakota, South Dakota, and Washington required a more complex pattern of 43 stars in six rows, 8–7–7–7–7–7:

Further Reading

Guenter, Scot M. *The American Flag, 1777–1924: Cultural Shifts from Creation to Codification.* Rutherford, NJ: Fairleigh Dickinson University Press, 1990.

Leepson, Marc. *Flag: An American Biography.* New York: Thomas Dunne/St. Martin's, 2005.

Marvin, Carolyn, and David W. Engle. *Blood Sacrifice and the Nation: Totem Rituals and the American Flag.* Cambridge, UK: Cambridge University Press, 1998.

American Society for the Prevention of Cruelty to Animals

The nation's first effort to protect animals from wanton hurt, the American Society for the Prevention of Cruelty to Animals (ASPCA) is the oldest animal welfare agency in America. On April 10, 1866, playwright Henry Bergh established the society in New York City, modeling its purpose and outreach on that of England's Royal Society for the Prevention of Cruelty to Animals.

During service to President Abraham Lincoln on a diplomatic mission to Russian Czar Alexander II, Bergh cringed at the abuse of horses in St. Petersburg. With the aid of Unitarian minister Henry Whitney Bellows, Bergh crusaded for the rest of his life on behalf of creatures tormented in cockfights, dogfights, and rat- and bear-baiting or tortured in slaughterhouses and circuses. Bergh's lecture at New York's Clinton Hall on February 8, 1866, presented statistics on animal suffering. The protest preceded the chartering of his organization and the circulation of a moral petition entitled "Declaration of the Rights of Animals."

Bergh tapped into widespread sentiment on issues of animal rights to humane care. Backing him were such prominent citizens as businessman John Jacob Astor III, newspaper editor Horace Greeley, and New York City Mayor Charles Godfrey Gunther.

Echoing Bergh's concepts, criminologist George Thorndike Angell, Boston's "Friend of Animals," proposed to raise public consciousness about human disrespect toward their bestial servants and companions, particularly racehorses. For the sake of public education, Angell edited and published the magazine *Our Dumb Animals* beginning in 1868; in the same year, he formed the Massachusetts Society for the Prevention of Cruelty to Animals.

Anticruelty Laws

On April 19, 1866, passage in New York State of the nation's first anticruelty legislation precipitated efforts by the first three ASPCA members to enforce the law, which protected only cattle, horses, oxen, and sheep. Members established headquarters at Broadway and Twelfth Street and quickly amassed donations.

Flashing a special badge, Bergh earned the nicknames "Animal Cop" and the "Great Meddler" for intervening in public episodes of horse lashing in traffic jams on Fifth Avenue. He drew crowds of both hecklers and supporters for emptying a butcher's van overloaded with stacks of live animals and for forcing stockmen to milk cows with distended udders. In 1871, after halting an overloaded horsecar before the team collapsed from exhaustion, Bergh caused a traffic jam until the company replaced the two-horse team with four fresh horses. During one stroll through the city, Bergh forced workmen to release a cat they had walled up in a newly constructed building as a form of amusement. In 1872, Bergh received support from Colonel William Babcock Hazen, a U.S. Army officer in the Civil War and Indian Wars, for protection of the buffalo in Kansas, where capricious slaughter endangered their survival.

Bergh carried his arrests through litigation, fining, and sentencing. In May 1866, he arrested a Florida boatman for carrying a live cargo of turtles pierced through the flippers with strings and forced to lie on their backs. Supporting Bergh's charge in court, the famed Harvard naturalist Louis Agassiz declared the transport an act of torture. In summer 1867, Bergh delivered a speech to 3,000 animal rights advocates in Putnam County, Florida, on "Our Dumb Chattels." Among his specifics of unnecessary harm, he named the use of dogs as dray animals, of primates in painful laboratory tests, and of live pigeons for target practice.

Thomas Nast, cartoonist for *Harper's Weekly,* ridiculed Bergh's efforts with satires of the rescuer insisting on winter coats and hats for animals and of Bergh intervening in a gorilla's tearful complaint about the defamation of primates in Charles Darwin's *On the Origin of Species.* Nast and his fellow caricaturists mocked Bergh for proposing fire escapes for animals and dubbed him the "Friend of the Brutes" and the "Moses of the ASPCA."

Systematic Intervention

Animal welfare workers focused on at-risk dogs, cats, and poultry and offered rewards for the apprehension of poisoners of animals. Members promoted animal adoption and ran an ambulance service from 1867 to rescue aged, sick, lashed, and injured dray horses left to die on the streets from exposure and starvation. In response to activists, New York City installed ten horse-watering fountains to protect carriage and van teams from dehydration and heat exhaustion. Guardians of the watering sites gathered evidence of need by counting the people, horses, mules, and dogs that drank from the troughs. ASPCA members denounced the salting of streets during icy weather due to the effect of salts on animals, devised a sling for saving horses from drowning at excavation sites, and operated a dispensary for medical care, where anesthetists eased suffering. Also in 1867, members reported the imprisonment of a man for bludgeoning a cat to death.

Bergh extended his campaign with legal prohibition of feeding cattle on distillery by-products called "swill milk," horse singeing and tail docking, vivisection, and the dipping of live fowl into boiling water for plucking elegant plumes for the hat industry. In curbside harangues, he arraigned coachmen who drove nails into horses' heads and who harnessed them with barbed or spiked bit-guards. In Union Square during blizzards, he turned back stagecoaches to save horse teams from floundering in snow.

When Bergh pressed his case in the U.S. Congress in 1873 for anticruelty laws covering interstate transportation, he sought the blanketing of horses carried on ferries and agitated for the feeding, watering, and exercising of livestock left in rail yards for extended periods. Unexpectedly, he found support from railroad laborers who protested the overcrowding of livestock cars. He spread his views on animal rights to lecture halls in Buffalo,

Chicago, Cincinnati, Cleveland, Columbus, Louisville, St. Louis, and Toledo and to an exhibit at the 1876 centennial celebration in Philadelphia.

Within two decades, the concept of a volunteer rescue agency for animals spread to 37 of the 38 states and to the cities of Boston, San Francisco, and Washington, D.C. ASPCA members employed constables to protect animals in markets, piers, and streets and publicized the result of court trials against flagrant animal abusers. The group distributed tracts to individual cabmen, carters, coachmen, and drovers and provided instructions to classrooms on pet care and the protection of wild bird nests and eggs.

In 1875, Bergh and attorney Elbridge Thomas Gerry expanded their mission of mercy with the formation of the Massachusetts Society for the Prevention of Cruelty to Children. At the urging of Methodist missionary Etta Angell Wheeler, Bergh interceded in the torment of Mary Ellen Wilson, a ten-year-old living barefoot in a New York City slum who had endured beatings, imprisonment in a dark room, ragged clothes, and a starvation diet while under the care of foster parents, Francis and Mary Connolly. After the girl's rescue on April 9, 1875, a court sentenced Mary Connolly to a year in jail. The case initiated the nation's child protection movement.

See also: Agassiz, Louis.

Further Reading

Beers, Diane L. *For the Prevention of Cruelty: The History and Legacy of Animal Rights Activism in the United States.* Athens: Ohio University Press, 2006.

Isenberg, Andrew C. *The Destruction of the Bison: An Environmental History, 1750–1920.* Cambridge, UK: Cambridge University Press, 2000.

Shamoo, Adil E., and David B. Resnik. *Responsible Conduct of Research.* New York: Oxford University Press, 2009.

Warren, Wilson J. *Tied to the Great Packing Machine: The Midwest and Meatpacking.* Iowa City: University of Iowa Press, 2007.

Anthony, Susan B. (1820–1906)

An agitator for gender equality, Susan Brownell Anthony put a public face on the early women's rights movement in America. A native of West Grove outside Adams, Massachusetts, she was born on February 15, 1820, to Quaker abolitionists Lucy Read, a women's rights advocate, and Daniel Anthony, a stern cotton manufacturer.

> Susan B. Anthony challenged concepts of child rearing that forced females to be submissive. In her address "Woman: The Great Unpaid Laborer" (1848), she asserted that females learned from birth to avoid aggressive roles: "Taught that a low voice is an excellent thing in woman, she has been trained to a subjugation of the vocal organs, and thus lost the benefit of loud tones and their well-known invigoration of the system."

In 1826, the family moved to Battenville, New York. Because of gender prejudice at the elementary school Susan attended, her father homeschooled her before boarding her at Deborah Moulson's Female Seminary in Philadelphia. At the Quaker meetinghouse, Anthony recognized that women worshipped equally with men but lacked opportunities in the secular world.

At age 19, she taught at Eunice Kenyon's Friends' Seminary in New Rochelle, New York, and for two years at the Canajoharie Academy in Amsterdam, New York, where she was promoted to headmistress. By age 28, she was a member of the Daughters of Temperance and an accomplished platform speaker. She contended that girls came of age without proper physical education.

A sober, clear-thinking reformer, Anthony set the tone for the suffrage movement by wearing a dark bonnet over a tight coil of hair at the nape and dark dresses edged in white collars and cuffs. In 1851, she partnered with idealogue Elizabeth Cady Stanton to champion temperance and to stimulate suffrage sympathies in Syracuse, New York. Beginning in 1852, Anthony addressed every subsequent National Woman's Rights Convention.

While remaining at home to rear her seven children, Stanton culled newspaper editorials, letters, and speeches for facts and opinions to undergird Anthony's addresses, which she delivered at the rate of nearly 100 annually at rallies, seminars, assembly halls, auditoriums, and street pulpits. Against the mores of the day, Anthony packed her alligator satchel and risked public humiliation and censure by traveling alone to venues by horse, stage, carriage, and river steamer.

Abolitionism and Suffrage

A member of the antislavery hierarchy, which included editor and speaker Frederick Douglass, lecturer Abby Kelley

Foster, and Boston philanthropist William Lloyd Garrison, Anthony joined the American Anti-Slavery Society in 1856 to coordinate its New York operations. She accepted as inevitable the long crusade for gender equality. From 1861 to 1865, she and Stanton joined the Grimké sisters, Angelina and Sarah, and Underground Railroad agent Harriet Tubman in an antislavery crusade that introduced them to grassroots political negotiation. On May 14, 1863, Anthony and Stanton met with Lucy Stone and other female abolitionists at the Church of the Puritans in New York City to launch the Women's National Loyal League, the first national women's political organization in America. Members collected 400,000 signatures on petitions demanding ratification of the Thirteenth Amendment to the U.S. Constitution to end human bondage and requesting relief for hardships faced by the families of Union soldiers.

In December 1866, at the New York City equal rights convention at the Cooper Institute, Anthony demanded impartiality and universality in the public forum. In 1868, with a donation of $4,000 from her cousin, Quaker philanthropist Anson Elisha Lapham, Anthony published *The Revolution,* a women's empowerment periodical edited by Parker Pillsbury and Stanton to generate discussion of gender issues. To support the expensive project, Anthony began a six-year circuit of public addresses to retire a debt of $10,000.

Returning to the suffrage movement in 1867, Anthony, accompanied by Stanton, the Reverend Olympia Brown, Lucy Stone, and Lucy's husband, Henry Brown "Harry" Blackwell, concentrated on securing female enfranchisement in Kansas by raising 9,000 votes for female suffrage. Anthony carried the campaign for state suffrage to eight other states. She opposed passage of the Fifteenth Amendment on the grounds that it perpetuated the dominance of males in government and public life by giving black men the ballot. During rallies in Portland, Oregon, Brown retreated from the catcalls and egg throwing that assaulted local suffragist Abigail Scott Duniway, publisher of the *New Northwest.* While speaking in Salt Lake City in Utah Territory in 1871, Anthony denounced Mormon polygamy, which placed one husband at the head of multiple wives and their children for domestic, religious, and financial support. On a second visit to the city, she applauded Mormon women for urging Utah lawmakers to include woman suffrage in the state constitution.

Confronting the Law

Anthony's demands for full citizenship rights invited arrest. The event followed the attempted voter registration on October 15, 1872, of Virginia Louisa Minor of St. Louis, Missouri. Attorneys Henry Rogers Selden and John Van Voorhis counseled Anthony on Victoria Claflin Woodhull's "New Departure Strategy," which held that, under the Fourteenth and Fifteenth amendments, women had the right to vote. On November 1, Anthony, her sisters—Mary Stafford Anthony, Guelma Penn Anthony McLean, and Hannah Lapham Anthony Mosher—and Rhoda DeGarmo sought the Eighth Ward polling place at a barbershop and coerced the registrars to grant them voting privileges. After registering in their home precinct, the five activists enlisted 50 more local women to do the same. On November 4, the *Rochester Union and Advertiser* called for the arrest and prosecution of the women and the registrars. The following day, Anthony cast her ballot.

On November 18, 1872, a U.S. marshal arrested Anthony and other suffragists for violating the Enforcement Act, which carried a penalty of three years in jail or $500. Anthony confided to Stanton that she had voted straight Republican and that the newspapers had turned the event into an all-winter battle. The officer declined to shackle her wrists, which she extended voluntarily, and escorted her to jail by horsecar. Fifteen lawbreakers appeared at the Madison County Courthouse for judgment:

Charlotte Bolles "Lottie" Anthony, teacher, 31

Mary Stafford Anthony, teacher, 45

Susan B. Anthony, orator, 52

Ellen S. Baker, teacher

Nancy M. Chapman, 22

Hannah M. Chatfield, seamstress, 63

Jane M. Cogswell, 69

Rhoda DeGarmo, activist, 74

Mary S. Hebard, activist

Susan M. Hough, 53

Margaret Leora Garrigues Leyden, 31

Guelma Penn Anthony McLean, housewife, 54

Hannah Lapham Anthony Mosher, housewife, 51

Mary Elizabeth Miller Pulver, 44

Sarah Cole Truesdale, housewife, 35

On December 23, Judge Ward Hunt set bail at $1,000 for Anthony as the instigator and $500 for the other female voters. To spare his client jail time, Selden paid bail.

According to a dramatic court record, *The Trial of Susan B. Anthony* (1874), at a presentencing hearing on June 17, 1873, Anthony lectured the audience and the media at Canandaigua Court House for one hour on the oppression of female citizens. To Judge Hunt, she lobbed a general remonstrance: "Robbed of the fundamental privilege of citizenship, I am degraded from the status of a citizen to that of a subject." The judge read a prepared statement finding her guilty. In hopes of carrying her case to the U.S. Supreme Court, Anthony refused to pay a $100 fine, which the court declined to collect.

Undaunted in her crusade, Anthony advocated women's equality in California, the Dakotas, Michigan, and Wyoming. In Denver, Colorado, she gained the support of Governor John Long Routt, whose wife, Eliza Franklin Pickerell Routt, became the state's first registered female voter. In prepared addresses, Anthony charged that the preamble to the Constitution promised the blessings of liberty to "we the people," yet offered them only to men. Scornful newspaper cartoons demeaned Anthony as a "husbandette" brandishing an umbrella against cowering males. The New York *Daily Graphic* pictured her striking a belligerent pose and wearing Uncle Sam's stovepipe hat.

Raising Public Awareness

As public opinion began to favor gender equity, Anthony co-authored the "Declaration of Rights for Women," which Stanton delivered at the Centennial Exposition in Philadelphia on July 4, 1876. The same day, Anthony and Matilda Joslyn Gage interrupted officials honoring the signing of the Declaration of Independence in Philadelphia.

In collaboration with Stanton and Gage, Anthony met at Stanton's home in Tenafly, New Jersey, to sort clippings, letters, notes, and speeches from international assemblies. They transformed the material into the first three volumes of the six-volume *History of Woman Suffrage* (1881–1922).

In 1877, Anthony's panegyric "Homes of Single Women" declared that women were justified in choosing to remain single rather than subject themselves to male tyranny. She added that the stable lives and efficient residences of single women proved them capable of homemaking for themselves. In the speech "Woman Wants Bread, Not the Ballot!" delivered in major American cities from 1870 to 1880, Anthony pointed out that 3 million American women supported themselves. She blamed the teaching profession for offering women degrading salaries and for elevating men to positions as headmasters, supervisors, superintendents, and school board members.

At age 72, Anthony presided over the National American Woman Suffrage Association, a position she held for 23 years. Upon Stanton's sudden death in New York from heart failure on October 28, 1902, Anthony wrote to newspaperwoman Ida Husted Harper on the end of the partnership: "Well, it is an awful hush—it seems impossible—that the voice is hushed." Without her colleague and speechwriter, Anthony spent four years alone rallying for political and social justice.

Before her death of pneumonia and cardiac disease on March 13, 1906, at age 86, Anthony directed her sister to leave fellow suffragist Anna Howard Shaw in charge of her savings, which Shaw pledged to the suffrage cause. Her followers wielded Anthony's life motto, "Failure is impossible." Upon ratification of the Nineteenth Amendment in August 1920, the media proclaimed the measure the "Anthony amendment." In 1979, the U.S. government recognized her selfless work with a new dollar coin, making her the first woman pictured on the nation's currency.

See also: Brown, Olympia; Gage, Matilda Joslyn; Stanton, Elizabeth Cady.

Further Reading

DuBois, Ellen Carol, ed. *Elizabeth Cady Stanton, Susan B. Anthony: Correspondence, Writings, Speeches.* New York: Schocken, 1981.

Gordon, Ann D., ed. *The Selected Papers of Elizabeth Cady Stanton and Susan B. Anthony.* 5 vols. New Brunswick, NJ: Rutgers University Press, 1997–2009.

Snodgrass, Mary Ellen. *Encyclopedia of Feminist Literature.* New York: Facts on File, 2006.

Wellman, Judith. *The Road to Seneca Falls: Elizabeth Cady Stanton and the First Woman's Rights Convention.* Urbana: University of Illinois Press, 2004.

Arizona

Arizona occupied prize territory between California and Texas and incurred an expansive Indian war over occupancy by Americans. The United States bought 9,000 square miles (23,300 square kilometers) of land in lower Arizona from Mexico for $10 million on July 25, 1853, by the terms of the Gadsden Purchase. President Franklin Pierce negotiated the deal to secure a southwestern rail route from Texas to San Diego, California. The purchase allotted Mexican land north of the Gila River to the United States and gave the Americans control of valuable copper deposits discovered in August 1854 at Ajo.

In 1856, citizens of western New Mexico Territory petitioned the U.S. Congress to separate them as Arizona Territory. President James Buchanan dispatched General Edward Fitzgerald "Ned" Beale to survey the expanse and to build the 1,000-mile (1,600-kilometer) Beale Wagon Road to aid immigrants journeying from Fort Defiance, New Mexico, to the Arizona–California border. Beale completed the task with the aid of 25 pack camels purchased in Tunis, providing pioneers adequate water along a level passage west.

More traffic crisscrossed the desert land twice weekly in 1858 with the extension of the Butterfield Overland Mail Route from Dragoon Springs through a main stop for beans and jerky at Tucson, the local headquarters. Storekeepers, butchers, and transporters prospered by supplying miners, soldiers, wagon trains, and Indian agencies. The Reverend William Henry Bacon arrived from St. Louis and opened a church and restaurant in Tucson.

At the same time, the growth of the Southwest presented the Eastern states with the problem of expanded slavery along the Mexican border. In facing the dilemma, President Abraham Lincoln chose the future admission of Arizona and New Mexico as slave states rather than see the Union disintegrate.

Autonomy

Arizonans met in Tucson in July 1860 to draft a state constitution, electing Granville Henderson Oury as their congressional delegate and physician Lewis Sumpter Owings as the provisional governor. Because of the area's proslavery leanings, Congress rejected Arizona's initial bid for statehood. On March 16, 1861, secessionists led by Confederate Colonel John Robert Baylor formally claimed the Territory of Arizona, which was still part of the vast, unwieldy New Mexico Territory. On August 1, he issued a proclamation identifying Arizona as part of the Confederacy and naming himself governor.

The onset of the Civil War on April 12, 1861, circumvented the immediate completion of a rail line and gave the Confederacy a route to the Pacific Coast and to a pro-South population in Southern California. The Union army curtailed service by the Overland Mail and abandoned forts in Arizona for battlefields in the east. Arizonans created their own law enforcement system until the opening of Fort Lowell in Tucson in 1866.

A triumph for the Confederacy, the formal proclamation of Arizona Territory in July 1861 coordinated citizens' pro-South efforts with those of Mesilla, the capital of New Mexico. Chiricahua Apache raiders took advantage of the absence of army patrols to oust settlers from the land. Colonel Baylor used liquor as a means of overcoming warriors, slaughtering villages, and kidnapping Apache children for enslavement. Confederate President Jefferson Davis disapproved of Baylor's savagery and, in 1862, stripped him of his rank.

The Arizona Rangers, 75 mounted frontiersmen commanded by Confederate Captain Sherod Hunter, headquartered at Tucson along the Butterfield Overland Mail Route and remained a rebel regiment until surrendering eight weeks after the fall of the Confederacy. Rangers fought off the California Column, Colonel James Henry Carleton's Union forces from Fort Yuma, and restored federal jurisdiction. The Arizona troops also attempted to exterminate the Chiricahua, Pinal, and White Mountain Apache by luring Chief Mangas Coloradas into captivity under a flag of truce and murdering and decapitating him. The loss of Mangas left at large Cochise, who wreaked terror on Arizona citizens.

To secure federal interests, the U.S. Army built Fort Bowie in July 1862. From January 6 to 22, 1864, Colonel Christopher "Kit" Carson led the 20-day Long Walk of the Navajo across central New Mexico toward Fort Sumner, forcing 9,000 Indians south through Four Corners—the geographic union of Arizona, Colorado, New Mexico, and Utah—and Canyon de Chelly and east to Bosque Redondo, New Mexico.

In May 1864, Arizona's first U.S. marshal, Milton B. Duffield, compiled the territory's first census. Subsequent demographics attest to the rapid growth of Arizona, with the population of Tucson increasing from 670 in 1860 to 3,224 by 1870. Boosting business and outside communications with the world was the first postwar mail delivery from California, which arrived at Tucson on September 1, 1865, and mail from the east, which the Barlow-Sanderson Overland Mail Company began delivering on August 24, 1866.

To suppress Indian attacks on stagecoaches, the California Column gave way to regular army patrols from Forts Apache, Mohave, Verde, and Whipple, which memoirist Martha W. Dunham Summerhayes described in *Vanished Arizona* (1908), an army wife's reflection on desert savagery.

Money-Making Prospects

As the Indian Wars raged in the mid-1800s, entrepreneurs began developing businesses in structures left from eras of Spanish and Mexico occupation. An English immigrant named Phillip Darrell Duppa partnered in ranching with John William "Jack" Swilling, a teamster for the Overland Mail and a prospector for gold near the Hassayampa Lynx Creek. Swilling joined the Gila Rangers, a vigilante company that guarded stage routes and protected miners against Cochise, Mangas Coloradas, and their Chiricahua Apache raiders.

At Pinos Altos, Swilling formalized the Arizona Rangers, a militia that later merged with the Confederate army. In 1863, he codified the first laws for the territorial capital at Prescott and for the Yavapai County mining district. Five years later, Duppa and Swilling founded the town of Phoenix, which Swilling supplied with water via his modern irrigation and canal company.

Under intense politicking by businessman Estevan Ochoa and Washington lobbying by explorer Charles Debrille Poston, known as the "Father of Arizona," the federalization of New Mexico Territory by President Lincoln on February 24, 1863, separated Arizona from New Mexico. The action assured Arizona's loyalty to the Union under Governor John Noble Goodwin and other appointed officials at Prescott.

The arrival of squatters John James Thompson and Margaret Parlee James "Maggie" Thompson, homesteaders on 80 acres (32 hectares), and of outlaw and hunter Jessie Jefferson "Bear" Howard in the Oak Creek Canyon established the satellite town of Sedona, named for settler Sedona Arabella Miller Schnebly. Governor Goodwin plotted court districts and conducted a census. The discovery of gold in the Bradshaw Mountains, along the Colorado and Gila rivers, and at Rich Hill and the Vulture Mine at Wickenburg increased the value of the territory to the Union. Tucson merchant and judge Charles Trumbull Hayden operated a freighter and mail service and ran a store near the mines at Tubac, the ruins of a town formerly occupied by Mexicans and Papago.

More Arizona towns emerged in promising spots. The erection of Fort McDowell at the confluence of the Upper Salt and Verde rivers in September 1865 required the hiring of Hispanic laborers and farmers. The workers' settlement grew into the city of Tempe, where Charles Hayden and Sally Calvert Davis Hayden invested in a store, three-story flour mill, warehouses, and cable ferry and promoted a school that developed into Arizona State University. In 1866, homesteader Esteban Ramírez founded Florence, which became a commercial center. When the crossroads exploded into a boomtown and a Wells Fargo station, prospector William Henry Long opened the adobe Silver King Hotel, named for the Silver King Mine; John Philip Clum, a liberal Indian agent, published newspapers in Florence and Tombstone. In 1867, citizens moved the capital to Tucson. Ethnologist John Wesley Powell explored the Grand Canyon in 1869 and used his close contact with the Ute as an opportunity to compile a dictionary of their language and to trade buckskin for artifacts.

By 1870, with silver prospecting drawing outsiders, Tucson's population reached 9,568. In 1877, Louis Cameron Hughes and partner Charles H. Tully supplied the town with an English newspaper, the *Daily Bulletin,* and a Spanish publication, *Los Dos Republicas.* Phoenix acquired its first paper, Charles E. McClintock's *Salt River Herald,* in 1878.

Pioneers and Colonists

Pioneers left Gila Bend in 1873 and established the town of Safford, named for the territory's third governor, attorney Anson Pacely Killen Safford. He is known especially for opening a public school system in March 1872, protecting the area from Indian raids and Mexican outlaws, and operating a bank to finance gold and silver mining and milling operations.

Arizona City, later called Yuma, founded by Jose María Redondo in 1865, relied on business brought upriver by Richard D. Chandler's Colorado Steam Navigation Company and overland by mule or ox train to supply food, hay, and firewood to areas beyond the range of rail service. The town supported a Methodist church, a Catholic parish, and two weekly newspapers, the *Sentinel* and the *Sun.*

Through Redondo's influence, the state opened a territorial penitentiary on July 1, 1876. The first seven prisoners lived in tents for five months while they constructed their own small cells from stone and strap iron. Over its 33-year history, the famous lockup, a typical prison of its day, provided unlighted stone-floored cells with wall chains to hold incorrigibles and ball-and-chain confinement for escapees. Most inmate deaths were the result of tuberculosis.

Mormon patriarch Brigham Young viewed northern Arizona as an opportune place to extend the religious communities of the utopian state of Deseret into an area remote from Protestant persecutors. In October 1876, 13 Mormon families volunteered for the venture. During the five-month passage, subsequent pioneers died along the way of attacks by Indians and Mexicans, drowning, accident, and desert exposure. In one party, Mormon settlers headed by 20-year-old Heber Jeddy Grant founded the Heber community in late 1876. A colonization party led by Daniel Webster Jones arrived in 1877 from St. George, Utah, to found the sectarian community of Lehi and to proselytize the Maricopa and Pima, a crusade Jones described in *Forty Years Among the Indians* (1890). The new settlement coincided with new copper strikes at Bisbee and the disclosure of a silver lode at Tombstone, the site of the area's first newspaper, *The Nugget.* More Latter Day Saints, superintended by apostles William Jordan Flake and Erastus Snow, established the community of Snowflake on July 21, 1878, where families built adobe homes.

The Desert Land Act of March 3, 1877, encouraged Mormon settlement in the Salt River Valley on free parcels of 640 acres (250 hectares) of arid land. With loans from Charles Hayden at Lehi, on September 14, 1877, the First Mesa Company, led by Charles Crismon and George Warren Sirrine, set out from Bear Lake and Paris, Idaho, and Salt Lake City, Utah. The pioneers joined Charles Inness Robson and Francis Marion Pomeroy and built Utahville, later called Mesa City.

In cooperation with the Maricopa and Pima, the Mormons watered the land with hand-dug irrigation canals that revived a 2,000-year-old water system originated by the Hohokam. The flow silted in the fields with soil nutrients suited to the pasturing cattle and sheep; to apple, peach, and pear orchards; and to the growing of alfalfa, beans, corn, cotton, grapes, melons, sorghum, squash, and wheat and flowers to nourish bee colonies. Children speared fish with pitchforks and sold them to Hispanic neighbors. Slowing the progress of the Mormon settlers were waves of disasters from flood, famine, and epidemics. They constructed their dirt-floored adobe homes of mud brick and cactus posts and added brush outbuildings to house stock. To survive intense heat, settlers slept among the trees and suspended wet sheets from the limbs to cool the air. Commerce developed through brick making, milling, and the ice industry.

In 1877, the Southern Pacific Railroad extended from Yuma to Los Angeles, California. Within four years, the line provided service to Tucson and El Paso on the Texas–Mexico border. Arizona became the forty-eighth state on February 14, 1912, the last addition to the continental United States.

See also: Cochise; Exploration; Four Corners Region; Geronimo; Long Walk of the Navajo; Mangas Coloradas; Mormons.

Further Reading

Acuña, Rodolfo F. *Occupied America: A History of Chicanos.* 6th ed. New York: Pearson Longman, 2007.

Anderson, Lisa A., Alice C. Jung, Jared A. Smith, and Thomas H. Wilson. *Mesa.* Charleston, SC: Arcadia, 2008.

Masich, Andrew E. *The Civil War in Arizona: The Story of the California Volunteers, 1861–1865.* Norman: University of Oklahoma Press, 2006.

Thompson, Jerry D., ed. *Civil War in the Southwest: Recollections of the Sibley Brigade.* College Station: Texas A&M University Press, 2001.

Arlington National Cemetery

A U.S. military burial ground plotted during the last year of the Civil War, Arlington National Cemetery occupies 624 acres (253 hectares) on the west bank of the Potomac River and the Alexandria Canal, in view of the nation's capital. In May 1861, General Irvin McDowell posted troops at Arlington House in Arlington County, Virginia, the former residence of Confederate General Robert Edward Lee and his wife, Mary Anna Custis Lee. The land became Union headquarters for 14,000 men; the environs housed Fort Whipple, army barracks, and military horse and mule stables on cleared timberland. In May 1865, at the proposal of Quartermaster General Montgomery Cunningham Meigs, a hostile anti-Confederate, the Union established Arlington Cemetery on a ridge above the Custis-Lee Mansion as a repository for the Union dead.

In the four years of transition from a Southern plantation, Arlington lost the grace and elegance of the original site, which the Lees had occupied for 30 years. After the First Battle of Bull Run at Manassas, Virginia, on July 21, 1861, Union soldiers seized Arlington Heights and began chopping Arlington Forest into logs to line trenches and rifle pits.

Although Mary Custis Lee held the deed to the 1,100-acre (445-hectare) estate, the U.S. government's confiscation of Arlington House on January 11, 1864, for back taxes of $92.07 and its sale for $26,800 served as punishment for General Lee's refusal of an appointment by President Abraham Lincoln on April 20, 1861, to head the federal army. In order to serve the Confederacy, Lee resigned from the U.S. Army and departed his home five days later. He never returned.

General Meigs selected the 200 acres (80 hectares) closest to Arlington House for a cemetery and located the first graves close to the front porch and rose garden to make the property uninhabitable for the traitorous Lees. The hallowed graveyard honored casketed or cremated remains of 1,500 war veterans and combat casualties as well as of 3,800 former slaves, members of the 180,000 U.S. Colored Troops, and reinterred heroes of antebellum battles as far back as the American Revolution.

Hallowed Ground

Administered by the U.S. Department of the Army and perpetually secured by an army honor guard, the cemetery, under the shade of red maples and white oaks, became a serene resting place for the dead, known and unknown. Under the direction of the nation's first professional undertakers, it received the first burial on May 13, 1864. A Union casualty of the Sixty-seventh Pennsylvania Infantry, 21-year-old Private William Henry Christman, a laborer from Lehigh County, Pennsylvania, had died in Washington, D.C., at Lincoln General Hospital of measles and peritonitis after nearly 14 months of service. To relieve the onslaught of corpses in Washington, the slope of Section 27 filled rapidly with 14 more burials by May 15, each overlooking the U.S. Capitol. A sawmill worker, William H. McKinney, a 17-year-old private in the Seventeenth Pennsylvania Cavalry who had died of pneumonia, was the first to have a family funeral; the third burial was 19-year-old William B. Blatt of the Forty-ninth Pennsylvania Infantry, who had succumbed from a shot through the head at the Battle of Spotsylvania, Virginia. On May 15, the first unknown Union dead went to their graves.

By war's end, Arlington held 16,000 of the total 620,000 combat victims, most from families too poor to afford embalming and transportation of remains. Crews monitored the graves and filled in sunken plots to produce a level greensward. The Washington, D.C., *Morning Chronicle* declared the creation of a dignified burial ground a "righteous use" of the Custis-Lee estate.

Like rows of fallen soldiers, the white-painted pine headboards with black lettering ranged from the Lee family rose garden over 200 acres (80 hectares) in regular array in contrast to the rolling slopes. A chaplain occupied the mansion to oversee operations. Officials opened the cemetery to all ranks of military, but prohibited the burial of veterans guilty of capital crimes.

Because of a shortage of ambulances and coffins, interments began with the arrival of a flag-draped corpse atop a caisson. (Before departing, equerries polished the brass studs on tack, oiled the rawhide reins, and washed the teams of six matched grays or blacks.) Soldiers in dress uniform rode the left three mounts. Attendants placed each deceased in a hand-dug grave, from which James Parks, a Lee family slave born on the property in 1843, removed 1.5 cubic yards (1.1 cubic meters) of clay soil. The ten-minute ceremony ended with three rounds of seven rifle salutes and the bugler playing "Taps," a 24-note cadence composed by General Daniel Adams Butterfield in July 1862 along the James River as a signal of "lights out." A stone vault in the Lee rose garden held 2,111 unidentified corpses of soldiers killed at the Battle of Bull Run.

Home for Freedmen

Beginning on May 5, 1863, 40 acres (16 hectares) on the stable grounds to the south of the Lee homestead served as Freedman's Village, a model town for 1,100 slaves liberated as contraband of war. While living cramped and unemployed in makeshift quarters at Camp Barker on the Maryland outskirts, runaways had died of epidemic disease at the rate of five per day from measles, scarlet fever, smallpox, and whooping cough. By contrast, at Arlington, for 27 years, slaves farmed individual plots, labored at fortifications for 40 cents per day, and improved their health by living in fresh air far from urban slums, a concept lauded in the May 7, 1864, edition of *Harper's Weekly*. Behind a pine board stockade and under the protection of the Freedmen's Bureau and U.S. Colored Troops, families were safe from recapture by kidnappers and army recruiters and raids by Maryland enslavers. A comment in the *Morning Chronicle* chortled that the use of a Southern plantation for ex-slaves chastened Lee for leading the Confederate army.

By 1864, Freedman's Village grew from 14 tenements to a town of 3,000 with an American Tract Society church, school for 900 pupils, adult training center, cobbleries and clothing factories, blacksmith and carpentry shops, four parks, pond, and retirement home. Canadian-trained black surgeon Anderson Ruffin Abbott superintended a staff of 14 who ran the 50-bed Abbott Hospital. Orator Sojourner Truth taught the freedmen and freedwomen cooking, knitting, and sewing and delivered pep talks on thrift.

Legacy

Mary Custis Lee returned in 1866 to visit Arlington House and found her family home debased and desecrated and the destruction of her rose garden indecent.

Mary Custis Lee's protests to Congress made government leaders cling more firmly to the hallowed resting place of Civil War patriots. Two years later, on Decoration Day—May 30, 1868—President Andrew Johnson proclaimed a federal day of respect for wreathing military graves with flowers. Inmates from the Soldiers' and Sailors' Orphan Asylum bore black satin sashes as signs of mourning and, over the Civil War dead, sang the anonymous ballad "Father Come Home" (1868).

General Lee quietly worked to restore family ownership of Arlington until his death at age 63 in 1870. Mary Custis Lee returned in June 1873, five months before her death. The transformation of her family's home convinced her that Arlington would never again be a residence. She died in November 1873.

Out of obligation to his heritage, Colonel George Washington Custis Lee, the eldest son of Mary Custis and Robert E. Lee, filed a lawsuit against the government in March 1877. The U.S. Supreme Court ruled 5–4 in 1882 that Mary Custis Lee held prior claim to land that had been unlawfully confiscated. Although his Custis grandparents were buried in the family plot, he sold the property to the Department of the Army for $150,000 in 1878.

General Meigs continued augmenting the former plantation with a wisteria-edged amphitheater, an arch honoring General George Brinton McClellan, and a border of canna and elephant ears. The nation's cemetery became a monument to military history and to the self-sacrifice of its martyrs. The land received the remains of John Lincoln Clem, a nine-year-old drummer at Chickamauga, Virginia Military Institute cadet Moses Jacob Ezekiel, medic Samuel Edwin Lewis of Chimborazo Hospital in Richmond, black Civil War recruiter Orindatus Simon Bolivar Wall, and Major Alexander Thomas Augusta, the army's first black surgeon. In addition, officials buried patriots and notables—Buffalo Soldiers and Indian fighters, "Mother of the Confederacy" Mary T. Thompson, Lincoln's stenographer James Tanner, Confederate army nurse Juliet Ann Opie Hopkins, U.S. Supreme Court Justice Oliver Wendell Holmes, Jr., and John Wesley Powell, the first white explorer of the Grand Canyon.

See also: Washington, D.C.

Further Reading

Dieterle, Lorraine Jacyno. *Arlington National Cemetery: A Nation's Story Carved in Stone.* San Francisco: Pomegranate, 2001.

Dodge, George W. *Arlington National Cemetery.* Charleston, SC: Arcadia, 2006.

Neff, John R. *Honoring the Civil War Dead: Commemoration and the Problem of Reconciliation.* Lawrence: University Press of Kansas, 2005.

Yalom, Marilyn. *The American Resting Place.* Boston: Houghton Mifflin, 2008.

Armour, Philip Danforth (1832–1901)

The founder of the Armour meatpacking dynasty, Philip Danforth "Phil" Armour applied rail technology and Western livestock know-how to the feeding of America. A native of Stockbridge, New York, he was born on May 16, 1832, and grew up on the family farm. His parents, Danforth and Juliana Ann Brooks Armour, sent him to Cazenovia Academy, but he abandoned education in favor of a job on the Chenango Canal, a towpath canal from Binghamton to Utica, New York.

At age 20, Armour began building his fortune by driving oxen and mining gold in California. In Milwaukee, Wisconsin, he opened a wholesale grocery house and rendered pork fat into soap. He partnered first with James J. Hill in the hide trade at St. Paul, then with Frederick B. Mills in merchandising fresh produce and grain, and later with John Plankinton in meatpacking in Milwaukee. A mark of his commercial acumen was his insistence on cash deals.

By the time Armour wed 20-year-old Malvina Belle Ogden in 1862, he had amassed $500,000. In addition to purchasing gold, he invested in the Baltimore & Ohio and the Chicago, Milwaukee & St. Paul railroads, as well as in the Northwestern Life Insurance Company, Kansas City streetcar companies in Kansas and Missouri, and the Illinois Trust and Savings, Metropolitan National, and National Trust banks.

Armour and his brothers, Herman Ossian Armour and Joseph Francis Armour, rejected the lumber industry as an investment and instead put their funds in grain and pork butchery. From his office in Chicago's first skyscraper—the Home Insurance Building on Adams and LaSalle streets—Phil Armour revolutionized the pork business by shipping live hogs to the city's sprawling stockyards for on-site killing and processing. In 1867, the trio incorporated as Armour and Company, the beginning of the world's largest slaughtering and food processing business. They located their abattoirs (slaughterhouses) along Wisconsin's Menomonee River Valley and competed with meat marketers in England,

France, and Germany. By the beginning of the Civil War, Armour had quadrupled his wealth.

Market Manipulation

With the fall of the Confederate capital at Richmond, Virginia, to Union forces on April 3, 1865, war profiteering ended. As the demand for military supplies decreased, pork prices tumbled from $40 per barrel to $18. Before the fall, while other meat czars were still speculating on military contracts, Armour signed deals to deliver at the higher price but waited for the 55 percent drop in price before purchasing meat. On the proceeds, he explored new business connections that retired his debts and boosted his prospects.

In 1870, Armour and Company added mutton to its line of beef and pork. Assisting the company's growth at the end of the cattle trails in Kansas City, Kansas, were two more brothers—Simeon Brooks Armour, who superintended trade, and the youngest sibling, Andrew Watson Armour, who opened Armour Brothers' Bank. In 1879, Phil Armour turned a $4 million profit on speculation in the pork market, which had rebounded in his favor.

To produce fresh, cured, smoked, and canned meats, the low-paid Armour packing staff worked on an assembly line, the first of its kind. As slaughtered animals suspended by their hind legs from a conveyor belt passed by each workstation, butchers, skinners, and de-boners risked serious injuries from cuts, pollutants, and disease arising from the blood-soaked killing floor. To decrease overhead costs, managers generally employed immigrants and nonwhite workers, who processed animals at a rate of 13 per minute. The sight of coordinated meat cutting drew visitors to the 1893 World's Columbian Exposition on excursions to the Union Stockyards.

Industrial Recycling

To recycle waste, Armour's research and development laboratories, located in 22 cities throughout the Midwest and Canada, found ways of turning previously discarded byproducts into bristle brushes, buttons, felt, fertilizer, gelatin, margarine, neatsfoot oil for leather conditioning, pepsin for cheese making, pork and beans, sugar, and tallow. He built Armour Glue Works in Bridgeport, Connecticut, and extended an industrial complex at Chicago's West 31st Street on the south fork of the Chicago River. He operated a horn and hoof recovery system as well as Armour Chemicals, Armour Ammonia Works, Armour Curled Hair Works, Armour Sandpaper Works, Armour Printing Works, and Armour Soap Works. Armour Leather Company processed rawhide and tanned skins.

Armour's innovations turned the conglomerate into Chicago's prime business and an employer of 20,000. In 1883, to outsell rival Gustavus Swift, the Armour Refrigerator Line, called the "Great Yellow Line," dispatched meats via 5,000 refrigerated cars built in the Armour rolling stock factory. In Milwaukee, he opened a ham house and the Armour Elevating Company to manage the grain enterprise and established the Armour and Company Icehouse in Memphis, Nebraska. In winter, 325 ice cutters stocked its lockers with blocks chopped from a 100-acre (40-hectare) man-made lake fed by Silver Creek.

Armour's reputation teetered between good deeds and scandal. While his enterprise reached an annual volume of $200 million from the slaughter of 1.8 million hogs and 800,000 steers, he lived simply and gave cash readily to the Armour Mission, a Chicago community center on West 33rd Street that offered free medical care, a library, and a kindergarten. With $1 million in profits, Armour founded the Armour Institute of Technology, a coeducational and racially integrated school that promoted the trades and the growing field of home economics. In his late seventies, Armour fought frivolous charges of bribing state legislators and of selling tainted canned beef that poisoned U.S. troops during the Spanish-American War. Soldiers scorned tinned meat as "embalmed beef" leftovers from the Civil War. Inspectors found no evidence of adulterants and attributed the loss of life in 1899 to kitchen neglect and careless handling and sanitation.

Armour suffered for two years from myocarditis (an inflammation of the heart muscle) and recuperated in Bad Nauheim, Germany, the Swiss Alps, and Pasadena, California. In 1900, the death of his heir and namesake depressed him. When the elder Armour died of pneumonia and heart failure on January 6, 1901, his estate approached $50 million. Chicago honored his memory with the opening of Armour Square Park on Lake Michigan to relieve miserable living conditions in the city's slums.

Further Reading

Horowitz, Roger. *Putting Meat on the American Table: Taste, Technology, Transformation.* Baltimore: Johns Hopkins University Press, 2006.

Smith, Andrew F., ed. *The Oxford Companion to American Food and Drink.* New York: Oxford University Press, 2007.

Wade, Louise Carroll. *Chicago's Pride: The Stockyards, Packingtown, and Environs in the Nineteenth Century.* Urbana: University of Illinois Press, 2002.

Warren, Wilson J. *Tied to the Great Packing Machine: The Midwest and Meatpacking.* Iowa City: University of Iowa Press, 2007.

Art and Architecture

American individualism evolved rapidly in the art and architecture of the 1860s and 1870s, as designers of buildings and interiors began to free themselves from slavish imitation of European styles and mannerisms. Municipal adornment still tended toward grandeur, as found in the towered courthouses of Nebraska; the Gothic spires that architect James Renwick, Jr., employed in St. Patrick's Cathedral in New York City in 1865; the High Victorian details that Henry Van Brunt and William Robert Ware incorporated in Memorial Hall at Harvard University in 1868; the Egyptian sphinx that Martin Milmore sculpted for the Mount Auburn Cemetery in Cambridge, Massachusetts, in 1872; and the Romanesque upthrust designed by Henry Hobson Richardson for Boston's Trinity Church in 1873. In Boston, Philadelphia, and Providence, Rhode Island, city halls displayed their self-importance and authority in the imperial baroque styling modeled in 1857 by the Louvre Museum in Paris.

The moneyed class used architecture as a badge of achievement. Capitalists Andrew Carnegie, John Pierpont Morgan, and John D. Rockefeller constructed palatial homes decorated with original art and artisanship in marble, mahogany paneling, and beveled glass. Stained glass expert Louis Comfort Tiffany refined interior design at the home of Cornelius Vanderbilt II (grandson of the shipping and railroad magnate) in New York City by incorporating glass tiles. Multimillionaire merchant Alexander Turney Stewart filled his Fifth Avenue mansion in New York City with Corinthian columns, elegant bubble-globed chandeliers, and classic statuary. His neighbor, financier Jay Gould, stocked his home with French paintings by Eugène Delacroix, Jean-François Millet, and other artists of the Belle Epoch. At his death, Gould's remains occupied a grand Ionic mausoleum at Woodlawn Cemetery in the Bronx.

American Tastes

Average home styles veered from the pompous to the serene. In Maine, colonial federal style dominated one- and two-story homes, with unvarying symmetry in sash windows, shutters, and chimneys at the gable ends. James R. Barber, a nitroglycerin maker in Titusville, Pennsylvania, chose subtle appointments—Gothic scrolled window caps and a circular attic window. To evidence the refinement of the heartlands, householders in Peoria, Illinois, and Toledo, Ohio, favored artistic touches imported from the Atlantic Coast—slender double columns, dentate edging, arched windows, mansard roofs, widow's walks, and ball-topped lightning rods.

In the semitropics, residents evolved the enlarged overhang of Florida cracker farmhouses and crafted cottages from coquina (sedimentary shellstone) or from tabby, an aggregate of lime, sand, and shell. New England missionaries on Kauai adapted to the extended lanais of Hawaiian architecture, which welcomed Pacific breezes.

English colonialism retained its hold on East Coast ports. In Savannah, Georgia, live oaks embraced homes, shutters framed shop windows, and English street lamps dotted narrow sidewalks and lighted cobbled alleyways. Along Battery Row in Charleston, South Carolina, landscaped gardens abandoned British geometrics. Builders created havens for gardening and entertaining by planting tall camellias alongside wrought iron and pergolas enlaced with Carolina jasmine and wisteria. Rebuilt after a 587-day bombardment by Union gunboats from 1863 to 1865, white columned homes in Charleston generated an aura of welcome with their porticos and port cocheres, shady verandas, awnings, and cupolas. The Gothic Revival church architecture of St. Matthew's German Lutheran Church, completed in 1871, and the Italianate design of the 24,000-square-foot (2,200-square-meter) mansion built by blockade runner George Walton Williams anchored the cosmopolitan blend common to a seaport.

The nation's most regionalized architecture enhanced the appeal of New Orleans, Louisiana, which suffered less damage from the Civil War than Savannah or Charleston. Antebellum Queen Anne mansions, uptown Creole townhouses edged in lacy wrought iron, and cottages outlined in gingerbread millwork shared space with double-gallery manses of the Garden District and Esplanade Ridge and the balconied ateliers and refurbished St. Louis Cathedral overlooking Jackson Square.

Farther inland, the infamous scorched-earth policy of Union General William Tecumseh Sherman left parts of the southern Piedmont in ashes. South Carolinians strove to make Columbia an economic cornerstone of the New South. Citizens anticipated the construction of a brick city market on Assembly Street and erected a statehouse and a governor's mansion on Arsenal Hill.

In Georgia, carpetbagger and builder Hannibal Kimball urged the legislature to move the capital from Milledgeville to Atlanta, Sherman's prize capture. To establish the heart of the New South, Kimball in 1868 erected the first capitol in four months and leveled 60 acres (24 hectares) of woodland to create Oglethorpe Park, site of the first International Cotton Exposition. He razed the remains of the car shed for a new Union Depot and replaced the Atlanta Hotel with the H.I. Kimball House, a six-story luxury hotel constructed from yellow brick.

Urban Planning

In a variety of locales—Indianapolis, Indiana; Nashville, Tennessee; Poultney, Vermont; and Richmond, Virginia—Americans paid tribute to the heroes of the Civil War with monuments to courage and gallantry. Cemeteries and town squares honored the fallen with obelisks and portrait statues of soldiers and sailors in uniform and officers on horseback.

During the postwar American Renaissance, sculptor Edmonia Lewis celebrated the black and native perspectives on the era's turmoil. She merited regard for depicting two aspects of her bloodline—*Forever Free* (1867), a glimpse of a black couple examining the Emancipation Proclamation, and *The Old Arrow Maker and His Daughter* (1872), depicting a scene from Henry Wadsworth Longfellow's epic poem *The Song of Hiawatha* (1855).

Looking toward the twentieth century, Frederick Law Olmsted's treatise *Public Parks and the Enlargement of Towns* (1870) envisioned the role of the urban planner as a harmonizer and reformer of the negative aspects of life, particularly discourtesy, debauchery, and violence. In addition to his work on 20 city parks and the Capitol grounds in Washington, D.C., in 1876, he finished landscaping New York City's 700-acre (280-hectare) Central Park, earning himself the title "Father of American Landscape Architecture" for setting the standard for peaceful, family-oriented spots of beauty.

Because private property in major cities brought premium prices, urban verticality replaced the horizontal flow of suburban terracing and rural lawns. With the aid of the foremost American architect, Richard Morris Hunt, co-founder of the American Institute of Architects, builder Rutherford Stuyvesant in 1869 erected Stuyvesant Place, a breakthrough in elegant city living. On four contiguous lots at 142 East Eighteenth Street between Irving Place and Third Avenue in New York City, Hunt's two five-story brick buildings in the classical French Renaissance style comprised 20 suites of seven to ten rooms, each leased for $1,200 to $1,800 a year. Spacious master suites featured fireplaces and wrought-iron balconies. Enhancing efficiency, live-in staff relied on dumbwaiters to deliver food and drink to parlors, public rooms, and dining rooms. In 1873, Hunt also designed the cast-iron Roosevelt Building at 478 Broadway and the Tribune Building on Park Row, the tallest structure in New York, which he topped with a massive clock tower.

After the Great Chicago Fire of October 8–10, 1871, Illinois residents determined to rebuild the city center finer and stronger than before. Because the fire incinerated 4 square miles (10 square kilometers) of prime lakefront property and business sites on both sides of the Chicago River, immediate building recycled accommodations, such as the water tank that housed the Chicago Library. At Mount Prospect, Archbishop Patrick Augustine Feehan remodeled the River Bent Knott Farm into a training school for Chicago orphans. Potter Palmer erected a second Palmer House hotel and billed it as the "World's First Fireproof Building." The reconstruction of the Chicago, Rock Island, & Pacific and Lake Shore & Michigan Southern rail depot at LaSalle and Van Buren streets gave Chicagoans a reason to host a city music festival. Philanthropists Sarah Tyson Hallowell and Bertha Palmer supported the city's resurgence in the arts by introducing French impressionists to the Midwest and by exhibiting local works.

Art for Everyone

During the postwar boom years, Americans began to respect the arts as essentials of everyday life. The Centennial Exposition of 1876 in Philadelphia introduced the middle-class householder to silver serving pieces, machine-made furnishings, drapes, fabrics, and Japanese wallpaper designed by William Burges and Edward William Godwin.

Lithograph copies of American art appealed to the masses, particularly the sporting scenes and folk life of printmakers Nathaniel T. Currier and James Merritt Ives. The Currier & Ives mail order business advertised 7,000 scenes. Their middle-class themes—carriage rides, waterwheels, farmyards, Mississippi paddle wheelers, people engaged in manual labor, churches, seasonal events—gained the approval of domestic mavens Catharine Beecher and Harriet Beecher Stowe, co-authors of the popular handbook *American Woman's Home* (1869), which condemned the tyranny of the tony art critic. By 1872, Currier & Ives prints clarified the Americana that typified the nation's perspectives and values.

Museums and historic sites instructed visitors on architecture, art, and history. Public repositories ranged from painting and sculpture museums to exhibits of anthropology and natural history, the focus of the Smithsonian Institution in Washington, D.C., founded in 1846, and the Pennsylvania Academy of the Fine Arts, which was completed in Philadelphia in 1876.

Responding to curiosity about American design and symbolism, the Metropolitan Museum of Art, founded in 1870, took shape on New York City's Fifth Avenue and exhibited the private collection of John Taylor Johnston, president of the Central Railroad of New Jersey. In 1871, architect Calvert Vaux designed a larger facility for the museum east of Central Park and decked it in High Victorian Gothic style, the same mode he used in 1877 for the American Museum of Natural History.

In Newark, New Jersey, Helena de Kay Gilder and Richard Watson Gilder in 1874 began organizing the Society of American Artists and the Art Students League, a tribute to national accomplishments. The consortium spotlighted works by muralist and stained glass expert John LaFarge and Augustus Saint-Gaudens, the founder of American portrait statuary and sculptor of a bronze monument to Union naval hero David Farragut.

The People's Art

Americans revered naturalism in native arts. Watercolorist Winslow Homer, an illustrator for *Harper's Weekly* during the Civil War, captured the exertions of ordinary people in outdoor settings, notably, *Thanksgiving in Camp* (1862), *A Game of Croquet* (1866), and the seascape *Two Are Company* (1872). His paintings featured former slaves during Reconstruction, lone riders on the Plains, and sailors and fishermen in vigorous seascapes tinged with the threat of harsh weather and rough water. American modernist painter and watercolorist James McNeill Whistler attained international stature with three masterworks, *Symphony in White, No. 1: The White Girl* (1862); *Arrangement in Grey and Black* (1871), a profile popularly titled "Whistler's Mother"; and *Arrangement in Black and Brown: The Fur Jacket* (1876). Impressionist Mary Cassatt established herself as a portraitist in gouache (a method of painting with opaque watercolors), favoring poses of mothers cuddling, nursing, and bathing children.

Frontier creativity demanded pragmatism and the use of local materials to express cultural traditions. These qualities describe the work of Navajo weaver Juanita, wife of Manuelito of Tohatchi, New Mexico, and of Washo basket maker

Albert Bierstadt's great landscapes of the American West—such as *Among the Sierra Nevada Mountains, California* (1868)—cast the wilderness in idyllic, romantic terms. The golden Western light, a frequent element, symbolized the promise of the future. *(The Granger Collection, New York)*

Ysabel Datsolali of Carson Valley, Nevada. Datsolali's intricately coiled and stitched geometrics on conical burden baskets and spherical ceremonial baskets achieved global notoriety from displays at the Smithsonian Institution.

Indian displacement produced a humanistic truism—that social chaos forces victims to express despair and nostalgia through art. At Fort Marion, Florida, following the 1874 Red River War in North Dakota, Captain Richard Henry Pratt distributed paper, pencils, crayons, pen and ink, and watercolors to imprisoned Arapaho, Cheyenne, and Kiowa, notably, Southern Cheyenne spiritual leader David Pendleton Oakerhater, also known as Medicine Maker. Caught in the decline of Indian culture, the artists drew scenes of ritual and dance, hunting, courtship, dreamscapes and visions, symbology, and the insurgency of whites on the Great Plains.

Simultaneously, white painters of desert scenes found beauty in the contrast of sky and light reflected from water and rocky surfaces, the basis of Thomas Moran's paintings *Children of the Mountain* (1867), *Cinnebar Mountain, Yellowstone River* (1871), *Colburn's Butte, South Utah* (1873), and *Chasm of the Colorado* (1873). Speed was the hallmark of quick-sketch artist Albert Bierstadt, who accompanied explorers to California and painted the luminous *Looking Down Yosemite Valley* (1865) and *Cathedral Rocks* (1872). In 1872, oil painter John Gast envisioned westering in an idyllic painting, *American Progress,* an allegory of Manifest Destiny. The setting epitomized the republic as a woman stretching telegraph wires west in the path of homesteaders, wagon trains, and railroads. Before her, Indians escape the intrusion of whites on traditional native lands.

Vernacular architecture made a similar compromise with desert and Plains conditions and materials, such as brush arbors, cave and sod dwellings, adobe ranchos along the Spanish frontier, and log cabins, such as the birthplace of autobiographer Laura Ingalls Wilder in 1867 near Pepin, Wisconsin, which she described in her *Little House on the Prairie* series. While men notched and stacked log walls, women and children trimmed branches, shaped hides into window coverings, stacked rocks for chimneys and hearths, and mixed mud, dung, and animal hair into sealants. Families crafted log bedsteads and tables and built chandeliers, chairs, and picture frames out of animal bones, antlers, and horns.

As the Atchison, Topeka, & Santa Fe Railroad moved southwest from Kansas to Texas, Arizona, and New Mexico, desert-rim depots and restaurants took the softened lines and Hispanic conventions of adobe missions and haciendas built from sun-fired earthen bricks around a central atrium. Elaborately fronted stores, hotels, and offices concealed the plain wood and brick boxes that dominated Western construction. In Cheyenne, Wyoming, amid plainer, less imposing structures, the workmanship of Barney Launcelot Ford's Interocean Hotel featured arched doorways and a corbeled roofline above a brick facade. During the 1870s, the rapidly urbanizing West reflected a greater sophistication of architecture and abandoned most of its crude wood corrals, bark-shingled barns, and mud brick forts to the elements.

See also: Centennial Celebration, U.S.; Olmsted, Frederick Law, Sr.; Photography; Stuyvesant, Rutherford.

Further Reading

Ellis, Edward Robb. *The Epic of New York City.* New York: Carroll & Graf, 2005.

Hornberger, Eric. *The Historical Atlas of New York City.* New York: Henry Holt, 2005.

Moore, William B., and Joshua F. Sherretts. *Oil Boom Architecture: Titusville, Pithole, and Petroleum Center.* Charleston, SC: Arcadia, 2008.

Plunz, Richard. *A History of Housing in New York City: Dwelling Type and Social Change in the American Metropolis.* New York: Columbia University Press, 1990.

Scheller, William G. *America, a History in Art: The American Journey Told by Painters, Sculptors, Photographers, and Architects.* New York: Black Dog & Leventhal, 2008.

Atchison, Topeka, & Santa Fe Railroad

Across a broad sweep of 6,069 miles (9,765 kilometers) from Chicago on Lake Michigan across Texas and the Southwest, the Atchison, Topeka, & Santa Fe Railroad (ATSF) followed the Santa Fe Trail. The railroad reaped reciprocal profits for shareholders and for investors in orchards, grazing land and cattle ranches, farms, mining camps, sheep herds, and cotton fields in its path.

Despite the sparse population of the unsettled West and the failure of two-thirds of railroads to show a profit at the time, Kansas Governor Samuel Medary chartered the ATSF on February 11, 1859. Congress underwrote the cost by conveying to the builders land grants of 6,400 acres (2,600 hectares) for every mile of track to sell to settlers at $1 per acre. By early 1873, the first leg of 469 miles (755 kilometers) from Atchison, Kansas, southwest to Topeka opened for business. The customer base ensured profits from the transport of freight, mail, and passengers.

Mapped in 1863 by Kansas state senator Cyrus K. Holliday, the founding father of Topeka and an organizer of the Republican Party, the railroad on paper extended to Mexico City, Galveston, and San Francisco. As an advertising ploy, the Atchison, Topeka, & Santa Fe carried the name of New Mexico's capital; however, because of engineering difficulties through bedrock, the western end of the railroad did not reach Santa Fe.

To doubters, Holliday reasoned that land that could support buffalo and Indians could also support white pioneers. A company advisory warned newcomers to be prepared for remote and desolate land. To save workers and their families from the squalor that accompanied railroad camps, the ATSF management supplied lodging, recreation, libraries, bathhouses, and hospital care.

The acquisition of rolling stock began with locomotives from Philadelphia's Baldwin Locomotive Works. With proceeds from the purchase and sale of Potawatomi lands, the ATSF crossed the Kaw River to Pauline, Kansas, in 1869, expanded to Dodge City, Kansas, in 1872, and reached Pueblo, Colorado, on March 1, 1876. Purchase of the Wichita & Southwestern spur in 1872 turned Wichita into a boomtown enriched by Texas cattle, stockyards, and a meatpacking plant.

Customer Demand

As the ATSF earned more profits than any competitor, the parallel exploitation of the frontier dispersed buffalo from their migratory patterns and scattered Indians. Rapid transit brought rich sportsmen and European sightseers, including Russian ambassador Grand Duke Alexis, who hunted in mid-January 1872 outside Fort Wallace, Kansas, with William Frederick "Buffalo Bill" Cody and generals George Armstrong Custer and Philip Sheridan. Legendary frontiersman William Barclay "Bat" Masterson and his older brother Ed joined the buffalo hunters in 1872. The onrush spawned outfitters along the ATSF tracks at Wichita, where expeditioners bought ammunition, Remington and Sharps sporting rifles, and skinning knives. Packing houses corned and smoked buffalo haunches for shipment east. Over a three-year period, ATSF cars hauled 32.4 million pounds (14.7 million kilograms) of buffalo bones, hide, and meat that formerly had been the province of the Arapaho, Cheyenne, and Kiowa. With the depletion of the herds, Masterson became an ATSF grader and detective.

The frontier began to rely on the ATSF for necessities. Westbound trains delivered personnel and fresh horses to Fort Union; eastbound trains carried coal to Kansans. Real estate speculators traveled the line at a reduced rate and received a rebate if they bought property. Unfortunately for the company's reputation, food at rail-side cafes tended toward beans, soda biscuits, and coffee gulped down on the run. Because of poor sanitation on counters, dishes, and utensils, passengers spread the word that travel aboard the ATSF lacked amenities.

At the Topeka depot in 1876, the ATSF began building a chain of 47 Harvey House eateries and inns. The company added a hotel in Florence, Kansas, and extended accommodations to the Pacific end of the line at San Bernardino, California. Managed by London-born Fred Harvey, the restaurants featured quality cuisine and ambience suitable for ladies. To fill in more remote segments, the ATSF became the first railroad to add dining cars, which Harvey also managed.

Changing the West

In 1877, ATSF planners moved west along the Arkansas River toward Royal Gorge, Colorado, where saboteurs from the Denver & Rio Grande impeded further construction. Stockholders turned their expansion goals toward Denver and Colorado Springs and consolidation with the Gulf, Colorado, & Santa Fe Railway. Chief Engineer Albert Alonzo Robinson chose a route to the coalfields of Trinidad, Colorado, as a source of engine fuel. In 1880, service to Albuquerque brought the first passenger train to New Mexico and ferried new residents to Raton, Maxwell, Springer, Santa Clara, La Junta, and Las Vegas. Gallup, New Mexico, became a central depot for Indian goods, Navajo wool, and alcohol. Train passengers amused themselves by shooting antelope and jackrabbits from the car windows and platforms.

Because the line bypassed Santa Fe and chugged through nearby Lamy, citizens of Santa Fe raised $150,000 on bonds to underwrite a spur to the ATSF. Arrival east of Santa Fe ended the demand for an overland trail and for Fort Union, where regiments had once shielded wagon trains from attacks by Comancheros, Jicarilla Apache, and Moache Ute.

Profits passed down the line. Engineers earned $3.50 per day, conductors $2. Smelters and metalworkers found steady work at the ATSF shops in Argentine, Kansas. The company encouraged industry and transported "lungers" (tuberculosis patients) to "health country." Dependable service to Phoenix, Arizona, made the city the area's agricultural center. Kansas City, Missouri, became the leading cattle and grain market in the trans-Mississippi West. In Southern California, citriculture flourished, boosting

Duarte and National City into lemon and orange packing and shipping centers.

In 1875, the company named famous locomotives the *Colorado Springs* and the *California Limited* and later honored the founder with the dubbing of the *Cyrus K. Holliday.* Holliday, the man who transformed the Southwest, directed the company until his death in 1900.

See also: Buffalo; Railroads.

Further Reading

Lewis, Allan C. *Railroads of the Pikes Peak Region, 1870–1900.* Charleston, SC: Arcadia, 2004.

Melzer, Richard. *Fred Harvey Houses of the Southwest.* Charleston, SC: Arcadia, 2008.

Smith, Randy D. *Heroes of the Santa Fe Trail, 1821–1900.* Raleigh, NC: Boson, 2006.

Atlanta, Georgia

Built on land formerly inhabited by Creek and Cherokee Indians, Atlanta, Georgia, retained its antebellum prominence as a nexus of agriculture, government, rail travel, munitions, medicine, and commerce. Founder Richard Peters, an agronomist and superintendent of the Georgia Railroad, foresaw greatness in the area and changed the provincial name of Marthasville to Atlanta in 1842. He purchased Downing Hill Nursery, built the steam-driven Peters Flour Mill and a lumberyard, and operated a stage line to Montgomery, Alabama. The stage line was replaced in 1851 by the Atlanta & West Point Railroad, which established service to Alexandria, Virginia.

By 1855, Atlanta called itself the "Gate City of the South." Its 6,000 citizens boasted a railcar factory, the Roswell Bridge over the Chattahoochee River, City Park, gas streetlights on cast-iron lampposts fueled by the Atlanta Gas Works, the Athenaeum Theater, Atlanta Medical College, a board of health, a Jewish Sabbath school, a depot, foundries, a red-light district at Five Points, a company of watchmen and three fire companies, Jonathan Norcross's Air Line Railroad, James Pinkney Hambleton's *Southern Confederacy* newspaper, the Oakland Cemetery, and the Atlanta Bank. To suppress a slave insurrection, a city ordinance imposed a $200 tax on freedmen living in Atlanta.

Lauded by John Steele and Jared Irwin Whitaker, prowar editors of the secessionist *Daily Intelligencer,* Atlanta's amenities served the Confederate army during the Civil War. The city council supported a militia of minutemen, compulsory smallpox vaccination, and the distribution of guns and uniforms to the rebel army. The Confederate government stored supplies and housed some 80,000 casualties at makeshift medical centers at the fairgrounds General Hospital and the Receiving and Distributing Hospital in the Gate City Hotel. The wounded received care at all civic buildings, as well as a contagion center at Markham's Farm and facilities at the American Hotel, Empire House, Mayson's Female Institute, Hayden's Hall, and Concert Hall. Burial crews interred 4,600 dead soldiers at Oakland Cemetery. Tacticians quartered near the Confederate nerve center, and a newly formed police force guarded a commissary stockpiled with food, ammunition, clothing, and hay for horses.

Outside the city center, the Confederate Rolling Mill and the Atlanta Rolling Mill produced iron rails, cannon, and plating for the ironclad steamer *Merrimac,* which was rebuilt as the CSS *Virginia.* The Withers Foundry and Machine Works and other metalsmiths manufactured shot, shells, knives, swords, pistols, and percussion caps for Colonel Moses H. Wright at the Atlanta arsenal, the largest south of Richmond, Virginia. The production of ordnance employed 5,500 men and women, the city's largest factory staff. Another 3,000 worked for Major George W. Cunningham at the Quartermaster's Depot making boots, uniforms, and hats for soldiers and sailors.

Wartime Changes

Atlanta lost its social gaiety after the onset of the Civil War. In May 1862, Colonel George Washington Custis Lee imposed a 9 P.M. curfew on blacks, restricted liquor sales, and closed poolrooms and gambling halls. Provisions trickled in via blockade runners and suppliers in Memphis, Tennessee. In winter, citizens dispatched supplies to the struggling Army of Tennessee and faced domestic shortages of hay, charcoal and firewood, potatoes, apples, butter, cheese, flour, and meat. On March 18, 1863, war widows rioted on Whitehall Street and seized bacon and flour. Mary Jane Thompson Peters, a volunteer with the St. Philip's Hospital Aid Society, made daily rounds to the poor with hampers of food and served coffee to soldiers. She tended to the dying and wrote consolatory letters home. A minority of Unionists smuggled supplies and spied for the North and distributed charity to 300 federal captives in the Fulton County Jail.

After the fall of Vicksburg, Mississippi, to the army of Union General Ulysses S. Grant in July 1863, Atlanta emerged as the next great war prize. Confederate General Howell Cobb headquartered the Georgia State Guard in the city. Throughout August, families dug holes in which to hide women and children and covered them with tin sheets or railroad ties; Marshal O.H. Jones fought crime by commandeering a force of elderly men and draft rejects.

Engineers found the fortification of Atlanta impossible. Strategists Lemuel Pratt Grant and Alexander McGehee Wallace realized the city's vulnerability and posted sharpshooters at Potter House. Using civilian and slave labor, they ringed the outskirts with 17 redoubts, trenches, wire traps, rifle pits, and earthworks to rebuff Union invaders and shelling. After the Union capture of Tennessee, Atlantans obeyed Confederate President Jefferson Davis by observing June 10, 1864, as a day of fasting and prayer for courage.

Siege of Atlanta

On July 17, 1864, federal troops under the command of General William Tecumseh Sherman, dubbed the "Father of Modern Warfare," approached Fulton County from the northwestern mountains and over the Coosa River. Sherman's company, consisting of 55,000 infantry, 5,000 cavalry, 2,000 artillerymen, and 64 guns, swept south to Jonesboro before reaching Atlanta on July 22. Union batteries fired artillery day and night and marched on a population that had swelled to 22,000 with the influx of displaced persons and field hands exiting plantation servitude.

On September 1, Confederate troops evacuated 12,000 civilians from the city by pressing the remaining noncombatants to follow the McDonough Road south to safety or to board the last train to Savannah. In the wake of the retreat, Confederate General John Bell Hood ordered the wrecking of equipment and the torching of public buildings and warehouses containing stores or machinery that might benefit the enemy.

On September 2, 1864, Sherman seized Atlanta, still occupied by some 50 families. He reconnected rail and telegraph lines and turned the city into a military garrison by ridding it of the hostile populace. Upon hearing of the city's capture, President Abraham Lincoln telegraphed his thanks.

When federal troops camped in City Park and Courthouse Square, citizens fed soldiers and tended the wounded of both armies. Mayor James Montgomery Calhoun oversaw the distribution of 2,000 sacks of corn, 7 hogsheads of sugar, and 170,000 pounds (77,000 kilograms) of bacon to the poor and to hospital kitchens. Following a ten-day truce, on September 11, Calhoun pled for mercy for pregnant women, children, and the elderly and handicapped; Sherman replied the next day that the South had to suffer the consequences of its rebellion. On September 12, General Hood begged for the city's preservation, which Sherman refused with an abrupt halt to their correspondence.

The Union army of General William Tecumseh Sherman left Atlanta in ashes in November 1864. "Behind us," he later wrote, "Atlanta lay smoldering and in ruins, the black smoke rising high in the air and hanging like a ball over the ruined city." *(MPI/Stringer/Getty Images)*

Upon Sherman's departure on his "March to the Sea" on November 11, 1864, he ordered his soldiers to burn the city. To raze brick and stone buildings, he dispatched sappers and battering rams to demolish the Macon & Western and Georgia railroad depots and to explode the Atlanta Gas Works and the magazines of forts. Before setting out for Savannah, the victorious "bummers" stripped coffins of decorative silver, removed skeletons from cemetery vaults, and placed the Union dead on catafalques.

Dr. Noel Pierre-Paul D'Alvigny saved the Atlanta Medical College by posing ward attendants on cots as though they were patients. Father Thomas O'Reilly, pastor of the Shrine of the Immaculate Conception, obtained an exemption for Catholic properties, City Hall, and hospitals, but little else of worth escaped devastation. Union soldiers burned the rail offices and roundhouse, dug up tracks and twisted crossties at West Point, demolished a college for women, and seized all but one fire engine. Two-thirds of the city's trees perished amid wrecked wagons and overturned tombstones. Packs of wild dogs and vultures fed on animal and human carcasses. The remaining citizens had no water pumps, armory, or jail in which to lock brigands.

From Despair to Hope

Mortality estimates reflect a pyrrhic victory, with approximately 20,000 killed on each side of the conflict. Of the 20 Atlanta civilians killed in the assault, freedman Solomon "Sam" Luckie died in August 1864 during the shelling of his barbershop and bathhouse at the Atlanta Hotel. Left standing amid 5,000 smoldering buildings were 400 residences, Masonic Hall, and the hospital at the Gate City Hotel. As horse thieves, child beggars, arsonists, and looters combed the debris for mules, hides, silverware, mirrors, pianos, and hidden valuables, the black population fled in large numbers to new starts on the frontier. At the collapse of Confederate currency, survivors and camp followers lived on scavenging and barter. Squatters commandeered the few fine houses that remained intact and collected wood scraps and bricolage to build shanties and fences.

The population of 10,940 whites and 9,288 blacks—including 928 widows and orphans—suffered a smallpox epidemic from winter 1864 into January 1865, which required the building of a temporary pesthouse to treat 100 victims. Ignorant paupers refused free treatment by Dr. Willis F. Westmoreland at the Atlanta Medical College because of rumors that the staff wanted more bodies for dissection.

Sister cities—Louisville, Kentucky, and St. Louis, Missouri—sent a total of $8,500 in relief funds. A trainload of supplies arrived from Decatur, Illinois, but Chicago sent only scorn for secessionists. The Northern press bombarded voters with the news of Atlanta's ruin and secured a landslide victory for President Abraham Lincoln.

After Union Colonel Beroth Ballard Eggleston and the First Ohio Cavalry restored order to the city in December 1864, Atlanta moved into recovery mode. Refugees straggled home throughout the winter. The city marshal authorized an 11 P.M. curfew and ordered burned-out buildings pulled down. Because of the overwhelming loss of fortunes and property, people shared a spirit of enterprise that boosted the value of real estate. The city formed four fire companies; congregations rebuilt Cumberland Presbyterian Church, the German Lutheran Church, and St. Luke's Episcopal Church. James R. Wylie established a wholesale grocery store; demand for replacement supplies set the city on its way to dominance of the dry goods market. Marshal O.H. Jones opened a livery stable. James R. Crew and Lemuel Grant began repairing railroads, which were operational by the following spring.

Until April 17, 1866, the U.S. military, under the command of General John Pope, quartered four companies of the Thirteenth Connecticut Regiment at McPherson Barracks to oversee Reconstruction in Fulton County, which included the rebuilding of bridges and the opening of the Atlanta Gas Light Company, Winship Iron Works, brass and iron foundries, W.C. Dodson's print shop, the Pitts & Cook planing mill and door and window factory, a new hardware distributor, and a rolling mill. Brothers Daniel, Emanuel, and Morris Rich operated M. Rich Dry Goods Store, the beginning of the Rich's Department Store chain. In December 1865, Alfred Austell opened the Atlanta National Bank.

Charities continued the work that preceded the siege of Atlanta. The Freedmen's Bureau and the American Missionary Association built a hospital and established relief stations to aid impoverished blacks. The Georgia Railroad and the Western & Atlantic Railroad donated trainloads of wood to the poor. Women held a charity fair on January 18 and 19, 1866, and raised $1,535.90 to relieve suffering among the destitute and victims of cholera. On April 26, the city celebrated the first Confederate Memorial Day, a legal holiday initiated by a war widow, Mary A. Howard Williams, and the Soldiers' Aid Society to honor the 6,900 graves of victims buried far from home and family; of the fallen, 3,000 remained unidentified.

Rising from the Ashes

Following the state's constitutional convention of December 9, 1867, and the departure of General John Pope on January 2, 1868, entrepreneurs George Washington Adair, Lemuel Pratt Grant, Richard Peters, and Hannibal Ingalls Kimball of Maine saw promise in Atlanta's revival. Grant engineered the relocation of Oglethorpe University to Atlanta. Kimball urged the Georgia legislature to move the state capital from Milledgeville to Atlanta; in 1868, he built the first capitol on land previously occupied by an opera house.

In 1869, Kimball and a group of investors formed the Atlanta Canal and Water Company to supply a sanitation system connected to the Chattahoochee River. The next year, Kimball leveled 60 acres (24 hectares) of woodland to create Oglethorpe Park, site of an agricultural fairground for the state Agricultural Society. He replaced the Atlanta Hotel with the H.I. Kimball House, a six-story luxury hotel constructed from yellow brick, and constructed a depot on the grounds of the car shed, which burned during the invasion. He enticed investors to the warehouse district by constructing 300 miles (480 kilometers) of track.

Contributing financial service, Grant founded the Bank of the State of Georgia; Joel Hurt organized the Atlanta Building and Loan Association. In 1871, Adair and Peters's horse-drawn streetcars stimulated growth in the city center and into the suburbs. Peters's eldest child, activist Mary Ellen "Nellie" Peters Black, rode her horse Diamond about the city to assist people in need. She fostered compulsory public education, free kindergartens, and the admission of women to the University of Georgia.

Refinements to commercial interests made Atlanta a world-class city. The Atlanta Literary Female Institution opened on July 1, 1871. In 1872, the state legislature appropriated funds for a federal courthouse and post office. Two years later, the Lakewood waterworks began supplying homes and businesses. At the National Surgical Institute, Dr. C.L. Wilson treated paralysis, chronic illness, and physical deformities. Louise King spearheaded the building of public fountains to water dray horses, a project of the Society for the Prevention of Cruelty to Animals. On March 14, 1874, journalist Henry Woodfin Grady, a city booster and reporter for the *Atlanta Daily Herald,* proposed building a "New South" through the synergy of local laborers with Northern financiers and industrialists. In 1876, the *Atlanta Constitution* emerged as a first-class political journal and a source of reconciliation from the wisdom of Joel Chandler Harris's Uncle Remus stories. By 1877, telephone service was available in the city.

A blot on Atlanta's history into the early twentieth century, leased labor kept ex-slaves bound to a life of drudgery. Throughout Georgia, as well as Alabama, Arkansas, the Carolinas, Florida, Mississippi, and Tennessee, the rise in the value of skilled workmen ages 20 to 45 began in 1864, when the cost of a single worker doubled from $120 to $240 per year for cutting timber or digging coal, iron ore, and limestone. The Chattahoochee Brick Company, owned by financier James Warren English, collaborated with a corrupt court system that intimidated black laborers, detained them for frivolous crimes, and charged them exorbitant court fees. Contracted to lumber mills, rail crews, and brickyards to pay their fines, black men and women occupied forced labor camps, where they survived on a starvation diet. They wore spiked shackles, suffered flogging by sadistic guards, and died in large numbers from tuberculosis.

See also: Literature.

Further Reading

Blackmon, Douglas A. *Slavery by Another Name: The Re-Enslavement of Black Americans from the Civil War to World War II.* New York: Anchor, 2009.

Chirhart, Ann Short, and Betty Wood, eds. *Georgia Women: Their Lives and Times.* Athens: University of Georgia Press, 2009.

Heidler, David S., and Jeanne T. Heidler, eds. *Encyclopedia of the American Civil War: A Political, Social, and Military History.* New York: W.W. Norton, 2000.

Kaemmerlen, Cathy J. *The Historic Oakland Cemetery of Atlanta: Speaking Stones.* Charleston, SC: History Press, 2007.

Weigley, Russell F. *A Great Civil War: A Military and Political History, 1861–1865.* Bloomington: Indiana University Press, 2000.

Atlantic Cable

See Field, Cyrus W.

B

Baltimore, Maryland

A seaport and commercial center from its founding in 1729, Baltimore, Maryland, commands a place in American history for its nearness to the nation's capital and for its dominance of the Chesapeake Bay.

Throughout the 1850s, slaveholders dropped to 1 percent of the white population, which owned 2,118 chattel. Free blacks and immigrants crowded into factories, ironworks, docks, shipyards, and urban housing on the west side of the nation's fourth-largest city. Some 4,300 black male laborers worked at 110 steam-powered factories, operated the Baltimore & Ohio Railroad, and freelanced oystering and crabbing in the bay. In homes and hotels, about 60 percent of black females served the rich as domestics.

As they had since colonial days, Baltimore's poor and homeless relied on economic relief from the Alms House. On a block bounded by Franklin, Lexington, Presstman, and Pulaski streets, the former Calverton estate sheltered the aged, mentally disabled, paralytic, and epileptic and farmed out orphans as apprentices to local business. City medical students practiced their skills on the sick and insane and valued unclaimed corpses as opportunities for anatomy labs and autopsies.

Amid a shifting voter base dominated by the secretive American or "Know-Nothing" Party, the city maintained a reputation for anti-immigrant rowdyism, lawlessness of street thugs, and corruption in law enforcement and the court system. In 1860, Baltimore Police Marshal George Proctor Kane began a modernization program to enhance citizen protection through peacekeeping, crime prevention, and investigation of political gangs.

Commercial leaders and Irish and German wage earners feared that a rumored Southern secession would disrupt trade with lucrative plantation markets and doom the city's economy, a concern shared by municipal leaders in New Orleans and St. Louis. On November 6, 1860, pro-South sympathies among the city's 212,000 citizens produced little support for the election of President Abraham Lincoln. Authorities allowed rebels to operate a Confederate enlistment center and cached weapons at a Baltimore municipal building.

Because of the city's ambivalence toward national loyalty, Baltimore was a likely spot for sectional conspiracy. On February 22, 1861, during Lincoln's 70-stop train trip from Springfield, Illinois, to Washington, D.C., for his inauguration as president, detective Allan Pinkerton, chief of the Union Intelligence Service, thwarted an assassination plot by a pro-Confederacy faction led by Corsican barber Cypriano Ferrandini. According to agent Kate Warne, the nation's first female detective, and her partner, investigator Hattie Lewis Lawton, the plot singled out the Camden Street train station for an attack by knife-wielding assassins when the president-elect, First Lady Mary Todd Lincoln, and sons Robert, Tad, and Willie changed from the Philadelphia, Wilmington, & Baltimore line to the Baltimore & Ohio Railroad. Suspecting both Mayor George William Brown and Police Marshall Kane—and possibly Maryland Governor Thomas Hicks—of engineering the assassination plot, Pinkerton cut telegraph wires to and from the city. He disguised Lincoln as an invalid and scheduled his passage through Baltimore after 3:30 A.M. To preserve appearances, Kane shepherded Mrs. Lincoln to John Gittings's mansion on Mount Vernon Square; Warne stayed on duty in the sleeping car to shield the future first lady until the train reached Washington, D.C., at 6 A.M.

First Bloodshed

Although Maryland did not choose secession along with the first seven states to leave the Union, a vocal bloc in the state validated the right to secede. Conflicting outlooks on slavery and civil war precipitated the Pratt Street Riot of April 19, 1861, a week after the rebel firing on Fort Sumter, South Carolina. Some 720 volunteers to the Union army's Sixth Massachusetts Regiment marched ten blocks from Baltimore's President Street Station, the nation's oldest city train depot, to the Camden Street station. Onlookers engaged in verbal harassment, looting, the brandishing of a South Carolina flag, a blockade, and attacks on railcars. Seven Union companies escaped, leaving four companies behind to face the fury of a mob intent on tearing up rails and crossties. Soldiers dropped their field packs and regimental band instruments and stripped insignia from their uniforms to conceal their enlistment in the Union army.

On foot, the 262 remaining soldiers, including the regimental marching band, quick-stepped the ten blocks through a gauntlet of marauders. Assailants fired shots and hurled rocks and bricks, which wounded 36 and killed 12 civilians and four enlistees. At the President Street Station, a secessionist lobbed a cobblestone that struck the skull of 33-year-old Corporal Sumner Henry Needham, the war's first Union casualty. Despite brain surgery, he died within hours at the Baltimore University Infirmary.

Regimental gunfire sparked an insurrection that threatened the USS *Allegheny,* an iron-hulled gunboat docked at Baltimore Harbor. The riot of some 8,000 people required intervention by a squad of 50 police officers and the medical assistance of nurses Dorothea Dix and Adeline Blanchard Tyler at the Holliday Street police station.

Lincoln and Civil Rights

Sectional animosities set in motion a month of skirmishes between police and brawlers and launched a four-year grudge against the Union. The U.S. Navy suspended harbor traffic to the south and began blockading Confederate ports. President Lincoln, the focus of hatred, suspended the writ of habeas corpus on April 27, the first infringement on constitutional rights and due process in the nation's history. Partisans stoned the house of a customs agent, Henry William Hoffman, a Lincoln appointee who chaired the Maryland Unconditional Union Central Committee and who kept watch for contraband ship propellers smuggled through Baltimore Harbor to the Confederate navy.

Government agents arrested editor Beale H. Richardson and the staff of the Baltimore *Republican* and editors E.F. Carter and W.H. Neilson of the *Daily Gazette* and the *Evening Transcript,* and they suppressed further pro-South publications of the *Evening Post* and *Evening Loyalist.* Only voters swearing an oath of loyalty to the Union could vote at city polls. Confederate spies, blockade runners, and contraband mail carriers faced prison at hard labor or the gallows. Amid mounting violence and arson, Rabbi David Einhorn, Republican Congressman Henry Winter Davis, and other prominent Unionists fled town.

To halt rail traffic at five bridges from Harrisburg and Philadelphia, Pennsylvania, Mayor Brown called out the 15,000-man pro-South state militia, which scavenged gun shops and armories for weapons. The Baltimore Steam Packet Company refused to transport Union soldiers to the Portsmouth, Virginia, naval yard.

Because of the hiatus in transportation from Baltimore, Mayor Brown was unable to ship the bodies of Union dead killed in the Pratt Street Riot to Boston to satisfy the request of John Albion Andrew, governor of Massachusetts. Andrew rebuked Baltimore citizens for their aggression against a peaceful military march that had earlier excited cheers among New Yorkers. A journalist for *Harper's Weekly* declared the killings murder and accused the Baltimore Vigilance Committee of terrorizing and detaining people seeking refuge in the North.

In anger at the encroachment of the Union military, banishment of dissidents, building of earthworks, and carousing of drunken soldiers, secessionists displayed pro-South baby clothes, badges, flags, neckties, photos, sheet music, and umbrellas, all of which the occupation force confiscated. Young rebels went south to join the Army of Northern Virginia. Teacher James Ryder Randall wrote a rebel song, "Maryland, My Maryland," which became the state anthem.

Strife and the City

On May 13, 1861, to save the nation's capital from being encircled by Confederate states, some 1,000 Union forces led by General Benjamin Franklin Butler placed Baltimore under martial law, seized powder stored at Greenmount Cemetery, and garrisoned the state. On Federal Hill south of the harbor, Butler surprised citizens by positioning artillery to protect the restringing of telegraph lines and to shield trains passing between Baltimore and Washington.

Detective Pinkerton, the head of security, detained pro-South state legislators, Mayor Brown, city councilmen, Police Commissioner Charles Howard, and Police Chief Kane at Fort McHenry, a federal prison for political dissidents and prisoners of war. Brown, Howard, and Kane remained in custody until March 26, 1865. The arrest of insurrectionist Ross Winans, an inventor and industrialist, resulted from fears that he had supplied rebels with munitions, including rapid-fire steam guns mounted atop armored carriages.

Although the Union stranglehold prevented Maryland from seceding, the four-year occupation by government troops encouraged sectionalism among dissidents and the radicalism of the Know-Nothings. In support of Lincoln,

Quaker businessman Johns Hopkins donated $500,000 for the arming of Baltimore against rebel invasion.

Throughout the mid-1860s, the Baltimore *Sun* survived censorship by maintaining objectivity. From correspondents at the nation's capital, the paper reported war news as well as stories about boating and ice skating in Druid Hill Park, the seizure of horses for military use, the building of the gunboat *Monocacy* by a local shipyard, the stocking of deer at the Baltimore Zoo, the construction of the Maryland Academy of Sciences in 1867, and the opening of the Maryland School for the Blind in 1872.

Black runaways commonly fled through the state, where bounty hunters profited from the movement of slaves along the Chesapeake Bay. Among the Underground Railroad agents who guided refugees to the North were mulatto mariner Norton Reynolds, drayman Thomas Skinner, and Harriet Tubman. Both Reynolds and Skinner served stiff sentences at the Maryland State Penitentiary in Baltimore for violating the Fugitive Slave Law of 1850.

In July 1863, a year before Maryland banned slavery, Colonel William Birney recruited 8,700 black inmates from slave jails to serve in colored regiments. As Union military camps ringed the city, Baltimore residents formed the Union Relief Association to distribute water and food and to provide quarters for the exhausted to rest. Sisters of Charity from Emmitsburg, Maryland, ran a skilled nurse corps; volunteers wrapped the suffering in blankets and applied hot bricks to their feet; the Adams Express Company established a hospital aide battalion to deliver supplies and ice to aid stations. As combat casualties increased, Washington hospitals dispatched caravans of ambulances bearing the overflow to Baltimore trauma centers. Among the earliest nursing staff to arrive was Clara Barton, who treated the wounded from Virginia battlefields. With a staff of volunteers, Thomas Sim operated a 380-bed convalescent center; volunteer women turned the Maryland Club House into the Freedman's Rest.

In April 1865, the city grieved the president's assassination by John Wilkes Booth, who had grown up in Baltimore and was buried in Greenmount Cemetery. The presidential funeral train arrived from Washington on April 21 and spent three hours in Baltimore. The city that had been so hostile to the president now welcomed the fallen leader. Swarms of residents lined the funeral route, and some 10,000 snaked past the coffin, on public display at the Mercantile Exchange. At the same time, occupation forces redoubled their efforts to suppress Confederate sympathies, particularly hero worship of Booth.

End of Reconstruction

While prisoners of war exited their cells and occupation forces withdrew on January 31, 1866, Baltimore provided care for victims at the Home for the Friendless, the Union Orphan Asylum, and the Soldiers' Home.

The city drew streams of freedmen and their families seeking new opportunities to throw off poverty. Freight and passenger service up the Chesapeake Bay enriched the Baltimore Steam Packet Company, the Chesapeake Steamship Company, and the Leary Line of luxury ships. At a consortium of trade unions in Baltimore on August 20, 1866, labor leaders established the National Labor Union, a federation led by William Sylvis representing 60,000 members of 50 local trade unions demanding an eight-hour day. On July 16, 1877, a wildcat strike erupted in the rail industry over the lowering of wages by the Baltimore & Ohio Railroad, fueling a national work stoppage. Violence and arson in the streets of Baltimore required President Rutherford B. Hayes to dispatch the military.

The legacy of Quaker financier and philanthropist Johns Hopkins, who had made his fortune from the Baltimore & Ohio Railroad, endowed the city with relief agencies and educational facilities. During recovery from the Civil War in 1875, two years after his death, Hopkins's will funded the House of Reformation and Instruction for Colored Children at Cheltenham Farm, 45 miles (72 kilometers) outside Baltimore. The staff tended orphans, crippled children, the offspring of alcoholics, and juvenile delinquents guilty of vagrancy and theft. The curriculum consisted of coursework on agriculture and domestic service. Male students raised pigs, grew hay for livestock, and raised and sold corn, oats, wheat, vegetables, and fruit.

Hopkins's bequest of $3.5 million, the largest in U.S. history to that time, endowed Johns Hopkins University, which opened on George Washington's birthday in the centennial year of 1876. To promote the sciences, the will provided for engineering and medical research under the German university system and awarded scholarships to indigent students, whom faculty groomed through seminars rather than lectures alone.

Also receiving an endowment of $3.5 million, the Johns Hopkins Hospital, built on a 13-acre (5-hectare) parcel bounded by Broadway, Jefferson, Monument, and

Wolfe streets, allied with the medical school as a research and teaching institution—the first medical center of its kind in the nation. Additional gifts to the city included Johns Hopkins University Press in 1878, the nation's oldest university press; the School of Nursing, established on the Nightingale method in 1889; and the Johns Hopkins School of Hygiene and Public Health in 1916.

See also: Catholicism; Judaism; Law and Courts; Lincoln, Abraham.

Further Reading

Cooper, Edward S. *Traitors: The Secession Period, November 1860–July 1861.* Madison-Teaneck, NJ: Fairleigh Dickinson University Press, 2008.

Rutkow, Ira M. *Bleeding Blue and Gray: Civil War Surgery and the Evolution of American Medicine.* New York: Random House, 2005.

Smith, C. Fraser. *Here Lies Jim Crow: Civil Rights in Maryland.* Baltimore: Johns Hopkins University Press, 2008.

Towers, Frank. *The Urban South and the Coming of the Civil War.* Charlottesville: University of Virginia Press, 2004.

Vorenberg, Michael. *Final Freedom: The Civil War, the Abolition of Slavery, and the Thirteenth Amendment.* Cambridge, UK: Cambridge University Press, 2001.

Bancroft, George (1800–1891)

Revered as the "Father of American History," writer, philosopher, and diplomat George Bancroft presided over the American Historical Association and promoted humanist education, democracy, and patriotism. The scion of a Revolutionary War hero, he was born in Worcester, Massachusetts, on October 3, 1800, the eighth of 13 children of Unitarian minister Aaron Bancroft and teacher Lucretia Chandler Bancroft. He studied at Phillips Exeter Academy and Harvard University and read Plato, Koine Greek, biblical history, modern European literature, Arabic and Hebrew history, and Roman classics at Berlin, Göttingen, and Heidelberg, Germany, where he absorbed German idealism while completing a doctoral degree.

Bancroft toyed with the idea of becoming a minister but instead eased into literary and educational pursuits. He taught Greek at his alma mater for a year, translated the verse of Friedrich Schiller, and published articles in the *American Quarterly,* New York *Ledger,* and *North American Review.* In partnership with progressive educator and librarian Joseph Green Cogswell, Bancroft administered the Round Hill School, an experimental school for boys in Northampton, Massachusetts.

After his marriage to Sarah Hopkins Dwight in 1827, Bancroft fathered two sons and two daughters. He began writing *The History of the United States* (1834–1875), which became his life's work. The first volume, *History of the Colonization of the United States* (1834), covered the period from 1492 to 1748. After his wife's death in 1837, he reared their children while collecting tariffs at Boston Harbor. As the appointee of President Martin Van Buren, Massachusetts's Democratic Party recognized Bancroft as its antislavery leader.

From Business to Politics

In 1838, Bancroft wed widow Elizabeth Davis Bliss, acquired two stepsons, and sired another daughter. He joined his father and brothers in work for the Bank of Michigan. After losing the 1844 Massachusetts gubernatorial election, Bancroft accepted appointment as secretary of the navy under President James K. Polk. In that capacity, he was responsible for conceiving and establishing the U.S. Naval Academy at Annapolis, Maryland. The facility opened on October 10, 1845, and enrolled 56 men.

Along with Secretary of State James Buchanan, Bancroft assumed prominence among the president's advisers. As temporary secretary of war, he ordered the seizure of California and the march of General Zachary Taylor's occupational troops into Texas, a move that precipitated war with Mexico and the ousting of Mexicans from territory north of the Rio Grande.

In 1846, he began a three-year posting as ambassador to Great Britain. In his free time, he researched primary documents on American history at the British Museum as well as in the national archives in Berlin and Paris and libraries in the Netherlands and Spain.

Upon settling in New York in 1849, Bancroft returned to his writing project and completed six volumes of his *History of the United States* by adhering to a rigorous daily schedule. His biographical writings included reflections on the lives of colonial theologian Jonathan Edwards, scholar Edward Everett, and presidents James K. Polk and Martin Van Buren. At a speech at New York's Cooper Institute on February 22, 1862, he urged the government to meet its obligations to democracy; the occasion marked the pinnacle of the author's patriotism. Throughout the war, Bancroft advised Lincoln on the historical precedent of insurrection.

On December 4, 1865, Bancroft wrote President Andrew Johnson's first message to Congress. On Lincoln's birthday, February 12, 1866, Bancroft addressed legislators, the Supreme Court, the cabinet, and President Ulysses S. Grant with a moving speech, "Memorial Address on the Life and Character of Abraham Lincoln," calling Lincoln the restorer of the republic.

Adviser to the Great

In 1867, Bancroft served as U.S. envoy to Germany and Prussia, where he promoted the rights of Europeans to expatriate from their birth countries. He clarified disputed North American boundaries with Great Britain and kept a close watch on the labors of Otto von Bismarck to establish the German Empire.

At age 75, Bancroft became a permanent resident of Washington, D.C., at a brownstone on H Street near the White House. He continued riding horseback during his summers at Newport, Rhode Island. After completing the tenth volume of his history in 1875, the following year, he honored the nation's centennial with a revised edition of his chronicle condensed into six volumes. In 1882, he issued the two-volume *History of the Formation of the Constitution of the United States,* which extols the influence of Thomas Jefferson. A widower for the last five years of his life, Bancroft lived with the family of his son, John Chandler Bancroft, and died of pneumonia on January 17, 1891.

Bancroft's legacy included scholarships to the city of Worcester and to Harvard University, honoring his parents and a former teacher. His personal, professional, and political correspondence preserved the events and opinions of his day, particularly his letters to President Abraham Lincoln, educator Louis Agassiz, Oliver Wendell Holmes, Sr., General Philip Henry Sheridan, and General Charles Sumner during the Civil War and Reconstruction. Bancroft's published papers established his beliefs that civil war was a test of the nation's vitality and that slavery would prove to be a temporary anomaly.

See also: Gettysburg Address; Johnson, Andrew.

Further Reading

Foner, Eric, ed. *The New American History.* Philadelphia: Temple University Press, 1997.

Heidler, David S., and Jeanne T. Heidler, eds. *Encyclopedia of the American Civil War: A Political, Social, and Military History.* New York: W.W. Norton, 2000.

Vorenberg, Michael. *Final Freedom: The Civil War, the Abolition of Slavery, and the Thirteenth Amendment.* Cambridge, UK: Cambridge University Press, 2001.

Banking and Finance

Like other aspects of American commerce, banking and finance suffered serious setbacks and disparities during the Civil War and its aftermath. Federal chartering of banks, mandated by the National Bank Act of February 26, 1863, standardized a national currency system based on federal bank notes. Secretary of the Treasury Salmon P. Chase recommended the system in 1861 to override state authority over the nation's economy. At the time, 2,600 banks issued money of their own design.

Chase targeted private coinage, such as that of silver miners in Nevada; attorney Anson Pacely Killen Safford's miners' bank in Gila Bend, Arizona; and stockman Joseph Geating McCoy's bank and stock trading office at the railhead in Abilene, Kansas. One private firm, Clark, Gruber, and Company of Leavenworth, Kansas, opened a branch bank in Denver, Colorado, and began minting $10 gold pieces. The company followed with $20, $5, and $2.50 coins and remained active until the U.S. Treasury bought the operation and turned it into an assay office. Overseeing the standardized federal system was the Office of the Comptroller of the Currency, a bureau of the Treasury Department headed by Hugh McCulloch, president of the Bank of Indiana.

Under the provisions of the National Bank Act, President Abraham Lincoln authorized the sale of federal bonds to finance the Civil War and the issuance of $450 million in greenbacks (paper bills not backed by treasury reserves of gold or silver). Comptroller McCulloch had the power to approve charters for new banks, issue lending and investment regulations, promote efficiency and innovative financial services, and penalize financial institutions that failed to comply with the law.

The first institution to adopt a national charter, the First National Bank of Pittsburgh, opened in 1863 under the presidency of James Laughlin with $400,000 in capital. The concept of federal banks took hold on the frontier at financier Jerome Bunty Chaffee's First National Bank of Denver, Colorado; the Stock Growers' National Bank in Cheyenne, Wyoming; and Stephen Elkins's Santa Fe National Bank in New Mexico. Defects in the system required Congress to pass the National Bank Act of 1864, which authorized internal regulation and audits.

Meanwhile, to pay the war debt, Congress enacted banking legislation on March 3, 1865, that levied a 10 percent tax on state bank notes as of July 1, 1866. The last of President Lincoln's financial moves, the act forced a confusing array of state currencies out of use and distributed

$150 million in circulating notes among states, territories, and the District of Columbia. The state banks declined in number, and 1,644 national banks dominated the national economy by October 1866.

Uncertainty and the Panic of 1873

Because of the emergence of barter, theft, and black marketeering, estimates of the era's trade and profits require guesswork. The dollar's value fluctuated from a low of $1.06 in 1861 to a wartime high of $1.96 in 1865 and back down to $1.26 in 1877. The late Reconstruction devaluation began a drop that remained steady until 1899, when the dollar reached a value of $1.

Passage of the British North America Act by the British Parliament on July 1, 1867, united the Canadian territories into a confederation. The unification of banking and currency fostered binational cooperation to enhance finance, commerce, and trade on both sides of the border.

As the United States became industrialized, the rise of a plutocracy attested to the control of banking, oil and coal, railroads, telegraph, and steel mills by monopolies and their unfair competition against small businesses. Newspapers sanctioned advertising that blamed high consumer costs and tight credit on financiers, land speculators, importers, and wholesalers.

A stock market crash in New York on September 18, 1873, triggered the Panic of 1873 and marked the beginning of the Long Depression, a five-year economic decline. Following demands for westward expansion and replacement of the national infrastructure after the Civil War, investors overindulged in risky railroad ventures, which resulted in overbuilding and delayed projects. The Coinage Act of 1873 dropped silver from federal currency standards and replaced a bimetal system with a gold standard. The shift reduced livelihoods in Colorado, Idaho, and Nevada, the primary silver-producing states.

The depressed money supply likewise jeopardized farms, mining operations, and small businesses and destabilized Jay Cooke & Company, a firm that overtaxed its credit to finance the Northern Pacific Railway through Duluth, Minnesota, to the Great Lakes. The collapse of Cooke's bank that same year had a disastrous domino effect, toppling other banks, 18,000 businesses, and 89 railroads, while deflating prices and real estate values.

The rapid drop shut down trading on the New York Stock Exchange for ten days. Manufacturers and steelmakers lost contracts and laid off workers, forcing the United States into a depression and generating an unemployment rate of 14 percent. War veterans migrated to potential job sites, earning the names "bum" and "tramp" for their ragged appearance on the road.

France and Germany slowed the U.S. economic recovery by placing tariffs on iron and rye. The economy lagged until the return of the U.S. gold standard in January 1879. During the lengthy slowdown, capitalists Andrew Carnegie, Cyrus McCormick, and John D. Rockefeller financed their individual projects and enriched themselves at the expense of competitors. The rise of U.S. plutocrats attested to the world that American banks had replaced European money markets as global financial centers.

Speculation and Distrust

During the presidency of Ulysses S. Grant, the media fostered an atmosphere of popular distrust of the reliance of big business on government favoritism. The Fisk-Gould Scandal of fall 1869 derived from the conspiracy of stockbroker James "Diamond Jim" Fisk, Jr., and investor Jason "Jay" Gould, owner of New York City's Tenth National Bank, to corner the gold market and enhance freight transport over the Erie Railroad. Gould displayed his power over the national economy by artificially elevating the gold market in March by purchasing $7 million in precious metals. On September 24, 1869, stock market speculation provoked the panic of Black Friday, when gold prices fell by 27 percent, ruining half of Wall Street and precipitating investor breakdowns and suicides. The hoarding of precious metals threatened American greenbacks, bonds, agricultural exports, and credit and launched a two-week market frenzy that stymied foreign trade.

At Indianapolis on November 25, 1874, backers of coin-based currency formed the Greenback Party (also known as the Greenback Labor Party), a populist bloc that opposed the National Bank Act of 1863. In Arkansas and Texas, prominent voices in the new party arose from former slaves and members of the Knights of Labor and the National Grange of the Order of Patrons of Husbandry, an agrarian society bent on economic and political self-betterment. James Baird Weaver, a malcontented Iowa politician, infused the party with disdain for Republican monetary policies and limited credit. He inflamed speculation concerning Grant's under-the-table dealings with railroads and banks.

The Greenback Party drew debtors, laborers, and farmers in the South and West who had lost income during the Panic of 1873. Members built a platform based on beliefs that hard money backed by precious metals benefited only wealthy financiers and banks. To return the struggling middle class to prosperity, Greenbackers promoted privately owned factories and banks and the free enterprise system of running the economy. The party's presidential candidate in 1876, inventor Peter Cooper of New York City, identified the gold standard and usury as the root causes of monetary deflation and the years-long depression.

Progress Preceding the Gilded Age

In addition to demanding the regulation of railroad hauling rates and the protection of natural resources, members of the Greenback Party demanded more cheap currency in circulation and fostered coinage of the silver dollar. They anticipated that inflated farm prices would ease agricultural debt and break the stranglehold that banks held over stockmen. Cooper won only 81,737 votes and no electoral votes, but 15 Greenbackers won seats in Congress and battered a pro-banking alliance with the perspectives of the agrarian and laboring classes.

On January 14, 1875, the Specie Resumption Act reduced the number of federal bank notes in circulation to $300 million and guaranteed the exchange of silver coins for Civil War paper "coins"—called "shin plasters," bills worth less than $1. While Greenbackers demanded repeal of the specie act, the federal offer of "hard money" eased suspicions of paper money and of government control of finances by returning power over currency to national banks. Because citizens declined the opportunity to demand gold for paperbacks, the Greenbackers gradually faded from the political scene.

Despite a perplexing economy, the 1860s and 1870s produced significant players on the financial scene for decades to come, including the Drexel, Morgan banking house, a Wall Street anchor for European investors. After the fall of Atlanta, Georgia, during General William Tecumseh Sherman's "March to the Sea," Alfred Austell in December 1865 opened the Atlanta National Bank, a sign of promise in a defeated and burned-out Southern capital. Francis Marion Coker founded the Bank of the State of Georgia, and Joel Hurt organized the Atlanta Building and Loan Association. In Utah, secular interests occupied Mormon financiers, who chartered Zion's Savings Bank & Trust Company in fall 1873.

Insuring Lives and Well-Being

The insurance industry got its start from entrepreneurial investment in risk management in the lives and welfare of ordinary citizens. While protecting orphans and widows from penury, insurance firms amassed capital to underwrite farm and factory expansion.

On April 21, 1862, Massachusetts Governor John Albion Andrew approved the establishment of the John Hancock Mutual Life Insurance, a Boston financial institution whose name honored a signer of the Declaration of Independence. In Chicago, entrepreneur Philip Danforth "Phil" Armour diversified his meatpacking conglomerate by investing in the Baltimore & Ohio Railroad, streetcar companies in Kansas and Missouri, and the Chicago, Milwaukee & St. Paul Railroad, as well as the Metropolitan National Bank, Illinois Trust and Savings, National Trust Bank, and Northwestern Mutual Life Insurance Company. In Hartford, Connecticut, in 1864, Travelers Insurance, led by stonecutter James Goodwin Batterson, offered accident policies covering travel by steamer or train, presaging America's first auto policies. In 1870, the firm chose a red umbrella as a recognizable symbol of personal security.

The Prudential Insurance Company, a large diversified financier, got its start in 1873 in the cellar of the State Bank in Newark, New Jersey. With $30,000 in capital, businessman John Fairfield Dryden, an investor in banks and street railways, founded the firm as the Widows and Orphans Friendly Society. Two years later, he changed the name to the Prudential Friendly Society. Dryden tailored his business model to the successful British Prudential Assurance Company, which insured laborers and dispatched agents to the home each week to collect payments. Dryden advertised his company as a source of industrial risk management, specifically, illness and disability relief, old age pensions, and burial funds for adults and children. For his insight into the needs of American immigrants and factory works, he earned $50 million and recognition as the "Father of Industrial Insurance."

See also: Chase, Salmon P.; Gould, Jay; Metropolitan Life Insurance.

Further Reading

Appleby, Joyce. *The Relentless Revolution: A History of Capitalism.* New York: W.W. Norton, 2010.

Bowers, Q. David. *Obsolete Paper Money Issued by Banks in the United States, 1782–1866: A Study and Appreciation for the Numismatist and Historian.* Atlanta, GA: Whitman, 2006.

Davis, Joseph Stancliffe. *Essays in the Earlier History of American Corporations.* 2 vols. Clark, NJ: Lawbook Exchange, 2006.

Hallett, Anthony, and Diane Hallett. *Entrepreneur Magazine: Encyclopedia of Entrepreneurs.* New York: Wiley, 1997.

Miller, Christine. *San Francisco's Financial District.* Charleston, SC: Arcadia, 2005.

Stanley, George E. *The Era of Reconstruction and Expansion, 1865–1900.* Milwaukee, WI: World Almanac Library, 2005.

Walton, Gary M., and Hugh Rockoff. *History of the American Economy.* 10th ed. Mason, OH: Thomas/South-Western, 2005.

Barnum, P.T. (1810–1891)

A master of publicity and showmanship, Phineas Taylor Barnum became a millionaire by assembling such popular culture phenomena as circuses, sideshows, and special collections of "curiosities." A native of Bethel, Connecticut, born on July 5, 1810, he was one of ten children of Irene Taylor and Philo Barnum, a merchant and hotelier.

Lazy but adept at numbers, Barnum sold lottery tickets at age 12 and learned the rudiments of bargaining and petty fraud while keeping a grocery store. In 1829, he married Charity "Chairy" Hallett, the mother of their four daughters. Barnum involved himself in auctioning, land speculation, lotteries, and the repeal of blue laws for infringing on the constitutional right of freedom of religion.

Barnum's weekly newspaper, *The Herald of Freedom,* earned him two months in the Danbury jail for libeling Seth Seelye, a pious Calvinist deacon at Bethel, for hypocrisy and usury and for defrauding an orphan boy of $17. The court silenced Barnum because he was a Universalist who did not believe he owed accountability to God. He turned the eight weeks of imprisonment into an opportunity for self-promotion. Upon his release on January 5, 1833, a band played "Home, Sweet Home."

At age 24, Barnum opened a sideshow at Niblo's Garden, a New York City theater on Broadway. He earned $1,500 per week from the exhibit of Joice Heth, a 78-year-old blind, paralytic slave women, for whom he had paid $1,000. He traveled across New England, advertising Heth as the 160-year-old nurse of George Washington. An autopsy at her death in 1836 proved her real age and earned Barnum the title "Prince of Humbugs."

Bored by selling tickets for Aaron Turner's traveling circus, Barnum assembled a variety act of his own, called Barnum's Grand Scientific and Musical Theater. In 1841, he and businessman John Scudder bought Scudder's American Museum, a garish five-story museum at Broadway and Ann Street in New York City. Acts featured such human anomalies as the conjoined twins Chang and Eng Bunker, Isaac W. "the Living Skeleton" Sprague, giants Arthur James Caley and Anna Haining Swan, the bearded Madame Clofullia, Constentenus the Tattooed Man, S.K.G. "the Armless Wonder" Nellis, and Zalumma the Circassion Beauty. In addition, Barnum presented automat and scientific gadgets, a tailless miniature horse, a flea circus, phrenology and taxidermy exhibits, Bohemian glassblowers, and minstrels in blackface. His hoaxes included a wax copy of the 10-foot-tall (3-meter-tall) petrified Cardiff Giant, Jo-Jo the Dog-Faced Boy, the Wild Men of Borneo, the Mammoth Infant, R.O. "the Living Phantom" Wickware, Mademoiselle Fanny, and William Henry "Zip the Pinhead" Johnson, a caged microcephalic ballyhooed as the "missing link" from Africa.

In the lecture hall, Barnum banned vulgarity and profanity and touted the wholesome nature and educational value of his lineup. To ensure the safety of women and children and the dignity of such visitors as the Prince of Wales, plainclothes detectives removed rowdy and drunken patrons. Within five years, 400,000 patrons per year visited the museum, which advertised 500,000 curiosities.

A Changed Man

Family and community, particularly the love of his daughters, altered Barnum's outlook. Contributing to his publicity was his eldest child, Caroline Cornelia Barnum, who often donned costumes and took part in exhibits. Charity Barnum rescued her husband from alcoholism in 1847 and steered him toward involvement in the temperance movement. He became a philanthropist and an abolitionist Republican, serving successfully as the mayor of Bridgeport and for two terms in the Connecticut legislature.

In September 1850, Barnum showcased a more cultural discovery, opera star Jenny Lind, the "Swedish Nightingale," at a cost of $187,500 for 150 concerts plus expenses. A second contract with Lind earned Barnum $500,000 from performances and the sale of "Jenny" souvenirs.

On a lowbrow note, Barnum's popular museum booths featured a desiccated monkey in a fish suit billed as the Fiji Mermaid, albinos, and the dwarves Leopold "Admiral Dot" Kahn, George Washington Morrison "Commodore" Nutt, Major Edward "General Grant, Jr." Newell, and General Tom Thumb, who debuted on January 1, 1842. Thumb, whose real name was Charles Sherwood Stratton, had stopped growing temporarily at age six months, when he was 25 inches (63 centimeters) tall. Over the next two decades, he grew to 2 feet, 11 inches (88.9 centimeters).

In 1862, President Abraham Lincoln invited Barnum and Thumb to the White House to meet his cabinet. The next year at Grace Church in New York City, Barnum created publicity at Thumb's wedding to dwarf Mercy

Lavinia Warren Bump. On a tour of Queen Victoria's court, Barnum profited from British curiosity about Thumb's imitations of Cain, Cupid, Frederick the Great, Hercules, King Arthur, Napoleon, Robinson Crusoe, Romulus, Samson, a Scots highlander, Tom Tit, and Yankee Doodle and from selling souvenirs of Thumb's wedding. During the couple's honeymoon in Europe, they dined with Emperor Napoleon III.

In addition to freak shows, Barnum's Moral Lecture room featured baby contests, dog and flower shows, tableaux, and scenes from the life of Dred Scott, as well as Shakespearean tragedy, the melodrama *Uncle Tom's Cabin,* and William Henry Smith's temperance play *The Drunkard; or, The Fallen Saved* (1844), which ran for 100 performances. Increasing Barnum's notoriety were his weekly paper, *Illustrated News,* and the first of four autobiographies, *Life of P.T. Barnum* (1854), which he distributed by mass printing.

Showman, impresario, and self-proclaimed "Prince of Humbugs," P.T. Barnum *(left)* poses in 1862 with the popular Commodore Nutt, whom Barnum billed as "the smallest man in the world." *(Hulton Archive/Getty Images)*

By 1856, however, unwise investments forced Barnum to the brink of bankruptcy, until Tom Thumb volunteered to make another tour to revive the promoter's finances. To his exhibits, Barnum added a sea lion and a beluga whale at the nation's first aquarium, a rogues' gallery, a display of the Seven Wonders of the World, and wax figures of James Buchanan and Franklin Pierce that brought his featured oddities to 850,000.

Over 24 years, the museum earned $9.5 million by charging a quarter admission to some 15,000 show-goers daily. When a Confederate arsonist burned the building on July 13, 1865, police shot an escaping tiger while firemen dragged wax figures toward safety. A second museum survived until 1868, when it, too, burned.

Innovators

On April 10, 1871, Barnum abandoned retirement and changed direction. He partnered with clown and horse manager Dan Costello and Wisconsin investor William Cameron Coup in opening a traveling entertainment, P.T. Barnum's Great Traveling Museum, Menagerie, Caravan, Hippodrome, and Circus. At the rate of 100 miles (160 kilometers) per night, the entourage traveled by rear-loading cars on the Pennsylvania Railroad. Barnum purchased his own train—custom-made sleepers, boxcars, and flatcars, designed by Coup and manufactured in Urbana, Ohio. To create public enthusiasm, the company ordered lithographed posters and sent clowns, acrobats, and bands on parades through small towns. An advance squadron preceded the train and drove tent stakes into the ground for rapid raising of the big top, which covered 5 acres (2 hectares) and offered seating for 10,000. On April 27, 1874, a performance at Madison Square Garden in New York City advertised chariot races, elephants, camels and llamas, acrobats, and high-wire walkers.

Barnum used some of his profits from the circus to endow Tufts University, to fund societies preventing animal cruelty, and to found Bridgeport Hospital, a cause to which Caroline Barnum contributed for the care of black patients. After the death of Charity Barnum in 1873, the 63-year-old showman married 22-year-old Nancy Fish.

By 1881, Barnum's traveling extravaganza billed itself as the world's first three-ring circus, the "Greatest Show on Earth." Barnum merged with London promoters James Anthony Bailey, James E. Cooper, and James Llewellyn

Hutchinson to form P.T. Barnum's Greatest Show on Earth, Sanger's Royal British Menagerie, the Great London Circus & Grand International Allied Shows. At a cost of $10,000, in 1882, the partners added a purchase from the London Zoo, the Sudanese bush elephant Jumbo, "Lord of Beasts." To cheering crowds, handlers marched the grand exhibit up Broadway and over the Brooklyn Bridge. Until Jumbo met a tragic end when crushed by a freight train in St. Thomas, Ontario, in 1885, he earned the partners $1 million, added the word "jumbo" to the English language, and earned Barnum the moniker "the Exhibition King." (Barnum sued the Grand Trunk Railway for $10,000 and free rail travel for a year.)

In 1886, Barnum's circus debuted in Philadelphia with four rings and a hippodrome. The performers toured the United States, England, France, Germany, Italy, Java, New Zealand, Russia, Scandinavia, Spain, and South America. Following a stroke, Barnum died in his sleep of heart failure on April 7, 1891. In 1919, his legacy survived in the Ringling Brothers and Barnum and Bailey Circus, the first modern circus.

Further Reading

Ashby, LeRoy. *With Amusement for All: A History of American Popular Culture Since 1830.* Lexington: University Press of Kentucky, 2006.

Barnum, Phineas T. *The Colossal P.T. Barnum Reader: Nothing Else Like It in the Universe.* Ed. James W. Cook. Urbana: University of Illinois Press, 2005.

Cook, James W. *The Arts of Deception: Playing with Fraud in the Age of Barnum.* Cambridge, MA: Harvard University Press, 2001.

Reiss, Benjamin. *The Showman and the Slave: Race, Death, and Memory in Barnum's America.* Cambridge, MA: Harvard University Press, 2001.

Vitale, Joe. *There's a Customer Born Every Minute: P.T. Barnum's Amazing 10 "Rings of Power" for Creating Fame, Fortune, and a Business Empire Today—Guaranteed!* Hoboken, NJ: Wiley, 2006.

Barton, Clara (1821–1912)

Among the 3,000 female volunteers to the Civil War effort, humanitarian Clarissa Harlowe Barton earned renown for extending emergency care in peacetime. A native of North Oxford, Massachusetts, she was born into a patriotic abolitionist family on December 25, 1821, and espoused the family's pacifism and Universalist faith.

She began practical nursing at age 11 after her brother David injured himself in a fall from a barn roof. After her homeschooling, at age 15, she taught at a subscription school in Bordentown, New Jersey, where she championed free public education for children whose parents could not afford the subscription fee.

In 1851, she took advanced courses at the Liberal Institute of Clinton, New York. Under appointment by President Franklin Pierce in September 1854, she became the first female on the staff of the U.S. Patent Office and the first female to receive the same pay as male clerks. However, gender harassment and malaria ended her employment in 1861.

In the aftermath of the Baltimore draft riots and the chaos resulting from the First Battle of Bull Run, Virginia, on July 21, 1861, Barton developed a sisterly affection for the Sixth Massachusetts Regiment, some members of which she knew personally. She advertised in the Worcester, Massachusetts, *Spy* for provisions, sewing supplies, serving utensils, salve, candles, and cash donations for the 3,000 wounded, whom she found bedded down on straw. Her independent relief program warehoused and distributed shirts, handkerchiefs, scarves, socks, and other personal and medical supplies to casualties. She also aided Frances Dana Gage in tending to the needs of freed slaves, who poured into the nation's capital with only the clothes on their backs.

On August 3, 1862, U.S. Surgeon General William A. Hammond licensed Barton to travel via army ambulance. She entered combat nursing six days later at the Battle of Cedar Mountain in Culpeper, Virginia, where she tended Union casualties and Confederate prisoners of war. She ate military fare and slept in tents without complaint. Behind military lines on battlefields from Camp Parole, Maryland, to Charleston and Fort Wagner, South Carolina, amid rifle and cannon fire, she brought water and comfort to the Confederate and Union fallen, solicited space in private homes, and helped the wounded board trains until typhoid fever overwhelmed her energies in mid-September 1862.

By January 1864, Barton was back in Washington, D.C., gathering supplies and superintending the diets of invalids at Point of Rocks, Virginia. On July 4, 1864, she aided a former domestic, the mother of 13. A personal letter contained the details:

> The rebel troops had taken her bedding and clothing and ours had taken her money, forty dollars in gold . . . I gave her all the food I had . . . and shall try to find employment for her.

Barton in Peacetime

By war's end, Barton's focus had shifted to the 22,000 missing soldiers and their anxious families. With the aid of 20-year-old veteran Dorence Atwater, she began collecting 13,000 names of those who had died at the notorious Andersonville Prison in Georgia, the largest Confederate military prison during the Civil War. Staff assumed that typhoid fever had caused the high death rate—about 100 per day—but a later investigation blamed malnutrition and epidemic pellagra. With facts recorded by Atwater, Barton began a letter-writing campaign to inform parents, widows, and orphans of soldiers' deaths.

With a company of woodworkers provided by Secretary of War Edwin M. Stanton and $15,000 to cover expenses, in July and August 1865, she identified soldiers' remains, directed landscaping and fencing, and corrected misspellings of names on grave markers at the 27-acre (11-hectare) stockade, where the dead had been dumped face down in trenches. Portrait photographer Mathew Brady captured her postwar efforts. On August 17, with the cemetery finished and only 460 graves unidentified, Barton raised the American flag and wept for the cruelties suffered by Union prisoners of war.

Because Atwater refused to surrender his list of Andersonville casualties to Union authorities, he was arrested, discharged from the army, and fined $300. Barton interceded on his behalf to gain amnesty from President Andrew Johnson and petitioned Horace Greeley, editor of the *New York Tribune,* to publish Atwater's compilation, which extended over five pages. She sent state lists to every national newspaper and requested free publication. Veterans replied to the lists with additional data on the survival and death of comrades and their places of burial.

Barton's energies served additional causes, including the honoring of Andersonville as a national cemetery. On February 21, 1866, she testified before Congress on the identification of soldiers' remains at Andersonville and on evidence of torture of some 34,000 prisoners of war.

In fall 1866, during a period of depression resulting from the end of her relationship with Colonel John H. Elwell of Cleveland, Ohio, Barton welcomed a chance to tour and lecture on volunteerism and "War Without the Tinsel" at 200 venues in Connecticut, Illinois, Indiana, Iowa, Kansas, Massachusetts, Michigan, Nebraska, New Jersey, New York, and Wisconsin. Arranging transportation and facilitating her appearances was Dorence Atwater, her secretary-companion, and fellow speakers Frederick Douglass, Ralph Waldo Emerson, William Lloyd Garrison, and Mark Twain. During the lengthy tour, she survived robbery in a sleeper car and a train wreck, but netted $12,000.

On November 30, 1867, Barton began assisting Susan B. Anthony and Elizabeth Cady Stanton in the woman suffrage drive by appealing to veterans to equalize opportunities for women and by writing essays for Lucy Stone's *The Woman's Journal.* Barton supported Frederick Douglass's civil rights initiative and campaigned for ratification of the Fifteenth Amendment to the U.S. Constitution, giving blacks the right to vote. In 1876, Anthony acknowledged Barton's exemplary career with a sketch in an encyclopedia of notable American women.

From Nurse to Lobbyist

In a state of nervous strain and near blindness in summer 1869, Barton completed her work for the U.S. Army's Office of Correspondence with Friends of the Missing Men. She had identified 22,000 missing soldiers and answered 68,132 letters about their identities and whereabouts. Reflecting on her altruism toward the grieving,

A schoolteacher and patent office clerk, Clara Barton began organizing relief efforts and caring for the wounded during the Civil War without an official organization or affiliation. In 1881, she founded the American Red Cross. *(Time & Life Pictures/Getty Images)*

the Reverend Olympia Brown remarked that Barton's "name is dear to soldiers and blessed in thousands of homes to which the soldier shall return no more."

On a medical vacation to Glasgow, London, Paris, Geneva, and Corsica during the Franco-Prussian War (1870–1871), Barton took up her aid station duties with the International Committee of the Red Cross, a neutral relief agency. With the aid of a translator, she opened sewing factories in Strasbourg, France, to employ women and supply clothing to refugees. Educating her on the principles of neutral relief stations in July 1870 was surgeon Louis Paul Appia, an eyewitness to the Battle of Solferino, Italy, on June 24, 1859, and a promoter of neutral relief efforts at Brescia, Milan, and Turin. The concept became Barton's crusade for the remainder of her 90 years.

In 1873, Barton returned to the United States to recuperate from a bleeding ulcer at a water cure sanitarium in Dansville, New York. In 1877, she wrote a pamphlet, *The Red Cross of the Geneva Convention: What It Is,* published the following year, in which she explained "the neutrality of all sanitary supplies, ambulances, surgeons, nurses, attendants, and the sick or wounded men, and their safe conduct, when they bear the sign of the organization." The text advocated the centralization of relief, preparation, impartiality, and international solidarity.

Barton urged President Rutherford B. Hayes and Congress to sign the Treaty of Geneva and to establish a standby national relief effort backed by a regimented cadre of volunteers and warehoused tents, wagons, and supplies. Her strategies for directing volunteers during floods, hurricanes, fires, epidemics, and disasters preceded the founding, on May 21, 1881, of the American Red Cross. By the time of her death from pneumonia on April 12, 1912, Clara Barton had become known as the "Florence Nightingale of America" and the "Angel of the Battlefields."

See also: Brady, Mathew; Brown, Olympia; Emancipation Proclamation.

Further Reading

Burton, David H. *Animating History: The Biographical Pulse.* Philadelphia: Saint Joseph's University Press, 2007.

Lurie, Maxine N., and Marc Mappen, eds. *Encyclopedia of New Jersey.* New Brunswick, NJ: Rutgers University Press, 2004.

McPherson, James M. *Battle Cry of Freedom: The Civil War Era.* Illustrated ed. New York: Oxford University Press, 1988.

Schultz, Jane E. *Women at the Front: Hospital Workers in Civil War America.* Chapel Hill: University of North Carolina Press, 2004.

Silber, Nina. *Daughters of the Union: Northern Women Fight the Civil War.* Cambridge, MA: Harvard University Press, 2005.

Bass, Sam (1851–1878)

Noted Texas desperado Sam Bass led his gang in horse thievery and train and stage robbery. An illiterate farm boy from Mitchell, Indiana, he was born on July 21, 1851, and orphaned in 1864. After five years of mistreatment by an uncle, Solomon Bass, and a slave driver, his maternal uncle David Sheeks, Bass fled at age 18 to St. Louis, Missouri. From there, he went by river steamer to Rosedale, Mississippi, where he worked in a mill and learned to shoot a pistol.

In 1871, in Denton, Texas, Bass found work as a cowboy and a teamster for Sheriff W.F. Eagan. In social contact with Frank "Blockey" Jackson, Jim Murphy, and Henry Underwood, Bass proved inept at gambling and, in 1874, at racing his mare Jenny. At the sheriff's insistence, Bass gave up driving wagons.

At Fort Sill, Oklahoma, in April 1875, Bass stole Indian ponies with the aid of accomplices John Hudson and Underwood and sold them in San Antonio. In 1876, he joined drover Joel Collins and Jack Davis in moving a herd of stolen longhorns to Sydney, Nebraska, and on to the Black Hills to sell them. Collins and Davis lost their illegal gains of $8,000 at poker dens in Deadwood, South Dakota, and Ogallala, Nebraska.

Bass failed to make a living in the freight business from Yankton and Dodge City, Kansas, to the Black Hills. He, Davis, and Tom Nixon took up stage robbery in the Dakotas, but they made little off their seven holdups. They reputedly waylaid the steel-lined coach of the Cheyenne & Black Hills Stage & Express Company five times in two months, killing driver Johnny Slaughter.

In summer 1876, Bass turned from holding up stages to robbing trains at Big Spring, Nebraska. On September 18, 1877, he formed a gang of six men—James Berry, Collins, Davis, William "Bad Bill" Heffridge (also known as Bill Heffery), and Nixon—who robbed a Union Pacific train en route to San Francisco. It would be their most lucrative heist—$60,000 in newly minted $20 gold pieces, plus $1,300 and four gold watches from passengers. The gang split the loot and separated.

Bass and five new gang members—Seaborn "Nubbins Colt" Barnes, Frank Jackson, Arkansas Johnson, James W. "Jim" Murphy, and Henry Underwood—holed up outside Dallas and stole amounts under $500 from stages and four trains. From the Fort Worth stage, they got so little cash that they returned a dollar to each passenger to pay for breakfast. A reward for $10,000 identified Bass and two accomplices, Davis and Heffridge.

Operating under the name Samuel Bushon, Bass remained at large from Pinkerton security agent Tooney Waits, Grayson County Sheriff William C. Everheart, and a group of Texas Rangers led by Captain Junius Peak, whom Governor Richard Coke had hired to track the Bass gang. Foiling a plot to rob the Williamson County Bank, gang member Jim Murphy betrayed the plan to John B. Jones, an Indian fighter and captain of the Texas Rangers. The robbers argued about shooting Murphy, until Jackson intervened in Murphy's favor.

On July 19, 1878, southeast of Dallas at Round Rock, Bass's bandits shot Deputy Sheriff Ahijah W. "Caige" Grimes, who attempted to disarm them at a dry goods store. Barnes died at the scene from a bullet to the head. Ranger George Harrell fatally wounded Bass, shooting him through the small of the back. Bass died on July 21, his twenty-seventh birthday. A lament believed to have been composed not long after his death, "The Ballad of Sam Bass," turned a short-lived thief into a Texas legend.

See also: Nebraska; Wyoming Territory.

Further Reading

Adams, Ramon F. *Burs Under the Saddle: A Second Look at Books and Histories of the West.* Norman: University of Oklahoma Press, 1989.

Harvey, Bill. *Texas Cemeteries: The Resting Places of Famous, Infamous, and Just Plain Interesting Texans.* Austin: University of Texas Press, 2003.

Martin, Charles L. *A Sketch of Sam Bass, the Bandit: A Graphic Narrative.* Norman: University of Oklahoma Press, 1997.

Baylor, John R. (1822–1894)

A Confederate war hero and Indian fighter, John Robert Baylor carved out and governed the Confederate Territory of Arizona. A native of Paris in Bourbon County, Kentucky, he was born on July 27, 1822, to army surgeon John Walker Baylor and Sophie Marie Weidner Baylor. As an adolescent, he lived in Second Creek outside Natchez, Mississippi, and, with his older brother, Henry Weidner Baylor, entered Woodward College in Cincinnati, Ohio, in 1835. Upon his return to the family in 1837, his widowed mother occupied a boardinghouse in Little Rock, Arkansas.

In 1840, the Baylor brothers moved to Rocky Creek south of La Grange, Texas, on the farm of their uncle, William Miller Baylor. John fought Comanche raiders and stoked a blood hatred of Indians. He joined Captain Nicholas Mosby Dawson's Texas cavalry and served during the 1842 Battle of Salado Creek, narrowly escaping the massacre.

Upon rejoining his mother at her boardinghouse at Fort Gibson, Oklahoma, Baylor taught at a school for Creek children. In company with his brother-in-law, Captain James Lowes Dawson, in July 1844, Baylor faced a false charge of abetting the murder of an Indian agent and trader, Seaborn Hill, for selling liquor to Indians, whom he exploited. With a reward of $750 on his head, Baylor fled over the Red River to Marshall, Texas.

In 1845, he wed Emily Jane Hanna, farmed and raised livestock at Ross Prairie, and fathered three daughters and seven sons. He gained prominence by studying law and serving in the Texas legislature. In 1855, while commissioned as special agent to the Brazos Comanche Agency at Clear Fork, he hunted buffalo with the Indians, yet promoted harsh treatment of raiders, arsonists, and pillagers. In a falling out with his supervisor, Robert Simpson Neighbors, Baylor lost his job after 18 months of service for making rash accusations against reservation Indians for raiding whites.

Embittered at his public humiliation, Baylor moved his family to a ranch in Parker County. In 1859, he led 1,000 vigilantes in a skirmish against the Comanche and, at Weatherford, issued the town's first newspaper, *The White Man.* As a result of mounting racism, General George Henry Thomas closed the Brazos agency and resettled the Comanche safely in Oklahoma. Subsequent raids to the south inspired Baylor, his 14-year-old son, Jack, and his younger brother, George Wythe Baylor, to lead 500 vigilantes in battles against the Indians. Flying a flag reading "Necessity Knows No Law," on June 11, 1860, the party shot 12 Indians to avenge an attack on brothers Frank and Josephus Browning while they searched for missing cattle. Josephus had died at the scene, where Apaches scalped him; Frank survived 17 arrow wounds by swimming Hubbard's Creek.

Following the election of President Abraham Lincoln in November 1860, Baylor joined the Knights of the Golden Circle, a secret society that sought the annexation of Mexico to the United States. At the Secession Convention in Austin, he agitated for the withdrawal of Texas from the Union. He recruited the Second Texas Mounted Rifles to oppose U.S. troops stationed in Texas. At the western edge of the state, he apportioned his 700 enlistees at Camp Hudson and at Forts Bliss, Clark, Davis, Lancaster, Quitman, and Stockton.

Baylor was aware that Confederate President Jefferson Davis planned a nation that included Southern states, New Mexico Territory, and California. Crucial to the financing of the Confederacy were the lead and silver mines at Mowry, Arizona. To achieve control over those resources, Baylor led a force of 250 over the Organ Mountains against Union Major Isaac Lynde at Mesilla, New Mexico, and captured Lynde's soldiers on July 27, 1861, at San Augustine Pass.

On August 1, Baylor reclaimed for the Confederate States of America the southern portion of Arizona and New Mexico as far west as the Colorado River. Promoted to lieutenant colonel, he became Arizona's first territorial governor and, within a week, established a court system. Baylor captured $9,500 from Fort Fillmore for the Confederate treasury and supervised the mining of gold and silver to conduct a war of liberation. He began consolidating militias to patrol the Rio Grande in order to prevent invasion by Union divisions, Sonoran bandits, and Apache raiders and struck Mexican outlaws deep in the Chihuahua Mountains. In response to media criticism by Robert P. Kelley, editor of the *Mesilla Times,* Baylor knocked him to the floor and shot him through the jaw. Kelley died three days later.

Chiricahua Apache raiders took advantage of the absence of army patrols to attack wagon trains and terrorize settlers of Pinos Altos, New Mexico, and Tubac and Tucson, Arizona. On January 25, 1862, Colonel Baylor raised a company of Arizona Rangers, led by Captain Sherod Hunter, and began negotiating treaties with the Papago and with Pima Chief Antonio Azul, enemies of the Apache. On March 20, Baylor issued orders for Indian genocide. He proposed slaughtering villages, kidnapping Apache children for enslavement, and distributing liquor and poisoned food as a means of executing Mescalero Apache warriors.

In March, Baylor attempted to raise more forces to stave off the California Column, a band of 2,350 Union troops, cavalry, and artillery led by Colonel James Henry Carleton. Jefferson Davis curtailed Baylor's savagery and stripped him of his command of the Arizona Brigade. Reinstated in March 1865, Baylor proposed recruiting Texans to retake Arizona Territory.

After the Confederate surrender at Appomattox Courthouse on April 9, Baylor dispersed rioters at Huntsville State Prison. He established a large ranch on the Nueces River at Montell, Texas, ran unsuccessfully for governor in 1873, and died on February 8, 1894.

See also: Davis, Jefferson.

Further Reading

Cool, Paul. *Salt Warriors: Insurgency on the Rio Grande.* College Station: Texas A&M University Press, 2008.

Lavash, Donald R. *A Journey Through New Mexico History.* Santa Fe, NM: Sunstone, 2006.

Masich, Andrew E. *The Civil War in Arizona: The Story of the California Volunteers, 1861–1865.* Norman: University of Oklahoma Press, 2006.

McChristian, Douglas C. *Fort Bowie, Arizona: Combat Post of the Southwest, 1858–1894.* Norman: University of Oklahoma Press, 2005.

Bell, Alexander Graham (1847–1922)

A Scots educator and communications technologist, Alexander Graham Bell engineered the first telephone system and shaped the way in which deaf-mutes learn to speak. Born in Edinburgh on March 3, 1847, to portrait miniaturist Eliza Grace Symonds and Alexander Melville Bell, a specialist in phonetics and speech defects, "Aleck" Bell received only five years of formal education and fleshed out his learning through observation and reading. Until age ten, he studied reading, writing, math, art, and piano under his mother's tutelage. He became an engineering whiz by age 12, when he invented for a local miller a wheat dehusker out of nail brushes and spinning paddles.

To assist his deaf mother with speech, Bell studied finger language and became the only family member to talk to her by aiming low tones at her forehead. From his father, he learned how to re-create Gaelic, Hindi, Latin, Persian, Sanskrit, and Urdu words on paper with complex symbols. After years of homeschooling, he achieved a mediocre record of attendance and performance in the classics at Royal High School.

On his own time, he learned photography; privately, he collected bird eggs, fossils, and dried plants and dissected the carcasses of mice, piglets, and rabbits. In 1862, he spent a year in London under the mentorship of his grandfather, elocutionist Alexander Bell. At age 16, he began teaching speech and piano at the Weston House Academy, a boys' school in Elgin, Scotland, where he simultaneously learned Greek and Latin; within a year, he enrolled at the University of Edinburgh to study the classics.

Bell resolved to replicate human speech through mechanical vibrations. From experiments with a tin and rubber talking robot and vocal manipulation of a Skye terrier named Trouve, he advanced to studies of vowel resonance using tuning forks. When the Bell family settled in London in 1865, he experimented with telegraphy and isolated the pitch of sounds in the oral cavities before taking to his bed from frustration and exhaustion. Bell taught at Somerset College in Bath and, while studying anatomy and physiology at London's University College, tutored deaf girls at Susanna E. Hull's school in South Kensington. A demanding schedule left him melancholy, sleepless, coughing, headachy, and underweight.

After he lost his younger and older brothers, 18-year-old Edward "Ted" and 20-year-old Melville "Melly" Bell, and Melly's infant son Edward to tuberculosis, Aleck settled their estates and fought the beginnings of the disease in his own lungs. In 1870, for the sake of the family's health, Bell moved his parents and widowed sister-in-law, Caroline Margaret Ottaway "Carrie" Bell, to Montreal, Canada, then to a small farm north of Lake Erie near Brantford, Ontario.

Bell in North America

In the Ontario carriage house, Bell continued his experiments and produced a written version of the previously unrecorded Canadian Mohawk language. His Mohawk friend, Chief George Henry Martin Johnson, made Bell an honorary chief.

In April 1871, Bell substituted for his father as educator at Sarah Fuller's School for Deaf Mutes in Boston, the first institution of its kind to teach speech to the hearing impaired. The *Boston Journal* and the *American Annals of the Deaf and Dumb* acknowledged Bell's revolutionary pedagogy and advice to special education teachers. He flourished as an instructor in visible speech and accepted more invitations to teach under the Reverend Thomas Gallaudet at the American Asylum for Deaf-Mutes in Hartford, Connecticut, and under Harriet Burbank Rogers at the Clarke School for the Deaf in Northampton, Massachusetts.

In October 1872, Bell taught 30 pupils at his own training center, the School of Vocal Physiology and Mechanics of Speech in Boston. He edited a pamphlet, *Visible Speech Pioneer* (1872), and assumed a professorship in vocal physiology at Boston University.

Because of the drain on his energy, in autumn 1873, he abandoned day and night classroom scheduling for full-time experimentation with sound, which businessman Thomas Sanders backed with the gift of a laboratory and quarters near Salem. Within months, the inventor perfected a harmonic telegraph that could send multiple messages simultaneously.

At the Massachusetts Institute of Technology in Cambridge, Bell analyzed electrical devices that transmitted sound in variant frequencies and transformed a replication of the original voice. In 1874, with a moving pen tracing lines on smoked glass, he used the phonautograph to capture the two-dimensional shapes of sound waves from the human voice and from musical instruments. While searching for a harp arrangement of harmonic reeds to vibrate a membrane, he received encouragement from Joseph Henry, director of the Smithsonian Institution.

On June 2, 1875, experimenting with acoustic telegraphy in collaboration with his assistant, electrical engineer Thomas Augustus Watson, Bell simplified the transmission of intelligible speech vibrations over a single reed and dropped his experiments with multiple vibrators. A year later, he improved the sulfuric acid and water microphone invented by Elisha Gray, a professor at Oberlin College in Ohio, that carried undulations through a needle. Bell foresaw using mercury as a conducting liquid to carry vocal waves over a wire. In August, he gave a live demonstration over 5 miles (8 kilometers) of stove wire strung over fences and telegraph poles and through a tunnel from Brantford to Mount Pleasant, Ontario.

From the Lab to the Public

Competition between Bell and Gray generated more than 600 lawsuits to determine the rights to the new technology. Bell relied on the legal advice of Marcellus Bailey and Anthony Pollok, patent attorneys hired by backer Gardiner Greene Hubbard, a former U.S. legislator. In the most protracted patent litigation in the United States to date, court appearances for 600 cases robbed Bell of time and energy as a web of lawsuits moved through the legal system to the U.S. Supreme Court. Both Gray and complainant Amos Emerson Dolbear admitted that Bell's breakthroughs in undulatory current preceded their discoveries of the basics of the telephone.

On June 25, 1876, at the Centennial Exposition in Philadelphia, Bell's recitation of a soliloquy from *Hamlet* over the "speaking telegraph" won global headlines, a contract for a telephone system from Emperor Dom Pedro of Brazil, and the admiration of Queen Victoria, who requested a private line connecting her residences in England and Scotland. Bell predicted that the system would spread from house to house by interconnecting wires and become as indispensable to domestic life as water or gas pipes. At Boston University, he engineered a device to capture human speech electronically in visible form as an educational tool for deaf-mutes.

On October 9, 1876, following a demonstration to the American Academy of Arts and Sciences involving the successful transmission of articulate speech over 2 miles (3 kilometers) of wire from Cambridge to Boston, Bell patented his sound conveyor and advanced to designing an electromagnetic telephone circuit that passed voices over a wire. William Orton, president of Western Union, proclaimed the device a toy and rejected Bell's offer to sell the patent for $100,000. By May 1877, the first switchboard dispatched messages to five Boston banks. Within two years, the telephone was worth $25 million.

In summer 1877, Bell formed the Bell Telephone Company, which made millions for his investors by opening commercial communications exchanges. Two days later, he married Mabel Gardiner "May" Hubbard, the mother of their two daughters and two sons. The couple left for a yearlong honeymoon to France and England. Combining relaxation with work, he intended to canvass for financial backing for a British telephone system. He augmented the system with the carbon button microphone, one of Thomas Edison's inventions that replaced the liquid transmitter with a hammered metal diaphragm and eliminated the need to shout into the receiver.

In 1878, Bell installed a telephone in the White House at the request of President Rutherford B. Hayes. That same year, Bell founded the New England Telephone Company and pioneered a community switchboard in New Haven, Connecticut. At age 68, Bell made the first transcontinental phone call over 3,400 miles (5,400 kilometers) of wire from New York to San Francisco. A naturalized U.S. citizen, he reared his family on L Street in Washington, D.C., and summered outside Baddeck on Cape Breton, Nova Scotia, where he set up a research lab.

A Profusion of Ideas

In 1880, Bell won France's Volta Prize for scientific achievements of 50,000 francs, which he used to finance the American Association to Promote the Teaching of Speech to the Deaf and to set up the Volta Laboratory in Washington, D.C. Using a mirror and a selenium crystal, he and his assistant, engineer Charles Sumner Tainter, produced a wireless photophone, a forerunner of fiber-optic technology. To the American Association for the Advancement of Science in Boston, Bell demonstrated the transmission of sound using a light ray rather than by electricity. He followed with a gramophone that played wax cylinders etched by a moving stylus, a hydrodrome and hydroplane, a metal detector, a prototype of the iron lung, sonar to detect icebergs at sea, and an audiometer to measure hearing acuity. He also surveyed methods of desalinization, solar distillation of water, alternative fuels, birth defects in sheep, and eugenics to prevent the birth of deaf children to deaf parents. When he invented a tetrahedral kite big enough to carry a person, the aileron to control airplane roll, and the tricycle aircraft landing gear, Mabel Hubbard Bell promoted his interest in flight by founding the Aerial Experiment Association, the first research organization endowed by a woman.

In six decades of scientific exploration, Bell obtained 30 patents and filled notebooks with memos and schematic drawings of inventions not yet realized in the lab, including the tape recorder, solar paneling, composting toilets, and air-conditioning. In 1880, three years after acquiring control of Western Electric Company to manufacture wiring and telephone receivers, Bell and his company managers created the first national long-distance network, which, in 1885, became the American Telephone and Telegraph Company (AT&T). Bell co-founded the National Geographic Society and *Science* and *National Geographic* magazines. He served on the board of the Smithsonian Institution, advised the U.S. Bureau of the Census on interviewing the deaf, and, in 1892, inaugurated telephone service from New York to Chicago.

At his death at age 75 in Baddeck on August 2, 1922, from diabetes and pernicious anemia, Bell held honorary doctorates from three American and three European universities. Americans silenced their telephones for one minute to honor the inventor.

Further Reading

Billington, David P., and David P. Billington, Jr. *Power, Speed, and Form: Engineers and the Making of the Twentieth Century.* Princeton, NJ: Princeton University Press, 2006.

Casson, Herbert N. *The History of the Telephone.* Middlesex, UK: Gardners, 2007.

Fang, Irving. *A History of Mass Communication: Six Information Revolutions.* Boston: Focal Press, 1997.

Gray, Charlotte. *Reluctant Genius: Alexander Graham Bell and the Passion for Invention.* New York: Arcade, 2006.

Benjamin, Judah P. (1811–1884)

One of America's most honored Jews, Judah Philip Benjamin, a British-born attorney and conservative statesman, supported Southern independence and secession, yet favored the abolition of slavery and the mustering of black forces to fight for the Confederacy. A former U.S. senator, he held several positions in the Confederate cabinet and advised President Jefferson Davis.

A native of Christiansted, St. Croix, in the British-occupied West Indies, Benjamin was born on August 6, 1811, to Sephardic Jewish immigrants, British fruit seller Phillip Benjamin and his wife Rebecca de Mendes, a

British-born Judah P. Benjamin of South Carolina, the first Jew elected to the U.S. Senate, resigned his seat to join the Confederate cabinet. He held several key positions and was a close adviser to President Jefferson Davis. *(The Granger Collection, New York)*

Dutch Portuguese resident on the way to New Orleans with her family. Circumstances forced her to give birth on the island while their ship delayed in the Caribbean as a result of the War of 1812.

In childhood, Judah and his siblings—Rebecca, Joseph, Solomon, Hannah, Judith, and Jacob—lived at the home of their uncle, auctioneer Jacob Levy, in Wilmington, North Carolina. In 1817, the Benjamins moved inland, where Judah attended Fayetteville Academy. Settling near the docks in Charleston, South Carolina, in 1832, his father made a living in produce and co-founded Beth Elohim, the nation's first Reform Jewish congregation.

Benjamin impressed his teachers, leading his class in the study of law at Yale College from 1825 to 1827, when he departed in disgrace for "ungentlemanly conduct." He completed his education in 1832 by clerking for a notary in New Orleans and established a lucrative practice in commercial law representing banks and railroads. One case involving the government of Lower California earned him the largest retainer for legal advice paid to that time.

At age 22, after tutoring a 16-year-old Creole Catholic aristocrat named Natalie Bauché de Saint-Martin, Benjamin married her in St. Louis Cathedral. Despite his refusal to convert to Catholicism, he settled amicably at 327 Bourbon Street with her parents, Auguste and Françoise Saint-Martin. Benjamin co-founded the Illinois Central Railroad and bought slaves to work his sugar plantation at Belle Chasse in Plaquemines Parish on the Mississippi Delta. To elude boredom and to escape rumors of infidelity, his wife left their rural Greek Revival mansion and raised their daughter Ninette in Paris.

Counsel to Lawmakers

In 1842, Benjamin served in the Louisiana state legislature as a Whig and, three years later, as a delegate to the Louisiana Constitutional Convention, where he envisioned a government run by planters and urban landowners. At age 39, he liquidated his plantation and 150 slaves. On the strength of his oratory, dedication, and skill at law, in 1852, he became the first Jew to win a seat in the U.S. Senate. To carry travelers and cargo to the Pacific Coast, he promoted a railroad across Mexico at Oaxaca, but the project failed.

In 1853, Benjamin declined President Millard Fillmore's nomination to a seat on the U.S. Supreme Court, which would have made Benjamin the first Jewish appointee to that body. A quarrel with Senator Jefferson Davis of Mississippi precipitated a challenge to a duel, which the two men settled without violence. Benjamin declined a second nomination to the Supreme Court extended by President Franklin Pierce in 1854.

In his second run for the U.S. Senate in 1859, Benjamin switched to the Democratic ticket. He chaired the Committee on Private Land Claims and supported Southern interests during Abraham Lincoln's campaign for the presidency. After Lincoln's victory, Benjamin advocated the secession of Louisiana from the Union, which legislators at Baton Rouge passed on January 26, 1861, by a vote of 113–17.

From February 25 to September 17, 1861, Benjamin served President Jefferson Davis at the capital in Richmond, Virginia, as the Confederacy's first attorney general. Thus, he was the nation's first Jew to hold cabinet-level office and the only key player in the Davis administration to own no slaves. As strategist, problem solver, and tactician, Benjamin conferred with the president sometimes 20 hours a day, advocating at length for persuading Kentucky to join the Southern cause. In fall 1861, Benjamin took LeRoy Pope Walker's post as secretary of war, an office he held until March 24, 1862. Among his duties, the most pressing was the purchase of ammunition and arms. In 1862, his picture adorned the Confederate $2 bill.

Public opinion in the South turned against Benjamin after he reprimanded generals P.G.T. Beauregard and Thomas "Stonewall" Jackson over the loss of Roanoke Island on February 8, 1862, to Union General Ambrose Burnside. To avoid public panic, Benjamin willingly took the blame and concealed from Southerners the severe shortage of soldiers and black powder that had forced the Confederate retreat from Roanoke Island. Benjamin resigned after Burnside's amphibious force halted some 80 percent of Confederate shipping from the North Carolina Outer Banks. The victory earned Burnside a field promotion to major general; the Confederate Congress censured Benjamin. Anti-Semites inflated charges against Benjamin by circulating false rumors that he had stolen from the Confederate treasury and banked illicit funds in Europe.

Fate of the Confederacy

In spring 1862, as New Orleans faced a Union assault from the Gulf of Mexico, Benjamin ordered the plating of 14 private steamers with iron and pressed foreign ambassadors to help defend the port. After spending $300,000 from the Confederate treasury for the city's defense, he received a reward for service. At the resignation of Secretary of State Robert Mercer Taliaferro Hunter in disgust over Davis's leadership, the president named Benjamin to that cabinet post. He held the position until May 10, 1865, a month after General Robert E. Lee surrendered to Union General Ulysses S. Grant at Appomattox, Virginia.

Following the issuance of the Emancipation Proclamation of January 1, 1863, Benjamin addressed a gathering of 10,000 people in Richmond to promote the freeing of any slave who enlisted in the Confederate army or navy. He used the plan as a selling point to the neutral British, who refused to back the Confederacy out of distaste for Southern slavery. Although General Lee supported the proposed mustering of black soldiers, planters rejected giving guns to former slaves until March 1865, during the rapid decline of hopes for a victory.

Upon the retreat of the Confederate president and cabinet from Richmond on April 2, 1865, Benjamin fled south in an attempt to consolidate forces in the trans-Mississippi West. Before the dissolution of the cabinet on May 5, he sheltered with a relative, Solomon Benjamin, in Ocala, Florida. As Union troops pursued, rumors of a plot formulated by a Canadian spy ring named Benjamin as the ringleader. Christian critics blamed Benjamin for being the Judas in President Abraham Lincoln's assassination on Good Friday.

Benjamin adopted an alias as a foreign peddler, burned documents and correspondence, and pushed farther south to Ellenton to the sugar plantation of Major Robert Gamble. Secessionist John Lesley of Tampa secured passage on an open yawl from Sarasota to Bimini. With the final $1,500 in gold that he owned, Benjamin traveled aboard a boatload of sponges to Nassau and by schooner to Havana.

After arranging steamer passage to Southampton, Benjamin remained socially unengaged during his residency in London. While amassing a second fortune, he avoided scurrilous scapegoating by carpetbaggers and never returned to the United States. He published a letter in a September 1865 issue of the London *Times* protesting the jailing of the failed Confederate president. To support Confederate First Lady Varina Howell Davis and her four children during her husband's imprisonment, Benjamin sent $12,000 to the family.

In June 1866, Benjamin joined the English legal system as a barrister. He compiled his *Treatise on the Law of Sale of Personal Property* (1868) and, in 1872, became Queen Victoria's personal counsel in 132 cases before the House of Lords. (He was the only non-native to hold that office for a British monarch.) On November 28, 1881, Benjamin composed a short letter refuting charges that he controlled $17 million in Confederate treasury funds deposited in the Bank of England and other European banks.

At his death from diabetes and heart attack at his Paris mansion on May 6, 1884, Benjamin's wife and daughter buried him in secret with Catholic rites among world notables at Père Lachaise Cemetery. A monument at the Gamble Mansion honors his service to the South. Historians continue to debate whether Benjamin failed the South or triumphed as the "brains of the Confederacy."

Further Reading

Bleser, Carol K., and Lesley Jill Gordon, eds. *Intimate Strategies of the Civil War: Military Commanders and Their Wives.* New York: Oxford University Press, 2001.

Evans, Eli N. *Judah P. Benjamin, the Jewish Confederate.* New York: Simon & Schuster, 1989.

Guterl, Matthew Pratt. *American Mediterranean: Southern Slaveholders in the Age of Emancipation.* Cambridge, MA: Harvard University Press, 2008.

Levine, Bruce C. *Confederate Emancipation: Southern Plans to Free and Arm Slaves During the Civil War.* New York: Oxford University Press, 2006.

Varon, Elizabeth R. *Southern Lady, Yankee Spy: The True Story of Elizabeth Van Lew, a Union Agent in the Heart of the Confederacy.* New York: Oxford University Press, 2003.

Woodworth, Steven E. *Davis and Lee at War.* Lawrence: University Press of Kansas, 1995.

Bethlehem Steel

In its nearly century and a half in existence, Bethlehem Steel emerged as the second-largest steelmaker in the United States, producing the raw material and parts for railroads, ships, and infrastructure and symbolizing to a competitive world the rise of American industry. As railroads crisscrossed North America, steel rails and trusses offered better, safer service than iron supports, which began breaking down within three months.

The giant steel manufacturer traced its origins to the Saucona Iron Company, founded in 1857 by merchant and realtor Augustus Wolle, a member of an entrepreneurial Moravian family in eastern Pennsylvania. Formed during the financial panic of that year with funding provided by rail magnate Asa Packer and civil engineer Robert Heysham Sayre, the operation company began with a single blast furnace on Saucon Creek south of the Lehigh River. The anthracite-fueled operation processed local ore extracted from Wolle's Gangewere Mine in Saucon Valley. The company made rails for Packer's Lehigh Valley Railroad, which connected Buffalo and Niagara Falls, New York, with Philadelphia, Pennsylvania, and Jersey City, New Jersey.

The iron factory evolved into the Bethlehem Rolling Mill & Iron Company, taking its name from the city of its location, a transportation hub. Under the presidency of industrialist Alfred Hunt, a Quaker from Philadelphia, the factory name changed once more on May 1, 1861, to the Bethlehem Iron Company.

The steelworks occupied 17 acres (6.9 hectares) served by the Lehigh Valley Railroad and received backing from the Moravian congregation and local businessmen—attorney Charles Brodhead, Charles Bartholomew Daniel, Ambrose H. Rauch, and Charles Walter Rauch. To serve as general manager and plant superintendent, Hunt hired ironmaster John Fritz, a self-educated inventor from Londonderry, Pennsylvania. A former employee of the Johnstown Cambria ironworks, Fritz had initiated a high-pressure blast operation and a three-high rolling mill to prevent the cracks that fouled machinery and to eliminate the cost and delay of a second rolling. For an annual salary of $5,000 and shares in the mill, he superintended the construction of a stone factory, but encountered a flood of the Lehigh River in fall 1861 that suspended building.

The early events of the Civil War slowed operations until July 1863, when cash and raw materials became more readily available. With the installation of rollers 1 foot (30 centimeters) in diameter, the company began smelting and processing brown hematite and magnetite from the Hibernian mine, which Quaker industrialist Joseph Wharton owned near Port Oram, New Jersey. The Lehigh Valley Railroad profited from having a local source of high-quality steel rails. Within ten months, the demand for rails required the construction of a second furnace.

During the Civil War, the profitable Bethlehem manufactory generated ingots, railroad tracks, gun mounts, caissons, projectiles, and armor plating for U.S. naval vessels. By 1865, the nation produced 19,000 tons (17,200 metric tons) of steel per year and began rerolling tracks that Confederate General Nathan Bedford Forrest had mangled to prevent trains from the North from delivering supplies to Union General William Tecumseh Sherman. After a merger with the Northampton Iron Company southeast of the complex in 1868, the Bethlehem Iron Company operated three blast furnaces, 14 puddle furnaces, and nine heating furnaces, as well as a foundry, rolling mill, blooming mill, hydraulic forging press, and machine shop.

In the 1870s, America grew to 40 million citizens, fueling rapid industrialization and hemispheric demand for goods and services. The Bethlehem factory spread over an area 1.25 miles (2 kilometers) long, with 25 acres (10 hectares) under one 30-foot (9-meter) roof. To shape 20,000 tons (18,100 metric tons) of rail annually, the factory's 700 employees, many of them German or Irish immigrants, worked 12-hour days.

The profitable enterprise generated stock dividends ranging as high as 20 percent. Bethlehem's steel magnates returned some of the profits to the community in April 1866 by founding Lehigh University, an Episcopal school that trained engineers, and by establishing South Bethlehem Moravian Church and, in 1872, St. Luke's Hospital to treat victims of industrial accidents.

Because American metallurgy lagged behind that of the British, Sayre and Wharton dispatched Fritz to England and Sweden to observe the innovative smelting method pioneered by Henry Bessemer in the 1850s. Under Fritz's direction, on October 4, 1873, the Bethlehem factory adopted the Bessemer-Mushet process, a means of decarburizing iron and reducing phosphorus and sulfur to harden the finished steel for longer life. Greater strength reduced metal fatigue that could result in fissures, cracks, or curls called "snakeheads," which could wreck trains. The pneumatic method of oxidizing impurities from molten pig iron endangered workers and machinery because of possible explosion, but it made possible mass production at a considerable reduction of manufacturing and labor costs.

The steelworks grew to contain hydraulic lifts, cast-iron molds, four Bessemer converters, and a 125-ton (113-metric-ton) vertical steam hammer, the largest ever built. Within the year, the company received orders for 2,000 tons (1,814 metric tons) of rails for the Jersey Central and Lehigh Valley railroads. In addition, the plant produced steel tubing, springs and axles, 100-caliber guns, steel shafts for propellers and pumps, and the heaviest armor plating required by the army and navy.

The quality of Bethlehem Steel products earned Fritz double his original salary and a place among the world's most renowned metallurgical and mechanical engineers. In 1876, he received a bronze medal at the U.S. Centennial Exposition for his engineering innovations, followed by the Bessemer Gold Medal of the Iron and Steel Institute, the Bronze Medal of the Louisiana Purchase Exposition, honorary doctorates from four universities, and the Gold Medal of the Franklin Institute of Philadelphia.

When the Bethlehem Rolling Mill and Iron Company became the Bethlehem Steel Company in 1899, the factory produced the nation's first wide-flange structural trusses for use in bridge, dam, prison, and skyscraper construction and shipbuilding. Under the command of steel titan Charles Michael Schwab, Bethlehem Steel competed with Krupp in Germany and Vickers' Sons & Maxim in England. The company endured until the twenty-first century, when more than $7 billion in debt forced it into bankruptcy in 2001.

Further Reading

Bianculli, Anthony J. *Trains and Technology: The American Railroad in the Nineteenth Century.* 4 vols. Newark: University of Delaware Press, 2001–2003.

Derbyshire, Wyn. *Six Tycoons: The Lives of John Jacob Astor, Cornelius Vanderbilt, Andrew Carnegie, John D. Rockefeller, Henry Ford, and Joseph P. Kennedy.* London: Spiramus, 2008.

Safford, Sean. *Why the Garden Club Couldn't Save Youngstown: The Transformation of the Rust Belt.* Cambridge, MA: Harvard University Press, 2009.

Warren, Kenneth. *Bethlehem Steel: Builder and Arsenal of America.* Pittsburgh: University of Pittsburgh Press, 2008.

Bicycles

Bicycles became an American fad around 1865 with the advancement of the wood-framed velocipede, a walking bicycle. The breakthrough was a rotary crank model made of iron and featuring a leather seat on a spring and wood treadles attached to the hub on the front wheel for pedaling. Developed in Paris, France, by blacksmith Pierre Michaux in the early 1860s, the bicycle entered mass production at 70 pounds (32 kilograms) and traveled at a rate of up to 12 miles (19 kilometers) per hour. It earned the nickname "boneshaker" for its jolting ride over cobblestones and rough terrain.

In July 1865, inventor Pierre Lallement, a manufacturer of baby carriages, introduced the *veloce* in Brooklyn, New York; he began assembling his product that fall in Ansonia, Connecticut. His exhibition ride to New Haven, Connecticut, in spring 1866 made the newspapers, which described his machine as "a curious frame sustained by two wheels, one before the other, and driven by foot cranks."

The bicycle sparked a craze in summer 1868, when a trio of New York gymnasts known as the Hanlon brothers—Alfred, George, and William—set out on bicycles of their own design from Boston Commons and raced across North America. After acquiring a U.S. patent, the Hanlons hired Calvin Witty, a Brooklyn carriage maker, to manufacture the vehicles. Sellers offered free lessons on mounting and dismounting, coasting, balancing at rest, and riding astride, sidesaddle, or with no hands. Purchasers rode in New York City's Central Park that September and at the Hanlon bicycle school at Broadway and Ninth Street. Among the elite who took classes was financier John Jacob Astor III.

On February 24, 1869, Thomas Green, a bicycle enthusiast in Lynn, Massachusetts, opened a riding rink under a giant circus tent. The *Lynn Reporter,* in anticipation of the venue, published a lighthearted article titled "Velocipedes" that predicted a time when "every man shall be his own horse." The essay opened with a four-line ditty:

> There was a man on a velocipede.
> Without oats or hay
> He will go all day;
> 'Tis a cheap thing to keep—a velocipede.

At the corner of Broadway and Twenty-Eighth Street in New York, the Pearsall brothers—Alva Adee Pearsall and George Frank E. Pearsall—established the 8,000-square-foot (745-square-meter) "Gymnacyclidium for Ladies and Gentlemen" on December 5, 1868, which featured band music and drew prominent men and women. For 15 cents admission plus a penny per minute, roller rinks called "riding academies" featured in the February 13, 1869, edition of *Harper's Weekly* enabled fans to ride bicycles indoors on a smooth surface and out of bad weather.

Cycling promptly took on the tone and intent of competitive athletics. In Portland, Maine, and Eau Claire, Wisconsin, in autumn 1869, promoters held races attended by crowds. Indoor racing drew fans in Chicago; Cincinnati, Ohio; and New Bedford, Massachusetts. Outdoors, endurance cyclists raced against other bicyclists and against horseback riders and sulkies. Acrobats in spangled costumes added thrills by pedaling across tightropes.

Moonlight cycling by velo clubs shifted the emphasis from competition to romance. Ladies rode on specially shaped bicycles that accommodated their skirts and petticoats. Newspaper cartoons pictured female riders as flirts who outrode males to gain attention and to display their shapely ankles. Creating scandal were female contenders in cycling tights; females wanting freedom of movement with more modesty wore bloomers, the trousers designed by feminist Amelia Bloomer. In 1871, ice skater Carrie Augusta Moore of Concord, Massachusetts, became known as the "Skatorial Queen" and the "Velocipede Queen," after adding gymnastics to her performance.

By the end of the 1860s, critics of the "velocipeding" fad saw it as a dangerous and expensive pastime that would soon fade. Anticyclers described biking as unsuitable for road traffic and potentially lethal to pedestrians and children playing on sidewalks. The device became the subject of such popular songs as Henry Atkins's "Velocipede Galop" (1868), S. Low Coach's "The Unlucky Velocipedist" (1869), and George Cooper's "The Gay Velocipede" (1869).

In New York City, the Reverend Henry Ward Beecher encouraged his congregation to ride bicycles—as they came to be called—for exercise; newspaperman Charles Anderson Dana promoted the construction of an elevated bike route across Manhattan. Temperance leaders predicted that bike riding would decrease opportunities for drinking and gambling and introduce tipplers to fresh air. Susan B. Anthony promoted the sport as a graceful outing for women and a source of privacy and independence during exercise. A journalist in Providence, Rhode Island, took a pragmatic approach by referring to the vehicle as a "feedless horse." Visionaries predicted that the bicycle was the forerunner of motorized personal transportation.

The high-wheeler became popular during America's post–Civil War bicycle (or "velocipede") craze. The larger front wheel increased biking speed but made riders vulnerable to sudden projection over the handlebars—referred to as "taking a header." *(Time & Life Pictures/Getty Images)*

Meanwhile, inventors bombarded the U.S. Patent Office with innovations, including special models for cycling on ice and a reclining bike that forced the rider to extend the legs straight ahead. Patent infringement suits demanded royalties from newcomers to the business. Thomas R. Pickering, an English immigrant to New York City, added a handlebar brake and lowered the total weight by crafting a frame from steel tubing. On June 12, 1869, *Scientific American* pictured the longer wire spokes engineered by New York inventor Virgil Price; inventor George L. Brownell of Worcester, Massachusetts, added cushiony, solid rubber tires. William Van Anden of Poughkeepsie, New York, equipped the Dexter bicycle with a ratcheted coasting mechanism that allowed the rider to rest the feet while the wheels continued to spin. Ball bearings, seats on metal coils, rear-wheel drive, grooved rims, leather suspension straps, saddlebags for tools, spare parts, and an oilcan, and a brake activated by the pressure of the backside against the bicycle seat diminished road shocks and eased the ride. Paired cyclists traveled tandem style on a duplex model.

To meet the demand for improved models, bicycle factories sprang up in Bridgeport, Connecticut; New Bedford, Massachusetts; and Newark, New Jersey. In 1870, James Starley and William Hillman of Coventry, England, changed the proportions of the front and back wheels on the "Ariel" high-mount model, which had a 50-inch (127-centimeter) front-drive wheel. The change increased cycling speed, but left riders vulnerable to sudden projection over the front axle—a fall known as "taking a header." Another problem was price. Because each bicycle was handmade, even the cheapest model cost a half year's salary for the average worker.

More patents—steel ball bearings, caliper brakes, pivoting frames, and epicycle gear changers—brought further improvements. According to Charles Spencer's 1876 handbook *The Modern Bicycle,* cyclists on the taller, high-mount models prevailed for races and cross-country rides. By 1877, a new burst of enthusiasm for bicycling in Boston launched the American cycling renaissance.

Further Reading

Ashby, LeRoy. *With Amusement for All: A History of American Popular Culture Since 1830.* Lexington: University Press of Kentucky, 2006.

Herlihy, David V. *Bicycle: The History.* New Haven, CT: Yale University Press, 2004.

Norcliffe, Glen, "Popeism and Fordism: Examining the Roots of Mass Production." *Regional Studies* 31:3 (May 1997): 267–280.

Black Codes

Southern Black Codes and Jim Crow "separate but equal" laws restricted freedmen from exercising their full citizen rights as voters, householders, and members of juries and militias. On February 8, 1865, Alabama passed a series of Black Codes a week after enactment of the Thirteenth Amendment, which outlawed slavery. Like the earlier slave codes, a deluge of local and state Black Codes whittled away personal rights, beginning in Tennessee in June, Florida in October, and Mississippi in November. In December 1865, South Carolina and Louisiana followed suit, with eminent jurist David L. Wardlaw codifying the first and sugar planter Duncan F. Kenner composing the latter.

The rush to restrict freedmen was slower in other states, with Virginia, North Carolina, Georgia, and Texas statutes passed in 1866 and Arkansas codes on February 6, 1867. Laws imposed capitation or poll taxes—$1 in Georgia and Louisiana, $2 in Alabama and Virginia, and $3 in Florida—character requirements, and literacy tests on black voters. The four-page Alabama registration form required oral reading and explanation of a passage of the U.S. Constitution, a task that stymied the illiterate.

To prevent black insurrections or postwar retribution against whites, state legislatures preempted behaviors by which majority blacks threatened minority whites. In Tennessee and Texas, these legalities also diminished the rights of Indians, who shared the political disenfranchisement of blacks. Florida's complex list of laws imposed a tax of $1 on black citizens to pay for freedmen's schools. In North Carolina, codes targeted sexual relations; black couples had to claim marital status by paying a 25-cent fee or else be fined for cohabitation and fornication, a misdemeanor. In both Carolinas, any black male who raped a white woman faced the death penalty.

New laws forbade holding assemblies, running for public office, filing lawsuits against whites, testifying against whites, leaving work without permission, owning of alcohol, firearms, ammunition, or knives, and even, in some cases, living in towns or cities. Horace Greeley, editor of the *New York Tribune,* branded these limitations on black citizenship "serfdom."

Blatant Injustice

Under the cloak of state and local statutes, Southern white supremacists persecuted the black underclass for unemployment, indebtedness, orphanhood, homelessness, loitering, traveling after dark, rude gestures and offensive language, "malicious mischief," and flirtation, seduction, or marriage with white women by black males. Vagrancy statutes condemned idle blacks to hard labor on chain gangs or to auctions to white planters for a period of servitude lasting up to one year. In Virginia, the punishment required convicts to labor at public works while confined to ball and chain or condemned them to jailing on bread and water.

Codes varied in details. Tennesseans could own only firearms issued by the army or navy; the law effectively excluded black gun ownership without mentioning race. Virginia allowed more personal freedoms for ex-slaves but increased the penalties for crimes committed by blacks. In Richmond, blacks could ride streetcars only on the outside platforms. In New Orleans, blacks could hire only "black star cars," special carriages marked with a star. The Louisiana Code Noir (Black Code) denied black laborers ownership of livestock. In Opelousas, whites patrolled the town after 10 P.M. to suppress black activities. New Orleans statutes dispersed church meetings at 9 P.M.—even memorial services for President Abraham Lincoln.

Mississippi Governor Benjamin Grubb Humphreys feared the thousands of blacks "turned loose" by the Civil War and remanded those under age 18 to a master or mistress for care and feeding, education, and medical care. His laws set aside areas in which blacks could reside and prohibited gun ownership, vagrancy, and property ownership or rental. Any worker who quit a job had to forfeit the year's wages. Calvin Holly, a black Union infantryman and agent of the Vicksburg Freedmen's Bureau, protested that whites robbed and shot black residents without fear of reprisal.

Alabama's blacks could not assemble at night and faced crackdowns in Montgomery for walking to church in groups. In farming out lawbreakers for punishment, county courts favored former slave owners as jailers until the convicted paid or worked off fines, which the sheriff of Birmingham coveted. Those residing in Mobile had to post a residency bond. In one court case, a group of women, arrested for arguing, spent ten days in the workhouse at the direction of Mobile's mayor, Mitchell Withers. In 1866, as a means of suppressing uprisings, the Florida state legislature, controlled by ex-Confederates, imposed stiff penalties. In convictions of black lawbreakers for crimes ranging from thievery to impudence, judges substituted pillorying or lashing for the fines and jailing exacted on white scofflaws for the same charges.

The Texas state legislature bound blacks by a tangle of discriminatory legislation. Nonwhites could not testify in court except against other blacks and could not apply for public land under state homestead laws. Statutes legitimized the quasi-bondage of apprentices learning a trade or farming under the control of a white master. Reluctant orphans and court remands risked lashing and forcible return if they fled their masters. Texas law regulated black laborers by requiring those who worked more than 30 days for one employer to sign a binding written contract, a statute that also applied in Florida, Mississippi, North and South Carolina, and Virginia. Deductions from negotiated remuneration were legal in cases of laziness, theft, broken equipment, absence without leave, debt, and disobedience. Meticulous exclusionary clauses such as those imposed in Florida, Georgia, and North Carolina defined people of color in Texas as anyone having at least one-eighth Negro blood. Although General Joseph Barr Kiddoo of the Freedmen's Bureau contravened against Black Codes on January 3, 1867, vigilantes murdered some 500 black Texans by ambush or lynching over the course of the next decade.

Public Response

The press worked both sides of the issue of civil rights. In the North, editors of the *New York Globe, Washington People's Advocate,* and *Cleveland Gazette* raged against the hypocrisy of emancipation. A letter in the *Chicago Tribune* condemned Black Codes as shameful. In the South, John Emory Bryant, editor of the *Augusta Loyal Georgian,* railed against the complicity of lawmakers in imposing unconstitutional regulations on some 500,000 black residents.

The *Charleston New Era* and the *Mobile Gazette* urged patience. In Macon, Georgia, an influential secessionist, Joseph Clisby, owner and editor of the *Daily Telegraph,* legitimized Black Codes on the grounds that blacks and whites did not share equal levels of intelligence and morality. Through scurrilous accusations, "Sioux," the anonymous editor of the Houston, Texas, *Freeman's Champion,* leaped from the bad manners and immoral partying of blacks to the freedom of laborers to negotiate for themselves as reasons for passing Black Codes. Rather than retaliate in kind, black journalists published reserved comments lest whites suppress their newspapers.

Horace White, the libertarian editor of the *Chicago Tribune,* chose South Carolina as a model of postwar status quo in the former Confederacy. South Carolinians chalked up maimings, shootings, and lynchings as warnings to all former slaves that cooperation with federal occupation forces could result in death. Laws required verbal courtesies from blacks toward whites and demanded written passes for servants leaving their employers' premises. Black Codes restricted immigration to South Carolina and imposed one-year licenses of $100 each on blacks pursuing a trade, peddling, or shopkeeping. For the worst offenses, such as horse stealing, South Carolina judges were more likely to impose the death sentence on black offenders than on white felons.

On December 1, 1865, Horace White, editor of the *Chicago Tribune,* vilified Mississippi's Black Codes as a thinly veiled re-enslavement of blacks: "We tell the white men of Mississippi that the men of the North will convert the State of Mississippi into a frog-pond before they allow any such law to disgrace one foot of soil in which the bones of our soldiers sleep and over which the flag of freedom waves."

See also: Civil Rights; Jim Crow; Reconstruction.

Further Reading

Dickerson, Donna Lee, ed. *The Reconstruction Era: Primary Documents on Events from 1865 to 1877.* Westport, CT: Greenwood, 2003.

Horton, James Oliver, and Lois E. Horton. *Slavery and the Making of America.* New York: Oxford University Press, 2005.

Rothenberg, Paula S., ed. *Race, Class, and Gender in the United States: An Integrated Study.* 7th ed. New York: Worth, 2007.

Wallenstein, Peter. *Blue Laws and Black Codes: Conflict, Courts, and Change in Twentieth-Century Virginia.* Charlottesville: University of Virginia Press, 2004.

Washburn, Patrick S. *The African American Newspaper: Voice of Freedom.* Evanston, IL: Northwestern University Press, 2006.

Black Communities

The growth of black communities in the 1860s and 1870s attests to the eagerness of former slaves to work and establish families in the safety and nurturance of other newly freed households.

Freedmen on the Move

On June 16, 1860, the *Brooklyn Eagle* reported a census listing 45,000 former slaves living in Canada West (present-day Ontario) and still arriving via the Underground Railroad at a rate of 10,000 per year. The newcomers settled Amherstburg, Buxton, Chatham, Colchester, Dresden, Sandwich, and Windsor. To the northeast, additional settlements took shape at London, Lucan, Port Burwell, and Port Stanley. Other communities in Canada included Kingston at the eastern end of Lake Ontario, Oro on Lake Simcoe, and Collingwood and Owen Sound on Georgian Bay, Lake Huron. The ambitious opened businesses as barbers and beauticians, cobblers, bricklayers, chimney sweeps, finish carpenters and builders, dressmakers, institutional launderers, jewelers and watch repairers, cabbies, bartenders and casino operators, and hotel keepers.

Inspired by articles in the *Saint Paul Broadax,* a black-owned paper, adventurers spread across Manitoba from Saskatoon to Thunder Bay; in 1874, Thomas Carney and William Fairbanks led 200 colonists over the Red River at the North Dakota boundary to Emerson, Manitoba's first city, which immigrants named for Underground Railroad backer Ralph Waldo Emerson. Hundreds shipped west to pioneer on the prairies at Amber Valley, Alberta, and Maidstone, Saskatchewan, or Victoria on Vancouver Island on the Pacific Coast. Some chose to colonize Velorio Trujano north of Oaxaca, Mexico, or parts of Cuba, Haiti, or Jamaica that were already predominantly black.

The rise of sharecropping for former Southern masters and the dishonesty of landlords forced some black farmers to look elsewhere for self-determination. Contributing to their desperation was the unwillingness of financiers to extend sufficient credit to tide over farmers during droughts, floods, or tornadoes. On January 16, 1865, Union General William Tecumseh Sherman issued Special Field Order 15, which offered former slaves 40-acre (16-hectare) plots and the loan of army mules to farm abandoned lands at Burnside, Butler, Cumberland, Hilton Head, Jekyll, Ossabaw, Port Royal, Sapelo, Skidaway, St. Catherines, St. Helena, St. Simons, Whitemarsh, and other of the 100 Sea Islands. Others farmed the rice fields 30 miles (48 kilometers) inland and extending south of the Santee River and Charleston, South Carolina, to the St. Johns River, Florida. That summer, 40,000 black farmers colonized 400,000 acres (162,000 hectares) along the South Carolina–Georgia coast, the former patrimony of the plantation aristocracy. The Atlantic Coast Eden survived until January 1866, when President Andrew Johnson reinstated the land claims of pardoned white owners, forcing the black farmers to become squatters, contract laborers, and sharecroppers.

Some blacks moved west to serve with the Buffalo Soldiers, scout for the army, guide wagon trains, open depots of the Pony Express, drive stagecoaches, break broncos on ranches, or homestead free or cheap federal land. Communities similar to those in Canada thrived in disparate parts of Texas, including Peyton Colony at Boardhouse in Blanco County, a community of former slaves from the William Roberts Plantation in Virginia, and Shankleville, founded by Jim and Winnie Brush Shankle, a married couple who had been separated by sale during slave times. Some 60 all-black towns lay within Indian Territory (Oklahoma), where black marriages to Cherokee, Chickasaw, Choctaw, Creek, and Seminole mates produced biracial families eligible for government allotments. In all, black communities spread from Alaska and New Hampshire to Arkansas, Florida, and Texas.

In James City, across the Trent River from New Bern in Craven County, North Carolina, black farmers resided for three decades from January 1, 1863, the date of the Emancipation Proclamation. Because Union officials distributed acreage to newly freed blacks as spoils of the Civil War, new landowners assumed legal possession of plots formerly deeded to whites. However, James City's order and prosperity proved ephemeral on April 19, 1893,

Black Communities Founded in the 1860s and 1870s

Town	Founded	Founder(s)
Africa, Ind.	1871	—
Andy, Tex.	1865	Andrew Bragg
Arkansas, Okla.	1860s	Black colonists
Bailey, Okla.	1860s	Henry E. Bailey
Beech Bottoms, N.C.	1870	Hampton Jackson
Bennettsville, S.C.	ca. 1865	Thomas Bennett, Jr.
Blackville, Ala.	1891	Pickens Black
Boardhouse, Tex.	1865	Peyton Roberts
Bookertee, Okla.	1860s	Black colonists
Canadian, Okla.	1860s	Black colonists
Centerville, Wash.	1875	George Washington
Chase, Okla.	1860s	Black colonists
Coit Mountain, N.H.	ca. 1830s	Vance Coit
Cologne, Tex.	1860s	Jim Smith, George Washington
Daufuskie, S.C.	1865	Gullah speakers from West Africa
Davis Bend, Miss.	1860	Ben Montgomery
Dempsey, Alaska	1868	Melvin Dempsey
Dunlap Colony, Kans.	1876	Benjamin Singleton, Columbus M. Johnson
East St. Louis, Mo.	1/17/1865	John B. Bowman
Ferguson, Okla.	1860s	Black colonists
Freedman's Town, Tex.	1866	—
Grayson, Okla.	1860s	Black colonists
Hall, Ky.	1862	Black army recruits
Hayti, N.C.	1877	Freedmen
Hill City, Kans.	12/1877	W.R. Hill, James P. Pomeroy
Immanuel, Ark.	1875	—
James City, N.C.	1863	Freedmen's camp
Kendleton, Tex.	1860s	Benjamin Franklin Williams
Leavenworth, Kans.	1866	Buffalo Soldiers
Liberty, Okla.	1860s	Edward Preston McCabe
Little Africa, Ark.	1875	—
Little Africa, Mo.	ca. 1860	Runaway slaves
Little California, N.C.	1863	Freedmen's Bureau
Little Hell, Del.	1870	Black farmers
Marshalltown, Okla.	1860s	—
Mitchelville, S.C.	1861	Samuel Francis DuPont, Thomas West Sherman
Morton City, Kans.	9/1877	Black immigrants
Mound Bayou, Miss.	1867	Isaiah Thornton Montgomery Green, Benjamin T. Green
Namrash, Miss.	1876	Black colonists
Nicodemus, Kans.	6/18/1877	Thomas Harris, W.R. Hill, Edward Preston McCabe, William Smith
North Fork, Okla.	1860s	—
Pennytown, Mo.	1870	Joseph Penny
Port Royal, S.C.	1862	Edward Lillie Pierce
Princeville, N.C.	1865	Freed slaves
Quindaro, Kans.	1859	Abelard Guthrie
Rhodes Creek, Idaho	1862	William Rhodes
Sedalia, N.C.	1870	Freedmen

(continued)

Black Communities Founded in the 1860s and 1870s *(continued)*

Town	Founded	Founder(s)
Shankleville, Tex.	1863	Jim Shankle, Winnie Brush Shankle
Singleton Colony, Kans.	1874	Benjamin Singleton
Skunk Hollow, N.J.	1860s	—
Three Creeks, Mo.	1863	John Jones
Tinkersville, W.Va.	1865	Lewis Rice
Wellston, Okla.	1860s	Black colonists
Westport, Mo.	1865	—
Wewoka, Okla.	1866	John Horse
White Pine, Nev.	1860s	Black miners
Wybark, Okla.	1860s	Black colonists

when Sheriff W.B. Lane and the state militia forced black citizens to sign three-year leases to property they thought they already owned.

Land of Opportunity

Because of legal quandaries in Southern claims courts over deeds, the American frontier beckoned to black go-getters. The West had the advantages of fewer grudge holders and less restraint on economic growth and greater demand for black-made and -managed goods and services.

Among sympathetic whites, abolitionist Horace Greeley, editor of the *New York Tribune,* made discreet donations to liberate slaves from bondage and sponsored the establishment of free black hamlets in the Midwest. He promoted colonies similar to Vinland, the emigrant community of Underground Railroad agent Amasa Soule in Lawrence, Kansas, and to a black community in Clarksburg, Indiana, called Africa. Greeley hired correspondent Samuel Forster Tappan to survey the successes of black homesteaders from Missouri to Nebraska. Additional information came from observers of black pioneers in Linn County, Kansas, and in Freeport, Illinois. Decades of mixed-race living among Asians, Indians, Spaniards, and whites lessened the hardships of black newcomers, particularly biracial couples from the East and South.

Spirituality furthered the concept of black municipalities. Wherever African Methodist Episcopal churches served black communities, ministers and their congregations obeyed the scriptural injunction in Matthew 25:36 to aid displaced and struggling outsiders as though they were Jesus Christ himself. Sanctuaries did double-duty as worship centers and as waystations, social welfare centers, and literacy training centers.

At Leavenworth, Kansas, by the end of the Civil War, 2,455 black settlers brought the state's total black influx to 12,000. The black populace burgeoned when Colonel Benjamin Henry Grierson began training the Tenth Cavalry of Buffalo Soldiers at Fort Leavenworth. At Quindaro, Kansas, education for black children was available from Eben Blachley, a Presbyterian teacher. In an abandoned brewery in September 1862, he founded Quindaro Freedman's School, the first black academy west of the Mississippi River and the nucleus of Western University. Charles Henry Langston, master of the Colored Masons and head of the Kansas Freedmen's Bureau, superintended the curriculum and spearheaded the state suffrage drive to bring Quindaro citizens into the state electorate.

The presence of moral leaders did not assure a family-centered town, however. East St. Louis, Missouri, incorporated in 1861, exhibited the worst of urbanism with its investment in gin dives, taverns, gambling and dance halls, and bordellos. Fueling vice in the area, a proliferation of liquor licenses attracted a dissolute element just passing through town.

The obverse of East St. Louis developed in 1867 in Mound Bayou, Mississippi. At a model plantation at Davis Bend in the Yazoo Delta of northwest Mississippi, Isaiah Thornton Montgomery and his cousin, Benjamin T. Green, colonized the nation's largest all-black town. The citizenry consisted of 300 former slaves of attorney Joseph Emory Davis, brother of Confederate President Jefferson Davis. Davis built his utopian concept on the philosophy of British reformer and industrialist Robert Dale Owen, a proponent of enlightened paternalism.

Montgomery gave speeches to recruit long-term settlers to a communitarian experiment based on self-segregation. Intent on racial pride, justice, and self-empowerment, the citizens bought 840 acres (340 hectares) at $7 per acre and opened a post office, banks and stores, schools, and six churches. They financed their investments from the proceeds of work in corn, cotton, and timber and from the marketing of railroad ties from the Mound Bayou sawmill. The town, officially incorporated on July 12, 1887, promoted morality and order by banning gambling and liquor sales. It needed no jail. The example spurred black ownership throughout Bolivar County. Out of admiration for the neighborhood effort, Scots philanthropist Andrew Carnegie donated $4,000 to build the Mound Bayou library.

Civil Rights

Some blacks terrorized by white supremacist groups such as the Knights of the White Camellia, Ku Klux Klan, Red Shirts, and White League favored expatriating former slaves to an all-black nation. In 1871, while the colonization or "Back to Africa" movement espoused resettlement of freedmen to Liberia in West Africa, the Freemen's Emigrant Aid Society of Elizabeth City, North Carolina, advised former slaves of the obstacles to living in Africa.

From an opposing perspective, orator Sojourner Truth encouraged the migration of freedmen to newly formed black communities in Kansas and Missouri, where newcomers could participate in democracy without fear of reprisal. In her seventies, she lobbied President Abraham Lincoln unsuccessfully for federal land grants for ex-slaves.

Another proponent of westering, freedman Benjamin "Pap" Singleton, a cabinetmaker and coffin maker from Nashville, Tennessee, doubted that former slaves could attain freedom while living under Jim Crow laws in the plantation South. In 1874, Singleton and the Reverend Columbus M. Johnson formed the Edgefield Real Estate and Homestead Association to locate affordable land for blacks in a Tennessee colony that excluded whites. The failure of their efforts precipitated a second proposal—blacks homesteading open land in the West as a means of independence.

In 1876, Johnson and Singleton surveyed land in Cherokee County, Kansas, and recruited families to colonize an all-black community. At Baxter Springs on the border with Missouri and Oklahoma, 73 settlers prepared to set up Singleton Colony in the land of John Brown, the martyred insurrectionist. Rumors declared that the government would underwrite transportation, property, tools, and supplies. The settlers chose acreage in Morris County obtained from the Missouri River, Fort Scott, & Gulf Railroad, but lead and zinc strikes boosted property values beyond their reach. Two years later, in March and April 1878, some 4,000 black colonists inflamed by "Kansas fever" swarmed through the city wharves at St. Louis, despite violation of the Civil Rights Act of 1875 by disgruntled planters, who forced steamboat captains to refuse passage to blacks.

Johnson and Singleton's pilgrims succeeded in launching the Dunlap Colony in east-central Kansas. The community grew to 2,400 settlers who resided temporarily in burrows and sod huts until they could build cabins. In 1879, Pap Singleton, the "Moses of the Colored Exodus," distributed posters and mustered the "Exodusters," 50,000 black colonists bound from Louisiana, Mississippi, and Texas. They journeyed by wagon, train, and steamer to Colorado, Illinois, Indiana, Kansas, and Oklahoma. With funds from the Colored Relief Board, they traveled west from St. Louis to build homes and businesses and to establish ranches in such black communities as Allensworth, California; Nicodemus and Singleton, Kansas; and Abelincoln, Boley, Clearview, Langston, Liberty, Taft, and Wewoka, Oklahoma. In 1874, Lelia Smith Foley won election as the mayor of Taft, making her the nation's first black female mayor.

Town Builders

On June 18, 1877, with colonizers from Kentucky, Louisiana, and Tennessee, land speculators W.R. Hill and Edward Preston McCabe, the father of the all-black town movement, founded a prairie settlement in the northwest corner of Kansas. They named it Nicodemus in honor of a runaway slave. Hill and McCabe distributed handbills setting a tone of welcome and camaraderie to adventurers Jenny Smith Fletcher and Zachary Taylor "Z.T." Fletcher and the Reverend Simon P. Roundtree. Families arrived by rail to Ellis, Kansas, and walked the remaining 55 miles (88 kilometers) to a stretch of dugout homes along the Solomon River. To finance their move to the austere territory, they collected buffalo bones to sell to fertilizer factories. Osage residents rescued newcomers from starvation by distributing firewood and food. More colonists followed. In September 1877, the Reverend M.M. Bell brought 300 settlers from Lexington, Kentucky; the Reverend Daniel Hickman fostered more Kentuckians in March 1878. The next spring, a partially identified "Reverend Goodwin" led 50 colonists from Mississippi to Nicodemus. The exodus of blacks to the Midwest earned commentary in the Jackson, Tennessee, *Afro-American Sentinel, Kansas City Times,* and *St. Louis Globe-Democrat.* An elderly interviewee compared the trek to the flight of the children of Israel from the tyranny of Pharaoh.

Within a decade, the self-governing populace increased to 500 black citizens, who flourished from the cultivation of 12 square miles (31 square kilometers) of farmland. Residents built a bank, two newspapers, a general store, post office, livery, lumberyard, four-room school, pharmacy, and a Baptist church, led by the Reverend Daniel Hickman and his wife, Williana Hickman. Jenny Fletcher served as postmistress and the first teacher and organizer of the African Methodist Episcopal Church. The first postmaster, Zachary Fletcher, built the first stable and inn, the St. Francis Hotel.

McCabe achieved consecutive terms as Kansas auditor, becoming the first black state officeholder. For the remainder of his life, he pursued the hope of an all-black state. In 1889, on the former homelands of the Fox, Iowa, Kiowa, and Sac, he founded the city of Langston, Oklahoma, and, with his wife, Sarah McCabe, established the *Langston City Herald,* a voice for the developer of black communities. An editorial challenged self-supporting black citizens to prove to whites that they were capable of building a city. Racists charged that ex-slaves intended to oust whites from Oklahoma.

McCabe alerted first-time homeowners that they had to make visible improvements on their acreage, such as plowing farmland, laying the foundation of a house, planting an orchard, fencing a corral, or digging a well. He warned that they should arrive with a Winchester rifle, frying pan, and a $15 filing fee. Within a year, Langston boasted 14 businesses, including a feed store, two blacksmith forges, two barbershops, two liquor stores, and seven groceries. By October 1892, businesses rose to a total of 25, including a cab line, two butcher shops, two brickyards, a saddlery, bakery, gristmill, banks and hotels, and volunteer fire company.

Liberated from the white majority, black settlers cultivated African American style in language, food, arts and crafts, and religion. On their land, they revived West African agrarian styles from the Gold Coast, Senegambia, and Sierra Leone and grew cotton, indigo, melons, okra, peanuts, rice, sorghum, sweet potatoes, and yams. From the training of educators, entrepreneurs, inventors, lawyers, ministers, and physicians came the black middle class and the identity formation of the African American.

See also: Greeley, Horace; Sojourner Truth; Thirteenth Amendment (1865).

Further Reading

Hine, Darlene Clark, and Jacqueline McLeod, eds. *Crossing Boundaries: Comparative History of Black People in Diaspora.* Bloomington: Indiana University Press, 1999.

Painter, Nell Irvin. *Creating Black Americans: African-American History and Its Meanings, 1619 to the Present.* New York: Oxford University Press, 2006.

Snodgrass, Mary Ellen. *The Underground Railroad: An Encyclopedia of People, Places, and Operations.* Armonk, NY: M.E. Sharpe, 2007.

Sowell, Thomas. *Ethnic America: A History.* New York: Basic Books, 2000.

Winks, Robin W. *The Blacks in Canada.* Montreal, Canada: McGill-Queen's University Press, 2005.

Black Kettle (ca. 1803–1868)

A Southern Cheyenne chief and peacemaker, Black Kettle was a martyr of U.S. Cavalry raids. Born in the Black Hills of South Dakota around 1803, Black Kettle, together with warrior society leader Roman Nose, mediated between hostile and peaceful Cheyenne after the arrival of prospectors and families to Colorado during the Pikes Peak Gold Rush of 1858–1859. On February 18, 1861, Black Kettle and five other chiefs joined the Arapaho in signing the Treaty of Fort Wise, which ceded native lands to whites and guaranteed peace on the Santa Fe Trail.

Contributing to increased violence were the predations of dog soldiers, renegade guerrilla warriors who refused settlement. The loss of the buffalo to hunters hired by the railroad and the U.S. Army forced braves into stealing cattle and food from settlers and wagon trains. In 1863, Black Kettle journeyed to Washington, D.C., to discuss conditions for Plains Indians with President Abraham Lincoln. The chief returned in spring 1864 to more vicious treatment at the Ash Creek Reservation, where soldiers shot his old friend, Lean Bear, who approached unarmed in welcome.

On November 29, 1864, Third Colorado Volunteers, armed with howitzers, led by Colonel John M. Chivington, and backed by Governor John Evans, precipitated a revenge war of Arapaho, Cheyenne, and Sioux against whites. A promoter of genocide, Chivington and his force of 700 attacked a Cheyenne settlement at Sand Creek near Fort Lyon in southeastern Colorado; they struck before dawn, while most of the braves were hunting. The soldiers slaughtered 133 Arapaho and Cheyenne, mostly women and children. Black Kettle raised a surrender flag alongside a U.S. flag, but he could not stop the cavalry assault, the burning of the village, or the sexual mutilation of women and children's corpses. His third wife, Medicine Woman, suffered nine bullet wounds but survived. After the slaughter, Chivington's men paraded drunk through Denver with skulls, scalps, and bloody limbs of their victims. On October 14, 1865, Black Kettle negotiated the Treaty of the Little Arkansas River with federal commissioners. The compromise lost more of his people's traditional hunting lands and cost him the respect of his most conservative followers.

The fallout from Chivington's massacre prompted Congress to condemn the savagery of the military and abruptly ended Black Kettle's hopes for peace. After the signing of the third Treaty of Medicine Lodge on October 28, 1867, he accepted assignment to Sand Creek Reservation in southeastern Colorado, but lost more authority to the belligerent dog soldiers. By mid-November, he had to enter negotiations with Arapaho Chief Big Mouth, Colonel William Babcock Hazen, and interpreter Henry Alvord of the Tenth Cavalry concerning a complex series of matters involving young hotheads on the prowl and families starving because federal beef allotments had not arrived.

In a snowstorm, Lieutenant Colonel George Armstrong Custer rode down and killed 103 Cheyenne on November 27, 1868, at the Washita River in Cheyenne, Oklahoma. U.S. soldiers slew 900 horses, attacked 51 lodges, scalped the dead, and captured 53 women and children. Before Arapaho and Kiowa warriors could intervene, Black Kettle and Medicine Woman died from bullets in the back as they forded the river. Hoofprints indicated that the cavalry rode over their remains and those of their dead horses.

See also: Washita Massacre.

Further Reading

Greene, Jerome A. *Washita: The U.S. Army and the Southern Cheyennes, 1867–1869.* Norman: University of Oklahoma Press, 2004.

Hatch, Thom. *Black Kettle: The Cheyenne Chief Who Sought Peace but Found War.* Hoboken, NJ: Wiley, 2004.

Johansen, Bruce E., and Donald A. Grinde, Jr. *The Encyclopedia of Native American Biography.* New York: Da Capo, 1998.

Lamar, Howard R., ed. *The New Encyclopedia of the American West.* New Haven, CT: Yale University Press, 1998.

Utley, Robert M. *Cavalier in Buckskin: George Armstrong Custer and the Western Military Frontier.* Rev. ed. Norman: University of Oklahoma Press, 2001.

Waldman, Carl. *Who Was Who in Native American History: Indians and Non-Indians from Early Contacts Through 1900.* New York: Facts on File, 1990.

Black Marketing

After the seaport blockade during the Civil War, the South suffered a rapid strangulation of supplies, morphine, liquor, raw materials, and foodstuffs. A black market flourished in cocaine, coffee, salt, sugar, and meat from blockade runners and speculators, who sold to panicked homemakers, surgical suppliers, and kitchen managers at hospitals, orphanages, schools, restaurants, and hotels.

Patrons of the black market encouraged the illegal sale of imported or stolen goods, often advertised as war surplus. Southern smugglers retrieved illicit goods from Northern speculators across military lines. After passage of the Confederate conscription act of March 28, 1862, forgers profited from the demand for exemption papers, which circulated on the black market. Military foragers boosted their income by selling stolen alcohol, farm goods, and livestock for cash or untraceable goods. Deserters and vagrants, fearful of capture, relied on black marketing for income. Collectors of donated clothing and bedding sold charitable contributions for cash.

At a Confederate cavalry camp near Austin, Arkansas, crop failures in 1861 and 1862 increased speculation at Little Rock, where black marketers profited from demand. Outside Fort Sumter, unloaders at the Chester, South Carolina, train station turned purloined freight loads of paint, varnish, iron rails, whale oil, and timber into easy money. At Hilton Head, South Carolina, smugglers stocked Savannah's black market shelves with drugs, whiskey, liquor, silk and ribbons, and luxury soaps. Florida watermen attempted a similar underground economy, but blockade running so destabilized the economy that the state was bankrupt at war's end.

By 1863, when the price of Kentucky bourbon had risen from 25 cents to $35 a gallon, the Confederate economy ranged out of control. In Memphis, Tennessee, where Union General James Clifford Veatch banned liquor sales and consumption in January 1863, black marketers exhibited an inventory of ale, beer, and wine. Among the best customers for prime whiskey were Union officers, who had more cash to spend than rebels of equivalent rank.

The Union made its own profits at Fort Pickens, Florida, by seizing and marketing cotton bales, an illegal trade with European buyers that flourished from Memphis to New Orleans to Galveston, Texas. In Alabama, guerrilla bands called "Partisan Rangers" engaged in banditry to steal horses, liquor, and cotton to stash or market on the underground. While European and Northern mills stood idle, hoarders and speculators boosted the price of cotton from 14 cents to 95 cents per pound.

Black marketing produced a climate of scapegoating. On December 17, 1862, General Ulysses S. Grant blamed Jewish merchants for cotton speculation and smuggling in Mississippi. He mistakenly labeled them traitors and ordered the ousting of Jewish families from military zones in Kentucky, Mississippi, and Tennessee.

In Jewish enclaves in Cincinnati, Ohio; Louisville, Kentucky; and St. Louis, Missouri, rabbis and congregations rallied against the outrage; they and others in Chicago, New York, and Philadelphia sent telegrams to the White House expressing their anger at being called underground profiteers. On January 3, 1863, U.S. Congressman John Addison Gurley defended Jewish merchants and persuaded President Abraham Lincoln to rescind Grant's banishment of Jews. Two days later, Rabbi Isaac Mayer Wise thanked President Lincoln for redeeming Jews of stereotyping as war exploiters.

At Libby Prison in Richmond, Virginia, black marketing relieved boredom while supplying prisoners of war with bartered foods or cash. Union inmates made hair chains and ornaments and bone rings, buttons, and toothpicks for barter with guards who sanctioned the internal prison economy. Outside Elmira Prison in southwestern New York, trustees performing prison labor traded inmate crafts for apples, cabbage, crackers, onions, and shellfish. They held whiskey allotments in their mouths to spit into cups and trade for quids of chewing tobacco or rat meat or hides to sew into gloves. Tobacco became a standard currency for underground purchases and trades. A similar survival system operated at Belle Isle, Virginia, where Corporal Ebenezer Seth "Eben" Ely operated a prison flatboat along the James River. He purchased tobacco, pies, and biscuits to sell or trade in camp to rescue Union prisoners of war from starvation, exposure, and illness. The upshot of the underground economy was more money for criminals and less for legitimate commerce.

The collapse of the South's monetary system produced further opportunities for grasping traders and criminals. In Chattanooga, Tennessee, at Christmas 1864, military administrators attempted to control price gouging for groceries, clothes, shoes, tobacco, and hardware by posting a fair price schedule in the *Gazette.* Union authorities enforced the price regimen by closing one black marketeer for selling illegal calico and women's finery, a favorite with camp followers. In Richmond, General John Winder, supervisor of martial law, attempted similar price controls but found them impossible to enforce. At Main and 17th streets along the James River and Shockoe Creek in Richmond at First Market, one of the nation's oldest farmers' markets, shoppers at the two-story brick emporium wrangled over prices and shortages with legitimate and illicit dealers. According to the memoir of Virginia resident Sallie A. Brock Putnam, to inflate prices, illicit traders jockeyed between cash-bearing citizens and military commissaries.

To survive increased surveillance and pilfering and to pay property taxes, participants in the free black underground risked arrest, lashings, and sentencing to a chain gang by selling stolen goods for black marketeers, thieves, and hustlers. In April 1864, smugglers of goods from the Cape Fear delta in Wilmington, North Carolina, squeezed buyers by charging $45 for a pound of corn and $250 for a pound of flour. To prevent Richmond's black merchants from prospering and gaining too much power, they became the targets of police and courts. Police increased market patrols from eight to 11 officers and beefed up the night watch; the Richmond City Council imposed a required certificate of good character from Mayor Joseph Carrington Mayo for licensing businesses.

Union profiteers were no less guilty of theft and deception. They thrived on the levee in Cincinnati, Ohio, and cheated black contrabands rescued by the army. With funding intended to equip black refugees for military service, disreputable commissioners engaged in underground commerce. At a government farm for refugees in Alabama and at the New England Freedman's Aid Society refuge at Beaufort, South Carolina, where up to 50 new arrivals appeared daily, quartermasters sold rations, medicine, and clothing allotments for cash. Black families scrambled for refuge in barns, sod huts, packing crates, and abandoned houses and sheds. Profiteering increased the death rate of black runaways to up to 50 percent at Helena, Arkansas; Memphis, Tennessee; and Davis Bend and Natchez, Mississippi.

To halt the underground economy, Secretary of War Edwin M. Stanton appointed William P. Wood as the first director of the U.S. Secret Service. Wood used black market contacts and a team of 30 agents to curtail war-related counterfeiting, forgery, and fraud.

See also: Law Enforcement.

Further Reading

Barnes, James J., and Patience P. Barnes. *The American Civil War Through British Eyes: February 1863–December 1865.* Kent, OH: Kent State University Press, 2005.

Frank, Lisa Tendrich, ed. *Civil War: People and Perspectives.* Santa Barbara, CA: ABC-CLIO, 2009.

Volo, Dorothy Denneen, and James M. Volo. *Daily Life in Civil War America.* 2nd ed. Santa Barbara, CA: Greenwood, 2009.

Black Migration

The liberation of 4 million slaves by the Emancipation Proclamation on January 1, 1863, and by the Thirteenth Amendment to the U.S. Constitution on December 6, 1865, enabled black Americans to choose their place of residency. At the end of the Civil War, 92 percent of blacks lived in the South; by 1870, the demographics remained disproportionately high in the former slave states.

Ostensibly, relocation allowed black citizens to escape racist violence by the Ku Klux Klan and to reclaim the freedoms denied their ancestors, the victims of a violent diaspora. Among those risk takers willing to migrate, former soldiers during the Civil War had a taste of adventure and knowledge of transportation via railroads and steamboats. In an astute assessment of the situation, the Reverend Houston Hartsfield Holloway, a blacksmith during his enslavement northwest of Macon, Georgia, foresaw the problems ahead for black migrants. He observed in his diary that the races had no experience with each other as equals. Blacks needed to learn about autonomy, and whites needed to acclimate to living and doing business with free blacks. Beginning in February 1865, the enactment of Black Codes demonstrated the intent of white elitists to maintain bondage through statutes that violated civil rights and disregarded universal emancipation.

Lacking mobility, cash, and travel experience, 89 percent of black Americans maintained Southern residency and continued to work in rural agriculture in a climate and terrain they understood. On September 23, 1865, William Joshua Falconer, editor of Alabama's *Daily Montgomery Ledger,* promoted the stereotype of the black farmer with the simplistic pronouncement that whites belonged in cities and blacks in the country. The statement ignored the urbanization of blacks in Baltimore, Boston, New York, and Philadelphia.

The black exodus did not begin in earnest until 1870, when 40,000 departed per decade. After cotton prices began to rise in 1870, a result of the worn-out soil in Alabama, the Carolinas, and Georgia, some 22,200 ex-slaves moved southwest to farm the rich alluvial crust of Meridian and Vicksburg in central Mississippi.

Until the collapse of Reconstruction in 1876–1877, movement within the South increased the black population of such cities as Corinth, Mississippi, and LaGrange and Memphis, Tennessee, which grew by 15,000 with an influx from the Mississippi Delta. Atlanta, Georgia, which elected two black members of the city council, experienced a 57 percent growth in population and a rise in black demographics from 21 percent to 46 percent of all residents. Conditions for immigrants to New Orleans improved in 1870, when the city staffed its police force with 28 percent black officers. In the outlying areas, the plunge of Louisiana land values by 70 percent made purchase of farmland more affordable for first-time buyers.

Black Population of Former Slave States, 1870

State	Number	Percentage of Total Population
Alabama	475,510	47.7
Arkansas	122,169	25.2
District of Columbia	43,404	33.0
Florida	91,689	48.8
Georgia	545,142	46.0
Louisiana	364,210	50.1
Mississippi	444,201	53.7
North Carolina	391,650	36.6
South Carolina	415,814	59.0
Tennessee	322,331	25.6
Texas	253,475	31.0
Virginia	512,841	41.9

Source: U.S. Census of 1870.

Adaptation to Change

Emigrants from the South met significant obstacles. The low percentage who could arrange long journeys reunited with families in the North and in Canada along the Great Lakes, a former destination for fugitives along Underground Railroad routes. At the eastern end of Lake Erie, migrants hurried through Niagara Falls, New York, to shelter at Fort Erie, Buffalo, and the Canadian side of Niagara Falls. At the juncture with Lake Ontario, blacks built communities at Hamilton, St. Catharines, and Toronto. Additional communities thrived at Kingston at the eastern end of Lake Ontario, Oro on Lake Simcoe, and Collingwood and Owen Sound on Georgian Bay, Lake Huron. Freed from the plow and the cotton gin, migrants found jobs cutting stone, whitewashing walls, keeping stores, cooking and serving at hotels and restaurants, repairing shoes and harnesses, dressmaking and fine hand laundry, tending the sick, driving delivery wagons, and crewing river barges and sloops.

White philanthropists broadened the options available to blacks by actively recruiting them to colonies and jobs in industry. Some 20,000 former slaves chose to leave the United States permanently. They joined the "Back to Africa" or colonization movement and settled on the Atlantic coast of the Horn of Africa. By 1867, the American Colonization Society had directed 13,000 freedmen to the black motherland. One group of 3,700 Virginians expatriated to Sierra Leone and Liberia, the continent's first republic. The most remunerative relocation occurred among Marylanders and Virginians headed for jobs in coal, coke, iron, steel, and tin in Pittsburgh, Pennsylvania. By 1870, their

Black migrants await departure at the wharves of Vicksburg, Mississippi, in the late 1870s. Some former slaves left the South during the Civil War, but the large-scale exodus north did not take place until Reconstruction and the years following. *(The Granger Collection, New York)*

numbers more than tripled to 6,136, or 7.1 percent of the city census.

Prejudice and Snobbery

Former slaves from the Lower Mississippi Valley incurred double-edged prejudice when they moved to the North. Those who sought to shift from agriculture to industry or skilled labor met disdain from a number of settled free-born blacks, as well as discrimination and segregation by whites. The two classes—slave-born and free-born blacks—developed separate neighborhoods, social clubs, and sports teams.

Church membership among Southern blacks flourished in African Methodist Episcopal (AME), African Methodist Episcopal Zion (AMEZ), Black Baptist and Presbyterian, and Colored Methodist Episcopal congregations. In Bronzeville, the black section of Milwaukee, Wisconsin, for three decades, St. Mark's AME offered the only choice for black worshippers. In Pittsburgh, black immigrant churchgoers chose between AME and AMEZ assemblies. More sophisticated blacks disdained the syncretic worship of migrants from the South, who added to standard Protestant elements of ritual voodoo, drumming, dance, and emotional outcries. Urban blues and folk songs recorded the sense of dislocation that accompanied exclusion and homesickness.

Trans-Mississippi territories beckoned to both blacks and whites. Some 70,000 black homesteaders chose Indiana, Kansas, and Oklahoma, where Jim Crow laws were less onerous and railroad jobs promised steady incomes. By 1870, the black population stood at a steady level in six Midwestern states.

Journalist Peter Anderson of San Francisco, founder of the *Mirror of the Times,* California's first black newspaper, enticed blacks to colonize either California or Sonora, Mexico, where he proposed founding an autonomous black republic. To stop the bleedout of cheap ex-slave labor, the Georgia legislature in 1876 imposed a $100 tax on labor recruiters for each county they canvassed. The Carolinas passed a similar law demanding a $1,000 per county fee, as did Alabama, where the licensing fee for labor agents was $5,000 per county. Despite intervention by municipalities to halt mass departure, from 1890 to 1920, the Great Migration enticed thousands to seek new lives in the urban Northeast and Midwest.

Black Population of Midwestern States, 1870

State	Number	Percentage of Total Population
Kansas	17,108	4.7
Ohio	63,213	2.4
Indiana	24,560	1.5
Illinois	28,762	1.1
Michigan	11,849	1.0
Iowa	5,762	0.5

Source: U.S. Census of 1870.

See also: Black Communities.

Further Reading

Hine, Darlene Clark, and Jacqueline McLeod, eds. *Crossing Boundaries: Comparative History of Black People in Diaspora.* Bloomington: Indiana University Press, 1999.

Painter, Nell Irvin. *Creating Black Americans: African-American History and Its Meanings, 1619 to the Present.* New York: Oxford University Press, 2006.

Snodgrass, Mary Ellen. *The Underground Railroad: An Encyclopedia of People, Places, and Operations.* Armonk, NY: M.E. Sharpe, 2007.

Sowell, Thomas. *Ethnic America: A History.* New York: Basic Books, 2000.

Winks, Robin W. *The Blacks in Canada: A History.* 2nd ed. Montreal, Canada: McGill-Queen's University Press, 2005.

Blackmore, William Henry (1827–1878)

English barrister and philanthropist William Henry Blackmore of Salisbury led British entrepreneurs in speculating on railroads, grazing land, and the cattle industry in the American West. Born into a respected ancestry on August 2, 1827, he completed King's College at Bruton and read law with solicitors Lambert and Norton. He began practicing business and maritime law in Liverpool as a partner with Duncan, Squarey, and Blackmore.

Mentored by American attorney Cyrus Martin Fisher in North American investment, Blackmore branched out to a finance office in London. At age 26, he collaborated in New York with politicians and financiers on land purchases and rail travel in Colorado and New Mexico. He extended his involvement in Dutch and German immigration by backing the United States Freehold Land and Emigration Company, which channeled settlers to the San Luis Valley in Colorado Territory.

Blackmore's fascination with the West inspired the founding of the Blackmore Museum in Salisbury in 1867. The collection featured ethnographic relics from Mississippi and Ohio Valley mound culture retrieved and catalogued by archaeologists Ephraim George Squier and Edwin Hamilton Davis. The exhibition documented the discovery in Peebles, Ohio, of Serpent Mound, the world's largest prehistoric effigy, first analyzed in Squier and Davis's text *Ancient Monuments of the Mississippi Valley* (1848).

During an initial survey of the trans-Mississippi West in autumn 1868, Blackmore hunted buffalo and traveled by the Kansas Pacific Railway to Laramie, Wyoming, and by stage to Salt Lake City, Utah, on a fact-finding mission for the British cabinet on the status of British Mormons in the Far West. On a subsequent expedition, his wife, Mary Sidford Blackmore, died of pneumonia in Bozeman, Montana, where he honored her by establishing a local cemetery.

In spring 1871, the philanthropist funded a survey of northwestern Wyoming led by geologist Ferdinand Vandeveer Hayden to document landmarks to be incorporated in Yellowstone National Park. The survey included the photos of William Henry Jackson and paintings by Thomas Moran.

To replace exhibits lost in a fire at the Smithsonian Institution in Washington, D.C., in 1865, Blackmore collected 1,282 photographic portraits of Native American men and women, six to eight per tribe, made by William Abraham Bell, Alexander Gardner, Antonio Zeno Shindler, and Orloff R. Westman. Among Blackmore's portfolio are close-ups of Oglala Lakota Sioux Chief Red Cloud, Lakota Sioux Chief Spotted Elk (Big Foot), and Spotted Elk's wife, White Hawk.

Blackmore was expert at financial ventures. In 1870, he and other British speculators bought up cheap real estate and established cattle ranches in New Mexico. For $100,000, he acquired more than 2 million acres (810,000 hectares) and employed his brother, sister, and cousin to superintend properties in Colorado and New Mexico.

In 1872, he proposed changing the name of Colorado Springs, Colorado, to Manitou, a reference to an Indian deity in Henry Wadsworth Longfellow's Ojibwa epic *The Song of Hiawatha* (1855). By 1880, the healing spa brought 30,000 outsiders, some out of curiosity, and others seeking relief from tuberculosis. With the refinement of the refrigerated railcar, Blackmore and other ranchers shipped thousands of pounds of fresh beef and mutton to England. As profits rose, so did property values and competition among big investors for grazing land and water rights.

Blackmore shot himself to death on April 12, 1878. His survivors distributed his artifacts and papers to the Birmingham Museum, the British Museum, the Historical Society of New Mexico, and the Smithsonian Institution.

After his death, publication of *The Hunting Grounds of the Great West* (1878), a concise overview authored by Blackmore and Richard Irving Dodge, preserved data on the game and first peoples of the North American desert. In the introduction, Blackmore classified tribes by nation and band, expressing pride in his acquaintance with great leaders of first peoples, including Spotted Tail, Ute Chief Ouray, Shoshone Chief Washakie, Arapaho Chief Little Raven,

Cheyenne Chief Little Robe, and warriors and leaders of the Apache, Comanche, Crow, Kiowa, Navajo, Osage, Pawnee, and Pueblo. At the end of Blackmore's introduction, he predicted the extermination of Indians, who would survive in history only as place-names on the map.

Further Reading

Grusin, Richard. *Culture, Technology, and the Creation of America's National Parks.* Cambridge, UK: Cambridge University Press, 2004.

Veenendahl, Augustus J., Jr. *Slow Train to Paradise: How Dutch Investment Helped Build American Railroads.* Stanford, CA: Stanford University Press, 1996.

Wyckoff, William. *Creating Colorado: The Making of a Western American Landscape, 1860–1940.* New Haven, CT: Yale University Press, 1999.

Bloomingdale's

A successful model of the one-stop, one-price department store, Bloomingdale's became a source of trendy merchandise in New York City. In 1861, 19-year-old Jewish merchant Joseph B. Bloomingdale, the son of Benjamin and Hannah Weil Bloomingdale, returned from a year's stint in California and formed a partnership with his 20-year-old brother, Lyman G. Bloomingdale, a veteran of the Union army. The two brothers advanced the sales style of their father, a peddler who had emigrated from Bavaria to America in 1837, and applied it to millinery, hosiery, blouses, pinafores, and nightshirts and other "gent's furnishings." Their featured item, hoop skirts, the wood-framed skirt shapers popularized by Empress Eugénie of France, outsold other goods.

At their Ladies' Notions Shop at 938 Third Avenue on the Lower East Side of Manhattan, Lyman and his wife, Hattie Collenberger Bloomingdale, and son Samuel occupied the second floor. On the first floor, they featured a variety of clothing—men's shirts for 48 cents, hoop skirts for 50 cents, six-ruffle bustles for $1.25, and overcoats for $9.98. Their business style combined quality goods, low prices, and courteous service.

In 1872, with women abandoning hoop skirts, the Bloomingdales opened the Great East Side Bazaar at Fifty-Sixth Street and Third Avenue with $6,000 in stock and two female clerks. The Bloomingdale brothers specialized in a wide array of European skirts, whalebone corsets, yard goods, and men's wear, which they imported from their buying office in Paris, France, and advertised in *Godey's Ladies' Book.* Their store profited from the construction of the Third Avenue elevated railway and competed with established dry goods and clothing merchants such as Macy's, Stern Brothers, B. Altman, and Siegel-Cooper.

The Bloomingdales' imaginative promotions buoyed their investment through the financial crash of 1873. As the population of the neighborhood changed from working class to privileged—a shift reflected by the new Metropolitan Museum of Art and St. Patrick's Cathedral near Central Park—wealthy residents invested in brownstones and patronized the store.

By 1880, Bloomingdale's occupied a five-story emporium. Employees enjoyed a paid two-week vacation at the seaside. The brothers advanced urban health and culture by donating to the American Museum of Natural History, B'nai Brith, Hebrew Orphan Asylum, Hebrew Technical Institute, Metropolitan Museum of Art, Montefiore Sanitarium, Mutual Relief Fund, New York Zoological Society, and Young Men's Hebrew Association.

After Joseph's retirement in 1896 and Lyman's death in 1905, the department store passed to Lyman's sons, Hiram Collenberger, Irving Ingersoll, and Samuel J. Bloomingdale.

See also: Department Stores.

Further Reading

Abelson, Elaine S. *When Ladies Go A-Thieving: Middle-Class Shoplifters in the Victorian Department Store.* New York: Oxford University Press, 1989.

Benson, Susan Porter. *Counter Cultures: Saleswomen, Managers, and Customers in American Department Stores, 1890–1940.* Urbana: University of Illinois Press, 1986.

Diner, Hasia R., and Beryl Lieff Benderly. *Her Works Praise Her: A History of Jewish Women in America from Colonial Times to the Present.* New York: Basic Books, 2002.

Williams, Ellen, and Steve Radlauer. *The Historic Shops and Restaurants of New York.* New York: New York Review of Books, 2002.

Booth, John Wilkes (1838–1865)

An American stage actor and vehement Confederate sympathizer, John Wilkes Booth martyred President Abraham Lincoln by gunning him down at Ford's Theatre in Washington, D.C., on April 14, 1865.

A first-generation Anglo-American born to Mary Ann Holms and the celebrated Shakespearean actor Junius Brutus Booth on May 10, 1838, Booth grew up among nine siblings on a farm outside Bel Air, Maryland. He disdained education at the Milton Boarding School in Sparks and at St. Timothy's Hall military academy in Catonsville. In his mid-teens, he memorized theatrical speeches and read the plays of Shakespeare.

In Baltimore in 1855, he debuted in a secondary role in *Richard III* and, under the stage name J.B. Wilkes, acted for a year in Philadelphia and later in Richmond, Virginia. To earn $20,000 a year, he played to female theatergoers by specializing in the suicide scene from *Romeo and Juliet* and in lusty villains and regicides, including portrayals of Brutus, Hamlet, and William Wallace.

On a year's tour from Boston to New Orleans in 1861–1862, Booth applauded the secession of slaveholding states and vilified President Lincoln. During a scene at Ford's Theatre in 1863, he aimed a menacing gesture at the president's box. Lincoln's reelection obsessed the actor, who doubted the Confederacy's chances of victory over the North. Booth attended the hanging of radical abolitionist John Brown and smuggled quinine to Southern field hospitals in Louisiana. The actor stalked the president and fantasized about kidnapping him from his summer residence at the Old Soldiers' Home, holding him in Richmond, and exchanging him for rebel prisoners of war. The dreamscape cast Booth as a Southern hero.

Actor John Wilkes Booth, the assassin of Abraham Lincoln, came from one of America's most famous theatrical families. A rabid Confederate sympathizer, Booth enlisted at least ten others in his plot to kill the president, vice president, and secretary of state. *(Library of Congress)*

Booth joined a Confederate spy cell in Maryland and enlisted a criminal, Samuel Bland Arnold, spy John Surratt, and Booth's boyhood friend, Michael O'Laughlen, as couriers for the Confederate Secret Service. After the South's surrender on April 12, 1865, the actor shifted his plot to assassination to retaliate against Lincoln's plans to extend the vote to freedmen.

Two days later, Booth plotted the shooting of the president during a performance of Tom Taylor's domestic farce *Our American Cousin* (1858). Accomplices accepted orders for the simultaneous murders of Secretary of State William Henry Seward and Vice President Andrew Johnson, both of whom eluded execution. Booth envisioned chaos in the capital and a chance for the Confederacy to seize control and reignite the war.

Around 9 P.M., Booth sneaked into the president's box. He shot Lincoln once in the back of the skull with a Derringer pistol and stabbed the presidential escort, Major Henry Reed Rathbone. Both the first lady, Mary Todd Lincoln, and Rathbone's fiancée, Clara Hamilton Harris, escaped injury. To dramatize his fantasy of regicide, Booth leaped to the stage, brandished a knife, and declared in Latin *Sic semper tyrannis* (thus always to tyrants).

During his escape by horse from the alley, Booth fractured his left fibula. He and accomplice David Edgar "Davy" Herold collected guns at Mary Surratt's Tavern south of Washington and halted at the residence of Dr. Samuel Alexander Mudd for setting and splinting of the broken leg. During Booth's treatment, on April 15, 1865, at 7:22 A.M., across from Ford's Theatre at the residence of William Petersen, Lincoln died.

In his diary, Booth jotted an exoneration of the killing as an act of patriotism. With a $10,000 reward on his head, he crept through the Maryland swamps and gleaned from newspapers that the nation, North and South, mourned the president's passing. Dismayed that the shooting had failed to elevate him to hero, the assassin hid among Maryland and Virginia Confederates. South of Port Royal near Fredericksburg, Virginia, he and Herold retreated to the farm of Richard Henry Garrett, the end of their 60-mile (96-kilometer) flight. Garrett deduced Booth's true identity and locked him and Herold in a tobacco barn, which federal cavalrymen surrounded before dawn on April 26. By setting the barn aflame, the troops forced the exit of Booth, who fell, fatally wounded through the neck and spinal cord by one shot from Sergeant Thomas Patrick "Boston" Corbett's Colt revolver.

A military court condemned to the gallows four plotters—George Andreas Atzerodt, David Edgar Herold, Lewis Thornton Powell (alias Lewis Paine), and boardinghouse owner Mary Elizabeth Jenkins Surratt, the first woman executed by federal command. Four others—Samuel Arnold, Samuel Mudd, Michael O'Laughlen, and Edmund Spangler—served prison sentences. Spangler and John Surratt escaped execution.

See also: Lincoln, Abraham; Seward, William Henry.

Further Reading

Evans, C. Wyatt. *The Legend of John Wilkes Booth: Myth, Memory, and a Mummy.* Lawrence: University Press of Kansas, 2004.

Goodrich, Thomas. *The Darkest Dawn: Lincoln, Booth, and the Great American Tragedy.* Bloomington: Indiana University Press, 2005.

McPherson, James M. *The Most Fearful Ordeal: Original Coverage of the Civil War by* The New York Times. New York: St. Martin's, 2004.

Steers, Edward, Jr. *Blood on the Moon: The Assassination of Abraham Lincoln.* Lexington: University Press of Kentucky, 2001.

Stephenson, Nathaniel W. *Abraham Lincoln and the Union.* New York: BiblioBazaar, 2008.

Borden, Gail (1801–1874)

Inventor Gail Borden, Jr., lengthened the shelf life of milk by selling condensed milk in tins. At the same time, he contributed to the upgrading of cleanliness standards in food processing and storage in America.

A native of Norwich, New York, he was born on November 9, 1801, to Gail and Philadelphia Wheeler Borden, a frontier family who lived in Kentucky, Indiana, and Ohio. Lacking a classroom education, he settled in Pearl River, Mississippi, to cure a chronic cough and supported himself for seven years as Amite County surveyor and federal cartographer. In Texas, he generated a topographical map of Galveston and Houston, before joining his brother, Thomas Henry Borden, in founding the *Telegraph and Texas Register,* a vehicle for the Republic of Texas and the state's second permanent newspaper. Gail helped draft the 1836 Constitution of the Republic of Texas; at age 36, he collected customs at Galveston.

The death of Borden's three-year-old daughter Mary in 1833 preceded the demise of his wife, Penelope Mercer Borden, during the yellow fever epidemic that killed 11 percent of Galveston's population in 1844. The dual loss piqued Borden's interest in refrigeration as a means of combating food poisoning and microbial contamination.

To the U.S. Army, hospitals, campers and sailors, and explorer Elisha Kane for the Grinnell Arctic expedition of 1850–1851, Borden marketed a "portable soup-bread" called the American Meat Biscuit. The dehydrated beef cracker, a packable, portable food, retained its nutritional properties after being reduced to 20 percent of its original volume. Borden varied the flavors with poultry, oysters, and veal and marketed the biscuits in airtight casks or soldered tin cases to protect them from moisture. The meat biscuit won the Council Medal at the 1851 World's Fair in London, Borden's honorary membership in the London Society, and a series of kudos from *Chambers, The Eclectic, The Lancet, Living Age, Newton's London Journal,* and *Scientific American* magazines. The *American Journal of Pharmacy* honored the biscuits for varying diets and for allowing one nation to transfer food gifts and surpluses to less fortunate countries.

On a transatlantic ship voyage in 1852, Borden observed that when cows in the hold became seasick, bottle-fed babies on board went hungry. The observation triggered an idea. Borden began studying the airtight condensation chamber used by Alonzo Giles Hollister to evaporate fruit juice into sugar at a Shaker community in New Lebanon, New York. In 1856, Borden patented a condensing process that evaporated and preserved milk in a vacuum without the addition of an antiseptic. With a steam jacket outside and steam coil inside his spherical copper vacuum chamber, he boiled the fluid at a temperature of 130 degrees Fahrenheit (54 degrees Celsius).

Borden began manufacturing the processed food with funds from New York financier Jeremiah Milbank. At the New York Condensed Milk Company, a factory in Burrville, Connecticut, he began pressing low-cost soluble milk cakes with pulverized sugar and canning tinned milk, which vendors sold from handcarts to Orthodox Jewish mothers in New York City. In 1861, to meet the needs of Union soldiers during the Civil War, Borden opened sanitary condensaries in Connecticut, Illinois, Maine, and New York; he insisted on milk contracts with hygienic dairies that monitored the health of cows. Employing a sterilized vacuum pan, he increased output to 5,000 gallons (19,000 liters) of condensed milk per day. Rebel soldiers who captured Union supply trains valued the recovery of Borden's Eagle Brand Condensed Milk and Peerless Brand Evaporated Cream. The Borden complex became the world's largest handler of milk products.

Two years before Louis Pasteur advanced his germ theory in 1864, Borden contributed to the science of food preservation by insisting on fresh, pure ingredients and by preventing decomposition or fermentation during processing. In 1862, he experimented with condensing beef extract, cider, cocoa, coffee, tea, and apple, currant, and grape juice. These products failed to outsell condensed milk, but their distribution to wounded soldiers by the U.S. Sanitary Commission helped rehydrate and revive combat victims.

During Reconstruction, while sons Henry Lee and John Gail Borden ran the milk manufactory, Gail operated a sawmill and copper factory at Bastrop, built a freedmen's school and Baptist mission, and informed dairiers of the need for sterile food handling. After his death while wintering in Borden, Texas, on January 11, 1874, Borden's wholesome vacuum-packed milk lowered the mortality rate for American infants and filled the emergency stocks of the American Red Cross.

See also: Children and Childhood.

Further Reading

Nelson, Scott Reynolds, and Carol Sheriff. *A People at War: Civilians and Soldiers in America's Civil War, 1854–1877.* New York: Oxford University Press, 2007.

Smith, Andrew F. *Eating History: 30 Turning Points in the Making of American Cuisine.* New York: Columbia University Press, 2009.

Snodgrass, Mary Ellen. *Encyclopedia of Kitchen History.* New York: Fitzroy Dearborn, 2004.

Steinberg, Ted. *Down to Earth: Nature's Role in American History.* 2nd ed. New York: Oxford University Press, 2009.

Boston, Massachusetts

A Puritan stronghold founded in 1630, Boston is one of the nation's oldest and most historic and culturally diverse cities. Established on the marshes and mudflats of Shawmut Peninsula, Massachusetts, it produced significant figures in business, education, government and law, religion, sports, and the arts. Those flourishing in the 1860s and 1870s include attorney Wendell Phillips, Bible scholar Theodore Parker, clergyman Edward Everett Hale, educator Amos Bronson Alcott, painter James Abbott McNeill Whistler, photographer Josiah Johnson Hawes, physician Lucy Sewall, poets Emily Dickinson and Julia Ward Howe, reformer Ezra Hervey Heywood, Senator Charles Sumner, suffragist Lucy Stone, and writer Louisa May Alcott.

Along with abolitionist Maria Weston Chapman of the Boston Female Anti-Slavery Society, orator Abby Kelley Foster of the American Anti-Slavery Society, and conductor William Cooper Nell of the Underground Railroad, equal rights agitators Harriet Bell Hayden and Lewis Hayden fostered rallies on Boston Common, where military units drilled in anticipation of the Civil War. From the civil liberties movement emerged heroes—watchmen Samuel Gridley Howe and Charles Lenox Remond of the Boston Vigilance Committee, agent Charlotte Forten of the Freedmen's Relief Association, and women's rights activist Lucy Stone of the American Woman Suffrage Association. Fierce reporters and editors furthered human rights through news and commentary published in John Albion Andrew's *Freedman's Record,* William Lloyd Garrison's *The Liberator,* and David and Lydia Maria Francis Child's *National Anti-Slavery Standard.*

Because of its prevailing spirit of humanitarianism, Boston became a city of nations where one-third of residents came from foreign shores. Following the increase of peasants fleeing Polish shtetls and surviving famines during Ireland's "Great Hunger" of the 1840s and 1850s, the city's cultural mix presented diverse perspectives on social and economic change. Those suffering from cholera, consumption, or typhus received care at the Deer Island hospital, built at the harbor's edge and later converted into an almshouse. By the time of the second immigrant wave in 1860, East Boston, composed of Armenian, Austrian, British, Canadian, German, Irish, Italian, Polish, Russian, and Scandinavian immigrants, developed into a waterfront community. Transporting Irish Catholics at a steady rate, the Galway steamers *Adriatic, Anglia, Columbia,* and *Hibernia* began service on March 26, 1861, to Boston and New York.

Immigrant carpenters and shipbuilders labored on Boston's prestigious homes, yachts, shops, banks, hotels, and churches as well as schools, factories, mills, warehouses, and schooners. Introduced by the tea trade, Oong Ar-showe opened the city's first Chinese tea and coffee shop in 1865 at 25 Union Street. Chinese laborers, admitted under the Burlingame Treaty of 1868, joined Jewish and Syrian workers at South Cove enclaves. In 1870, the district opened the nation's first public library branch.

Settling In

Instigated by the behavioral and monetary divide between the nouveau riche and the urban poor, ethnic and religious clashes created tensions between Beacon Hill aristocrats and the "unwashed." At the center of the city's growing pains stood the bumptious, energetic Irish

Americans of Charlestown and South Boston. A fire at Clark and North streets and around Boston Harbor on February 24, 1862, that left thousands homeless brought Bostonians together in a challenge to restore commerce and employment.

To improve medical care, philanthropist Andrew Carney in 1863 donated $75,000 to the Daughters of Charity of St. Vincent de Paul. Mother Superior Ann Alexis Shorb built the 40-bed Carney Hospital, the first such Catholic facility in New England, and began admitting Civil War casualties. At the outpatient clinic, the sick paid 10 cents for treatment. Shorb and ten nuns also held fairs at Concert Hall to fund schools and St. Vincent's Orphan Asylum at Camden Street. To provide spiritual leadership, Catholic fathers chartered Boston College in 1863, the first Jesuit school in the city.

Between 1860 and 1870, Boston's population ballooned by 41 percent, from 177,840 to 250,526, forcing rapid annexation of Breed's Island, Brighton, Charlestown, Dorchester, Roxbury, and West Roxbury. Roxbury became the home of Italian Catholics and of German, Polish, and Russian Jews, who operated clothing and shoe factories and paint and tin shops. During the Civil War, to guard against a Confederate raid on Boston Harbor, the Union army established a camp at Gallops Island. Uniformed police kept order by wielding nightsticks. By 1869, the Cochituate Stand Pipe supplied water to the city's fire companies. In the mid-1870s, municipal authorities funded mounted patrols and a steam-powered harbor boat, the *Protector.* Soup kitchens at station houses and the distribution of Thanksgiving turkeys increased respect for police among the poor.

"Hub of the Universe"

During Mayor Frederick Walker Lincoln, Jr.'s seven years in office (1858–1860; 1863–1866), Boston engineers continued filling in the lowlands and expanding commerce. Horse-drawn trolley car lines crisscrossed major streets, bringing suburbanites into the city center within seven minutes. By land, construction of the Broadway Bridge, Congress Street Bridge, and West Fourth Street Drawbridge improved city access and relieved congestion.

From the sea, ferry passengers and freight arrived along Fort Point Channel to Rowes Wharf, the nation's oldest functioning landing, which received shipments of brick, coal, granite, timber, and wool as early as 1630. Park Square Station, built in 1872, received arrivals aboard the New York, New Haven & Hartford Railroad, which brought tourists to the Old Boston Tavern, a favorite gathering spot since 1712. When the Boston, Revere Beach, & Lynn Railroad entered service in 1875, passengers could ride for 3 cents.

Citizens seeking the Western experience could travel across the Mississippi River aboard the Adams Express Stage, which, until 1880, operated coaches to New Orleans and St. Louis. The Pacific Mail Steamship Company and Wells Fargo expressed freight as far west as Shanghai, China, and Kobe and Yokohama, Japan. The *Niagara* carried European travelers aboard the Cunard line to Liverpool from Boston Harbor; the Leyland Line offered similar transport aboard the *Istrian.* In 1869, Donald McKay's clipper ship the *Glory of the Seas* emerged from his East Boston shipyard to carry goods between Asia and the Atlantic seaboard. The *Daily American Eagle* faulted shippers for luring non-English-speaking paupers to Boston at the rate of 500 per day.

Civil Libertarians

Bostonians treasured their connections to American freedom. They made strides toward full citizenship for blacks, whether freedmen or runaways. As early as 1854, to safeguard Beacon Hill, clothier and gambler John P. Coburn, a transporter on the Underground Railroad and officer of the New England Freedom Association, formed the Massasoit Guards, a black volunteer security force that he paid from private funds. Into the mid-1860s, he and his patrolmen warded off kidnappers, posses, and bounty hunters, making safe people who otherwise were "not secure on the soil where the Declaration of Independence was written."

On March 31, 1863, a turning point in the history of the American military, Colonel Robert Gould Shaw, a veteran of the Battle of Antietam, Maryland, began readying for service the Fifty-fourth Massachusetts Volunteer Infantry, the nation's first regiment of freedmen. His professional example drew 40 percent of black men of military age in Boston, who risked sale into slavery if captured by rebel forces. Among the enlistees were Massasoit Guardsmen and two prominent brothers—Private Charles Douglass and Sergeant Major Lewis Douglass—the sons of former slaves Anna Murray and orator Frederick Douglass, a major recruiter of black soldiers.

Colonel Shaw set standards of fairness by orchestrating the boycott of a pay scale that reimbursed black soldiers $7 per month, a lower rate than the $10 payment to white recruits. His family and that of Frederick Douglass, along with nearly 2,000 black Bostonians, attended the May 18 presentation of regimental flags. Before the

Fifty-fourth's departure from Boston Harbor to Hilton Head, South Carolina, on May 28, 1863, a parade through Boston elicited bouquets and the admiration of Harriet Jacobs, author of *Incidents in the Life of a Slave Girl* (1861).

In anger at the notoriety of black soldiers, the Irish laboring class mocked their competitors for jobs and issued in the *Boston Pilot* racial slurs at black males in Union uniforms. After Shaw's martyrdom at the assault on Fort Wagner, South Carolina, he lay among the 1,515 black troops interred in a common grave on the Atlantic shore. Confederate General Johnson Hagood refused to separate Shaw's remains for a dignified officer's burial, because Shaw had chosen to lead nonwhite soldiers.

Improved Health Care

The Home for Aged Men in Boston's South End served Civil War veterans until 1869, when it shifted emphasis to indigent retirees. Improved medical conditions reduced outbreaks of contagion. Boston City Hospital, established in the South End in April 1864, equipped a "foul ward," a lazarette for smallpox victims. In 1866, trustees moved the contagion ward to more comfortable quarters on Albany Street and opened a cholera building at the wharf. In September 1867, the hospital pioneered the disinfection of wounds with phenol (carbolic acid) and, in 1869, began circulating an in-house clinical publication, the *Boston Medical and Surgical Journal.* Its commentaries attested to the predominance of Irish poor in the 350-bed facility. By 1877, the city added new medical and surgical pavilions, a trauma room, ambulance service, and outpatient clinics in dermatology, gynecology, laryngology, neurology, and otology.

In the South End at Rutland Street, in 1868, Adeline Blanchard Tyler administered Children's Hospital, a 20-bed facility treating the Irish poor and superintended by Sister Theresa of the Anglican Order of the Sisters of St. Margaret. The staff, led by Civil War surgeon Francis Henry Brown, specialized in trauma medicine and tuberculosis treatment and published findings in the *Boston Medical and Surgical Journal.*

In 1862, Berlin-born physician Maria Elizabeth Zakrzewska founded the New England Hospital for Women and Children and staffed it with female professionals. She and an associate, surgeon Susan Dimock, extended opportunities to white and black women seeking training in nursing and midwifery. They graduated the first certified nurse, Linda Richards, in 1873, and the first certified black nurse, Mary Eliza Mahoney, in 1879.

Scientific Breakthroughs

Boston became a center for technological advancement that connected the city to the rest of the world. On June 1, 1869, inventor Thomas Alva Edison obtained a U.S. patent for his electric vote recorder, an in-house method of recording legislative votes with the flick of a switch. His stock ticker, installed in 25 Boston investment firms, printed paper messages from the New York Stock Exchange. William Orton, president of Western Union, paid Edison $10,000 for a quadruplex telegraphy system, which Orton ballyhooed on July 10, 1873, in *The New York Times.* By October 3, the four-message system went into commercial operation, linking Boston with New York City.

Simultaneous with Edison's varied lab creations, Alexander Graham Bell, a Scots teacher of the deaf and professor at Boston University, studied electrical devices that replicated or transmitted sound. In 1874, his phonautograph captured the two-dimensional shapes of sound waves with a moving pen scratching lines on smoked glass. While experimenting with acoustic telegraphy in collaboration with his assistant, Thomas Augustus Watson, on June 2, 1875, Bell simplified the transmission of speech vibrations over a single reed. Following the successful transmission of sound from Cambridge to Boston on October 9, 1876, Bell patented the telephonic mechanism and advanced to designing an electromagnetic telephone circuit. That same year, as an educational tool for deaf-mutes, Bell invented a machine that mimicked human speech electronically in visible form.

Citizen Cooperation

Events both positive and negative brought out community pride and fervor in Bostonians. Carrying forward traditions begun during the American Revolution, they regularly fired the Molly Stark Cannon on the Fourth of July and gathered at the Great Elm on Boston Common to note a current event. On June 17, 1875, citizens in military dress celebrated the centennial of the Battle of Bunker Hill. On September 17, 1877, sculptor Martin Milmore, a graduate of Boston Latin School, adorned Flagstaff Hill of Boston Common with a $75,000 monument to Lady Liberty honoring all Union sailors and soldiers. The ceremony brought together two Confederate officers with Union generals Joseph Hooker and George Brinton McClellan.

The Great Boston Fire of November 9–10, 1872, erupted at 7 P.M. in a four-story hoopskirt factory and warehouse at Kingston and Summer streets and engulfed 65 acres (26 hectares) east of Washington Street. Firefighters failed to halt the advance by exploding combustibles in the path with kegs of gunpowder. In the course of two days, flames destroyed 1,500 businesses in 776 buildings and much of the financial district, at a cost of $100 million in damage. Included in the loss were Trinity Church and the offices of the *Boston Globe* and the *Boston Herald*; dozens of insurers were bankrupted.

Keeping order during and after the cataclysm, the National Lancers posted a home guard. Within months, architect George A. Clough oversaw the erection of five-story office buildings, financed primarily by commercial interests.

Recovery

As the city pulled itself out of personal and financial loss, opportunities beckoned the young and drew scholars to local schools, the Boston Museum of Fine Arts, yacht and sailboat racing clubs, the Young Men's Christian Union, and the Natural History Museum, a storehouse of dinosaur eggs and animal exhibits. In 1861, the incorporation of the Massachusetts Institute of Technology at Back Bay on Boylston and Clarendon streets proposed a curriculum of economics, English, history, law, and modern languages. Following the chartering of Boston University in 1869 to train students of all races, genders, and beliefs for the ministry, the school received its first applicants at 23 Pinckney Street. In addition to the Theological School, located in the five-story Wesleyan Building on Bromfield Street, trustees Lee Claflin, Isaac Rich, and Jacob Sleeper in 1872 established the College of Music, which collaborated with the New England Conservatory of Music at Franklin Square. Simultaneously, the School of Law made higher education history with the nation's first nine-semester curriculum and the first required entrance exam. The following winter, the university opened a coeducational School of Medicine and the College of Liberal Arts, which trained language students in Greek, Latin, and Sanskrit. At the School of Oratory, Alexander Graham Bell taught elocution and physiology. By 1874, the trustees increased the range of studies with the School of All Sciences. For the city's dedication to scholarship, it earned the nickname "Athens of America."

See also: Agassiz, Louis; Alcott, Louisa May; Dewey, Melvil; Dickinson, Emily; Everett, Edward; *Godey's Lady's Book*; Home Economics; Labor and Labor Unions; Stanton, Elizabeth Cady.

Further Reading

Baltzell, E. Digby. *Puritan Boston and Quaker Philadelphia.* New York: Free Press, 1979.

Duncan, Russell. *Where Death and Glory Meet: Colonel Robert Gould Shaw and the 54th Massachusetts Infantry.* Athens: University of Georgia Press, 1999.

Freemon, Frank R. *Gangrene and Glory: Medical Care During the American Civil War.* Urbana: University of Illinois Press, 2001.

Horton, James Oliver, and Lois E. Horton. *Slavery and the Making of America.* New York: Oxford University Press, 2005.

Sarna, Jonathan D., Ellen Smith, and Scott-Martin Kosofsky. *The Jews of Boston.* New Haven, CT: Yale University Press, 2005.

Bozeman Trail

On June 24, 1862, simultaneous with a gold strike outside Drummond at Gold Creek, Montana, explorer John Marion Bozeman and guide and cattle trader John M. Jacobs initiated the Bozeman Trail. In May 1863, traveling west to east, the trail makers scouted the historic detour from the Oregon Trail. The Bozeman Trail followed a dangerous course southwest toward Fort Bridger, in Utah Territory, over land guaranteed by treaty to Indians. On the way from the Yellowstone River, the duo encountered 75 to 80 Indians, who robbed them of food and mounts.

The unmarked route linked Fort Laramie, Wyoming, with Fort Reno on the Powder River, country embedded with trails that Arapaho, Blackfeet, Cheyenne, Crow, Lakota, and Shoshone had traveled for centuries to their hunting grounds. Jacobs drew the first map:

> From the North Platte River in Nebraska, the trail ran west to Fort Laramie, Wyoming.
>
> It continued over three crossings of Powder River forks to Fort Phil Kearny in the Big Horn Mountains.
>
> On an even arc, the route led northwest over the Bighorn River to Fort C.F. Smith, Montana.
>
> Through Bozeman Pass in the Gallatin Mountains, the route passed over the Yellowstone River to Fort Ellis, Montana.
>
> The trail crossed the Gallatin River, a branch of the Missouri River, and ended at Virginia City, Montana.

In southwestern Montana, Bozeman established the town of Bozeman, which drew miners from played-out claims in Colorado and Idaho to Bannack, the "land of gold." The enactment of the Homestead Act, which went into effect on January 1, 1863, aroused interest in free land among pioneers, adventurers, and speculators.

As more Easterners and immigrants claimed America's "Manifest Destiny," combined travel by ox-drawn wagons over the main route and its side trails reached 400,000. According to the *Montana Post,* the new trail saved travelers 700 miles (1,100 kilometers) and rewarded them with sufficient buffalo and elk, water, and grass to feed large trains.

By 1864, Bozeman, Jacobs, and Jacobs's eight-year-old Emma, daughter of his Flathead wife, had led 1,500 to 2,000 emigrants in four wagon trains over the 540-mile (870-kilometer) route. Despite road agents and hostile Indians, at 15 miles (24 kilometers) per day, the pioneers completed the trip in 36 days. The Townsend train involved more than 150 wagons and 450 journeyers, including memoirist Rosa Beall, who reported Lakota terrorism against settlers.

By February 1865, telegraph crews of the Missouri River and Rocky Mountain Road and Telegraph Company and the Fort Laramie Wagon Road and Telegraph Company merged to link the Montana backcountry with the East and West coasts. A ferry builder proposed a crossing of the Yellowstone River and the Bridger Cutoff, influencing the *Montana Post* to proclaim the Bozeman Trail the best road to Montana.

Whites on Indian Land

The influx of settlers and engineers displaced Indians and aroused native vengeance. Over six months, the Lakota and Northern Cheyenne stepped up attacks on three forts. To protect routes to the sacred Black Hills, Chief Gall, a leader of the Hunkpapa Sioux and a lieutenant of Sitting Bull, applied blockades, decoys, and guerrilla tactics. Guide and scout George Ray protected his caravan along the Bozeman Trail by picking off Lakota with a Henry rifle.

The army closed the thoroughfare to all but military traffic and chose maximum punishment as a way of ridding the route of marauders. Marching from Fort Laramie along the trail and the Powder River Road, General Patrick Edward Connor, a proven Indian fighter and commander of the Utah district, attempted to end forays on westerers, freighters, and mail carriers.

In north-central Wyoming on August 29, 1865, Connor's 400-man Powder River Expedition, led by mountain man Jim Bridger, half-breed interpreter Mitch Boyer, and 80 Pawnee scouts, won the Battle of the Tongue River. At a 600-acre (240-acre) Arapaho camp on an oxbow of the river, the cavalry lobbed Spencer rifle and howitzer fire against a coalition of 500 Arapaho and Lakota subsistence hunters led by Northern Arapaho chiefs Black Bear, Friday, and Medicine Man and Yankton Sioux leader Wolf Moccasin. Black Bear stopped the cavalry from advancing along Wolf Creek, but he could not avoid heavy losses, including the death of his son. The battle resulted in the shooting of 63 braves and 12 soldiers, the slaughter of 1,000 Indian mounts, and the capture of 18 Arapaho women and children, who later gained their release. A headline in the *Rocky Mountain News* exonerated soldiers who burned native corpses along with the camp, 250 lodges, and supplies of buffalo meat and robes.

Travel Restored

With the Plains Indian threat subdued and the establishment of Fort Connor at Sussex, Wyoming, in May 1866, pioneer traffic resumed with the departure of the Thomas O. Miles wagon train. Two weeks later, his party crossed the Yellowstone ford, where John Bozeman strung a ferry line. One of the few women among 1,000 travelers, Ellen Gordon "Nellie" Fletcher, offered a female perspective in her diary, *A Bride on the Bozeman Trail* (1870). English diarist Richard Lockey's party followed and engaged in amicable barter with the Arapaho, trading food for buckskin, buffalo robes, moccasins, and blankets.

On July 3, a hint of hostility emerged among Chief Neva's Southern Arapaho at the Bighorn River crossing. He appeared to have received news of Red Cloud's move against the white invasion that threatened Sioux dependence on the dwindling buffalo.

Conflict ensued within two weeks. On July 17, Red Cloud seized the Bighorn ferry, destroyed a trading post, and stole the ferryman's horses and mules. On July 21, army engineer James A. Sawyers's road-building expedition, traveling from Nebraska to the Montana goldfields, negotiated a military escort for his 80 wagons, 300 cattle, and 73 prospectors. Along the way through Sioux territory to the Powder River, through half-breed interpreter George Brent, Sawyers pacified Northern Cheyenne Chief Dull Knife and Oglala Lakota Chief Red Cloud with gifts of coffee, flour, sugar, and tobacco. At the Bighorn River crossing, Sawyers hurried on to Virginia City by pioneering a shortcut, the Clarks Fork cutoff.

The U.S. Army ended free travel the next week and combined trains into a single 350-wagon expedition for departure on August 2 led by Jim Bridger at the head of two cavalry companies. At the Bighorn ferry, they encountered a traffic jam—200 wagoneers waiting to cross via the restored service.

Plains Indians Versus the Army

As the U.S. Army constructed three forts to protect the Bozeman Trail, the Arapaho sought revenge by allying with the Cheyenne and Lakota. Red Cloud forged a coalition of 2,000 Indians to fight a war against the army for possession of the Powder River Valley. By September 1866, his warriors had curtailed pioneer travel.

On December 21, 1866, to discourage the desecration of the sacred Black Hills of South Dakota and to halt prospecting on traditional lands, Red Cloud abetted Crazy Horse, Miniconjou Chief Hump, Hunkpapa chiefs Gall and Rain-in-the-face, and Northern Cheyenne Chief Little Wolf, and war society leader Roman Nose in luring Captain William Judd Fetterman and some 80 soldiers out of Fort Phil Kearny, Wyoming, to an ambush of 2,000 Arapaho, Cheyenne, and Lakota. In 20 minutes, the Indians massacred the entire military party. On April 20, 1867, on the Yellowstone River outside Livingston, Montana, five Blackfeet Indians murdered trailblazer John Bozeman.

Red Cloud persisted in his war against the U.S. Army. Outside Fort Phil Kearny on August 2, 1867, he again led the Lakota against a party of woodcutters, who hid behind upended wagons. Although the attackers suffered greater loss than the soldiers, Red Cloud demanded that the government abandon forts on the Bozeman Trail and along the Powder River before treaty negotiations could begin. During the term of Seneca engineer Ely Samuel Parker as commissioner of Indian affairs, the army agreed to the Treaty of Fort Laramie of 1868, which guaranteed Lakota ownership of the Black Hills, extending from western South Dakota into Wyoming.

See also: Crazy Horse; Fetterman Massacre; Montana Territory; Red Cloud; Wyoming Territory.

Further Reading

Johansen, Bruce E., and Donald A. Grinde, Jr. *The Encyclopedia of Native American Biography.* New York: Da Capo, 1998.

Lamar, Howard R., ed. *The New Encyclopedia of the American West.* New Haven, CT: Yale University Press, 1998.

McDermott, John D. *Circle of Fire: The Indian War of 1865.* Mechanicsburg, PA: Stackpole, 2003.

Sherow, James E. *The Grasslands of the United States: An Environmental History.* Santa Barbara, CA: ABC-CLIO, 2007.

Waldman, Carl. *Who Was Who in Native American History: Indians and Non-Indians from Early Contacts Through 1900.* New York: Facts on File, 1990.

Brady, Mathew (1822?–1896)

A portrait artist and recorder of American history, photographer Mathew Bertram Brady was a pioneering figure in the field of photojournalism. An Irish American born near Lake George in Warren County, New York, he began drawing with crayons belonging to artist William Page.

He required treatment at age 12 for eye inflammation, a harbinger of his diminished vision in middle age. In his mid- to late teens, he clerked in a department store and manufactured jewelry cases. In 1844, he apprenticed in daguerreotype portraiture at a Washington Square studio under Samuel F.B. Morse, then publisher of the *New York Observer.*

At Brady's first business locations—the Daguerran Miniature Gallery at 205–207 Broadway and Fulton streets in New York City, and the Mathew Brady Photographic Studio at Pennsylvania Avenue and Seventh Street in Washington, D.C.—and at later venues, he exhibited photographic portraits of such notable figures as Dolley Madison, John Quincy Adams, Walt Whitman, Andrew Jackson, Abraham and Mary Todd Lincoln, Robert E. Lee, Emperor Napoleon III, Zachary Taylor, Washington Irving, Tom Thumb, John Charles Frémont, Edgar Allan Poe, Jenny Lind, John Wilkes Booth, Frederick Douglass, and John James Audubon. Along with the famous, Brady also photographed slaves, Indians, and inmates at Blackwell's Island Prison, the subject of the second edition of Marmaduke Sampson's *Rationale of Crime and Its Appropriate Treatment* (1846). Brady collected 12 of his distinguished celebrity photos for *The Gallery of Illustrious Americans* (1850), which posed abolitionist theologian William Ellery Channing alongside proslavery politician John C. Calhoun and Henry Clay, orchestrator of the Missouri Compromise.

Brady developed a following for historical photography that reached the galleries of London, Naples, and Rome. His theme, which Mark Twain described as "the expiring mighty period of American men," stressed the centrality of forceful personalities on events and of character and morals on political controversy. He won a medal for 48 portraits shown at the 1851 Crystal Palace Exhibition in London, the first international photographic competition. In his thirties, Brady mastered ambrotype photography on glass and the French process of albumen printing on paper, and he offered his services to the public in unique newspaper ads.

His work appeared in *Harper's Weekly,* including news of Frederick Law Olmsted's plans for Central Park and an inauguration portrait of President Lincoln as cover art. In 1860, Brady received visits from the first Japanese envoys posted in the United States and from Edward, Prince of Wales, the first English royalty to make a state visit. The envious asked their peers, "Have you been Bradyed yet?"

Caught Up in the Moment

Brady felt compelled to photograph the Lincoln presidency and the Civil War in a pastiche that he described as "like a rich newspaper." He posed Lincoln for a campaign photo after the famed Cooper Union address of February 27, 1860. Lincoln later credited the picture and the speech with clinching the election.

Brady risked death and capture during the First Battle of Bull Run at Manassas, Virginia, on July 21, 1861, by transporting his cameras in two horse-drawn wagons and by setting up mobile darkrooms manned by 23 photographers. In the Union rout that followed, Brady—who required assistance because of his failing eyesight—was lost for three days. He arrived in Washington, D.C., with damaged equipment, but still in possession of the faces and panoramas of war. Within weeks of the Battle of Antietam, Maryland, on September 17, 1862, Brady's images featured a stark battlefield exhibit devoid of heroics. The gallery introduced mass communication to the media.

Rapidly, Brady earned a reputation for artistry. His photos appeared in *Harper's Weekly* and won the respect of the New York *World,* which described his immersion in combat as "distinct and omnipresent." *The New York Times* called Brady a realist who laid corpses on the doorsteps of noncombatants. Viewers and purchasers of his stereographs, mounted prints, and album cards discovered the intimate details of suffering and gore, as well as the ruin of ships and rail lines and the service of drummer boys, tenters, grave diggers, military surgeons, and nurses.

During the course of the war, Brady invested $100,000 in 10,000 negatives, capturing images of the Battle of Gettysburg, Pennsylvania, on July 3–4, 1863, and of Cold Harbor, Virginia, which raged from May 31 to June 12, 1864; he came under fire at the Battles of Fredericksburg, Chancellorsville, and Petersburg. In spring 1864, Brady broadened his coverage by dispatching assistant Andrew Burgess to Mexico City to record the uprising led by Benito Juárez against the Emperor Maximilian I.

Lost Momentum

During the Reconstruction period, Brady continued documenting America's growth and turmoil. With the help of Mary Anna Custis Lee, he captured a somber Robert E. Lee on his back porch after the Confederate surrender on April 9, 1865, at Appomattox, Virginia. Brady followed Lincoln's funeral cortege to Springfield, Illinois.

Early in 1866, Brady exhibited his collection of war images on Park Avenue at the New-York Historical Society. Of its accuracy and honesty, General Ulysses S. Grant noted that the scenes were well chosen to serve the student, artist, and future generations, implying that Brady's photos could shape attitudes toward sedition and war.

Brady's camera immortalized the arrival in Washington of Ponca and Ute ambassadors, of the Sioux war chiefs Red Cloud and Spotted Tail, of nurse Clara Barton and the survivors of the Andersonville Prison, and of South Carolina politician Joseph Hayne Rainey, the first black U.S. congressman. Brady collaborated with painter Alonzo Chappel and publisher John Bachelder to create a commemorative tableau, "The Last Hours of Lincoln" (1865), depicting the witnesses who kept bedside vigil for the wounded president.

Brady tried unsuccessfully to sell his collection to the U.S. government in March 1869 and was forced to sell his New York studio. Brady's declining years were beset by theft and financial ruin resulting from the depression of 1867 and the Panic of 1873. After his plan to sell his images to the War Department failed, he retreated to a rented room in poor health, having broken a leg in a horsecar accident. On April 15, 1875, Congressman James A. Garfield and General Benjamin Franklin Butler commiserated with Brady and negotiated the purchase of the war negatives for $25,000—but the money was too little to rescue Brady from penury. In the 1880s, violators of his copyright profited from selling postcards and stereopticon views of the war years. Novelist Stephen Crane referred to the pictures in his classic war novel *The Red Badge of Courage* (1895).

At Brady's death on January 15, 1896, in a pauper's ward of Presbyterian Hospital in New York City, he was bankrupt, widowed, and nearly blind. Edward Bailey Eaton published Brady's studies of President Lincoln and field portraits of Confederate and Union combatants in *The Photographic History of the Civil War* (1912), the first direct visual record of war.

See also: Harper's Weekly; Olmsted, Frederick Law, Sr.

Further Reading

Brown, Joshua. *Beyond the Lines: Pictorial Reporting, Everyday Life and the Crisis of Gilded Age America.* Berkeley: University of California Press, 2006.

Marien, Mary Warner. *Photography: A Cultural History.* 2nd ed. Upper Saddle River, NJ: Prentice Hall, 2006.

Palmquist, Peter E., and Thomas R. Kailbourn. *Pioneer Photographers of the Far West: A Biographical Dictionary, 1840–1865.* Stanford, CA: Stanford University Press, 2000.

Trachtenberg, Alan. *Reading American Photographs: Images as History, Mathew Brady to Walker Evans.* New York: Hill and Wang, 1989.

Brewing

An American tradition from colonial times, fermenting grain into beer provided citizens with a low-alcohol, bacteria-free beverage brewed according to northwestern European tradition. Cities honored their maltsters, brewmasters, and coopers for distributing local beers, a mark of civic distinction.

In Poughkeepsie, New York, the Vassar Brewery, among the nation's largest, employed 50 brewers and dispensed 30,000 barrels per year. Some complexes, such as Bernhard Stroh's brewery in Detroit, Michigan; George Koenig Master Brewers in Cincinnati, Ohio; and Canandaigua in Victor, New York, sold by-products and made related products, including cider, cola, fruit ades, ice blocks, ice cream, malt extract, near-beer (beer with an alcohol content of 1 percent or less), and vinegar.

To ensure a saleable product, at Benton Park in St. Louis, Missouri, several breweries stored beer above a system of sinkholes and natural limestone caverns in an ideal temperature that stayed constant at 55 degrees Fahrenheit (12 degrees Celsius). A similar system of cooling at the Albion Ale and Porter Brewery in San Francisco, California, drew water from a spring under Hunter's Point Hill and stored brewed products in natural caverns. In Sheboygan County, Michigan, German brewer Gustave Seidemann of Saxe-Weimar dug a beer cave into a hill on the river and lined it with brick to keep casks cool during storage.

After the Civil War, increased immigration of ale, lager, malt liquor, pilsner, porter, steam beer, and stout drinkers from Czechoslovakia, Germany, Great Britain, and Poland created a beer culture. Consumption rose to an average of 3.4 gallons (12.9 liters) per capita. To protect their interests, while congressmen debated the immediate and long-term effects of drinking beer, lager, brandy, and whiskey on the populace, beer makers formed the U.S. Brewers' Association (USBA), a lobbying consortium. At their first meeting in New York City at Pythagoras Hall on August 21, 1862, members chose as president Frederick Lauer, a lager maker from Reading, Pennsylvania.

At war's end, Congress repealed other taxes but, in 1868, retained those on alcohol. The USBA facilitated the industrialists' relationship with the U.S. Bureau of Internal Revenue, which declared beer and distilled liquor luxuries or indulgences, like tobacco smoking. To finance the Union army debt, lawmakers imposed excise and liquor taxes at the rate of a yearly $50 license fee for each brewer and distiller, 20 cents per gallon on liquor, and $1 dollar per 31-gallon (117-liter) barrel of ale, beer, lager, and porter. By 1889, brewers had paid $295,311,185 to the U.S. Treasury.

To satisfy local demand, German farmers in Pennsylvania planted barley, hops, and soapwort or bouncing bet (*Saponaria officinalis*), a common herb that generated foamy heads. From 1682 to the 1890s, the prosperity of German beer makers turned Philadelphia into the nation's prime brewing center. In 1864, Frederick August Poth of Rheinfalz, Germany, established F.A. Poth & Sons Brewing Company on Jefferson Street in Brewerytown on the Schuylkill River in Philadelphia. His six-story malt house stored bins of barley and malt, steeping tanks, and a kiln house. Wort masters left barrels of hops, malt, and water open in the brew house to encourage yeast to convert sugar into alcohol, the chemical change that determines flavor and alcohol content. Poth's Brewerytown competitor, Bergner & Engel, founded in 1870, produced half the city's beer and won the Grand Prize at the 1876 Centennial Exposition. Advertisements featured gold seals indicating a later prize from the 1878 Paris Exposition for Bergner & Engel's brewing process.

The first giant beer houses began appearing in the late 1870s with Pabst in Milwaukee, Wisconsin, and Anheuser-Busch in St. Louis. The operations ensured jobs for brewmasters, keg builders, sugar refiners, grain vendors, bottle makers, yeast sellers, and van drivers, who delivered kegs directly to saloons and hotels.

In Milwaukee, aggressive beer marketing contributed to urban culture. Pabst, the manufacturer of 100,000 barrels per year, opened the Pabst Theater, the nation's fourth largest, and the 8-acre (3-hectare) Pabst Park, a *biergarten* (beer garden) equipped with a roller coaster, Katzenjammer Palace funhouse, and music pavilion that featured Wild West shows and orchestral concerts. In addition to selling tickets, beer baron Frederick Pabst touted 5-cent schooners of brew. A competitor, the Schlitz Brewing Company, built the Schlitz Park Theater, Schlitz

Bergner & Engel's Brewery in Philadelphia produced half of the city's beer in the 1870s. A heavy influx of German farmers and brewers in and around Philadelphia made the city the nation's leading beer producer. *(Kean Collection/Getty Images)*

Palm Garden, and Schlitz amusement park. Another rival, Valentin Blatz, owner of the Val Blatz Brewing Company, Milwaukee's third-largest brewery, erected the Blatz Hotel, a five-story city landmark featuring an elegant taproom.

In St. Louis, Eberhard Anheuser, a prosperous German-born candle and soap manufacturer from Bad Kreuznach, established another U.S. beer dynasty. He bought the struggling Bavarian Brewery in 1860 and, seven years later, introduced pasteurization to keep liquids fresh. In 1871, as his production grew, he began marketing Budweiser, a light Czech pilsner lager. His partner, Adolphus Busch of Kastel, Hesse, husband of Anheuser's daughter Lily, trained in the brewery business at Collegiate Institute in Belgium. Busch popularized King Cola in 1877 and chaired the company when Anheuser died in 1880. After purchasing the trademark of Budweiser, he extended his company with railroad icehouses and iced freight cars for nationwide distribution. He introduced bottled beer, an innovative packaging that withstood humidity and climatic change. By 1891, Busch's vans delivered over 1 million barrels per year. He used profits of $60 million to build Adolphus Busch Hall, a Germanic museum at Harvard University.

In 1870, at the height of the small-scale operation, 3,286 breweries nationwide satisfied a beer-drinking public that downed 6.6 million barrels at the average rate of 5.3 gallons (20 liters) per person. Within five years, the numbers had risen to 9.5 million barrels per year from 2,783 brewers, who produced an average of 6.6 gallons (25 liters) per drinker. By 1890, the average beer drinker put away 13.6 gallons (51.5 liters) per year, produced by 1,256 breweries.

The proliferation of urban beer gardens, pubs, and saloons produced a parallel phenomenon in the emergence of temperance groups, the most organized lobbying effort of the times. They faced down the USBA, which challenged the thinking that beer, like whiskey, addicted drinkers and encouraged alcohol abuse. At Chicago, where alcohol generated one-quarter of city revenues, the Anti-Saloon League and the Women's Christian Temperance Union kept up their crusade for 70 years. With the exception of Prohibition from 1920 to 1933, the backlash against a primarily male social outlet did little to halt public consumption of alcohol.

See also: Temperance Movement.

Further Reading

Kleber, John E. *The Encyclopedia of Louisville, Volume 2000.* Lexington: University Press of Kentucky, 2001.
Mittelman, Amy. *Brewing Battles: A History of American Beer.* New York: Algora, 2008.
Smith, Andrew F., ed. *The Oxford Companion to American Food and Drink.* New York: Oxford University Press, 2007.

Brown, Olympia (1835–1926)

Suffragist writer and preacher Olympia Brown set a record of firsts in women's history. Born on the frontier at Prairie Ronde, Michigan, on January 5, 1835, to Asa Briggs Brown and Lephia Olympia Brown, she profited from a strict upbringing. Lephia insisted that homework came before chores and that the family discuss the events of the day from reports in the *New York Weekly Tribune.*

Olympia completed her studies at the local elementary school, organized a school on her father's land for neighboring children, and taught classes at age 15. Profiting from the insistence of her parents that she acquire a university degree, she advanced to Mount Holyoke Female Seminary in Massachusetts. The college disappointed her with its staunch Calvinism and its low expectations for women.

While studying at Antioch College, a coeducational school in Yellow Springs, Ohio, and, in 1863, at St. Lawrence University Theological School in Canton, New York, Brown preached on holidays and during vacation at Heuvelton and Ogdensburg, New York. Battling the diminution of females by professors and faculty wives, she became the first American woman to earn a degree in theology.

School was Brown's first gender hurdle, but more followed. After ordination by hesitant Universalists in Malone, New York, on June 25, 1863, she served as the nation's first ordained female minister for the next 24 years. During that time, she held pulpits in Montpelier, Vermont; Weymouth Landing, Massachusetts; Bridgeport, Connecticut; and Racine, Wisconsin. Her parishioners generally approved her liberal beliefs, particularly her espousal of free religious thought, denial of eternal damnation, crusade for women's rights at colleges and universities, and refusal to take the surname of her husband, printer John Henry Willis, owner of the *Racine Times-Call,* whom she wed in 1873. Among her mentors was Antoinette Brown Blackwell, a prominent suffragist and libertarian orator.

Champion of Equality

After her first meeting with crusaders Susan B. Anthony and Elizabeth Cady Stanton in 1866 at the American Equal Rights Association convention in New York City, achieving full citizenship for women occupied Brown's spare time. She recognized a postwar turnabout in social advocacy: "The old abolitionists . . . imagined that with the freeing of the slaves the whole battle for equal rights in this country was fought out," she later wrote. Brown reasoned that the education and enfranchisement of women would elevate females as wives, mothers, professionals, and citizens.

In summer 1867, after suffrage tacticians moved their focus to state elections in the Midwest, Brown, along with Lucy Stone and her husband, hardware dealer Henry Brown "Harry" Blackwell, crusaded in Lawrence, Leavenworth, and Topeka, Kansas, for changes to the state constitution reflecting women's right to the ballot. During a four-month leave from the pulpit, Brown delivered 300 addresses on gender equality, traveling with "rough men, Indians, or negroes, anybody that would go."

The next year, Brown, following the example of civil rights orators Abby Kelley Foster and Lucretia Mott, joined Julia Ward Howe and Lucy Stone in establishing the New England Woman Suffrage Association, the nation's first suffrage organization. To mobilize their synergy, Brown brought Anthony, Howe, and Stanton to Racine to speak to the community. Stanton described Brown as a formidable debater for facing down Kansas Judge T.C. Sears, who abased women. In 1869, when suffrage theorists split into the American Woman Suffrage Association (AWSA) and the National Woman Suffrage Association (NWSA), Brown maintained her support of both factions. In a transcendent passage in her memoir, she exulted in female strengths: "Would that the women of today might catch the immortal fire that was in them!"

In 1877, Brown resigned the pulpit at Good Shepherd Racine Universalist Church to preach part-time in Columbus, Mukwonago, and Neenah, Wisconsin. The change left her more time for the suffrage campaign and for opening educational institutions to women. Her mother assisted Brown by caring for her two children.

A Long Crusade

The coming of middle age did little to compromise Brown's campaigning. She realized the gift of a long life that encompassed second-wave suffrage and influence on "young women who today are entering upon fields of remunerative activity which have been opened to them by the labors of those who have gone before." In 1882, she coformed the Wisconsin Woman Suffrage Association and chaired the group for the next 20 years.

In 1887, following passage of the School Suffrage Law and her resignation from the ministry, Brown attempted to vote and carried her challenge to the Wisconsin Supreme Court, which rejected her argument for woman suffrage. In 1892, she abandoned AWSA and NWSA and, in Chicago, organized the Federal Suffrage Association, which revived the effort to persuade Congress to alter the U.S. Constitution.

In widowhood in 1893, Brown continued operating her husband's publishing business. In her eighties, she joined Alice Paul and Lucy Barnes in a yearlong picket of the White House, where Brown burned the speeches of President Woodrow Wilson. After passage of the Nineteenth Amendment to the Constitution on August 25, 1920, Brown voted for the first time.

Living half time in Racine and Baltimore to be near her daughter, Brown promoted the American Civil Liberties Union and co-founded the Women's International League for Peace and Freedom. Publication of a memoir, *Acquaintances Old and New Among Reformers* (1911), and a biography, *Democratic Ideals: A Memorial Sketch of Clara Bewick Colby* (1917), preceded her death on October 23, 1926, in Baltimore, following a lengthy tour of France, Italy, and Switzerland. Her tombstone in Racine, Wisconsin, reads "Mother Olympia Brown."

See also: Anthony, Susan B.; Douglass, Frederick; Howe, Julia Ward; Stanton, Elizabeth Cady; Stone, Lucy.

Further Reading

Bressler, Ann Lee. *The Universalist Movement in America, 1770–1880.* New York: Oxford University Press, 2001.

McMillen, Sally. *Seneca Falls and the Origins of the Women's Rights Movement.* New York: Oxford University Press, 2008.

Sneider, Allison L. *Suffragists in an Imperial Age: U.S. Expansion and the Woman Question, 1870–1929.* New York: Oxford University Press, 2007.

Streitmatter, Rodger. *Voices of Revolution: The Dissident Press in America.* New York: Columbia University Press, 2001.

Buffalo

Until 1845, the American bison, popularly known as the buffalo, was the most numerous species of wild mammal on Earth. It thrived on American prairie grass and sedge, ranging along the Great Bison Belt from Mexico to Canada, as far north as Alaska and as far east as the Appalachian Mountains. Natural attrition—by drowning, falls, prairie fire, and lightning—killed some 9 percent of buffalo annually; Indians and explorers followed herd trails in Indiana, Kentucky, Ohio, and Virginia, increasing the loss of life through hunting.

Viewing the buffalo as a spiritual animal, Pawnee arranged skulls in geometric figures along the Platte River in Nebraska as a token of respect and reverence. In the Missouri Valley, the Arikara stuffed sage into the eyeholes of buffalo skulls and placed them in rows on the prairie as icons of worship and as a warning to approaching herds. In the 1870s, Jesuit missionary Father Jerome D'Aste complained that the Flathead risked infringing on Blackfeet territory for the rare opportunity to bag buffalo: "The passion for buffalo is a regular fever among them and could not be stopped."

Simultaneous with the natives' adoration of the huge beasts, pragmatic white settlers valued the herds as sources of chips and bones as fuel for cooking and heating. Farmers pulverized bones into fertilizer to enrich the soil. Indians dug up the grounds around buffalo jumps and sold whole skeletons to fertilizer and carbon factories.

The introduction of firearms and the expertise of horse riders threatened the species as early as the 1830s. On a summer journey in 1859 via the Leavenworth & Pikes Peak Express, Horace Greeley, editor of the *New York Tribune,* viewed millions of buffalo out the window of the stagecoach and mourned the human folly of exterminating "nature's children." During an 18-year drought that ended in the 1860s, herds diminished. The attrition coincided with the rise in demand for buffalo meat to feed pioneers and railway crews. Hastening the animal's disappearance was the fashion trend on the East Coast and in Europe toward hide rugs, robes, and belts and the display of horned skulls as trophies. Restaurants featured buffalo tongue on their menus. In May 1871, dealer William C. Lobenstein of Leavenworth, Kansas, the first major merchant to profit from the kills, supplied 500 hides to an English tanner who manufactured leather goods for British soldiers.

Around 1872, hunting teams armed with .50–.90 Sharps and Springfield buffalo rifles and bandoleers holding 42 rounds set out from Dodge City, Kansas. Staking out territory north of the Arkansas River and around the Canadian, Cimarron, and Red rivers, they targeted herds and felled hundreds of animals per day to be skinned and beheaded. Butchers left the remains of the carcasses to rot. Vigorous buffalo hunters such as William Frederick "Buffalo Bill" Cody in Nebraska, Frank Emmett in Montana, Vic Smith in North Dakota and Wyoming, Frank Mayor in Colorado, Pawnee Bill Lillie and J.C. Settles in Oklahoma, Leo Teton in Idaho, William "Billy" Dixon and "Plainsman Charley" Rath in Texas, and Wyatt Earp, Pat Garrett, and William Barclay "Bat" Masterson in Kansas could earn up to $50 per pelt. Historian Steven Rinella accounts for the need of loners to slaughter:

They were Confederate soldiers escaping the shame of Reconstruction. They were Union soldiers escaping the boredom of victory. They were orphans. They were wanted alive for fraud here, wanted dead for murder there.

Because Plains Indians relied on the buffalo for food and shelter, President Ulysses S. Grant refused to sign a congressional bill in 1874 to shield herds from stalkers. In October 1876, Scots American hunter J. Wright Mooar, the shooter of some 20,000 buffalo, boasted of killing his second albino buffalo in Scurry County, Texas, a coup that impressed fellow hunter Teddy Roosevelt. As Mooar saw the buffalo decline in number to the north, in 1873, with his brother, hide trader John Wesley Mooar, he established the Mooar Brothers Ranch in Scurry County, Texas, where herds were more plentiful.

The deliberate extinction of wild buffalo herds by army scouts and railroad planners hastened the end of nomadic Indian life on the Great Plains. On October 21 and 28, 1867, the Arapaho, Southern Cheyenne, Comanche, Kiowa, and Kiowa-Apache signed the Treaty of Medicine Lodge, an idealistic accord under which the U.S. government promised protection of herds south of the Arkansas River. With impunity from federal marshals, however, railway officials laid lines along buffalo trails and demanded that the great shaggy beasts be removed from tracks to halt damage to engines and delay of shipments.

Outraged at the waste, Cheyenne, Comanche, and Kiowa marauders plundered the Texas Panhandle in 1874 and launched the Second Battle of Adobe Walls on June 27, 1874. Braves openly flouted the treaty by abandoning Oklahoma reservations to raid Texas ranches and trading posts. In 1875, General Philip Sheridan violated the terms of the Medicine Lodge accord by urging federal authorities to slaughter herds to starve out Plains tribes. Under his direction, the U.S. Army ended the uprising in late September 1875 at Palo Duro Canyon, Texas.

The Buffalo Hunters' War brought malnourished Comanche warriors into confrontation with Texas hunters. In December 1876, Chief Black Horse directed a war party of 170 from the Fort Sill Reservation in Oklahoma to the arid Llano Estacado (Staked Plains) on the Red River of the Texas Panhandle to end the wholesale slaughter of herds. On February 1, 1877, the warriors shot hunters and stole horses before withdrawing to Yellow Horse Canyon outside Lubbock.

An attack by the hunters on March 4, 1877, cost the Comanche 35 casualties before they escaped. Quanah Parker convinced the renegades to return to Fort Sill. A parallel confinement of the Nez Percé of Idaho ended that year with the people's last buffalo hunt in Yellowstone National Park and their immurement on reservations. By 1884, except on federal parkland at Yellowstone, the buffalo, numbering 1,200–2,000, neared annihilation.

See also: Joseph, Chief; Medicine Lodge Treaty (1867); Yellowstone National Park.

By 1878, buffalo herds were too sparse to warrant tracking. British entrepreneur and philanthropist William Henry Blackmore, co-author of *The Hunting Grounds of the Great West* (1878), viewed grazing grounds between the Arkansas and Cimarron rivers and around Fort Dodge, Iowa, and estimated the death of the buffalo at the rate of 1 million per year. He lamented the near extinction of migratory buffalo herds:

> When One reads of the total destruction during the three years (1872–3 and 4) of four millions and a half of the "Black Cattle of Illinois," out of which number upwards of three millions have been killed for the mere sake of their hides, it is at first almost impossible to realise what this slaughter represents, and how much good and nutritious animal food, which would have fed the red men as well as the hardy settlers of the "Great West," has been wasted.

Blackmore also regretted that the Department of Revenue taxed Alaskan seal kills but did not tax buffalo hunts, which might have enriched federal coffers by $15 million.

Further Reading

Franke, Mary Ann. *To Save the Wild Bison: Life on the Edge in Yellowstone.* Norman: University of Oklahoma Press, 2005.

Hamalainen, Pekka. *The Comanche Empire.* New Haven, CT: Yale University Press, 2009.

Isenberg, Andrew C. *The Destruction of the Bison: An Environmental History, 1750–1920.* Cambridge, UK: Cambridge University Press, 2001.

Rinella, Steven. *American Buffalo: In Search of a Lost Icon.* New York: Spiegel & Grau, 2008.

Sherow, James E. *The Grasslands of the United States: An Environmental History.* Santa Barbara, CA: ABC-CLIO, 2007.

Buffalo Soldiers

After the Civil War, the U.S. Army undertook a plan to subdue the West that led to the reorganization of black Union troops into Indian fighters. The creation of standing regiments of blacks was the work of General Ulysses S. Grant, who, after the Civil War, served as a military adviser on the pacification of the South. Immediately, Lieutenant Colonel George Armstrong Custer refused to lead a black regiment, an assignment that he and other white officers considered an insult and a demotion.

Colonel Edward Hatch of Bangor, Maine, a cavalry hero of Grant's Mississippi campaign during the war, began enrolling 818 men for the Ninth Cavalry, which headquartered at Greenville, Louisiana. Volunteers, hoping for a better life and career opportunities, came from demobilized Union regiments, farms, semiskilled labor, and unemployment lines at a time when labor unions rejected nonwhite members. As soldiers, ambitious black men could establish a career that provided food, board, clothing, medical and dental care, and retirement benefits. Stymieing Hatch's efforts, the recruitment of white officers slowed to a trickle before stabilizing at only 11, some of them brutal racists.

The U.S. military equipped black soldiers with substandard saddles, tack, uniforms, Spencer repeater rifles, and the .36 Colt Navy revolver, which was standard issue. Within weeks, soldiers living in abandoned presses in a stuffy cotton baling plant came down with cholera and required removal southeast to Carrollton, a suburb west of New Orleans. To ease problems with paperwork, chaplains attended to spiritual and educational needs of former slaves, most of whom were illiterate.

On March 29, 1867, the 885 men of the Ninth Cavalry moved out by steamer to Indianola, Texas, on the Gulf of Mexico. Some remained at Brownsville on the coast; the rest marched 150 miles (240 kilometers) to San Pedro Springs outside San Antonio for training. A mutiny erupted over the soldiers' prejudicial treatment under Lieutenant Edward Heyl, resulting in the shooting deaths of Lieutenant Seth E. Griffin and Sergeant Harrison Bradford. Black dissidents went to prison, but gained pardon and reinstatement for justifiable revolt against cruelty.

In July 1867, the Ninth Cavalry began patrolling the frontier at Fort Clark west of Corpus Christi on the coast and at Fort Davis and Fort Stockton north of the Rio Grande. Among Southern settlers, former Confederate rebels harbored hatred for uniformed blacks. On September 17, 1868, black troopers proved their worth at the Battle of Beecher Island, Colorado, on the Arikaree River, the north fork of the Republic River, where 48 soldiers halted the advance of Cheyenne warrior society leader Roman Nose and an allied band of 600 Arapaho, Brulé and Oglala Sioux, and Northern Cheyenne.

At Fort Garland, Colorado, in 1876, skirmishes in the La Plata region between Ute raiders and miners proved that the Ninth Cavalry had spirit and skill. On January 24, 1877, Clinton Greaves, a former Virginia slave, won a Medal of Honor for fighting his way through 50 Apaches in the Florida Mountains and rescuing his unit. Near Deming, New Mexico, in 1877, Lieutenant Henry Wright earned a Congressional Medal of Honor for leading his scouting party from Fort Bayard into an armed camp of some 50 Chiricahua Apaches.

Tenth Cavalry

Simultaneous with the formation of the Ninth Cavalry, Colonel Benjamin Henry Grierson, a hero of the Vicksburg and Port Hudson campaigns in 1863, began mustering men from Connecticut, Massachusetts, New York, and Pennsylvania for the Tenth Cavalry. On September 21, 1866, black recruits arrived at Fort Leavenworth, Kansas, where the men billeted in unheated barracks. Because of poor sanitation and drainage, the first arrival, William Beauman, came down with malaria; dozens died of contagion. Grierson defended his men from the racism of General Philip Henry Sheridan and kept regiments out of view of marching whites.

Within ten months, the U.S. Army had recruited eight companies of black volunteers from Arkansas, Kentucky, Louisiana, and Missouri. Despite a problem with substandard mounts, under the motto "Ready and Forward," the Tenth Cavalry rode the Southwestern Great Plains to combat heightened violence. During his 25 years heading black forces, Colonel Grierson predicted that his horse soldiers would one day gain recognition for their service, which involved exploring vast expanses of territory seven days a week, threatened by thirst, extremes of heat and cold, rattlesnakes, renegade Indians, and desperados.

Deployed in August 1867, the Tenth Cavalry moved to Fort Riley, Kansas, and to Fort Gibson in eastern Oklahoma, where tensions between nomadic tribes and settlers reached a boil. By August 2, Sergeant William Christy lay dead of a bullet to the head, the first of the regiment to die in action. For $13 per month, men in the Tenth Calvary countered bootleggers and kidnappers of women and children and guarded mail, payroll, and stagecoach routes. In winter 1867–1868, Grierson's regiment fought Arapaho, Cheyenne, Comanche, Kiowa, and Kiowa-Apache. Soldiers shielded builders of corduroy roads and workers on the Kansas Pacific Railway, which hostile Arapaho, Cheyenne, and Sioux raided to halt the laying of rails over Indian Territory (Oklahoma). Soldiers strung telegraph wire, protected the Chickasaw and Choctaw from Plains Indian ambush, rebuilt Fort Arbuckle, Oklahoma, and constructed stone buildings at Fort Sill in southwestern Oklahoma.

After 90 cavalrymen held off 800 Cheyenne braves, the Cheyenne named the shaggy-haired black troops "Buffalo Soldiers," a backhanded compliment to their tenacity by comparing them to the fierce, sacred animals.

Military Achievement

Representing 20 percent of the Plains force and, in remote locales, half of the available manpower, Buffalo Soldiers earned a reputation for doing the army's dirty work, including the impossible task of patrolling 1,300 miles (2,100 kilometers) of Texas frontier and 400 miles (640 kilometers) of the Rio Grande.

When General William Tecumseh Sherman arrived at Fort Griffin, Texas, in April 1870, he dismissed reports of harrowing escapes from Indians, until his own entourage narrowly eluded a Kiowa ambush led by Chief Satanta in mid-May on Salt Creek Prairie, which concluded in his men being scalped, mutilated, and roasted alive. The next month, Sergeant Emanuel Stance, formerly a Louisiana sharecropper, earned commendation for retrieving two kidnap victims and stolen horses and for halting an attack on a wagon train at Kickapoo Springs, Texas. At Fort Griffin, Texas, Lieutenant Edward P. Turner of Pennsylvania led troops on the trail of 20 outlaws.

In 1874, the regiment chased Comanche and Kiowa marauders in New Mexico until the removal of natives to Indian reservations in Oklahoma. That winter, troops opened the Llano Estacado (Staked Plains) of north and west Texas and eastern New Mexico to pioneers. Headquartered at Fort Concho, Texas, in 1875, the regiment established law and order, hunted outlaws, maintained trade routes, protected survey teams, and combated Mexican and Comanchero banditry and rebellion. In 1877, Lieutenant Henry Ossian Flipper, West Point's first black graduate, commanded Troop A at Fort Sill. To prevent outbreaks of malaria, he engineered a drainage system called "Flipper's ditch."

By the end of the Indian Wars in the early 1890s, the Buffalo Soldiers had fought in the Cheyenne War (1867–1869), the Red River War (1874–1875), the Apache Wars (1875–1876), and the Sioux War (1890–1891). They never lost a battle. Throughout, black enlistees maintained a higher retention rate and a lower desertion rate than whites, and earned a reputation for good humor, sobriety, and endurance. For acts of courage and self-sacrifice, 19 Buffalo Soldiers earned the Congressional Medal of Honor for gallantry and courage in the Indian Wars.

See also: Weapons.

Further Reading

Carlson, Paul H. *The Buffalo Soldier Tragedy of 1877.* College Station: Texas A&M University Press, 2003.

Glasrud, Bruce A., and Michael N. Searles, eds. *Buffalo Soldiers in the West: A Black Soldiers Anthology.* College Station: Texas A&M University Press, 2007.

Leckie, William H., and Shirley A. Leckie. *The Buffalo Soldiers: A Narrative of the Black Cavalry in the West.* Rev. ed. Norman: University of Oklahoma Press, 2003.

Schubert, Frank N., ed. *Voices of the Buffalo Soldier: Records, Reports, and Recollections of Military Life and Service in the West.* Albuquerque: University of New Mexico Press, 2003.

Burbank, Luther (1849–1926)

Agronomist, geneticist, and plant hybridizer Luther Burbank pioneered 800 innovations in truck farming and orchardry to increase the supply and quality of the world's food. A farm boy known as "Little Lute," he was reared on a 200-acre (80-hectare) farm outside Lancaster, Massachusetts, where he was born into a Unitarian family on March 7, 1849.

Burbank ended his formal education after a year at Lancaster Academy, where he studied drawing and painting and pondered a career in medicine. Largely self-trained, he admired the works of transcendentalist essayist Ralph Waldo Emerson and of glaciologist Louis Agassiz. At age 16, he worked for the Ames Plow Company at Worcester, doing woodturning and pattern making.

In 1870, to support his widowed mother, Burbank purchased a 17-acre (6.9-hectare) truck farm outside Lunenburg and began marketing vegetables and seeds, including an improved variety of table grape. After a two-year process of selection, he developed from a rare seedpod the Russet Burbank potato, a white-fleshed staple crop and the predecessor of the Idaho Russet. He sold the rights to his improved potato in 1874 for $150.

Burbank moved to the West Coast in 1875, before California was a garden spot. He found work in Petaluma at the W.H. Pepper nursery and fended off the effects of a fever acquired during his work in damp environments. Surveying the indigenous plants, particularly the wild yam, unusual nuts, and *yerba buena,* a curative herb, Burbank exulted, "I firmly believe from what I have seen that it is the chosen spot of all this earth as far as Nature is concerned."

On October 31, 1877, he settled on 4 acres (1.5 hectares) in Santa Rosa, California, near the home of his brother Alfred. Working as a carpenter, Burbank supported himself; his mother, Olive Burpee Ross Burbank; and his sister, Emma Louisa Burbank. Meanwhile, he built a greenhouse, raised bedding plants, established a nursery, and perfected methods of hand pollination.

He bought foreign seeds and crossbred squash, berries, and lawn grasses, using the methods advocated by British naturalist Charles Darwin in *The Variation of Animals and Plants Under Domestication* (1868). Destroying sometimes all but two examples from a field of 1,000 test plants, he followed his faith in the environment as the architect of acquired traits. In the process, he developed frost-resistant plum trees, low-acid tomatoes, elephant garlic, and spineless cacti.

A humble amateur scientist devoid of cant, Burbank followed pragmatic trial-and-error methods to satisfy market needs. His potato relieved the Irish of future famines by combating blight. In his mid-fifties, he spent two $10,000 grants from the Carnegie Institution of Washington on such trial improvements as the hybrid white blackberry, royal walnut, pineapple quince, elephant heart plum, winter rhubarb, super wheat, rainbow grass, and thornless rose.

Outside Sebastopol, California, in 1885, he extended his plant selection on an 18-acre (7.3-hectare) spread called Gold Ridge Farm, which needed no irrigation. There, he monitored 3,000 trials at a time and invented the square-edged Burbank shovel. In 1893, his catalog *New Creations in Fruits and Flowers* enticed growers to try new varieties.

Burbank sparked controversy by recommending that children mature naturally like plants, thus they should remain unschooled until at least age ten. Among agronomists, he incited sneers and rebuttals for his belief that he could propagate mutations, "fixed races" that maintained nonchanging traits, such as the tasty fruit resulting from hybridizing the stubble berry with rabbit weed. Despite his unorthodox methods, farmers as far away as Europe and South Africa planted his new varieties. Americans dubbed him the "Plant Wizard."

Scholars scorned Burbank for his intuitive propagation of new strains—the Shasta daisy, Elberta peach, Indian corn, quick-maturing chestnut, dwarf sunflower, and fire poppy—yet thousands of naturalists visited his test fields to observe. For the American Breeders' Association, he issued articles on heredity, variation, species formation, and evolution. The Luther Burbank Press, which he helped found to promote his discoveries, published *The Training of the Human Plant* (1907), the 12-volume *Luther Burbank: His Methods and Discoveries and Their Practical Application* (1915), the eight-volume *How Plants Are Trained to Work for Man* (1921), *The Harvest of the Years* (1927), and *Partner of Nature* (1939). Burbank's commentaries trained other experimenters in his theories and functional methods, including multigrafting and the crossbreeding of species, such as the plumcot, a cross of the apricot and plum.

Suffering gastric complaint and a heart attack, Burbank died on April 11, 1926. Four years later, Congress passed legislation to patent hybrids such as those he had propagated.

Further Reading

Isely, Duane. *One Hundred and One Botanists.* Ames: Iowa State University Press, 1994.

Pauly, Philip J. *Biologists and the Promise of American Life from Meriwether Lewis to Alfred Kinsey.* Princeton, NJ: Princeton University Press, 2002.

Sackman, Douglas Cazaux. *Orange Empire: California and the Fruits of Eden.* Berkeley: University of California Press, 2005.

Smith, Jane S. *The Garden of Invention: Luther Burbank and the Business of Breeding Plants.* New York: Penguin, 2009.

Stansfield, William D. "Luther Burbank: Honorary Member of the American Breeders' Association." *Journal of Heredity* 97:2 (March/April 2006): 95–99.

Bureau of Agriculture, U.S.

A crucial scientific agency during America's rise to agrarian greatness, the U.S. Bureau of Agriculture increased profits for farmers and ranchers while ensuring food safety and availability throughout the country. The agricultural unit expanded in 1836, from the work of attorney Henry Leavitt Ellsworth, the first commissioner of the U.S. Patent Office. With a budget of $1,000, he aimed to salvage and preserve plants and seeds, purchase seeds from foreign countries, and compile statistics concerning where and under what conditions crops flourished.

Isaac Newton, a Quaker dairyman, member of the U.S. Agricultural Society, and former chief of the Agricultural Division of the Patent Office, took up Ellsworth's crusade and lobbied presidents James Buchanan and Abraham Lincoln to establish a federal department of agriculture. Farm journals lobbied for a scientific agency devoid of political influence. The formal elevation of the department to the executive cabinet level in 1889 secured for Ellsworth the title of "Father of the U.S. Department of Agriculture."

To ensure prosperity for some 33 million citizens, President Abraham Lincoln on May 15, 1862, created the independent Bureau of Agriculture within the U.S. Department of the Interior. Newton led the agrarian division and published its monthly and annual reports, a vehicle for issuing results from the laboratory directly to farmers and legislators. As part of his federal duties to conduct physical scientific research, Newton partnered with meteorologist Joseph Henry of the Smithsonian Institution in developing theories of weather and climate. Newton also found time to amass 1,000 volumes in an agricultural library directed by Aaron B. Grosh, a chaplain and a founder of the Grange Movement (National Grange of the Order of Patrons of Husbandry).

Newton launched the Economic Museum of Agriculture, a 5,000-square-foot (464-square-meter) space in Washington, D.C., that he stocked with varieties of grains, farm and forest produce, livestock breeds, and explanations of the impact of soil and climate on crop yields. To facilitate his compilation of statistics, introduction of new plants and livestock, testing of farm implements, soil analysis, answering citizens' questions, and forecasting of farm needs, his office hired a staff of 29 scientists, including Scots botanist and gardener William Saunders and entomologist Townend Glover, the first lepidopterist (a specialist in butterflies and moths) to hold a federal office, plus a horticulturist, an editor, and an internationally respected statistician, Jacob R. Dodge.

With the original budget of $80,000, the Bureau of Agriculture began scrutinizing the vast field of food plant and animal science. In a block bounded by Adams and Madison drives and Fourth and Sixth streets, the staff propagated experimental gardens. Their needs required another block, a former army cattle yard at Constitution and Independence avenues and Twelfth and Fourteenth streets.

Chemist Charles M. Wetherill analyzed sorghum, sorghum sugar, and sorghum syrup. He also compiled and issued the bureau's first leaflet, "Report on the Chemical Analysis of Grapes" (1862), which found American wine grapes to be equal to those grown in Europe. Saunders tested cultivation variables on cinchona (the source of quinine), coffee, figs, nuts, olives, oranges, silk, and tea. As a landscape architect and an advocate of land reclamation and reforestation, he planted 80,000 trees in Washington, imported camphor trees, and introduced seedless and navel oranges from Brazil to California citrus growers.

In 1866, Swiss organic chemist Henri Erni investigated soil, fertilizer, sugar beets, and fermentation. Vintners requested analysis of blackberry and rhubarb wine. Miners bombarded Erni's one-room lab in the basement of the Patent Office with silver ore from Nevada, copper from Maryland, oil shale from Indiana, and assay samples from California, New Jersey, Utah, and Washington. He published extracts of his work for the *Sunday Morning Chronicle.*

Meanwhile, Newton, a practical farmer, concentrated on experiments on 67 varieties of potatoes and on 55 types of spring and fall wheat. He died in office in 1867 from the effects of a sunstroke suffered when he ran to an experimental field to rescue wheat samples from a looming thunderstorm.

Subsequent holders of the commission included John W. Stokes (1867), Horace Capron, (1867–1871), Frederick Watts (1871–1877), and William G. LeDuc (1877–1881). Capron secured more space for the bureau in 1868, when he moved operations from the Patent Office. To cut costs on field labor and dray animals, he rallied farmers to invest in steam plowing. Under Capron's Division of Botany and Entomology, Irish chemist Thomas Antisell studied glauconite (greensand), clays and marls, phosphates, fish culture, and leather tanning methods. In his 1869 survey of meat extracts, peanuts, and sweet potatoes, Antisell warned that fertilizers adulterated foods. His successor, physician Ryland T. Brown, extended Antisell's work with assessments of the effects of sewage on farmlands.

Frederick Watts, the division commissioner in 1871, established the Division of Microscopy under Scots physician Thomas Taylor, a specialist in mushroom culture. Taylor studied the adulteration of butter and lard and appraised agricultural disasters caused by cranberry rot, grape mildew, peach yellowing, and plum disease. In 1873, chemist William McMurtrie ventured into cereals and sugar corn and the effects of bat guano, insecticides, mildew, and rot on grain. He also collected data on sumac and animal fibers and on the oil, silk, sugar, and wine industries.

In 1877, physician Peter Collier introduced inquiries on sugar and fodder, grasses, and veterinary remedies. He anticipated the work of the U.S. Food and Drug

Administration with his analyses of mineral and well water, baking powder, butter and margarine, and coffee and tea substitutes. LeDuc's projects included a tea farm and investigations of insect infestations, stock feed, irrigation methods, and animal deaths from pleuropneumonia.

Research under these technicians preceded the founding of a Bureau of Animal Industry and the Division of Veterinary Science. Bureau regimens established the need for laws prohibiting the use of certain chemicals, other forms of polluting public water sources, and the adulteration of food and drugs.

See also: Grange Movement.

Further Reading

Barron, Hal S. *Mixed Harvest: The Second Great Transformation in the Rural North, 1870–1930.* Chapel Hill: University of North Carolina Press, 1997.

Bradley, Raymond S., and Philip D. Jones, eds. *Climate Since* A.D. 1500. New York: Routledge, 1992.

Conlin, Joseph R. *The American Past: A Survey of American History.* 9th ed. Boston: Wadsworth/Cengage Learning, 2009.

Sherow, James E. *The Grasslands of the United States: An Environmental History.* Santa Barbara, CA: ABC-CLIO, 2007.

Woods, Thomas A. *Knights of the Plow: Oliver H. Kelley and the Origins of the Grange in Republican Ideology.* Ames: Iowa State University Press, 1991.

Bureau of Indian Affairs

A U.S. federal agency within the Department of the Interior, the Bureau of Indian Affairs (BIA)—originally called the Office of Indian Affairs—superintends 87,000 square miles (225,000 square kilometers) of Native American land and coordinates educational, sanitation, and medical services to American Indians. Organized in 1824, the BIA received its first commission in 1869 with the appointment of Brigadier General Ely Samuel Parker, a bilingual Seneca and veteran of the Civil War who was dubbed "Little Father of Indians."

The need for intervention in clashes between settlers and natives arose in 1862, when open warfare broke out between Minnesota homesteaders and the Dakota Sioux. The situation worsened in Colorado Territory on November 29, 1864, after Major John M. Chivington and 700 troops of the Third Colorado Volunteers attacked the Sand Creek Reservation near Fort Lyon just after dawn, while most of the braves were out hunting, and slaughtered 133 Arapaho and Cheyenne, mostly women and children. Losing only 15 militiamen, the attackers plundered and burned tepees, stole horses, and took scalps, fingers, fetuses, and genitals from the corpses to flaunt as war plunder.

At the end of the Civil War, increased traffic to the frontier over the Bozeman Trail from Nebraska to Montana aroused greater Sioux belligerence against outsiders, who desecrated the sacred Black Hills of South Dakota. During demobilization of the Union army in summer 1865, Parker counseled the Catawba, Cherokee, Choctaw, Creek, and Seminole, the five tribes that had allied with the Southern Confederacy. In 1866, he traveled the Missouri River to isolate problems at Fort Phil Kearny, Wyoming, after the Fetterman Massacre, in which Arapaho, Cheyenne, and Lakota warriors ambushed and slew 80 soldiers of a woodcutting detail, mutilating most of the bodies.

In January 1867, according to *The Diary of Gideon Welles,* secretary of the navy under presidents Abraham Lincoln and Andrew Johnson (1911), the U.S. Army wrangled with the Department of the Interior over military control of the Indian bureau. Welles described the military as "sojourners, not residents" and championed the status quo. "The old, single-hearted agents studied the character of the Indian, studied his habits, and interested themselves in his welfare," he wrote, while soldiers generalized that all Indians were enemies.

Parker agreed to speak for some 2,500 Brulé and Oglala Sioux, but he introduced himself as spokesman for President Johnson's call for "permanent homes," a euphemism for reservations. He further distanced himself as a native ambassador on Christmas Eve 1867 by marrying a white woman, Minnie Orton Sackett. General Ulysses S. Grant gave her away at the altar.

By 1868, President Johnson and General Grant restrained the U.S. Cavalry from intensifying hostilities, which cost the government $1 million in army readiness for every Indian death. From a Seneca viewpoint, General Parker, the subsequent commissioner of Indian affairs, alerted whites to a native fear: "The Indian races are more seriously threatened with a speedy extermination than ever before in the history of the country." To ensure the survival of native peoples, he drafted Grant's "Peace Policy," discussed the feasibility of outfitting Indian hunters with rifles and ammunition, and purged corrupt politicians, profiteers, and Indian agents from the BIA as a means of restoring order on the frontier. In 1870, he hosted Lakota chiefs Red Cloud and Spotted Tail in Washington, D.C., to discuss the founding of reservations and the ousting of mining firms from native lands.

While visiting with Secretary of the Interior Jacob Cox in 1870, Oglala Lakota Sioux Chief Red Cloud directly addressed the issues of race and equality and commented on the Office of Indian Affairs:

> My face is red; yours is white. The Great Spirit has made you to read and write, but not me. I have not learned. I come here to tell my Great Father what I do not like in my country. You are all close to the Great Father, and are a great many chiefs. The men the Great Father sends to us have no sense—no heart.

When famine threatened the efforts to establish peace, Parker spent personal funds on shipments of food to the Black Hills. He risked his credibility by calling out the cavalry against the Piegan in 1870 for killing and robbing white settlers. His enemies weakened his discretionary powers. A charge of fraud ended Parker's patience withinept bureaucracy. He resigned his post on August 1, 1871.

Racial warfare revived in 1874 in the Black Hills of South Dakota. The conflict prefaced the Battle of the Little Bighorn on June 25, 1876, a startling massacre of Lieutenant Colonel George Armstrong Custer and the U.S. Seventh Cavalry by Lakota chiefs Sitting Bull and Crazy Horse and Cheyenne war commander Two Moons. The federal retaliation in 1877 dispersed tribes of the Northwest, Great Plains, and Southwest to reservations established on arid lands and ended all efforts to recognize Indian sovereignty in treaty negotiations.

The BIA—comprising superintendencies in Arizona, California, Colorado, Dakota, Idaho, Montana, Nevada, New Mexico, Oregon, Utah, Washington, and the Central, Northern, and Southern divisions—enforced fish and game regulations as well as water rights and access for hunter-gatherers of native plants and healing herbs. The resignation of Secretary of the Interior Columbus Delano on October 5, 1875, and the appointment of Zachariah Chandler to Grant's cabinet resulted in the immediate firing of corrupt officials and of attorneys hired to represent Indian tribes.

Fraud and wrangling continued to disrupt the smooth operation of the BIA, as Catholics squabbled with Quakers and mainline Protestants over mission rights, entrepreneurs schemed to gain control of mining rights, and epidemics decimated suffering tribes. By 1882, federal authorities had jettisoned the Peace Policy.

See also: Black Kettle; Fetterman Massacre; Geronimo; Indian Reservations; Lincoln, Abraham; Little Bighorn, Battle of the; Parker, Ely; Sand Creek Massacre; Washita Massacre.

Further Reading

Armstrong, William H. *Warrior in Two Camps: Ely S. Parker, Union General and Seneca Chief.* Syracuse, NY: Syracuse University Press, 1990.

Heidler, David S., Jeanne T. Heidler, and David J. Coles. *Encyclopedia of the American Civil War: A Political, Social, and Military History.* New York: W.W. Norton, 2000.

Jacoby, Karl. *Crimes Against Nature: Squatters, Poachers, Thieves, and the Hidden History of American Conservation.* Berkeley: University of California Press, 2001.

Johansen, Bruce E., and Donald A. Grinde, Jr. *The Encyclopedia of Native American Biography.* New York: Da Capo, 1998.

Lamar, Howard R., ed. *The New Encyclopedia of the American West.* New Haven, CT: Yale University Press, 1998.

Utley, Robert M. *The Indian Frontier, 1846–1890.* Rev. ed. Albuquerque: University of New Mexico Press, 2003.

California

In the 1860s, on a continent still only half settled, California bore an aura of wealth and promise. In the pre–gold rush days of 1848, the isolated outpost hosted just 15,000 non-native American residents. The blazing of the California Trail southwest from the Oregon Trail at Fort Hall, Idaho, and subsequent toll roads over the Sierra Nevada kept wagon trains moving along the Humboldt River until rail travel became feasible.

In the aftermath of the California Gold Rush, American-style merchandising enabled vendors to engage buyers with a variety of goods previously unavailable on the frontier. San Francisco, a natural port city, was the home of S&G Gump's four-story home furnishings gallery, the I. Magnin luxury department store, the R.H. M'Donald dental supply house, the dry goods business of Levi Strauss & Company, and floating miners' emporiums operating in San Francisco Bay. From the democratized commercial style of the West Coast came Macy's in Marysville, Lipman Wolfe & Company in Sacramento, and the May Company and Goldwater's Department Stores in Los Angeles.

By mid-century, of the 300,000 people living in the trans-Mississippi West, 200,000 dwelled in California, which entered the Union as the thirty-first state on September 9, 1850. The population rose by almost 68 percent, from 380,000 in 1860 to more than 560,000 a decade later. In the *New York Tribune,* Horace Greeley's editorials glowed with admiration for the state's unspoiled natural beauty, particularly the Yosemite Valley and the Mariposa Grove, the nation's first state parks, which he visited in 1859.

To relieve Hispanic residents of overtaxation and minority status and to counter state tax exemptions for miners, on February 5, 1859, Don Andrés Pico, a state senator and Californio (Californian of Latin American descent) rancher in the San Fernando Valley, proposed dividing the state into Klamath to the north and the Territory of Colorado, a slaveholding municipality. Under the patronage of President James Buchanan, a plebiscite disclosed 76 percent support among Old Californians in Los Angeles, but only 9.5 percent in Tulare and San Luis Obispo counties. In March 1860, U.S. Senator Milton Slocum Latham promoted the separation in Congress, but the movement died during the political crisis leading up to the Civil War.

Secessionism on the Frontier

Exacerbating the need to communicate with the West in the first year of the Civil War was the impetus to promote Unionism among San Francisco's Southern Democrats, Californios, and militiamen in the Los Angeles Mounted Rifles. Jefferson Davis, president of the Confederate States of America, planned a secessionist sweep across the South through Texas to New Mexico Territory and California. Via a network of forts and the U.S. Pacific Squadron, President Abraham Lincoln kept close watch on insurgency, which threatened a permanent dissolution of states.

On April 6, 1861, *Harper's Weekly* reported on a secessionist conspiracy in San Francisco led by financier Asbury Harpending and the Knights of the Golden Circle, who abetted Colonel John Robert Baylor in the seizure of southern New Mexico for the Confederacy. At the insistence of Federal Marshal Henry Dwight Barrows, Colonel James Henry Carleton arrested San Francisco Undersheriff Andrew Jackson King for using his elective office to promote secessionism in public processions. By a plurality, Californians squashed Democratic demagoguery by electing Republican Leland Stanford as governor on September 4, 1861. From April to August 1862, the California Column of 2,350 soldiers, led by Carleton, marched 900 miles (1,450 kilometers) to the Rio Grande in Texas to drive Confederates out of Arizona and New Mexico. Carleton posted spies in Apache and Navajo territory to inform the Union of subsequent attempts to suborn patriotism in the Southwest.

Another threat to California approached from the shore: Pro-South privateers aboard the schooner *J.M. Chapman* on marine transport by the Pacific Mail Steamship Company. On March 15, 1863, the night of the pirates' first raid, San

Francisco police and U.S. treasury agents on board the war sloop USS *Cyane* seized the *Chapman* and its contraband cargo of Bowie knives and navy revolvers. Without incident, officers imprisoned three Confederate plotters in solitary confinement at Alcatraz and imposed ten-year sentences. The *Chapman* became a war prize sold at public auction.

To display support for President Lincoln and the Union, Czar Alexander II of Russia in September 1862 dispatched six men-of-war from the Imperial Fleet in the Baltic Sea to moor in San Francisco Bay. Under the command of Admiral Andrei Alexandrovich Popov on a second cruise, the arrival of the *Abrek, Bogatyr, Gaidamak, Kalevala, Novik,* and *Rynda* on October 12, 1863, elicited cheers from shoremen and blessings from U.S. Secretary of the Navy Gideon Welles. Russia's imperial challenge helped to dissuade England and France from intervening on the Confederate side.

Progress in the West

Until mechanized travel was available, travelers depended on horse- and mule-drawn coaches, beginning in 1849 with James E. Birch and Frank Stevens's California Stage Company, which traveled between Deadwood, South Dakota, and Oroville, California. In 1860, Alexander Majors, William H. Russell, and William Waddell initiated a route from Missouri via the Central Overland California & Pikes Peak Express.

To finance the Civil War, President Lincoln on July 1, 1862, promoted east–west transportation from the Atlantic Coast to the goldfields of the West by signing the Pacific Railway Act. His intent was to connect the Mississippi Valley to the Pacific Coast, a potential gateway to trade in Hawaii, Australia, New Zealand, Japan, and China. The linkage of tracks promised a safer route for gold and silver shipments, which the Confederate navy stalked over the long sea route from frontier mines to federal mints on the East Coast.

By 1863, the San Francisco Railroad carried passengers across California; telegraph wires bore messages east to New York City and news items to the West. Financiers profited from dealings with the Pacific Stock Exchange, Fireman's Fund Insurance Company, and Bank of California, the most powerful financial firm on the U.S. Pacific shore. In a reelection bid on November 8, 1864, Lincoln won an overwhelming majority of the popular vote—58.6 percent—from the country's westernmost state.

In early March 1865, four weeks before the Confederate surrender at Appomattox, Virginia, a three-year engineering survey, the Western Union Telegraph Expedition, led by Smithsonian Institution naturalist Major Robert Kennicott, began mapping the coastline from California, Oregon, and Washington Territory north and west into British Columbia. The project preceded Lincoln's plan to add resource-endowed Western states to the salvaged Union. Freighting and travel throughout the frontier improved in 1866 with John Mullen's California & Idaho Stage Line and Benjamin Franklin and Henry Winslow Corbett's California & Oregon Stage Company.

Investing in Change

The frantic rush to complete rail travel to the Pacific required a significant alteration in California's economy and demographics. Under the Burlingame Treaty with China, which President Lincoln signed on July 28, 1868, unrestricted Chinese immigration supplied cheap labor to mines and rail construction camps. In 1867, 400 members of the anti-Chinese Workingmen's Party attacked Asians in San Francisco. When crews connected the Union Pacific to the Central Pacific Railroad on May 10, 1869, the unified track reduced travel time from New York to San Francisco from three weeks to eight days. The direct route brought thousands of travelers, miners, farmers, traders, and speculators, as well as students to the University of California, which opened in Oakland in 1868.

In 1870, developer John Wesley North led a colony of refined, pious colonists from Knoxville, Tennessee, to Riverside in San Bernardino County. On the Santa Ana River, he established a utopian agricultural commune, located along the Southern Pacific rail lines. Investor Collis Huntington's plan to turn Santa Monica into a deepwater port failed, as did activist Georgiana Bruce Kirby's Santa Cruz suffragist society, which, in 1871, challenged the state law prohibiting full citizenship for women. Improving trade and tourism in 1872, a regular steamship service, the Occidental & Oriental shipping lines from Australia through the Hawaiian Islands to California, increased the flow of visitors and investors. The writings of Ambrose Bierce, Bret Harte, and Mark Twain inspired legends about the Pacific Coast lifestyle, drawing more people to the state.

In the Mojave Desert, mining proved lucrative in Death Valley after the Panamint City copper and silver strike of 1872. To outwit robbers lurking in Surprise Canyon, owners John Percival Jones and William Morris Stewart—known as the "Silver Senators"—cast silver ore into 450-pound (990-kilogram) spheres for hauling to

Los Angeles. The freight driver named his wagon the "Cannonball Express." Mining revived the Monterey economy in July 1875 with the Guadalupe Mine Company's discovery of the Cinnabar Creek Lode, a vein of mercury. In the early 1880s, the unearthing of borates returned Death Valley to prominence as a source of quick fortunes.

Blended People

The state's population diversity precipitated cultural clashes. From 1848 to 1871, Californians targeted Mexicans and killed off 50,000 Native Americans from 70 different tribes. Conditions worsened for Californios in 1862, when a three-year drought killed thousands of cattle and bankrupted Los Angeles traders. At Oxnard, sheep replaced cattle as moneymaking livestock for meat and tanning. Lacking credit from white-owned banks, unemployed vaqueros (herdsmen) abandoned bankrupt cattle and horse farms to become itinerant sheep shearers.

Racists incited strife against Chinese workers, who competed with California nativists for jobs and housing by breaking the strike of white workers and working for subsistence wages. Asian laborers formed six "tongs," secret societies that flourished in San Francisco, and prospered as farmers and stoop laborers. In Monterey, the Chinese shared the commercial fishing industry with an influx of Genoese seamen. To protect their property, coolie workers sent their earnings home to China, shipping $50,000 in gold dust in 1867.

Editorials in the *Union* and the *Yreka Journal* denigrated the Chinese as unclean, leprosy-ridden pagans who did not deserve citizenship among Christians. Asian dominance lessened in the delta of west-central California in 1875, after John Ferris's clamshell dredge replaced manual digging with mechanized dirt removal. In Sacramento, the Chinese labor force found jobs in a salmon cannery and, in 1876, at Joseph Routier's fruit cannery, where tin cans were handmade and soldered.

In April 1876, some 4,000 disgruntled members of the Sacramento Supreme Order of Caucasians demanded an all-white labor force in private and civil service jobs. On Trout Creek outside Truckee, raiders burned tents of Chinese woodcutters and shot at the men as they fled the fire. In early October of that year, the *Sacramento Daily Union* and the *Reno Evening Gazette* shamed Truckee citizens for harboring killers. On October 29, 1877, former sailor Dennis Kearney, a 30-year-old drayman and rabble-rouser from Oakmount, Ireland, rallied thousands of protesters to Nob Hill in San Francisco. He denounced the wealth of rail and realty tycoons and charged the Central Pacific Railroad with unfair employment of cheap Asian laborers.

Pioneering in the late 1870s brought more settlers, most of them white. In his inaugural address on March 5, 1877, President Rutherford B. Hayes promised to foster settlement and irrigation of the nation's deserts. Passage of the Desert Land Act of 1877 offered public property in allotments of 320 acres (130 hectares) per person or 640 acres (260 hectares) per married couple, a larger parcel than lands offered by the Homestead Act of 1862. California farmers and livestock men petitioned for plots and free water for growing wheat, vegetables, cotton, vineyards, and fruit and nut orchards. Chief among the 10 million acres (4 million hectares) open for purchase were California's Imperial Valley and Owens Valley.

Within days of the bill's passage, William B. Carr and James Ben-Ali Haggin of San Francisco hired surrogates to buy 100,000 acres (40,500 hectares) along the Southern Pacific tracks outside Bakersfield. The vast claim suppressed population growth and stripped the area of community and recreational access to waterways. Federal investigators assessing land improvements in California found only 5 percent of the land claims to be lawful.

See also: Post Office and Postal Service; San Francisco, California.

Further Reading

Fehrenbacher, Don E. *The Slaveholding Republic: An Account of the United States Government's Relations to Slavery.* Ed. Ward M. McAfee. Oxford, UK: Oxford University Press, 2002.

Gifford, Terry, ed. *John Muir: His Life and Letters and Other Writings.* London: Baton Wicks, 1996.

Hunt, Aurora. *Army of the Pacific: Its Operations in California, Texas, Arizona, New Mexico, Utah, Nevada, Oregon, Washington, Plains Region, Mexico, etc., 1860–1866.* Mechanicsville, PA: Stackpole, 2004.

Isenberg, Andrew C. *Mining California: An Ecological History.* New York: Hill and Wang, 2005.

Lingenfelter, Richard E. *Death Valley and the Amargosa: A Land of Illusion.* Berkeley: University of California Press, 1986.

Moore, James G. *Exploring the Highest Sierra.* Stanford, CA: Stanford University Press, 2000.

———. *King of the 40th Parallel: Discovery in the American West.* Stanford, CA: Stanford University Press, 2006.

Pomeroy, Earl S. *The Pacific Slope: A History of California, Oregon, Washington, Idaho, Utah, and Nevada.* Lincoln: University of Nebraska Press, 1991.

Capitol, U.S.

The assembly building of Congress and a functioning symbol of bicameral government in America, the U.S. Capitol in Washington, D.C., united the Senate chamber in the south wing with the House of Representatives chamber in the north wing. Designed in 1792–1793 by architect William Thornton, a physician from the British West Indies, the building featured Roman elements to associate American democracy with that of ancient Rome.

The floor plan of 540 rooms underwent extensive scrutiny and modification by architects Benjamin Henry Latrobe and Charles Bulfinch before its completion in 1864. Congress paid slave owners $5 per month for each bondsman who worked on the project. Crews received free blankets and lived in shacks thrown together on the Capitol lawn.

The opening of the Senate chamber in 1859 allowed half of the legislature to put the building to use. The following year, the U.S. Supreme Court vacated its room in the Capitol and held sessions in the former Senate chamber. At the Capitol's East Portico, presidents took the oath of office and delivered their inaugural addresses. While roofers were replacing the Capitol's copper dome with a cast iron model, senators from Alabama, Arkansas, Florida, Georgia, Louisiana, Mississippi, and Texas gathered in the House of Representatives on January 5, 1861, to demand states' rights and to pledge themselves to secessionism. During the Civil War, Capitol Hill built up with row houses and mansions, federal townhouses, markets, hospitals, and the Thomas Jefferson Building of the Library of Congress.

The Rotunda honored the first deceased president for the state funeral of Abraham Lincoln on April 19, 1865. A queue of thousands wound past the bier to mourn a beloved president who had steadied the reins of power during the Civil War. The pine catafalque returned to service for the lying in state of U.S. Congressman Thaddeus Stevens in 1868, Senator Charles Sumner in 1874, and Vice President Henry Wilson in 1875.

The Capitol remained functional throughout the various building stages. The final phase of construction expanded the original design to 754 feet by 350 feet (230 meters by 107 meters), equal to more than four football fields. Manpower required black slaves to hew logs, cut and lay stone, dig trenches, and bake bricks for the structure. To accommodate the growing Congress, architect Thomas Ustick Walter and his assistant, August Schoenborn, doubled the size of the chambers and added the Rotunda and the 180-foot (55-meter) cast iron double dome and cupola.

Atop the Capitol Dome poses the bronze statue *Freedom Triumphant in War and Peace,* designed by sculptor Thomas Gibson Crawford and hoisted into place on a spherical plinth on December 2, 1863. The female figure, standing nearly 20 feet (6 meters) tall and weighing 7.5 tons (6.8 metric tons), wears a crested helmet, classic chiton and fringed stola, and brooch. Crawford enhanced the figure with symbolism—an eagle on the crest, the letters "U.S." on the brooch, a sheathed sword in her right hand, and a laurel wreath and shield of the nation in her left. Around the globe he incised *E pluribus unum* (One out of many) to indicate the union of states into a single nation. The completed piece was the work of Philip Reid, a mulatto slave who superintended the Clark Mills Foundry in Bladensburg, Maryland, and oversaw the assembly of segments on the Capitol lawn. In 1874, landscape artist Frederick Law Olmsted planned the walkways, drives, terracing, and groves surrounding Capitol Hill.

Inside adornment by government painter Constantino Brumidi, an Italian Greek immigrant, decorated the 4,664-square-foot (434-square-meter) oculus (eye) of the Capitol Dome with the *Apotheosis of George Washington,* an allegorical fresco. The circular scene depicts classic characters proclaiming the godhood of the first president. A second ring of action figures represents the military, science, navy, commerce, mechanics, and agriculture. Historical events honor inventors Benjamin Franklin, Robert Fulton, and Samuel Morse; the transatlantic telegraph cable; an ironclad warship; financier Robert Morris, who bankrolled the American Revolution; ironworker Charles Thomas; and Cyrus McCormick's mechanical reaper.

Below the 36-window clerestory stands the *Frieze of American History,* a fresco imitating monochromatic carved stone bas relief. Begun by Brumidi and completed by Roman artist Filippo Costaggini and American muralist Allyn Cox in 1951, the 19 scenes personify America as Miss Liberty and dramatize the historical significance of Christopher Columbus; conquistadors Hernán Cortés, Francisco Pizarro, and Hernando de Soto; Captain John Smith and Pocahontas; William Brewster and the Pilgrims of Plymouth Colony; New England settlers; Georgia Governor James Oglethorpe and the Muskogee; Major John Pitcairn at the Battle of Lexington; the founding fathers authoring the Declaration of Independence; the surrender of Lord Cornwallis at Yorktown, Virginia; the death of Shawnee Chief Tecumseh;

General Winfield Scott claiming Mexico City; the end of the Civil War; sailors fighting the Spanish-American War; and the Wright brothers' plane at Kitty Hawk, North Carolina.

In 1864, Congressman Justin Smith Morrill (R-VT) proposed the creation of the semicircular National Statuary Hall, a repository of two statues from each of the states. The cutting, loading, and polishing of marble columns fell to slaves living at the quarry at Noland's Ferry, Maryland. Their pay enriched their owners, who supplied each worker with clothing. New Yorkers sent models of Governor George Clinton and diplomat Robert R. Livingston. Rhode Island contributed images of General Nathanael Greene and theologian Roger Williams. In 1876, the state of Massachusetts presented marble likenesses of statesman Samuel Adams and Governor John Winthrop. Vermont chose a marble statue of Ethan Allen, hero of the Revolutionary War. Over time, the crowding of statues and stress on the Rotunda floor required the construction of display annexes in the Crypt and the Hall of Columns on the first floor and the Capitol Visitor Center to house the images of nine women and 91 men who had an impact on the nation's history.

See also: Washington, D.C.

Further Reading

Field, Cynthia R. *Paris on the Potomac: The French Influence on the Architecture and Art of Washington, D.C.* Athens: Ohio University Press, 2007.

Holland, Jesse J. *Black Men Built the Capitol: Discovering African-American History In and Around Washington, D.C.* Guilford, CT: Globe Pequot, 2007.

Kennon, Donald R., ed. *The United States Capitol: Designing and Decorating a National Icon.* Athens: Ohio University Press, 2000.

Captain Jack (ca. 1837–1873)

The guerrilla war chief of the Modoc tribe at Tule Lake on the California–Oregon border, Captain Jack plotted an 11-month conflict, known as the Modoc War, that cost the U.S. Army $4 million. The son of a Modoc chief, he was born around 1837 and named Kintpuash.

In 1864, the encroachment of white settlers prompted the removal of 250 Modoc along with members of the Klamath, Snake, and Yahuskin tribes to the Klamath Reservation at Chiloquin in southwestern Oregon. Subsequently, the Modoc ceded to U.S. Superintendent of Indian Affairs Alfred Benjamin Meacham their territory on Lower Klamath Lake, Lost River, and Tule Lake.

Life in Oregon among the rival Klamath at the Yainax Reserve on the Sprague River was a constant battle. Hunger forced the Modoc to kill and eat their own horses. In 1865, Captain Jack chose to live off fishing, trapping, and hunting at Tule Lake rather than starve on government rations. In January 1868, he and Curly Headed Doctor, the tribe's shaman, led 32 disgruntled Modoc warriors south to Lost River and Clear Lake, California.

In 1869, the U.S. Army forced the Modoc back to the Yainax Reserve, where lax discipline allowed soldiers to cheat natives at gambling and to prostitute their wives. Refusing to be forced into farming and herding, Captain Jack directed 180 followers to Tule Lake in April 1870 to resume the traditional Modoc lifestyle of hunting and gathering on the lava beds. The following spring, a local sheriff issued an arrest warrant for Captain Jack after he killed a Klamath shaman who had failed to cure a sick child.

Major John Green, an emissary of the U.S. Office of Indian Affairs, resolved to force the Modoc back into captivity. In the Battle of Lost River on November 29, 1872, Captain Jack assembled 50 of his people at a stronghold of caves and trenches in the lava beds south of Tule Lake; the Modoc fended off federal forces ten times their number. On January 17, 1873, Colonel Frank Wheaton, 225 troops, and 107 civilian vigilantes lost a siege against 51 Modoc.

After a hard winter, the band surrendered to the U.S. Army on April 11 and entered mediation. At the formal caucus, Captain Jack shot General Edward Richard Sprigg Canby between the eyes, making Canby the only general killed in the Indian Wars. An accomplice, Boston Charley, severely wounded Superintendent Meacham and killed the Reverend Eleazar Cady Thomas, a Methodist peace commissioner.

Captain Jack miscalculated the effects of the shootings on the U.S. Army. The murders precipitated a face-off at Dry Lake, where the U.S. Army sent General Jefferson Columbus Davis with 1,000 troops to apprehend the Modoc band. A second engagement on April 15 involved capture of the Modoc water supply and blocking their escape route to Tule Lake. The pursuit required the complicity of Modoc traitors, who aided the army in exchange for amnesty.

On June 4, 1873, pursuers seized Captain Jack and five Modoc warriors at Langell Valley, Oregon, just north of the California border. President Ulysses S. Grant approved the execution of Captain Jack, Black Jim, Boston

Charley, and John Schonchin. Two others, Brancho and Slolux, entered Alcatraz prison to serve life sentences. Editor and propagandist Lydia Maria Child commiserated with the Modoc and quoted Captain Jack's lament, "To die by bullets not hurt much; but it hurts a heap to die by hunger."

The hanging of Captain Jack and his three aides at Fort Klamath on October 3, 1873, ended the Modoc War. The victims' skulls were displayed at the Smithsonian Institution. The army transferred the surviving 163 Modoc in unheated cattle cars to the Quapaw Reserve in northeastern Oklahoma.

See also: Child, Lydia Maria

Further Reading

Blake, Tupper Ansel, Madeleine Graham Blake, and William Kittredge. *Balancing Water: Restoring the Klamath Basin.* Berkeley: University of California Press, 2000.

Brown, Dee. *The American West.* New York: Simon & Schuster, 1995.

Cozzens, Peter, ed. *Eyewitnesses to the Indian Wars, 1865–1890.* 5 vols. Mechanicsburg, PA: Stackpole, 2001–2005.

Hall, Roger A. *Performing the American Frontier, 1870–1906.* Cambridge, UK: Cambridge University Press, 2001.

Palmquist, Peter E., and Thomas R. Kailbourn. *Pioneer Photographers of the Far West: A Biographical Dictionary, 1840–1865.* Stanford, CA: Stanford University Press, 2000.

Personifying the American myth of the "self-made man," Andrew Carnegie began work as a 13-year-old bobbin boy at a Pennsylvania cotton mill, advanced his career as a telegraph and railroad operator, and founded his own steel company at age 30. *(Hulton Archive/Stringer/Getty Images)*

Carnegie, Andrew (1835–1919)

Iron and steel magnate and philanthropist Andrew Carnegie exhibited the zeal of an immigrant for the freedoms and capitalist opportunities of America. At his birth to shoe binder Margaret Morrison Carnegie on November 25, 1835, in a one-room cottage in Dunfermline, Scotland, he became the namesake of his paternal grandfather, an irrepressible wit. His father, weaver William "Will" Carnegie, specialized in making damask fabric until the steam-powered loom put him out of a job. In order to support Margaret, Andrew, and four-year-old Thomas Morrison "Tom" Carnegie, Will moved the household to Allegheny City, Pennsylvania, in 1848 to live with extended family. He found work in local cotton factories.

At Anchor Mills, 13-year-old Andy Carnegie walked a mile to work for $1.20 a week as a bobbin boy. At Pittsburgh in 1850, he more than doubled his previous wages delivering messages for the Atlantic & Ohio Telegraph Company. By age 16, he worked as a telegrapher, while educating himself at night by reading newspapers and borrowed books. Within two years, he advanced to a salary of $20 per month in the employ of the Pennsylvania Railroad as the personal telegrapher, accountant, and secretary to Superintendent Thomas Alexander Scott, his mentor. At Will Carnegie's death in 1855, Andrew supported himself, his mother, and 12-year-old Tom.

While supervising the Pittsburgh division of the railroad, Carnegie mastered the basics of business management and finance. He opened the telegraph office 24 hours a day and burned wrecked railcars to clear the tracks following a collision. Rumors of a strike gave him time to have labor leaders fired and to suppress the work stoppage in the planning stage.

With insider information, he mortgaged the family house for $500 and invested in Adams Express, a freight and cargo transport company, which earned him $5,000 in annual dividends. Subsequent shares in Theodore Tuttle Woodruff's Knight Sleeping Car Company and in bridges, iron, and rails generated capital for buying into Woodruff's merger with George M. Pullman's sleeper factory.

Enrichment in Boom Times

At the outbreak of the Civil War, Carnegie made money out of patriotism. He superintended military rail and telegraph lines between Washington, D.C., and Alexandria, Virginia, relayed munitions, and repaired sabotaged tracks at Annapolis, Maryland, to circumvent a rebel invasion of the capital. On July 21, 1861, he transported Union soldiers from the Battle of Bull Run and reported the debacle to the *Pittsburgh Chronicle.* His stock in a steel rolling mill and in the Columbia Oil Company at Titusville, Pennsylvania, in 1864 profited from military demands for shells and for cannon and gunboat lubricants. On an outlay of $11,000, he earned a 162 percent return the first year and reinvested in oil at Duck Creek and Pithole Creek, as well as in companies supplying the military with coal, wood, bridges, grading, and rolling stock. Upon his conscription in February 1864, Carnegie paid an Irish immigrant $850 to join the Union army in his place.

At war's end, Carnegie sold his rail interests and took a year's vacation in Europe. Upon his return, he concentrated on buying iron ore veins and steamer lines on Lake Superior. In Pittsburgh, an industrial center in the mid-1860s, he formed the Union Ironworks, Keystone Telegraph Company, and Keystone Bridge Works, the nucleus of Carnegie Steel.

In 1870, after settling with his mother at the St. Nicholas Hotel in New York City, he moved his office from Wall Street to Broadway. He began courting Louise Whitfield, whom he wed in 1887, a year after he suffered a debilitating bout of typhoid fever. He bought control of the Pacific & Atlantic Telegraph Company and began stringing wire from St. Louis, Missouri, to Indianapolis, Indiana. During the lengthy economic slowdown of 1873, Carnegie and capitalists Cyrus McCormick and John D. Rockefeller financed their individual projects and enriched themselves at the expense of competitors.

By studying Henry Bessemer's steelmaking process, Carnegie determined that steel would replace iron in the national infrastructure. In 1875, Carnegie's first steel plant, the Edgar Thomson Works in Braddock, Pennsylvania, began processing 2,000 rails for the Pennsylvania Railroad. The completion of the Eads Bridge over the Mississippi River at St. Louis and the construction of the Centennial Palace for the 1876 Philadelphia Exposition demonstrated the grace and strength of Carnegie's most advanced steel products.

He retired in 1897 and settled his wife and infant daughter Margaret at Skibo Castle, a 20,000-acre (8,100-hectare) estate on Loch Evelix in northern Scotland. By 1901, the sale of Carnegie's steel mill to J. Pierpont Morgan resulted in the nation's largest corporate buyout and the formation of U.S. Steel, the nation's first corporation worth more than $1 billion.

From Greed to Good Deeds

Carnegie's good works brought him greatness. In December 1868, he pledged any amount of personal income in excess of $50,000 per year to charity. He honored his old friend Edwin M. Stanton, former secretary of war, by endowing the chair of political economy at Kenyon College in his name. In 1877, Carnegie treated his hometown to a commodious swimming pool and bathhouses and a lending library; he awarded Pittsburgh a library and Allegheny City a library and music hall. Botanist Luther Burbank spent two $10,000 grants from the Carnegie Institution of Washington on hybridizing white blackberry, royal walnuts, pineapple quince, elephant heart plums, winter rhubarb, super wheat, rainbow grass, and thornless roses. Carnegie invested in a laboratory for Bellevue Hospital Medical College in New York City.

To the end of the nineteenth century, one-on-one efforts at Carnegie learning centers and at church schools, freedmen's societies, and public libraries elevated public literacy. The overall distribution of $350 million underwrote the Carnegie Foundation of New York, Carnegie Foundation for the Advancement of Teaching, Carnegie Hall, Carnegie Institution of Washington, the beginnings of Carnegie Mellon University, Carnegie Trust for the Universities of Scotland, Carnegie United Kingdom Trust, Central American Court of Justice, Hero Fund, and the Peace Palace at the Temple of Peace in Holland. Carnegie's donations to blacks went to the National Negro Business League and to the Tuskegee Institute. Out of admiration for the builders of black communities, he donated $4,000 for the construction of a library in Mound Bayou, Mississippi.

Enemy and Advocate

Carnegie antagonized Americans and the British with his outspoken opinions about ruthless business tactics, organized religion, and liberty. His writings espoused the need for underselling, cost cutting, and employee pensions and denounced the minimum wage, income taxes, and the eight-hour workday. He bought and directed newspapers in the British Isles to endorse the ouster of the monarchy and the installation of an American-style republic. In the United States, he defied Unionists and hired Pinkerton detectives to halt labor organization. He demonized American imperialists for annexing the Philippines and for considering a similar seizure of Cuba. His donations to colleges required a severance of connection with churches. He is best remembered as the enemy of the privileged class and as an advocate of free enterprise and lifelong education.

When Carnegie died of bronchial pneumonia at Shadowbrook Estate in Lenox, Massachusetts, on August 11, 1919, he had built 3,000 public libraries in 47 states. He left only $30 million to his family, servants, and legatees, which included the Cooper Union, Hampton Institute, St. Andrew's Society, and surviving former U.S. presidents and their widows.

Further Reading

Beckert, Sven. *The Monied Metropolis: New York City and the Consolidation of the American Bourgeoisie, 1850–1896.* Cambridge, UK: Cambridge University Press, 2001.

Derbyshire, Wyn. *Six Tycoons: The Lives of John Jacob Astor, Cornelius Vanderbilt, Andrew Carnegie, John D. Rockefeller, Henry Ford, and Joseph P. Kennedy.* London: Spiramus, 2008.

Morris, Charles R. *The Tycoons: How Andrew Carnegie, John D. Rockefeller, Jay Gould, and J. P. Morgan Invented the American Supereconomy.* New York: Henry Holt, 2005.

Nasaw, David. *Andrew Carnegie.* New York: Penguin, 2006.

Smil, Vaclav. *Creating the Twentieth Century: Technical Innovations of 1867–1914 and Their Lasting Impact.* New York: Oxford University Press, 2005.

Carpetbaggers and Scalawags

The bane of Southern conservatives from 1862 to 1877, carpetbaggers and scalawags were scornful nicknames for the politicians and opportunists who furthered the aims of Republicans to extend civil rights to former slaves. Disgruntled rebels named the newcomers "carpetbaggers" for their rapid move south after the Civil War to prey on the collapsing oligarchy and to disenfranchise white Southerners by denying them the vote. In league with freedmen and scalawags—renegade Southerners who supported the dismantling of the plantation system—carpetbaggers swayed the votes of naive and trusting blacks.

The influx of temporary residents began in 1862 with the arrival of humanitarian teachers and missionaries, whom Southerners vilified as do-gooders and meddlers for teaching blacks to read and encouraging them to demand their rights. One of these idealists, author Harriet Beecher Stowe, left Hartford, Connecticut, to run a cotton plantation in Florida to give jobs to freedmen. At her home in Mandarin on the St. Johns River, she opened a school and taught children and adults word skills from primers and spellers.

Rich Northern speculators and former Union army officers purchased prime land, tracts of hardwoods, and railroads from cash-strapped Southern aristocrats and hired freedmen to supervise cotton planting and harvesting and to restore rail lines uprooted during combat. Over a 12-year period, carpetbaggers gained 10 governors' seats, 17 U.S. Senate positions, and 45 terms in the U.S. House of Representatives. When civil uprisings threatened the peace after the election of Ulysses S. Grant to the White House in 1868, federal troops restored order and placed carpetbaggers and scalawags in positions of authority.

The term "carpetbagger" was a Southern epithet for Northerners who arrived in the former Confederate states, with no more belongings than could fit in a cloth traveling bag, seeking political power and personal fortune in Reconstruction governments. *(The Granger Collection, New York)*

The establishment of the Freedmen's Bureau on March 3, 1865, put federal clout behind President Abraham Lincoln's plan to establish racial equality while rebuilding the war-torn South. Some 50 benevolent and relief organizations, including African Methodist Episcopal, African Methodist Episcopal Zion, and American Missionary Association outreaches, cooperated with federal agents to bring immediate relief to the poor and homeless. For the bureau's 45 hospitals and 4,000 schools, the government spent $5 million and printed an agency textbook for educating 100,000 pupils. By 1870, 250,000 blacks had attended bureau schools, which were staffed primarily by Northern volunteers and evangelists. By the middle of Reconstruction, in June 1872, Congress had spent a total of $20 million on uplifting blacks from bondage to full citizenship.

The altruistic aims of Reconstruction foundered amid the turmoil created by infiltrators such as General Milton Smith Littlefield of Brooklyn, New York, dubbed the "Prince of Carpetbaggers." His taxation and railroad schemes in North Carolina and the manipulation of $4 million in public funds and railroad bonds by his partner, scalawag George William Swepson of Virginia, inflamed the Ku Klux Klan, which had formed in Pulaski, Tennessee, on December 24, 1864. Less pernicious but also hated, Harrison Reed of Massachusetts, a former U.S. treasury agent, began serving as governor of Florida in 1868, but he lacked the political savvy to control wrangling in the Republican Party.

At Galveston, Texas, in 1869, George Thompson Ruby, a militant black journalist and teacher from New York, outraged business owners by organizing dockworkers into the Labor Union of Colored Men and by incorporating insurance firms and railroads. Moses Bascom Walker, a Yale Law School graduate and Texas Supreme Court justice from Ohio, assisted the occupation by federal forces; he struggled to settle conflicting claims to the governorship before being ousted from the bench in 1873. In Louisiana, Henry Clay Warmoth, a scandal-ridden Illinois lawyer, muscled into the gubernatorial election and enforced a liberal desegregation policy that resulted in his impeachment in 1872. He purchased a sugar plantation and lobbied for higher sugar tariffs to augment his profits.

In South Carolina, under a cloud of irregularities, carpetbagger Daniel Henry Chamberlain of Massachusetts, another Yale graduate and federal law expert, drew up a new state constitution. His election as governor in 1874 raised questions of election tampering in areas where the vote count exceeded the number of registered residents. In Alabama, over a period of 11 years, U.S. Senator George Eliphaz Spencer of Champion, New York, faced charges of intimidating citizens, vote buying, embezzling state funds, and influence peddling. Similar corruption attached to the reputations of other interlopers who gained control of the South.

The ongoing differences between North and South fueled racism and diminished the efficiency of honest outsiders trying to enforce federal laws. In 1868, Congress named as governor of Arkansas and Mississippi General Adelbert Ames of Maine, a West Point graduate and Union hero at the First Battle of Bull Run. By filling civil offices with former slaves in Vicksburg on December 7, 1874, he roused white supremacists in the Red Shirts and the White League to riot against 120 black militiamen. Whites accused black sheriff Peter Crosby of forgery and embezzlement and drove him from office.

The upheaval resulted in 20 executions without trials, an injustice that stirred the wrath of British journalist Harriet Martineau. According to the federal investigation of U.S. Congressman Stephen Augustus Hurlbut, a Southerner from Charleston, South Carolina, Yankee carpetbaggers ridiculed evidence of murder. Southerners retaliated that white citizens had no choice but to fight the larceny, plunder, and fraud of Northern intruders and black secret societies. White planter James Madison "Mad" Batchelder, a veteran of the Battle of Gettysburg, referred to the suppression of Vicksburg's black protesters as "taking charge of Sambo and colonizing him."

Violence damaged the Republican Party and fueled a resurgence of Democrats, who regained legislative power in November 1875. Within months, the Mississippi legislature forced Ames to resign, along with his appointees. U.S. Senator Hiram Revels, the nation's first black senator, informed President Grant of the duplicity of carpetbaggers such as Ames, whose intent was self-empowerment through demagoguery, but the call for help came too late.

The election of President Rutherford B. Hayes in 1876 and his curtailment of Reconstruction effectively disenfranchised black Republicans. One by one, states replaced Democrats with more effective Republican officials, including U.S. Senator Blanche Kelso Bruce of Mississippi, who favored development of the Mississippi Valley and clothing allotments to black pioneers who established communities in Kansas. Democrats supplanted the glad-handing of carpetbaggers with strict Black Codes that eroded freedmen's liberties, particularly ownership of knives and guns. The withdrawal of federal troops and the return north of carpetbaggers and scalawags heightened the menace of Jim Crow laws to black citizens in the South.

See also: Freedmen's Bureau; Jim Crow; Ku Klux Klan; Reconstruction.

Further Reading

Hahn, Steven. *A Nation Under Our Feet: Black Political Struggles in the Rural South, from Slavery to the Great Migration.* Cambridge, MA: Belknap Press, 2003.

Martinez, J. Michael. *Carpetbaggers, Cavalry, and the Ku Klux Klan: Exposing the Invisible Empire.* Lanham, MD: Rowman & Littlefield, 2007.

Rable, George C. *But There Was No Peace: The Role of Violence in the Politics of Reconstruction.* Athens: University of Georgia Press, 2007.

Valelly, Richard M. *The Two Reconstructions: The Struggle for Black Enfranchisement.* Chicago: University of Chicago Press, 2004.

Waldrep, Christopher, and Michael A. Bellesiles, eds. *Documenting American Violence: A Sourcebook.* Oxford, UK: Oxford University Press, 2006.

Catholicism

Roman Catholicism, the world's largest Christian denomination, influenced patterns of worship, values, and folkways in immigrant, black, and Indian communities throughout the Americas in the 1860s and 1870s. Traditional teachings and rituals suited the needs of the humble, such as the singing of Catholic hymns and songs at the Jesuit school for freedmen in Bardstown, Kentucky; Benedictine Father Bede Marty's work at the Lakota Sioux Mission in South Dakota; and the medical clinic of Mother Mary Xavier Mehegan in Peoria, Illinois, for the sick poor.

In the archdiocese of New Orleans, missionaries dispatched by Archbishop Jean-Marie Odin evangelized and educated enslaved Africans. In Bismarck, South Dakota, Father John Chrysostom Foffa, a Swiss Benedictine, began teaching local grade schoolers at St. Mary's Academy. In Bourbon County, Kentucky, the parish eased the concern of devout survivors by burying deceased members in sanctified earth at Olivet Catholic Cemetery.

On the Atlantic Coast, the number of Roman Catholics burgeoned as non-English-speaking immigrants from Bavaria, Bohemia, Germany, Ireland, Italy, Poland, Prussia, Russia, Sicily, and Spain passed through Ellis Island, New York, Boston, and Baltimore. Boosting their numbers was the Emigrant Aid Act of 1864, which sanctioned the recruitment of skilled workers abroad. Pittsburgh grew from 20 Catholic households from Eastern and Central Europe to become a major Pennsylvania diocese. Baltimore became the nation's first archdiocese and the location of the first religious order of black women, the Oblate Sisters of Providence. Between 1860 and the 1870s, Boston's population ballooned 41 percent, from 177,840 to 250,546, forcing the annexation of Roxbury, the nation's largest enclave of Italian Catholics.

In 1863, the Roman Catholic Church hesitated to condemn slavery or to establish mission schools on plantations, where states outlawed literacy for blacks. One abolitionist in Cincinnati, Ohio, Archbishop John Baptist Purcell of Mallow, Ireland, issued an editorial in the *Catholic Telegraph* declaring human bondage a deterrent to the faith. To incite patriotism among parishioners, he flew the American flag from the cathedral spire and led German and Irish Catholics in a clash against the Know-Nothing or American Party, nativists who opposed European immigration as a source of crime, slums, and welfare taxation.

James Augustine Healy, a former slave from Macon, Georgia, and the nation's first black Catholic priest, spearheaded a protest against taxation of Boston churches and defended Catholicism as a source of socialization and education. After his promotion to bishop in Portland, Maine, Healy avoided political commentary on racism but continued to establish parishes, missions, and schools. His sister, Mother Superior Mary Magdalen (Eliza Healy), co-founded Notre Dame College, a women's institution on Staten Island, New York.

In National Conflict

During the Civil War, Catholic priests and nuns cooperated with Protestant volunteers in serving the nation with a broad range of skills. Catholic and Anglican motherhouses dispatched medical workers who debrided and sutured wounds while counseling casualties against blasphemy, obscene language, gambling, and tippling.

From New Orleans, a cadre of Daughters of Charity fanned out to battlefield work in Alabama, Florida, Mississippi, and Virginia. To increase staffing, Archbishop Jean-Marie Odin issued pleas for volunteers in the parish newspaper, *The Morning Star,* and received help from 40 seminarians and five European Ursulines. The nuns opened the Ursuline Academy of Galveston, the first parochial school for girls in Texas.

In Indianapolis, Indiana, on May 17, 1861, Mother Superior Mary Cecilia Bailly, at the request of Governor Oliver Hazard Perry Morton, organized the Sisters of Providence at City Hospital to bandage, feed, cook, clean, and launder for the wounded. At Terre Haute, the nuns took charge of soldiers at Camp Morton who were quarantined with measles. As flatboats delivered combat victims to the hospital and to medical centers in Vincennes, Bailly's partner, Sister Athanasius Margaret Fogarty of Roscommon, Ireland, carried a small basket of supplies to a log pier and risked contagion while treating enteritis, measles, and typhoid. Despite advancing arthritis, she continued convalescent care until 1871.

As medical demands increased, the Woman's Central Association of Relief chastised Dorothea Dix, head of the U.S. Sanitary Commission, for stereotyping Catholic sisters as proselytizers. Against Dix's orders, surgeons and medics welcomed convent residents for their cleanliness, humanitarianism, and obedience to orders.

In Dorchester, Massachusetts, in 1863, Irish philanthropist Andrew Carney donated $75,000 to the Daughters of Charity of St. Vincent de Paul for the establishment of Carney Hospital, New England's first Catholic Hospital. Mother Superior Ann Alexis Shorb built the 40-bed facility and began admitting Civil War casualties. Against a tide of anti-Catholic sentiment, she and ten nuns also held fund-raisers at the Dorchester Concert Hall to underwrite the education of homeless children at St. Vincent's Orphan Asylum at Camden Street.

At Emmittsburg, Maryland, Mary Euphemia Blenkinsop of Dublin, Ireland, mother superior of the Sisters of Charity, staffed an enlistment service and recruited skilled and unskilled women to volunteer for the war effort. Mother Mary of St. Angela (Eliza Maria Gillespie) and 80 Sisters of the Holy Cross staffed army facilities in Louisville and Paducah, Kentucky; Mound City, Illinois; Memphis, Tennessee; and Washington, D.C. In 1862, the Holy Cross corps worked for General Ulysses S. Grant in forming a navy nurse corps aboard the *Red Rover,* America's first "sanitary steamer." Headquartered at Cairo, Illinois, they equipped the floating hospital with an amputation theater, latrines, laundry, icebox, and kitchens and treated an average of 1,000 surgical patients per year.

The clergy and laypeople became everyday heroes by superintending charity clinics, field hospitals, and emergency wards. Nuns volunteered to approach enemy dressing stations under flags of truce and to staff refugee camps and recuperation centers for invalids and amputees. One Daughter of Charity, Sister Valentine Latouraudais, the head nurse of St. John's Infirmary in Milwaukee, Wisconsin, took as her mission the profoundly wounded, to whom she administered last rites.

In May 1864, Father Thomas O'Reilly, a Catholic chaplain for the Confederacy, ministered to army camps and hospitals in LaGrange, Marietta, and Newnan, Georgia. During the Battle of Atlanta on July 22, 1864, he superintended a sprawl of 40,000 rebel and Yankee wounded in churches, homes, hospitals, and parks. In November, he threatened to lead a mutiny of Catholic soldiers if General William Tecumseh Sherman's troops raided the Church of the Immaculate Conception or the city's Baptist, Episcopal, Methodist, and Presbyterian sanctuaries. At his urging, soldiers of the Second Massachusetts Regiment guarded his parsonage and the rest of the block to prevent arson.

Postwar Missions

For some volunteers, the end of war initiated new assignments. On May 23–24, 1865, at the Grand Review of the Armies in Washington, D.C., the Irish Brigade, inspired by Chaplain William Corby, instilled pride by marching in the parade and acknowledging their victories with a Gaelic battle cry, *fág an bealach* (clear the way).

In Baltimore, Father James Gibbons enlisted in the Union army as a volunteer chaplain to criminals and prisoners of war incarcerated at Fort Marshall and Fort McHenry, Maryland, and remained involved in Catholic missions. He secured food and medical care for rebel captives and for Union deserters and interceded in the death sentences of Confederates accused of blockade running and spying. After the war, he aided Bohemian, Irish, Italian, Polish, and Scandinavian immigrants with settlement and language problems and supported Catholic immigrant communities in the Dakotas, Illinois, Iowa, Minnesota, Nebraska, and Wisconsin. Gibbons promoted the Knights of Labor for their peaceful methods of settling labor and safety issues, and he helped Americanize and unify native and immigrant Catholics and to ease racism in labor unions.

The upsurge of the faithful fueled bigotry among Americans who demonized cities and discounted foreigners, especially Catholics and Jews, as true citizens. Old-stock American nativists feared that "papists" intended to usurp schools and the republican government and to run both according to the dictates of Pope Pius IX. Xenophobes boosted membership in the Ku Klux Klan and other pseudo-patriotic secret societies and mobilized mobs with cries of "No popery!" Rumors asserted that Catholics would proselytize freedmen and immigrants and overrun factory crews, forcing white natives out of work.

Temperance leaders targeted German and Irish Catholics for their preference for alcohol and for using saloons as bastions of male bonding against anti-immigrant persecution. St. Patrick's Day processions and demonstrations became political rallies celebrating Catholic solidarity. Newcomers lacking a command of written and spoken

English clung to the parish priest or mutual aid societies such as the Polish Roman Catholic Union of America in Chicago, the nation's oldest Polish American organization. Founded by Vincent Barzynski and Theodore Gieryk, the organization aided the semiliterate in interpreting laws and contracts. The society offered insurance and death benefits for widows and orphans, sports and recreation for children, and a source of ethnic identity for some 10,000 Polish Catholics. Aggressive Irishmen turned to more belligerent organizations, including Clan na Gael, an offshoot of the Irish Fenian Brotherhood formed in New York City in 1867, and the Molly Maguires, an agrarian fraternity that emerged from the Ancient Order of Hibernians to fight exploitation of Catholic laborers in the Pennsylvania coalfields.

Educating the Faithful

The clergy vigorously shielded children and youth from social and economic changes. Caseworkers ensured the rearing of the unwanted according to Christian principles through the work of the Society for the Protection of Destitute Roman Catholic Children in New York City. Because of the dominance of Protestant staff in public schools, illiterate Catholic parents often kept their children home. Irish Catholics in Sacramento, California, revered schools operated by Irish nuns and Christian Brothers, who taught literacy through lessons on Irish history and poetry. Such curriculums isolated rather than democratized.

A similar respect for the traditional culture in South Bend, Indiana, influenced nuns to teach classes at a girls' grade school in German rather than in English. At Warwick, Rhode Island, the village priest accommodated French and Irish Catholics with separate curricula taught in French and English. The Sisters of Charity, an apostolic order, founded bilingual academies in New England, New Jersey, New York, and Washington State.

To provide spiritual leadership, Catholic fathers chartered Boston College in 1863, the first Jesuit school in the city. For the seven-year course, students focused on Greek, Latin, philosophy, and theology. In the District of Columbia at Georgetown University, the nation's largest Catholic college, Jesuit priest Patrick Francis Healy, the first black American to earn a doctorate, taught philosophy in 1866 and liberalized professional offerings in chemistry, law, medicine, and physics. Mother Mary of St. Angela opened colleges in Austin, Texas; Baltimore, Maryland; Columbus, Ohio; Salt Lake City, Utah; and Washington, D.C. She produced two series of readers and spellers for training catechized children in elocution through essays on monasteries, Joan of Arc, "The Martyrdom of St. Agnes," the "Hymn of St. Francis," and religious liberty in Maryland.

In an anti-Catholic environment, curriculum became a religious battleground. Archbishop Martin John Spalding vilified public classrooms as godless. He extended relief funds for the war-torn South, welcomed social workers from the French Little Sisters of the Poor, and opened St. Mary's Industrial School for delinquent boys and the Association of St. Joseph to receive homeless girls, both in Baltimore. At the Second Plenary Council of Baltimore in 1866, Spalding pressed for the building of schools for black and white pupils in every parish. He instituted catechism for children attending public schools and envisioned the foundation of a Catholic university.

The Plenary Council charged parents with guarding children against anti-Catholic reading material. Councilmen promoted the purging of textbooks of antichurch doctrine and the reading of such Catholic periodicals as Baltimore's *Catholic Youth's Magazine,* Boston's *Spare Hours,* Chicago's *Young Catholic's Guide* and the *Sunday School Messenger,* New York City's *Children's Catholic Magazine* and *Youth's Temperance Banner,* and the German-language *Der Schutzengel* (The Guardian Angel). Adults had a wider choice of reading matter—the *Gazetta Polska Katolicka* (Polish Catholic Gazette) in Detroit, *Central Magazine* in St. Louis, Boston's the *Pilot,* New York City's *Metropolitan Record,* Baltimore's *Katholische Kirchenzeitung* (Catholic Church News), and Philadelphia's *The Catholic Herald and Visitor* and *The Catholic Standard.*

In 1875, President Ulysses S. Grant banned public funding of parochial education and mandated nonsectarian schooling to promote intelligence and patriotism rather than superstition and adherence to priests. To suppress religious agitation during political campaigns, Speaker of the House Gillespie Blaine (R-ME) proposed the Blaine Amendment, a constitutional separation of church and state to ban sectarianism but allow instruction in global religious history. With support from Baptists, Congregationalists, and Methodists, the House passed the bill 180-7, but the amendment failed by four votes in the Senate. States enacted the proposal, with the exception of Arkansas, Connecticut, Louisiana, Maine, Maryland, New Jersey, North Carolina, Rhode Island, Tennessee, Vermont, and West Virginia.

On the Frontier

After committing themselves to succor Indians and settlers, the clergy faced multiple dilemmas in evangelism, including the sanctioning of biracial marriage. The publication in German of *Der Wanderer,* a Catholic newspaper in St. Paul, Minnesota, raised questions about perpetuating Old World languages rather than fostering proficiency in English. Missionaries carried Catholicism to Hispanics, who made up 52 percent of the population of Phoenix, Arizona, to Wyoming Catholics in Cheyenne, to the Tohono O'odham of Arizona's Sonoran Desert, and to the Grand Ronde Reservation of Kalapuya and Upper Chinook in Oregon. Eugene Casimir Chirouse, a Catholic missionary at Everett, Washington, ministered to the Tulalip Reservation, translated scripture and a dictionary into Salish dialects, and vaccinated thousands during a smallpox outbreak in March 1862 among Pacific Coast and Puget Sound Haida and Tsimshian. In San Francisco, California, Mother Superior Mary Baptist Russell of Newry, Ireland, opened the region's first Catholic hospital, which received victims of the 1868 smallpox epidemic. She and the Sisters of Mercy also formed a visiting nurse program and established a soup kitchen and a hospice for the terminally ill.

A deadly smallpox epidemic in May 1866 at the Menominee reservation at Keshena, Wisconsin, required immediate burial of victims to maintain health standards. Non-Christians fled to the woods. Because an immigrant priest, the Reverend A.M. Joseph Mazeaud of Belgium, insisted on orthodox funerals for Christians, the disease infected 79 mourners, most of them Catholic converts. The priest went to jail for ignoring anticontagion regulations, for exhuming a corpse, and for sanctioning public wakes for the dead that spread infection to 150 victims. Although Indian Agent Moses M. Davis inoculated 800 Indians, the Menominee declined in number to 1,800. A revival of the mission by two Capuchin friars, Cajetan Krauhahn and Lucius Fuchs, subjected both men to hunger and exposure to extreme cold. The Menominee remained vulnerable to smallpox until the missionaries, Indian agents, and traders began a vaccination program in 1869.

During a failure of the Bureau of Indian Affairs to rescue prairie Indians from starvation, epidemics, and illiteracy, Catholics joined Quakers and mainline Protestants in extending missions and medical care across the West and Southwest. In 1864, the Sisters of Charity built St. John's Hospital in Leavenworth, Kansas, becoming the first females to operate a trans-Mississippi medical center.

The decline of the faithful in Tucson, Arizona, required a campaign to reconvert lapsed Catholic Mexicans, Papago, and Pima by pioneer priest Joseph Projectus Machebeuf of Lorraine, France. A missionary to New Mexico, Ohio, and Texas, he stripped orthodox ritual of pagan elements. With the aid of Father Jean-Baptiste Lamy, Machebeuf refined church work and fought depravity around Santa Fe, New Mexico. Machebeuf later built the first Catholic church in Denver, Colorado. The establishment of the Roman Catholic see at Santa Fe in 1875 with Lamy as archbishop eased tensions between Anglos and Hispanics and fostered education at parochial schools in Albuquerque, Bernalillo, Las Vegas, Mora, Santa Fe, and Taos.

See also: Damien, Father; Missions and Missionaries; Nursing.

Further Reading

Bergquist, James M. *Daily Life in Immigrant America, 1820–1870.* Westport, CT: Greenwood, 2008.

Blum, Edward J. *Reforging the White Republic: Race, Religion, and American Nationalism, 1865–1898.* Baton Rouge: Louisiana State University Press, 2005.

Butler, Jon, Grant Wacker, and Randall Balmer. *Religion in American Life: A Short History.* New York: Oxford University Press, 2007.

Dolan, Jay P. *In Search of an American Catholicism: A History of Religion and Culture in Tension.* New York: Oxford University Press, 2002.

Shea, William M. *The Lion and the Lamb: Evangelicals and Catholics in America.* Oxford, UK: Oxford University Press, 2004.

Cattle and Livestock

From Fort Myers, Florida, to Southern California, northern Montana, and parts of Hawaii, ranching and stockbreeding fostered America's first billion-dollar industry.

The financial risk was considerable to entrepreneurs such as Samuel "Burk" Burnett, a stockman and breeder of American quarter horses after 1870 at the Four Sixes Ranch at Guthrie, Texas, one of the most successful spreads in the northern part of the state. During the Panic of 1873, Burnett retained 1,100 cattle in Kansas for a year and sold the herd at a profit of $10,000. In Hawaii, the establishment of ranches required the importation of Spanish vaqueros (herdsmen), who taught cowboy skills to islanders.

In California after the Gold Rush of 1849, investment in ranches put cash-strapped breeders in an unstable financial situation. Threats to herds from flooding in 1861 and from drought during 1862 and 1864 forced Southern stockmen to reevaluate their cash flows after losing

3 million steers. Impoverished ranchers sold acreage at a cut-rate price to pay land taxes. The California economic base switched from ranching and stock to orchardry, truck farming, and tourism.

Native Americans looked on ranch stock as available meat to replace dwindling buffalo herds. Among the Southern Cheyenne of Colorado in 1861, Chief Black Kettle could not stop renegade dog soldiers from raiding corrals and barns to forage for food to supply the starving tribe. In this same period, Indians on the Owyhee River south of Boise, Idaho, stole some 450 cattle, horses, oxen, and sheep from white pioneers.

Rustling in Arizona threatened Cochise, an Apache chief and cattleman. On February 4, 1861, false arrest for allegedly running off 20 head of cattle from Sonoita Creek sent three Apaches to the gallows, including Cochise's brother Coyuntura. Resentful of white intruders on Apache land, Geronimo continued scrounging with Mangas Coloradas, Cochise's father-in-law, driving Mexican stock north across the U.S. border and pilfering supplies from townspeople.

On April 10, 1865, Black Hawk and 16 Ute warriors attacked the settlement at Manti, Utah, and drove off 40 cattle. For the next two years, Black Hawk, with aid from Colorado Utes, New Mexico Apaches, and Navajo Chief Manuelito from Four Corners, extended forays against Mormons along the Arizona–Utah border and stole 350 cattle in Scipio, Utah.

War and Profit

War raised the demand for beef. In New Mexico, Civil War sympathies goaded Texas rebels into rustling herds from Mesilla until the intervention of a Colorado regiment of miners and pioneers called "Pikes Peakers." At Lawrence, Kansas, marauder William Clarke Quantrill stole cattle and robbed farmers before becoming a Confederate guerrilla leader in Kentucky, Missouri, and Texas during the Civil War.

In Brownsville, Texas, in 1874, rustler Juan Nepomuceno Cortina, the "Red Robber of the Rio Grande," outraged cattle magnate Richard King by stealing cattle from the 860,000-acre (350,000-hectare) King Ranch. King overcame the challenge of rustlers and cyclical drought and upbred the Santa Gertrudis strain, the nation's first indigenous beef cattle.

In 1870, British attorney William Henry Blackmore and other British speculators drove out smallholders by buying up cheap land in New Mexico and turning the cattle business into easy money. For $100,000, Blackmore grabbed 2 million acres (810,000 hectares) and employed his brother, sister, and cousin to superintend cattle ranches in Colorado and New Mexico.

Because of the scarcity of herds in the East and North, cattlemen in Kansas, New Mexico, Oklahoma, and Texas could sell a steer for $40—ten times its worth in the Southwest. By the mid-nineteenth century, Texas drovers had pushed some 200,000 Spanish longhorns via the Shawnee Trail to Missouri. The cattle traveled by steamboat down the Mississippi River and over the Gulf of Mexico to New Orleans. Because many stockbreeders enlisted to fight in the Civil War, herds were left unattended. When the Texas cattlemen returned, they found their livestock doubled in number and ranging over the plains unbranded.

In isolated Montana Territory in 1860, drovers hired 20 cowboys, several wagoneers, and wranglers to tend 40 horses to complete a drive of 2,500 cattle. Active from sunrise to sunset and throughout the night on patrol, they moved at a rate of 10 miles (16 kilometers) per day, requiring two months to complete a 600-mile (960-kilometer) drive. The railhead at Abilene, Kansas, opened on September 2, 1867, and supplied beef to Chicago abattoirs and to restaurants in the Atlantic states. Oliver Loving, a blazer of the Goodnight-Loving Trail, was the first drover to herd longhorns from Texas to Chicago's cattle pens.

By the late 1860s and early 1870s, the availability of free-flowing water determined the success of the stock business, which favored former Crow lands for pasturage. Overgrazing by dairy herds and sheep forced mountain Montana stockmen to the Sun River Valley at the center of the territory. At Deer Lodge, Conrad "Con" Kohrs and John Bielenberg settled their Herefords south of the Sun River and drove marketable stock over Wyoming and Nebraska to dealers in Omaha and Chicago; Robert S. Ford and Thomas Dunn tended 1,000 head outside Fort Shaw at the Sun River Crossing and sold beef in Canada to the Royal Canadian Mounted Police.

In the mid-1870s, brothers John T., Perry J., and Sanford Moore preferred the upper Musselshell Valley. In late September 1877, Robert Coburn's herd grazed along Flatwillow Creek, where Chief Joseph and the Nez Percé bartered for meat on their flight from General Nelson A. Miles.

From Local to Eastern Markets

Cattle breeders evolved methods of increasing profitability. In Montana, to defend cattle from thievery by Blackfeet and white outlaws, Coburn joined Kohrs, Bielenberg, and other area cattlemen in coordinating mass roundups and cattle drives.

In Texas, the stringing of barbed wire fences and the use of well drills and windmills to irrigate land enabled farmers to settle on grasslands that had been too arid in the previous era of settlement.

A fabled Texan, John Simpson "Cow John" Chisum, known as the "Cattle King of the Pecos," made his mark as the owner of some 80,000 head in Paris, Texas, and Roswell, New Mexico. While outsmarting Mescalero thieves with regular herd patrols, he marketed beef to the Union army and to Apache agencies in Arizona and New Mexico. As the owner of the Jingle-Bob spread at South Spring outside Lincoln, New Mexico, he drove 600 head in spring 1867 up the Pecos River along the Goodnight-Loving Trail to sell to government contractors at Fort Sumner. When an outbreak of splenic tick fever (bovine babesiosis) required quarantines of cattle in western Missouri and eastern Kansas, Chisum became one of the first breeders to drive his herds over the Chisholm Trail to Abilene, Kansas. His face-off against land baron Major Lawrence G. Murphy involved an 18-year-old cowboy and gunman, William Henry "Billy the Kid" McCarty, and turned the Lincoln County range war into a Western myth of democracy versus greed.

In Colorado, the incorporation of open-range stockmen produced a predictable boom. Speculators profited from ample water and grassland along the South Platte River, as well as from cheap cowboy labor. The first cattle king, John Wesley Iliff, went into business in 1861 on 15,000 acres (6,100 hectares) and negotiated contracts to provide beef for crews of the Union Pacific Railroad. John Wesley Prowers built his fortune on 400,000 acres (162,000 hectares) on the Arkansas River, which supported 10,000 short-horned Herefords. In 1872, the territorial legislature passed a roundup law scheduling seasonal roundups. By 1877, the Arkansas Valley event involved 500 cowboys, 50 chuck wagons, and 3,500 mounts. Statutes covered distribution of mavericks (motherless calves). The favoritism of federal legislators toward beef barons angered smallholders by halting the fencing of small farms. By the 1880s, however, greed destroyed corporate ranching by promoting overstocking and overgrazing.

A pioneer of the meatpacking industry, Gustavus Franklin Swift developed meat cutting and distribution into a model of mass production. Trained in the butcher's trade in 1853 on Cape Cod, Massachusetts, he bought his own abattoir and meat market at age 16. In 1875, at a rail nexus of Chicago's Union Stock Yard & Transit Company, Swift set up the nation's most successful meat business. Within days of slaughtering, he dispatched fresh cuts via vans to Eastern markets. Engineer Andrew Chase extended the shelf life of cheap beef by shipping it in ice-cooled and ventilated railcars to branch meat supply markets along the Atlantic seaboard for sale to butcher shops, grocers, institutions, and steak houses. Middlemen completed the connection to small towns with personal delivery to mom-and-pop stores and delis. In addition, Swift recycled meat by-products into buttons, fertilizer, glue, knife handles, margarine, medicines, and soap. He donated profits to Northwestern University, the University of Chicago, Methodist churches, and the Young Men's Christian Association.

See also: Chisholm Trail; Colorado; Dodge City, Kansas; Goodnight-Loving Trail; Horse Breeding; Law Enforcement; Oklahoma Territory; Ranching; Range Wars; Stetson, John Batterson; Weapons.

Further Reading

Brown, Dee. *The American West.* New York: Simon & Schuster, 1995.

Cypher, John. *Bob Kleberg and the King Ranch: A Worldwide Sea of Grass.* Austin: University of Texas Press, 1995.

Hagan, William T. *Charles Goodnight: Father of the Texas Panhandle.* Norman: University of Oklahoma Press, 2007.

Lea, Tom. *The King Ranch.* Boston: Little, Brown, 1974.

Malone, Michael P., Richard B. Roeder, and William L. Lang. *Montana: A History of Two Centuries.* Rev. ed. Seattle: University of Washington Press, 1991.

Moehring, Eugene P. *Urbanism and Empire in the Far West, 1840–1890.* Reno: University of Nevada Press, 2004.

Scott, Paula A. *Santa Monica: A History on the Edge.* Charleston, SC: Arcadia, 2004.

Starrs, Paul F. *Let the Cowboy Ride: Cattle Ranching in the American West.* Baltimore: Johns Hopkins University Press, 1998.

Centennial Celebration, U.S.

At the Centennial International Exhibition of 1876, the first World's Fair in the United States, Americans celebrated independence in Philadelphia, the nation's "cradle of liberty." Throughout 1876, Americans took an interest in maps, memorabilia, and the history of the role of General George Washington and Valley Forge in the American Revolution.

Holiday planners at Windsor, Connecticut, marked sunrise on the Fourth of July with a 13-gun salute to the colonies. In Portsmouth Harbor, New Hampshire, retired

The Main Exhibition Hall at Philadelphia's Centennial Exhibition in 1876 was the largest building in the world at the time. The exposition, America's first world's fair, attracted more than 10 million visitors from May to November. *(Kean Collection/Getty Images)*

sailors posed in period uniform for a centennial photo aboard the USS *Hartford,* a sloop of war that had served during the Civil War as the flagship of Admiral David Farragut. Presbyterians in Montclair, New Jersey, hosted a display of Revolutionary War artifacts and concluded with the lighting of barrels of tar. Boys in Gloucester, Massachusetts, and in towns across the country dressed as minutemen and enjoyed a parade.

Civic and domestic elements colored observation of the centennial. Crafters in Transylvania County, North Carolina, revived colonial-style weaving and handmade furniture. In Sandusky, Ohio, residents draped their homes and trees in the national colors, held a boat race in the bay, and featured a high-wire acrobat crossing Columbus Avenue. In Clinton County, Iowa, celebrants planted the Centennial Elm. Citizens at Red Oak, Iowa, held a year-end ball based on the theme of 100 years of history. At Cape May, New Jerseyites took an interest in historical preservation; at the mouth of the Cohansey River, officials inaugurated the Ship John Shoal Lighthouse. At Newburgh, New York, thousands cheered the Fourth of July at General George Washington's headquarters at the home of Isaac Potts, a favorite site of General Benjamin Franklin Butler and veterans from the Grand Army of the Republic to reunite for regimental parades and pageantry. At Huron County, Michigan, sawmills competed to produce the largest pine planks; in Washington, D.C., rivals raced bicycles through the Palisades along the Potomac River.

To the West, citizens took pride in being part of the Union. Cities and towns strung flags across Main Street and hosted parades. Sam Cary, editor of the *West Plains* (Missouri) *Journal* issued a city history. At Cleveland, Ohio, oil baron John D. Rockefeller donated cash and land to supply the city with a park. At Stockton, California grain merchant J.D. Peters designed and erected a centennial arch proclaiming *E pluribus unum* (one out of many).

Andrew Jackson Bryant, the mayor of San Francisco, welcomed the year 1876 with a midnight ringing of 100 fire alarm bells, flag displays, rifle salutes at the armory, and rocket showers and bonfires at Brenham Place Fire Alarm Office. Banks, stock exchanges, courts, and public offices closed; ministers delivered patriotic sermons. The Master Mariner's Benevolent Association held a sailboat race from the Presidio to North Beach. Sailors conducted a mock sea battle at Harbor View. A German band marched through a triumphal arch honoring George Washington and the Marquis de Lafayette and performed "La Marseillaise," the French national anthem.

Centennial Expo

In 1866, the nation's ninetieth year, John Lyle Campbell, an astronomy and math professor at Wabash College in Crawfordsville, Indiana, proposed to Philadelphia Mayor Alexander Henry a centennial birthday party showcasing the nation's cultural and industrial achievements. Planners from the Franklin Institute, Pennsylvania General Assembly, and Philadelphia City Council welcomed the opportunity to affirm American accomplishments alongside foreign exhibits.

In 1871, Congressman William Darrah Kelley (R-PA) and industrialist Daniel Johnson Morrell stirred interest in the exposition in Congress. Joseph Roswell Hawley, a Civil War general and former governor of Connecticut, chaired the planning commission; merchant John Welsh solicited donations for the massive construction. Elizabeth Duane Gillespie, the great-granddaughter of Benjamin Franklin and a fund-raiser for the U.S. Sanitary Commission, chaired the Women's Centennial Executive Committee, which showcased a century of women's accomplishments. The powerhouses of the suffragist movement staffed the Chestnut Street headquarters.

A transportation committee scheduled the Haddington streetcar line and special Pennsylvania Railroad cars to direct people in Baltimore, New York, and Pittsburgh to 2,000 hotels and boardinghouses in Philadelphia. At the depot on Elm Avenue, passengers disembarked at the entrance to the 200 prefabricated or permanent exhibition halls and barns. Within the complex, a comfort station offered cloakrooms, lunch counters, lavatories, a parlor and a reading room, a barbershop, and the rental of wheelchairs for 60 cents an hour. For 3 cents round-trip, an elevated railway moved people from the Agricultural Hall to the Horticultural Hall. For American readers, *Harper's Weekly* posted a hot air balloon overhead and, on September 30, issued a two-page spread of attractions.

The Nation's Pride

Opening on May 10, 1876, at Fairmount Park on grounds that German American engineer Hermann J. Schwarzmann designed on the banks of the Schuylkill River, the event began with an appearance by President Ulysses S. Grant and First Lady Julia Grant. In the presence of Brazilian Emperor Dom Pedro II and Empress Teresa Christina Maria, the first couple switched on the Corliss Centennial Engine, the world's largest steam engine. Designed by inventor George Henry Corliss in Providence, Rhode Island, at a cost of $100,000, the 1,500-horsepower beam engine stood 70 feet (21 meters) tall and, with pulleys and leather belts, powered the entire show.

At the five-story headquarters on Walnut Street, bunting decorated windows. Individual exhibits enhanced the theme of "Arts, Manufactures and Products of the Soil and Mine," including an expanse of shrubs and trees from three continents—Asia, Europe, and North America—planted in the 27-acre (11-hectare) Centennial Arboretum.

The hundredth anniversary of the American republic coincided with a broad range of events: the endowment of Johns Hopkins University, Henry Bergh's organization of the American Society for the Prevention of Cruelty to Animals, evangelist Dwight Lyman Moody's revivals, the formation of the first national professional baseball league, and the admission to the Union of Colorado, which became known as the Centennial State. Most troubling to fairgoers was the Battle of the Little Bighorn, a significant American military defeat by Plains Indians on June 25, 1876. To foreign critics, the news defeated national efforts to separate citizens from charges of barbarity and to foster an atmosphere of refinement and advancement.

A total of 10,164,489 visitors paid 50 cents each to walk the 450-acre (182-hectare) fair site. Daily attendance fluctuated from a low of 12,720 to 274,919 on September 28, Pennsylvania Day. The Singer Sewing Company transported its employees free of charge to the firm's exhibit house. Visitors viewed a range of advances—Charles and Maximilian Fleischmann's yeast cakes, H.J. Heinz ketchup, John McCann's oatmeal, Chapman Maltby's dried coconut, James W. Tufts's ice cream sodas, and Charles Hires's root beer, a blend of carbonated water with 25 berries, herbs, and roots. Exhibitors popularized sugared popcorn and introduced the banana to shoppers. Wrapped in tinfoil, each banana cost a dime.

Sporting events included an international rowing match, prizefight, horse and dog shows, and Scottish games. For the occasion, the National Rifle Association held an international competition and outshot contenders from Australia, Canada, Ireland, and Scotland.

Fairgoers climbed to the telescope atop the 300-foot (91-meter) Iron Observatory on George's Hill, the nation's tallest manmade structure. Using the telescope, they got close-up views of high-wheel bicycles, mechanical reapers, Turkish marijuana, Remington typewriters, Waltham watches, an American eagle called "Old Abe," a parade of the Knights Templar, Tlingit totem poles, and the right arm and torch of the Statue of Liberty. Black attendees admired Francesco Pezzicar's *The Freed Slave,* a semi-nude image of a black man in broken shackles holding a copy of the Emancipation Proclamation.

An Educational Assemblage

The National Academy of Sciences in Washington, D.C., invited notable world scientists and dominated the entourage by hosting 8,175 of the 30,854 displays, including a model of the fishing village at Cape Ann, Massachusetts, and the nucleus of the nation's first zoo. China chose a medical show of folk cures—betel nuts, lizards, opium, seahorses, and Spanish fly. Meticulous displays of dinosaur fossils showcased the expertise of paleontologist Edward Drinker Cope. Zoologist George Brown Goode mounted stuffed specimens of North American mammals, including an elk, musk ox, polar bear, and a 15-foot (4.6-meter) walrus. The Smithsonian Institution provided exhibits focused on natural phenomena, including explorer James Gilchrist Swann's collection of Alaskan biota, botanist Mary Agnes Chase's collection of grasses, and live and painted displays of birds and fish, arranged by naturalist Spencer Fullerton Baird, the Smithsonian's secretary.

Alexander Graham Bell's "speaking telegraph" amazed visitors on June 25, 1876, when he recited a soliloquy from *Hamlet,* utilizing the device. Two models of American technology, the Gatling machine gun and the Rodman gun, a durable, 80-ton (73-metric-ton) cannon firing a half-ton (0.45-metric-ton) shot, drew viewers to the U.S. Government Building. From a network of narrow-gauge rail lines of the Denver & Rio Grande Railroad, investor James Graham Fair determined to supply Los Gatos, California, with a similar light rail system. John Fritz's contributions to the Bessemer steel process received a bronze medal. John Batterson Stetson won the Philadelphia Centennial Exposition gold medal for business acumen in shaping and marketing the Stetson hat. Other prizewinners included the Yale lock, Colgate and Pfizer chemicals, Henry Daniel Justi's line of porcelain teeth, Fairbanks scales, John Deere farm equipment, Kentucky bourbon, Campbell soups, Tiffany silver, Durner pipe organs, and Steinway pianos.

In acknowledgment of the arts, the fair committee opened on 1,000 voices singing Georg Friedrich Handel's *Hallelujah Chorus* (1741), church chimes, factory whistles, and a 100-gun salvo. German romanticist Richard Wagner composed the orchestral *Centennial Inauguration March.* Poet and musician Sidney Lanier of Macon, Georgia, wrote the cantata "Centennial Meditation of Columbia," which extolled art, science, law, and religion in American history; poet John Greenleaf Whittier produced his "Centennial Hymn," a six-stanza tribute to virtue and freedom. Johann Strauss II, the Viennese waltz king, wrote for piano "The American Exposition Waltz."

Italian Americans made a gesture to their heritage by displaying Emanuele Caroni's statue of Christopher Columbus, the nation's first honorarium to the discoverer of the Americas; Jews contributed the *Religious Liberty* statue, executed by Moses Jacob Ezekiel, a veteran of the Confederate army. Historical painter Archibald MacNeal Willard of Bedford, Ohio, mounted *The Spirit of '76,* a classic canvas featuring colonial fervor. Painter and photographer William Henry Jackson displayed photos of vanished Indian culture from Canyon de Chelly, Arizona, and shaped scale model clay and plaster casts of Anasazi petroglyphs, watchtowers, and worship kivas at the ruined Canyon of the Ancients in southwestern Colorado.

The Fair's Influence

Amid exhibits from 24 states and 37 nations, until the fair's closing on November 10, 1876, presentations of the American flag on objects and buildings reinvigorated patriotic ideals and respect for U.S. history, particularly that of the 13 original colonies. For scholars, Quaker archivists from the Friends Historical Association assembled manuscripts, tracts, and religious heirlooms to recognize the doctrinal advances and contributions of the sect to the nation's first century. For publishers, a collection of 8,000 newspapers impressed outsiders with the job of keeping the nation abreast of current events and of forming a national identity.

The fair offered suffragists a platform for protesting the limitations on women's citizenship. At Independence Hall, orator Susan B. Anthony joined Matilda Joslyn Gage in disrupting officials honoring the signing of the Declaration of Independence. Researcher and organizer Elizabeth Cady Stanton presented the "Declaration of Rights for Women," co-written by Anthony. Lucy Stone charged that female Americans ranked below rebels, freedmen, retardates, lunatics, and criminals.

Retrospectives of the Centennial Exhibition declared it a financial failure, but a boost to America's stature among nations. Foreign visitors expected to find a nation of pioneers, but came away admiring North American inventions and mechanics, including prototypes of electric dynamos, Baldwin locomotives, the cylinder press, the Line-Wolf ammonia compressor for refrigeration and ice-making, and Nikolaus Otto's internal combustion engine.

A variety of positive outcomes made the exhibition seem worthwhile. Publisher Frank Leslie took the opportunity to recycle pictures and text for an expensive commemorative or souvenir book, *Frank Leslie's Illustrated Historical Register of the United States Centennial Exposition* (1876). The London *Times* marveled at the growth of American industrial genius. British engineer John Anderson stated that Americans led the world in technological know-how. Argentina, Brazil, Chile, and Colombia chose the American system on which to model free trade. Within the year, the balance of trade favored U.S. exports and made New York City, the chief port, the nation's financial center. To achieve the same economic upsurge, Atlanta, Louisville, New Orleans, Charleston, and South Carolina, organized city fairs.

See also: Philadelphia, Pennsylvania.

Further Reading

Giberti, Bruno. *Designing the Centennial: A History of the 1876 International Exhibition in Philadelphia.* Lexington: University Press of Kentucky, 2002.

Gross, Linda P., and Theresa R. Snyder. *Philadelphia's 1876 Centennial Exhibition.* Charleston, SC: Arcadia, 2005.

Heinzen, Nancy M. *The Perfect Square: A History of Rittenhouse Square.* Philadelphia: Temple University Press, 2009.

Palmquist, Peter E., and Thomas R. Kailbourn. *Pioneer Photographers of the Far West: A Biographical Dictionary, 1840–1865.* Stanford, CA: Stanford University Press, 2000.

Central Pacific Railroad

At the beginning of the era of mechanized construction, the Central Pacific constituted the last civil engineering feat completed by manual labor. In July 1862, chief engineer Theodore Judah and his assistant, Lewis Clement, surveyed the 764-mile (1,229-kilometer) route of the Central Pacific from San Francisco through Sacramento to north-central Utah Territory. The chief, called "Crazy Judah" for his persistence, issued a monograph, *A Practical Plan for Building the Pacific Railroad* (1857), a succinct prophecy of the effects of streamlining on transportation and the railway's profitability.

Judah lobbied the project through the U.S. Congress and secured financing from the "Big Four"—Charles Crocker, Mark Hopkins, Jr., Collis Potter Huntington, and Leland Stanford, the governor of California. They faced six years of shipping equipment, rails, spikes, and blasting powder by schooner on an eight-month journey 17,000 miles (27,300 kilometers) around Cape Horn and through San Francisco. The Goss & Lombard Sacramento Iron Works assembled the first locomotives. A skilled mechanic, Andrew Jackson Stevens, became a city legend for his mastery of train engine construction.

Before the laying of the first rails in Sacramento on October 26, 1863, President Abraham Lincoln signed the Pacific Railway Act on July 1, 1862. The legislation guaranteed the Central Pacific and Union Pacific railroads public lands and timber rights for building stations, rail sidings, and machine shops. Congress allotted the builders $16 per mile of track, with a rate of $48 per mile for track laid through mountain routes. The project required the dynamiting of steep grades and the construction of water tanks, service yards, trestles, retaining walls, and culverts.

The Pacific Railway Act angered San Francisco Mayor Henry Perrin Coon, who refused to issue the required $650,000 in government bonds. The *Sacramento Daily Union* demonized the railroad as a land grab and an enslaver of the local labor force to the tyrant Stanford. Nonetheless, Sacramento profited from the complex of produce storehouses and maintenance and repair shops and from the construction of freight cars, cabooses, tankers, dining cars, and passenger coaches. The work boosted the economy with 4,378 jobs, paying $2,300 per year. The payroll of $10 million represented 48 percent of the city's annual industrial income.

Chinese Labor

Despite the imposition of a $2.50 per month tax on Chinese workers under the California Anti-Coolie Act of April 26, 1862, some 12,000 laborers emigrated from the farms of Guangdong Province in southern China to construction camps east of Sacramento. The mammoth project required rappelling down bluffs in baskets or on seats suspended from ropes, boring holes and footholds by hand with mauls and steel drills, and filling crevices with black powder at the rate of 500 kegs per day. Each mile of track consisted of 400 rails, each rail weighing 500 pounds (225 kilograms) and requiring 10 spikes to secure it.

The work plunged the men into desert heat and on sledges and two-wheeled carts over the Sierra Nevada summit. Most onerous for crews was the coring of the Sierra Madre with 42 tunnels totaling 6,213 feet (1,894 meters). In winter 1866–1867, they endured 44 blizzards leaving drifts as high as 40 feet (12 meters). Crocker bought 12-foot (3.7-meter) snowplows for the locomotives, which jumped the tracks because of ice. To protect the investment, at a cost of $12 million, he erected snow sheds over the 40 miles (64 kilometers) of track crossing the Sierras, which enabled crews to work through the winter.

For $30 per month, the Chinese, called "celestials," lived above abysses and within range of rockslides and slept in 34 miles (54 kilometers) of bunkers yards deep in snow. Using shoulder yokes, the men balanced loads of rubble left and right. When granite summits at Cisco proved too hard for dynamite, engineers resorted to Alfred Nobel's "blasting oil" (nitroglycerine), introduced in 1867.

Overall, 1,200 workers died from falls, crushing injuries, and explosions. To treat injured crewmen, the company in November 1868 opened the four-story, 125-bed Central Pacific Hospital in Sacramento and subsidized worker casualty insurance. Because white laborers earned higher wages than Asian workers, 2,000 coolie tunnelers organized a sit-down strike in June 1867 and negotiated a raise to $35 per month. Thomas Nast, cartoonist for *Harper's Weekly,* satirized the brutality of white Californians against a peaceable, unarmed race.

Obstacles to Progress

Samuel S. Montague succeeded Judah as chief engineer after the latter died of yellow fever, contracted on a trip to Panama in November 1863—barely a month after the project began. Progress was steady as the rails inched northeast from Sacramento, reaching Truckee River, Nevada, by April 1868 and Promontory Summit, Utah, a year later. In the arid stretches across the Great Basin, crews occupied tent cities and rationed water. In the last miles of the Central Pacific, Utah Territory provided Mormon laborers to grade cuts and slopes.

Efficient labor methods pushed the project seven years ahead of schedule. The territory gained prominence in transportation history on May 10, 1869, when the Transcontinental Railroad reached completion at Promontory Summit. Eight years and four months after its incorporation, a gold spike joined the Central Pacific line with the Union Pacific Railroad. Stanford presided over the driving of the ceremonial spike in the united rails. Four months later, on September 6, the final leg of the railway connected Sacramento to the seaport of Oakland, California.

The nation celebrated the transcontinental feat with speeches, bonfires and fireworks, cannon salutes and parades, and, in Philadelphia, the ringing of the Liberty Bell. Streamlined transportation replaced wagon trains and long sea journeys and reduced overland travel from New York to San Francisco from 21 days to 8 days. Fare for the 3,350-mile (5,390-kilometer) route was $65. With the influx of settlers, prospectors, and investors, the population of Utah reached 86,800 by 1870, more than twice the 40,275 counted in 1860.

For its control of labor and transportation, the Central Pacific dominated the California economy and political scene. The Central Pacific Railroad named its first locomotive the *Governor Stanford,* a subsequent engine the *C.P. Huntington,* and a freight hauler *El Gobernador* after the ex-governor, who chaired the rail company. The Central Pacific monopoly relocated its headquarters from Sacramento to San Francisco and absorbed river barges, stage and freight lines, ferries, riverboats, cable cars, realty, and oil and timber firms. The Occidental & Oriental Steamship Company extended international trade by hauling Central Pacific freight and passengers to Hawaii, China, and Japan.

See also: Stanford, Leland.

Further Reading

Ambrose, Stephen E. *Nothing Like It in the World: The Men Who Built the Transcontinental Railroad, 1863–1869.* New York: Simon & Schuster, 2001.

Avella, Steven M. *Sacramento: Indomitable City.* Charleston, SC: Arcadia, 2003.

Bianculli, Anthony J. *Trains and Technology: The American Railroad in the Nineteenth Century.* Vol. 3, *Track and Structures.* Newark: University of Delaware Press, 2003.

Cox, Don, and Paula Boghosian. *Sacramento's Boulevard Park.* Charleston, SC: Arcadia, 2006.

Palmquist, Peter E., and Thomas R. Kailbourn. *Pioneer Photographers of the Far West: A Biographical Dictionary, 1840–1865.* Stanford, CA: Stanford University Press, 2000.

Cereals and Grains

From prehistory, the harvesting of grain assured agrarian communities satisfying meals as well as forage for herds and a portable trade commodity. In the 1860s, the home economics movement in the United States focused on whole-grain bread making, a daily task that became a symbol of dedicated domesticity. According to the cookbooks of the day, loaves and dinner rolls provided the family with a compact form of nutrition and protected individuals from dyspepsia.

Domestic mavens Catharine Beecher and Harriet Beecher Stowe, authors of *The American Woman's Home, or Principles of Domestic Science* (1869), warned housewives to buy the purest flour and yeast, to protect their staples from vermin and adulterants, and to alternate the use of wheat with barley, buckwheat, corn meal, oats, rice, and rye. In Boston cooking schools, women from tenements learned to invest in inexpensive whole grains and dried legumes rather than costly meats to feed their families. The advent of dietetics lionized grain for its diversity in feeding infants and nursing mothers, invalids, the elderly, and victims of chronic disease.

The Civil War threatened grain farming by raising the price of implements and seed, and by reducing cash-strapped farmers to cultivation of less acreage. After the 1862 military draft in both the North and the South pulled men from their land, women as far south as Ocala, Florida, superintended wheat planting and harvesting to meet the demands of their families and the military for bread. Slaves maintained small patches of millet and corn for their families' consumption and built corncribs to store the harvest for use in winter. For sweeteners, they valued sorghum, a plant imported from Africa and grown in the South, and made molasses, the standard accompaniment to cornbread.

The freeing of slaves on January 1, 1863, ended labor-intensive riziculture (cultivation of rice) from Wilmington, North Carolina, to northern Florida. Simultaneously, the importation of coolie laborers from Guangdong Province, China, to build the Transcontinental Railroad revived interest in rice as an alternative to corn, oats, and wheat. Demand for rice resituated cultivation from the Atlantic Coast Lowcountry and Louisiana to the Sacramento Valley, the nation's new rice bowl.

To avoid the concentration of a single grain in one area, railcars, elevators, and silos moved and housed supplies. The combined effect of such technology and improved farming methods made possible the exportation to Great Britain of an unparalleled 50 million bushels (1.76 trillion liters) of grain.

On the Frontier

As wagon trains moved west, the transport and protection of grain proved onerous to families beset by Indian attacks, insect plagues, and daily fording of rivers. Settlers of the frontier left behind ready supplies of pearl millet and buckwheat for cereal, vetch from Maryland and Virginia, and clover and timothy for hay from New England, New York, and Pennsylvania. After crossing the Continental Divide, they depended on bulk shipments of buckwheat, oatmeal, corn meal, rice, and wheat flour, as well as salt, dried beef, whiskey and medicines, fruit, and delicacies to ease the monotony of the frontier diet of game, fish, and wild greens.

In lieu of regular deliveries, families relied on such preserved foodstuffs as salt pork, jerky, dried peas, and hardtack, a tasteless, thrice-baked wheat cracker made palatable by soaking in water, milk, or gravy. For scouts and Pony Express riders, saddlebag meals of jerky with pone or biscuits required only one hand for dining on the gallop. Bakers and innkeepers struck a bonanza in mining, timber, and railway camps by providing prospectors and crew with loaves of bread, biscuits, cookies, and cakes.

For variety, along the Great Lakes, traders obtained from the Anishinabe, Menominee, Ojibwa, and Winnebago traditional wild rice, a perennial grass seed that Indian women dried in the sun, winnowed in baskets, and cooked with maple sugar and blueberries. Idaho developed a reputation among farmers for dry, cold weather suited to stock pasturing, orchards, and the harvesting of grains, wild grasses, and wild rye. Wisconsin farmers experimented with alfalfa, a digestible fiber for stock; the Dakotas and Minnesota dominated trade in flaxseed, a source of linseed oil. Sonoma, California, dominated the growing of hops for brewing beer. Farther south in New Mexico, log flumes irrigated the San Juan Valley into lush pastures and grain fields. Despite violent outbreaks among the Santee Dakota in the Dakotas and Minnesota, the flatlands drew grain farmers, who plowed virgin prairie to raise wheat. From Nebraska to Oklahoma and Texas, livestock depended on fields of sorghum, a forage crop suited to southern heat. A related seed plant, broomcorn enriched Oklahomans with a crop that supplied dry bristles for brooms and household brushes.

The Great Plains states quickly adapted to Indian corn as a staple. Farm communities profited from rapid settlement and the demand for grain from railroad crews, the military, Indian agents, trading posts, and missions. Pragmatic frontierswomen varied their corn-based meals with breakfasts of johnnycakes or cooked cereal, packable lunches of roasted ears, snacks of parched corn, and suppers of hominy, corn and potato chowder, or corn mush and milk.

In 1863, the demand for grain in Canyon de Chelly, Arizona, caused the Navajo to revolt against General James Henry Carleton over army control of grazing land and the government's failed delivery of promised grain and hay supplies. Hungry Plains nations, in lieu of living off of the dwindling buffalo herds, stole grain from whites. Members of tribes bound by the Medicine Lodge Treaty of 1867 deserted reservations to hunt and to loot corrals, barns, and grain sheds. The Kiowa and Kwahadi Comanche raided west Texas as far south as the Red River and seized grain to prevent malnutrition and starvation.

By 1870, as corn developed into the world's top feed grain, the nation's yield reached 1 million bushels (35 million liters). Two years later, the United States led the world in the increase of grain production. In 1873, corn cultivation expanded to more than 34 million acres (13.8 million hectares). According to estimates published by the U.S. Department of Agriculture, harvests of the six major grains thrived and increased from 1871 to 1876 (in number of bushels):

Grain	1871	1876	Percentage Increase
Barley	31,014,098	40,169,195	29.5
Buckwheat	8,479,720	11,970,031	41.2
Corn	1,037,621,700	1,455,988,117	40.3
Oats	278,503,300	384,500,652	38.1
Rye	15,621,820	23,113,596	48.0
Wheat	272,442,580	404,195,909	48.4
Total:	**1,643,683,218**	**2,319,937,500**	41.1

Members of the Grange (National Grange of the Order of Patrons of Husbandry), led by Oliver Hudson Kelley, a staff member of the U.S. Department of Agriculture, protected grain and forage farmers by promoting Granger laws in Illinois, Iowa, Minnesota, and Wisconsin. The legislation fought corrupt middlemen by regulating stockyards, warehousing, grain elevators, cooperative silos, and freight rates.

See also: Armour, Philip Danforth; Brewing; Grange Movement.

Further Reading

Barron, Hal S. *Mixed Harvest: The Second Great Transformation in the Rural North, 1870–1930.* Chapel Hill: University of North Carolina Press, 1997.

Conlin, Joseph R. *The American Past: A Survey of American History.* 9th ed. Boston: Wadsworth/Cengage Learning, 2009.

Sherow, James E. *The Grasslands of the United States: An Environmental History.* Santa Barbara, CA: ABC-CLIO, 2007.

Smith, Andrew F., ed. *The Oxford Companion to American Food and Drink.* New York: Oxford University Press, 2007.

Snodgrass, Mary Ellen. *Encyclopedia of Kitchen History.* New York: Fitzroy Dearborn, 2004.

Charleston, South Carolina

In the 1860s and 1870s, Charleston, South Carolina, experienced extremes of Southern social and economic restructuring. In 1860, the city, a major Atlantic Coast slave exchange, exemplified the worst of the plantation economy. At the confluence of the Ashley and Cooper rivers, its merchants traded in fresh produce and seafood, sweetgrass baskets, and cotton, phosphate, and salt exports, all produced by slave labor.

The plutocracy, consisting of the upper 5 percent of the population, allowed interracial marriage but rejected economic diversification. They vilified industry as a disruption of domestic peace and social order, which they maintained by slave patrols. While white aristocrats south of Broad Street enjoyed gracious living and leisure, blacks toiled. In violation of the law, free blacks organized secret schools to advance the cause of literacy. Because of their vigor, people of African heritage influenced Lowcountry cookery, music, gardening, and storytelling in the Gold Coast dialect known as Gullah.

Secession put the population in danger and idled clerks, mechanics, merchants, and stevedores. The election of Republican President Abraham Lincoln in 1860 enraged white Charlestonians. Lincoln's threat to the Southern economy prompted South Carolina to withdraw from the Union on December 20. The defection triggered a domino effect among ten other proslavery states in the South.

On January 9, 1861, as the steamer *Star of the West* delivered supplies to Fort Sumter, white cadets at the exclusive Citadel military academy, alerted by Cadet William Stewart Simkins and led by Cadet John Marshall Whilden, fired cannon at U.S. Army recruits, the first Union soldiers to dodge rebel shots. The attack was one of eight engagements involving the academy. The

Robert Barnwell Rhett, Jr., proslavery editor of the extremist *Charleston Mercury* and the "Father of Secession," declared that the Confederacy could not survive emancipation: "Hack at the root of the Confederacy—our institutions—our civilization—and you kill the cause as dead as a boiled crab." Rhett smeared the era's most controversial figure, President Abraham Lincoln, as a proponent of miscegenation and biracial families and charged that his vice president, Hannibal Hamlin, was a mulatto.

school sent 36 cadets to war in June 1862 and lost one-third of the combatants to the conflict.

Harbor War

Before the firing on Fort Sumter on April 9, 1861, P.G.T. Beauregard, the Confederacy's first general, inspected the harbor and, in conference with Governor Francis Wilkinson Pickens, planned upgrades to redoubts and coastal defenses. Completed with 153 black volunteers, the munitions and earthworks extended to the bay with cannon emplacements and a signal outpost at the White Point Gardens bathhouse, located at the city's southern tip.

Because Lincoln refused to grant an audience to Southern emissaries, on April 12, Confederate President Jefferson Davis plotted the bombardment of Fort Sumter in Charleston Harbor, the first official engagement of the Civil War. After the rebel seizure of the island fort, Charleston residents took a front-row seat to Civil War harbor blockading and the smuggling of munitions, supplies, and mail to the Confederacy. Memoirist Mary Chesnut made a meticulous record of events, some of which she observed from the roof of her house.

Teeming with free persons of color, the city became a bulwark of Southern stoicism and of race and class consciousness. Historian Benjamin Arthur Quarles dubbed Charleston the "Confederate Holy of Holies." Of the white men aged 15–50 who departed to war, one-quarter died in the conflict. Of necessity, white women turned their hedged gardens into vegetable patches; blacks took over civil jobs, particularly in fire companies, a shield against Union attack.

On September 18, 1861, Castle Pinckney, a mile off the coast on Folly Island, housed the first 156 prisoners of war. Under guard by the city's Zouave (light infantry) cadets, Union soldiers captured at the First Battle of Bull Run on July 21 lived well in clean surroundings, compared to the unspeakable conditions at Andersonville and Libby prisons.

In summer 1862, yellow fever spread up the Atlantic Coast by ship, killing 42 percent of those infected. Increasing fear, the Union capture of the Sea Islands, Beaufort, Hilton Head, and Port Royal forced white families to move from the coast to the interior in order to avoid invasion or an insurrection of some 15,000 black refugees seeking freedom behind enemy lines. To defend Charleston, the Confederate navy began constructing ironclad ships, including the CSS *Chicora* and *Palmetto State.*

Liberating Conflict

Whites could not overlook the temptation that lured their slaves to flee bondage. Fearing sale and permanent separation from his wife, steamboatman and former slave William Summerson in late April 1862 arranged with a vegetable vendor to hide him in a rice cask and drive him past sentries. The next day, Anne Summerson joined her husband north of the Ashley River. They paddled a boat to the Stono River and surrendered to a Union flagship, the USS *Pawnee,* where Summerson offered information that led to the capture of two Southern ships. In response to such opportunities to run, slave owners increased curfew vigilance and restricted black congregations from holding prayer meetings and fishermen from venturing into the bay.

A boost to black pride came on May 12, 1862, when black navigator Robert Smalls loaded his family—his wife Hannah and their children, Elizabeth and Robert, Jr.; Smalls's brother, engineer John Smalls; and John's two children—on the steamer *Planter.* Smalls piloted the ship through Charleston Harbor past sentries at Fort Moultrie and Fort Sumter to the clipper USS *Onward* and hoisted a white truce flag. With the detailed information he provided about torpedo placement, the Union navy plotted an assault on James Island.

As casualties increased, field medics turned the Methodist church at Bennett and Hibben streets and Mount Pleasant Presbyterian Church into hospitals. On October 4, 1862, pro-Union barber Thomas Brown helped Northern officers escape Roper Hospital by supplying the patients with Confederate uniforms. Black rescuers concealed the escapees for a month until the officers could flee the South.

In April 1863, the Union navy began carpeting Charleston with a 587-day bombardment by gunboats. Shelling with grapeshot and canisters left Meeting Street in ruins. Business owners, doctors, and bankers retrenched out of cannon range; families retreated inland to Camden and Columbia. By late October 1863, the *Charleston Mercury* predicted a slim chance of Thanksgiving dinner for Confederate soldiers, whose rations were limited by irregular supply.

William Henry Shelton published in *The Century Magazine* "A Hard Road to Travel out of Dixie" (1890), a memoir of his flight from a Charleston prison in December 1863 with Albert T. Lamson and Edward E. Sill. On their way to the Great Smoky Mountains, a black community spread a feast in a barn, offering an array of farm specialties—pork pie, sausage, yams, biscuits with sorghum, and milk. In reference to escaping prisoners, General Beauregard summarized the difficulties of port control in his *Report on the Defense of Charleston* (1864) and indicated the value of Fort Wagner to guard the main shipping channel into the city. The threat of harbor breach demanded constant military and civilian surveillance, which staved off an amphibious assault on Johns Island in July 1864.

After the capture of Columbia, Union General William Tecumseh Sherman chose to let Charleston collapse from attrition. In fall 1864, his field order awarded the islands south of Charleston to the newly liberated, who settled on abandoned rice plantations. On November 9, slaves aided Lieutenant James M. Fales and two other Union officers in escaping a city prison to the safety of an abandoned barn. Black families donated food and kept watch for pickets while the weary men slept. Out of vengeance, Confederate soldiers deliberately shot disloyal blacks who fought for the enemy.

A New Charleston

By 1865, white Charlestonians despaired for the antebellum South. On February 17, 1865, General William J. Hardee evacuated rebel troops, leaving the city to Union General Alexander Schimmelfennig, who freed all slaves. Fewer than 12,000, or 30 percent of city residents, remained behind. As a gesture of defiance, departing soldiers exploded the artillery that guarded Battery Row, spiked heavy guns to render them useless, and burned cotton sheds, warehouses, torpedo boats, and shipyards.

In the last weeks of the war, as thousands of whites boarded trains to the northwest, federal forces confiscated the Citadel and ruled the city. Marching north from Savannah, Sherman considered Charleston the birthplace of the war and a combat prize. He burned the city but missed the historic College of Charleston. One of the first nurses to arrive was Susie King Taylor, an escapee from slavery in Savannah, Georgia, who observed defeated whites sneering at black insurgents.

Before war's end, widows began working alone or in groups at the regular tending of gravesites, which involved pulling grass, planting violets and other perennials, and sweeping away dead leaves. By 1865, docking at Charleston, South Carolina, slowed to light traffic because of the debris of 30 ships wrecked by the Union navy. After the Confederate surrender at Appomattox, Virginia, blacks fired the harbor guns in celebration. Black soldiers returned to their former homes with an eye toward vengeance, especially against white police officers. Skirmishing and street brawls marred the city's attempt at restoring peace.

During Reconstruction, Charlestonians faced hunger and waves of rootless freedmen, who turned for aid to the city's vigorous black populace. The 3,232 freedmen formed nearly 20 percent of the citizenry. Of particular attraction for former male slaves were young freedwomen, who outnumbered free males two to one. Many of them had been the concubines of planters and were the mothers of mulatto children.

Without servants, the city of gardens suffered damage and neglect, but the harbor once more accommodated pleasure boats and ferries from the dock at Ferry Street to Mount Pleasant across the bay. Blockade running turned merchant and financier George Walton Williams into a millionaire. With the proceeds, he became the first homeowner to rebuild after the war, constructing a 24,000-square-foot (2,230-square-meter) Italianate mansion at 16 Meeting Street, the largest example of Charleston grandeur. The post office reinstated mail service and advertised in the newspapers the arrival of mail for residents of outlying villages.

Trade flourished from wagons parked across from the Charleston Hotel; horse-drawn trollies carried sightseers past architectural treasures. Sweetgrass weavers set up stands on heavily traveled roads and performed their craft for the curious. Others sold flowers, herbs, and potions. Many found work mining phosphate rock or raising cotton on James Island tenant farms. White planters controlled tenant farmers' profits by forming the James Island Agricultural Society.

Politics seethed with jealousies and desire for revenge. Charlestonians of all colors disdained the arrival of carpetbaggers from New England. After passage of the Fourteenth and Fifteenth amendments, blacks joined the Republican Party and elected 124 delegates to the state constitutional convention, 57 percent of whom were black males. For the next decade, half of the 18-man Charleston city council was black. Divisions among Republicans arose from the wavering loyalty of mulattos—Benjamin A. Boseman, the Reverend Francis Lewis Cardozo, Robert Carlos DeLarge, William McKinlay, and Edward P. Wall—because they were kin to white aristocrats. Darker politicians, led by Martin Robinson Delany, known as the "Father of Black Nationalism," resented the pomposity of mulattos who held high positions in government. John Scanlon and others bought abandoned plantations and formed black communities east of the city at Phillip and Remley's Point, a cooperative run by the black-owned Charleston Land Company. The Longshoremen's Protective Association struck on city wharves to demand higher wages.

In a populace that was three-quarters black, Northern missionaries aided former slaves in forming their own churches and schools. At the Avery Normal Institute, the American Missionary Association, led by Francis Cardozo, prepared 400 students for college and trained teachers for classrooms.

White supremacists, backed by the paramilitary Red Shirts, fought back in 1876 through election fraud to select the first postwar Democratic governor, Wade Hampton, hailed as the "Savior of South Carolina." The foundering of the Republican Party allowed Democratic legislators to suppress black civil rights and create Black Codes and Jim Crow laws that segregated black citizens from Charleston schools, fire and police battalions, hospitals, and cemeteries.

See also: Jim Crow.

Further Reading

Coakley, Joyce V. *Sweetgrass Baskets and the Gullah Tradition.* Charleston, SC: Arcadia, 2005.

Horton, James Oliver, and Lois E. Horton. *Slavery and the Making of America.* New York: Oxford University Press, 2005.

Jenkins, Wilbert L. *Seizing the New Day: African Americans in Post–Civil War Charleston.* Bloomington: Indiana University Press, 2003.

Spruill, Marjorie Julian, Valinda W. Littlefield, and Joan Marie Johnson. *South Carolina Women: Their Lives and Times.* 2 vols. Athens: University of Georgia Press, 2009.

Chase, Salmon P. (1808–1873)

A lifelong libertarian, Salmon Portland Chase had a distinguished career in politics and law, serving as a U.S. senator and governor of Ohio, secretary of the treasury in the cabinet of President Abraham Lincoln, and chief justice of the United States.

A scion of New England patriots, he was born on January 13, 1808, in Cornish, New Hampshire, to farmer and taverner Ithamar Chase and Janette Ralston Chase, a Scots immigrant. After his father's death from paralysis in 1817, his mother supported Salmon and his nine surviving siblings. Salmon attended a private elementary school taught by his sister in Keene and studied Latin for three years at Colonel Dunham's school in Windsor, Vermont. With guidance from his mother, he absorbed accounts of federal politics in the *Columbian* and the *Washingtonian.*

In 1820, he lived with an aunt and uncle, Sophia May Ingraham Chase and Philander Chase, the Episcopal bishop of Ohio and founder of Kenyon College, and studied New Testament Greek at a parochial school in Worthington. When the uncle became president of Cincinnati College in 1822, Salmon spent his sophomore year there. He then returned to New Hampshire, taught in Vermont at Roxbury and at Royalton Academy for boys, and studied law at Dartmouth College in New Hampshire, graduating Phi Beta Kappa in 1826.

At 18, Chase moved to Washington, D.C., and taught at a classical seminary. With an introduction to law from U.S. Attorney General William Wirt, he was admitted to the bar in 1829, set up a practice at Cincinnati in 1830, and began compiling a three-volume annotated collection, *The Statutes of Ohio and of the Northwestern Territory* (1833–1835).

The death of his first wife, Katherine Jane Garmiss, from puerperal fever in 1835 inspired Chase to do good works. During his marriage to Eliza Ann Smith, he joined the Cincinnati Anti-Slavery Society, founded by journalist Gamaliel Bailey. With fellow attorney Rutherford B. Hayes, Chase offered pro bono legal counsel to fugitive slaves and Underground Railroad agents.

After his second wife died of tuberculosis in 1845, Chase became more involved in slave rescue and earned the nickname "Attorney General for Fugitive Slaves." Before the U.S. Supreme Court, he contested the constitutionality of the Fugitive Slave Law of 1850, which forced citizens to assist in the recapture of runaways. His third wife, Sarah Bella Dunlop Ludlow, also died from tuberculosis in 1852, leaving daughters Katherine "Kate" and Janette "Nettie" Ralston in his care.

Chase partnered with lawyers Francis Jackson, Samuel Gridley Howe, Horace Mann, Robert Morris, and Samuel Edmund Sewall in defending Captain Daniel Drayton, who attempted the rescue of 77 runaways aboard the sloop *Pearl* from Georgetown to New Jersey. In efforts to stop the spread of slavery to the frontier, Chase co-founded both the Liberty and Free-Soil parties.

A Presence in Politics

In 1849, Chase led the abolitionist contingent in the U.S. Senate and introduced the Pacific Railway Act, which ultimately produced the Transcontinental Railroad. He joined attorney Abraham Lincoln and Congressman Joshua Reed Giddings, a slave rescuer, in outlining the abolition of slavery in the District of Columbia. After passage of the Fugitive Slave Law, Chase and colleagues John Parker

Hale, Charles Sumner, and Benjamin Wade publicly denounced the statute, which made abolitionists complicit in slave recapture.

In 1855, Ohioans elected Chase to the first of two terms as governor, making him the first state executive to be elected from the Republican Party. From this position, he advocated prison reform, public schools, treatment of the mentally ill, and woman suffrage. On May 24, 1859, he joined attorney John Mercer Langston in convincing an audience in Cleveland, Ohio, of President James Buchanan's favoritism toward the slaveholding South. In 1860, Chase won reelection to the Senate.

Upon Lincoln's election to the presidency, Chase vacated his Senate seat to join the cabinet as secretary of the treasury. Secretary of State William Henry Seward collaborated with Chase and Secretary of War Edwin M. Stanton on a survey of Washington politicians for evidence of disloyalty to the Union. Chase urged Lincoln to defy slavers and end the Civil War by enlisting blacks in the Union army. In 1862, he appealed to pragmatism by reminding the president that the military would not suffer the absence of a few Quaker conscientious objectors.

Chase levied the nation's first income tax and oversaw the federal chartering of banks, mandated by the National Bank Act of February 26, 1863, which standardized a national currency system based on federal bank notes. He printed paper money and negotiated with Jay Cooke & Company for the sale of government bonds to pay a war debt of more than $20 billion. In 1864, Chase added the words "In God We Trust" to all U.S. currency. Because his picture appeared on dollar bills, people nicknamed him "Old Greenbacks."

Chief Justice

In the mid-1860s, Horace Greeley, editor of the *New York Tribune,* made a tentative nomination of Chase for president, an office that Chase coveted. In December 1865, after Lincoln appointed Chase to the U.S. Supreme Court as chief justice, the jurist became an activist for the judicial branch of government during a tangle of litigation, judging cases concerning threats to the Union and to civil rights posed by Reconstruction and loyalty oaths. He immediately named John Rock, an attorney from Massachusetts, as the court's first black advocate. On April 3, 1866, Chase freed four condemned men from prison for involvement in an assassination plot. Historians lauded the action as a triumph for constitutional liberty over extreme overreaching by the War Department, which made 13,535 political arrests during the Civil War without due process.

The first chief justice to head the impeachment trial of a president, Chase presided over an 1867 hearing that charged President Andrew Johnson with contempt of Congress and exceeding executive authority. Under Johnson's general amnesty to secessionists, Chase freed former Confederate President Jefferson Davis, who had been jailed on charges of treason. In 1869, Chase delivered landmark decisions that outlawed secession by individual states (*Texas v. White*) and defended a 10 percent tax on state bank notes (*Veazie Banks v. Fenno*).

After suffering a stroke and heart attack in 1870, Chase slowly resumed responsibilities to the bench. He continued supporting full citizenship for blacks and, in 1872, co-founded the Liberal Republican Party. He died of paralytic stroke on May 7, 1873, in New York City. In 1934, the U.S. Treasury honored Chase by placing his portrait on the $10,000 bill.

See also: Ex Parte Milligan (1866).

Further Reading

Davis, David Brion, and Steven Mintz, eds. *The Boisterous Sea of Liberty: A Documentary History of America from Discovery Through the Civil War.* New York: Oxford University Press, 1998.

Goodwin, Doris Kearns. *Team of Rivals: The Political Genius of Abraham Lincoln.* New York: Simon & Schuster, 2005.

Graber, Mark A. *Dred Scott and the Problem of Constitutional Evil.* Cambridge, UK: Cambridge University Press, 2006.

Towers, Frank. *The Urban South and the Coming of the Civil War.* Charlottesville: University of Virginia Press, 2004.

Chesnut, Mary (1823–1886)

As an antidote to fear and depression, diarist Mary Boykin Miller Chesnut of South Carolina captured the panic and stoicism of noncombatants as the Civil War swept over the Confederacy. Born on March 31, 1823, in Statesburg, she was the eldest of four children of Mary Whitaker Boykin and Stephen Decatur Miller, South Carolina's governor. She bore the name of her mother and maternal grandmother, Mary Whitaker Boykin, a matriarch of the Southern aristocracy.

She learned reading from her paternal grandmother, Margaret Moore White Miller, and basic skills at a day school several miles away in Camden. In fall 1835, she began studying French, German, history, literature, music, rhetoric, and science at Madame Talvande's French School for Young Ladies on Legare Street, an elite academy in the heart of the Charleston Battery. During a month-long trip to Mississippi, she developed sympathy for blacks and realized that Charlestonians dismissed bondage as a harmless institution. At age 17, she married attorney James Chesnut, Jr., a future U.S. senator and secessionist, and lived in Camden at Kamchatka, a three-story mansion.

At the heart of her plaint lay a denunciation of patriarchy and the hypocrisy of male monogamy, including that of her husband James, whose career moves determined her destiny. On the eve of war, the Chesnuts settled in Charleston while James served as aide-de-camp to Confederate General P.G.T. Beauregard. On April 12, 1861, while staying at the John Rutledge household at 116 Broad Street on Battery Row, Mary observed the Confederate predawn firing on Fort Sumter and knelt to pray for the South.

On April 23, she retreated to Mulberry Plantation, the Chesnut homestead on the Wateree River south of Camden, but she continued to receive reports on Charleston, where privateers dared breach the Union blockade. She summarized foundry and clothing factory production of armor and uniforms and, initially, believed that coastal defense would suffice against the Union. Her faith wavered on December 13, 1861, while a fire of suspicious origin consumed Charleston from East Bay and down Broad Street river to river.

War's Specter

With her frequent moves and daily reading of the press from Charleston, New York, Richmond, and Washington, D.C., Mary Chesnut acquired a liberal view of the South's ruin. While her husband served as chief of staff to Confederate President Jefferson Davis in Richmond, she befriended first lady Varina Howell Davis.

The diarist's dozen volumes summarized the end of slavery and the funerals of relatives and friends killed in the conflict. To those infected with typhoid fever at a Charlottesville hospital, Chesnut sent a supply of white sugar. In late August 1861 at Robertson Hospital on Main and Third streets in Richmond, she delivered peaches and grapes to administrator Captain Sally Louisa Tompkins, the only woman holding an officer's rank in the Confederate army.

While fever—probably malaria—kept Chesnut housebound for part of 1862, she reported on military scuttlebutt and on the snobbery within Charleston women's auxiliaries, which the upper crust left to lower-class females. From August 1862 to October 1863, she was too busy as a volunteer feeder of wounded men at Wayside Hospital at Columbia Junction to keep up her journal.

Fearing a Union invasion, Chesnut kept luggage packed for retreat to inland safe zones. Her opinions poured out in her daily retrospectives. She railed against author Harriet Beecher Stowe as a Northern agitator, disapproved of the concubinage of females by white slave owners, and grieved over the pillage at Mulberry. By 1864, when rail service halted, she held little hope of a Confederate triumph. While society disintegrated and currency devalued, she partnered with her maid Molly in selling butter and eggs to generate cash. During General William Tecumseh Sherman's "March to the Sea," she left Columbia on February 16, 1865, the eve of the Union torching of the capital, and hurried by train through Charlotte, North Carolina, to the relative safety of Lincolnton.

Reduced Circumstance

Homelessness tested Chesnut's ability to cope. She paid $30 a day for squalid accommodations and lived on the contents of a food box packed with coffee, flour, rice, and sugar. While Sherman's march devastated homes and fields and Yankee carpetbaggers occupied South Carolina, Chesnut lapsed into hysterical weeping at the family's humbling. With no certain direction, among streams of displaced persons, she accepted handouts from friends of chicken, preserves, and sausages. In mid-March 1865, she moved back to her home state and reunited with James at a three-room accommodation in Chester, South Carolina.

After Varina Davis fled Union cavalry and boarded a wagon to leave Charlotte, North Carolina, with her children—ten-year-old Margaret Howell, eight-year-old Jefferson, Jr., three-year-old William Howell, and nine-month-old Varina Anne—Chesnut received them. Meanwhile, Union forces trailed Jefferson Davis and immured him at Fort Monroe, Maryland, under a charge of treason. Throughout April, the Chesnut house became a magnet for elite Southern refugees, who bedded down on pallets. At Kamchatka, the Chesnuts turned to reading for escape from pessimism. In July, Mary ceased her journal.

In 1866, she looked for a job. With Molly, she again sold eggs and reinitiated the butter and milk operation by retrieving cows from the swamp. With James Chesnut resuming his political career, poor kin and returning former slaves increased her responsibility as plantation mistress.

Reconstruction reduced Chesnut to penury. At Sarsfield, built in 1873, she lived on $100 a year plus $144 income from the sale of dairy goods and eggs. Varina Davis recognized the strain on Chesnut's failing heart and urged her to support herself by publishing the war diaries.

In 1881, Chesnut reorganized the 460 notebooks of her journal and submitted one episode, "The Arrest of a Spy," to the *Charleston Weekly News and Courier.* Her financial situation worsened in 1885, in part because her husband's family entailed his estate to a male heir. She died of heart disease on November 22, 1886. Nearly a century later, publication of the complete diary, *Mary Chesnut's Civil War* (1981), earned editor C. Vann Woodward a Pulitzer Prize for history.

See also: Charleston, South Carolina; Columbia, South Carolina.

Further Reading

Chesnut, Mary Boykin. *Mary Chesnut's Civil War.* Ed. C. Vann Woodward. New Haven, CT: Yale University Press, 1981.

———. *The Private Mary Chesnut: The Unpublished Civil War Diaries.* Oxford, UK: Oxford University Press, 1984.

Snodgrass, Mary Ellen. *Encyclopedia of Feminist Literature.* New York: Facts on File, 2006.

Spruill, Marjorie Julian, Valinda W. Littlefield, and Joan Marie Johnson. *South Carolina Women: Their Lives and Times.* 2 vols. Athens: University of Georgia Press, 2009.

Stern, Julia A. *Mary Chesnut's Civil War Epic.* Chicago: University of Chicago Press, 2010.

Chicago, Illinois

In the 1860s and 1870s, Chicago, the largest city in the Midwest, served as a point of connection between Easterners and the frontier and as an anchor for rail, banking, mercantile, lumber, grain, and livestock empires. Freedmen had long operated depots of the Underground Railroad, beginning with printer Zebina Eastman, publisher of Chicago's first abolitionist newspaper, the *Western Citizen.* On May 18, 1860, the Republican Party met and nominated antislavery attorney Abraham Lincoln for his first term as U.S. president. Copperheads (Southern sympathizers) supported slavery and turned the *Chicago Times* into an anti-Lincoln, anti-emancipation conduit of the Democratic Party.

Partisan defiance of slavery intensified in the early 1860s. In 1864, Afro-German tailor and realtor John Jones, together with Joseph Medill, publisher of the *Chicago Tribune,* issued a pamphlet, *The Black Laws of Illinois and a Few Reasons Why They Could Be Repealed,* refuting Black Codes issue by issue; the Illinois legislature rescinded the codes the following year. After appointment to the school board and election as a county commissioner, Jones became the first black elected to office in the United States.

The Republican faction raised $325,000 at sanitary fairs organized by Jane Currie Blaikie Hoge and Mary Ashton Rice Livermore, enlisted 22,436 army volunteers, and dispatched Sisters of Mercy to tend to combat casualties at Mercy Hospital on Calumet Avenue. The Chicago Soldiers' Home on Lake Park Avenue admitted 700 wounded and, under the direction of the Sisters of Carondelet, tended orphans and handicapped children.

On February 21, 1862, on Lake Michigan, the Union turned the training fields of Camp Douglas into its westernmost war prison. The 60-acre (24-hectare) lockup, spread over foul, swampy ground, gained notoriety as a death camp for 20 percent of the 30,000 rebels confined to it. Built for 6,000 captives, it held more than twice that many at a time. Vindictive guards tortured inmates, withheld rations and blankets in freezing weather, and executed rebels arbitrarily. Confederate prisoners died of enteritis, pneumonia, scurvy, smallpox, and typhoid. Against the cold, naked men turned burlap bags into garments. In winter 1864, 1,091 died over a four-month period. The total, some 6,000 corpses, lay in a common grave, the largest mass burial in the Western Hemisphere. At least 30 percent remained unidentified because of lax record keeping. At war's end, the military dismantled the camp. After citizens banded in mourning on May 1, 1865, when Lincoln's funeral train passed through town, acrimony decreased among partisans.

War and Profits

With the war terminating Mississippi River trade to supply army camps, the demand for beef and leather turned Chicago into the world's largest meat processor. Military contracts enriched Nelson Morris, one of the earliest meatpackers to profit from the industry. For on-site slaughter and rendering of livestock, entrepreneur Philip Danforth Armour revolutionized the pork business. He shipped live hogs to the Union Stock Yard & Transit Company, a 320-acre (130-hectare) complex that founder John B. Sherman built and transportation baron Timothy Blackstone chaired at the juncture of nine rail lines south of the city. In 1867, the incorporation of Armour and Company initiated the world's largest slaughtering and butchering business. To facilitate meat distribution, the conglomerate invested in the Baltimore & Ohio and the Chicago, Milwaukee, & St. Paul railroads, as well as the Metropolitan National Bank, Illinois Trust and Savings, National Trust Bank, and Northwestern Mutual Life Insurance Company.

After stockman Charles Goodnight and freighter Oliver Loving established the Goodnight-Loving Trail in 1866, they herded longhorns from Texas, Oklahoma, and Kansas to the cattle pens of Chicago. Investor John Wesley Iliff bought 800 Texas longhorns from Goodnight and negotiated beef contracts with the Union Pacific Railroad. As 100,000 Texas longhorns entered open range per year, cattlemen relayed their fattened stock to Chicago from the railhead at Ogallala, Nebraska. Innovator Gustavus Franklin Swift engineered ice-cooled railcars to keep meat fresh. Iliff shipped beef to Chicago in Swift's iced railcars and supplied Indian reservations with beef as well. At his death in 1878, wife Elizabeth Sarah Iliff continued their livestock operation.

By 1870, the Chicago stockyard received 3 million animals per year. Cornelius Vanderbilt channeled the fresh meat to the Atlantic Coast via railroad, laying tracks between Chicago and New York City.

To redirect prodigious cattle pen and distillery waste, garbage, and sewage away from Lake Michigan, the source of drinking water, Commissioner Samuel D. Lockwood hired engineers to dig the Illinois and Michigan Canal. On July 18, 1871, the complex water system reversed the flow of the Chicago River toward the Mississippi River and stemmed recurrent outbreaks of typhoid.

Urban Progress

As the antipollution campaign improved conditions, Chicago gained esteem as a merchandising center. Visitors and newcomers arrived aboard sidewheelers. Lighthouses, breakwaters, and the U.S. Life-Saving Service protected freighters and outsiders in transit. In 1865, the installation of fire alarm boxes reduced the travel time of firefighters and pumpers to urban emergencies. Construction of Cook County Hospital, opened in 1866, extended medical treatment to an exploding population.

The LaSalle and Washington street tunnels under the Chicago River and the construction of the Montgomery Ward mail-order business enticed pedestrian and carriage traffic to the commercial strip. Anchoring department store service, Marshall Field & Company, the world's second-largest department store, became a landmark at 111 North State Street in 1868. In competition with Macy's and Montgomery Ward, Field and store manager Harry Selfridge cultivated urban female shoppers by displaying upscale goods for home and table. Completion of the Chicago & Eastern Illinois Railroad in 1869 attracted new industry. By 1870, the city extended 3 miles by 6 miles (4.8 kilometers by 9.7 kilometers) along the southern tip of Lake Michigan.

The Great Fire of October 8–10, 1871, destroyed most of the downtown, excluding the city's water tower on North Michigan Avenue, and left one-third of residents homeless. Chicagoans received immediate aid from the Chicago Relief and Aid Society, which managed $5 million in donations. Rallied by Mayor Roswell B. Mason, a former manager of the Illinois Central Railroad, the citizenry determined to rebuild the metropolis bigger and safer than before. Workers dumped debris into Lake Michigan, extending the shoreline. The city council revived the Fire Patrol; the Illinois Central expanded suburban routes for 650 passengers per day. The arrival of Chinese laborers initiated Chicago's Chinatown. Architects formulated modern methods of increasing urban density by building concrete and steel skyscrapers, a model for other vertical metropolises. By 1877, with connections to the Union Pacific, the Missouri, Kansas, and Texas Railroad—the nation's longest rails-to-trails project—routed city freight as far south as Havana, Cuba, and Mexico.

Metropolitan Center

The city flourished in publishing as well as the arts, sports, medicine, and education. The first city museum, the Academy of Sciences, founded by herpetologist Robert Kennicott, opened in 1865 with a scholarly natural history collection. Two years later, the area acquired a ballpark for its baseball team; the following year, a pair of swans and a bear cub formed the nucleus of the Lincoln Park Zoo.

Also in 1868, printers William H. Rand and Andrew McNally formed a partnership to produce the *Chicago Tribune* and to publish guides, tickets, and timetables for local railroads. By 1870, the partners were issuing an illustrated paper, the *People's Weekly,* followed later in the decade by wax-engraved maps, business atlases, and trade books. City council members established a board of education and, in 1874, banned classroom segregation. Industrialist John D. Rockefeller, the world's richest man, channeled his profits of $500 million into the founding of the University of Chicago.

Lake Michigan became the city's prime draw. The Chicago Yacht Club organized pleasure boating. Bohemian,

Irish, and Polish lumbermen hustled boards and planks down the Chicago River from schooners arriving from the Upper Great Lakes to the Lumber Exchange at Wolf Point, north of the city center. Immigrant laborers and socialists rioted on July 26, 1877, in an upheaval called the Great Uprising. Violence required the combined intervention by police and the U.S. militia.

As revivalists targeted sailors on the Great Lakes and fought the proliferation of saloons and casinos, Chicago emerged as the nation's fastest-growing city. At the opening of the World's Columbian Exposition—also known as the Chicago World's Fair—in 1893, the city offered accommodations in 1,400 hotels, most constructed after the great fire.

See also: Armour, Philip Danforth; Chicago Fire; Great Lakes; Jones, Mother; Montgomery Ward; Sports.

Further Reading

Bernstein, Arnie. *The Hoofs and Guns of the Storm: Chicago's Civil War Connections.* Chicago: Lake Claremont, 2003.

Cutler, Irving. *Jewish Chicago: A Pictorial History.* Charleston, SC: Arcadia, 2000.

Genzen, Jonathan. *The Chicago River: A History in Photographs.* Englewood, CO: Westcliffe, 2007.

Levy, George. *To Die in Chicago: Confederate Prisoners at Camp Douglas, 1862–65.* 2nd ed. Gretna, LA: Pelican, 1999.

Lewis, Robert D. *Chicago Made: Factory Networks in the Industrial Metropolis.* Chicago: University of Chicago Press, 2008.

Chicago Fire

The Great Chicago Fire of October 8–10, 1871, incinerated 4 square miles (10.4 square kilometers) of prime property on Lake Michigan. The conflagration began at 9 P.M. in a shed at 137 DeKoven Street and gained strength as it consumed log piles and plank sidewalks.

Daniel "Pegleg" Sullivan turned in the alarm and tried to free his mother's cow from danger. Some urbanites observed from a distance and felt safe until flames jumped two branches of the Chicago River and spread northeast among German and Scandinavian immigrant communities. In the 34-block sweep, covering 2,100 acres (850 hectares), the fires consumed the courthouse, post office, customs house, and Booksellers' Row. Only rubble remained of grain elevators, wooden bridges, riverboats, and shipyards. The sudden loss obliterated grave markers and left one-third of residents homeless.

In stiff winds that propelled the fire at speeds of more than 65 acres (26 hectares) per hour, showers of sparks and shingles rained destruction on the former livery stable that warehoused Montgomery Ward's merchandise, grain-filled elevators, and dock property and shipments. Schooners burned to the water line. The grand Palmer House hotel, a nuptial gift to the owner's bride, Bertha Honoré Palmer, vanished in cinders 13 days after its opening. Winds directed the fire toward the *Navarino,* a new $50,000 steamer of the Goodrich Transportation Company, owned by Captain Albert Edgar Goodrich and moored at the North Pier. The smolder from 17,500 buildings and ships generated smoke and ash that imperiled navigation for weeks.

The collapse of the waterworks halted the flow of water to the 185 professional firefighters, who could do little to control the devastation. As mansions, hotels, tenements, and shanties blazed to the north, trains stopped miles from the city. Lumberyards ignited in a red flash. Panicked residents blackened by soot fled under the Chicago River via the LaSalle and Washington street tunnels, rushed through graves in Potter's Field, and sheltered at Lincoln Park. A light rain fell for 25 hours, keeping the park safe. Others ran east, cowered under a viaduct, or stood shoulder-deep in the cold lake. Free passes took others from the chaos by train.

The Sisters of Charity superintended emergency services. Searchers recovered fewer than half the 300 victims for burial in a mass grave, which prevented the spread of disease. Volunteers vaccinated the vulnerable against a possible outbreak of smallpox. Of the original civic buildings, only the 154-foot (47-meter) water tower on North Michigan Avenue and the Chicago Avenue pump station survived. Photographer Jex Bardwell hurried to the scene to capture the historic loss.

Frederick W. Pelton, the mayor of Cleveland, Ohio, organized a mass meeting to muster aid; Cincinnati set up two soup kitchens. At the *New York Herald,* people thronged the office for news of loved ones. New York rail tycoon James "Diamond Jim" Fisk loaded contributions on a freight wagon and drove it to a train headed for Chicago.

Until the restoration of water service, a city ordinance outlawed the lighting of matches and the smoking of cigars and pipes. The first spurt of water from city pumps spread contamination and illness.

Civic Authority

Citizens blamed the fire on Catherine "Cate" O'Leary, the wife of farmer Patrick O'Leary and a vulnerable target as an Irish Catholic female. A later reconstruction of

The Great Chicago Fire of October 8–10, 1871, left much of the downtown area in ruins. A strong wind carried the flames across the city, razing 17,500 buildings—many of them made of wood—and leaving one-third of the population homeless. *(Archive Photos/Stringer/Getty Images)*

events pointed to Pegleg Sullivan and his accomplice, Dennis Regan, as the culprits, or possibly to importer Louis M. Cohn, treasurer of the board of trustees of the Chicago Elks, and a party of craps shooters gambling in the O'Leary's barn. In November, the police and fire commissioners deposed 50 people and recorded 1,100 pages of testimony, but came to no conclusion as to the cause of the catastrophe.

At the request of Mayor Roswell B. Mason, a former manager of the Illinois Central Railroad, General Philip Sheridan coordinated infantry companies and imposed martial law with the aid of 5,000 emergency police and militia. He commandeered regiments from Omaha, Nebraska, and, to the south, ordered rations from St. Louis, Missouri, and tents from Jeffersonville, Illinois. Sentries patrolled the streets after dark and guarded the gas works and lumberyards against looting. Sheridan closed saloons and accosted innkeepers for charging exorbitant rates. Orderly civilians piled rubble to free streets for horsecars and wagons. Street stalls began selling apples, cider, grapes, and tobacco. Temporary storefront operations secured credit and new inventory.

The mayor trusted Henry King, president of the Chicago Relief and Aid Society, to distribute $5 million in donations, including gifts from Levi Strauss, founder of a San Francisco mercantile and manufactory; $100,000 from Alexander Turney Stewart, the nation's leading importer; and the first $30 earned by the Fisk Jubilee Singers. Schools and churches received the homeless. While Quaker women sewed clothing, Thomas Clarkson Hill of Western Springs directed 75 Quakers in the distribution of garments, bedding, food, and cash. Donations paid for the construction of temporary barracks to house 1,000 families and of 5,200 cottages.

A wagon from Field, Leiter & Company distributed bread and meat in the streets. Schlitz breweries in Milwaukee shipped barrels of beer and fresh water to survivors. John A. Anderson, superintendent of the Belvidere Delaware Railroad in New Hope, Pennsylvania, delivered relief packages and a day's wages from each employee. The A&P food chain dispatched a trainload of relief supplies and employees to distribute it. Seamstresses received 5,300 free Singer sewing machines to produce replacement clothing. Skilled laborers received tools. By May 1873, the Chicago Relief and Aid Society had helped 156,968 individuals, almost half the city's population, and had rooted out obvious frauds seeking free support.

A City Revived

Rallied by Mayor Mason, the citizenry determined to rebuild the metropolis bigger and safer than before. By the Tuesday morning after the three-day disaster, while ruins crumbled as they cooled, lumber was already arriving at the docks. A Northbrook, Illinois, brickyard sent building supplies. In an editorial published on October 11, Joseph Medill and Horace White, owners of the *Chicago Tribune,* urged cheer and determination. Two weeks later, the *Chicago Weekly Post* issued a one-word headline: "Resurgam" (Latin for "I shall rise again").

Women opened a clothes closet at the Michigan Avenue Baptist Church. The German Relief Society doled out cash to pay rent for the homeless. Workers dumped debris into Lake Michigan, extending the shoreline with loads of charred remains worth $222 million. The first reconstructed office was the realty firm of William D. Kerfoot. Potter Palmer erected a second Palmer House and billed it as the "World's First Fireproof Building." Thomas Hughes, a member of the British Parliament, collected 7,000 books and housed them in a water tank at Adams and LaSalle streets to replace the lost Chicago Library. Safecrackers came into demand to open vaults and restore cash to the destitute. The survival of 878 Diebold safes made the company name famous. The loss bankrupted Gurdon Saltonstall Hubbard, the city's first underwriter. A war hero, Arthur Ducat, Sr., spearheaded fire prevention standards for the insurance industry.

A temporary city hall conducted business adjacent to the water tank. To escape the blaze, the owners of Rand McNally & Company had buried their printing equipment in the sand on the shores of Lake Michigan; a few days later, they resumed business. Skilled and semiskilled Czech and German laborers found job opportunities. German Jews opened Michael Reese Hospital and B'nai Brith lodges. At Mount Prospect, Archbishop Patrick Augustine Feehan remodeled the River Bent Knott Farm into a training school for Chicago orphans.

The reconstruction of the Chicago, Rock Island, & Pacific and Lake Shore & Michigan Southern rail depot at LaSalle and Van Buren streets produced jubilation and a city music festival. Philanthropist Sarah Tyson Hallowell supported the city's resurgence in the arts by introducing French masters to the Midwest and by exhibiting local works.

Business dominated the next decades of urban recovery. Promoting the city's resurgence, Gilman and Hartford, founders of the A&P chain, established an anchor store in Chicago. George Martin II of Naperville made a fortune quarrying brick tile and limestone for Chicago's building projects. At South Bend, Indiana, ironworker James Oliver bought up cast iron from the Chicago ruins and recycled it into sewing machine stands. East of Chicago, Oak Park experienced a residential boom, as did Winnetka to the south. Construction of the Chicago, Milwaukee, St. Paul, & Pacific Railroad in 1872 established commerce with Wisconsin. In 1873, a series of trade shows at the Inter-State Exposition Building solicited industry and business that catapulted Chicago into modernity.

See also: Chicago, Illinois.

Further Reading

Genzen, Jonathan. *The Chicago River: A History in Photographs.* Englewood, CO: Westcliffe, 2007.

Miller, Ross. *The Great Chicago Fire.* Urbana: University of Illinois Press, 2000.

Sawislak, Karen. *Smoldering City: Chicagoans and the Great Fire, 1871–1874.* Chicago: University of Chicago Press, 1995.

Smith, Carl. *Urban Disorder and the Shape of Belief: The Great Chicago Fire, the Haymarket Bomb, and the Model Town of Pullman.* 2nd ed. Chicago: University of Chicago Press, 2007.

Vale, Lawrence J., and Thomas J. Campanella, eds. *The Resilient City: How Modern Cities Recover from Disaster.* New York: Oxford University Press, 2005.

Child, Lydia Maria (1802–1880)

Publisher and propagandist Lydia Maria Francis Child, the nation's first female journalist, wrote and edited humanistic works favoring the rights of women, children, slaves, and Indians. Born on February 11, 1802, in Medford, Massachusetts, she grew up in a Calvinist household, attended "Ma'am Betty's" dame school and Miss Swan's Seminary, and selected books from the library of the parish minister. She developed reformist beliefs from her brother, Convers Francis, Jr., a Unitarian theologian at Harvard University, and from transcendentalist writer, editor, and critic Margaret Fuller.

After the death of her mother, Susannah Rand Francis, from tuberculosis in 1814, her father, Convers Francis, Sr., sent her to live with her married sister, Mary Francis Preston, in Norridgewock, Maine. There, she befriended members of a Penobscot community. At age 17, she taught school at Gardiner, Maine. By age 20, she had cultivated friendships with antislavery activists Ralph Waldo Emerson, Abigail Goodwin, the Reverend Theodore Parker, and poet John Greenleaf Whittier.

At age 22, she published the nation's first historical novel, *Hobomok: A Tale of Early Times* (1824), a romance about wedlock between the title character, a Pequot, and Mary Conant, a rebellious Puritan. In 1828, she wed David Lee Child of West Boylston, Massachusetts, an abolitionist lawyer and the editor of the *Massachusetts Journal.* After they settled at Wayland, Massachusetts, Child encouraged his wife's membership in the Boston Female Anti-Slavery Society and her essays for *The Liberator* and for his own newspaper.

Lydia Maria Child founded a bimonthly publication, *Juvenile Miscellany,* America's first youth magazine, in 1826, and published several books: *The Frugal Housewife: Dedicated to Those Who Are Not Ashamed of Economy* (1829), a handbook on domestic economy; *The Mother's Book* (1831); *Good Wives* (1833); and *The Family Nurse* (1838), a guide to first aid. Through these efforts, Child funded the family's involvement in the Underground Railroad. Abandoning the *Juvenile Miscellany* in 1840, she launched a family reform weekly, the *National Anti-Slavery Standard,* which aired the outrage of runaway slaves at their former owners and tormentors.

Controversy

Mentored by polemicist William Lloyd Garrison, Child published civil rights essays in the *Liberty Bell, New York Tribune, Boston Courier,* and Edgar Allan Poe's *Broadway Journal.* She also issued a bold libertarian manifesto, *An Appeal in Favor of That Class of Americans Called Africans* (1833). The radical essay enlisted a young Charles Sumner (future senator from Massachusetts) to the cause of immediate emancipation, but it also angered conservative friends and Christian subscribers to her magazine, as well as the board of the Boston Athenaeum, which confiscated her library card.

Child championed the centrality of women to civilization in *History of the Condition of Women, in Various Ages and Nations* (1835) and rebutted religious superstitions with a three-volume treatise titled *The Progress of Religious Ideas Through Successive Ages* (1854). The election of Child, Maria Weston Chapman, and Lucretia Mott to the executive board of the American Anti-Slavery Society generated an antifeminist backlash that led to the resignation of James Gillespie Birney, Gerrit Smith, Arthur Tappan, and Lewis Tappan from the organization.

Following the execution of John Brown and his conspirators for their raid on the federal arsenal at Harpers Ferry, Virginia, in 1859, Child heightened her activism as an antislavery tractarian. She guided Harriet Jacobs in compiling the memoir *Incidents in the Life of a Slave Girl: Written by Herself* (1860), an exposé of the sexual bondage of black women by white men. Child composed "The Duty of Disobedience to the Fugitive Slave Act" (1860), a directive on violating federal law by aiding escapees.

During the Civil War, she gathered supplies for the rescue of contrabands (escaped slaves) and donated to the literacy school of the Port Royal Experiment, in which former slaves worked on land abandoned by plantation owners on the Sea Islands of South Carolina. In reference to volunteer nurses, she marveled that "Ladies, who had been accustomed to while away the hours of life with fancy work, manifested a degree of executive ability in the sanitary commission, and in the hospitals."

Woman Suffrage and Native Rights

After the Civil War, Child fostered humanism and full citizenship for women. She established the Massachusetts Woman Suffrage Association, denounced the Fifteenth Amendment granting the vote to black males only, and wrote pro-woman articles for *The Independent* and *The Woman's Journal,* charging the church with condoning the silencing of females. Women, she railed, "have been trained to consider it unfeminine to think, unladylike to work, and who spend their days in decorating their persons to catch the eye of purchasers." In an essay titled "Physical Strength of Women," published in *The Woman's Journal* on March 15, 1873, she lauded females for stamina and cited as models the Abenaki and Penobscot women she had observed in Maine.

In *The Freedmen's Book* (1865), a common primer in literacy classes, Child gathered writings by Frederick Douglass, Charlotte Forten, William Lloyd Garrison, Frances Ellen Watkins Harper, and Phillis Wheatley, America's first black author. In fictional mode, Child composed a social novel on human bondage, *A Romance of the Republic* (1867), which foresaw miscegenation as an answer to racism.

As the U.S. military pressed the Plains Indians into confinement, Child penned *An Appeal for the Indians* (1868), a reflection on the uprooting of native peoples that influenced the "Peace Policy" of President Ulysses S. Grant. She lobbied for the right of Indians to their language, culture, and religion, including polygamy. With a cry of outrage, she denounced the actions of President Andrew Jackson and the Indian Removal Act of 1830 in displacing the peaceful Cherokee from the Carolinas and the Seminole from Florida: "God of heaven grant me patience! . . . I am so tired of shams!"

Disabled in widowhood by arthritis, Child compiled *Aspirations of the World* (1878), an anthology of spiritual and moral citations by world authors. She died of heart disease on October 20, 1880.

See also: Abolitionism; Douglass, Frederick; Fifteenth Amendment; Forten, Charlotte; Jacobs, Harriet.

Further Reading

Karcher, Carolyn L. *First Woman in the Republic: A Cultural Biography of Lydia Maria Child.* Durham, NC: Duke University Press, 1998.

———, ed. *A Lydia Maria Child Reader.* Durham, NC: Duke University Press, 1997.

Sneider, Allison L. *Suffragists in an Imperial Age: U.S. Expansion and the Woman Question, 1870–1929.* New York: Oxford University Press, 2008.

Snodgrass, Mary Ellen. *Encyclopedia of Feminist Literature.* New York: Facts on File, 2006.

———. *The Underground Railroad: An Encyclopedia of People, Places, and Operations.* Armonk, NY: M.E. Sharpe, 2007.

Children and Childhood

The safety and nurturance of children during the 1860s and 1870s varied by location, ethnicity, religion, and economic status. Privileged households, such as Hurricane Plantation, the home of U.S. Senator Jefferson Davis at Davis Bend, Mississippi, and Butler Island and St. Simons Island, the Georgia plantation homes of the daughters of actor Fanny Kemble, provided servants and nannies. Ample funds paid for seaside homes, boarding schools, and European travel, the training ground of landscaper Frederick Law Olmsted. In-house tutoring in art, music, and foreign language offered specialized skills, such as the French lessons that readied statesman Hamilton Fish for politics and the instruction in Greek and romance languages that prepared poet Julia Ward Howe for writing and lecturing.

Scholarly families encouraged perusing in their private libraries. The press offered subscriptions to such children's magazines as Frank Leslie's *Boys' and Girls' Weekly* and *Boys of America* and the Mormon *The Juvenile Instructor.* Products for children ranged from Baron Justus von Liebig and Henri Nestlé's infant formulas to imported dolls and mechanical games and toys sold in New York City at Macy's, Alexander Turney Stewart's Marble Palace, and Frederick August Otto Schwarz's Toy Bazaar, which opened on Broadway in 1862.

Refined parents enrolled their children in the best schools, such as Boston Latin School, the alma mater of orator Edward Everett; Salem Normal School, attended by educator Charlotte Forten; Clinton Liberal Institute, the choice of lecturer Matilda Joslyn Gage and railroad magnate Leland Stanford; Monmouth Academy, the elementary school of General Oliver Otis Howard; and Stockbridge Academy, the preparatory school of capitalist Cyrus W. Field. Southern planters and oil and railroad barons established dynasties that passed inherited wealth to sons, such as the South Carolina plantations that politician James Chesnut, Jr., received from his father and grandfather and the $90 million inheritance that rail and shipping magnate Cornelius Vanderbilt left to his son William.

The Average Child

Before the advent of universal public education, middle-class Americans relied on parochial and public day schools and home care. Instruction varied markedly in substance and classroom method, as with the gendered training that suffragist Susan B. Anthony received at Deborah Moulson's Female Seminary in Philadelphia; the memorization of Catholic hymns and songs at the Jesuit school for former slaves in Bardstown, Kentucky; and the introduction to Hebrew and Torah at the yeshivas that Rabbi Isaac Mayer Wise opened at the Lodge Street Synagogue in Cincinnati, Ohio. Truancy officers prevented the idle and vagrant from getting into trouble on the streets.

Nutrition improved at the family table after railroad companies began delivering varieties of fresh meat, fruit, and vegetables. Suffragists urged mothers to rally communities against adulterated food and over-the-counter nostrums, particularly milk whitened with chalk dust, preserved fruit and vegetables colored with copper sulfate, bread permeated with sawdust, and cough syrup and fever reducers laced with alcohol and opium. In the 1860s, Gail Borden's vacuum-packed condensed milk lowered the infant mortality rate by shielding children from food poisoning and microbial contaminants.

As early as the 1860s, to escape high unemployment, housing shortages, inflated prices, and the temptations of smoking, drinking, gangs, and petty crime to their children, many middle-class parents chose to move to the countryside. Those who could not afford relocation sometimes chose vacations or respites for youth with grandparents or other relatives in rural areas, the decision of the parents of Indian fighter John Robert Taylor of Little Rock, Arkansas.

Apprenticeships situated bright children in promising futures, such as attorney Abraham Lincoln's assistance to a Sangamon County surveyor in Illinois, hatmaker John

Batterson Stetson's training in felt buying, merchant Rowland Hussey Macy's apprenticeship aboard the New Bedford whaler *Emily Morgan,* and the pharmaceutical instruction at the Good Samaritan Pharmacy in Lafayette, Indiana, that equipped Eli Lilly for medical research. Others trained themselves through reading and self-education, the choice of chemist Thaddeus Lowe, illustrator Thomas Nast, suffragist Elizabeth Cady Stanton, poet Walt Whitman, theologian Mary Baker Eddy, and conservationist John Muir. The cagy showman P.T. Barnum sold lottery tickets at age 12 and learned the rudiments of bargaining and fraud while keeping a grocery store.

Child Survival

Among immigrants, children acclimated more rapidly than adults to the new culture and language. In Chicago in 1860, 56 percent of deaths occurred among children under the age of five. Those living in congested tenements shared subdivided apartments and formed social networks with street gangs of the same racial, cultural, and religious background. Unsupervised, they played ringolevio, marbles, stickball, and hide-and-seek in vacant lots, abandoned buildings, and the streets amid wheeled vehicles, horse dung, and garbage, until their families could put them to work. Trade skills became a rite of passage for boys, who learned from their fathers, uncles, and grandfathers. Females learned traditional mothering and housewifery, which included sewing, cooking, cleaning, nursing, and midwifery.

During the Industrial Revolution, employers favored underage laborers, who could easily climb among cotton looms and bandsaws and down mine shafts. At Anchor Mills in Allegheny City, Pennsylvania, 13-year-old Andrew Carnegie, the son of a Scots weaver from Dunfermline, walked a mile to work for $1.20 a week as a bobbin boy. At the Sauquoit Silk Mill in Scranton, Pennsylvania, girls in their mid-teens took poor-paying jobs as reelers, spinners, and winders. Females reached marriageable age at ten and bore children in their preteen years.

Outbreaks of enteritis, trachoma, diphtheria, smallpox, and yellow fever decimated populations from birth to age three, the fate of the four Irish American children of Mary Harris "Mother" Jones. Without appropriate prenatal and pediatric care, older children suffered physical deformities from birth defects, rickets, and tuberculosis.

On the frontier, child mortality reached its highest levels. The Mormons in Utah suffered more premature births and heavy loss of children because of child marriage to polygamists, early and frequent pregnancies, and pregnancy among older women. Families incurred high child mortality rates, particularly from cholera, dysentery, erysipelas, milk sickness, and typhoid. Infection came in waves, such as the rise of scarlet fever in 1875 in Owens

Child mortality, poverty, and delinquency troubled American society in the decades after the Civil War, especially in urban areas. Evangelist Dwight L. Moody poses with a group of orphans at one of his Chicago mission houses in 1870. *(MPI/Stringer/Getty Images)*

Valley, California, that left children weakened by damage to heart valves. Malaria and parasites proliferated from increases in roaches, ants, flies, and the anopheles mosquito from poor yard sanitation and ignorance of hygiene. Quinine relieved fever and ague, but not the sources of infection. After cabin dwellers built solid residences, sealed floors and screened windows reduced the incidence of sickness, especially for crawling babies.

Growing up in the West had its advantages. Farmers in Iowa, Minnesota, and Wisconsin abandoned planting in exhausted soil and turned to dairying, adding milk, butter, and cheese to a family diet rich in wild greens, fish, and game. Boys and girls learned to ride bareback and to use firearms for hunting and self-protection, the background of lawman James Butler "Wild Bill" Hickok and boy riders for the Pony Express. On farms, to the detriment of education, children such as orator Lucy Stone and agriculturist Luther Burbank took a vital part in herding, planting, reaping, and food preservation and transport to market.

During the Civil War, the military accepted boys as young as ten, some fleeing slavery or the tedium of agriculture for adventure in combat. They made themselves useful as lookouts, drummers, grooms, messengers, burial crews, stretcher bearers, and hospital orderlies. However, because two-thirds of war deaths resulted from contagion, boy soldiers shared mortality risks with adults, who tended to die of dysentery, measles, pneumonia, and scurvy.

Heightened Risks

Black slave children were often victims of fetal infection, malnutrition, crib death, hookworm, heat stroke, and such accidents as the unintended head injury incurred by slave rescuer Harriet Tubman. Slave mothers tended to conceive too young and bear underweight infants. Life in the slave quarters in vermin-ridden environments and dirt-floored cabins such as those at Boone Hall Plantation in Charleston, South Carolina, increased incidents of infection by intestinal and respiratory microbes and by typhus, especially in Virginia. Demographers estimate that 35 percent died in the first 12 months of life.

Those who survived to age four increased their chances of longevity by 15 percent. Slaves attempted to shield their children from lashings, enforced matings, and sale on the auction block, the fate of Sojourner Truth, who shared a negotiated sale with a flock of sheep. In their preteens, slave children caught up in height and weight, perhaps because owners improved rations to produce stronger field hands or saleable commodities, whom overseers listed in farm records along with livestock.

Where possible, workers such as ship's caulker Frederick Douglass hired themselves out to tradesmen to increase their vocational education. After emancipation on January 1, 1863, parents promoted opportunities by sending daughters and sons to freedmen's schools, such as the model system set up by Northern missionary Ellen Murray and social worker Nelly Winsor at Port Royal, South Carolina.

For the bottom socioeconomic echelon, suffering and need in foundling homes, asylums, juvenile reformatories, and almshouses spread hopelessness from one generation to another. Among lepers at Father Damien's colony in Kalaupapa, Molokai, Hawaiian orphans faced certain death from contagion. In urban areas, child mortality rose among large families living in cramped, unhygienic spaces. In New York City, unmarried women gave birth to fatherless infants at the charity hospital on Blackwell's Island.

In Ohio in 1871, authorities committed 29 girls and 182 boys to madhouses. Illinois instituted the Chicago Reform School at Pontiac, Michigan, to punish and reshape budding criminals. In lieu of homes for delinquents, Michigan judges in 1873 remanded 100 girls and 377 boys to jail, where they developed coping skills for life among hardened criminals.

Those waifs who escaped institutions survived by their wits. They scavenged in urban trash and slept in coal cellars and on piers, dodging predators and scorn as "gutter children" or "wharf rats." Dependents placed in orphanages lived in barracks and worked as domestics or farmhands to earn money or foodstuffs for the institution. Child prostitution sold a vulnerable commodity to callous pedophiles who spread gonorrhea and syphilis to the young. Some delinquents avoided adult jails by apprenticing in the trades or joining the navy. *The New York Times* opened a floating hospital in 1866 as a respite for newsboys in need of medical treatment and fresh air along the East River.

Native American Children

After the demise of the buffalo, the greatest want pervaded Indian reservations in the Plains states and the Great Basin. Historians estimate that half of all native children failed to reach adulthood. In California, the Common School Act of 1860 barred native pupils from classrooms. At the Rincon Reservation in San Diego County, California, Mission Indians taught their offspring the basics of living, but not the curriculum preferred by whites. Instead of math and spelling, they learned how to avoid kidnap, indenturing to whites, exile to forts, jailing, and hanging.

Subsistence marked the daily activities of old and young, among them Crow Foot, the 14-year-old son of Hunkpapa Sioux shaman Sitting Bull, who died in a skirmish with reservation police in Fort Buford, North Dakota. Comanche leader Quanah Parker and his brother Peenah Pecos Parker suffered the double ruination of mixed white and Indian blood and orphaning in 1860 after their father's murder and their mother's recapture. During the incarceration of Lakota war chief Crazy Horse in Montana on the Great Sioux Reservation, his wife Black Shawl suffered from tuberculosis. Their only child, They Are Afraid of Her, died in 1873.

In a period of rapid socioeconomic decline, young natives lost touch with tribal traditions, the fate of Seneca General Ely Samuel Parker, and came under the power of corrupt Indian agents, missionaries, and military authorities. Mangas Coloradas, on a peace mission with his son Mangus to Fort McLane, New Mexico, died in 1863 under torture and left Mangus to carry on the Chiricahua Apache struggle for freedom. In winter 1877, Chief Joseph of the Wallowa band of Nez Percé fled the American cavalry and struggled through snow toward the U.S.–Canadian border. He witnessed the rapid decline of the young and old to exposure from lack of blankets.

Two decades later, assimilation academies, notably, the Chilocco Indian School on the Cherokee Strip in Oklahoma, Quaker White's Manual Labor Institute at Wabash, Indiana, and the Carlisle Indian Industrial School in Pennsylvania, forced native children into a concentration camp existence. Under Carlisle headmaster, Richard Henry Pratt, in 1873, 10,606 children of 140 tribes wore the clothes and shoes of whites. When the school barber cut their hair, the Lakota mourned and wailed into the night. Forced to speak English and abandon their native deities, 269 Apache children pined for home and died in large numbers of heartbreak. Student Zitkala-Sa accused the staff of imposing evangelism on her and the others and of marching them to meals and classes, washing them in lye soap, and locking them in cells. Left among the 192 grave markers were bead and shell necklaces, sage and sweetgrass bundles, and prayer cloths.

Protective Services

Following the Confederate surrender at Appomattox, Virginia, American society adopted a more paternal attitude toward the vulnerable. The formation of animal protective agencies under the American Society for the Prevention of Cruelty to Animals (ASPCA) in 1866 led to community rescue of neglected and abused children. One documented case in 1869, the imprisonment of Samuel Fletcher, Jr., revealed that the blind boy lived in a basement. After his escape, a court fined his parents $300 and set a precedent of defending children's rights. As a result, Massachusetts hired agents of the state board of charities to attend trials involving juveniles and to place them in homes and make follow-up visits.

ASPCA founder Henry Bergh and attorney Elbridge Gerry intervened in a pathetic case in 1875. At the urging of Methodist missionary Etta Angell Wheeler, rescuers removed Mary Ellen Wilson, an undersized ten-year-old, from a tenement at 341 West 41st Street in New York City. Bruised and gashed on her legs and face with scissors, she lived in rags in a dark room and endured torment. Her foster parents, Francis and Mary Connolly, claimed custody illegally and fed the child a diet of bread and water. After the girl's seizure on April 9, 1875, a court placed her in an orphanage and sentenced Mary Connolly to a year in jail.

The Wilson case initiated the nation's child protection movement, supported by shipping and railroad magnate Cornelius Vanderbilt. Quaker philanthropist John D. Wright bought land in Eatontown, New Jersey, to house the Society for Friendless and Cruelly Treated Children summer camp, a project superintended by the American Female Guardian Society of New York. Volunteers established the New York Society for the Prevention of Cruelty to Children in 1874, involving constables in the deliverance of endangered minors, especially infants left unattended in public in their carriages. In 1877, the state legal system trained police in the investigation of child endangerment. Officers called "Gerrymen" intervened in the sale of alcohol, drugs, and weapons to children and prohibited the hiring of children in saloons.

Subsequent laws freed youth from labor in factories and sweatshops and protected boys hired by telegraphers and messenger services. Additional legislation banned children from frequenting or begging in brothels, opium dens, gaming parlors, and stores selling tobacco and pornography. In Austin, Texas, teacher Helen Maria Gerrells Stoddard lobbied to raise the age of girls' sexual consent from 12 to 15. By 1890, social agencies received and placed 15,000 poor and endangered children per year in secure lodgings.

In the late 1860s, awareness of child endangerment fueled humanitarian reform, beginning with the Knights of Labor, Philadelphia street missions, and German labor unions in Milwaukee, Wisconsin, and furthered by such media advocates as Desha Breckinridge, editor of the Lexington, Kentucky, *Morning Herald.* The effort was a two-pronged improvement of family life—the removal of children from industry—including Warner Brothers garment mills in Bridgeport, Connecticut; Pennsylvania coal mines; fruit canneries in Dixon, California; and glassworks in Alton, Illinois—and the curtailment of adult competition with young workers, who depressed the wages of their elders.

The situation worsened among poor whites in cotton mills throughout Alabama, Georgia, and the Carolinas, where 23 percent of the labor force was underage. Children lost fingers to whirling belts, pulleys, and shafts and vision to metal slivers and glass shards. Between 1870 and 1880, the percentage of child employees rose from 16 percent to 16.6 percent of all children aged 10–14. In 1876, the Working Men's Party proposed banning the hiring of children under the age of 14. The following year, the New York Society for the Prevention of Cruelty to Children and cells of the ASPCA united to form the American Humane Association, an umbrella agency that battled domestic violence, neglect, and exploitation.

Coupled with immunization campaigns, city drainage and sanitation efforts, temperance crusades, and the pasteurization of milk, protection of children in the last quarter of the nineteenth century boosted the well-being and life expectancy of babies and children.

See also: American Society for the Prevention of Cruelty to Animals; Forten, Charlotte; Frontier Life; Hospitals and Asylums; Literacy; Mormons.

Further Reading

Burlingame, Dwight F., ed. *Philanthropy in America: A Comprehensive Historical Encyclopedia.* Santa Barbara, CA: ABC-CLIO, 2004.

Crenson, Matthew A. *Building the Invisible Orphanage: A Prehistory of the American Welfare System.* Cambridge, MA: Harvard University Press, 1998.

Forman-Brunell, Miriam, ed. *Girlhood in America: An Encyclopedia.* Santa Barbara, CA: ABC-CLIO, 2001.

Hindman, Hugh D. *Child Labor: An American History.* Armonk, NY: M.E. Sharpe, 2002.

Horton, James Oliver, and Lois E. Horton. *Slavery and the Making of America.* New York: Oxford University Press, 2005.

Smith, Eve P., and Lisa A. Merkel-Holguín, eds. *A History of Child Welfare.* New Brunswick, NJ: Transaction, 1996.

Chisholm Trail

The Chisholm Trail began as a humble route to serve the nation's first billion-dollar industry—cattle. The route bore the surname of Cherokee Scots guide and interpreter Jesse Chisholm, a builder of Oklahoma trading posts in Cleveland, Hughes, and Oklahoma counties and an instigator of the Treaty of Medicine Lodge, signed on October 21 and 28, 1876. Originally followed by Wichita Indian hunters and warriors over migratory north–south buffalo courses, the route eased supply trains of the Confederate army north to Kansas during the Civil War.

During the absence of stockmen throughout the war, cattle multiplied into a frontier bonanza. In spring 1865, Chisholm, along with partner James Richard Mead, followed the way north on a trading venture past Council Grove and drove 3,000 steers to the Fox and Sac Reserve. Chisholm returned in April 1866 with 250 steers and wagons loaded with furs and trade goods, which he peddled as far south as Fort Sill.

Stockman and buyer Joseph Geating "Joe" McCoy blazed the route as a summer cattle trail from San Antonio, Texas, over the Red River to the Union Pacific (later Kansas Pacific) stockyards in Abilene, Kansas. From July 1 to September 1, 1867, on 480 acres (195 hectares), he invested in the eight-week construction of a bank, hotel, corrals, chutes, and stock trading office. He intended to trade in Texas longhorns, a wild Spanish breed from northern Mexico and southern Texas that was known for warding off predators with horn and hoof and for its resistance to drought.

Unfortunately, the longhorns were susceptible to epizootics of splenic tick fever (bovine babesiosis, or Spanish fever). In 1868, the disease that the animals carried in their kidneys, livers, and spleens killed 15,000 steers in Illinois and Indiana. Charley Gross, McCoy's assistant, exclaimed, "Hell was to pay. . . . To see their small stock of cattle die off was to them almost unbearable, it was almost open gun war."

When tick fever caused stockmen in west-central Missouri and eastern Kansas to reject an influx of Texas longhorns, McCoy avoided the easterly Shawnee Trail by traversing central Oklahoma. By establishing that overwintered longhorns were immune to the fever, he had them exempted from the ban and promised to cover any stock lost to disease. To woo dubious Illinois stock buyers, he imported a Wild West show to Chicago and sponsored a buffalo hunt and lavish entertainment in Abilene.

Ease of travel along the Chisholm Trail enriched Oklahomans and turned the scruffy log village of Abilene into a wealthy trading center. In 1867, Colonel Oliver W. Wheeler funneled 100 cow ponies and 2,400 steers for two months from San Antonio along a feeder trail over the North Canadian River on the famous track north, which lay outside the Kansas animal quarantine. Indian toll collectors demanded a dime per head for access to Indian Territory (Oklahoma); cholera epidemics exacted a toll in human lives.

On September 5, 1867, McCoy filled 20 railcars with steers bound for Chicago abattoirs. By June 1868, his operation required 1,000 railcars per month, more rolling stock than the railroad could provide.

Boom Times

By 1870, drovers preferred the Chisholm Trail, which McCoy and his agent, W.W. Sugg, advertised at a cost of $5,000 in circulars throughout Texas, and rerouted herds to Kansas from as far south as the King Ranch in Brownsville on the Gulf of Mexico. The fliers promised higher profits and fewer losses on the drive north. The first printed reference appeared in the *Kansas Daily Commonwealth* in May 1870. Within the year, McCoy's shipping operation managed 600,000 cattle, some of them "wet cattle" (stolen) from Mexico for ear-cropping and branding.

According to the *Texas Handbook,* for a cost of 60 to 75 cents per head, a team—trail boss, wrangler, cook, and 10 to 14 cowboys—could complete the drive from southern Texas through central Kansas at the rate of 10 miles (16 kilometers) per day. The drovers were advised to avoid stampedes by keeping the cattle well watered and grazed.

High traffic transformed Abilene. According to McCoy's *Cattle Trade of the West and Southwest* (1874), idle cattlemen there enjoyed sophisticated entertainment, lodged at the Drovers' Cottage, and received the kindness and nurse care of Lou Gore, the innkeeper. Mounted on mustangs, some 5,000 youthful cowboys per day, cash salaries in hand, turned the trail end into a blazing den of violence. McCoy summarized the town's attractions as "the barroom, the theater, the gambling room, the bawdy house, the dance house. . . . Such is the manner in which the cowboy spends his hard-earned dollars."

When the crime rate burgeoned almost overnight, rowdies faced tough law enforcement by such renowned marshals as Thomas James "Tom Bear River" Smith, who was martyred in the line of duty, and his replacement, James Butler "Wild Bill" Hickok. Smith encountered two assassination attempts when he tried to enforce a gun ban in the city limits. Hickok disarmed shooter John Wesley Hardin. In a later melee, Hickok accidentally shot his own deputy.

During its heyday, the 800-mile (1,300-kilometer) hoof-scarred Chisholm Trail directed 4 million mustangs and 7 million beeves from Fort Worth to Abilene. As nesters and land speculators crowded into eastern Kansas, the monopoly of cattle shipment gradually moved west, in part to avoid tick fever on quarantined routes.

After completion of the Atchison, Topeka, & Santa Fe Railroad in 1872, alternate routes pressed drovers to Caldwell, Dodge City, Ellsworth, Junction City, Newton, and Wichita, Kansas. The financial boom held firm for nearly 17 years, when the fencing of open grazing range with barbed wire and the extension of the Missouri, Kansas, & Texas Railroad (known as the "Katy") into Texas ended overland trail herding.

See also: Buffalo; Cattle and Livestock; Dodge City, Kansas; Hickok, James Butler "Wild Bill"; Law Enforcement; Oklahoma Territory; Weapons.

Further Reading

Brown, Dee. *The American West.* New York: Simon & Schuster, 1995.

Massey, Sara R., ed. *Black Cowboys of Texas.* College Station: Texas A&M University Press, 2005.

———, ed. *Texas Women on the Cattle Trails.* College Station: Texas A&M University Press, 2006.

Smallwood, James M. *The Feud That Wasn't: The Taylor Ring, Bill Sutton, John Wesley Hardin, and Violence in Texas.* College Station: Texas A&M University Press, 2008.

Wishart, David J., ed. *Encyclopedia of the Great Plains.* Lincoln: University of Nebraska Press, 2004.

Christian Science

Christian Science derived from the physical experience and philosophy of Mary Baker Eddy, America's most prominent nineteenth-century female theologian. A native of Bow, New Hampshire, she was born on July 16, 1821, to Abigail and Mark Baker. She internalized in girlhood the Congregationalist concepts of original sin, predestination, and eternal damnation but disclaimed them in adulthood. Because of her tenuous state of health, her scriptural readings concentrated on suffering and healing. At age 23, she returned home in widowhood after the death of her husband, George Washington Glover, from yellow fever. Plagued by neurasthenia, she supported her infant son by teaching kindergarten and writing for the New Hampshire *Patriot,* but had to put the boy in foster care.

In 1852, she married Daniel Patterson, an itinerant dentist, and recovered from depression under the care of Phineas Quimby, a mesmerist from Portland, Maine, specializing in psychosomatic ills. While she recuperated from a back injury after a fall on ice in 1866, study of Jesus's healing of a paralytic through forgiveness introduced her to metaphysics, the basis of Christian Science. She became the original Christian Science practitioner and received her first disciple, spiritualist Hiram Stevens Crafts, a piano maker, the next year while boarding with his family at Lynn, Massachusetts.

Over a three-year immersion in scripture, she acknowledged a supreme deity above the Christian Trinity and valorized godly healing above hygiene, surgery, and material medicine. At age 29, she published her first leaflet, *Science of Man,* on the role of the mind and spirit in Christian healing. In 1875, she issued *Science and Health, With Key to the Scriptures,* a text for her followers covering atonement, redemption, medicine, and physiology.

In 1877, after a divorce, she wed Asa Gilbert Eddy, a sewing machine salesman and fellow believer in the concepts of earthly illusion and spiritual truth. They cofounded the Christian Science Associations and the Church of Christ, Scientist, a religion chartered in June 1879 by the state of Massachusetts.

From 1881 to 1889, Mary Baker Eddy taught methods of prayer and healing techniques at the Massachusetts Metaphysical College in Boston. Over a three-week term, her 800 pupils completed a six-lecture curriculum costing $300 per individual or couple. Students also could opt for six lectures on metaphysical obstetrics for $100. Simultaneously, Eddy edited the *Christian Science Journal, Christian Science Quarterly,* and *Christian Science Sentinel.*

In 1908, members initiated the *Christian Science Monitor,* a respected daily commenting on current events. At her death in Newton, Massachusetts, on December 10, 1910, Eddy's writings on the worth of transcendent wisdom, divine grace, natural harmony, and antimaterialism held the respect of scholars and theologians.

Further Reading

Eddy, Mary Baker. *Manual of the Mother Church: The First Church of Christ Scientist.* Boston: First Church of Christ, Scientist, 1920.

———. *Science and Health, With Key to the Scriptures.* Boston: First Church of Christ, Scientist, 1971.

Gallagher, Eugene V., and W. Michael Ashcraft, eds. *Introduction to New and Alternative Religions in America.* Westport, CT: Greenwood, 2006.

Schaefer, Richard T., and William W. Zellner. *Extraordinary Groups: An Examination of Unconventional Lifestyles.* 8th ed. New York: Worth, 2008.

Whorton, James C. *Nature Cures: The History of Alternative Medicine in America.* New York: Oxford University Press, 2002.

Cincinnati, Ohio

In the 1860s and 1870s, Cincinnati became a bastion of liberalism in the American Midwest. Located north of the Ohio River adjacent to the slave states of Kentucky and Virginia (now West Virginia), the city furthered the rescue efforts of the Underground Railroad with the hideaway and disguise closet at the home of Levi and Catherine White Coffin, the Reverend Charles Brandon Boynton's generosity at the Vine Street Congregational Church, and the niche retreat in the floor of real estate speculator John T. Crawford. At College Hill near Farmers' College and the Ohio Female College, Mary Jane Wilson Pyle concealed passengers in the cellar while her neighbors, Dr. John Witherspoon Scott and his wife, Mary Potts Neal Scott, excavated tunnels and chambers for concealing refugees.

In opposition to the Fugitive Slave Law of 1850 and to the caning of John Joliffe, the Cincinnati attorney for the Underground Railroad, lawyer and future president Rutherford B. Hayes offered free court defense of black runaways. In partnership with attorney Salmon P. Chase, Hayes crusaded for emancipation and vilified the forced extradition of slaves from free territory. And at Lane Theological Seminary, where Theodore Dwight Weld had helped launch the abolitionist movement in the 1830s, students and faculty continued to promote immediate emancipation by aiding runaways.

Civil War Era

As the Civil War implicated the Midwest, control of Ohio's waterways became crucial to food suppliers, especially the rationers of some 50,000 soldiers at Camp Dennison. According to Joseph Hartwell Barnett, editor of the *Cincinnati Daily Gazette,* on June 12, 1861, a federal embargo on Mississippi River traffic deprived families of corn, flour, hay, livestock, oats, pork, and wheat, a restriction that forced groceries and feed stores to close.

In collusion with residents of southern Illinois and Missouri, Cincinnatians relied on a covert barter system in contraband items. A parallel flow of coal, corn, flour, and wheat through the Chesapeake and Ohio Canal kept local households supplied. Profiteers fattened their purses through theft and fraud along the Cincinnati levee by cheating black contrabands.

Copperheads (Southern sympathizers) and General John Hunt Morgan's rogue Confederate cavalry threatened the peace. General Ambrose Burnside imposed martial law on July 11, 1863, an extreme move aided by Governor David Tod, who supplied the city militia with 5,000 guns to defend the riverfront. Until the embargo ended on August 29, 1865, scalawags continued to skim war profits.

To keep the peace, Mayor George Hatch and Union General Lewis Wallace enlisted 706 men in the Black Brigade of Cincinnati, the nation's first formal regimentation of black peacekeepers. One of the brigade, Powhatan Beaty, received the Congressional Medal of Honor for bravery in combat.

Volunteerism proliferated among civilians, who mustered the Ninth Ohio Infantry, the first German regiment in the Union army, and outfitted them with a donation of $250,000. Local women and the Sisters of Charity staffed the casualty wards of the Good Samaritan Hospital and provided rehabilitation for the disabled at the 150-bed Soldiers' Home at Main and Third streets.

A Cincinnati native, herbalist and nurse-dietitian Mary Ann Bickerdyke, managed to rescue combat victims and ferry cows and hens downriver to supply Union casualties with fresh milk, butter, and eggs. On June 9, 1861, she traveled by train to Cairo, Illinois, for river passage to the hospital corps of General William Tecumseh Sherman. As his head nurse, she sheltered escaping slaves and set them to work in the Union army laundry and kitchen.

Reconstruction

In the mid-1860s, Cincinnati increased its generosity and compassion for the needy, beginning with Levi Coffin's direction of the Western Freedmen's Aid Society and, in 1866, with the enrollment of medical and nursing students in the teaching unit at Good Samaritan Hospital. City planners purchased land for Washington Park, a locus of cultural gatherings and Civil War monuments. Burnet Woods at Clifton Avenue added the pleasures of lake boating and trail hiking north of town. To aid those who could not read English, the city's 14 transportation companies coded horsecars and street maps with primary colors. At a time when reporters earned as little as $10 per week, the *Cincinnati Commercial* abandoned party press tactics to institute balanced reporting that favored ex-slaves and immigrants.

Laborers found work at sausage factories, meatpacking plants at Union Stock Yard, granaries and distilleries, Queen City Varnishes & Japans, Cincinnati Coal & Coke, Lion Brewery, Lunkenheimer machine company, and Cincinnati Coffin Company. Skilled workers found jobs on the Ohio River building the John Augustus Roebling Bridge, the nation's first and the world's longest suspension bridge to that time, which ironworkers completed in December 1866.

Recreation and education dominated much of the postwar period with such outlets as an archery range, Bohemian culture society, swimming clubs, and Chester Driving Park, a race course on Spring Grove Avenue. Philanthropist Sarah Worthington formed the Ladies' Academy of Fine Arts, where classes in painting encouraged female students. Artisan Benn Pitman set up workshops at McMicken School of Design to teach ceramics and woodcarving. To promote civic spirit, backers founded the Cincinnati Red Stockings baseball team on June 23, 1866, and introduced player salaries and knickerbocker-style club uniforms. At the end of its first season, the team held a record of 57 wins and one tie.

The following year, Clara Baur and her niece, Bertha Baur, enrolled female students in flute, piano, violin, and voice as well as training in French, German, and Italian at the Conservatory of Music, the city's first music school. Tipplers from the University of Cincinnati gathered at the beer garden established by taverner Louis Mecklenburg. Diners could partake of fried potatoes, wiener schnitzel, rye bread, and beer at Henry Wielert's pavilion, a venue for Michael Brand's orchestra.

In 1875, starch manufacturer Andreas Erkenbrecher donated 60 acres (24 hectares) for the Cincinnati Zoological Garden. To increase songbird varieties with European species, he founded the Society for the Acclimatization of Birds. His philanthropy honored immigrant contributions to the area, where German newcomers made up one-third of the citizenry.

Urban Reform

Cincinnati's Republican Party engaged prestigious jurists, reporters, and woman suffrage advocates. In spring 1861, residents began patronizing the Fourth Street office of the world's first degreed female dentist, Lucy Hobbs Taylor, who paid for her apprenticeship by taking in sewing.

In March 1874, evangelical ministers, led by the Reverend Henry Thane Miller, banded to combat drink and found women eager to prohibit the sale of beer at hotels and saloons. The female contingent, backed in their endeavors by Columbus Mayor James G. Bull, encountered mockery, jeers, screams, and spitting as they lobbied for a city temperance ordinance in Cincinnati. The next month, seven city policemen arrested 43 temperance workers for praying in front of a saloon on Baymiller Street in the southeastern part of town. Male officials embarrassed themselves by cross-examining the mothers, wives, and daughters of prominent men, including Emily Leavitt, wife of a Baptist minister. Charged with obstructing the sidewalk, the women reminded the judge that authorities targeted female "drys" rather than German immigrant drinkers and loafers. After the judge dismissed the case, the women retreated to front yards and church property to rail against alcohol.

Simultaneous with liberality toward freedmen and women, the German Jewish community originated the American Reform Judaism movement. At temple services, worship leaders introduced instrumental accompaniment to hymns and read from German texts rather than the traditional Hebrew. The movement introduced new rituals—confirmation and the bat mitzvah, a coming-of-age ceremony for girls. In 1866, the opening of the Plum Street Temple across from Cincinnati's City Hall made Rabbi Isaac Mayer Wise's Reform congregation the nation's second largest. In 1873, reformers began uniting the American Hebrew Congregations and, two years later, established Hebrew Union College, the nation's first Jewish seminary, with funding provided by industrialist Henry Adler of Lawrenceburg, Indiana. Rabbi Wise presided over the teaching of Torah and classical texts and the ordination of rabbis entering the ministry.

See also: Hayes, Rutherford B.

Further Reading

Griffler, Keith P. *Front Line of Freedom: African Americans and the Forging of the Underground Railroad in the Ohio Valley.* Lexington: University Press of Kentucky, 2004.

Middleton, Stephen. *The Black Laws: Race and the Legal Process in Early Ohio.* Athens: Ohio University Press, 2005.

Snodgrass, Mary Ellen. *The Underground Railroad: An Encyclopedia of People, Places, and Operations.* Armonk, NY: M.E. Sharpe, 2007.

Stradling, David. *Cincinnati: From River City to Highway Metropolis.* Charleston, SC: Arcadia, 2003.

Taylor, Nikki Marie. *Frontiers of Freedom: Cincinnati's Black Community, 1802–1868.* Athens: Ohio University Press, 2005.

Cinco de Mayo

A focal patriotic holiday for Chicanos and sympathetic Latinos, especially those in Texas and the Southwest, Cinco de Mayo (Fifth of May) celebrates Mexico's victory over the French invasion force at Puebla north of Veracruz on May 5, 1862. The holiday honors General Ignacio Zaragoza, who led 4,000 troops against some 8,000 French insurgents of Maximilian I, the archduke of Austria and emperor of Mexico. Maximilian had resolved to conquer and control part of North America and to support the Confederacy during the Civil War.

Since the defeat, people throughout the Southwest celebrate Mexican culture, arts and crafts, and heritage, much as other ethnic American groups enjoy Chinese New Year, Oktoberfest, and St. Patrick's Day. The fiesta reaffirms the historic bond that Chicanos hold with Mexico and asserts ethnic pride.

Gatherings begin with traditional mariachi music, with eight instrumentalists playing Tejano and *conjunto* tunes on guitar, trumpet, and violins. Contributing a festive air, costumed performers dress in sequined skirts and shawls, sombreros, and leather jackets with embroidery and silver buttons. Hosts distribute barbecue, tacos, and Mexican beer; guests participate in horse parades, speeches, and folkloric street dances featuring the bolero, corrido, mambo, ranchera, polka, and waltz. Children smash piñatas filled with sweets, wave Mexican flags, sing Spanish songs, and enjoy fairs, foot races, and fireworks.

Amid secular merrymaking, Roman Catholic observances focus on the Virgen de Guadalupe, a sixteenth-century manifestation of the Virgin Mary and her indigenous Mexican counterpart.

Further Reading

Castro, Rafael A. *Chicano Folklore: A Guide to the Folktales, Traditions, Rituals and Religious Practices of Mexican Americans.* New York: Oxford University Press, 2001.

Estrada, William David. *The Los Angeles Plaza: Sacred and Contested Space.* Austin: University of Texas Press, 2008.

Marley, David F. *Historic Cities of the Americas: An Illustrated Encyclopedia.* Santa Barbara, CA: ABC-CLIO, 2005.

Citizenship

Throughout the second half of the nineteenth century, questions of citizenship provoked wrangling over the constitutional definition of human rights in American democracy. From the Civil War through Reconstruction, the U.S. court system set precedents for a significant broadening of national laws governing immigration, citizenship, and civil rights.

In 1848, in speeches around Rochester, New York, suffragist Elizabeth Cady Stanton censured obstacles to full citizenship for women. The campaign for female enfranchisement continued in state legislatures and Congress for some 75 years until women attained citizens' privileges and fair representation in government.

During the presidential campaign of 1860, Abraham Lincoln promoted government programs to enhance citizen welfare through higher education and free public land for homesteading. When these programs became a reality with the establishment of land-grant colleges and passage of the Homestead Act of 1862, a wave of European immigrants contributed foreign cultures and religions to the citizenry. Newcomers forced native-born Americans to reexamine their willingness to accept aliens in American society and to honor the freedoms guaranteed by the Bill of Rights. The surge in homesteading aroused bigotry among Americans who did not count foreigners, especially Catholics and Jews, as worthy citizens.

An inevitable clash over slavery further challenged the predominant white male concept of who deserved full membership in democracy. The outbreak of civil war on April 12, 1861, aroused the ire of Senator Charles Sumner of Massachusetts and others, who blamed secessionist states for abandoning their national loyalty to protect slavery, an inhumane institution that fostered the breeding of black children for sale.

Obligations to the U.S. military resurrected citizens' rights concerns that dated to colonial days. During the four-year conflict, draft quotas of the nation's first federal military conscription heightened dissension among both patriots and pacifists. In the South, newspaper editors mocked the North, where bribes to enlistees suggested that patriotism was less fervid in the Union than in the Confederacy. During public discussion of national emancipation for slaves, libertarians demanded the mustering of black soldiers as well as the enfranchisement of blacks as citizens.

On January 1, 1863, President Lincoln initiated the dismantling of the bondage system by issuing the Emancipation Proclamation. Simultaneously, Thaddeus Stevens, floor manager of the U.S. Congress, advocated harsh punishments for secessionists for abandoning their fidelity to the Union.

In this same period, author Edward Everett Hale composed an allegory, "The Man Without a Country," published anonymously in the *Atlantic Monthly* in December 1863. The classic short story mused on the statelessness of a Philip Nolan, a fictional character who chooses to strip himself of national belonging. The popularity of Hale's story reflected readers' serious consideration of their allegiance to the nation and its government.

Demands for Rights

The issues of peacemaking, enfranchising women and blacks, and restoring citizenship to secessionists dominated American politics for the next 14 years. At the height of war, on December 8, 1863, President Lincoln looked past the military conflict to the concerns of noncombatants. He introduced the concept of clemency for traitors by granting amnesty to Southerners who reclaimed their U.S. citizenship and freed their slaves.

In summer 1864, Lincoln pocketed a bill proposed by Congressman Stevens and senators Sumner and Benjamin Wade that called for a majority of residents in each of the 11 rebel states to swear that they had never condoned disaffiliation with the Union. With more forgiveness toward the rebels, Lincoln crafted an alternative—the Ten Percent Plan, by which the Union reclaimed Southern states in which one-tenth of the citizens declared themselves loyal, regardless of their past allegiance. His landslide victory at the polls proved his assumption correct—most Americans favored mercy and peace over extended grudge bearing.

On March 8, 1865, Lincoln's Second Inaugural address congratulated Americans for conducting the nation's business, despite four years of civil and governmental turmoil. On May 10, 1865, federal agents imprisoned Confederate President Jefferson Davis in irons at Fort Monroe, Virginia, and charged him with treason. He incurred bankruptcy and the confiscation of his home at Davis Bend south of Vicksburg, Mississippi. Along with former Confederate General Robert E. Lee, Davis suffered expatriation, a diminution of voting privileges that posed a severe humiliation for a former U.S. senator.

Meanwhile, the nation's first black field commander, Martin Robinson Delany, the grandson of African abductees, advised the president on the needs of ex-slaves and aided the work of the Freedmen's Bureau in introducing former bondsmen to citizens' rights and responsibilities. After the bureau set up the Theological School for Freemen in Richmond, Virginia, the school began the process of educating blacks to become full-fledged Americans.

Violence and Resentment

Nearly eight months after Lincoln's assassination, on December 6, 1865, the 38th Congress altered the U.S.

Constitution by adopting the Thirteenth Amendment, which prohibited slavery. As a result, white Southerners, angered by the wreckage of their economy and society and the nullification of state elections and constitutions, fomented resentment and reprisals. Racist crime and guerrilla militias cowed freedmen in the Carolinas, Florida, Louisiana, and Mississippi. The Ku Klux Klan, Red Shirts, White League, and Knights of the White Camellia lynched blacks for purchasing land, operating schools and businesses, and owning guns, all evidence of the rise of former slaves toward equality with white Americans. To ensure obedience to federal law and to suppress the Ku Klux Klan and the passage of racist Black Codes, Congress instituted a federal enforcement agency within the Freedmen's Bureau.

Congressional passage of the Civil Rights Act of April 9, 1866, over President Andrew Johnson's veto, established the citizenship of all native-born Americans, excluding Indians. The law introduced a period of Radical Reconstruction and guaranteed federal protection of black rights to housing and jobs. Most offensive to entrenched Southern racists, the third section of the Fourteenth Amendment, adopted on July 9, 1868, excluded former rebels from appointment or election to state and federal offices.

At the May 12, 1869, American Equal Rights Convention in New York City, black orator Frederick Douglass declared that Reconstruction-era violence against black males made their enfranchisement more urgent than that of women. He reasoned that white females already possessed more social and economic privileges than blacks of either gender. Seeking to curtail the exclusion of women from the law's protection, on May 15, 1869, tactician Elizabeth Cady Stanton co-founded the National Woman Suffrage Association.

As Stanton anticipated, after Congress ratified the Fifteenth Amendment on February 3, 1870, the new constitutional laws conferred on black males both civil rights and the vote, but denied full citizenship to Asians, Native Americans, and women. These landmark laws overruled states' rights and nullified Black Codes that had restricted the free movement of blacks and forbade them from testifying against whites in court. Delayed ratification in the Confederate states sent a message to the Republican-controlled Congress that secessionist Democrats would not tolerate a federalized central government elected by black illiterates with no background in civics.

President Ulysses S. Grant bolstered the justice system with the Ku Klux Klan Act of 1871, which gave him military power to enforce citizen rights. On May 22, he restored full citizenship to all but 500 Confederates still aggrieved at the failure of "the cause." By the middle of Reconstruction, in June 1872, Congress had spent a total of $20 million on uplifting blacks from bondage into equality.

Expansion of Civil Rights

The Civil Rights Act of March 1, 1875, co-written by Senator Sumner and Congressman Benjamin Franklin Butler, both of Massachusetts, looked beyond the Constitution to the spirit of democracy stated and implied in the Declaration of Independence. The intent was to expunge the social injustices that had marred the early years of the republic. The legislation ensured unimpeded citizenship for ex-slaves in the North and South and indirectly rebuked President Grant for failing to shield freedmen from a backlash of Southern bigots. The wording guaranteed all citizens access to public transportation, recreation and amusement, and hotels and inns, but not to schools and cemeteries or service on juries, a privilege that remained limited to white males.

In reality, the law made little impact on social and economic racism grounded in plantation slavery and white supremacy. Even though black males advanced toward full citizenship, they faced hindrances similar to the constraints of their forebears. During settlement of the contested presidential election of 1876, the Compromise of 1877 lessened federal powers by removing Union occupation forces from the South. The U.S. government abandoned its efforts to ensure racial equality, enabling former Confederate states to deprive freedmen of their newly won liberty.

To the West, citizens took pride in being part of the Union. In an extension of human rights to the Southwest, legislators in 1868 banned the sale of female and child slaves among the Navajo, a glimmer of hope for Indian rights. The Bureau of Immigration, a division of the U.S. Treasury, monitored the recruitment of Asian coolie labor. Although the Naturalization Act of 1870 barred Asians from full Americanization, the influx of foreigners doubled.

On March 3, 1875, Congress passed the Page Act, which prohibited the recruitment of Asian slave laborers, convicts, and prostitutes. The act also placed Indian negotiations in the hands of a guardian, Columbus Delano, head of the U.S. Department of the Interior. By phasing out past treaties and dismantling the tribal structure, the law reclassified Indians as federal wards under the U.S. Constitution and demoted hereditary chiefs of state from positions of influence and authority. The legislation implied that Indians were incapable of solving ethnic educational, medical, and relational dilemmas, particularly the problematic legal status of the Native American in the United States. The law recognized the nation's need to ensure the well-being of individual Indians and foretokened the enstatement of natives under the Indian Citizenship Act of 1924.

See also: Fifteenth Amendment; Fourteenth Amendment; Thirteenth Amendment (1865).

Further Reading

Gardner, Martha. *The Qualities of a Citizen: Women, Immigration, and Citizenship, 1870–1965.* Princeton, NJ: Princeton University Press, 2005.

Heald, Bruce D. *Main Street, New Hampshire.* Charleston, SC: Arcadia, 2003.

Keyssar, Alexander. *The Right to Vote: The Contested History of Democracy in the United States.* New York: Basic Books, 2000.

Rothenberg, Paula S., ed. *Race, Class, and Gender in the United States: An Integrated Study.* 7th ed. New York: Worth, 2007.

Smith, Rogers M. *Civic Ideals: Conflicting Visions of Citizenship in U.S. History.* New Haven, CT: Yale University Press, 1997.

Civil Rights

In the 1860s and 1870s, abolitionism and citizen rights dominated the thinking of Americans. Freedmen found support from President Abraham Lincoln, orator Frederick Douglass, and Salmon P. Chase, chief justice of the U.S. Supreme Court. One event in particular, General Ambrose Burnside's suppression of Confederate sympathizers in Ohio, outraged former Ohio congressman Clement Laird Vallandigham, the lead agitator for the Copperheads (Southern sympathizers) and a defender of free speech. In Dayton on May 1, 1863, he challenged the pro-Union majority by demanding the ouster of "King" Abraham Lincoln for waging war to liberate blacks and by maligning the president for enslaving whites.

Convicted by a military tribunal of disloyalty to the Union, Vallandigham began a two-year sentence at a military prison in Cincinnati. The Northern Democratic press excoriated the Lincoln administration for coercing war protesters. The U.S. Supreme Court refused to hear Vallandigham's appeal. To prevent Vallandigham from becoming a pacifist cause célèbre, Lincoln on May 19 commuted his sentence to exile behind enemy lines in Tennessee.

At war's end, despite the obstructionism of President Andrew Johnson, the 39th Congress refused to seat Southern representatives. A Republican majority of 70 percent passed civil rights legislation guaranteeing full citizenship to residents born in the United States. The law recognized black citizenship, but continued to exclude Native Americans from political enfranchisement.

In Lexington, Kentucky, the press for human rights legalized black and mulatto slave marriages and offspring for a 50-cent fee. During Reconstruction, Congressman Lyman Trumbull of Illinois, chair of the Senate Judiciary Committee, led Republicans in a crusade for black human rights.

Civil Rights Act of 1866

On April 9, 1866, Congress passed the first Civil Rights Act, which prohibited job and housing discrimination by prejudicial state laws. It was the first major legislation passed over a presidential veto, that of Andrew Johnson. The law vitiated Southern Black Codes and Jim Crow statutes, badges of servitude that imposed poll taxes and literacy tests on black voters and forbade freedmen from holding public office, filing lawsuits against whites, and owning alcohol and weapons. Violators of the Civil Rights Act faced a $1,000 fine and/or a year's imprisonment for persecuting the black underclass.

The U.S. Army took an aggressive stance against white vigilantism, which punished blacks for unemployment, possessing money, loitering, or flirtation or seduction of white women. The Freedmen's Bureau intervened in deceptive labor practices by helping former slaves negotiate contracts. Additional enactments in January 1867 extended voting rights to blacks in the District of Columbia and the territories. The liberality toward voting rights angered the National Woman Suffrage Association, which elected Elizabeth Cady Stanton and Susan B. Anthony to promote equivalent rights for women.

A flaw in the Civil Rights Act of 1866—the absence of aid for people too poor to press suit in court and too weak and outnumbered to combat the Ku Klux Klan—allowed racist terrorism to continue. Arousing fear among Southern whites, the registration of 703,000 black voters produced majorities in Alabama, Florida, Louisiana, Mississippi, and South Carolina. Riots erupted in Memphis, Tennessee, and New Orleans, Louisiana, giving Republicans an opportunity to increase the power of Reconstruction laws to protect freedmen from civil uprisings. However, in Bertie County, North Carolina, arson, crop destruction, and the rape of black women

Freedmen in New Orleans line up to vote in 1867. Several Southern states enfranchised ex-slaves, but it took the Fifteenth Amendment in 1870 to guarantee federal black suffrage. Even so, racists found ways to suppress black citizenship. *(The Granger Collection, New York)*

intimidated Republicans and allowed Democrats to regain control of the state.

In 1868, Georgia's refusal to acknowledge black civil rights forced the 40th Congress to revoke the state's readmission to the Union and to reimpose martial law. On September 3, Henry McNeal Turner, the state's first black legislator, defied the authority of whites to withhold representation from elected officials.

Executing Federal Law

On May 31, 1870, the 41st Congress passed the Enforcement Act of 1870, which legalized the use of force to prohibit bribery, coercion, or terrorism from impeding voters from casting their ballots. Prosecution of the law brought to justice thousands of Klansmen and threatened the survival of their brutal citizen militia. To further counter election fraud, a supplemental bill, the Force Act of February 28, 1871, allowed federal scrutiny of voter registration and congressional elections by the regional U.S. circuit court and federal marshals in each district. More than 5,000 violators appeared before federal judges, who convicted one-quarter of conspiracy to interfere with rights of citizenship. The U.S. Supreme Court later overturned indictments under the Force Act of 1871 on the grounds that the federal government had usurped states' authority to oversee the voting process.

In a later strike for civil rights, on April 20, 1871, the 42nd Congress targeted paramilitary fanatics with the Ku Klux Klan Act, which enforced the Fourteenth Amendment. The legislation empowered President Ulysses S. Grant to dispatch federal troops to states infiltrated with Klansmen and to suspend habeas corpus by jailing offenders without due process of law. In October 1871, the implementation of the act in ten South Carolina counties resulted in the banning of racist conspirators from service on juries. Federal empowerment in Corpus Christi, Texas, reduced the Klan's public profile. By removing trials from local courtrooms, federal authorities ensured fair hearings under impartial judges no longer intimidated by Klansmen.

In Lynchburg, Virginia, federal authorities formed a public school system financed by fines for civil rights infractions. In Poughkeepsie, New York, a black couple, Joseph Rhodes and his wife Sadie, used the law as a springboard for integration. They forced the issue of segregation by launching a test litigation demanding federal civil rights. In fall 1874, Josephine Rhodes, the eldest of their five children, and younger sisters Marietta and Sarah integrated public schools.

Civil Rights Act of 1875

In February 1875, the biracial 43rd Congress passed the Civil Rights Act of 1875; President Ulysses S. Grant signed it into law on March 1. A bold declaration of social rights, the legislation outlawed racial discrimination on juries and in public accommodations—hotels, saloons, theaters, buses, and trains. Drafted by Republican congressmen from Massachusetts—Benjamin Franklin Butler, a crusader against terrorists, and Charles Sumner, a champion of voting rights—the legislation rebuked President Grant for failing to protect freedmen from a backlash of Southern elitists. Sumner wanted the law to require equal accommodation in churches, cemeteries, and schools, but Republicans feared that his vision of fairness would wreak havoc in the South. Infringements of black citizenship merited fines of $500 to $1,000 and jail sentences of one to 12 months. Another provision charged law enforcement officers with civil and criminal noncompliance if they failed to protect black citizens from racism.

While state courts awaited a ruling on constitutionality by the U.S. Supreme Court, the law lacked sufficient backing for universal defiance of racial prejudice. On October 15, 1883, in a consolidated decision on five cases—collectively referred to as the Civil Rights Cases—the Supreme Court held 8–1 that the legislation was unconstitutional for overreaching powers belonging to the states. As a result, Alabama, Arkansas, Florida, Georgia, Kentucky, Louisiana, Mississippi, and Texas passed state laws segregating public transportation. Similar decisions from state benches condoned separate but equal accommodations in Delaware, Maryland, Missouri, and North Carolina. In retaliation, two black newspapers, the *New York Globe* and the Boston *Hub,* charged that the judicial branch of government refused to respect equal rights.

See also: Black Codes; Department of Justice, U.S.; Fifteenth Amendment; Fourteenth Amendment; Ku Klux Klan; Reconstruction.

Further Reading

Grofman, Bernard, Lisa Handley, and Richard G. Niemi. *Minority Representation and the Quest for Voting Equality.* Cambridge, UK: Cambridge University Press, 1992.

Kaczorowski, Robert J. *The Politics of Judicial Interpretation: The Federal Courts, Department of Justice, and Civil Rights, 1866–1876.* New York: Fordham University Press, 2005.

Olson, Lynne. *Freedom's Daughters: The Unsung Heroines of the Civil Rights Movement from 1830 to 1970.* New York: Scribner's, 2001.

Rothenberg, Paula S., ed. *Race, Class, and Gender in the United States: An Integrated Study.* 7th ed. New York: Worth, 2007.

Utter, Glenn H., and Ruth Ann Strickland. *Campaign and Election Reform: A Reference Handbook.* 2nd ed. Santa Barbara, CA: ABC-CLIO, 2008.

Clothes and Fashion

The rise of print media and factory mechanization in the 1860s changed Americans' thinking on fashion from need to "must have." The difference between Western European fashion and that of the United States embarrassed Americans at the Paris Universal Exposition of 1867, at which France hosted 219 booths and the Americans only nine. Fashion commentators used the dowdiness of American women as a goad to adopt conspicuous consumption in clothing.

For the tasteful American woman, *Godey's Lady's Book,* the "Queen of Household Magazines," set the standard for 1 million readers as far west as California, Hawaii, Texas, Washington Territory, and Wisconsin. Garment layouts highlighted luxury items—the morning negligee and nightgown, matinee skirt, Josephine shawl, ball gown, wedding gown and mantilla, opera hood, hairpiece, fichu, and Zouave jacket. Craft-minded women saved patterns for crochet, embroidery, knitting, and ornate monogramming, a job commandeered by mothers of the bride and other female relatives of engaged girls.

Readers in remote locales freshened stale outfits with mail-order hair ornaments, pins, bracelets, necklaces, earrings, yarn, scarves, feathers, and yard goods. Factory girls and Irish servant girls bought cheap ginghams and calico and copied the ornate fashions that originated in brocade and velvet.

Retail Trends

In the early stage of industrialization, fashion became an ever-changing series of trends exploited in print advertisements by merchants such as Marshall Field in Chicago and Rowland Hussey Macy in Manhattan. Clothing critics in *Arthur's Illustrated Home Magazine, Potter's American Monthly,* and *Ladies' Repository* stressed European dominance of the fashion world with such terms as *décolletage, en suite, matellassé, moiré, peignoir, plissé, polonaise,* and *tablier.*

After the invention of the domestic sewing machine, sweatshops staffed primarily by immigrant women generated modish items. These were sold in such upscale New York City department stores as Alexander Turney Stewart's Iron Palace on Broadway and Joseph B. and Lyman G. Bloomingdale's chain, begun in 1872 on the Lower East Side.

In contrast to the conservative austerity of men's attire, women's fashions shifted rapidly in cut, color, and ornamentation. To promote rapid turnover in chic wardrobes, Jordan Marsh in Boston, Rich's in Atlanta, Wanamaker's in Philadelphia, and Meier & Frank in Portland, Oregon, decked window displays in the latest designs and fabrics. At I. Magnin in San Francisco, seamstress Mary Ann Magnin turned clothes shopping into a personalized fashion show by seating shoppers on couches while sales associates paraded garments one by one for inspection.

Department stores and apothecary shops added sidelines of cosmetics and hair care and hygiene products hyped with illustrations of swank belles and their beauty secrets. In 1870, the American Pharmaceutical Association warned of heavy metals in hair lotions, complexion soap, and face powder. The *American Journal of Pharmacy* and the *American Chemist* alerted readers to the danger of palsy and facial paralysis caused by lead salts in freckle lotions, pomade, and hair dyes and restorers, as well as convulsions, kidney failure, and hallucinations caused by bismuth and lead carbonate in pearl powder for whitening teeth. Articles in the *Medical and Surgical Reporter* declared toxic all fashionable concoctions for skin, hair, teeth, and nails containing mercury salts, prussic acid, and arsenic, a common ingredient in skin whiteners.

The Feminist Debate

The suffrage movement expressed the ire of female reformers toward voguish, conspicuous styles that pleased and titillated men. In a culture governed by male wealth, dynasty, and prestige, the shaping of the body into upthrust bust, flat abdomen, and protruding derriere forced women into decorative passivity. Gamblers, racetrack touts, and politicians seeking notoriety adorned their arms in public with fetching women clad in body-revealing array and oversized hats.

In an era marked by high rates of tuberculosis, women's rights agitators charged the boned corset with restraining women's spines and ribs into grotesque shapes that limited flexibility and breathing. The editors of *Health and Beauty, Health Reformer, Herald of Health, North American Review,* and *Transactions of the American Institute of Homeopathy* advocated well-being over fashion, as it applied to binding baby layettes, hoop skirts weighted with fringe and ruching, six to eight layers of petticoats, thin-soled shoes, cramped gaiter boots, and tight lacings. Ellen Gould White, founder of the Seventh-Day Adventist Water Cure in Battle Creek, Michigan, modeled a reform outfit in 1865 and counseled Christian women to dress modestly and to shorten skirts enough to avoid contagion by street and gutter filth.

An antidote to crippling fashion came from the sick. At hydropathy (water cure) spas, patients enjoyed the Oneida costume—"Turkish trousers" (pantaloons) and ballet-length tunic dresses similar to those worn by Islamic women. Iconoclasts—such as nurse Clara Barton, reformers Angelina and Sarah Grimké, actor Fanny Kemble, suffragist Elizabeth Cady Stanton, and Civil War physician Mary Edwards Walker—introduced the revolutionary outfits to the public, inspiring jingles, catcalls, and snide caricatures. According to *Laws of Life and Women's Health Journal,* the nonrestrictive harem pants

Fashion plates from *Godey's Lady's Book* in 1863 illustrate the styles of the day in women's luxury attire, featuring full skirts supported by hoops and crinolines. Print media heightened the nation's fashion sense and accelerated the pace of change. *(Transcendental Graphics/ Getty Images)*

enabled women to garden, cycle, ice-skate, and play lawn tennis and croquet. Hydropathist Lydia Sayer Hasbrouck, publisher of *The Sibyl: A Review of the Tastes, Errors & Fashions of Society,* popularized trousers as a socially acceptable comfort.

The National Dress Reform Association, headquartered in Glen Haven, New York, won stronger support in the Midwest. Susan B. Anthony, the leader and role model of the Northeastern women's rights movement, considered fashion too great a battleground and retreated to issues of full citizenship for women. Dress reformers riposted that women's rights advocates were Benedict Arnolds to the cause; however, the dress reform movement lost steam by 1864.

A decade later, the debate revived. In Painesville, Ohio, journalist Mary Ella Tillotson, author of *Progress vs. Fashion: An Essay on the Sanitary and Social Influences of Women's Dress* (1873) and *Woman's Way Out* (1876), organized the short-lived American Free Dress League (AFDL). AFDL member Susan Pecker Fowler advocated the "freedom suit," "science costume," or "American suit," a female costume suited to the autonomy of the New Woman rather than the arbitrary rule of male designers. In defense of the trousered costume, Fowler spent a night in jail for supposedly violating a nonexistent Jersey City ordinance. At an AFDL convention in Philadelphia, Tillotson lambasted as ignorant the hecklers who ridiculed pants for women. Members demonstrated such labor-alleviating attire at the 1876 Centennial Exposition in Philadelphia, winning a medal for the Alice Fletcher Depot.

The Rugged West

On the frontier, exigency and climate defined clothing styles for both men and women, which tended toward unisex outfits of buckskin chaps and leggings, denim jeans, flannel shifts, leather boots, and Stetson hats. Fur coats, hats, and gloves made bearable the severe cold of the Dakotas, the Yellowstone River Valley, and the Continental Divide. California miners replaced tattered garments at floating emporiums operating in San Francisco Bay. Some sold recycled articles made by "shoddy factories," which tore rags into thread for reweaving.

After John Warren Butterfield launched the Butterfield Stage, his standard dress set a pattern that stage conductors and drivers such as Henry "Hank" Monk copied—a long yellow linen duster, high leather boots, a vest and white shirt, and a flat-brimmed hat. In 1876, union suits—cotton or cotton-wool one-piece underwear from Manhattan manufacturers Bradley, Voorhees, and Day—introduced warmth and stretch with knitted undergarments that covered the arms and legs. Women generally preferred woolly stockings. As whites coerced Indians onto reservations, the suppressors demonstrated their empowerment by forcing Native Americans to abandon their traditional dress and to adopt the prevalent white attire.

See also: Bloomingdale's; *Godey's Lady's Book*; Stetson, John Batterson; Strauss, Levi.

Further Reading

Crane, Diana. *Fashion and Its Social Agendas: Class, Gender, and Identity in Clothing.* Chicago: University of Chicago Press, 2000.

Cunningham, Patricia A. *Reforming Women's Fashion, 1850–1920: Politics, Health and Art.* Kent, OH: Kent State University Press, 2003.

Davis, Fred. *Fashion, Culture, and Identity.* Chicago: University of Chicago Press, 1992.

Fischer, Gayle V. *Pantaloons and Power: A Nineteenth-Century Dress Reform in the United States.* Kent, OH: Kent State University Press, 2001.

Zakim, Michael. *Ready-Made Democracy: A History of Men's Dress in the American Republic.* Chicago: University of Chicago Press, 2003.

Coal and Coal Mining

During the Industrial Revolution, coal, the most abundant fossil fuel in the United States, undergirded the mining, rail, and steel industries and served as a catalyst for labor reform. In 1864, *Harper's* monthly magazine reported that the country had approximately 1 square mile (2.6 square kilometers) of coalfield for every 15 square miles (39 square kilometers) of surface, a ratio twice that of Great Britain. Of 197,000 square miles (510,000 square kilometers) of U.S. coalfields, about two-thirds flourished in the Arkansas, Iowa, and Missouri Basin and the Appalachian Basin (Kentucky, Pennsylvania, and Virginia); others spread across the Midwest and into Oklahoma and Texas. The report concluded that coal mining and the transport of coal by hoist to rail turned a profit at the expense of human toil. Workers accepted danger, compromised health, and shortened lifespan as the cost of earning their wages.

The mining industry developed a symbiotic relationship with railway companies, which imported workers to sparsely populated mountain coalfields. In the mid-1800s, fossilized carbon replaced wood as the primary fuel for homes and industry. A native force of miners and emigrants from England, Ireland, Scotland, and Wales dug deposits of bituminous (soft) coal in 15 states. The 50 collieries in the Allegheny Mountains of West Virginia exploited rich lodes of fat coking coal for steel production, oily cannel coal (oil shale) for lighting, gassy bituminous grade for industry, and hot-burning splint for home heating.

The wealth of the Lehigh mines at the Mammoth coalfields of southwestern Pennsylvania extended 30 acres (12 hectares) in a stratum 70 feet (21 meters) thick. At West Overton, industrialist Henry Clay Frick, a future partner of Andrew Carnegie, got his start turning coal into coke in a beehive oven for use in steel mills. Frick eventually controlled 80 percent of the Pennsylvania mines.

An American Industry

During the last year of the Civil War, *The Bankers' Magazine and Statistical Register, Journal of the Money Market, and Commercial Digest* reported on the increased demand for coal and the expansion of the mining industry. According to the trade periodicals *Engineering and Mining Journal* and *Transactions of the American Institute of Mining Engineers,* the largest veins, some nearly a half mile (800 meters) deep, anchored the economies of Ohio, Pennsylvania, and West Virginia. Despite wartime embargoes, the flow of coal through the Chesapeake and Ohio Canal and along the Cleveland, Columbus, & Cincinnati and the Lake Short & Tuscarawas Valley railroads kept local families supplied. On the Great Lakes, freighters sped coal, iron ore, and limestone to steel mills and to railheads in Erie, Pennsylvania, and Ashtabula, Ohio. Coal traffic from the anthracite (hard coal) fields of Pennsylvania centered on coal docks in Erie and Cleveland. In 1862, a successful startup in Shamokin, the Cameron Colliery, operated on three slopes at three entrances and produced 66,114 tons (59,965 metric tons) per year. Within a decade, the company comprised four drifts and a labor force of 151 miners.

On October 3, 1863, President Abraham Lincoln composed a Thanksgiving proclamation thanking God for the gifts of America's natural resources. He specified the mining of natural deposits of coal, iron, and precious metals in the West, a section of the country he intended to turn into productive states of the Union.

On the frontier, mining attracted farmers away from agriculture to nonseasonal work that guaranteed a steady cash income. In Kansas, a small operation at Pittsburg enriched William Core, who dug coal from outcroppings in a ravine on his land and ferried it to blacksmiths across the Kansas–Missouri line in Carthage. With railroad access, a smelting operation grew in 1876 with the importation of laborers from Wisconsin to load some 48 coal-fired kilns.

Along the Powder River and at Carbon and Rock Springs, Wyoming, lump or steamboat coal for blast furnaces brought higher rewards than chestnut, pea, or bag coal for stoking kitchen and parlor stoves, puddling furnaces, and blacksmith forges. In 1860, farther west along the Columbia River in Washington Territory, David Mowery and Erasmus M. Smithers tunneled into a seam of lignite, a soft brown coal. The resultant Renton, Seattle, and Talbot mines produced coke and lignite for home and industrial steam engine use.

Merchant Charles Plummer streamlined the process of loading coal by laying narrow-gauge train tracks from Lake Washington to Seattle Harbor piers. From James O'Loughlin's Coal Mountain farther north at Hamilton, coal made a precarious journey by canoe before being transferred from Puget Sound to south-central California. By 1876, coal miners loaded 26,707 tons (24,223 metric tons) of coal aboard barges to convey from Seattle to San Francisco. To convince miners to remain in the area, the first shipment of "Mercer girls" (mail-order brides) began turning an all-male mining district into a family-centered community in 1864.

Reducing Costs and Raising Profits

At war's end, global shipping became an attainable goal for U.S. merchants. Government surveyors explored the Midway Islands for development into a coaling depot for North Pacific steamships. On March 30, 1867, Congress and President Andrew Johnson commissioned Secretary of State William Henry Seward to purchase Alaska in the hope of reaping profits from deposits of coal, gold, graphite, and iron.

As the United States became less agrarian and more industrialized, the rise of a plutocracy attested to the control of banking, oil and coal, and railroads by shrewd monopolists. To man the digging operations in central Pennsylvania, mine owners recruited immigrants from Poland and Lithuania, whose eagerness to escape Russian domination influenced them to work for low wages. At Port Johnston in Bayonne, New Jersey, some 300 workers used a steam shovel and crowbars to load coal at a half-mile-long wharf for 8 cents per hour. Topmen shoved coal from railcars down chutes, trimmers wielded boards or spades to direct the lumps into bins, and wheelers directed pea coal into barrows from shore to the holds of ships and canal barges.

A strike against the Lehigh-Wilkesbarre Railroad in fall 1876 resulted after management dropped pay by one-third. A second strike on July 26, 1877, aired wheelers' complaints that they worked 13-hour days for $1 in pay. Lehigh fired the strikers and brought in German dockworkers, who also refused to labor for so little remuneration. According to the *Bayonne Herald,* a Catholic priest, Thomas M. Killeen, involved Mayor Henry Meigs and Councilman Steven K. Lane in negotiation with Lehigh owners, who agreed to a bonus pay system.

In the South, as leaders of the New South built an industrial base, coal and coke mining began to replace agriculture as a major employer of unskilled labor. Author John D. Imboden predicted in *Coal and Iron Resources in Virginia* (1872) that mines at Stone Mountain would outstrip Pittsburgh in production. After the repair of war-torn rail lines, Southerners reconstructed penitentiaries to fill their needs for cheap labor. To restore lucrative trade with the North, unscrupulous sheriffs leased convicts to lumber yards, turpentine camps, and coal mines. The Nashville *Republican Banner* rationalized that working felons in mines taught them a trade that would support them for a lifetime. In Alabama and Georgia, mine owners paid $19 per month for convict upkeep as opposed to the cost of $2 per day to employ a free laborer. Birmingham investors profited from a steady head count of penal laborers, who ensured negotiable contracts with iron furnaces and steel mills.

Investigators found former slaves serving sentences for petty larceny, vagrancy, and trespassing and suffering lashing, malnutrition, and shackling to cots in unsanitary prison camps. Miners in Kentucky and Tennessee complained that convict leasing competed unfairly with free labor, reducing wages by up to 20 percent.

Human Costs

Vast changes in the Midwest accompanied the arrival of the railroad. In 1865, the opening of the Missouri, Kansas, & Texas Railroad south to Galveston, Texas, eased coal transports through remote territory. With the completion of the Transcontinental Railroad in 1869, John Edgar Thomas, head of the Pennsylvania Railroad, extended rail service over the Allegheny Mountains, converted wood-burning steam locomotives to coal, and invested in coal mines to fuel engines.

The Denver smelting operation of Meyer Guggenheim, a Swiss émigré, stimulated the coal industry at Trinidad, Colorado, thus ending the scramble for wood as furnace fuel. At Jimmy Camp Creek, Matt France negotiated shipping aboard the gondolas of the Denver & New Orleans Railroad to transport coal to Colorado Springs and Denver.

In 1868, the Union Pacific opened a coal mine at Rock Springs, Wyoming, and established the Wyoming Coal and Mining Company as operators. When laborers struck for better pay, management hired Scandinavian immigrants at the rate of $2 a day and stationed U.S. troops at the mine to prevent a clash. A second strike at Sweetwater and Washakie, Wyoming, in 1875 prompted the Union Pacific Coal Department to hire 150 Chinese strikebreakers, who proved dependable and hardworking. In Indian Territory (Oklahoma) in 1872, freighter James Jackson "J.J." McAlester opened the first coal mine, the McAlester Coal Mining Company, at Bucklucksy (later named McAlester). In 1876, Nebraska's fortunes rose after rail lines linked Missouri River traffic with Burlington & Missouri River railcars at Plattsmouth, offering jobs in regional lumber and coal yards. Into the late 1870s, the Southwest began to rely on the Atchison, Topeka, & Santa Fe Railroad for necessities. Westbound trains delivered personnel and fresh horses to Fort Union; the eastbound route carried coal to Kansans.

Coal took on an ethnic, folkloric, and gendered significance among miners. Appalachian mining communities assembled for Baptist hymn sings, storytelling, dancing, baseball and horseshoes, and athletic contests displaying strength and agility. Their superstitions focused on dogs, mules, and horses that pulled tramcars and warned miners of danger ahead. At union rallies, miners harmonized on "The Avondale Mine Disaster" (1869), the ballad of a coal mine fire near Wilkes-Barre, Pennsylvania, and "Down in the Coal Mine" (1872), a tune composed by anthracite diggers about gloom and culm (coal dust) dumps. In 1876, a come-all-ye song, "Two-Cent Coal," memorialized the freezing of the Monongahela River and the slicing of miners' wages from 3 cents to 2 cents per bushel. When ice jams thawed and flooded the owner's property, miners celebrated the disaster.

Strength in Unity

Oppressed diggers and loaders grasped at solidarity and collective bargaining. Despite such management ploys as the outlawing of mining unions in Illinois in February 1863, colliery employees collaborated to secure steady employment and wages and to reduce the dangers of such hazards as cave-ins, flooding, collapsing gob (waste) piles, runaway trams, and methane gas explosions. The least

Poet John Wallace Crawford, a Scots immigrant, mourned the coal industry's disregard for suffering in "Only a Miner Killed" (1877). Music historians interpret the lyrics as a contrast between the lavish funeral for Cornelius Vanderbilt with the ragtag procession following a miner's coffin:

Only a miner killed—oh! is that all?
One of the timbers caved, great was the fall,
Crushing another one shaped like his God.
Only a miner lad—under the sod.
Only a miner killed, just one more dead.
Who will provide for them—who earn their bread?
Wife and little ones: pity them, God,
Their earthly father is under the sod.
Only a miner killed, dead on the spot,
Poor hearts are breaking in yonder lone cot.
He died at his post, a hero as brave
As any who sleeps in a marble top grave.
Only a miner killed! God, if thou wilt,
Just introduce him to Vanderbilt,
Who, with his millions, if he is there,
Can't buy one interest—even one share.
Only a miner, bury him quick;
Just write his name on a piece of a stick.
Though humble and plain be the poor miner's grave
Beyond, all are equal, the master and slave.

deadly jobs involved open-cut or surface mining of a basset (horizontal stratum or outcrop).

For depth, miners resorted to benching or cutting through a column of steps or strata. Drift mining or undercutting followed a seam across a contiguous valley or ravine below a breast or slope. Thick deposits required shute or chamber mining of whole rooms, which engineers supported with tall pillars of coal to protect "manways" (tunnels). Underground laborers illuminated their work with candlesticks and bug lights, candles surrounded by tin reflectors. Trolley or tram boys fastened themselves by breast straps to crawl along tracks and pull loaded cars to dump sites.

As a source of comfort, isolated mountain communities shared housing, stores, pubs, and churches and relied on gossip to warn of threats to their income by mine closures and the hiring of scabs (strike breakers). To maintain order in coal regions in Beaver, Indiana, Luzerne, Schuylkill, Somerset, and Westmoreland counties, the Pennsylvania legislature authorized a private force of Coal and Iron Police, a militia of gunmen and thugs who trounced miners' civil rights by enforcing vigilante law that favored mine owners. By 1866, 7,632 officers called "yellow dogs" spied on workers and their families and reported damage and theft of company equipment and endangerment of profits.

In 1873, labor agitator Mary Harris "Mother" Jones met illiterate "coal crackers" who risked their lives because of their inability to read safety instructions. She witnessed appalling conditions in Pennsylvania among spindly child miners as young as age eight. While they worked for pennies as "breaker boys" or "cracker boys" removing slate and dirt from coal, toothed iron rollers endangered their limbs and clouds of coal dust threatened their lungs and eyes. During the Long Strike of 1874–1875 in western Pennsylvania, Jones educated laborers on the faults of capitalists, who lashed wages by 80 percent and crushed collective bargaining. To fight starvation, exploitation, and a pro-management court system in Reading, she coached uneducated immigrants to combat anti-union owners and managers of canals, coal mines, docks, and shipping. As a result, the U.S. Senate investigated miners' complaints about working conditions and mine safety.

In 1877, cultural and language difficulties made unionizing difficult, but not impossible. The demand for tunnelers and smelters lured Austrian, Croat, Italian, Serb, and Slovene workers to the Midwest. At Des Moines, Iowa, coal mines relied on blacks, Czechs, Greeks, Mexicans, Russians, and Scandinavians. Low-paid Knights of Labor at Leadville, Colorado, walked off the job to force issues of safety, pay, and freedom of assembly.

The Desert Land Act of 1877 tended to enrich land and water monopolies to the detriment of homesteaders. Fraudulent claims derived from mining concerns greedy for coal and iron veins. Muckraking journalist Henry Demarest Lloyd began investigating big business for the *Chicago Tribune* and alerted readers to the corrupt land grabs and conspiracies of monopolists and empire builders such as Andrew Carnegie, James Jerome Hill, Andrew W. Mellon, J. Pierpont Morgan, and John D. Rockefeller.

Laws reined in slipshod operations that threatened workers. Pennsylvania statutes raised the employment age for boys to 12 and required safety lamps, speaking tubes, inspection records and accident reports, and firefighting teams. In Illinois, legislation passed on May 16, 1877, imposed regulations on drainage ditches from mines and compensated abutting properties for damage due to mining operations. Engineers had to map collieries, ventilate drifts, provide escape shafts, drain flooding, mark boundaries, and bore holes to vent firedamp (flammable methane vapor), blackdamp (carbon dioxide), and afterdamp (carbon monoxide). Additional rules protected workers from debris falling on hoist cages and required shaft fencing, safety valves, and signals of cave-ins. Engineers and inspectors risked fines up to $100 or imprisonment for negligence causing injury or death. Widows and orphans could claim compensation for loss of life.

See also: Labor and Labor Unions; Molly Maguires.

Further Reading

Gorn, Elliott J. *Mother Jones: The Most Dangerous Woman in America.* New York: Hill and Wang, 2002.

Murrin, John M., et al. *Liberty, Equality, Power: A History of the American People.* 4th ed. Belmont, CA: Thomson/Wadsworth, 2009.

Palladino, Grace. *Another Civil War: Labor, Capital, and the State in the Anthracite Regions of Pennsylvania, 1840–1868.* New York: Fordham University Press, 2006.

Sadler, Spencer J. *Pennsylvania's Coal and Iron Police.* Charleston, SC: Arcadia, 2009.

Wolff, David A. *Industrializing the Rockies: Growth, Competition, and Turmoil in the Coalfields of Colorado and Wyoming, 1868–1914.* Boulder: University Press of Colorado, 2003.

Cochise (1812–1874)

A Chiricahua Apache chief and freedom fighter, Cochise battled the intrusion of settlers, prospectors, and the U.S. Cavalry on native lands from 1861 to 1872. A model of strength and probity, he was born in northern Mexico or southeastern Arizona, grew up in Arizona, and succeeded his father as chief of the Chokonen-Chiricahua Apache. At age 36, he cut wood for the Butterfield Overland Mail Company at the Apache Pass Station east of Tucson.

On February 4, 1861, Lieutenant George Nicholas Bascom arrested Cochise and several of his relatives for allegedly rustling 20 head of cattle at Sonoita Creek and for abducting the 12-year-old stepson of rancher John Ward. When subsequent information proved the perpetrators to be Pinal Apache, not Chiricahua, the captives gained their release.

Cochise, accompanied by his principal wife, younger brother Coyuntura, two nephews, and his sons, 26-year-old Taza and four-year-old Naiche (or Natchez), rode under a truce flag to Bascom's headquarters at Fort Buchanan to offer assistance in returning the abducted boy to his parents. Bascom hanged Cochise's brother and two nephews. Denied a trial to clear his name, Cochise killed hostages and escaped to Sonora, despite three bullet wounds. The debacle, known as the Bascom Affair, precipitated a quarter century of violence called the Apache Wars.

At a turning point in his tolerance of white incursion on traditional lands, Cochise took advantage of a shortage of U.S. Army personnel, many of whom had gone east to fight in the Civil War. On July 15, 1862, he collaborated with his father-in-law, 70-year-old Mangas Coloradas, a unifier of the Coyotero and Mimbreño Apache. Cochise, backed by Geronimo's band, attacked a wagon train and raided the Butterfield station. Leading 200 warriors to Apache Pass, he ambushed some 100 California volunteers. General James Henry Carleton directed 3,000 California volunteers against Cochise, who raised a stronghold as a trap for the army. Faced with rifles and cannon, Cochise retreated and transported his wounded father-in-law to a surgeon in Janos, Mexico.

Cochise hid out in the Dragoon Mountains of southern Arizona for a decade. During this time, he slew 150 settlers of Cooke's Canyon, Arizona. After Mangas Coloradas surrendered on January 17, 1863, soldiers shot him during an alleged escape attempt and sent his skull to a New York phrenologist. The decapitation galvanized Cochise into action to retaliate in the name of his people. Using hit-and-run tactics, he savaged American and Mexican homesteaders on the Butterfield Trail.

When Colonel George Crook settled the Apache outside Fort Tularosa, New Mexico, Cochise remained at large, dodging the Indian scouts and informers whom Crook sent into the mountains. After his capture in September 1871, he escaped the following spring and plotted new incursions against settlers in southern Arizona and New Mexico.

In fall 1872, Cochise met with General Oliver Otis Howard, a legate from President Ulysses S. Grant, and with scout Thomas Jefferson Jeffords, Cochise's blood brother. After 11 days of negotiation, Cochise convinced the delegation to create a Chiricahua reservation at Apache Pass and to name Jeffords the Indian agent. In 1873, Howard brokered a peace initiative with the Apache Nation. Cochise surrendered with 200 followers and volunteered to keep the peace.

Cochise lived out the remaining months of his life at the Chiricahua Reservation. He died of natural causes on June 8, 1874, and was interred in an undisclosed location in the Dragoon Mountains. His eldest son, 39-year-old

Taza, took his father's place as peacekeeper, but lacked the authority over disparate bands that Cochise had displayed. Taza died of pneumonia two years later. His younger brother, Naiche, a 19-year-old militant and follower of Geronimo, succeeded him as spokesman for the Apache.

See also: Geronimo; Mangas Coloradas.

Further Reading

Brown, Dee. *The American West.* New York: Simon & Schuster, 1995.

———. *Bury My Heart at Wounded Knee: An Indian History of the American West.* New York: Holt, Rinehart and Winston, 1970.

Johansen, Bruce E., and Donald A. Grinde, Jr. *The Encyclopedia of Native American Biography.* New York: Da Capo, 1998.

Lamar, Howard R., ed. *The New Encyclopedia of the American West.* New Haven, CT: Yale University Press, 1998.

Roberts, David. *Once They Moved Like the Wind: Cochise, Geronimo, and the Apache Wars.* New York: Simon & Schuster, 1994.

Sweeney, Edwin R. *Cochise: Chiricahua Apache Chief.* Norman: University of Oklahoma Press, 1991.

Waldman, Carl. *Who Was Who in Native American History: Indians and Non-Indians from Early Contacts Through 1900.* New York: Facts on File, 1990.

Coinage Act of 1873

See Banking and Finance

Colfax, Schuyler (1823–1885)

Journalist, abolitionist, and politician Schuyler Colfax, Jr., served his country for nearly two decades as a U.S. congressman from Indiana (1855–1869, including six years as Speaker of the House) and as the seventeenth vice president of the United States (1869–1873) under President Ulysses S. Grant. The Crédit Mobilier scandal ended his political career.

Born on March 23, 1823, near the Battery in New York City, he was the son of Hannah Delamater Stryker and Schuyler Colfax, Sr., a bank teller on Wall Street who had succumbed to tuberculosis five months earlier. He traced his ancestry to the American Revolution, when his English grandfather, William Colfax, served in the colonial military under General George Washington. A 17-year-old widow, Hannah Colfax turned their North Moore Street home into a boardinghouse. After education at Forrest and Mulligan's school and Dr. Griscom's Boys' High School, ten-year-old Colfax quit school to clerk in a retail store to help support his mother and maternal grandmother, also named Hannah Delamater Stryker.

At age 13, Colfax traveled by wagon with his mother and stepfather, merchant George Washington Matthews, to New Carlisle, Indiana, where they operated a Sabbath school. While educating himself by reading borrowed books and newspapers at the post office, Colfax worked for editor Horace Greeley as a journalist for the *New York Tribune.* Colfax reported political news for the *Indiana State Journal* and served St. Joseph County as deputy auditor. In 1842, he edited a Whig paper, the *South Bend Free Press,* which he renamed the *St. Joseph Valley Register.* At the Indiana Constitutional Convention of 1849, he represented Whigs and opposed barring blacks from settling in Indiana. For his amiability and tact, he earned the nickname "Smiler."

Rise to Power

After losing a first run for Congress as a Whig in 1850, Colfax won the 1854 election for a seat in the U.S. House of Representatives on a platform opposing the Kansas-Nebraska Act, which allowed Western homesteaders to vote on the expansion of slavery to the West. Although President Abraham Lincoln suspected Colfax of intrigue, the congressman befriended Republicans during the 34th Congress and chaired the Committee on Post Offices and Post Roads.

In 1863, Colfax energized antislavery representatives as Speaker of the House of the 38th Congress. In that capacity, he promoted passage of the Thirteenth Amendment, which legislators ratified on December 6, 1865. In summer 1865, he toured mining country and inspected progress on the Union Pacific Railroad. With three journalists, the congressman traveled west the next year to inspect progress on the Transcontinental Railroad. In his honor, capitalist and railroad builder Leland Stanford renamed Illinoistown "Colfax."

In the hope of advancing his career, Colfax declined to run for the U.S. Senate or for governor of Indiana. At the Republican presidential convention in Chicago on May 21, 1868, he joined Ulysses S. Grant on the presidential ticket. The first House Speaker to rise to the executive level, Colfax became vice president on March 4, 1869.

Colfax presided over the U.S. Senate at a crucial point during Reconstruction. On February 25, 1870, he administered the oath of office to U.S. Senator Hiram Revels of Mississippi, the first black U.S. congressman. The following year, the vice president declined President Grant's proposal that Colfax resign his office to replace Hamilton Fish as secretary of state. The press turned against Colfax for his insincerity and for accepting a bribe from a stationer seeking a government contract for envelopes. At the Republican presidential convention in Philadelphia on June 5, 1872, to Grant's relief, delegates rejected Colfax as a subsequent candidate for national office.

In the meantime, Colfax had gained a reputation for accepting expensive gifts. The New York *Sun* shamed him for diverting $23,336,319.81 in Union Pacific Railroad funds for personal use during the Crédit Mobilier scandal. Under chief counsel Aaron F. Perry, the Poland Committee, a federal investigation conducted by the 42nd Congress from December 1872 to February 18, 1873, censured Colfax, mastermind Congressman Oakes Ames of Massachusetts, and 11 accomplices for influence peddling through the illicit distribution of rail stock to 30 politicians. To Ames's claims that he had bought 20 shares of stock for Colfax in December 1867 and paid him $1,200 in dividends, Colfax denied profiteering on Crédit Mobilier or Union Pacific stock. A bank deposit signed by Colfax on June 22, 1868, for $1,200 shocked his friends and aroused the New York *Evening Mail* to impugn and ridicule the former vice president's lame excuses.

Until his death from heart attack at a railroad depot in Mankato, Minnesota, on January 13, 1885, Colfax earned $2,500 per speech as a lecturer on the statesmanship of Abraham Lincoln.

See also: Election of 1868; Election of 1872.

Further Reading

Harris, William C. *Lincoln's Last Months.* Cambridge, MA: Harvard University Press, 2004.

Sirgiovanni, George S. "Dumping the Vice President: An Historical Overview and Analysis." *Presidential Studies Quarterly* 24 (Fall 1994): 765–782.

Smith, Adam I.P. *No Party Now: Politics in the Civil War North.* Oxford, UK: Oxford University Press, 2006.

Colleges and Universities

The Civil War altered the policies of America's college and universities, which struggled to remain solvent. As the army and navy drained the general population of young men, institutions recruited conscientious objectors and ill-prepared students whom the military rejected. In the South in 1861, South Carolina College, the University of Georgia, and an academic preparatory academy in Mobile, Alabama, filled empty seats by enrolling preteen boys. By 1865, more than 60,000 pupils were studying at the nation's 563 postsecondary institutions—an average student population of only 107 per school. In class, pedagogy consisted primarily of lecture, note taking, and recitation. Because college professors followed standard academic course outlines, tutors groomed the young for learning abstract concepts and research methods.

Citizen activism involved college students in public debate, especially on secessionism, abolitionism, and slave rescue. At Oberlin College in Ohio, a campus station of the Underground Railroad collaborated with local conductors to relay refugees by boat or steamer to waterfront depots at Cleveland, Huron, or Sandusky, Ohio, and across Lake Erie to freedom. In South Carolina on January 9, 1861, as a steamer delivered supplies to Fort Sumter, white cadets at the exclusive Citadel military academy fired cannon at U.S. Army recruits, the first Union soldiers to dodge rebel shots. The attack was one of eight engagements involving the academy.

At the demise of slavery, missionaries created educational opportunities for freedmen at Atlanta University and Berea College in 1865 and, in the following years, encouraged black entry into the professions through studies at Fisk University in Nashville, Tennessee, and the Lincoln Normal School in Marion, Alabama. In 1866, General Oliver Otis Howard proposed a progressive idea to white educators—the building of Howard University in Washington, D.C., to train a black professional class of attorneys, dentists, doctors, ministers, and teachers.

Under provisions of the Morrill Land-Grant Act of 1862, every state received public lands to sell; the proceeds were applied to land-grant colleges across the nation that promoted agriculture, engineering, and military science. The founding of Kansas State Normal School at Emporia, Lincoln College at Topeka, and the Kansas state university at Lawrence coincided in 1866 with the demand for surveyors and engineers employed in railway construction. In 1870, Ohio Governor Rutherford B. Hayes founded the Agricultural and Mechanical College, the beginning of Ohio State University.

Some months before the completion of the Transcontinental Railroad in May 1869, educators merged the College of California with the Agricultural, Mining and Mechanical Arts College to form the University of

California, Berkeley, a leader in higher education in the American West. In San Francisco in 1873, the University of California added its first medical school. In the Pacific Northwest, enrollment at the University of Oregon stopped the bleed-out of talented students and researchers to Eastern universities.

Hands-On Instruction

Research and laboratory experimentation introduced Americans to thinking skills based on problem solving rather than rote memorization of theory. The first U.S. hospital allied with a medical school, the Bellevue Hospital Medical College in New York City, received premed students in March 1861. The 13-man faculty taught anatomy, chemistry, clinical medicine, obstetrics and gynecology, orthopedics, physiology and hygiene, surgery, therapeutics, and toxicology.

For a broader choice in coursework, Eastern colleges incorporated the German philosophy of academic freedom and Charles Darwin's theories of evolution, which sectarians censured. Evolution became a battleground in fundamentalist institutions such as Vanderbilt University, but expanded in influence at Brown, Princeton, and Yale universities. At Yale, researcher Othniel Charles Marsh introduced pupils to fieldwork in paleontology, a subject that demanded objectivity toward creationism and the timeline of animal life on planet Earth. At Cornell University, President Andrew Dickson White championed preparation for specialized occupations. For the sake of pragmatism, he rejected pedantry that reduced learning to historical dates, scientific formulas, and literary gerund grinding.

At Harvard University, beginning in 1869, President Charles William Eliot, an education reformer and editor of the Harvard Classics, charged theology with bigotry and cruelty and resolved to end the dominance of theological interpretations over pure science. He coordinated high school curricula with college coursework and elevated the criteria for admission to advanced studies. In "The New Education: Its Organization" (1869), the first of a two-part treatise published in the *Atlantic Monthly,* Eliot validated the need for balance between the classics and practical subjects—mathematics, modern languages, and pure and applied science, which required hands-on experience. In place of lockstep requirements in ethics, Greek, Latin, and philosophy, he pioneered a flexible elective system that allowed students to individualize their courses of study to suit their interests and skills. The resulting trend in college requirements raised academic and professional expectations and fostered specialization and independent laboratory research at Cornell and Johns Hopkins, the nation's first research university. At the Massachusetts Institute of Technology, founder William Barton Rogers supported Eliot's stringent standards by refusing to award empty diplomas to the wealthy for the sake of donations to the school. Yale alumnus William Walter Phelps voiced student dissatisfaction with the limited variety of teachers and demanded the hiring of staff with a broader range of backgrounds.

Women's Intellectualism

The women's rights movement fostered the inclusion of women in higher learning and the professions. Influential writer and editor Sarah Josepha Hale advocated the idea that young women should receive the same opportunities and training that their brothers received at Brown, Harvard, and Yale, including medical education and preparation for the pulpit ministry. From theories of equal educational opportunities for women, a community of well-endowed, rigorously academic female colleges emerged.

In 1861, brewer Matthew Vassar in Poughkeepsie, New York, founded Vassar College, a prototype of the woman's college taught by a female faculty. The other "Seven Sister" schools—Barnard, Bryn Mawr, Mount Holyoke, Radcliffe, Smith, and Wellesley—likewise favored female professors and encouraged pride in women's accomplishment. In New York City in 1863, Dr. Clemence Sophia Lozier opened the New York Medical College and Hospital for Women at 724 Broadway. In 1868, sisters Elizabeth and Emily Blackwell aided parturient women and their infants by establishing the Women's Medical College of New York City.

With the aid of philanthropists such as Sarah Babcock, Queen Emma of Hawaii, Fanny Jackson Coppin, Dorothea Dix, Sarah Josepha Hale, and Sophia Smith, women students in 1870 accounted for 21 percent of enrollment in U.S. institutions of higher education. The employability of female professionals improved with the opening of Hunter College in New York City and the addition of homemaking curriculum at Iowa State Agricultural College, Kansas State Agricultural College, and Illinois Industrial University at Urbana.

At Boston College Hospital, Linda Richards, the nation's first professional nurse, introduced curriculum suited to the first generation of registered nurses. At Oberlin College, a progressive campus for all races and both genders, Mary Jane Patterson, a classics major, became the first black female to earn a bachelor's degree. Educator Frances Willard accepted the presidency of Evanston College for Ladies and a deanship in 1873 at Northwestern University. In 1876, the first woman entered the San Francisco Medical College of the Pacific.

College Sponsorship

Religious institutions offered students both theology and social skills. Quakers trained pupils in literature and logic at Swarthmore College, a coeducational liberal arts school in Delaware County, Pennsylvania. Quaker physician and educator Ann Preston opened Woman's Hospital in Philadelphia in 1862 and became the nation's first female dean of a medical college. In Kansas, Eben Blachley, a Presbyterian teacher, founded the Quindaro Freedman's School, the first black academy west of the Mississippi River and the nucleus of Western University. Daughters of Charity opened the Ursuline Academy of Galveston, the first parochial preparatory school for girls in Texas. Mother Superior Mary Magdalen (Eliza Healy) cofounded Notre Dame College, a women's institution on Staten Island, New York. Catholic fathers chartered Boston College in 1863, the first Jesuit school in the city. At Georgetown University, the nation's largest Catholic college, Jesuit father Patrick Francis Healy, the first black American to earn a doctorate, taught philosophy in 1866 and liberalized professional offerings in chemistry, law, medicine, and physics. In 1875 in Cincinnati, Ohio, the Union of American Hebrew Congregations founded Hebrew Union College, the nation's first Jewish seminary, with funding provided by industrialist Henry Adler of Lawrenceburg, Indiana.

The generosity of businessmen and philanthropists such as Adler, Ezra Cornell, Frederick Law Olmsted, Rutherford Stuyvesant, Levi Strauss, and Montgomery Ward democratized campuses with a broader socioeconomic range of students that included blacks, Indians, Jews, and women. To boost media professionalism, at Washington College in Lexington, Virginia, President Robert E. Lee offered financial aid to 50 students majoring in journalism. In a gesture toward postwar healing of sectionalism, shipping and railroad magnate Cornelius Vanderbilt bankrolled New York City's College of Physicians and Surgeons and Vanderbilt University in Nashville, Tennessee; oil magnate John D. Rockefeller channeled his profits of $500 million into the University of Chicago and the Rockefeller Institute for Medical Research. Iron and steel magnate Andrew Carnegie underwrote Cooper Union, a laboratory for Bellevue Hospital Medical College, and Hampton Institute for freedmen and honored an old friend by endowing the Edwin M. Stanton Chair of Political Economy at Kenyon College in Ohio. Hatmaker John Batterson Stetson invested his profits in DeLand Academy, Temple University, Stetson University Law School, and the beginnings of San José State University. Leland Stanford, former governor of California, established Stanford University, a nonsectarian coeducational agricultural school built on the family's Palo Alto estate.

See also: Cornell, Ezra; Dewey, Melvil; Gibbs, Josiah Willard; Land-Grant Colleges; Smith, Sophia; Sports.

Further Reading

Angulo, A.J. *William Barton Rogers and the Idea of MIT.* Baltimore: Johns Hopkins University Press, 2009.

Cross, Coy F., II. *Justin Smith Morrill: Father of the Land-Grant Colleges.* East Lansing: Michigan State University Press, 1999.

Geiger, Roger L., ed. *Perspectives on the History of Higher Education, 2007.* New Brunswick, NJ: Transaction, 2007.

Stratton, Julius A., and Loretta H. Mannix. *Mind and Hand: The Birth of MIT.* Cambridge, MA: MIT Press, 2005.

Williams, Roger L. *The Origins of Federal Support for Higher Education: George W. Atherton and the Land-Grant College Movement.* University Park: Pennsylvania State University Press, 1991.

Colorado

Following the 1858–1859 Gold Rush at Pikes Peak, Colorado, settlers formed the extralegal state of Jefferson, on land formerly owned by Mexico. They based their claim to the territory on "squatter sovereignty." The unofficial boundaries of the state enclosed parts of present-day Kansas, Nebraska, New Mexico, Utah, and Washington, governed by Robert Williamson Steele, known as the "Father of Colorado."

The rogue state lost support in summer 1860, primarily because of an unpopular poll tax. As abolitionism in the North hastened a clash with states' rights advocates in the South, Coloradans clung to sectionalism and channeled political concerns into defense against Indians.

On February 28, 1861, Congress created Colorado Territory, which encompassed a prosperous gold-mining area. The Union needed the precious metal to finance the Civil War, which erupted five weeks later. The legislation, signed by outgoing President James Buchanan, replaced the provisional territory of Jefferson and established William

Gilpin, a Colorado booster, as the first governor of what Gilpin hoped would be a Western utopia.

According to the 1860 U.S. census, at the height of trade in buffalo hides, Colorado's population reached 34,277. Within five years, the supplying of Coloradans brought 100 million pounds (45 million kilograms) of freight to the area by wagon. Toilsome grades over the Rocky Mountains required the routing of ox teams that pulled heavy wagons some 600 miles (960 kilometers) from Missouri River steamers. Slowing deliveries of mail and driving up the price of supplies were scarce pasturage and water for dray teams, as well as Indian raids, bandits, and unpredictable weather over the Continental Divide. The region connected to the rest of the country in 1863, with the stringing of telegraph wires from Julesburg to Denver. By 1870, Colorado's population had risen to 90,923.

Growth skyrocketed in the 1870s with the beginning of the silver era, introduced by the Caribou Mine in Boulder County, successfully operated by Jerome Bunty Chaffee, founder of the First National Bank of Denver, and industrialist David Halliday Moffat. Following a veto by President Andrew Johnson, but through the advocacy of President Ulysses S. Grant, Colorado entered the Union as the thirty-eighth state on August 1, 1876. Because the nation had just celebrated its hundredth anniversary, Colorado earned the nickname "Centennial State."

Indian Wars

Territorial clashes between white prospectors and the Arapaho, Cheyenne, Comanche, Kiowa-Apache, and Lakota provoked the Colorado War (1863–1865), which erupted to the south along the Arkansas River. The nullification of the 1851 Treaty of Fort Laramie and enforced residency of tribes at the Sand Creek Reservation and at Fort Lyon raised tensions among tribes, who retaliated by disrupting mail and supply deliveries. In autumn 1863, Indians were cool to invitations to a treaty session. The following spring, rustling and harassment escalated to strikes against stages and wagons.

The Arapaho slaughter of 29-year-old ranch hand Nathan Ward Hungate; the rape and stabbing of his wife, Ellen Eliza Decker Hungate; and the scalping and mutilation and near decapitation of their two daughters, the infant Florence V. and three-year-old Laura B. Hungate, on June 11, 1864, 25 miles (40 kilometers) southeast of Denver, was the turning point in white tolerance. The raiders compounded the crime by tossing the woman and her children in the well, rustling cattle, and burning the ranch. Church bells drew settlers to view a display of the maimed and scalped corpses in a Denver store window and to plot vengeance. An obituary in the *Rocky Mountain News* spread outrage.

On June 27, 1864, Governor John Evans, functioning as superintendent of Indian affairs, tempered his anger by offering shelter to friendly tribes at federal forts. A terrorist retort—the murder of one of the governor's cavalrymen, Conrad Moschel, shot in the back and head the following August 21—brought the total of victims to 208.

Because the garrisoning of Fort Garland and Fort Lyon proved inadequate to the threat, Governor Evans mustered the First Regiment of Colorado Infantry. In eastern Colorado, the more belligerent ranchers and farmers proposed a preemptive strike to rid the area of Indians for good. The plan foundered after Arapaho and Cheyenne, led by Chief Black Kettle, retreated to Fort Lyon.

Colonel John Milton Chivington promised safe conduct to Sand Creek for Black Kettle's band. The predawn assault on November 29, 1864, conducted by 700 troops of the Third Colorado Volunteers armed with howitzers, ended with the mutilation and scalping of 133 Cheyenne men, women, and children.

News of mass genocide by out-of-control whites alerted Arapaho, Lakota, and Northern Cheyenne to a war on the Central Plains. In a peace settlement, Arapaho, Cheyenne, Comanche, and Kiowa-Apache agreed to live in southwestern Oklahoma. Black Kettle accepted assignment to the Sand Creek Reservation in southeastern Colorado.

Despite these agreements, around 1,500 Cheyenne dog soldiers and Arapaho and Lakota renegades wreaked post–Sand Creek vengeance on the town of Julesburg. They sacked the town on January 7, 1865, and returned on February 2 to steal sacks of corn, down telegraph poles and chop lines, and burn buildings to the ground.

The white backlash worsened in mid-September 1868, when Southern Cheyenne chief war society leader Roman Nose and Oglala Chief Pawnee Killer led 1,000 warriors against the 48 army scouts of Major George Alexander Forsyth at the Battle of Beecher Island along the Arikaree Fork of the Republican River near Wray, Colorado, on the Kansas border. After Roman Nose died in the third charge, Cheyenne Chief Dull Knife led the third foray. Surviving army scouts dug rifle pits in the sand and called for military backup from Fort Wallace, Kansas, 100 miles (160 kilometers) away. The Indians kept up attacks for seven days, killing their enemies' horses and mules and isolating the cavalry without food. Help arrived on the ninth day.

The army took hope from the brave confrontation against superior numbers that whites would eventually overcome Plains Indians. To save money and military lives, during his State of the Union address on December 4, 1871, President Ulysses S. Grant proposed a "Peace Policy" that required the reorganization of the Office of Indian Affairs and the hiring of religious leaders to supervise agencies and Christian schools to ready Indians for citizenship.

Prosperity

In rivalry with Golden, the capital city of Denver prospered from eastern links to the Colorado Central, Denver Pacific, Kansas Pacific, and Denver & Rio Grande railroads. Supporting the miners in land disputes was a string of pro-mining governors, beginning with John Long Routt, who suppressed an insurrection of squatters at Creede. Otto Mears, a Russian émigré and translator, facilitated the removal of the Ute from the ore-rich San Juan Mountains and directed toll roads and narrow gauge lines to isolated silver strikes around Silverton, Oro City, Ouray, and Leadville, the state's fastest-growing city. Passing over the Continental Divide after the Panic of 1873, rails transported gold and silver ores to processing centers, but plunged the territory into rail control wars. Transportation brought students to the University of Denver in 1867, to the School of Mines at Golden and the Congregationalist Colorado College in Colorado Springs in 1874, and to the University of Colorado at Boulder in 1877.

The incorporation of open-range stockmen contributed to Colorado's wealth. Major investors profited from ample water and grassland along the South Platte River, as well as from cheap cowboy labor.

The first cattle king, self-made Colorado millionaire John Wesley Iliff, went into business in 1861 as a grocer and invested in 15,000 acres (6,100 hectares) of land on the South Platte River. He swapped produce and clothing for cattle, bought 800 Texas longhorns from Charles Goodnight, and negotiated contracts to provide beef for crews of the Union Pacific Railroad. In 1870, Iliff shipped beef to Chicago in ice-cooled railcars and supplied Indian reservations as well. At his death in 1878 from gallbladder inflammation, his wife, Singer sewing machine agent Elizabeth Sarah Fraser Iliff, continued his livestock operation.

Another livestock breeder and beef magnate, John Wesley Prowers, also began as a mercantile clerk. After peddling goods to Fort Laramie, Fort Union, and Fort Lyon, he married Amache "Amy" Ochinee, daughter of the Cheyenne Chief Ochinee, and built his fortune on 400,000 acres (162,000 hectares) at Boggsville on 40 miles (64 kilometers) along the Arkansas River, which supported 10,000 short-horned Herefords.

By 1868, the introduction of merino sheep to Weld County and South Park complicated issues of open grazing and heightened racial tensions between Anglo beef raisers and Hispanic shepherds. The Pueblo *Colorado Chieftain* reported a total population of sheep at 317,500.

In 1872, a roundup law authorized the scheduling of spring and fall cattle roundups. By 1877, the Arkansas Valley event involved 500 cowboys, 50 chuck wagons, and 3,500 mounts. Statutes covered the details of ownership and the distribution of mavericks (motherless calves).

During periods of hostility between beef barons and nesters, the Grange (National Grange of the Patrons of Husbandry) spoke for farmers. Against Grangers' political clout, the Colorado Stock Growers' Association promoted branding as proof of ownership and lobbied Congress to set aside the open range from homestead laws that allowed smallholders to fence their acreage. However, greed and arrogance destroyed corporate ranching in the 1880s by promoting overstocking and overgrazing.

See also: Agriculture; Black Kettle; Indian Reservations; Statehood.

Further Reading

Abbott, Carl, Stephen J. Leonard, and Thomas J. Noel. *Colorado: A History of the Centennial State.* 4th ed. Boulder: University Press of Colorado, 2005.

Leyendecker, Liston E., Christine A. Bradley, and Duane A. Smith. *The Rise of the Silver Queen: Georgetown, Colorado, 1859–1896.* Boulder: University Press of Colorado, 2005.

MacKell, Jan. *Brothels, Bordellos, and Bad Girls: Prostitution in Colorado, 1860–1930.* Santa Fe: University of New Mexico Press, 2004.

Ubbelohde, Carl, Maxine Benson, and Duane A. Smith. *A Colorado History.* 9th ed. Boulder, CO: Pruett, 2006.

Wolff, David A. *Industrializing the Rockies: Growth, Competition, and Turmoil in the Coalfields of Colorado and Wyoming, 1868–1914.* Boulder: University Press of Colorado, 2003.

Columbia, South Carolina

The capital of South Carolina, Columbia figured in a series of historic events during the Civil War and Reconstruction periods. Founded in 1786 and named for Christopher Columbus, it was the nation's first planned city, which engineers laid out in grids on the Congaree River. Contributing to its prosperity were cheap waterpower and the South Carolina Central Railroad, which connected the environs with two ports, Charleston and Wilmington, North Carolina.

By 1860, slave ownership placed the state's white population at 43 percent, with more than 402,000 residents classified as slaves and 10,000 as free blacks. The predominance of black residents caused Columbians to fear the enfranchisement of vengeful bondsmen. To suppress insurrections, whites sought to keep Northern and abolitionist newspapers out of the hands of literate blacks.

War brought partisans into face-to-face confrontation. The South's first secession convention met at the First Baptist Church on December 17, 1860—roughly four months before the outbreak of the Civil War—to proclaim the Republic of South Carolina.

Following the firing on Fort Sumter in Charleston Harbor on April 12, 1861, the confinement of 150 Union prisoners at Castle Sorghum on the Saluda River in November of that year made a mockery of humane conditions. When the prison population rose to 1,400, the lack of latrines, soap, blankets, and clean clothes increased discontent and outbreaks of disease. According to a journal kept by a Union prisoner, Captain Willard Worcester Glazier of Albany, New York, inmates, barefoot and sickly, occupied lean-tos and tent shelters or holes in the ground and ate little more than cornmeal cakes and sorghum molasses, the cause of chronic diarrhea. Enthusiasm for "The Cause" buoyed Southern hopes of a quick end to war prisons; in the meantime, Columbian women complained that the inmates were vulgar and impudent to passersby.

In mid-war, the population of Columbia doubled from its peacetime census of 8,000. A paper shortage reduced the *Daily Southern Guardian* and the *Tri-Weekly South Carolinian* to one sheet each. Because General George Brinton McClellan's Union forces menaced the Confederate capital at Richmond, Virginia, in May 1862, authorities moved the treasury to Columbia and imported skilled platemakers and lithographers from England to print Confederate treasury notes.

The closure of Columbia College left a spacious campus for use as the second home of the Fair Grounds Hospital. There, Joseph Le Conte and James Woodrow formulated alcohol, chloroform, ether, and silver nitrate for the medical corps. The city also manufactured buttons, gunpowder, ink, matches, niter, socks, and swords. In lieu of cotton, silk, and woolens, Columbia's women turned homespun into a patriotic fashion statement.

Grace Elmore organized a three-day bazaar beginning on January 17, 1865. She collected contributions, sewed tasseled cushions, and made tobacco sacks and smoking caps for hospital patients. The fund-raiser earned a total of $24,936.50. The high spot of the bazaar was real coffee available by the gallon.

Under the Gun

General James Chesnut, Jr., husband of Mary Boykin Miller Chesnut, recorder of the Pulitzer Prize–winning *A Diary of Dixie* (1905), remained in the capital for much of the war. He co-wrote the Confederate constitution and chaired the Executive Council of Five, a wartime board that regulated travel and food distribution. No longer involved in a sparkling social life, Mary Chesnut nursed some of the 75,000 wounded who passed through Wayside Hospital near the railroad. She fell ill with fever that kept her housebound for much of 1862. By 1864, rail service had halted, but dinners, cotillions, parties, and barbecues continued. The Chesnuts hosted General Wade Hampton and, on October 4, 1864, served truffle-stuffed turkey to Confederate President Jefferson Davis, who rallied Columbia citizens from the front porch of the Chesnuts' story-and-a-half cottage on Hampton Street. By late winter, letters and diaries by Mary Chesnut and others held little hope of a Confederate victory.

On General William Tecumseh Sherman's march to the sea, he punished arch-secessionists with scorched-earth tactics. After his departure from his headquarters at McBride's Plantation, his troops incinerated the property, crossed the Broad and Saluda rivers into Richland County, and marched on Columbia. Amid civic chaos, on February 17, 1865, men in blue set fire to stashes of cotton bales and bundles of pitch and straw. Joining the ranks of Sherman's "bummers" were escapees from Camp Sorghum. Destruction included the Arsenal Military Academy, the Congaree River Bridge, two rail depots, the city jail and courthouse, the Robert Wilson Gibbes collection of historic documents, General Wade Hampton's plantation at Millwood, the Confederate Printing Plant, the Episcopal, Lutheran, and Methodist churches, and the slave-based plantation economy. To save the Confederate Post Office, employees dumped lithography plates of postage stamps into the Congaree River. On April 8, a sketch in *Harper's Weekly* pictured city panic and Union delight in the conflagration.

While freedmen served rowdy soldiers liquor in buckets and bottles, a stream of white refugees from Beaufort, Charleston, and Sumter fled Sherman's atrocities. Because of the devout Catholicism of his wife, Ellen Mary Ewing Sherman, the general tried to spare the Ursuline Convent School for Girls, a campus housing 200 pupils. When he failed, Mother Baptista sheltered the girls overnight in a Catholic graveyard and moved them the next day to the former Union headquarters at the Hampton-Preston Mansion on Blanding Street.

Surviving the war were the cottage of freedwoman midwife Celia Mann on Richland Street, the home of insurance magnate Edwin Whipple Seibels at Pickens and Richland streets, the Presbyterian seminary on Blanding Street, and Trinity Episcopal Church at Gervais and Sumter streets. By March 1865, martial rule pacified Columbia.

The New South

While clinging to Jim Crow laws and restricting freedmen to domestic and field labor, white South Carolinians strove to make Columbia an economic cornerstone of the New South. Eight weeks after the fall of the South, grocery prices stabilized, with meat at 10 cents per pound, coffee hovering between 50 and 75 cents per pound, and green tea at $2.50 per pound. Citizens anticipated the construction of a brick city market on Assembly Street. Whites tolerated self-government by black freedmen and the formation of two black volunteer fire companies. Train service to Charleston returned in January 1866 and, in April, to Charlotte, North Carolina, boosting Columbia into a rail hub.

The state repatriated to the Union on July 9, 1868, but, because of the burning of courthouse records, citizens labored in legal turmoil to establish land rights. Richland County increased in population from 18,307 in 1860 to 23,025 a decade later. Columbians grew in number by 700 and erected a statehouse and a governor's mansion on Arsenal Hill for Governor Robert Kingston Scott. In two years, the city supported 69 factories and produced $500,000 in goods. By 1871, the addition of a broom factory, cottonseed refinery, planing mills and sawmills, foundries, and railroad shops put 500 people to work.

The racial situation improved for city dwellers. While elite white supremacists complained of law but no justice in rule by Yankee soldiers, black and white rail workers competed to lay new track and restore connection to the outside world. General Alfred Stedman Hartwell published a letter in the *Daily Phoenix* urging freedmen to become literate and to uphold the family rather than wander the countryside in idle self-indulgence. As Confederate soldiers straggled home, on July 4, 1865, some 5,000 black males processed up Marion and Blanding streets to hear a reading of the Declaration of Independence at the college chapel, an event followed by an integrated barbecue and picnic with fireworks.

The passage of civil rights legislation in March 1867 assured blacks of their place in local and national government. Wade Hampton, chairman of the state Democratic Party, encouraged racial cooperation and unity, but secretly looked for means to placate blacks without capitulating to their demands. On January 1, 1870, Governor Scott presided over a black celebration of the Emancipation Proclamation, which began with a brass band leading marchers in a parade to the capitol. In 1870, widow Bathsheba Adams Barber Benedict of Pawtucket, Rhode Island, bought an 80-acre (32-hectare) plantation in eastern Columbia and established Benedict College, a black Baptist liberal arts institution, in the former residence of a slave master.

Goodwill did not suppress violent racists, however. Late in 1870, the Ku Klux Klan, calling themselves the "Cotton Town Rangers" and the "Knights of the Black Circle," grew to 1,000 members in York County northwest of the capital. Klansmen infiltrated Columbia following rumors that black radicals had burned white-owned stores and a mill and murdered whites at the depot. Joining a violent city brotherhood known as "The Ring" were 12 legislators and other state officials.

Despite the reputation of Reconstruction for upheaval and graft, Columbia realized universal public education, uniform tax codes, civil rights, an end to dueling and to debtor's prison, and the reform of city government and the court system. The city annexed parts of the suburbs and, in 1871, began erecting a penitentiary with convict labor. The boyhood home of future president Woodrow Wilson took shape on Hampton Street near Columbia College, which reopened in 1872.

Media coverage of the seating of former slaves in the state legislature underscored the North's delight in humiliating the South. Among black Columbians in the House of Representatives were tailor Robert John Palmer, carpenter Israel Smith, grocer Augustus Cooper, farmer Uriah Portee, and William Beverly Nash, a waiter at a Columbia hotel. The integration of male and female students of both races at the University of South Carolina in October 1873 caused white faculty to resign and white students to leave until the re-segregation of the campus four years later. The first black professor, Richard Theodore Greener, a Harvard-trained classical scholar and philosopher, repaired vandalism at the 27,000-volume college library.

In 1876, attorney James Chesnut, Jr., chaired a convention of Democrats who protested the postwar military rule and demanded a return to home rule. During a vicious and corrupt election, Democrats promoted the gubernatorial candidacy of Wade Hampton. The disputed outcome resulted in dual state governments for Columbia until April 1877, when Hampton prevailed as governor.

Under a compromise negotiated by President Rutherford B. Hayes, Republicans ended Reconstruction and exited the state. Key to the city's political and economic growth was the replacement of the federal courthouse, jail, post office, and rail lines, which offered first-class freight fees of a dollar per hundredweight to Baltimore and New York.

See also: Ku Klux Klan; Reconstruction; Slaves and Slavery.

Further Reading

Deas-Moore, Vennie. *Columbia, South Carolina.* Charleston, SC: Arcadia, 2000.

Edgar, Walter B., ed. *The South Carolina Encyclopedia.* Columbia: University of South Carolina Press, 2006.

Moore, John Hammond. *Columbia and Richland County: A South Carolina Community, 1740–1990.* Columbia, SC: University of South Carolina Press, 1993.

Rable, George C. *But There Was No Peace: The Role of Violence in the Politics of Reconstruction.* Athens: University of Georgia Press, 2007.

Weigley, Russell F. *A Great Civil War: A Military and Political History, 1861–1865.* Bloomington: Indiana University Press, 2000.

Comstock Act (1873)

In 1873, a conservative backlash against women's rights and freedom of the press resulted in an increase in censorship, suppression of the purchase and use of birth control devices and medications, and intrusive investigation of private sexual acts between consenting adults. On March 3, 1873, Congress passed the Comstock Act, a codification of priggish dicta to halt promiscuity, masturbation, voyeurism, and sexual solicitation. The Comstock law arose from a state precedent, New York's anticontraception legislation of 1868, which banned birth control and abortion.

Launched into the spotlight by the Young Men's Christian Association crusade against public debauchery and wanton amusements, Anthony Comstock, a moralist from New Canaan, Connecticut, advocated no tolerance of bawdiness or impurity. He and his organization, the New York Society for the Suppression of Vice, led a puritanical campaign that infiltrated classrooms and snooped on clinics to circumvent public access to information on human reproduction. His followers lobbied to ban sketches and photos, leaflets, books, letters, postcards, and sexually explicit advertisements and birthing instructions that they deemed lewd, indecent, or obscene. In New York City, Comstock single-handedly inveighed against immorality by alerting authorities to bordellos and abortion mills. As a lone agent, he seized banned materials and arrested promoters and purchasers of pornography, which he believed fostered lechery and debauched youth.

The Comstock Act targeted distributors of contraception advice, medications, or devices by criminalizing them for transmitting prurient material through the U.S. mail. The proscription ranged from birth control to paintings, statues, nudie magazines, and posters, and entrapped dealers in anatomy textbooks, condoms, pessaries and diaphragms, spermicidal gels, foaming tablets, aspirin suppositories, and abortifacients. Challenging the ban were spermicidal douche solutions based on iodine, opium, prussic acid, strychnine, or tanin. Dealers risked a fine of $5,000 and a five-year prison sentence for lending, disseminating, vending, issuing, or owning literature on human sexuality or birth control devices or drugs.

The United States became the butt of jokes among Europeans for being the only Western nation to charge purveyors of birth control with felony. Editor Angela Fiducia Tilton Heywood, publisher of *The Word,* a liberal journal, accused Comstock of fraud and claimed that he threatened women's rights by harassing proponents of contraception, by demonizing private expressions of sensuality, and by stalking opponents and raiding their medicine cabinets and closets.

Threats to Privacy

The groundswell of prudery in New York influenced a Connecticut ban on the sale and use of birth control methods. Feminists and contraceptive manufacturers opposed sexual ignorance and contested male control over female health. Anatomy teachers, midwives, and physicians faced arraignment by advocating women's knowledge and control of their own bodies. Violators risked a 12-month prison sentence for such acts as lecturing on female reproductive health, coitus, and venereal disease.

The conservatism of the Northeast spread to 24 states that reclassified contraception as erotic and unlawful.

Only New Mexico refused to condemn the private intimacies of consenting adults. Taking a pragmatic approach to new legislation, police departments hesitated to monitor sexually active couples in favor of investigating violent crime.

In the New York City post office, Comstock turned into a zealous demonizer of sex. He armed himself and flashed a badge to sanction the commandeering of letters, publications, and packages. Moving underground, sellers of pornography and vendors of contraceptives ignored his diatribes against anatomical knowledge as an inducement to sinful, bestial acts. Comstock spied freely, searched without a warrant, and impounded mail and such evidence as the rubber contraceptives that pharmacist Morris Glattstine sold at his Broadway drugstore. In 1872, Comstock tracked contraceptive manufacturer Morris Sickel from New Haven, Connecticut, to Montreal, Canada, and from Chicago, St. Louis, and Memphis to New Orleans and Havana, Cuba, before making an arrest. Charged with "trafficking in debauchery," Sickel paid a $500 fine and served 12 months in jail. On March 6, 1872, Comstock nabbed Charles Mancher, a New York doctor who sold rubber contraceptives.

Other violators of the Comstock Act warehoused contraband goods at concealed locations and sold them under assumed names. Euphemistic ads presented merchandise under equivocal copy, which depicted cervical caps as uterine supports, vaginal syringes as agents of female hygiene, and condoms as penile shields against venereal infection. False claims featured birth control methods as cures for barren wombs.

Comstock Versus Feminists

On November 2, 1872, under the Post Office Act of June 8 of that year, Comstock led U.S. marshals on a raid of the first women prosecuted—social reformers and free love advocates Victoria Claflin Woodhull and her younger sister, Tennessee Celeste "Tennie C" Claflin, who allegedly issued taboo articles in *Woodhull & Claflin's Weekly* and distributed them through the U.S. mail. Their most salacious piece, published on October 28, 1872, divulged the affair between the Reverend Henry Ward Beecher and Elizabeth Tilton, a married member of Beecher's congregation. The exposé lambasted Beecher for hypocrisy and cowardice. The sisters alerted readers to clandestine adultery in marriage and endorsed reproductive education, reliable contraception, licensed prostitution, and divorce rights and sexual freedom for both genders. After defending the pair in court, author George Francis Train of Boston incurred cell time for blasphemy and lewdness. Public snickering prompted Thomas Nast, the cartoonist for *Harper's Weekly,* to depict Woodhull as a satanic siren.

Although Comstock became a laughingstock, his persistent inquiries and innuendoes ruined reputations. In New York in 1874, he confiscated the rubber shields sold by Morris Bass, a Bavarian immigrant to Detroit. In 1876, marshals charged H. Gustavus Farr of Indiana with immorality for advertising vaginal diaphragms in popular magazines. In Princeton, Massachusetts, on November 3, 1877, a federal judge cited editor Ezra Hervey Heywood, issuer of the pamphlet *Cupid's Yokes,* a clinical treatise on marital sex and birth control, and New York attorney Robert Green Ingersoll for publishing opinions on contraception and seduction in *The Word* and for dispatching them through the U.S. mail. Heywood went to prison at hard labor in Dedham, Massachusetts.

Pounded by complaints from 6,000 suffragists and defenders of the civil right to free speech, President Rutherford B. Hayes pardoned Heywood after he had served six months of a two-year sentence. In defiance of his critics and in condemnation of President Hayes, Comstock collected petitions from church school teachers and ministers supporting the continued enforcement of prudish injunctions. Free speech proponents topped Comstock's backing with 70,000 signatures on a petition demanding repeal of the Comstock Act.

Further Reading

Brodie, Janet Farrell. *Contraception and Abortion in Nineteenth-Century America.* Ithaca, NY: Cornell University Press, 1994.

Frisken, Amanda. *Victoria Woodhull's Sexual Revolution: Political Theater and the Popular Press in Nineteenth-Century America.* Philadelphia: University of Pennsylvania Press, 2003.

Gorney, Cynthia. *Articles of Faith: A Frontline History of the Abortion Wars.* New York: Simon & Schuster, 1998.

Morone, James A. *Hellfire Nation: The Politics of Sin in American History.* New Haven, CT: Yale University Press, 2004.

Cooke, Jay (1821–1905)

Financier and rail speculator Jay Cooke raised funds to finance the Civil War and introduced the concept of price stabilization through the sale of municipal bonds. A native of Sandusky, Ohio, he was born on August 10, 1821, to U.S. Congressman Eleutheros Cooke and Martha Caswell Cooke, the daughter of a Canadian prisoner of war during the American Revolution.

Homeschooled and educated in trading at the firm of Seymour & Bool in St. Louis, Missouri, Cooke worked his way up to a partnership at the Philadelphia brokerage E.W. Clark & Company, which helped finance the Mexican-American War. After redirecting his career at age 37, he reorganized failing canal, rail, and telegraph projects from his office on Wall Street.

On January 1, 1861, the banker incorporated Jay Cooke & Company, the nation's first "wire" brokerage house and its most powerful financial institution. In addition to dealing in gold, brokering notes from state banks, and trading in foreign exchange, Cooke loaned the state of Pennsylvania $3 million to equip troops for the Civil War. After the Union's surprise loss at the First Battle of Bull Run on July 21, 1861, within hours of the release of the news in the *Philadelphia Inquirer,* Cooke raised $1.75 million in pledges to the military.

On February 25, 1862, U.S. Secretary of the Treasury Salmon P. Chase negotiated with Cooke for the sale of a half billion dollars in government bonds to buy more than $20 billion worth of guns, mounts, and equipment for the Union army. Through telegraphic communication from his offices in New York, Philadelphia, and Washington, D.C., Cooke, the official subscription agent for national loan, hired 2,500 bankers, realtors, and insurance clerks as assistants to sell $511 million in bonds to 1 million buyers. The field agents raised the funds at the rate of $3 million per day. Cooke also advised the government on realizing President Abraham Lincoln's concept of national banks, which quickly opened in Philadelphia and Washington.

Throughout the Civil War, Cooke's worldwide reputation for fiscal responsibility made him invaluable to U.S. finance. In 1863, at the breaking point in national fiscal health, Senator William Pitt Fessenden battled cash shortfalls by negotiating short-term loans from Cooke.

Under the National Currency Act of 1863, the U.S. Secret Service worked with local police forces to protect government bonds, checks, stamps, securities, and federal vaults from counterfeit bills. Felons such as bond forger William E. "Long Bill" Brockway endangered one-third of the nation's currency, threatened the stability of the banking system, and cheated the U.S. Treasury of $75,000. Jay Cooke & Company offered a $20,000 reward for the prosecution of Brockway's gang.

Near the end of the Civil War, Cooke again hawked bonds in towns, military posts, mining camps, and even pacifist Quaker communities by persuading the press to back the bond business. By July 1865, he had sold $830 million in bonds that raised cash for military supplies and soldier pay.

During Reconstruction, Cooke invested in the Northern Pacific Railway, which he redeemed from 30 months of mismanagement. The Coinage Act of 1873 depressed the money supply and jeopardized his company, which overtaxed its credit to finance the Northern Pacific Railway through Duluth, Minnesota, to Tacoma, Washington. On September 18, 1873, because of demands for westward advancement and national infrastructure replacement after the Civil War, a stock market crash triggered the Panic of 1873. The collapse of Cooke's bank toppled other banks, 18,000 businesses, and 89 railroads while deflating prices and real estate values. Some 5,000 business failures slashed incomes, especially among unemployed workers, and crushed unions by 73 percent, a setback that lasted for five years.

By 1875, shrewd investments with mine owners and with the Mormon Church in the North Horn Silver Mining Company at Frisco, Utah, restored Cooke's wealth. He died on February 8, 1905, in Cheltenham, Pennsylvania, where his philanthropy built the Ogontz School for Girls.

Further Reading

Beckert, Sven. *The Monied Metropolis: New York City and the Consolidation of the American Bourgeoisie, 1850–1896.* Cambridge, UK: Cambridge University Press, 2003.

Lane, Charles. *The Day Freedom Died: The Colfax Massacre, the Supreme Court, and the Betrayal of Reconstruction.* New York: Henry Holt, 2008.

Lubetkin, M. John. *Jay Cooke's Gamble: The Northern Pacific Railroad, the Sioux, and the Panic of 1873.* Norman: University of Oklahoma Press, 2006.

Morris, Charles R. *The Tycoons: How Andrew Carnegie, John D. Rockefeller, Jay Gould, and J.P. Morgan Invented the American Supereconomy.* New York: Henry Holt, 2005.

Renehan, Edward J., Jr. *The Dark Genius of Wall Street: The Misunderstood Life of Jay Gould, King of the Robber Barons.* New York: Basic Books, 2005.

Cook's Tours

An innovator of the tourist trade at battle sites and on global frontiers, Thomas Cook pioneered affordable world travel and conceived the idea of traveler's checks. Born in Derbyshire, England, on November 22, 1808, he worked in gardening of market fruits and vegetables and apprenticed in carpentry before beginning a career as a cabinetmaker and itinerant Baptist evangelist and temperance leader.

Accessing vendors by telegraph, he began organizing tours in 1841 by chartering a train trip for 570 temperance workers aboard the Midland Counties Railway from Leicester to Loughborough, England. He branched out to family-style pleasure traveling in Scotland, London, and Paris and then to grand European excursions, which he merchandised in the *Exhibition Herald and Excursion Advertiser.* Cook's itineraries launched mass domestic tourism, budget hotel and train fares, and coastal resorts.

In the 1860s, Cook's tours added the United States to a new list of destinations that included Egypt, Italy, and Switzerland. Travelers to North America could choose independent routes for a fixed period and paid the Cook Travel Agency for coupon books covering the costs of travel, rooms, and meals.

On Fleet Street in London, Thomas Cook partnered with John Mason Cook under the name Thomas Cook and Son. More adventuresome than his father, John Mason Cook reconnoitered itineraries personally and merchandized maps and guidebooks, hiking shoes, luggage, and telescopes. In 1865, he organized tours of Civil War battlefields and introduced a 222-day global tour beginning with a steamer from Europe to North America and including a stagecoach ride across the frontier, a Pacific paddlewheeler voyage to Japan, and a concluding trek through China and India to Europe.

The first U.S. tour in May 1866 put travelers under the personal guidance of John Mason Cook. For $250 for a month's stay, the group visited Central Park, Madison Avenue, and the Hudson River in New York City. The journey continued at the travelers' own pace with rail excursions to Niagara Falls, the Great Lakes, Montreal, Toronto, and Mammoth Cave, Kentucky. Outside Richmond, Virginia, they viewed Civil War battlefields in disarray, as military grave crews dug trenches to receive piles of sun-bleached animal and human skeletons. The itinerary returned the travelers up the Atlantic Coast via Washington, D.C., and departed from Vermont. The travel company gained particular notoriety from the satisfaction of two of its customers, Mark Twain and President Ulysses S. Grant.

To relieve travelers of worries about lost or stolen money, the company in 1874 initiated circular notes (traveler's checks), a preprinted book of checks in fixed amounts guaranteed by the Thomas Cook Agency. Thomas Cook retired in 1879 and died on July 18, 1892. John Mason Cook expanded the world tour business with the help of his sons, Ernest Edward, Frank Henry, and Thomas Albert "Bert" Cook.

Further Reading

Rojek, Chris. "Tourism and Citizenship." *International Journal of Cultural Policy* 4:2 (April 1998): 291–310.

Withey, Lynne. *Grand Tours and Cook's Tours: A History of Leisure Travel, 1750 to 1915.* New York: William Morrow, 1997.

Copperheads

Zealous Northern Democrats—or Peace Democrats—who sympathized with Southern secessionists and advocated a negotiated settlement of differences earned the derogatory nicknames "butternuts" and "copperheads." Membership in this faction included U.S. Senator Daniel Voorhees, New York Governor Horatio Seymour, and New York City Mayor Fernando Wood, along with racist propagandists, states' rights defenders, anti-industrial farmers, and German and Irish Catholics. Merchants impoverished by the curtailment of trade with the plantation South along the Mississippi River raged at railroad owners for raising shipping rates during the national conflict. Antiwar Copperheads gained temporary control of the Indiana legislature and the Illinois House of Representatives. In Cambria and Clearfield counties of west-central Pennsylvania, armed Copperheads promoted draft resistance among some 1,800 deserters.

Historians accord covert operators a cachet they shared with the Ku Klux Klan and the Knights of the White Camellia for incendiary speech and malicious plots. A secret society, the Knights of the Golden Circle (later known as the Order of American Knights and the Order of the Sons of Liberty) flourished in Indiana, Iowa, Missouri, Ohio, and Wisconsin among negrophobes and supporters of secession. Led by a white supremacist, George W.L. Bickley, a physician and journalist in Cincinnati, Ohio, the Knights promoted the spread of slavery through Texas into Mexico and the Caribbean. President Abraham Lincoln retaliated by prohibiting the distribution of Copperhead newspapers through the U.S. mail and by suspending habeas corpus and arbitrarily rounding up Copperheads as underminers of Union enlistment and material backers of the Confederacy.

Insurgency

On February 15, 1861, two months before the outbreak of Civil War, Texas Ranger Ben McCulloch, later a Confederate war martyr, led a 550-man cavalry on a Copperhead-inspired assault on the federal arsenal at San Antonio, Texas. The following May 13, at midnight, Confederate

Rangers and Knights set fire to the triweekly *Alamo Express* and wrecked the press. The next morning, officials discovered a plot to exile or hang 150 prominent loyalists.

Unionist Republicans reviled the Copperheads for concealing their duplicity and virulence. Confederate sympathizers responded by blaming abolitionism and President Lincoln for forcing the nation into a state of anarchy. As a token of their beliefs, they sliced the image of Liberty from copper pennies and wore the icons on their lapels.

Journalists Wilbur F. Storey, proprietor of the *Chicago Times*; Charles Henry Lanphier of the *Illinois State Register*; Samuel Medary, editor of the Columbus, Ohio, *Crisis*; and Edward G. Roddy, publisher of the Uniontown, Pennsylvania, *Genius of Liberty,* circulated scurrilous charges that Lincoln was a tyrant and a tool of black slaves, members of an inferior race. Marcus Mills "Brick" Pomeroy, a Wisconsin editor of the Lacrosse *Democratic,* labeled Lincoln a bigot and a butcher and encouraged an assassin to strike the president to the heart. On August 14, 1862, a federal marshal seized Dennis A. Mahoney, the Irish-born publisher of the Dubuque, Iowa, *Herald,* who was sent to prison in Washington, D.C., for his virulent antiwar editorials.

When the war extended into a lengthy struggle, covert insurgents, spies, and bushwhackers threatened violent opposition, particularly in southern Illinois. Armed stalkers seized Unionists from their homes and lashed or shot them. At Mattoon, renegades clashed with Union infantrymen on furlough, forcing constables and sheriffs to place such political hotbeds under martial law. Copperheads and General John Hunt Morgan's rogue Confederate cavalry threatened the peace. At San Antonio, Texas, strength in numbers forced Union General David E. Twiggs to surrender the federal arsenal to the Knights of the Golden Circle on February 16, 1862.

At the height of Confederate victories, Copperheads acted on their beliefs by urging Union forces to desert. Fueling discontent, the Emancipation Proclamation of January 1, 1863, stirred alarm that free blacks and Radical Republicans would overrun the North, elevating the rates of unemployment and crime.

The most outspoken of Southern sympathizers languished in military stockades for interfering with soldier recruitment. On the order of Union General Ambrose Burnside, former congressman and Copperhead agitator Clement Laird Vallandigham of Dayton, Ohio, went to prison on May 7, 1863, for inciting resistance to the war. Burnside labeled Vallandigham a pernicious shirker and traitor for choosing pacifism over military service.

Printer Harrison Henry Dodd, founder and grand commander of the Order of the Sons of Liberty in Indianapolis, spread rumors of launching an uprising of Confederate prisoners of war at Camp Morton, Indiana. Spies into the secret knighthood, emboldened by the support of Indiana Governor Oliver Hazard Perry Morton, leaked the traitors' intent to aid Confederate prisoners in overthrowing the state governments of Indiana, Ohio, and Michigan.

Lost Cause

More Copperhead press coverage accompanied the uncertainties of 1863, generating hints that Lincoln favored miscegenation. Pro-South, proslavery publisher J.F. Peeks maligned President Lincoln as "Africanus I," the widow-maker, and issued a campaign pamphlet charging the president with a suspicious past. The Belfast-born editor of the Catholic *Metropolitan Record,* John Mullaly of the Bronx, New York, shifted loyalties by advising Irish males to evade the Union military draft.

In July, Union victories at Gettysburg, Pennsylvania, and Vicksburg, Mississippi, deflated Copperhead bombast. Without attaining his dream of becoming emperor of Mexico, on August 18, 1863, Bickley entered solitary confinement at Ohio Penitentiary in Columbus for spying on Indiana Unionists and for soliciting funds from Confederate agents to aid Morgan's Raiders, the Confederate marauders who invaded Indiana and Ohio in July 1863.

Agitation between loyalists and Copperheads peaked on March 28, 1864, at a riot around the courthouse in Charleston, Illinois. The lawlessness resulted in the deaths of Copperhead leaders John Cooper and Nelson Wells and in the escape of John O'Hair, the pro-South sheriff of Coles County, Illinois. Republicans charged Peace Democrats with conducting a civil war within a civil war.

Before the Confederate surrender at Appomattox, Virginia, on April 9, 1865, liberals and Unionists crushed Copperhead rhetoric and threats. On July 30, 1864, the Indianapolis *Daily Journal* exposed the secret rites and constitution of the covert Sons of Liberty. In summer 1864, Union General William Tecumseh Sherman's advance on Atlanta, Georgia, eroded sympathy for the South. The liberation of Northern prisoners of war from Andersonville Prison in western Georgia heightened outrage against barbaric treatment of fellow Americans fighting on the opposite side of secessionism.

The arrest of Dodd and his co-conspirator, William A. Bowles, on August 20, 1864, disclosed a cache of revolvers and ammunition intended to support Morgan's Raiders. Federal authorities held Bowles for treason until May 31, 1865, when President Andrew Johnson commuted his capital sentence to life imprisonment.

See also: Baylor, John R.; Civil Rights; *Ex Parte Milligan* (1866); Habeas Corpus, Suspension of.

Further Reading

Heidler, David S., and Jeanne T. Heidler, eds. *Encyclopedia of the American Civil War: A Political, Social, and Military History.* New York: W.W. Norton, 2000.

Lurie, Maxine N., and Marc Mappen, eds. *Encyclopedia of New Jersey.* New Brunswick, NJ: Rutgers University Press, 2004.

Smith, Adam I.P. *No Party Now: Politics in the Civil War North.* Oxford, UK: Oxford University Press, 2006.

Weigley, Russell F. *A Great Civil War: A Military and Political History, 1861–1865.* Bloomington: Indiana University Press, 2000.

Cornell, Ezra (1807–1874)

With wealth amassed from the telegraph industry, machinist Ezra Cornell achieved his lifetime dream of founding a university—Cornell University in Ithaca, New York—in 1865. Born on January 11, 1807, in Westchester County, New York, he was related to Benjamin Franklin and the eldest of 11 children of Quaker potter Elijah Cornell and Eunice Barnard Cornell.

Largely self-educated, Cornell worked in carpentry in Syracuse and mechanics in Homer and managed Jeremiah S. Beebe's plaster mill at Fall Creek. Traveling on foot, he sold Barnaby and Mooers side hill plows in Georgia in winter and in Maine in summer. In collaboration with inventor Samuel F.B. Morse, Cornell co-founded the Western Union Telegraph Company in 1855.

Cornell's fortune derived from decades of work in the telegraph industry. He earned Morse's trust and eventual collaboration by laying wire from Baltimore to Washington, D.C., and from Buffalo, New York, to Milwaukee, Wisconsin. In 1847, after recovering from a bout with typhus, he directed the spread of telegraph lines from Troy, New York, through Vermont to Montreal, Canada. After the merger of two companies to create Western Union, Cornell became the chief stockholder for the next 15 years.

He abandoned his work in telegraphy in 1860, after suffering five breaks in his arm and three in his fingers while leaning on a train car window. He began investing in photo-lithography and coal oil in Kentucky and Ohio and raising cattle and sheep at his farm, called Forest Park, in upstate New York. At age 55, he began the first of two consecutive terms in the New York State Assembly as a Republican and traveled to Austria, France, Germany, Great Britain, Holland, and Switzerland. In 1863, with money from his investments, he gave $60,000 for the establishment of the Cornell Library at Ithaca, a meeting place for civic, religious, and social groups. In May 1864, he answered a call from President Abraham Lincoln and rendered aid to the Union wounded from the First Battle of Bull Run.

As chairman of the state Committee on Agriculture, Cornell involved himself in higher education during a period of progressive innovation. In 1865, under the Morrill Land-Grant Act, passed three years earlier, he co-founded Cornell University, a practical professional school chartered through the efforts of its first president, Andrew Dickson White, a Yale University–educated teacher of English and history. White suggested that, with Cornell's $500,000 and $600,000 from the state of New York, they could establish a nonsectarian school of agriculture, biology, and mechanics at Ithaca on Cornell's land overlooking Cayuga Lake. Cornell declared that Ithaca would become America's seat of learning. In a letter to his five-year-old granddaughter, Eunice Cornell, in 1867, he promised that girls and boys would receive equal education at Cornell University.

Cornell and White collected ideas about academics from noteworthy sources. Naturalist Louis Agassiz suggested candidates for professors of science and sources of available shell collections. While Cornell oversaw construction, White superintended the campus's architectural style. White spent $15,000 abroad for books and chemicals and endowed the campus with his personal library, a world-class collection. On a European tour, he surveyed the instructional freedom at the Royal Agricultural College at Hohenheim, Germany, and hired professors of English, history, and veterinary medicine in England. White personally combed the Latin Quarter in Paris for books and anatomical models and bought lab equipment in Berlin, Darmstadt, and Heidelberg, Germany.

The university opened on October 7, 1868, with an enrollment of 412, more than any other institution of higher learning in the United States. The school initiated the elective system, a means of individualizing courses of study that influenced the teaching style at Harvard University. In 1872, timber magnate Henry W.

Sage, chairman of Cornell's board of trustees, donated $250,000 to build a women's dormitory for the first equal opportunity coeducational Ivy League school in America. Cornell University accepted freedmen and initiated scholarships for women.

Cornell traveled Europe and maintained an extensive correspondence. The Panic of 1873 diminished his fortune and limited his philanthropy shortly before his death in Ithaca on December 9, 1874.

See also: Colleges and Universities.

Further Reading

Geiger, Roger L., ed. *Perspectives on the History of Higher Education, 2007.* New Brunswick, NJ: Transaction, 2007.

Oliver, John William, Jr., Charles L. Cherry, and Caroline L. Cherry, eds. *Founded by Friends: The Quaker Heritage of Fifteen American Colleges and Universities.* Lanham, MD: Scarecrow, 2007.

Rhodes, Frank H.T. *The Creation of the Future: The Role of the American University.* Ithaca, NY: Cornell University Press, 2001.

Cotton

Long-staple cotton, the mainstay of the Southern economy, both blessed and cursed Americans. The southeastern quadrant of the nation represented the world's largest cotton-growing region. By 1860, some 2 million U.S. farms annually raised more than 5 million bales of raw cotton, a labor-intensive crop requiring hand separation of fiber from seed by two-thirds of the nation's 4 million slaves. Georgia led the region in textile manufacturing, which employed 2,800 laborers. Profits at Natchez, Mississippi, produced more millionaires per capita than any other U.S. town.

Shippers from the ports of Charleston, Galveston, New Orleans, and Savannah benefited from the steady flow of bales to the North and Great Britain. Trade with the North turned river towns from Pawtucket, Rhode Island, to Worcester, Massachusetts, into milling centers. The quality of American *Gossypium barbadense* and *Gossypium hirsutum* suited the looms of British fabric factories at a time when India's farmers lagged behind global demand. Plantations supplied client nations with low-cost fiber cultivated and harvested by field hands at the cost of wretched toil and damage to fingers from prickly bolls and to health from bent backs and heat stroke.

Libertarians could not ignore the brutality of cotton farming. Congregationalists, Mennonites, Methodist Episcopalians, Presbyterians, Quakers, Shakers, Unitarians, and evangelicals protested profiteering from the flesh trade and the financial exploitation of slave-planted, slave-harvested cotton. Following an extensive tour of the South and Texas, Frederick Law Olmsted published *Journeys and Explorations in the Cotton Kingdom: A Traveler's Observations on Cotton and Slavery in the American Slave States* (1861), a three-volume abolitionist treatise that demonized as immoral the inherited wealth from human bondage. In the introduction to the third volume, Olmsted noted the role of Eli Whitney's cotton gin in promoting the slave culture and in turning planters into a plutocracy lavished in comfort and luxury. From his observations in Virginia, Olmsted warned that slavery made the cotton economy an illusionary and self-defeating agricultural windfall. The text proclaimed such a one-crop economy to be counterproductive to the nation's future.

War and Profits

As conflict loomed over states' rights, New York capitalists anticipated the loss of cotton imports and shipping from Southern plantations. The South, on the other hand, used cotton as an economic tool in its diplomatic negotiations with European nations to persuade them to finance the Confederate army. The secession of South Carolina from the Union in December 1860 prompted Union trade embargoes. President Abraham Lincoln sought a peaceful solution by limiting the sale of fiber crops to the North, but his plan to choke off profits to the Confederate war machine took longer to succeed than he had anticipated.

Harbor blockades and the Confederate embargo on May 21, 1861, suppressed the export of cotton valued at $300 million, but invigorated the immensely profitable business of blockade running along the Atlantic Coast and from Tampa Bay, Florida, into the Gulf of Mexico. At Memphis, Tennessee, and Yorktown, Virginia, soldiers recycled unsold bales into an effective waterfront barricade; at Paducah, Kentucky, harbor fortification turned cotton transports into iron-plated naval vessels. Because of strong secessionist sympathy in Kentucky, federal revenue agents doubled the suppression of trade. Merchants disguised boxes as loads of wood and continued trafficking in cotton to southern Illinois and over the Mississippi River into Missouri and south through bayous and creeks to Confederate mills.

In April 1861, the outbreak of the Civil War curtailed trade in cotton yarn and fabric to the outside world, forcing farmers to ship west over the Rio Grande into Mexico. In Bertie County, North Carolina, agrarians turned to peanuts and tobacco as ready cash crops. As a wise investment, Alexander Turney Stewart of New York bought up cotton before prices rose; he sold it at a loss to Union manufacturers of uniforms, blankets, and hospital linens, which he donated to the forces of General Ulysses S. Grant. A similar operation on the Chattahoochee River at Roswell, Georgia, turned fibers into Confederate pants and shirts, dyed "Roswell gray," until a Union regiment burned the mills and cotton house on July 6, 1864. Merchant Marshall Field foresaw shortages in cotton and woolen goods and invested his cash in warehousing merchandise that earned him $2.5 million over the course of four years. Globally, agrarian experiments in cotton growing in Egypt and Tahiti failed to replicate the profits that "King Cotton" generated in the American South.

Human Cost

Cash income from cotton goods continued to generate human misery. One of the most published photos of whipping scars featured Peter, a field hand on Captain John Lyon's Atchafalaya cotton plantation outside Washington, Louisiana, who suffered a severe lashing in 1863. *Frank Leslie's Illustrated Newspaper* followed the seasonal cycle of hoeing, harvesting, cleaning, and weighing bags of fiber. Artist Alfred Waud, on assignment from *Harper's Weekly,* moved with the Army of the Potomac and illustrated the dangers to enslaved cotton harvesters.

In Ocala and Tallahassee and along Florida's sea islands, the loss of 90 percent of eligible males to the Civil War forced women, elderly men, the disabled, and children to superintend planting and harvesting. At Waxahachie, Texas, a similar wartime cadre produced 4,000 bales per year but lacked the cash to pay for shipping. After enactment of the Homestead Act in 1862, cultivation spread west to California, where farmers and livestock

Cotton remained king in the South after the Civil War, with foreign and domestic demand rising sharply. Sharecroppers and low-wage laborers, many of them women and children, tended the fields and operated the mills. *(MPI/Stringer/Getty Images)*

men petitioned for plots and free water for cotton fields in the 10 million acres (4 million hectares) available in Imperial Valley and Owens Valley.

With the advance of Union forces, Confederate residents fleeing their plantations outside Charleston, Memphis, and Nashville and cotton warehouses at Monroeville, Alabama, and along the Mississippi River burned cotton sheds and warehouses to prevent the enemy from seizing and selling stored bales. Occupation forces hanged planters who defied Union orders to leave harvests intact.

Cotton and Recovery

During Reconstruction, cotton remained a focus of contention. After emancipation, freedmen despised cotton culture, a crop symbolic of bondage. To invigorate self-sustaining farms, reformer Oliver Hudson Kelley, a staff member at the U.S. Bureau of Agriculture, led the Grange Movement (National Grange of the Order of Patrons of Husbandry) as an antidote to a stymied regional agriculture, especially in Alabama and Mississippi.

Overall, 89 percent of black farmers maintained Southern residency and continued to work in rural agriculture in a climate and terrain they understood. Rich Northern speculators and former Union army officers purchased prime land and imported laborers to supervise cotton planting and harvesting on tenant farms and to restore rail lines for shipping to Northern factories. To give jobs to former slaves, author Harriet Beecher Stowe left Hartford, Connecticut, to run a cotton plantation on the St. Johns River in Mandarin, Florida. Mississippi recreated a microcosm of slavery by leasing black convicts as a source of cheap labor. A brutal punishment for minor crimes such as vagrancy and trespass, forced labor mimicked the plantation system.

In the postwar market surge, U.S. production of cotton bales rose by 65 percent. After Arkansans and Texans began cultivating cotton fields, residents of Jacksonville, Arkansas, and the Brazos bottoms outside Houston and north of Tyler and Waco, Texas, recovered rapidly from wartime despair. They hauled their crop via mule- or ox-drawn wagons toward Nachitoches, Louisiana, over the Red and Sabine rivers. As the Cotton Belt extended farther west, the Southern Pacific Railroad bought up lines through North Texas to the Plains states.

At the Sea Island plantations and the cotton processing towns of Athens, Augusta, Columbus, Macon, Marietta, and Thomaston, Georgia, scientific methods produced an all-time bonanza in 1870 of 726,406 bales. The Augusta Cotton Exchange, organized in 1871, trafficked daily in raw fibers carried by wagons and unloaded from boats. The state's processing plants rose in number to 34 and its cloth, burlap, and bleached yarn production earned $12.6 million. Petersburg, Virginia, pulled itself out of postwar despair by building six cotton mills, which employed 500 workers. At Port Royal, South Carolina, investors in cotton built the world's largest fiber compress, which turned 1,500 pounds (680 kilograms) of raw cotton into a 500-pound (230-kilogram) bale and more than 200 pounds (90 kilograms) of seed. The pressing of cotton seed oil, which was used as the basis for processed foods, turned waste into additional profit.

Reconstruction Economy

Politicians anticipated that inflated farm prices would ease agricultural debts and break the stranglehold that banks and rail barons held over cotton dealers. By coercing sharecroppers and shackled chain gangs to cultivate cotton, Southern profiteers enriched themselves on the increased demand generated by such industrialists as Seth L. Milliken, founder of the Deering-Milliken & Company in Portland, Maine. Milliken promoted the postwar agricultural resources of the South by importing cotton for processing in New England. In 1868, he established headquarters to New York City and patented trademark bleached cotton goods—Bermuda Lily, Bianco, Mother's Choice, and Progress. In Gadsden, Alabama, the Georgia and Alabama Steamboat Company constructed the *Magnolia,* a steamer that carried cotton goods to market. At the Memphis Cotton Exchange, incorporated in 1874, an association settled controversies between cotton factors in Tennessee and northern Mississippi with classification standards and transaction rules that decreased risks to farmers.

As before emancipation, the cotton economy affected lives in myriad ways. The booming cloth and yarn business enriched the Houston & Texas Central Railroad, which transported 300,000 bales in 1877. To prevent smokestacks from showering cotton lint with sparks, engineers chose to push trains rather than head them.

At cotton mills, employers favored underage laborers, who could easily climb among carding and spinning machines, overhead pulleys, rope and twine rollers, and looms. Triggering respiratory illness among weavers, cotton fluff filled the air around flywheels; bleaching fumes exacerbated lung disorders. Sparks from metal parts threatened flash fires in oily lint. The situation worsened among "lintheads" and "cracker girls" (poor white mill hands) in cotton mills throughout Alabama, Georgia, and the Carolinas, where 23 percent of the labor force was underage.

Children lost fingers to whirling belts, pulleys, and shafts and vision to slivers and boll debris. Between 1870 and 1880, the proportion of child employees rose from 16 percent to 16.6 percent of all children aged 10 to 14. The introduction of Levi Strauss's denim factory in San Francisco in 1873 increased demand for fibers to make cotton duck fabric for jeans and jackets. With the merchandizing of the sewing machine and the influx of Bohemian, Italian, Lithuanian, and Russian Jews in the 1870s, female labor at sweatshops doubled the nation's annual production of cotton goods to $420 million.

See also: Deering-Milliken & Company.

Further Reading

Albion, Robert Greenhalgh. *Square-Riggers on Schedule: The New York Sailing Packets to England, France, and the Cotton Ports.* Princeton, NJ: Princeton University Press, 2001.

Horton, James Oliver, and Lois E. Horton. *Slavery and the Making of America.* New York: Oxford University Press, 2005.

Lakwete, Angela. *Inventing the Cotton Gin: Machine and Myth in Antebellum America.* Baltimore: Johns Hopkins University Press, 2003.

Myers, Peter C. *Frederick Douglass: Race and the Rebirth of American Liberalism.* Lawrence: University Press of Kansas, 2008.

Noll, Mark A. *God and Race in American Politics: A Short History.* Princeton, NJ: Princeton University Press, 2008.

Crazy Horse (ca. 1842–1877)

A chief of the Oglala Lakota, the majority branch of the Sioux, Crazy Horse assisted his people by devising inventive war strategies. Born near Rapid City, South Dakota, to Crazy Horse and Rattle Blanket Woman, daughter of the famed Miniconjou warrior Black Buffalo, the younger Crazy Horse inherited a family pride in resilience and loyalty. He experienced visions in the Black Hills of South Dakota that predicted his future as a protector of his people.

He gained a warrior's reputation during combat with the Arikara, Blackfeet, Crow, Pawnee, and Shoshone. He and other Lakota backed the Southern Cheyenne of Colorado after 133 died at the Sand Creek Massacre of November 29, 1864. Crazy Horse fought at the Battle of Red Buttes and faced U.S. Cavalry from Kansas and Ohio at the Platte River Bridge Station at Mills, Wyoming, in July 1865, when Indians attacked a wagon train and slew most of its military escort. As a result, the army abandoned Fort Caspar in east-central Wyoming and regrouped farther east at Fort Fetterman. The Lakota rewarded Crazy Horse by naming him "Shirt Wearer," a title of military greatness.

> Shortly before his death, Crazy Horse regretted that the native Plains lifestyle ended with the decimation of the buffalo:
>
> > We preferred hunting to a life of idleness on the reservations, where we were driven against our will. At times, we did not get enough to eat, and we were not allowed to leave the reservation to hunt. We preferred our own way of life.

During the Fetterman Massacre on December 21, 1866, at Fort Phil Kearny, halfway along the Bozeman Trail, Crazy Horse, Miniconjou Chief Hump, and Hunkpapa chiefs Gall and Rain-in-the-face enticed men of the U.S. Eighteenth Infantry to Massacre Hill in north-central Wyoming. Meanwhile, Cheyenne Chief Little Wolf waited in ambush at Peno Creek, while Oglala Lakota Sioux Chief Red Cloud lurked beyond Lodge Trail Ridge. Boxed in by some 2,000 Arapaho, Cheyenne, and Sioux braves, 78 soldiers armed with seven-shot Spencer rifles and two scouts armed with Henry rapid-fire repeater rifles suffered a massive defeat that concluded with the mutilation of 79 bodies. The Indians intended the slaughter to discourage the desecration of the sacred Black Hills on the South Dakota border and to halt prospecting on traditional lands.

On August 2, Crazy Horse and nearly 2,000 braves met a woodcutting detail outside the same fort and lost 120 men to soldiers equipped with Henry rifles. When Lieutenant Colonel George Armstrong Custer led prospectors into the Black Hills in 1874 and located gold along French Creek in the Badlands, Crazy Horse left the Great Sioux Reservation to defend his people's territory.

At the beginning of the Great Sioux War, on June 17, 1876, at the six-hour Battle of Rosebud Creek at Big Horn County in southeastern Montana, Crazy Horse and an army of 1,800 Northern Cheyenne and Lakota outmaneuvered General George Crook and 1,000 soldiers led by 260 Crow and Shoshone scouts. The triumph preceded the Lakota union with the Cheyenne and Sioux for the Battle of the Little Bighorn in south-central Montana, in which Crazy Horse, Sitting Bull, and Chief Gall led the attack on June 25. Eyewitnesses among the Arapaho and Hunkpapa Sioux proclaimed Crazy Horse a major force against Custer and 225 men of the U.S. Seventh

Cavalry. Despite the Indian victory, the Sioux remained stymied by the loss of the buffalo, the linchpin of the Indian economy.

After a defeat on January 8, 1877, by U.S. troops at Wolf Mountain, Montana, on February 28, Crazy Horse witnessed the removal of the Black Hills and 7 million acres (2.8 million hectares) from the Great Sioux Reservation. On May 6, he led a band of 800 followers, along with He Dog, Iron Crow, and Little Big Man, to Fort Robinson at Pine Ridge, Nebraska, to surrender at the Red Cloud Agency to General Crook.

During incarceration, Crazy Horse left the reserve to locate treatment for his consumptive wife Black Shawl, the second of his three wives and the mother of his only child. Crook feared that Crazy Horse was plotting an insurrection. To avoid trouble, Spotted Tail convinced the warrior to return voluntarily. Crazy Horse died on September 5, 1877, of a bayonet wound inflicted by a guard, William Gentles.

See also: Black Kettle; Buffalo; Dakota Territory; Little Bighorn, Battle of the; Red Cloud; Weapons.

Further Reading

Brown, Dee. *The American West.* New York: Simon & Schuster, 1995.

———. *Bury My Heart at Wounded Knee: An Indian History of the American West.* New York: Holt, Rinehart and Winston, 1970.

Calloway, Colin G., ed. *Our Hearts Fell to the Ground: Plains Indian Views of How the West Was Lost.* Boston: Bedford/St. Martin's, 1996.

Cozzens, Peter, ed. *Eyewitnesses to the Indian Wars, 1865–1890.* 5 vols. Mechanicsburg, PA: Stackpole, 2001–2005.

Johansen, Bruce E., and Donald A. Grinde, Jr. *The Encyclopedia of Native American Biography.* New York: Da Capo, 1998.

Lamar, Howard R., ed. *The New Encyclopedia of the American West.* New Haven, CT: Yale University Press, 1998.

Crime and Punishment

The expansion of the United States in the 1860s and 1870s produced both urban and frontier models of crime and punishment. To the east of the Mississippi River, an influx of Chinese, German, Irish, and Italian immigrants after the Civil War filled inner cities with slum dwellers left jobless after the Civil War. Crime rates increased. Cities developed professional uniformed police to prevent misdemeanors and felonies and to disband gangs, such as the Mississippi Valley riverboat gamblers who preyed on Mobile and Natchez, Mississippi, and Cincinnati, Ohio.

Prisons filled with corrupt guards and ungovernable inmates who brutalized each other. Severe lashing, manacling, and starvation diets encouraged recidivism and put the public at risk of career felons. To stem prison violence, wardens channeled inmates' energies into work. At the Maine State Prison in 1864, prisoners performed $2,000 worth of work by blacksmithing, cabinetmaking, chair making, painting, and tailoring.

During this period, the issuance of state currencies encouraged counterfeiting. To suppress fake bills, under the National Currency Act of 1863, U.S. Treasury Agents tracked perpetrators of 200 operations. The U.S. Secret Service captured engraver Benjamin F. Boyd, leader of a counterfeiting gang in Cincinnati, who served time at the Illinois State Penitentiary at Joliet. In Philadelphia, agents collared bond forger William E. "Long Bill" Brockway, who spent a decade in the New York State Prison for robbing the nation of $75,000.

Trains and banks, another growing temptation, presented thieves with wealth concentrated in a small space. The first train robbery occurred on May 5, 1865, at North Bend, Ohio; the first daylight bank robbery took place in Liberty, Missouri, on February 13, 1866. In Indiana, the Reno Gang invaded passenger cars of the Ohio & Mississippi Railroad at Seymour in October 1866 and in May 1868 at Brownstown. At Chicago, Allan Pinkerton's agents organized a posse to crush the gang, whom masked vigilantes hanged.

Before constitutional guarantees of suspects' rights, police and jailers routinely used in-house violence and coercion to threaten and intimidate alleged offenders. As a punishment and a protection of the citizenry, states built penitentiaries to retain wrongdoers. At the new prison in Pittsburgh, Pennsylvania, inmates during the 1860s faced solitary confinement under the Philadelphia System, which theorized that the absence of distractions afforded inmates time to meditate on their wrongdoings and to choose a lawful path. Meanwhile, corporate crime by railroad and mining barons, insider traders, and land speculators went unpunished.

Mounting Concerns

At a time when the penal system consisted of 40 state prisons, 25 houses of correction, and 2,000 jails, the inequities of the justice system provoked citizen complaints. On October 13, 1870, in Cincinnati, activists Zebulon Reed Brockway and Enoch Cobb Wines rallied prison reformers, including the governors of Indiana, New Jersey, and Ohio, at the National Prison Congress. Wines noted that the incarceration of some 120,000 inmates did not stop crime rates from rising. Delegates from 24 states and from Canada, Denmark, England, and South America proposed replacing punishment with reformation of convicts and supervision of newly released inmates as they returned to home and work. The application of indeterminate sentences allowed lawmakers to determine whether criminals should serve part or all of their prison sentences. Prison staff based parole decisions on observation of inmate behavior.

A parallel movement in Indiana, Massachusetts, and New York crusaded for separate facilities for women guarded by female wardens. Idealists envisioned the upgrading of attitudes and behaviors of "wayward" women. The first test of the theory, the Indiana Reformatory Institution for Women and Girls, opened at Indianapolis on October 8, 1873. Visitors from Massachusetts, New York, Ohio, Pennsylvania, and Wisconsin noted the high percentage of women who returned to productive lives. A Massachusetts commission urged a similar statewide experiment.

In the South, violence during the Civil War and Reconstruction resulted in illegal revenge assaults and slayings. Home guard units hunted down deserters, forgers of furlough papers, and Unionists—and hanged them. To punish carpetbaggers, mobs seized Northern intruders, stripped them, and made spectacles of them by tarring and feathering and riding on a rail. Whites targeted blacks for being the cause of war deaths and loss of family fortunes and for 12 years of military occupation of the former Confederacy. In Selma, Alabama, the justice system rounded up blacks for selling produce within the town and for cursing whites. Convicts wore striped suits and labored in shackles by day, while living in filthy cages by night.

The Ku Klux Klan, Red Shirts, White League, and Knights of the White Camellia lynched blacks for purchasing land, operating schools, owning guns, voting, and running for public office, all evidence of the rise of former slaves toward full citizenship. In 1868, the massacre of 1,300 voters from South Carolina to Arkansas preceded adoption of the Fourteenth and Fifteenth amendments to the U.S. Constitution. Although President Ulysses S. Grant retaliated with federal acts and martial law over counties infested by Klan terrorists, racist crime and election fraud burgeoned in the Carolinas, Florida, Louisiana, and Mississippi.

Frontier Crime

In the trans-Mississippi West, lawlessness on sparsely populated land increased because of the temptation to steal. Clashes between stockmen and settlers of the American West grew into vicious wars over the sharing of open grassland, water and mineral rights, carry laws, and fencing. Nomadic bandits used hit-and-run tactics to flee out of range of peace officers and U.S. marshals. The Colfax County War, a series of revenge killings over corrupt land monopolies in New Mexico Territory, required the intervention of Buffalo Soldiers and territorial militia, dispatched by Governor William A. Pile.

In mining territory in Kansas and Nebraska, claim disputes over unsurveyed land precipitated the formation of squatter courts, extralegal claim associations governed by a marshal. Punishment of claim jumpers consisted of beatings, arson, and scattered and broken mining equipment. At Vulture City, Arizona, owners of the Vulture Gold Mine hanged 18 thieves of high-grade ore. To impose order, federal agents replaced claims clubs with government land offices.

Outlaws such as Texas desperado Cullen Baker and the Quantrill Gang used the Civil War and Reconstruction as justification to raid and murder. Families in remote locales relied on guns rather than warrants for self-protection from shooters, armed robbers, and thieves. During the open range period, cattle grazed freely. The increase in untraceable theft from Texas to Montana required branding and possession of bills of sale, two proofs of ownership that lawmen respected. In Texas, laws prohibited the possession of straight and curved irons used to alter brands. The theft and slaughter of a single cow brought minor punishment, but stealing a horse was a capital crime. Ranchers in Mexico and Texas armed for danger as they pushed herds to rail centers in Kansas. To combat blatant rustling, settlers formed posses or quasi-military groups called Moderators, Minutemen, Regulators, and White Caps. In Tex-Mex communities along the Rio Grande, the *corrido,* a folkloric oral journalism, such as "El Corrido de Kiansis" (Ballad of Kansas, ca. 1860), bewailed the rough justice of lynch mobs and celebrated pistoleers who outshot and outrode Texas Rangers.

Cyclical assaults on Pony Express riders, wagon trains, stagecoaches, and railways required intervention by U.S. Cavalry patrols or by rail detectives. Beginning in July 1875 in Sonora, California, Wells Fargo detective J.W. Thacker issued reward posters offering $250 for stagecoach bandit Charles E. "Black Bart" Boles; Texas Rangers led by John B. Jones tracked the Sam Bass Gang and, following a bank heist, shot the leader to death outside Round Rock. After the James Gang plotted the first successful train robbery in the American West on July 21, 1873, at Adair, Iowa, and stole $3,000 from the Rock Island Express, the Pinkerton National Detective Agency began a manhunt that resulted in the shooting death of Jesse James in 1882. Posses weakened the gang by shooting members, killing some and wounding others. Some of the law enforcers, such as Wyatt Earp and William Barclay "Bat" Masterson, operated on both sides of the law, as brigands and sworn officers.

Crime Fighting

Western fortune hunting lured con artists as well as greedy entrepreneurs. In 1871, two frauds, cousins Philip Arnold and John Slack, created a pyramid scheme called the Great Diamond Hoax. They spread reports around San Francisco of a diamond field rumored to lie in Arizona or near Ralston City, New Mexico. On a butte in northwestern Wyoming Territory called Diamond Peak, the tricksters salted the actual treasure into anthills with sticks. Curious speculators, who contributed $35,000 each in earnest money, followed the con men to property containing some $150,000 in South African gemstones acquired from gem cutters in Amsterdam and London. Among the interested parties were Horace Greeley, editor of the *New York Tribune*; former Union army generals Benjamin Franklin Butler and George Brinton McClellan; William Chapman Ralston, founder of the Bank of Colorado; and jewelry magnate Charles Lewis Tiffany.

The company traveled by train from Lathrop, California, to Rawlins, Wyoming, for a four-day ride into the hills and arrived on June 4, 1872. Upon inspection by mountain man Clarence King, a federal geologist educated at Yale University, the placement of industrial-grade diamonds, emeralds, garnets, rubies, and sapphires attested to a swindle. After the *San Francisco Chronicle* exposed the grifters, Slack fled to St. Louis, Missouri, to build caskets; Arnold, who netted $550,000 from the plot, settled a lawsuit for fraud and died in 1878 of complications from a shootout.

Historic frontier towns—Tombstone, Arizona; Deadwood, South Dakota; San Francisco, California; Virginia City, Montana; and Abilene, Caldwell, Dodge City, Ellsworth, Hays, and Wichita, Kansas—hired sheriffs to control public drunkenness and gunplay, the crime that sent John Henry "Doc" Holliday to jail in Dallas, Texas, in 1875. One-on-one issues, such as petty thievery, "thimblerigging" (con games), and cheating at blackjack, faro, or poker, resulted in personal settlement of issues with fists. As towns incorporated, businessmen and traders opted for city ordinances against brothels and rowdy casinos. In the 1870s, Missouri law shut down cardsharps Bob Potee and Albert Showers, who cheated cowboys and ranchers in Kansas City. In Abilene, Kansas, town marshal James Butler "Wild Bill" Hickok enforced statutes forbidding public display of weapons, despite his notoriety for killing members of the McCanles Gang in 1865. The most feared criminals usually served time in prison for their misdeeds or died violently.

The legendary West grew in popular culture in subsequent years from pulp fiction in *Beadle's Dime Novels, Harper's Monthly, National Police Gazette, Pacific Monthly,* and *Saturday Journal.* Readers preferred grisly narratives, such as the charge that Jack Slade tied outlaw Jules Beni to a post, shot him 22 times, and cut off his ears for souvenirs. Buffalo Bill's Wild West Show carried into the twentieth century expanded episodes of Indian raids, walk-downs on Main Street, and stagecoach holdups exploited for the amusement of Easterners and Europeans.

Capital Punishment

The gallows awaited frontier criminals in the 1860s. At the end of the Dakota War in 1862, some 2,000 Indians surrendered. Of 303 raiders convicted of murder and rape, President Abraham Lincoln pardoned all but 38 from execution. The nation's largest mass execution occurred at their hanging in Mankato, Minnesota, on December 26, 1862. The rest of the captives served three-year prison terms at Fort Snelling. The military exiled the prisoners' families to Nebraska. In 1864, the murder of Warden Richard Tinker at Thomaston, Maine, resulted in the hanging of his killer and in three subsequent executions until the state legislature outlawed capital punishment in 1876.

After the death of President Lincoln from an assassin's bullet on April 15, 1865, a military court condemned to the gallows four male plotters and boardinghouse owner Mary Surratt, the first woman executed by federal command. The hangings occurred at the Old Arsenal Penitentiary at Fort McNair in Washington, D.C., on July 7, 1865. On November 10, 1865, a Confederate major, Henry Wirz, the only Civil War soldier convicted of war crimes, went to the gallows for plotting the murder of Union prisoners of war at Andersonville, Georgia.

On the frontier, capture of offenders tended toward an on-the-spot discussion of the evidence and a folk hanging, the doom of killer Jack Slade, whom vigilantes executed at Virginia City, Nevada. In 1876, vigilantes from Bannack, Montana, pursued the Plummer Gang across the plains and slew some 80 rustlers. On a ride to Nebraska, they hanged 13 thieves in a single morning from a railway bridge. Members exonerated the "lynch law" as efficient and cheap, because it avoided the complexities of lawyers, judges, courts, juries, and jails.

In the 1870s, although prison wardens and criminologists found no link between the death penalty and suppression of crime, Southern and Western states and territories favored capital punishment. In 1859, Southerners applauded the hanging of John Brown for plotting a raid on the federal arsenal at Harpers Ferry, Virginia. The execution generated the first flurry over breaking news in American history.

Following four years of bloody civil war, parts of the country began to lose enthusiasm for public retribution. Wisconsin ended executions before it began record keeping; Michigan retained the penalty only for acts of treason. Tennessee discontinued executions. Colorado, Iowa, Maine, Oregon, Rhode Island, and Washington abolished the death penalty, but later reinstated it at citizen demand. Maine whittled down application of the penalty until, by 1875, executions ceased. In courts in Illinois, Indiana, Louisiana, and Minnesota, criminals were not eligible for the death penalty unless the jury agreed unanimously. Other states—Kansas, New Hampshire, New York, Vermont—delayed sentencing and encouraged juries to set penalties of life imprisonment.

See also: Comstock Act (1873); James Gang; Law Enforcement; Quantrill, William; Range Wars; Stagecoach Travel; Tweed, William Magear.

Further Reading

Edge, Laura B. *Locked Up: A History of the U.S. Prison System.* Minneapolis, MN: Twenty-First Century Books, 2009.

Kaczorowski, Robert J. *The Politics of Judicial Interpretation: The Federal Courts, Department of Justice, and Civil Rights, 1866–1876.* New York: Fordham University Press, 2005.

MacKell, Jan. *Brothels, Bordellos, and Bad Girls: Prostitution in Colorado, 1860–1930.* Santa Fe: University of New Mexico Press, 2004.

Steelwater, Eliza. *The Hangman's Knot: Lynching, Legal Execution, and America's Struggle with the Death Penalty.* Boulder, CO: Westview, 2003.

Custer, George Armstrong (1839–1876)

One of the most controversial military figures of the American West, cavalry officer George Armstrong Custer earned a reputation for racism and grandstanding. He is best remembered for the humiliating defeat of his U.S. Seventh Cavalry regiment at the hands of Sioux and Cheyenne warriors at the Battle of the Little Bighorn in Montana on June 25, 1876.

Born of English and Hessian ancestry in New Rumley, Ohio, on December 5, 1839, Custer was the son of blacksmith Emanuel Henry Custer and Marie Ward Kirkpatrick Custer. Educated at public schools in Monroe, Michigan, and at Hopedale Normal College in Ohio, he taught classes at New Rumley in 1856 before entering the U.S. Military Academy at West Point.

After graduating from West Point in 1861—last in his class—he gained combat experience in the Civil War at the Battles of Bull Run, Chickahominy, and Chancellorsville. At age 23, Custer rose to the rank of brigadier general. He favored grandiose ceremonial dress decorated on the sleeve with some 10 inches (25 centimeters) of braid. His flair in battle cost him 257 cavalrymen at the Battle of Gettysburg, the gravest loss of the Army of the Potomac.

Following a year's break from soldiering, Custer campaigned for Andrew Johnson and refused to lead a black regiment, which he deemed an insult and demotion. He accepted the post of lieutenant colonel of the Seventh Cavalry, which pursued hostile Cheyenne from their headquarters at Fort Riley, Kansas. He incurred a 12-month suspension for leaving without permission to visit his wife, memoirist Elizabeth Bacon "Libbie" Custer. On April 19, 1867, at Pawnee Fork, he burned an abandoned enclave of dissident Cheyenne and Sioux, who had torched a wagon station at Smoky Hill. The destruction of 140 lodges, 420 buffalo robes, 226 saddles, cookware, and tools established his notoriety for extremism.

On November 27, 1868, Custer led a murderous raid on a peaceful Arapaho and Cheyenne winter village on the Washita River outside Cheyenne, Oklahoma. In foot-deep snow, the hasty dawn attack pitted 250 Indians against 660 troopers, who overran, killed, and scalped 103 villagers. The cavalry either shot or slit the throats of 875 ponies and mules, attacked and burned 51 lodges, slew Council Chief Little Rock, and captured 53 women and children.

The *Leavenworth* (Kansas) *Evening Bulletin, The New York Times,* and the *New York Tribune* quickly vilified

Cavalry officer George Armstrong Custer, famous for his "last stand" against Indian attack at the Battle of the Little Bighorn in June 1876, had earned a reputation for flamboyance, daring, and disobeying orders—as well as for his vicious treatment of native peoples. *(Buyenlarge/Getty Images)*

Custer for his vicious maltreatment of peaceable Indians and for inflating the Cheyenne body count to 140. The genocidal attack divided opinion on the quality of leadership of the Seventh Cavalry. Depicted at an inquiry as a sadistic butcher, Custer faced charges lodged by soldiers Frederick Benteen and Ben Clark that he had taken as his concubine one of the captives, Little Rock's daughter, 19-year-old Monahsetah, then seven months pregnant. In reply, Custer's memoirs, *My Life on the Plains; or, Personal Experiences with Indians* (1874), ridiculed those who branded him a child killer and self-aggrandizer. He did not deny claims of fathering a subsequent child of Monahsetah.

The need for military protection in 1873 brought Custer and 12 companies of the Seventh Cavalry to Mandan, North Dakota, in the Black Hills, where Crazy Horse, chief of the Oglala Lakota Sioux, led hostile bands against white miners and settlers. By 1876, the Sioux had fomented war to drive out intrusive whites and joined Arapaho and Northern Cheyenne to form an unprecedented army of 1,800 plains warriors. Headed by Crazy Horse and Hunkpapa chiefs Gall and Sitting Bull, the combined force annihilated Custer and his 267 troops and officers on June 25, 1876, east of Billings in south-central Montana at the Battle of the Little Big Horn.

The landmark American military defeat—informally known as Custer's Last Stand or the Battle of the Greasy Grass—coincided with preparations for the celebration of the nation's centennial. Against the advice of Arikara and Crow scouts, Custer disobeyed orders to wait until June 26 and attacked at noon. Along with 225 of his men, Colonel Myles Keogh, and their mounts, Custer and his brother, Lieutenant Thomas Ward Custer, died at Last Stand Hill from head and chest wounds.

Libbie Custer spent her widowhood defending her husband from posthumous shame with the books *Boots and Saddles* (1885), *Following the Guidon* (1890), and *Tenting on the Plains* (1893). The press romanticized her husband until the twentieth century, when film and history reviewed the less noteworthy details of Custer's military record.

See also: Bureau of Indian Affairs; Crazy Horse; Little Bighorn, Battle of the; Montana Territory; Sitting Bull; Weapons.

Further Reading

Calloway, Colin G., ed. *Our Hearts Fell to the Ground: Plains Indian Views of How the West Was Lost.* Boston: Bedford, 1996.

Cozzens, Peter, ed. *Eyewitnesses to the Indian Wars, 1865–1890.* 5 vols. Mechanicsburg, PA: Stackpole, 2001–2005.

Donovan, James. *A Terrible Glory: Custer and the Little Bighorn, the Last Great Battle of the American West.* New York: Back Bay, 2008.

Greene, Jerome A. *Washita: The U.S. Army and the Southern Cheyennes, 1867–1869.* Norman: University of Oklahoma Press, 2004.

Lamar, Howard R., ed. *The New Encyclopedia of the American West.* New Haven, CT: Yale University Press, 1998.

Utley, Robert M. *The Lance and the Shield: The Life and Times of Sitting Bull.* New York: Ballantine, 1994.

D

Dakota Territory

On March 2, 1861, the U.S. Congress, at the urging of President James Buchanan, incorporated the Territory of Dakota, which had grown to a population of 4,829 by 1860. Controlled from the capitol at Yankton, it consisted of the northernmost segment of the Louisiana Purchase, a landmass comprising parts of the current states of Montana, Nebraska, North Dakota, South Dakota, and Wyoming.

Despite outbreaks of violence among the Santee Dakota in neighboring Minnesota, the eastern section of the territory drew grain farmers, who plowed virgin prairie to raise wheat. After the governorship passed from William A. Jayne, personal physician to President Abraham Lincoln, to Dakota resident Newton Edmunds in 1865, the creation of a revenue system and public schools, peacemaking with the Lakota, and the promotion of sheepherding attracted more settlers.

The territory's third governor, Andrew Jackson Faulk, coveted Sioux lands that promised prosperity from mining and pine harvesting. His collusion with entrepreneurs in 1868 precipitated bitter fighting with Indians over possession of the sacred Black Hills. Worse for Indian claims was the appointment of scandal-ridden Governor John A. Burbank in 1869. Because Burbank encouraged patronage and speculation in real estate on native land, President Ulysses S. Grant replaced him with John L. Pennington, an ineffectual authority figure during the face-off between the Sioux and gold prospectors. Leading the insurgents was Charles Collins, editor of the *Sioux City Times,* who violated treaties in 1872 by launching the Black Hills Mining and Exploration Association.

At the border of Iowa, Nebraska, and South Dakota, the first European settlers chose the confluence of the Big Sioux and Missouri rivers as a site to dig their sod huts, which they shored up with poles transported north by water. In July 1862, Mahlon Gore, a printer from Orlando, Florida, and his brother Albert preceded a stream of pioneers from Michigan to the Sioux Valley and readied 10 acres (4 hectares) of prairie with ox teams for planting.

In 1863, memoirist Elizabeth Bacon "Libbie" Custer followed her husband, Brigadier General George Armstrong Custer, to Mandan, North Dakota, as the regiment's only woman. She wrote of her life as an army wife in *Boots and Saddles* (1885), *Following the Guidon* (1890), and *Tenting on the Plains* (1893).

In Vermillion, Mahlon Gore opened a print shop, edited the *Dakota Republican,* and administered the Homestead Act of 1862 by deeding plots to frontier families. He served as legislative clerk at Yankton in 1863 and returned to his vegetable plot to raise cabbage, onions, potatoes, and squash to sell to soldiers at Fort Randall some 60 miles (96 kilometers) to the northwest. After an infestation of grasshoppers destroyed his crop in 1864, he managed the *Sioux City Journal.*

By 1869, the Grange Movement in the southeastern counties had begun organizing homesteaders along the Big Sioux and Missouri rivers into an economic and political bloc to raise the attainments of farm families.

Law and Order

Between the territory's eastern front and the Missouri River, General Alfred Sully pacified thousands of Lakota in 1864. The tense situation called for the building of Fort Buford on June 15, 1866, at the juncture of the Missouri and Yellowstone rivers at Williston, North Dakota. A prairie fire at Fort Ransom in southeastern North Dakota on October 26, 1867, threatened an uncompleted structure housing the U.S. Eighth Cavalry. A rolling blaze engulfed livestock and wood supplies, threatened a store of black powder, and killed four residents of a camp of mixed-race natives, many of whom suffered grotesque burns.

After the signing of the Fort Laramie Treaty of 1868, completion of the Dakota Southern Railroad in 1872 improved transportation from Vermillion to Sioux City, Iowa. On August 24, 1872, the first telegram sent from Fort Hancock carried greetings from Linda Slaughter, the organizer of North Dakota's first Sunday school and the area's first school superintendent, postmaster, and writer.

In 1874, a territorial history identified parties of Hutterites from Russia as well as three female settlers: a black military cook, Sarah "Aunt Sally" Campbell; Martha "Calamity Jane" Canary, a military escort in 1875 and a nurse during a smallpox epidemic in 1876; and memoirist Annie Donna Fraser Tallent, the first white woman to view the Black Hills. Tallent was the only female member of John Gordon's party of 28 prospectors arriving at French Creek on December 21, 1874. She survived the first winter in a sod hut shored up by hemlock boughs and finished with flour sack windows and a coffee bag door. At Sturgis, she served as superintendent of schools and president of the board of education and composed *The Black Hills; or, The Last Hunting Ground of the Dakotahs* (1899), which reported the condition of the Custer Trail, freight and postal service to the Dakotas, horse thievery, smutty jokes and lewd songs from a Deadwood dance hall, and her meeting with James Butler "Wild Bill" Hickok in Deadwood only months before his death.

The settlers' need for military protection in 1873 brought Custer and 12 companies of the U.S. Seventh Cavalry to the Black Hills, where Crazy Horse, chief of the Oglala Lakota, led hostile bands of Indians against whites. Accompanying the military were more miners and geologists, who converged at Deadwood Gulch, a settlement of tents and shanties founded in 1875.

By 1876, the Sioux fomented war to drive out intrusive whites and joined the Arapaho and Northern Cheyenne to form an unprecedented army of 1,800 Plains warriors. Headed by Crazy Horse, Chief Gall, and Sitting Bull, the combined force annihilated Custer and his troops on June 25, 1876, east of Billings in south-central Montana at the Battle of the Little Bighorn.

Following the gold rush in the Black Hills on April 9, 1876, the fortune of brothers Fred and Moses Manuel and their partners, Alexander Eng and Henry "Hank" Harney, at the Homestake Mine near Lead, South Dakota, lured get-rich-quick prospectors. Subsequent strikes—at the Manuel brothers' Golden Terra quartz mine and Old Abe Mine, M. Cavanaugh's Highland Chief Mine, and Smokey Jones's Golden Star Mine—required hearty workers and ore millers plus the administrative skills of Ludwig D. Kellogg, an expert on commercial-grade ore.

With the enrichment of mine speculators, the region acquired an unsavory reputation for gambling, crime, prostitution, and claim jumping, until the arrival of Sheriff Seth Bullock from Helena, Montana. On August 1, 1876, Wild Bill Hickok angered Jack McCall during a poker game at Deadwood in Nuttal & Mann's Saloon No. 10. McCall shot Hickok in the back of the skull, thus giving Deadwood the reputation of being among the Midwest's rowdiest towns.

More violence followed the removal of the Black Hills in a parcel of 7 million acres (2.8 million hectares) from the Great Sioux Reservation on February 28, 1877. The murder of Crazy Horse on September 5 of that year at Fort Robinson, Nebraska, shifted control of Dakota Territory permanently from the Sioux to whites.

See also: Crazy Horse; Grange Movement; Hickok, James Butler "Wild Bill"; Hutterites; Law Enforcement; Little Bighorn, Battle of the; Sitting Bull; Wyoming Territory.

Further Reading

Glasrud, Bruce A., and Michael N. Searles, eds. *Buffalo Soldiers in the West: A Black Soldiers Anthology.* College Station: Texas A&M University Press, 2007.

Greene, Jerome A. *Washita: The U.S. Army and the Southern Cheyennes, 1867–1869.* Norman: University of Oklahoma Press, 2004.

Lamar, Howard R., ed. *The New Encyclopedia of the American West.* New Haven, CT: Yale University Press, 1998.

Ostler, Jeffrey. *The Plains Sioux and U.S. Colonialism from Lewis and Clark to Wounded Knee.* Cambridge, UK: Cambridge University Press, 2004.

Wardhaugh, Robert Alexander. *Toward Defining the Prairies: Region, Culture and History.* Winnipeg, Canada: University of Manitoba Press, 2001.

Damien, Father (1840–1889)

Father Damien, a Flemish volunteer nurse and missionary, ministered to Hawaii's outcast lepers and their families from 1864 until his death from leprosy 25 years later. He was born Jozef de Veuster in Tremeloo, Belgium, on January 3, 1840.

The 1863 leprosy epidemic in Hawaii, introduced by Chinese immigrants, forced King Kamehameha V to sequester the sick. Two years later, the king criminalized and exiled 140 lepers at gunpoint to a lifetime quarantine at Kalawao, a 2,500-acre (1,000-hectare) compound on the Kalaupapa Peninsula on Molokai, a virtual living graveyard, surrounded on three sides by ocean and on the fourth by escarpments devoid of fresh water.

Provisioners approached by mule track or tossed their supplies into the sea for swimmers to retrieve. Some of the lepers drowned in the surf. At the medical colony, patients entered quarters segregated by race and received no visits from doctors or nurses. To relieve their suffering, De Veuster learned to speak Hawaiian and, after his ordination as a father of the Sacred Heart in Louvain, committed himself to the care of Hawaii's lepers.

Upon his arrival in Honolulu on March 19, 1864, Father Damien began treating public health problems on Oahu and refuting superstitions that leprosy was a visitation of God's anger. His parishioners endured an eruption of Mauna Loa Volcano to the southwest on March 27, 1868, followed on April 2 by an earthquake that destabilized rock walls.

On May 10, 1873, Father Damien accepted certain death by beginning a mission to the commune of Kalaupapa, Molokai, where 80 inmates lay moribund in the hospital. He arrived by boat with 50 additional patients and his supervisor, Bishop Louis Maigret. Damien found filthy, abandoned patients living on wild fruit in caves or in damp government-issue huts made from sugarcane, *ki* leaves, and *pili* grass.

Because physicians refused to handle lepers, Father Damien brought medicines and bandages with which he rinsed fevered bodies, treated lesions, and reduced parasite infestations. He planted vegetable gardens, piped in fresh water for drinking and washing, constructed two orphanages, and built beds and coffins. Lacking assistance, he performed last rites, dug graves, and split rails for a cemetery fence to keep animals from digging up the corpses. In 1874, King Lunalilo increased the population of the colony by arresting and secluding another 500 lepers.

Much of Father Damien's efforts heartened the living. He arranged footraces and taught children and adults to ride horseback, sing, and play the organ and other musical instruments. At mass, he preached sermons about the transfiguration of the diseased body after death. On November 20, 1874, after a three-day cyclone called Die Deutsche Seewarte III destroyed 23 huts and damaged 50 more, he rebuilt shelters that had been blown apart by the wind and soaked by the rain.

In 1884, when he, too, was infected, Franciscan sisters and Ira Barnes Dutton of the Sacred Hearts Brotherhood treated Father Damien until his death at age 49 on April 15, 1889. Two monuments—at the Hawaiian state capitol in Honolulu and in the National Statuary Hall in Washington, D.C.—honor his service. On October 11, 2009, Pope Benedict XVI canonized De Veuster as Saint Damien, the apostle to lepers.

Further Reading

Daws, Gavan. *Holy Man: Father Damien of Molokai.* Honolulu: University of Hawai'i Press, 1973.

Lal, Brij V., and Kate Fortune, eds. *The Pacific Islands: An Encyclopedia.* Honolulu: University of Hawai'i Press, 2000.

Stewart, Richard. *Leper Priest of Moloka'i: The Father Damien Story.* Honolulu: University of Hawai'i Press, 2000.

Davis, Jefferson (1808–1889)

U.S. Senator Jefferson Davis of Mississippi led the Confederate States of America as its only president. He was second only to General Robert E. Lee in the affection of Southerners.

A native of Christian County, Kentucky, he was born on June 3, 1808, to a Welsh American family of patriots who fought in the American Revolution and the War of 1812. He graduated from West Point in 1828 and married the daughter of future president Zachary Taylor, Sarah Knox Taylor, who died just 12 weeks later of malaria.

Departing from his estate, Davis Bend, a model plantation community of 350 slaves, Davis gained infantry experience leading the Mississippi Rifles during the Mexican-American War. He also served his country as a U.S. representative (1845–1846), senator (1847–1851, 1857–1861), and secretary of war (1853–1857) under President Franklin Pierce. The secession of South Carolina from the Union precipitated Davis's resignation from Congress on January 21, 1861, on account of his loyalty to the South and to the principle of states' rights.

Davis returned to Mississippi to head its militia. At a constitutional convention in Montgomery, Alabama, the Confederate capital, he assumed the provisional presidency on February 9, 1861. He opposed Mississippi's secession from the Union and established a Peace Commission to negotiate a truce with Northern abolitionists. Because President Abraham Lincoln refused to grant an audience to Southern emissaries, Davis plotted the bombardment of Fort Sumter in the harbor of Charleston, South Carolina, on April 12, 1861, the first engagement of the Civil War.

By May 20, 1861, Davis's domain consisted of South

Jefferson Davis based his arguments for states' rights on Article IV of the U.S. Constitution:

> Within the purview of this article of the Constitution, the States are independent, distinct, and sovereign bodies—that is, in their reserved powers they are as sovereign, separate, and supreme as the Government of the United States in its delegated powers. One of these reserved powers is the right of the people to alter or abolish any form of government, and to institute a new one such as to them shall seem most likely to effect their safety and happiness.

A political cartoon from May 1865 depicts the capture of Confederate President Jefferson Davis. He allegedly donned his wife's overcoat to elude Union officers, setting off rumors that he attempted to flee in women's clothes. *(MPI/Stringer/Getty Images)*

Carolina, Mississippi, Florida, Alabama, Georgia, Louisiana, Texas, Virginia, Arkansas, and North Carolina, the last state to secede. He set up a capital at Richmond, Virginia, and installed his government in the Virginia State Capitol to be nearer Washington, D.C. On June 8, Tennessee became the eleventh state to join the Confederacy. His official election to a six-year term as president on November 6, 1861, and the appointment of General Robert E. Lee to command the Confederate army established Davis's lead in strategizing the war effort.

Davis and the Confederacy

Contributing to the difficulty of creating a new country was the South's lack of factories, navy, railroads, shipyards, and armaments and the need to ensure the well-being of a white populace that was one-fourth the size of the Northern citizenry. After engineering secession in 11 states, Davis vied for control of Kentucky and Missouri.

Failing to raise funds, arms, and ammunition from the English and French to win the war, he planned a Confederate sweep across the South, including Texas, New Mexico Territory, and California. Crucial to the independence of the Confederacy were Southwestern gold and silver lodes in former Spanish lands, particularly around Mowry, Arizona. Davis's persistence persuaded John Robert Baylor, the military governor of Arizona, to identify the territory as a Confederate possession. The addition became official on February 14, 1862, with Baylor as the first governor.

Deficient as a leader and administrator, Davis acknowledged the lack of cohesion in his cabinet. With little monetary support, he struggled on against the devaluation of Confederate currency, the liberation of slaves, increasing starvation in Southern states, and the disastrous turn of the war to the Union's favor in July 1863. After Lee's surrender to General Ulysses S. Grant at Appomattox, Virginia, on April 9, 1865, Davis dissolved his rebel government on May 5 and fled south in an attempt to consolidate forces in the trans-Mississippi West.

Upon the predawn capture of Davis and his family at a camp in Irwinville, Georgia, on May 10, 1865, federal troops imprisoned him in irons in a gun emplacement at Fort Monroe, Virginia. He faced charges of treason and complicity in the assassination of President Abraham Lincoln.

Postwar Life

After the war, Davis suffered bankruptcy and the loss of Brierfield, his home at Davis Bend south of Vicksburg, as well as his U.S. citizenship. Ironically, his former Senate seat passed to Hiram Rhodes Revels of Natchez, Mississippi, the first black elected to the U.S. Senate. During Jefferson's incarceration, his second wife, Varina Howell Davis, known as the "Widow of the Confederacy," supported the family with freelance writing.

In 1867, editor Horace Greeley, abolitionist Gerrit Smith, and investor Cornelius Vanderbilt raised the $100,000 bail for Davis. He left the country to join his family in Montreal, Canada, where his four children were enrolled in school. With the winter endangering his frail health, he embarked on a tour of Cuba, England, Scotland, and France. He never came to trial and received amnesty in December 1868, but he bore the brunt of national outrage over starvation and cruelty to prisoners of war at the Confederate prison in Andersonville, Georgia.

Davis returned to private life with enthusiasm and energy. He sold Davis Bend to a former slave, merchant and inventor Benjamin T. Montgomery. In 1869, Davis lost money in a capital venture, the Carolina Life Insurance Company of Memphis, Tennessee. At the same time, he advised Southern politicians to maintain their belief in state sovereignty and to profit from their natural resources. After settling at Beauvoir in Biloxi, Mississippi, in his sixties, he promoted the Southern Pacific Railroad and proposed siphoning off English trade with Brazil to U.S. consortia on the Gulf of Mexico.

Following the signing of the Amnesty Act on May 22, 1872, by President Ulysses S. Grant, Davis remained among the 500 secessionists still considered outlaws. In 1875, he traveled to Iowa to deliver a speech but was rebuffed as a traitor. Over a five-year period, he composed a comprehensive memoir and apologia for states' rights, *The Rise and Fall of the Confederate Government* (1881).

At Davis's death in New Orleans from bronchitis on December 5, 1889, loyal Southerners paid their respects by lowering flags and leading a funeral cortege to his burial in Richmond.

Further Reading

Berkin, Carol. *Civil War Wives: The Lives and Times of Angelina Grimké Weld, Varina Howell Davis, and Julia Dent Grant.* New York: Alfred A. Knopf, 2009.

Chadwick, Bruce. *The Two American Presidents: A Dual Biography of Abraham Lincoln and Jefferson Davis.* Secaucus, NJ: Carol, 1998.

Cooper, William J., Jr. *Jefferson Davis, American.* New York: Random House, 2001.

Glatthaar, Joseph T. *General Lee's Army: From Victory to Collapse.* New York: Simon & Schuster, 2009.

Yearns, Wilfred Buck. *The Confederate Congress.* Athens: University of Georgia Press, 1960.

Deering-Milliken & Company

A woolens manufacturer in Portland, Maine, Deering-Milliken & Company contributed to U.S. success in the world textile market. Industrialists William Deering and Seth Llewellyn Milliken founded the firm in 1865.

Deering, of South Paris, Maine, settled in Portland in 1861 to manufacture uniforms for the Union army. Of Scots ancestry, Milliken, a former court clerk and congressman from Maine's Third District, gained fame for orations on behalf of the Republican Party and for helping to establish railway service in his home state. He promoted the postwar agricultural resources of the South by importing cotton for processing in New England.

The textile firm, one of the largest of its kind, sold woolens from several mills in Maine: Mayo & Son in Foxcroft, Cowan Woolen and Cumberland Mills in Lewiston, Farnsworth and Worumbo Manufacturing in Lisbon, Madison Woolen in Madison, North Berwick in York County, Cascade Woolen Mill in Oakland, Robinson Mills in South Windham, and F.S. Mackenzie in Bridgewater. In 1868, after Deering left the firm to found a harvester company in Plano, Illinois, Milliken headquartered his business in New York City and patented trademark bleached cotton goods—Bianco, Mother's Choice, Bermuda Lily, and Progress.

The company weathered the Panic of 1873 and prospered by purchasing financially shaky textile mills in New England and the South. As a result, Deering-Milliken became the nation's largest textile manufacturer.

Further Reading

Andrews, Mildred Gwin. *The Men and the Mills: A History of the Southern Textile Industry.* Macon, GA: Mercer University Press, 1987.

Edgar, Walter B., ed. *The South Carolina Encyclopedia.* Columbia: University of South Carolina Press, 2006.

Link, William A. *Roots of Secession: Slavery and Politics in Antebellum Virginia.* Chapel Hill: University of North Carolina Press, 2003.

Democratic Party

The Democratic Party evolved in the late 1780s out of a faction promoting the civil rights of the individual as declared in the U.S. Constitution. Proponents favored state sovereignty over a strong federal government and, in the 1850s, encouraged the spread of slavery across the frontier. Democrats celebrated the U.S. Supreme Court's decision of March 6, 1857, for denying the civil rights of slave Dred Scott.

As the citizenry fragmented over slavery and economic issues before the presidential election of 1860,

Democrats split along the lines of North and South and war and peace. U.S. Senator Stephen A. Douglas, opponent of former Illinois congressman Abraham Lincoln, upheld the concept of popular sovereignty. U.S. Senator Jefferson Davis of Mississippi harangued the pro-South leadership to preserve the Southern plantation system by championing states' rights. The first of three critical elections, the 1860 vote polarized political loyalties and initiated a two-party system. Fueled by New Englanders and Midwesterners, the overwhelming Republican victory that year forced Democrats, who had dominated the presidency for seven decades, to reexamine their tactics.

After abandoning the party that had failed to protect their rights of property, slave owners formed the Southern Democratic Party, which advocated withdrawal from the Union. At a convention held at South Carolina Institute Hall in Charleston from April 23 to May 3, 1860, Southern "fire-eaters," led by orator William Lowndes Yancey of Alabama, proposed a federal slave code for the frontier territories. Quashed by moderates, who supported Douglas, Yancey and the Southern Democrats vacated the assembly hall. The remaining delegates adjourned until June 18, extending the party schism for four weeks. An attempt at amelioration failed after the two party extremes met in Baltimore at separate conventions.

Southern Democrats pinned their hopes on John C. Breckinridge of Kentucky, then the U.S. vice president, who advocated federal protection of slaveholders' rights to conduct their purchase, sale, and employment of slaves in a Western territory. At a speech in Wilmington, Delaware, Yancey warned that blacks threatened to marry the daughters of whites. Southern Democrats asserted their primacy after Breckinridge carried 11 slave states, but they conceded the election to Abraham Lincoln.

Fracture

As a result of the resounding Democratic defeat, South Carolina seceded from the Union on December 20, 1860, initiating a domino effect across the Deep South and catapulting party leader Davis to the presidency of the Confederate States of America. The expulsion of 11 Democratic leaders from Alabama, Arkansas, the Carolinas, Florida, Georgia, Louisiana, Mississippi, Tennessee, Texas, and Virginia ensured Republican control of Congress.

The Northern Democratic Party denounced the Lincoln administration for silencing war protesters and for abandoning the civil rights of Copperheads (Southern sympathizers in the North), who endorsed the spread of slavery across the frontier, Mexico, and the Caribbean. Pro-South factions in Iowa, Illinois, Indiana, Missouri, Ohio, and Wisconsin encouraged draft evasion and desertion from the Union army.

At the height of the Civil War, Democrats anticipated that strong opposition would defeat President Lincoln's bid for a second term. On August 29, 1864, Union General George Brinton McClellan headed the badly splintered Democratic Party, which demanded a cease-fire and an immediate negotiation to end the war. He vilified the Emancipation Proclamation and censured the president for inept military command. Republicans retaliated by stigmatizing Democrats as traitors to the Union. The electoral landslide that returned Lincoln to the presidency devastated the Democratic Party.

Fight for Control

Passage of civil rights legislation on March 27, 1866, overriding the veto of President Andrew Johnson, assured blacks of their place in local and national government. Democrats opposed the extension of the Freedmen's Bureau on February 19, 1866, and the Reconstruction Act of March 2, 1867, which prohibited Confederate soldiers from voting. The party looked for means to placate blacks without capitulating to their demands for equality.

The Democratic bloc known as the "Solid South" rallied against passage of the Enforcement Act of 1870 and the Force Act of 1871, by which federal observers scrutinized congressional elections for fraud. During Senate debates on the Ku Klux Klan Act of 1871, Democrats promoted extremism as a means of restoring whites to power. When members of the violent wing of the party assassinated hundreds of black electees and destroyed black sections of Rosewood, Florida; Greenwood, Oklahoma; and Wilmington, North Carolina, criminal politics forced moderate Democrats to ally with Republicans.

Throughout two terms under President Ulysses S. Grant, the Democratic Party honed an entrenched hatred of moneyed interests, fiscal favoritism toward banks and railroads, and governance of the South by carpetbaggers and scalawags. By opening day of the 44th Congress on March 4, 1875, Democrats once more controlled the House of Representatives and plotted the end of Reconstruction.

Democrats allied with urban immigrants and exploited the piety of Catholics, Episcopalians, and German Lutherans with appeals to morals. The anti-Republican underground and white supremacist press prodded the racist paramilitary to spread terrorism and murder across the

South. Militants sent the Ku Klux Klan, Red Shirts, and White Leaguers to intimidate voters and to disrupt political rallies and strategy sessions. Louisiana alone incurred the deaths of 1,300 freedmen by political assassins.

By 1876, the mishandling of Reconstruction, rising debt and taxes, and the repatriation of the 11 secessionist states triggered a Republican comedown. While Democratic "Redeemers" promised to speed up the Reconstruction process, the anti-Grant press reviled the former Union general as a drunkard and a waster of tax revenues. White supremacists in South Carolina, backed by the paramilitary Red Shirts, perpetrated election fraud to select the first postwar Democratic governor, Wade Hampton, hailed as the state's savior.

The party moved its annual convention to Missouri and demanded reform of the federal executive branch. The Democratic platform called for the ousting of carpetbaggers from the South, tariff reform, limited immigration of Asian aliens, and curtailment of government land deals with railroad moguls. The return of full enfranchisement to former secessionists allowed Democratic legislators to suppress black civil rights and to create Black Codes and Jim Crow laws that initiated a century of racial discrimination.

See also: Election of 1860; Election of 1864; Election of 1868; Election of 1872; Republican Party.

Further Reading

Richardson, Darcy G. *Others: Third-Party Politics from the Nation's Founding to the Rise and Fall of the Greenback-Labor Party.* New York: iUniverse, 2004.

Richardson, Heather Cox. *The Death of Reconstruction: Race, Labor, and Politics in the Post–Civil War North, 1865–1901.* Cambridge, MA: Harvard University Press, 2001.

Sachsman, David B., S. Kittrell Rushing, and Roy Morris, Jr., eds. *Seeking a Voice: Images of Race and Gender in the 19th Century Press.* West Lafayette, IN: Purdue University Press, 2009.

Smith, Adam I.P. *No Party Now: Politics in the Civil War North.* Oxford, UK: Oxford University Press, 2006.

Weigley, Russell F. *A Great Civil War: A Military and Political History, 1861–1865.* Bloomington: Indiana University Press, 2000.

Dentistry

American dentistry in the post–Civil War era profited from the liberalization of dental practice and from technological advancement.

In 1854, Emiline Roberts became the nation's first female dentist by learning the profession of her husband, Dr. Daniel Albion Jones of Danielson, Connecticut. In widowhood ten years later, she assumed his practice and remained at work for six decades. The world's first degreed female dentist, Lucy Hobbs Taylor, completed a private tutorial at the Ohio College of Dental Surgery and, in 1861, opened an office in Cincinnati, Ohio, and later moved her practice to Lawrence, Kansas. In 1869, a son of former slaves, Robert Tanner Freeman of Washington, D.C., graduated from Harvard University Dental School and became the first degreed black practitioner.

Throughout this period, patents improved dental instruments and methods, beginning in 1864 with Sanford C. Barnum's rubber dam to isolate the teeth, and continuing with the automatic cavity pluggers of J.C. Dean and I.A. Salmon of Boston in 1865 and the pneumatic one-shot plugger of George B. Snow and Theo G. Lewis of Buffalo, New York, in 1866. The following year, William G.A. Bonwill of Dover, Delaware, designed a labor-saving automatic mallet for filling teeth. The value of treatment resulted in the appointment in 1872 of the first army dentist, William Saunders, a steward at the hospital of the U.S. Military Academy at West Point.

In 1868, a machinist in Kalamazoo, Michigan, George F. Green of Montreal, ended the agony of manual drilling by creating a 5.5-inch (14-centimeter) pneumatic bur drill powered by a bellows operated with a pedal, which the Samuel S. White Company manufactured in New York City in 1872. In 1875, Green revolutionized rapid tooth filling by perfecting the electric dental drill and fan. At first, the electromagnetic motor fit directly into the handpiece, called the "dental engine." For maneuverability, reengineering extended the handpiece on a cord from the motor. Until electric power became available a quarter century later, most dentists relied on Green's treadle-powered model.

The streamlining of tooth repair involved Julius A. Bidwell's soft-metal mallet in 1870, the dental engine of J.B. Morrison in 1871, and the improved drill of G.V. Black in 1871. Further development of ceiling pulleys by Charles Merry of St. Louis, Missouri, enabled dentists to adjust brackets and to shift positions of the drill and lights. Eli T. Starr of Philadelphia eased patient discomfort in 1875 with a chair headrest; Andrew A. Hazeltine of New Bedford, Massachusetts, added sponges and a spout to dampen grinding wheels. Electric cavity pluggers developed by Joaquin Bishop and F.A. Bonwill came on the market in 1875, as did the vulcanized rubber handle patented by R.B. Donaldson of Washington, D.C., and polishing tools designed by L.F. Locke of Nashua, New Hampshire.

In 1876, John Fry of Johnstown, Pennsylvania, patented a cavity filling from an amalgam of mercury, platinum, silver, tin, and zinc. Cornelius Reagles of Schenectady, New York, replaced ivory and gutta-percha in dental plates with a pyroxyline compound. In 1877, the Wilkerson chair applied pump hydraulics to raising and lowering the patient, thereby relieving stress on the dentist's back.

On the West Coast, the R.H. M'Donald & Company supply house in San Francisco, California, shipped a variety of goods—surgical instruments, forceps, scalers and pluggers, excavators, drill burs, nerve bits and sockets, dental lathes, vulcanite, gold foil, mirrors, and chairs. Shipments traveled as far west as Honolulu, where John Morgan Whitney, formerly of Vermont, set up a practice in September 1869. He treated islanders and the royal household of kings Kamehameha V and David Kalakaua. Increasing the need for dental care in Hawaii was the introduction of chewing tobacco, hard bread, and hot meals. Subsequent island dentists advertised gas anesthesia—nitrous oxide, ether, and chloroform—to ease pain.

Further Reading

Jordan, Diann. *Sisters in Science: Conversations with Black Women Scientists on Race, Gender, and Their Passion for Science.* West Lafayette, IN: Purdue University Press, 2006.

Lurie, Maxine N., and Marc Mappen, eds. *Encyclopedia of New Jersey.* New Brunswick, NJ: Rutgers University Press, 2004.

Weisz, George. *Divide and Conquer: A Comparative History of Medical Specialization.* New York: Oxford University Press, 2006.

Wishart, David J., ed. *Encyclopedia of the Great Plains.* Lincoln: University of Nebraska Press, 2004.

Department of Justice, U.S.

Since its creation in 1870, the U.S. Department of Justice has regulated the enforcement of federal law and the administration of justice.

In 1867, Congressman William Lawrence (R-OH), a judge and chair of the legislative Committee on the Judiciary, studied the office of U.S. Attorney General Henry Stanbery and his staff of solicitors and district attorneys. Stanbery advised Lawrence that the attorney general was unable to prepare opinions on legal questions without the aid of a solicitor general to secure a uniform decision on matters of justice in all federal courts. Prefatory to the impeachment of President Andrew Johnson in 1868, Lawrence submitted a bill to Congress proposing the creation of a department of justice. The bill failed, but Congress approved the Committee on Retrenchment's request that the government no longer engage private counsel to plead federal cases.

With Lawrence's backing, Congressman Thomas Allen Jenckes of Rhode Island resubmitted the proposal to organize a justice department in order to unify decisions on jurisprudence. President Ulysses S. Grant signed the bill on June 22, 1870, establishing the new bureau of federal advocacy to deter dilatory court action, reduce judicial jealousies, and coordinate federal issues in lower courts nationwide.

The Department of Justice began operating on July 1, 1870, after the presidential appointment of Solicitor General Benjamin Helm Bristow, the former district attorney of Louisville, Kentucky, as principal deputy of the attorney general. For two years, Bristow scheduled and superintended 47 legal suits in federal appellate courts and aggressively prosecuted cases involving terrorism by the Ku Klux Klan. To resolve miscarriages of justice, he argued new evidence before the U.S. Supreme Court and filed amicus curiae (friend of the court) briefs in cases with constitutional significance, such as the disarming of freedmen in South Carolina and Texas to prevent them from fighting off racist attackers. To safeguard the civil rights of former slaves, Bristow instructed authorities of the Freedmen's Bureau to transfer local cases involving blacks to federal court.

Bristow also raided and prosecuted the "Whiskey Ring," a syndicate of distillers, distributors, and revenue agents in St. Louis, Missouri, who defrauded the federal government of liquor tax on some millions of gallons of whiskey each year. Litigation required Bristow to charge Orville Elias Babcock, the personal secretary of President Grant. When the perpetrators came to court in October 1875, 110 convictions of the 200 defendants resulted in the recovery of $3,362,295 in tax revenue. By smashing the ring, Bristow returned $2 million in taxes per year to the U.S. Treasury.

In November 1872, Samuel Field Phillips (R-NC), a former speaker of the North Carolina House and Supreme Court reporter, became Grant's second appointee as solicitor general. Edwin B. Smith and Thomas Simons served as Phillips's assistants. An able debater, Phillips earned respect for cutting court time by discarding minor issues and focusing on the overriding question of legality and justice. He denounced the "separate but equal" doctrine as racist and pressed for conviction of members of the Ku Klux Klan for usurping the rights of black voters by scaring them away from the polls. To support the Civil Rights Act of 1875, Phillips expanded federal control of elections.

See also: Civil Rights.

Further Reading

Kaczorowski, Robert J. *The Politics of Judicial Interpretation: The Federal Courts, Department of Justice, and Civil Rights, 1866–1876.* New York: Fordham University Press, 2005.

Klinkner, Philip A., and Rogers M. Smith. *The Unsteady March: The Rise and Decline of Racial Equality in America.* Chicago: University of Chicago Press, 2002.

Nelson, William E. *The Fourteenth Amendment: From Political Principle to Judicial Doctrine.* Cambridge, MA: Harvard University Press, 1988.

Rable, George C. *But There Was No Peace: The Role of Violence in the Politics of Reconstruction.* Athens: University of Georgia Press, 2007.

Valelly, Richard M. *The Two Reconstructions: The Struggle for Black Enfranchisement.* Chicago: University of Chicago Press, 2004.

Department Stores

In the aftermath of the privations of the Civil War, department stores satisfied consumer demand for a variety of quality retail goods in a customer-friendly atmosphere. On Broadway in Manhattan in 1846, Irish American merchant Alexander Turney Stewart stocked his Marble Palace with Irish laces and linens, silks, embroidered garments, and quality women's clothes. He sold his wares at fixed prices and allowed customers free access to aisles and counters. The open atmosphere generated an aura of privilege and choice, both antidotes to low moods.

In 1862, Stewart built the Iron Palace, an eight-story department store covering a full city block on Broadway. He expanded his stock from dress goods to include upholstery material, carpets, bedding and table linens, glass and china, gift items, toys, and sports equipment. The outlay of the department store grew in quality and variety in proportion to the rise of the urban middle class, who had both leisure time and the funds for discretionary and impulse buying. Stewart cultivated goodwill by offering complementary services to the carriage trade, including ladies' lounges featuring luxury appointments and home delivery of merchandise by uniformed van drivers.

Gender and status appeal invigorated Stewart's competitors, whose storefronts formed the "Ladies Mile," a New York shopping experience that entertained affluent white female consumers. By appealing to their sense of order and adventure, merchants blended shopping with convenience and recreation, generating the atmosphere of a social club with an ever-changing bazaar. The concept of the departmentalized commercial display suited other New York magnates, who refined marketing to such wealthy customers at Abraham & Straus, B. Altman, Macy's, and McCreary's and engaged in price wars. The slogan "the customer is always right" summarized the psychology that made Macy's, and other full-service stores, a success. At the same time, the hiring of young working-class women offered new opportunities for women beyond the grubby factory job or the heavy burdens of laundry or waitressing.

On Fifth Avenue, Lord & Taylor appealed to patriotism and the winter holiday spirit by opening the business day with a playing of "The Star-Spangled Banner" and by anticipating Christmas and Hanukkah shopping and decoration needs with elaborate seasonal window displays. The chain expanded to Long Island, Philadelphia, and Washington, D.C.

In 1872 on Third Avenue in Manhattan's Lower East Side, brothers Joseph B. and Lyman Gustavus Bloomingdale situated their trade in hoop skirts, corsets, European fashions, and gentlemen's furnishings. The placement of the Third Avenue elevated railway sped customers from uptown to the attractive store, which specialized in trendy European fashions and home decor.

Urban Trend

Rival cities produced clusters of department stores in downtown areas. From 1841, Eben Dyer Jordan and Benjamin L. Marsh thrived in Boston with the establishment of Jordan Marsh. After the Civil War, they expanded their trade in linen and silk by adding clothing, gift items, and baked goods, and they courted refined clientele with a regular schedule of afternoon concerts and art shows.

In Louisville, Kentucky, in 1845, auctioneer Jeremiah Bacon and his sons, Edwin, Jeremiah, Jr., and John Bacon, established J. Bacon's & Sons, the oldest department store in the South, which grew to 63 departments in a six-story emporium by 1876. Bacon's & Sons competed with the Levy Brothers stores, which Henry and Moses Levy, dry goods suppliers during the Civil War, opened in 1861. Levy Brothers boasted a full line of goods, as well as men's and children's barbershops.

Atlantans patronized M. Rich Dry Goods, the nucleus of Rich's Department Store, a boon to the city in 1867, only two years after General William Tecumseh Sherman burned the commercial and warehouse districts on his march through Georgia. The company was the idea of Morris Rich, a Hungarian Jew who set up shop on Whitehall Street.

Anchoring department store service in Chicago, Marshall Field & Company, the world's second-largest department store after Macy's, became a landmark at 111 North State Street in 1868. In competition with Macy's and Montgomery Ward, Field and his store manager, Harry Selfridge, cultivated urban female shoppers, the wives of rising businessmen who complemented their husband's ambitions with upscale purchases for home and table.

Philadelphia shoppers enjoyed a remarkable array of goods offered on a single floor. In 1861, John Nelson Wanamaker, the father of modern advertising, opened Wanamaker's, the forerunner of a chain that spread to New York, London, and Paris. In 1876, he advanced from a seller of men's and boys' clothing to dry goods merchant and restaurateur at a Pennsylvania Railroad freight warehouse, a venue he remodeled into the Grand Depot of John Wanamaker & Company. Under skylights, the one-floor interior housed 129 semicircular counters, ranging outward from a center statue. Signage pointed shoppers to linens, sheeting, laces, gloves, ribbons, and ladies' furnishings. Technology aided mercantile trade with the replacement of gas lamps with electric lights and the mechanized cash carrier system, a pulley and wire apparatus that David Brown of Lebanon, New Jersey, invented in 1875. Wanamaker's orderly arrangement of goods influenced the floor plan of the Philadelphia Centennial Exhibition of 1876.

Shopping Coast to Coast

Store builders on the frontier imitated East Coast marketing by placing multiple departments under one roof and stocking shelves with goods suited to the needs of pioneers, farm families, miners, cowboys, and railroaders. In 1850, at the height of the California Gold Rush, Lipman Wolfe & Company got its start in Sacramento by replacing the peddler's tray with a centralized store. Owners Solomon Lipman and his nephew Adolphe Wolfe took advantage of the Comstock Lode silver strike in 1859 and set up a branch mercantile in Virginia City, Nevada. Their branch in Portland, Oregon, competed with Charles William King, William Parker Olds, and Hardy Christian Wortman, founders of Olds, Wortman & King, one of the oldest commercial enterprises on the Pacific Coast.

On Front Street in Portland in 1857, another competitor, Bavarian immigrants Aaron Meier and Jeanette Hirsch Meier, turned a mule-drawn wagon of housewares, notions, and sundries into a dry goods store. After partnering with Emil Frank in 1873, the firm of Meier & Frank prospered as a central commercial source for clothing, sewing needs, candy, hardware, and tools. In early widowhood, Jeanette Meier managed the business and headed Portland's philanthropists in charitable donations.

On March 1, 1869, Mormons in Salt Lake City, Utah, supported the opening of Zion's Cooperative Mercantile, a community retail outlet. Located on Main Street, the cooperative sold home goods, sewing machines, clothes, draperies and carpet, canning needs, and locally made boots, as well as liquor and beer by the case. Within months, it became the nation's first incorporated department store.

In 1871, San Franciscans patronized S&G Gump's, a four-story gallery on Market Street specializing in furniture, decorative accents, and statuary. Founded by Gustave Gump and his brother Solomon Gump, German Jewish immigrants from Heidelberg, the store got its start selling art, bronzes, cornices, etchings, gilt moldings, jade, mantels, mirrors, porcelain, rugs, sideboards, and woodwork imported from Austria, England, France, Germany, and Italy. The owners operated a four-story factory on Jessie Street, where they produced fine wood detailing for homes and offices.

Merchants made the most of their innovations through commerce in outlying areas, such as Lipman Wolfe & Company's establishments in California and Nevada and the Gump brothers' branch in Portland, Oregon. To support her family, dressmaker Sarah Nathan Goldwater opened Goldwater's Department Stores, a chain introduced in Los Angeles and, in 1868, in San Francisco and Arizona.

In 1877, in Leadville during the Colorado silver rush, David May appealed to prospectors by selling red wool long johns and Levis, denim pants made rugged with copper rivets at stress points. The May Company invested in full-service branches in Cleveland, St. Louis, and Los Angeles.

For the more refined customer, that same year, Mary Ann Cohen Magnin, a Dutch seamstress specializing in bridal gowns and infant clothes, improvised the salon concept of retailing at her store in San Francisco. She named it I. Magnin in honor of her husband, Isaac Magnin, who gilded frames in Solomon Gump's Oakland workshop. Shoppers sat on couches while sales associates tempted them with garments. For the convenience of shoppers, department chains such as the May Company and I. Magnin were the impetus for the mass production of clothing and domestic items and of installment credit, democratized marketing, and shopping centers. To make the most of prime urban space, builders promoted verticality in the design of the first skyscrapers.

See also: Macy's; Marshall Field; Stewart, Alexander Turney; Strauss, Levi.

Further Reading

Abelson, Elaine S. *When Ladies Go A-Thieving: Middle-Class Shoplifters in the Victorian Department Store.* New York: Oxford University Press, 1989.

Benson, Susan Porter. *Counter Cultures: Saleswomen, Managers, and Customers in American Department Stores, 1890–1940.* Urbana: University of Illinois Press, 1986.

Bjelopera, Jerome P. *City of Clerks: Office and Sales Workers in Philadelphia, 1870–1920.* Urbana: University of Illinois Press, 2005.

Diner, Hasia R., and Beryl Lieff Benderly. *Her Works Praise Her: A History of Jewish Women in America from Colonial Times to the Present.* New York: Basic Books, 2002.

Depression of 1873–1878

A financial collapse in Vienna, Austria, and a stock market crash on September 18, 1873, triggered the Panic of 1873. Losses initiated the Long Depression in the United States, Great Britain, and Europe, increasing the stream of immigrants from Austria-Hungary, Italy, Russia, and Spain. The rapid drop in trading shuttered the New York Stock Exchange for ten days.

The crash derived from the overindulgence of postwar investors, who pledged 20 percent of U.S. capital to high-risk dock and railroad ventures. Imprudent expansionism resulted in overbuilding, cutthroat competition, and delayed projects. Tight money destabilized Jay Cooke & Company, a powerful financial firm that had strained its credit to extend the Northern Pacific Railway through Duluth, Minnesota, to the Great Lakes. The limited money supply bankrupted 18,000 businesses and 89 railroads, crushed construction and home building, and imperiled private schools and small factories and businesses.

In Pennsylvania and West Virginia, the onset of the depression forced miners to combat a 20 percent pay cut by initiating strikes. In Chicago, the nation's first permanent working class suffered irregular employment and 3 million lost jobs. Manufacturers and steelmakers lost contracts and laid off workers, raising the unemployment rate to 14 percent. Owners of small factories responded to mechanized overproduction by cutting wages and workers' hours. In scandals marring the two-term presidency of President Ulysses S. Grant, the press promoted popular distrust of big business and condemnation of the commercial policies of the Republican Party.

While national productivity slowed and borrowers defaulted on more than $1 billion in loans, the depression spread as far west as San Francisco, and Virginia City, Nevada. It destroyed the Freedman's Savings Bank (established by the U.S. government to support economic development among freed slaves) and idled 1 million workers in winter 1873–1874, many in the lumber business. A meager congressional response, the Inflation Bill of 1874, earned a presidential veto, because it failed to inject enough dollars into circulation to stabilize falling prices.

Organized labor rapidly lost influence with management. The panic crushed unions by 73 percent, a setback that lasted until 1878. In cities, the jobless organized rallies demanding relief and joined solidarity demonstrations for unions, most prominently the Great Railroad Strike of 1877, the first nationwide industrial job action. Commercial failures slashed incomes, increasing hunger and homelessness among the jobless. During decades of worker panic, humanitarian labor organizer Mary Harris "Mother" Jones traveled to major strike zones and lived among the poor in tents and lean-tos. She organized work stoppages and educated laborers about class war and the hereditary nature of "involuntary poverty."

As gloom descended on the Grant administration, the public demonized rampant greed. Creditors benefited from the deflation caused by federal reliance on gold as a medium of exchange. Rail owners transporting gold and silver ores to processing centers ignited rail control wars. Shrewd speculators—Andrew Carnegie, Thomas Edison, Henry J. Heinz, Rowland Hussey Macy, Cyrus McCormick, John D. Rockefeller, and Cornelius Vanderbilt—enriched themselves by financing projects at the expense of cash-poor competitors. In the midst of the 1873 depression, capitalist Jason "Jay" Gould, president of the Atlantic and Pacific Telegraph Company, coveted Western Union's telecommunications monopoly and unrivaled legislative cronyism and invested in a merger of the companies. Collaborators Mark Twain and Charles Dudley

Warner produced a novel, *The Gilded Age* (1874), a parody of unprincipled affluence and manipulation of labor.

As the financial collapse radiated distress nationwide, rural America suffered a significant setback. Inflation strangled debtors, mainly factory workers and Southern and Western agrarians. Cotton profits fell by half and grain by two-thirds. Planters and ranchers lacked cash to pay inflated fertilizer and seed prices and freight rates, to repair fences and outbuildings, and to replenish diminishing herds. They favored higher prices to increase their liquidity to requite loans. The depression lowered family buying power by 25 percent to 50 percent and deflated food prices and the value of pasturage and farm and ranch equipment. War veterans migrated to potential harvest sites, earning the names "bum" and "tramp" for their ragged appearance on the road during winter months of joblessness. France and Germany slowed the U.S. economic recovery by placing protective tariffs on iron and rye.

While the economy tilted dangerously toward the wealthy few, white and black populists pressured Congress to combat unemployment and indigence by restricting big business. Protesters focused on bankers' control of the money supply and labeled the demonetization of silver the "Crime of 1873." To save paper money, on June 10, 1874, Midwesterners coordinated state conventions in Illinois and Indiana and advocated the circulation of paper currency and federal control of loans. Because Democrats ignored the issue of usury, a small consortium met on November 25 at Indianapolis to fight the debt-based economy. Rural protesters from Connecticut, Illinois, New York, Ohio, Pennsylvania, and West Virginia formed the Greenback Party, an antimonopolist revolt that produced the largest unsuccessful third-party movement in American history. Led by New York industrialist Peter Cooper and former Democratic Congressman Samuel Fenton Cary of Ohio, the coalition resolved to break the private bank monopoly of the cash supply. Thomas Nast, illustrator for *Harper's Weekly,* used his cartoons and lectures to endorse a return to the gold standard to reduce citizen insolvency.

Philanthropists pitied smallholders caught in the financial crunch. The Charity Organization Society distributed relief to the underclass. Begun in the Germantown neighborhood of Philadelphia in 1873, the first citywide society took shape in Buffalo, New York, in December 1877. The charity's creator, the Reverend Stephen Humphreys Gurteen, led the elite members of St. Paul's Guild in providing working mothers with child day care. The model bureau created standards that separated the indolent and undeserving from unemployed immigrants, widows, war veterans, invalids and the handicapped, and the elderly. Altruistic directors, in cooperation with members of Hebrew Charities and Societies of St. Vincent de Paul, formed a "charity clearinghouse." The society's model spread over urban America and parts of Europe.

The economy lagged until the return of the U.S. gold standard in January 1879. That year, the depression ended and gave way to the Gilded Age, the greatest period of economic growth to that time. Economists reflected on the disparate causes and remedies for the panic and depression. The treatise *Progress and Poverty: An Inquiry into the Cause of Industrial Depressions and of Increase of Want with Increase of Wealth, the Remedy* (1879), by political economist Henry George, condemned low wages and denounced the Homestead Act of 1862 for enabling land speculators to raise realty prices. As a leveler of class differences, George proposed the abolition of tariffs and a federal tax on large properties. To relieve the relentless toil among the working poor, the founder of the Christian Labor Union, the Reverend Jesse Henry Jones, a Massachusetts Congregationalist, advocated limiting the workday to eight hours.

See also: Banking and Finance; Gold Standard; Poverty and Wealth.

Further Reading

Beckert, Sven. *The Monied Metropolis: New York City and the Consolidation of the American Bourgeoisie, 1850–1896.* Cambridge, UK: Cambridge University Press, 2001.

Lane, Charles. *The Day Freedom Died: The Colfax Massacre, the Supreme Court, and the Betrayal of Reconstruction.* New York: Henry Holt, 2008.

Lubetkin, M. John. *Jay Cooke's Gamble: The Northern Pacific Railroad, the Sioux, and the Panic of 1873.* Norman: University of Oklahoma Press, 2006.

Morris, Charles R. *The Tycoons: How Andrew Carnegie, John D. Rockefeller, Jay Gould, and J.P. Morgan Invented the American Supereconomy.* New York: Henry Holt, 2005.

Renehan, Edward J., Jr. *The Dark Genius of Wall Street: The Misunderstood Life of Jay Gould, King of the Robber Barons.* New York: Basic Books, 2006.

Desert Land Act (1877)

On March 3, 1877, the U.S. Congress encouraged the settlement of states and territories in the Far West by passing the Desert Land Act. In his inaugural address on March 5 of that year, President Rutherford B. Hayes likewise promised to serve national interests by fostering the settlement and irrigation of desert lands in the West, which federal surveyors began mapping in the 1850s.

Enactment of the bill offered public land in allotments of 320 acres (130 hectares) per person, a larger parcel than that granted by the Homestead Act. Farmers and livestock men could petition for plots and free water for agrarian use in Arizona, California, the Dakotas, Idaho, Montana, Nevada, New Mexico, Oregon, Utah, Washington, and Wyoming, but not Colorado. Chief among the 10 million acres (4 million hectares) open for purchase were lands in the Gallatin Valley of Montana, the Imperial and Owens valleys of California, the Salt River Valley of Arizona, the Snake River Valley of Idaho, and the Yakima River Valley of Washington. To boost the availability of farm produce to mining camps, the offer excluded mining and lumbering as sources of income on allotted property.

Married pioneers could buy 640-acre (260-hectare) parcels at $1.25 per acre; single men were eligible only for 320-acre plots. A down payment of 25 cents per acre held the claim for three years. At the end of a 36-month period, homesteaders had to prove that they had watered at least one-eighth of their plot. They paid the remaining $1 per acre and obtained deeds to rugged home sites in the High Plains that were threatened by drought, wind, prairie fire, and insect infestation. Immediately, ambitious Oregon ranchers took advantage of the act in areas receiving limited rainfall.

In less accessible parts of the frontier, the legislation encouraged the sharing of resources and the growth of sheepherding, lumbering, and ranching. In Arizona, Mormon colonists welcomed the legislation as a boon to proselytizing. At Lehi, on September 14, 1877, the First Mesa Company built Utahville, later called Mesa City, in south-central Arizona. The newcomers constructed dirt-floor adobe homes of mud brick and cactus posts and added brush outbuildings to the housing stock. In cooperation with the Maricopa and Pima tribes, the Mormons irrigated the land with hand-dug canals that revived a 2,000-year-old Hohokam water system and silted in the fields. Soil nutrients improved pasturage for cattle and sheep; apple, peach, and pear orchards; clover and flowers to nourish bee colonies; and fields of alfalfa, beans, corn, cotton, grapes, melons, sorghum, squash, and wheat. Commerce developed through brick making, milling, and the ice industry.

Despite the success of a few settlers in turning the Great American Desert into prime farmland, the Desert Land Act tended to enrich land and water monopolies to the detriment of homesteaders. In Wyoming, only 4,148 or 26 percent of the claims succeeded in directing artificial water flow to a total of 15,898 plots.

The U.S. General Land Office took only months to discover the faulty logic of the Desert Land Act and the corruption of land grabbers and monopolizers of natural resources. Fraudulent claims came from lumberers, who concealed the prime fir and pine on their claims on the Pacific slope; from mining concerns greedy for coal and iron veins; and from range barons, who hired applicants to stake claims and made no effort to irrigate cheap grazing land. For example, U.S. Senator Joseph Maull Carey and Governor Francis Emroy Warren robbed the American people of thousands of acres in Laramie County, Wyoming, on which they grazed 80,000 sheep.

Within days of the bill's passage, William B. Carr and James Ben-Ali Haggin of San Francisco, California, hired surrogates to buy 100,000 acres (40,500 hectares) along the Southern Pacific tracks outside Bakersfield. The vast claim suppressed population growth and stripped the area of community and recreational access to waterways. While the Bakersfield Grange opposed the monopoly and demanded the repeal of the Desert Land Act, Carr and Haggin manipulated the *Bakersfield Californian* as a company mouthpiece. Farther south in New Mexico Territory, the Pecos Irrigation and Investment Company bought consecutive parcels from individual settlers at bargain prices.

To stave off loss to drought, the General Land Office suspended purchases and reported land fraud to Secretary of the Interior Carl Schurz. Federal investigators assessing land improvements in California found only 5 percent of the land claims lawful. Two years after the enactment of the Desert Land Act, Congress adjusted the generous distribution of dry lands by conducting land surveys at the request of the secretary of the interior and the commissioner of public lands.

The governor of Idaho Territory, John Philo Hoyt, disagreed with federal agents and proclaimed the act to be the salvation of the parched Snake River Valley. The governor of Montana Territory, Benjamin Franklin Potts, found 95 percent of the land claims working to the good of settlers and their farms. The governor of Wyoming Territory, John Wesley Hoyt, applauded the prosperity of cattlemen and assisted them in obtaining large desert tracts.

See also: Hayes, Rutherford B.; Homestead Act (1862).

Further Reading

Bogener, Steve. *Ditches Across the Desert: Irrigation in the Lower Pecos Valley.* Lubbock: Texas Tech University Press, 2003.

Klein, Maury. *The Genesis of Industrial America, 1870–1920.* Oxford, UK: Oxford University Press, 2007.

Pisani, Donald J. *From the Family Farm to Agribusiness: The Irrigation Crusade in California and the West, 1850–1931.* Berkeley: University of California Press, 1984.

Worster, Donald. *A River Running West: The Life of John Wesley Powell.* New York: Oxford University Press, 2002.

Dewey, Melvil (1851–1931)

A skilled cataloguer of books, Melvil Louis Kossuth Dewey, known as the "Father of Modern Librarianship," created the Dewey decimal library classification system. A native of Adams Center, New York, he was born into a devout Baptist family on December 10, 1851. He became enamored with books and reading and, to enhance local intellectual opportunities, organized a Young People's Lyceum. With money that he earned chopping wood and herding cattle, he bought an unabridged dictionary. On January 29, 1868, he endangered his lungs by rescuing texts from a burning school library at Hungerford Collegiate Institute. At age 18, he entered the Oneida Institute, a Free Will Baptist seminary in Oneida, New York.

In 1872, while a junior at Amherst College, Dewey kept accounts at the college library to pay his tuition and despaired at the lack of a consistent shelving system. The staff either arranged books alphabetically by title or on numbered shelves and assigned volumes a place located from a master list. The awkward systems and the remarking of books wasted time and labor. At the end of the year, Dewey became acting librarian for the college.

While Dewey attended graduate school at Amherst from 1874 to 1877, he studied general liberal arts—art, philosophy, psychology, and science. He promoted simplified spelling, shorthand, metric weights and measures, and other efficient arrangements of information. He studied a flawed library shelving system proposed in 1856 by Nathaniel Bradstreet Shurtleff, the mayor of Boston, that relied on decimal arrangement. At age 25, Dewey invented a similar method of shelving print material in a ten-section hierarchy that expanded numerically to an infinite number of places and alphabetically under the primary author's last name. He published his initial idea as *Classification and Subject Index for Cataloguing and Arranging the Books and Pamphlets of a Library* (1876).

He co-founded the American Library Association at 32 Hawley Street in Boston and issued the *American Library Journal.* He organized the first library conference on October 6, 1876, in Philadelphia, where 13 women and 90 men gathered at the Pennsylvania Historical Society. His proposed system of informational services upgraded the librarian's post from a job to a profession.

The Dewey numbering system begins with informational and general works at 000, and rises by hundreds to philosophy, occultism, and psychology (100); religion (200); social sciences (300); language (400); science and mathematics (500); technology and applied science (600); fine arts, decorative arts, and recreation (700); literature and rhetoric (800); and history, geography, and biography (900). Subtopics follow an arbitrary pattern. Literature breaks into American (810), English (820), German (830), French (840), Italian (850), Spanish (860), Latin (870), Greek (880), and minor languages (890). A further specification of topic divides English literature into poetry (821), drama (822), fiction (823), essay (824), oratory (825), letters (826), satire and humor (827), miscellaneous (828), and Anglo-Saxon or Old English (829).

Recurring numbers assist in locating particular subclassifications; for example, the number 73 refers to the United States, whether in cooking, medicine, or mountain climbing. As the permanent collection grows, shelvers shift rows of books, keeping them in Dewey's numerical order. The organization method became standard for public and scholarly libraries in 130 countries.

Before his death from cerebral hemorrhage on December 26, 1931, Dewey also invented hanging vertical files, designed a school of library science, and directed the Columbia University library and the New York State Library, the beginning of a state library development service.

Further Reading

Giberti, Bruno. *Designing the Centennial: A History of the 1876 International Exhibition in Philadelphia.* Lexington: University Press of Kentucky, 2002.

Humez, Alexander, and Nicholas D. Humez. *On the Dot: The Speck That Changed the World.* New York: Oxford University Press, 2008.

Manguel, Alberto. *The Library at Night.* New Haven, CT: Yale University Press, 2008.

Wiegand, Wayne A. *Irrepressible Reformer: A Biography of Melvil Dewey.* Chicago: American Library Association, 1996.

Dickinson, Emily (1830–1886)

An introverted, enigmatic individualist, poet Emily Elizabeth Dickinson crafted intuitive images of a repressed woman's yearnings and misgivings. Dubbed the "Belle of Amherst," the "Myth," and the "New England Mystic," she was born on December 10, 1830, on Main Street in the Dickinson brick homeplace built by her grandfather, the founder of Amherst College. Of New England Puritan stock, she developed from toddlerhood an affinity for music and verbal virtuosity. She spent most of her 55 years in her Massachusetts hometown as a spinster, self-cloistered in her residence on North Pleasant Street.

Dominated by her unaffectionate mother, Emily Norcross Dickinson, and her grim Calvinist father, U.S. legislator Edward Dickinson, she developed into a child prodigy. Except for her older brother, William Austin Dickinson, she earned little male approval in childhood for her brilliance. In mid-life (ca. 1862), Dickinson looked back on standard Victorian child psychology, which demanded the silencing of females:

> when a little Girl
> They put me in the Closet—
> Because they liked me "still"

Recalling her training at Amherst Academy and Mount Holyoke Female Seminary, Dickinson summarized the prejudice against competitive female intellectuals in "We lose—because we win" (ca. 1858). Before entering her most fruitful writing period, she suffered a distaste for evangelical zeal, bouts of depression, and fears of damnation and death. She described herself as small and wren-like, and retreated into caring for her dog Carlo and revealing letter writing.

Dickinson rebelled against religious intolerance and gender bias in witty, first-person verse, demanding to know "Why—do they shut Me out of Heaven?" (ca. 1861). She examined evanescence and the afterlife as well as provocative themes and motifs offering glimpses of her friendships and ambitions, which she described in "Hope Is the Thing with Feathers" (ca. 1861). She recognized the interiority of her inspiration in "It is easy to work when the soul is at play" (ca. 1861). Of an undeclared love, she vowed "Where Thou art—that—is Home" (ca. 1863). In anguish at undisclosed obstacles, she hinted at rage in "My Life had stood—a Loaded Gun" (1863).

At an emotional plateau in 1864, Dickinson sequestered herself in an upstairs room to write vigorous, rhapsodic lyrics and prim elegies in an idiosyncratic style that was misunderstood and unappreciated by her contemporaries. She made frequent reference to herself as a bee gathering nectar and recognized in "The Poets light but Lamps" (ca. 1864) that her immortality hinged on the survival of her verse. As indicated by "Bind me—I still can sing" (ca. 1865), she fought household suppression by writing private poetry.

By 1867, she spoke to outsiders through the door but interacted only with nieces, nephews, and neighborhood children. She collected sweet peas for pressing in notebooks and proclaimed "Exhilaration is the Breeze" (1868). She captured the torments of social restraint in "Tell All the Truth But Tell It Slant" (ca. 1868) and scolded herself, "I should not dare to be so sad" (1871), a reference to the grief of losing family members and friends.

In 1872, eyestrain and nephritis complicated the burden of doing the family baking and nursing her mother through senility and paralytic stroke. The poet retreated further from society, reading the works of Charlotte and Emily Brontë, Elizabeth Barrett Browning, Lydia Maria Child, and George Eliot, her literary companions. She mourned, "So much of Heaven has gone from Earth" (ca. 1872), a hint at her state of mind.

Dickinson's writing style violated literary standards of the day for capitalization, punctuation, and versification. A clash with the editors of her first seven poems submitted for publication ended her ventures into the critical market. Secluded in a private world, she generated prose and verse that defied categorization, such as the lament "How lonesome the Wind must feel Nights" (ca. 1877) and the admissions "I have no Life but this" and "They might not need me—yet they might" (ca. 1877).

At the poet's death on May 15, 1886, her younger sister, Lavinia Norcross Dickinson, disobeyed Emily's directions to burn 1,775 poems and 300 letters to Susan Huntington Gilbert Dickinson, her brother Austin's wife. Dickinson's canon, which reached print in 1955 in its original form, has influenced the later feminist writings of Jean Rhys, Adrienne Rich, and May Sarton.

Further Reading

Farr, Judith. *The Passion of Emily Dickinson.* Cambridge, MA: Harvard University Press, 1992.

Juhasz, Suzanne, and Christanne Miller, eds. *Emily Dickinson: A Celebration for Readers.* New York: Gordon and Breach, 1989.

Mitchell, Domhnall. *Emily Dickinson: Monarch of Perception.* Amherst: University of Massachusetts Press, 2000.

Pollak, Vivian R., ed. *A Historical Guide to Emily Dickinson.* New York: Oxford University Press, 2004.

Snodgrass, Mary Ellen. *Encyclopedia of Feminist Literature.* New York: Facts on File, 2006.

Diseases and Epidemics

The settlement of the United States introduced soldiers, pioneers, ranchers, and indigenous populations to European diseases, thus inadvertently reducing Indian tribes and, in some cases, exterminating them. At the outbreak of the Civil War, the flight of pro-Union tribes from Indian Territory (Oklahoma) to Kansas and Colorado threatened refugees of the Wichita with epidemic cholera, measles, and smallpox. An outbreak of smallpox in a virgin-soil population in Santa Monica, California, in 1861 killed cattleman and vintner José Ysidro Reyes, founder of Rancho Boca de Santa Monica, a Mexican land grant of 6,656 acres (2,694 hectares). The loss of the vigorous stockman generated inheritance squabbles and boundary disputes requiring more than two decades to settle.

In the winter of that same year, a frontier legend and ballad from Alma in central Colorado lionized Lady Silver Heels, an employee of the Buckskin Joe dance hall who performed in silver shoes. After the death of her fiancé, Jack Herndon, during a smallpox epidemic, she turned the saloon into a contagion ward and nursed miners and sheepherders from Bayou Salado. Because the disease scarred and disfigured her, in spring 1862, she disappeared before the miners could thank her with a collection of $5,000. In her honor, they named a local peak at Fairplay, Colorado, Mount Silverheels. A ghost story romanticized the heroine as a veiled woman garbed in black and wandering the Buckskin Joe cemetery to weep at the graves of the dead.

More realistic is the history of a smallpox outbreak on March 12, 1862, among Pacific Coast and Puget Sound Haida and Tsimshian, later reported by Eugene Casimir Chirouse, a Catholic missionary at Everett, Washington, and by Indian agent Henry Webster at the Makah Reservation in Clallam County, Washington. After promoters advertised for hearty lumbermen and sturdy women and families to settle Washington Territory, the influx of outsiders increased. Contagion spread following the docking of *Brother Jonathan,* a steamer carrying 350 gold prospectors to Victoria, British Columbia, from San Francisco, where smallpox overran the region.

In the same month, another epidemic slew 150 citizens of San Luis Obispo, the northern military headquarters of California, and killed Chief Juan Antonio and thousands of Cahuilla when the disease overran San Bernardino. Outsiders journeying from the southern coast of California into Washington Territory carried microbes into grog shops and bordellos run by native prostitutes.

In Vancouver, the *Daily British Colonist* blamed the first smallpox case on the squalor of Indian camps rather than the susceptibility of native peoples to diseases for which they had no natural immunity. Compounding the danger, on March 24, 1862, the arrival of the steamer *Oregon* introduced another infected traveler into the population. In *The Coming of the Spirit of Pestilence: Introduced Infectious Diseases and Population Decline Among Northwest Coast Indians, 1774–1874* (1999), author Robert Thomas Boyd declared the outbreak the fault of racists and opportunists for failing to quarantine and vaccinate natives and for making hospitalization voluntary.

To stem the death rate outside Vancouver, Victoria Islanders drove away the Salish and Songhee and torched their homes. The Indians paddled canoes up the Pacific Coast and carried the pathogen to Sitka, Alaska. Doctors vaccinated whites, but only a few Songhee.

In spring 1863 at Fort Victoria, John Sebastian Helmcken, the Hudson's Bay Company physician, injected toxin via an ivory blade into 500 natives, most of them Songhee, including Chief Freezy and his wife and daughter. To the *Daily Press* on March 27, 1863, Helmcken explained the low turnout for inoculation: "It was pretty hard at first to convince them of the benefit arising from this simple operation, but after a while they were made to believe that the threatened sickness, the smallpox, was far worse than their great enemy, the measles." More than a year after the outbreak, Father Leon Fouquet vaccinated 3,400 Kootenay of Washington to prevent a similar tragedy in Northwest Territory.

Smallpox followed migrant populations, including an influx of liberated slaves to St. Helena Island, South Carolina, in fall 1862. The Reverend William Duncan, a Church of England missionary, led 58 Tsimshian followers from Fort Simpson toward his compound at Metlakhatla in southern Alaska. Five days later, smallpox felled 300 Tsimshian. Two days later, the Songhee moved on, bearing infection to Discovery Island and the San Juan Islands in Washington Territory. Helmcken reported that nearly every infected patient succumbed to the pox, with or without inoculation.

Those who advocated a traditional sweating-and-cooling regimen hastened death by subjecting patients to steam baths, then throwing them into the bay, where they died from shock. Villagers drove the sick into the forest, where naked shamans tied delirious children to trees and danced in a frenzy, hoping for a cure. Left untended with only a blanket, water, and salmon, the young expired and decayed in the open air, raising the stench of corruption.

When burial parties lagged behind the death count, they tied rocks to corpses and threw them into the bay.

By December 1862, the Songhee and the Nootsack of the Tulalip Reservation in the mid–Puget Sound area survived in isolation. The death toll rose to 14,000 among the Bella Bella, Haida, Kwakiutl, Makah, Skallam, Tlingit, and Tsimshian, threatening the extermination of the Bella Bella, Skallam, and Tsimshian. Of the total population of 30,000 natives, only half survived the Pacific Coast epidemic.

Institutional Epidemics

In a letter, British actor and diarist Fanny Kemble noted the value of malaria and swamp fever to the Confederates, who were acclimated to epidemics in the humid South.

In August 1863, the Union army opened a pesthouse on the Mississippi River outside West Alton, Illinois, at Sunflower Island, later known as Smallpox Island. The facility housed the sick and dying from the contagion introduced on October 15, 1862, by prisoners of war from Colonel John S. Poindexter's Missouri Regiment. When smallpox raged, more than 1,260 Confederate prisoners of war shared quarantine with Union soldiers and noncombatants. The sick died at the rate of six to ten per day. According to Confederate Captain Griffin Frost, a newspaper publisher from Palmyra, Missouri, and the author of *A Camp and Prison Journal* (1867), victims came primarily from Arkansas, Mississippi, Missouri, and Tennessee. Confusing an accurate epidemiological account were infections from dysentery, malaria, measles, pneumonia, tuberculosis, and typhoid. Staff buried some 2,200 corpses at the Confederate Soldiers' Cemetery in North Alton and interred the rest in unmarked trenches.

Similarly pressing, the emergence of smallpox in May 1865 among the Menominee on a reservation at Keshena, Wisconsin, required the immediate burial of victims to maintain health standards. Non-Christians fled to the woods. When a Belgian priest, the Reverend A.M. Joseph Mazeaud, refused secular orders and insisted on orthodox funerals for Christians, the disease infected 79 mourners, most of them Catholic converts, including Menominee Chief Pegah Kenah. The priest went to jail for ignoring anticontagion regulations, for exhuming a corpse, and for sanctioning public gatherings that spread infection to 150 victims. Although Indian agent Moses M. Davis inoculated 800 Indians, the Menominee declined in number to 1,800. They remained vulnerable to smallpox until Indian agents, missionaries, and traders began a vaccination program in 1869.

Late 1860s Epidemics

In 1868, while Indian agents concealed epidemics and starvation from their superiors in Washington, D.C., Southwestern Indians battled tuberculosis, smallpox, spinal meningitis, trachoma, and venereal diseases. In July, Sarah Winnemucca, a Northern Paiute interpreter and scout for agent Calvin Bateman and General Oliver Otis Howard at Camp McDermit in northeastern Nevada, discovered that her tribe at Pyramid Lake Reservation in the western part of the state was dwindling from hunger, measles, and smallpox. The infections appear to have come from secondhand clothing donated to the Paiute, though some natives feared that whites had poisoned the Humboldt River.

At the Cheyenne and Arapaho Reservation in southwestern Kansas, malaria struck a virgin population, generating alarming mortality rates among resident women and children of the Apache, Arapaho, Cheyenne, and Kiowa. The same disease, called "ague" or "intermittent fever," assailed Clackamas, Kalapuya, and Molalla in the Columbia and Willamette valleys of Washington Territory. Because Indians lacked experience with European disease, shamans treated unfamiliar symptoms with limited native pharmacopoeia.

The outbreak of a seven-year smallpox pandemic in late 1868 in Philadelphia and New York coincided with the threat of the Franco-Prussian War, which began on July 19, 1870. The disease infected 3,100, killing 26 percent. Most of the dead were uninoculated immigrant children from France and Germany who were living in slums amid poor sanitation and ignorance. In May 1869, the staff of the New York City board of health visited the residences of 700,000 newcomers to examine unhygienic conditions. Some slum dwellers hid sick relatives rather than send them to metropolitan isolation wards to suffer alone. Uneducated adults rejected doctors as sources of pestilence and accused the medical profession of profiteering.

To the west, during a period of diminishing buffalo herds and increased whiskey trade and outbreaks of measles and influenza, in September 1869, thousands of Northern Plains Indians and Métis in the United States and Canada succumbed to smallpox. They acquired the disease from bartering at trading posts along the upper Missouri River.

According to Alonzo S. Reed, the Indian agent at Milk River, Montana, the Upper Assiniboine at the Fort Peck Reservation near Wolf Point, Montana, were the first infected; next, the Gros Ventre and Métis; and, in

January 1870, the Blackfeet and Cree. In northern Montana, the Gros Ventre lost 741 members, 57 percent of their original 1,300. Many survived as invalids, blind, disfigured, and crippled.

Historians blame the Assiniboine for digging up the remains of a crewman of the steamer *Utah* to steal his burial clothes. The disease migrated from Fort Belknap in northern Montana to white corpse robbers, who pilfered bone bundles wrapped in pelts and tied in treetops. To escape illness, the River Crow fled southwest to the Musselshell River of central Montana; the Blackfeet resettled north in central Alberta, Canada. Chief Red Stone led the Lower Assiniboine east to safety among the Yankton Sioux at Standing Rock in Dakota Territory.

According to British entrepreneur and philanthropist William Henry Blackmore, co-author of *The Hunting Grounds of the Great West* (1878), the Arapaho suffered from close association with whites by the loss of 8,500 Indians, reducing the tribe's population to 1,500.

Yellow Fever

Like smallpox, yellow fever traveled rapidly via water traffic. According to privateer Thomas Edward Taylor, author of *Running the Blockade: A Personal Narrative of Adventures, Risks, and Escapes during the Civil War* (1896), the disease engulfed Nassau in summer 1862, filling the Caribbean port with the sick, dying, and grieving. Fever spread up the Atlantic Coast by ship to Charleston, South Carolina, and Wilmington, North Carolina, where 42 percent of victims died.

In the late 1860s and 1870s, Memphis, Tennessee, a cotton trade center on the Mississippi River, incurred a series of yellow fever outbreaks. Several thousand died; others abandoned the area, causing a collapse of the local economy. The epidemic ended with improved sanitation and revived port city business with new cotton and lumber mills, stockyards, and small businesses employing whites and former slaves.

In spring 1864, Southern sympathizers headquartered in Canada plotted biological terrorism in Northern cities. A cavalryman from Woodford County, Kentucky, Luke Pryor Blackburn, a field surgeon under General Sterling Price, claimed to be a New Orleans physician. In mid-April 1864, he sped from Halifax, Nova Scotia, to Bermuda to treat fever victims and won a citation from the Queen's Admiralty for altruism. A month later, Blackburn loaded eight steamer trunks with bedding, gowns, and bandages contaminated by fever patients and shipped the containers to Union territory. On July 12, London-born cobbler Godfrey Joseph Hyams, a former rebel agent and spy stationed in Montreal and Toronto, transported the trunks from the steamer *Alphia* to New York City, Philadelphia, and Washington, D.C., to sell at auction. He dispatched contaminated goods to Union headquarters at Norfolk, Virginia, and New Bern, North Carolina. Charles M. Allen, the U.S. consul to Bermuda, arrested Hyams for sedition. Because 2,000 died at New Bern from yellow fever, Blackburn erroneously concluded that Hyams's actions had caused the plot to succeed.

On September 4, 1864, Blackburn returned to Bermuda to collect three trunks of infected bedding and towels to warehouse on St. George Island, until he could transport the lot to New York in spring 1865. The trial of the assassins of Abraham Lincoln disclosed the bioterrorism plot after Hyams revealed the intent to introduce septic hospital laundry in the urban North. The *Montreal Gazette* proclaimed Blackburn an inhumane villain. At his trial in Toronto for violating the Neutrality Act, evidence revealed bioterrorism in the New Bern epidemic and disclosed a scheme by Southern agents to mail President Abraham Lincoln infected dress shirts. Investigators located the trunks stashed on St. George Island, but the court exonerated Blackburn for plotting mass murder. New York newspapers, the Philadelphia *Enquirer,* and the Washington *Intelligencer* vilified Blackburn as a fiend. Ironically, he and his conspirators were unaware that only the bite of a disease-bearing mosquito can transmit yellow fever.

On August 21, 1876, the arrival of Spanish cargo ships carrying ballast and lumber from Havana, Cuba, to the Atlantic & Gulf Railroad wharves of coastal Georgia introduced yellow fever at Brunswick, Doboy Island, and Savannah. Officials wrestled with the problem of cyclical fever outbreaks in the Caribbean and contagion arriving through trading vessels. Post office employees fumigated letters but could not slow the plague, which gained strength from exposed sewage. The outbreak was particularly devastating to Catholic priests and nuns who treated the poor.

Dr. Louis A. Falligant composed a monograph describing his use of aconite, arsenic, belladonna, brandy in cracked ice, ipecac, mustard footbaths, *nux vomica,* and quinine to relieve symptoms. A biological study connected the runoff from slaughterhouses and drainage from hospitals with the corruption of fresh water creeks and adjacent marshland. The conclusion blamed night air as the vehicle for the pathogen. It was not until 1881 that Carlos

Finlay, a Cuban researcher, connected the "yellow jack" to mosquito infestation.

The Southern Border

The Gulf of Mexico suffered a similar coastal outbreak of yellow fever. In July 3, 1867, following the death from the "black vomit" of a German traveler from Indianola to Galveston, Texas, residents incurred a "yellow jack" epidemic. A local physician suppressed the diagnosis by a Confederate surgeon, Greensville S. Dowell, founder of the Galveston Medical Society and the *Galveston Medical Journal,* who conducted an autopsy on a victim and located telltale black matter in the stomach. Worsening the situation were heavy rains and puddles of stagnant water that bred germ-carrying mosquitoes. The fever infected one-quarter of the citizenry and killed nearly one-tenth of the population.

Officials could do little more than fumigate with burning tar and import ice to cool patients' fevers. The Howard Association, composed of volunteers who were immune to yellow fever, offered medicine, nurse care, and home visits, which they underwrote with $1,120 in donations. The flight of 5,000 people after an August 2, 1867, alert in the *Galveston Daily News* sent the disease inland with travelers on stagecoaches and trains. By September, the death toll had risen to 1,150, with the daily rate as high as 20 per day. On October 3, 1867, Galveston was nearing the end of four months of sickness when a hurricane killed more citizens, smashed homes and businesses, and endangered convalescing patients with relapse.

A thick infestation of mosquitoes carried infection along the Gulf of Mexico 125 miles (200 kilometers) southwest to Corpus Christi, where 12 percent of the populace succumbed to the scourge. The Howard Association collected donations, built a pesthouse and coffins, and employed undertakers to prepare the corpses of paupers. On August 27, 1867, the group's president, the Reverend Jesse P. Perham, died of fever.

Pharmacist William DeRyee, a Bavarian immigrant from Würzburg who ran a drugstore on Chaparral Street, accepted the role of contagion expert and created a fever treatment following the deaths of two local doctors and his 17-year-old son, Emil DeRyee. The pharmacist suppressed convulsions with morphia, used creosote and chlorinated water as an antiseptic, and dosed feverish patients with potassium salicylate. He packed the sick in hot ash and brought down fever with cold towels. According to the Brownsville, Texas, *Daily Ranchero,* by August 30, "The fever was abating for want of material."

Cholera

Unlike yellow fever, cholera moved rapidly via contaminated water. In the Midwest in summer 1864, treatment for epidemic cholera consisted of sweating patients in blankets and applying mustard plasters to the torso and feet.

Through Sioux territory along the Platte River in eastern Nebraska, Mormon patriarch Samuel Kendall Gifford gave sanitation instructions to wagon trains on abandoning septic wells and drawing water from free-flowing currents. He insisted that pioneers boil water for use during overland travel. Along the trail west to a Mormon enclave in Salt Lake Valley, Utah, Gifford observed fresh graves, jettisoned deathbeds, and miners hurrying east to escape contagion.

At Leavenworth, Kansas, in 1864, Mother Xavier Ross, leader of the Sisters of Charity, put Sister Joanna Bruner in charge of the first civilian hospital at Fort Harker, where 200 died of cholera. Bruner, the first woman to administer a hospital west of the Mississippi River, began teaching classes in nursing. For children orphaned by the epidemic, the nuns sought adoptive parents.

Newspapers urged boiling drinking water and disinfecting dishes and laundry. Bacteriologist George Miller Sternberg, a general in the U.S. Army, treated the sick and improved drainage and sanitation. His data for the Army Medical Museum summarized the outbreak's demographics, which included his 25-year-old bride, Louisa Russell Sternberg, who died of the disease on July 15, 1865.

When cholera struck Louisville, Kentucky, in 1865, authorities fought the waterborne cholera pathogen by declaring public health everyone's responsibility. The city council passed ordinances requiring that poultry and livestock remain in pens and that garbage be burned. A board of health hired street sweepers and garbage collectors to keep drinking water pure.

The forced movement of tribes across the Midwest introduced more virgin populations to the scourge. During the resettlement of the Whitebead Caddo and Hasinai or Tejas from Colorado, Kansas, and Texas to Indian Territory (Oklahoma) in 1865, Indians rebelled against military escorts. Upon reaching Oklahoma, Chief Showe-tat led the Caddo along with the Delaware and Shawnee during a cholera outbreak. Outside the Washita

River valley in west-central Oklahoma, 107 died before their arrival at Fort Washita in south-central Oklahoma.

In winter 1866, cholera spread over the Great Plains, infecting the Caddo, Pima, and Wichita. Contagion took some 1,500 lives as it swept from Carlisle Barracks and Governor's Island into eastern Kansas, perhaps carried by the Buffalo Soldiers of the Thirty-Eighth Infantry Regiment on their arrival from Jefferson Barracks, Missouri, on the way to New Mexico Territory.

Joseph Janvier Woodward's *Report on Epidemic Cholera and Yellow Fever in the Army of the United States, During the Year 1867* (1868) paralleled transportation routes with the advance of sickness. He charted the infection along the western branch of the Union Pacific Railroad to rail crews and army outposts. Pathogens advanced northward and menaced Canada. During a political journey with President Andrew Johnson and General Ulysses S. Grant around the West, Secretary of State William Henry Seward became so depleted by cholera that he rode a special railcar back to Washington, D.C.

Epidemic Conditions

In the early 1860s, rudimentary knowledge of threats to public health from infestations of vermin and unhygienic air, water, and earth inhibited control and treatment of disease. In the agrarian South, the spread of hookworms contributed to two decades of declining productivity among people who might otherwise have flourished.

After the onset of the Civil War in April 1861, makeshift hospitals in churches, hotels, government buildings, residences, schools, tent cities, and warehouses clustered the wounded alongside those felled by contagious disease. Improvised clinics treated a gamut of ailments—chicken pox, dengue fever, dysentery, enteritis, hepatitis, malaria, measles, mumps, pertussis, pneumonia, and typhoid—all of which migrated from attendants to their families and neighbors. The job of treatment and rehabilitation passed to amateurs at an ingathering of beds and linens, pillows and mattresses, bandages, dishes, and cutlery. Heightening the death toll were catastrophic erysipelas, gangrene, pyaemia, and tetanus from septic residents, unsterilized kitchens, infectious privies, and shallow wells.

Teams transferred patients to civilian outposts and organized kitchens to concoct invalid diets, poultices, and tonics. In Washington, D.C., untrained volunteers laundered bedding and nightshirts, boiled lice and nits from blankets, and hand-fed invalids. Limited pharmacopoeia consisted of palliative quinine, coffee, and sherry. Poet and medic Walt Whitman, author of *Memoranda During the War* (1876), cheered the sick with gifts of citrus fruit, dried fruit, jams and fruit syrup, pickles, and rice pudding, a digestible treat for fever victims.

The lack of fruit and vegetables in the summer of 1864 produced massive death from dysentery and scurvy, particularly among Georgia residents during General William Tecumseh Sherman's assault on Atlanta. Farther west at Fort Larned, Kansas, an army outpost on Pawnee Fork 8 miles (13 kilometers) from the Arkansas River, on July 6, 1864, venereal disease ravaged soldiers.

To the west, the privations of soldiers threatened the strength and speed of the military guarding wagon trains, mail delivery, and settlements on the frontier. Sergeant John Spring reported on an unusual scourge, an outbreak of malaria at Camp Wallen in Cochise County near Huachuca City, Arizona. On May 4, 1867, according to Elizabeth Bacon "Libbie" Custer's autobiographical account *Boots and Saddles* (1885), Lieutenant Colonel George Armstrong Custer's riders battled cholera at Fort Hays, Kansas. Soldiers deserted because of cold, hunger, illness, mud, and soggy tent grounds. Their diet of bacon and moldy hardtack produced rampant scurvy, which General Winfield Scott Hancock countered with onions and potatoes as antiscorbutics.

In 1869, diphtheria gathered strength in Gila and Graham east of Phoenix, Arizona. Victims blamed peddlers for spreading the plague. In 1874, a party of 18,000 Hutterite immigrants from Radichev, Russia, encountered 37 deaths from dysentery at a stopover in Lincoln, Nebraska.

See also: Chisholm Trail; Forten, Charlotte; Hospitals and Asylums; Oklahoma Territory; Panama Canal; Seward, William Henry; Stanton, Edwin M.

Further Reading

Boyd, Robert Thomas. *The Coming of the Spirit of Pestilence: Introduced Infectious Diseases and Population Decline Among Northwest Coast Indians, 1774–1874.* Seattle: University of Washington Press, 1999.

MacKell, Jan. *Brothels, Bordellos, and Bad Girls: Prostitution in Colorado, 1860–1930.* Santa Fe: University of New Mexico Press, 2004.

Scott, Paula A. *Santa Monica: A History on the Edge.* Charleston, SC: Arcadia, 2004.

Snodgrass, Mary Ellen. *World Epidemics: A Cultural Chronology of Disease from Prehistory to the Era of SARS.* Jefferson, NC: McFarland, 2003.

Dix, Dorothea (1802–1887)

A humanitarian lobbyist and the Union army's head nurse during the Civil War, Dorothea Lynde Dix was the first female to receive appointment to a federal post. Born in Hampden, Maine, on April 4, 1802, she reared her brothers, Charles Wesley and Joseph Dix, Jr., the sons of Mary Bigelow, an unstable mother, and Joseph Dix, an itinerant Methodist evangelist. "Dolly" Dix spent her childhood pasting and sewing religious leaflets for her father to promote his fanaticism.

Like her grandfather, Elijah Dix, who operated a pharmacy south of Faneuil Hall in Boston, she displayed a fierce initiative and vigor for aiding society's outcasts. She fled the family home in Worcester, Massachusetts, in 1814 and lived in Boston with her widowed grandmother, Dorothy Lynde Dix, and a great aunt, Sarah Lynde Fiske. Dix educated herself through attendance at lectures by Harvard professors and reading in libraries. In 1819, she enrolled in a girls' academy in Dorchester.

After operating a dame school for 16 girls and teaching classes for neighborhood children in the family stable, Dix gave up her profession to recuperate from a tubercular disease at the home of public health reformer William Rathbone in Liverpool, England. Returning to the United States, she taught needlework and attended the Unitarian church in Boston of William Ellery Channing, who became her mentor.

Dix came under the influence of Channing's friends, libertarians Ralph Waldo Emerson, Samuel Gridley Howe, Horace Mann, and John Greenleaf Whittier. She tended Channing's children—12-year-old Mary and 10-year-old William Francis Channing—in Portsmouth, Rhode Island. During winter 1830–1831, on vacation with the Channings in St. Croix, she first encountered cane field slaves. At Channing's suggestion, she taught Sunday school at the East Cambridge House of Correction in Massachusetts and wrote devotional and children's literature.

In her thirties, at a time when some 17,435 mentally ill inmates occupied cruel, filthy madhouses and city prisons, Dix's labors toward medical and social reform took her to every sanitarium, jail, and poorhouse in Massachusetts. The investigation, funded by an inheritance from her grandmother, took Dix to 14 states, as well as Italy; New Brunswick, Newfoundland, and Nova Scotia, Canada; and Scotland. Her alliance with U.S. Vice President Millard Fillmore led Congress in 1852 to approve the construction of St. Elizabeth's Hospital in Washington, D.C. To maintain an active schedule, Dix worked daily from 5 A.M. to 1 A.M.

During a rest cure with Quakers in Liverpool, England, in September 1854, she studied the Quaker concept of social welfare. She endangered her lungs by shaming and railing at legislators to rescue poor mental patients from incarceration with criminals in cages and pens, where they lived chained to walls and received lashings on their naked flesh to subdue their ravings. In 1856, Dix petitioned Pope Pius IX to succor the mentally ill in substandard asylums in Rome.

Patriotic Duty

Within days of the onset of the Civil War, Dix led a troop of volunteer nurses in a march on Washington, D.C., to demand a gender-neutral military medical corps. She already had displayed her skill in trauma nursing at Baltimore following the Pratt Street Riot of April 19, 1861, which killed 12 and wounded 36. On June 1, 1861, at age 59, Dix accepted appointment by Secretary of War Simon Cameron and acting Union Surgeon General Robert Crooke Wood to an unpaid job as supervisor of wartime nurse care. Wood dictated that Union facilities would receive 30 percent female nurses.

Dix's bureaucratic post, supervising 3,000 members of the U.S. Sanitary Commission, demanded that she exercise patience with a disorganized system and undisciplined staff. During the day, at her office a block from the White House at 14th Street and New York Avenue, she screened interviewees and recruited qualified people for ward duty and stretcher bearing. She rejected fashion plates and hired plain women who wore no hoop skirts, ringlets, or jewelry.

Dix passed 31 probationary nurses to Dr. Elizabeth Blackwell for training in New York City at Bellevue Hospital before they were sent on assignment to hospitals in Alexandria, Georgetown, and Washington. Cameron reported to President Abraham Lincoln that he trusted Dix with the complex relief effort, which also involved shipping heavy supplies to field aid stations. Blackwell, however, disagreed with Cameron and claimed that Dix was a disorganized meddler. History remains undecided as to Dix's value to the war effort.

An admirer of Florence Nightingale, heroine of the Crimean War, Dix challenged society to accept women's roles in medicine. Mocked as "Dragon Dix," she gained a reputation for angering dilatory nurses and surgeons who lacked her attention to detail. She modeled the basics of her profession—self-control, sobriety, hygiene, idealism, zeal, and unbiased treatment of all in need of care. She labored to solicit supplies, set up aid stations and field surgeries, and prevent cases of sunstroke by petitioning women to sew havelocks to attach to military caps and cover the neck. At night, she volunteered at the Seminary Hospital at N and 30th streets to manage the linen service and dress wounds. For staffing field hospitals and ambulances, she preferred women between the ages of 30 and 45 to minister to men in their teens and twenties and to weather the sniping of misogynistic surgeons and aides.

To her detriment, Dix angered the Woman's Central Association of Relief by refusing the services of mothers and sweethearts of soldiers and by rejecting Catholic sisters or girls of marriageable age. Dix remanded nurses to their rooms at 9 P.M. and denied them any evening amusement or fraternization with military men. She lobbed tactless criticism at workers whom she deemed unfit for medical work, particularly doctors who drank on the job, consorted with prostitutes, and neglected sanitation. One of her nurses, Hannah Ropes, carried complaints to Secretary of War Edwin M. Stanton, who fired the surgeon and assistant in question for brutalizing patients. Out of loyalty to the military medical team, Dix defended the nurse corps and interceded on behalf of individuals needing rest and treatment for exhaustion. She annoyed nurses with her arbitrary opinions and decisions, yet she addressed each as "my child" and rewarded good service with small gifts, flowers, or a cup of tea.

Over the next four years, Dix made do on four or five hours of sleep per night, while scrambling to sort out the needs of staffs. She assigned "respectable" white women to nursing tasks and sent black and white laboring-class women to work in commissaries, laundries, and linen rooms. She favored Sophronia Bucklin, a doughty triage nurse and a worker in tent wards who insisted that the military serve nutritious meals to the sick and wounded. At Point Lookout, Maryland, a tent village for prisoners of war, Dix overruled Union surgeons on the issue of ministering to Confederate casualties; she dispatched Ella Louise Wolcott to see to their needs. After the Battle of Bull Run on July 21, 1861, Dix was forced to relax her high standards when faced with a deluge of 1,124 Union casualties from Manassas, Virginia.

To organize patient care on the Virginia peninsula at Yorktown, she commandeered homes, churches, schools, inns, warehouses, and even the U.S. Patent Office. Newspaper accounts of the influx drew hundreds of volunteers, many from the families of congressmen and capital officials. By October, the Union humanitarian network had collapsed because of internal feuds.

During the winter, Dix declined President Lincoln's offer of a one-horse wagon and driver to assist her trudges to government bureaus and hospitals. She reciprocated his kind gesture by assigning a nurse to attend Tad Lincoln within hours of the death of his brother, 11-year-old "Willie" Lincoln, on February 20, 1862, from typhoid fever.

A Failed Mission

In late April 1862, Surgeon General William Alexander Hammond usurped Dix's power to hire and fire nurses. Following the Battle of Gettysburg on July 4, 1863, she and her corps of 40 "Dixies" found 5,000 rebel casualties left untended on the field. From the rigors of battlefield nursing, her weight fell from 139 pounds (53 kilograms) to less than 100 pounds (45 kilograms).

By early October 1863, while Dix organized a medical center on the Outer Banks of North Carolina, officials stripped her of control of staffing hospitals. An assignment to the Virginia Eastern Lunatic Asylum at Williamsburg in late winter 1864 returned her to the familiar work of inspecting institutions and making recommendations. In spring, she debriefed returning soldiers on prison conditions in the South.

After an assassin's attack on Secretary of State William Henry Seward on April 14, 1865 (the same night President Lincoln was murdered), Dix attended Seward personally with home-cooked meals. She remained at her Washington post night and day without furlough until September 1, 1866. Upon her departure from the capital, she dispatched a postwar staff to nurture and rehabilitate men from Andersonville and Libby prisons for return home. As a civilian, she raised funds for veterans, widows, and orphans; for the American Society for Prevention of Cruelty to Animals and temperance crusades; for scholarships to Vassar College; and for a monument to the dead at Fort Monroe, Virginia.

In later years, Dix abandoned professional nursing and distanced herself from reminiscences of wartime practice, which she deemed a failure. She reclaimed her moral vision of humane care of the insane and extended her outreach to orphans and to education for the blind. Ailing from arthritis, bronchitis, and malaria, she conducted surprise inspections of asylums and toured the ruins of the South. Her tours of the United States, Canada,

Europe, and Japan resulted in the establishment or upgrading of professional care at 32 institutions.

At age 78, her sight and hearing began to decline, forcing her to retire to Trenton State Hospital in New Jersey, an institution she had founded. Until her death on July 17, 1887, she continued corresponding with officials and friends in support of humanitarian causes.

Further Reading

Brown, Thomas J. *Dorothea Dix: New England Reformer.* Cambridge, MA: Harvard University Press, 1998.

Giesberg, Judith Ann. *Civil War Sisterhood: The U.S. Sanitary Commission and Women's Politics in Transition.* Boston: Northeastern University Press, 2000.

Lurie, Maxine N., and Marc Mappen, eds. *Encyclopedia of New Jersey.* New Brunswick, NJ: Rutgers University Press, 2004.

Schultz, Jane E. *Women at the Front: Hospital Workers in Civil War America.* Chapel Hill: University of North Carolina Press, 2004.

Snodgrass, Mary Ellen. *Historical Encyclopedia of Nursing.* Santa Barbara, CA: ABC-CLIO, 1999.

Dodge City, Kansas

The seat of Ford County in northwest Kansas, Dodge City became a frontier legend as the center of lawlessness and trade. Established in 1847 as Fort Mann, a shield for pioneers traveling the Santa Fe Trail, the site became Fort Atkinson in 1850.

During the Cheyenne uprisings of 1865, the outpost became Fort Dodge, which worked in tandem with Fort Larned to protect mail service, military supply routes, and pioneers on their way up the Arkansas River to Colorado. Contributing to traffic were the 10 million longhorn steers driven northeast into Kansas over the Shawnee and Chisholm trails from 1866 to 1890. Moving from Santa Fe, New Mexico, to buyers in Franklin, Missouri, steers were tempting to Cheyenne and Kiowa rustlers as the herds passed through Cherokee, Chickasaw, and Choctaw land in Indian Territory (Oklahoma).

The town originated in 1871 with the three-room sod hut of cattleman and government woodcutter Henry Laughlin Sitler of Crawford County, Pennsylvania. The area, known as the "Deadwood of Kansas," already had earned a forbidding reputation after the shooting of three wagoneers driving a government supply train on March 18, 1871. The rest stop for travelers preceded Charles Myer's trading post and George M. Hoover's tent tavern, a watering hole for soldiers, buffalo hunters and traders, and crews from the Atchison, Topeka, & Santa Fe Railroad, which brought service to the town in September 1872.

In the final years of the buffalo trade, shipper Charles Rath of Rath and Company and his competitors dispatched some 100 million hides north and east, and sold skulls and bones to fertilizer and china factories. Rambunctious businesses opened on Front Street, a double thoroughfare on each side of the railroad. City officials hired Marshal William L. "Buffalo Bill" Brooks to cleanse the area of reckless shooters and killers, but his career ended on July 29, 1874, when he went to the gallows for stock thievery from the Southwestern Stage Company, for which he drove. He and his ilk found resting places in Boot Hill Cemetery.

A quarantine imposed in 1866 to halt the spread of anthrax from Texas cattle eased in 1876. The human population hovered at 1,200. As drives swung west, Dodge City surpassed the livestock centers at Abilene, Caldwell, Ellsworth, Newton, and Wichita, Kansas, to become the "Queen of Cow Towns." When herders such as black cowboy Nat Love and Charlie A. Siringo, a wrangler at the LX ranch, pushed off the Chisholm Trail into Dodge City, bordellos and stockyards thrived from young men looking to spend their cash and "whoop 'em up Liza Jane."

Frank Loving and other cardsharps played poker and chuck-a-luck in gambling halls; Deputy Marshal William Barclay "Bat" Masterson patrolled the streets; "Big Nose" Kate Elder performed in a sporting house; her lover, John Henry "Doc" Holliday, who practiced dentistry, knifed Ed Bailey for violating the rules against looking at discards from a poker hand. After Holliday entered a hotel room on house arrest, Elder bluffed guards into fighting a fire and helped Holliday escape.

William Harris's famed Long Branch Saloon became the site of gunfights and walk-downs, such as the shooting of Marshal Ed Masterson, the argument between Loving and gunman Levi Richardson, and the 1877 confrontation between gunman Clay Allison and Marshal Wyatt Earp. Barkeep Charlie Bassett and his deputies, James C. Earp and James Masterson, succeeded Wyatt Earp as keepers of the peace.

See also: Bass, Sam; Chisholm Trail; Law Enforcement.

Further Reading

Lamar, Howard R., ed. *The New Encyclopedia of the American West.* New Haven, CT: Yale University Press, 1998.

Shortridge, James R. *Cities on the Plains: The Evolution of Urban Kansas.* Lawrence: University Press of Kansas, 2004.

Dodge City, Kansas, settled in 1872, emerged as a notorious Wild West town and cattle drive destination on the Santa Fe Trail. With the coming of the railroad, dealers shipped Texas longhorns and the hides of slaughtered buffalo en masse to Eastern markets. *(Fotosearch/Stringer/Getty Images)*

Vestal, Stanley. *Dodge City, Queen of Cowtowns: "The Wickedest Little City in America," 1872–1886.* Lincoln: University of Nebraska Press, 1998.

Wishart, David J., ed. *Encyclopedia of the Great Plains.* Lincoln: University of Nebraska Press, 2004.

Douglass, Frederick (1817–1895)

A platform orator and advocate of the abolitionist, antilynching, temperance, and, later, suffragist movements, organizer Frederick Douglass became the nation's first black adviser to presidents. After escaping slavery at Tuckahoe in Talbot County, Maryland, and fleeing to New York City, he lived with Underground Railroad conductors and learned to read and write.

The change in his outlook attested to the collusion of whites to keep blacks ignorant of freedom and critical thinking, which would make them unfit for bondage. He worked as a shipyard caulker in New Bedford, Massachusetts, where he married runaway Anna Murray.

Under the influence of abolitionist editor William Lloyd Garrison, Douglass joined the speakers' union of the American Anti-Slavery Society and published an autobiography, *Narrative of the Life of Frederick Douglass, an American Slave* (1845) and an abolitionist newspaper, *The North Star.* He applauded the skills of suffragist speaker Lucy Stone, but castigated her for blending antislavery sentiments with women's rights.

Douglass campaigned against Senator Stephen A. Douglas for the election of Abraham Lincoln as in 1860. Upon Lincoln's swearing in as president, Douglass urged him to recruit former slaves for the Union army.

While living in Washington, D.C., Douglass advised President Andrew Johnson, who insulted the orator and his wife with a sneer at the inauguration on March 5, 1865. In July 1867, Douglass rejected a commission to chair the Freedmen's Bureau, which he viewed as a short-term means of placating former slaves.

In defiance of the Jim Crow caste system, he condemned the convict lease system and lynch laws as double infamies of class legislation. To the rise of minstrel Thomas Dartmouth "Daddy" Rice and his imitators, singers of "Jump, Jim Crow," Douglass declared blackface shows disgusting and their distorted stereotypes corrupt. He defended former slaves from charges of laziness and lack of ambition by reminding whites that overcoming war was just the beginning. Blacks had faced such other hurdles as lack of

After the martyrdom of Colonel Robert Gould Shaw and the Fifty-fourth Massachusetts Volunteer Infantry, the U.S. Army's first black regiment, at Fort Wagner, South Carolina, Frederick Douglass reminded the nation that devotion to duty proved the black man a patriot:

> In that terrible battle, under the wing of night, more cavils in respect of the quality of negro manhood were set at rest than could have been during a century of ordinary life and observation. . . . Talk of his ability to meet the foe in the open field, and of his equal fitness with the white man to stop a bullet, then began to prevail.

education, poverty, prejudice, and violence, all of which promised a burnishing of character and resolve.

In 1868, he lectured on the right to vote and edited the weekly *New National Era.* The following year in New Orleans, he presided over the National Convention of Colored Citizens and promoted membership in the Republican Party.

The advancement of blacks occupied Douglass's time and talents. At the May 1869 National Woman's Rights Convention in New York City, he declared that post–Civil War violence against black males made their enfranchisement more urgent than that of women. He faced down angry women's rights leaders, particularly Elizabeth Cady Stanton, president of the National Woman Suffrage Association, who opposed the Fifteenth Amendment to the U.S. Constitution on the grounds that it perpetuated male rights to equality and legislation. Nonetheless, Congress voted to adopt the amendment on February 3, 1870.

Throughout the 1870s, Douglass chaired the Freedmen's Savings and Trust Company, which disappointed him with the disappearance of $40,000 embezzled by dishonest agents. Douglass issued statements of innocence and demanded that the unscrupulous take the blame for missing funds. In 1871, he accepted appointment as assistant secretary of the Santo Domingo Commission, followed by an honorary doctorate from Howard University.

Douglass made memorable comments marking several significant occasions. On April 14, 1876, at the unveiling of the Freedmen's Monument in Washington, D.C., he delivered a tribute to the martyred President Lincoln for signing the Emancipation Proclamation, recognizing that "because of his fidelity to union and liberty, he is doubly dear to us, and his memory will be precious for ever." During the suffrage campaign of the Reverend Olympia Brown, Lucy Stone, and Stone's husband, hardware dealer Henry Brown "Harry" Blackwell, in summer 1876 in Lawrence, Leavenworth, and Topeka, Kansas, Douglass lambasted women's rights advocates for rating women's needs over those of black males. "There are no Ku Klux Clans seeking the lives of women," he thundered. In opposition to Richard Theodore Greener, a Harvard-trained classical scholar and philosopher and the first black professor at the University of South Carolina, Douglass rebuked blacks for migrating to the North in search of better lives.

He advanced to U.S. marshal of the District of Columbia in 1877 and, in 1884, aroused public denunciation of miscegenation by marrying a white woman, Helen Pitts, his second wife. Douglass remained active until his last days on February 20, 1895, when he collapsed while delivering a speech promoting women's rights.

See also: Brown, Olympia; Child, Lydia Maria; Education; Emancipation Proclamation; Fifteenth Amendment; Jim Crow; Lincoln, Abraham; Stanton, Elizabeth Cady; Stone, Lucy.

Further Reading

Horton, James Oliver, and Lois E. Horton. *Slavery and the Making of America.* New York: Oxford University Press, 2005.

McFeely, William S. *Frederick Douglass.* New York: W.W. Norton, 1991.

Myers, Peter C. *Frederick Douglass: Race and the Rebirth of American Liberalism.* Lawrence: University Press of Kansas, 2008.

Noll, Mark A. *God and Race in American Politics: A Short History.* Princeton, NJ: Princeton University Press, 2008.

Oakes, James. *The Radical and the Republican: Frederick Douglass, Abraham Lincoln, and the Triumph of Antislavery Politics.* New York: W.W. Norton, 2007.

Sneider, Allison L. *Suffragists in an Imperial Age: U.S. Expansion and the Woman Question, 1870–1929.* New York: Oxford University Press, 2008.

Snodgrass, Mary Ellen. *The Underground Railroad: An Encyclopedia of People, Places, and Operations.* Armonk, NY: M.E. Sharpe, 2007.

Draft and Draft Riots

During the Civil War, obligatory military service heightened dissension among a citizenry divided over the nation's first federal military conscription. The compulsory enrollment of men for service in the U.S. Army and U.S. Navy generated dissension among states over quotas to fill in the shortfall of volunteer enlistment. The greatest animosity over draft evasion and civil disobedience to draft law occurred in states with large populations of Catholic males, particularly Irishmen.

Confederate Draft

In the Confederacy, during the first year of the conflict, President Jefferson Davis relied on volunteers. Amid the parades and sectional fervor, most marchers in gray tended to reenlist in exchange for a $50 bounty and a two-month furlough. Soldiers had a choice of cavalry, infantry, or navy service and could change companies on request and elect their own officers.

Southern newspapers jeered at the North, where fears of a rebel invasion and bribes to enlistees indicated less patriotism and diminished manhood. Editorials overlooked the Southern commutation fee of $1,000, by which rich Southerners could pay poor whites to take their place. News reporters also concealed the revolt of deserters and layabouts in the Carolinas, Georgia, and Tennessee who formed gangs that assassinated draft agents and state troopers.

Enthusiasm for the Southern cause quickly waned, particularly in agrarian areas, where seasonal harvests ensured family survival. Around Fort Myers, Florida, clutches of draft dodgers hid out on the range and rustled steers for food. In the Kissimmee River Valley, the Cow Cavalry forced men into the regular army or the reserves, as a home guard to round up shirkers and as drovers of scrub cattle and hogs to Southern encampments and starving townships as far north as Virginia.

To shift from volunteer minutemen to a professional military, Davis began drafting soldiers on April 16, 1862, for a one-year term of service. To keep veterans in the line, the law arbitrarily extended terms of enlistment, depending on need. Resisters declared coercive military service a form of tyranny or bondage and charged the Confederate Congress with favoring any stay-at-home male owning 20 or more slaves. In five Texas counties, German Americans protested the draft, forcing a period of martial law until tempers cooled.

Simultaneously, to meet regimental quotas, conscription expanded eligibility from ages 18–35 to 17–50. The need for replacement troops raised the number of draftees to more than 30 percent of the Southern armies. The call-up in February 1864 left to Davis's discretion the exemption of factory workers.

Union Draft

After President Abraham Lincoln's initial call for 500,000 men, Union states operated individual enlistment systems and formed state regiments, which procured men for three months of service. After the disastrous Battle of Bull Run on July 21, 1861, citizens realized that the war

July 25, 1863.] THE NEW-YORK ILLUSTRAED NEWS. 201

THE MOB TEARING DOWN A PICKET FENCE TO SUPPLY THEM WITH SHILLELAHS ON MONDAY, JULY 13.

MOB MURDERING THE POLICE ON MONDAY, JULY 13.

BRUTAL MURDER OF A NEGRO MAN IN CLARKSON STREET BY THE RIOTERS, WHO STRIPPED OFF HIS CLOTHES AND HUNG HIM TO A TREE, AFTERWARDS BURNING THE BODY, ON MONDAY, JULY 13.

PILLAGING THE ORPHAN ASYLUM, CORNER FORTY-THIRD STREET AND FIFTH AVENUE ON MONDAY, JULY 13.

Engravings from the *New York Illustrated News* dramatize the anti-draft rioting that erupted in that city in June 1863. Working-class protesters objected to draft exemptions for wealthier men who could afford to pay a commutation fee of $300. *(MPI/Stringer/Getty Images)*

would require thousands more men. At New Haven, Connecticut, officers restructured regiments and offered $100 city bounties to accompany $250 in federal compensation and up to $200 from the state for men to leave their families.

In April 1862, at the end of the first twelve months of combat, Secretary of War Edwin M. Stanton, in anticipation of a quick victory, closed recruitment offices, including a tent complex at Independence Square in Philadelphia. By May, he corrected his optimistic evaluation of need and pressed state governors to mobilize more infantry regiments.

In the coming weeks, President Lincoln reevaluated ground strength and petitioned states to answer the nation's call for more soldiers, whether they be citizens or immigrants. He established state quotas, to be filled by July 7, 1862, with fighters obligated to enlistments of three years:

State	Quota (Regiments per State)	Total Regiments
New York	28	28
Pennsylvania	21	21
Ohio	17	17
Massachusetts	12	12
Illinois, Indiana	9	18
Michigan	6	6
Connecticut, Iowa, Maine, New Jersey, Wisconsin	5	25
Kentucky, Maryland, Missouri	4	12
New Hampshire, Tennessee, Vermont, Virginia	2	8
Delaware, Minnesota, Rhode Island	1	3
Total:		**150**

Indiana Governor Oliver Hazard Perry Morton urged President Lincoln to abandon the state quotas and institute a national draft. Out of concern for factory employment, Governor John Albion Andrew of Massachusetts proposed enlisting men west of New England or in Europe. On July 15, 1862, Congress passed the Federal Militia Act, which required 300,000 enlistees. The bill apportioned quotas by state population and limited service to nine months. By August 4, Lincoln demanded 300,000 more recruits.

State systems began with a roll call by the county tax collector and recommendations to the county sheriff, which excluded drunks, madmen, the mentally retarded, paupers, and felons. Hundred-dollar federal bounties and state enticements as high as $450 coaxed men into uniform. A commissioner and surgeon assessed each inductee and exempted those with disabilities, those supporting widows or motherless children, and those in crucial jobs—telegraphy, railroad or ferries, powder mills, government work, teaching, the ministry, medicine and pharmacy, or judgeships. Those eluding call-up by fleeing to Canada or Mexico faced federal arrest warrants. Con artists collected cash deposits by promising immunity from the draft.

Media interest in the state-by-state outcome reported the success or failure of various methods of enlisting soldiers:

State	Quota	Total Conscripted	Percentage Filled
New York	59,705	1,781	3
Pennsylvania	45,321	32,215	71.1
Ohio	36,858	0	0
Illinois	26,148	0	0
Indiana	21,250	337	1.6
Massachusetts	19,080	16,685	87.4
Minnesota	17,269	0	0
Wisconsin	11,904	958	8
Michigan	11,686	0	0
New Jersey	10,478	10,787	103
Maine	9,609	7,620	79.3
Maryland	8,532	0	0
Connecticut	7,145	5,602	78.4
New Hampshire	5,053	1,736	34.4
Vermont	4,898	4,781	97.6
Rhode Island	2,712	2,059	76.0
Delaware	1,720	1,799	104.6
Total:	**299,368**	**86,360**	**28.8**

By September 3, 1862, new regiments marched south from Connecticut, Massachusetts, New Jersey, New York, and Pennsylvania. Meanwhile, complaints of elitism echoed through Maryland, Pennsylvania, and Wisconsin. At Port Washington, Wisconsin, on November 10, a throng of 1,000 Belgian Catholic men and women wielded pitchforks and a ceremonial cannon at the residence of Draft Commissioner William A. Pors, a German Protestant and Republican from Hamburg. The mob burned draft rolls and stoned Pors on the courthouse steps until he was able to take shelter in the post office cellar. Six companies of the state militia arrived by steamer over Lake Michigan from Milwaukee and arrested 130 draft resisters, who served 12-month prison sentences at Camp Randall in Madison.

President Abraham Lincoln's National Conscription Act (or Enrollment Act) of February 16, 1863, called up able-bodied single white males ages 20–45 and married men ages 20–35 to register for the draft by May 3. A *New York Times* editorial applauded the troop levy as proof that the Union intended to prevail over secessionists or over any foreign power daring to threaten the United States. The law offered a bounty—$25 at the time of recruitment and the remaining $75 upon mustering out—and permitted a commutation fee of $300, by which draftees could hire substitute soldiers, usually poor men or immigrants.

The quota system proved unwieldy and inequitable to Irish immigrants, who protested both abolition and the draft. The opposition interpreted the call-up as a class-, faith-, and race-based sacrifice of Irish males to free black slaves. Out of nearly 250,000 men chosen for examination, 94 percent escaped service. Corrupt physicians classed healthy men as unfit for combat. Legal loopholes allowed shirkers to claim medical or occupational exemptions. Of the 2.1 million soldiers in the Union army, 92 percent enlisted; of the remaining 8 percent, three-fourths accepted pay to fight for draft resisters.

In the ranks, volunteers suspected conscripts, who lowered morale by their poor attitude toward the military and patriotism. In response to the uneven enrollment of social classes for national service, officers battled desertion, self-mutilation of fingers and toes to escape service, bounty jumping, and requests for nullification of enlistment.

Draft Riots

During summer 1863, antidraft riots, abetted by rabble-rousing in the *New York Daily News,* erupted across the North, sparking the nation's largest and bloodiest civil insurrection to that time. Irrationally, some 70,000 lawless whites led by Irish workers blamed blacks for causing national disunity and worker exploitation and for competing for jobs at the custom house, docks, Staten Island Ferry, and tobacco warehouses. In the absence of the Seventh and Seventy-first New York militias, anarchists had free rein to brawl in the streets with cart staves, angle irons, and clubs. Worsening the situation, the repeal of exemptions for volunteer firefighters struck directly at the Irish.

At an emotional peak two days after the state draft lottery, mobs erupted in tenements along Third Avenue in the Five Points district of Lower Manhattan, where two-thirds of the residents were immigrants. Over July 13–16, insurrectionists from foundries, machine shops, railroads, shipyards, and street gangs stopped trains, ransacked draft offices, and looted and burned the Colored Orphan Asylum, the Black Joke Engine Company, Grand Central Station, and a boardinghouse for black sailors.

In a show of class hatred, gangs of unskilled workers—barbers, bootblacks, brick makers, coachmen, cooks, hod carriers, launderers, longshoremen, porters, stablemen, waiters, and whitewashers—aimed to control the city. They set their sights on seizing the U.S. Treasury vaults, banks, communications centers, forts, shipyards, and major roadways. Individuals stoned rich Republicans and their Fifth Avenue mansions, and vented anger against the Internal Revenue office and the *New York Tribune* building on Park Row. Raiders set fire to the high-toned Brooks Brothers clothing store. Bands demolished rail lines and telegraph wires, slew black pedestrians, and lynched blacks, police, and the "$300 men" who had paid their way out of the draft. Vindictive marauders drowned black longshoremen and set fire to corpses dangling from trees and lampposts. A prime target, Police Superintendent John Alexander Kennedy, suffered a beating that left him with 72 gashes and a crippled leg. At Oliver's Livery Stable on the East River, Colonel Henry T. O'Brien suffered choking with a stick and died of a shot to the skull for discharging a howitzer down Second Avenue and killing a woman and child.

On the second day, throngs gained strength and audacity. To protect the city's financial nerve center and, by extension, national security, the U.S. Navy anchored a warship off Wall Street and loaded cannon with grapeshot. The Bank Note Company stirred vats of sulfuric acid; custom house employees made bombs. William Magear "Boss" Tweed, the grand sachem of Tammany Hall, calmed angry Irish workmen and patrolled the streets to halt violence and arson, which left 3,000 homeless and destitute.

In addition to buying positive media coverage, Tweed earned respect for devising draft exemptions for firemen, militia, and police. To equalize the war's burden on all eligible men, Tweed proposed establishing a lottery system involving the spin of a wooden wheel to select draftees. Mayor George Opdyke pressed the city council to appropriate $2 million to buy draft exemptions for the underclass. Irish slum dwellers, realizing their numerical clout, turned Tammany Hall into a powerful political machine.

While 20 percent of nonwhite residents fled the city, a British-style metropolitan police force of 1,500 and fire departments battled the class and ethnic war. Arson and threats against the *New York Tribune,* Armory, and residences of prominent Republicans required the mounting of Gatling guns on wagons. Four regiments of federal troops and three of state militia battled the final foray on the evening of July 16, when the riot converged on Gramercy Park. Some 120 insurgents died. Police, aided by militia and cadets from West Point, could not halt the burning of 50 buildings and the loss of $5 million in private property. By the time 10,000 Union troops from Gettysburg, Pennsylvania, enforced peace, the death count had reached 125.

Assistant Provost Marshal Robert Nugent published in the press the suspension of the draft in Manhattan and Brooklyn. Upon returning, black residents formed "Little Africa," a protective enclave in Greenwich Village. A week later, editorial commentary in *Harper's Weekly* charged ignorant slum dwellers with misconstruing exemptions for business owners, whose loss to the city would result in widespread unemployment. Long after the riot, Americans stigmatized the Irish as thugs.

Spreading Discontent

To the north and northwest, more rumblings sparked threats and violence at Albany, New York; Jersey City and Newark, New Jersey; Toledo, Ohio; Evansville, Illinois; Boston, Massachusetts; and Watertown, Wisconsin. To prevent the economic collapse of Yorktown, New York, men eligible for the draft paid $30 each to a mutual treasury to persuade farmhands and carpenters to serve in place of the town's more prestigious males. In southern Illinois, Indiana, and Missouri, factions resisted the draft and grumbled at inflation and the waste of the federal treasury on war debts. The Michigan frigate *Georgian* landed squads of marines at Buffalo and Milwaukee in August 1863 to quell 7,000 draft rioters, who attempted to torch grain elevators.

While Northern volunteers rallied to the recruiting song "We Are Coming, Father Abraham, Three Hundred Thousand More," Mennonite preachers denounced conscription from the pulpit. In December, Kentucky recruiters coerced several Shaker draftees into service at Bowling Green. Pacifism also set Quakers apart from mainline faiths, but allied them with the Amish, Dunkards, Hutterites, and nonreligious pacifists, who faced derision and barbarity for their refusal to arm and fight in the Civil War.

At the request of prominent Philadelphia Quakers, Lincoln intervened in death sentences and paroled dissenters from daily torment. On December 30, 1863, he communicated through Secretary of War Edwin M. Stanton the reclassification of Mennonites, Quakers, and Shakers as conscientious objectors. Stanton paroled all Union pacifist prisoners of war who declined to pay a fine. By February 24, 1864, when an amended Conscription Act declared conscientious objectors official noncombatants, President Lincoln expressed his sympathy for pacifists and allowed them to keep their military mounts.

At an upturn of Union victories in March 1864, Lincoln drafted 200,000 more men, reorganized the pension program, and launched a series of national cemeteries for interment of fallen soldiers. Secretary of the Treasury William Pitt Fessenden advised Lincoln to accept fugitive blacks in the military; he also denounced the recruitment of Irish and German immigrants, while rich white males paid as much as $800 to escape the draft.

For a new call-up of 500,000 draftees on July 18, 1864, Congress rid the process of elitism by repealing commutation fees, which the Confederacy had abandoned six months earlier. Because of the rise in draft-age male converts, hawks accused Dunkard, Mennonite, and Quaker congregations of harboring cowards. Military leaders advocated prison at hard labor for men they called slackers, malingerers, and combat evaders.

See also: Lincoln, Abraham; New York City.

Further Reading

Beckert, Sven. *The Monied Metropolis: New York City and the Consolidation of the American Bourgeoisie, 1850–1896.* Cambridge, UK: Cambridge University Press, 2003.

Bruce, Susannah Ural. *The Harp and the Eagle: Irish-American Volunteers and the Union Army: 1861–1865.* New York: New York University Press, 2006.

Smith, Adam I.P. *No Party Now: Politics in the Civil War North.* Oxford, UK: Oxford University Press, 2006.

Snodgrass, Mary Ellen. *Civil Disobedience: An Encyclopedic History of Dissidence in the United States.* Armonk, NY: M.E. Sharpe, 2009.

Stephenson, Nathaniel W. *Abraham Lincoln and the Union.* New York: BiblioBazaar, 2008.

E

Education

By the 1860s, Americans expected to meet the demands of the Industrial Revolution and modernization through universal education. After the Civil War drained communities of staff and principals, postwar enthusiasts reopened and enlarged schools.

The steady influx of non-English-speaking immigrants required a different type of coursework to acclimate newcomers to civic and industrial pluralism. To avoid the assimilative goals of public systems, Irish and Slavic Catholics and German Lutherans founded parochial institutions such as St. Patrick High School in Chicago; the Daughters of Charity school in Virginia City, Nevada; and Gwynedd Mercy Academy in Gwynedd Valley, Pennsylvania. In Guilford County, North Carolina, Quakers typically homeschooled their children, producing a respectable reading comprehension rate among the devout. In 1874, the Young Men's Hebrew Association in Manhattan offered youth lectures, Bible and Hebrew classes, a library, and coursework in bookkeeping, drafting, physical education, and shorthand.

Newcomers to America invested in foreign-language teaching and scriptural lessons as molders of character and pride. Textbooks maintained the dialect, ethics, and mores of their motherlands, such as the philosophy and language at Greek Orthodox schools and the German stories read at the nation's first kindergarten, which opened with a German faculty in St. Louis, Missouri, in 1873. The same attitude prevailed in Hawaii, where missionaries taught from textbooks in the Kanaka language. After-school programs in California taught Chinese American children Mandarin and brush writing. In Cincinnati, Ohio, Moritz Loth, founder of the Union of American Hebrew Congregations, energized plans for opening Jewish preparatory schools and outlined Torah curricula that preserved Jewish identity. To shield Hasidic culture and beliefs from Americanization, ultraconservative Jews built neighborhood day schools where the Hebrew language dominated. In large Catholic parishes, schools allowed only one ethnicity, such as German, Greek, Irish, Lithuanian, or Polish. In Detroit, Michigan, Father Joseph Dabrowski published in Polish a reader and math and geography texts. These curricula isolated rather than democratized first-generation citizens.

New initiatives for the disabled normalized an underserved population. In 1868 at the Maryland School for the Deaf and Dumb in Frederick, teachers offered both academics and life-based lessons in lip reading and speech as requirements for a high school diploma. Compassion for the deaf expanded to black children in North Carolina after the establishment in 1869 of the Governor Morehead School at Raleigh, the first institution in the nation to train former slaves.

In April 1871, educator Alexander Graham Bell taught at Sarah Fuller's School for Deaf Mutes in Boston, the first to impart speech to the hearing impaired. The *Boston Journal* and the *American Annals of the Deaf and Dumb* acknowledged Bell's revolutionary pedagogy and advice to special education teachers on developing language skills in young pupils. In October 1872, he applied the methods outlined in his pamphlet *Visible Speech Pioneer* (1872) to educating 30 pupils at the School of Vocal Physiology and Mechanics of Speech, his training center in Boston.

Schools for the blind incorporated textbooks in embossed letters and raised dots, the hybridization of a French system known as American Braille. Congress subsidized printing houses that produced books for the blind.

Less advanced philosophies of education for the deaf-blind and for the learning-impaired reduced classroom opportunities to the kindergarten level and to vocational centers such as the Cincinnati Workhouse; a state asylum in Glenwood, Iowa; and the Institute for Deaf and Dumb, and Blind at Romney, West Virginia. Students learned to be brick and broom makers, caners, cobblers, cooks, knitters, launderers, and seamstresses.

Revised Curricula

American towns increased standards for youth by extending the number of years of schooling with more high schools and curricula that offered both traditional subjects—arithmetic, geography, grammar, history, Latin, reading, writing—and utilitarian training. On the frontier, missionaries brought literacy to Indians at trading posts and remote outposts, such as the Methodist training center of the Reverend James Harvey Wilbur and Lucretia Ann Wilbur at Yakima, Washington, and classes for Chickasaw and Choctaw at Elliot Academy in Smithville, Oklahoma. Community-minded areas such as Westerville, Ohio; Boulder, Colorado; and Fargo, North Dakota, set high standards for one-room schools. In Sioux Falls, South Dakota, students made do with a sod shanty; in Phoenix, Arizona, 21 local children assembled in a single-room adobe house.

In the South, learning varied by pedigree, race, and gender. Rich planters hired tutors for homeschooling and sent their sons and, with less frequency, their daughters to private academies. Because poor white children received no schooling, the state of Georgia launched a literacy initiative in 1870 that more than quadrupled enrollment and opened schools for six months a year.

Where states prohibited education for slaves, clandestine efforts brought literacy to blacks. In Macon, Georgia, groups of 50 clustered around a single teacher in unheated buildings lacking books, seats, and slates. Before the end of the Civil War, white volunteers, black preachers, members of the American Missionary Association, and freedmen established literacy classes in areas where ex-slaves flocked to embrace liberty. During the transition, the Freedmen's Bureau, headed by General Oliver Otis Howard, nourished and shielded blacks while training them for citizenship. In 1866, during an era of racial separation in classrooms, New Orleans set an example of desegregation. By contrast, in 1871, the board of education in Lynchburg, Virginia, carried separation to the extreme by dividing children according to gender, race, and religion.

By 1876, the demand for free, tax-supported public education for all Americans spread to rural areas, the least served by state systems. Rather than preparation of the elite for universities, progressive educators sought methods of meeting universal needs. A more democratic process balanced readings from the classics with vocational training based on technological and scientific advancements in chemistry, psychology, public sanitation, and immunology. In Boston and Philadelphia, tenement workers welcomed immigrant women to home economics classes that enlightened mothers to the nutritional needs of children, the elderly, and invalids and to foods and cooking styles that made the most of limited budgets. Enlightened teachers valued the individuality of each child and created classroom environments that addressed different interests, talents, and abilities, including those of handicapped children.

Beginning in 1866, the Freedmen's Bureau spent $5 million in federal funds to open schools for former slaves—for whom education had been forbidden. By 1870, there were more than 1,000 schools for free blacks across the South. *(The Granger Collection, New York)*

Controversy

Shifts in educational theory generated debate among leaders of the field. Reformer William Torrey Harris, superintendent of the St. Louis public schools in 1868, denounced the narrow formalism of traditional classical instruction and proposed educating the whole child to produce independent thinkers. Advocating the German idealism of Georg Hegel, Harris's oratory opposed manual training and practical education and defended the cultural and spiritual values of classical education that introduced youths to the cultural riches of the past.

Philosopher John Dewey advocated "instrumentalism" (learning through problem solving) and promoted individual research, such as cultivating seeds and plants and fostering creativity through writing workshops and laboratory experiments. Dewey advocated training a cadre of more flexible teachers at schools of education and envisioned preparing boys for the construction industry through trade schools that taught bricklaying, carpentry, plastering, and plumbing.

Geography professor Daniel Coit Gilman, president of Johns Hopkins University, opposed traditional lectures, notebook copying, and rote recitation. He supported instruction in the sciences and social sciences in Connecticut grammar schools and high schools and advocated ongoing teacher education through journals and professional associations.

Charles William Eliot, a chemistry professor at the Massachusetts Institute of Technology and later president of Harvard University, redefined the public school curriculum to prepare students for higher learning. He advanced uniform guidelines for college preparation and outlined free electives to allow students to select courses that interested them. Labor activist Washington Gladden embraced flexible education for validating the working classes, especially nonwhite citizens. Felix Adler, founder of the Ethical Culture Movement, stripped superstitious traditions from Jewish education and focused on ethical behavior.

As women learned about self-assertion from the abolitionist movement, female education increased dramatically by 1865. Under the Morrill Land-Grant Act of 1862, women broadened their personal goals to include public and private education and a choice of professions. The expansion of public education in the South, West, and rural areas everywhere created a need for teachers. Forward-thinking females chose coeducational colleges, such as California State Normal School in San José and Swarthmore at Pendle Hill, Pennsylvania. Overall, coeds found curricula lacking in preparation for the classroom and gender prejudiced in barring them from such courses as anatomy and human reproduction, considered indelicate for girls. All-female colleges, especially the "Seven Sisters"—Barnard, Bryn Mawr, Mount Holyoke, Radcliffe, Smith, Vassar, and Wellesley—opened coursework to women and prepared them to teach open-minded lessons to boys and girls. Defying the trend toward intellectual advancement in women, Edward H. Clarke's treatise *Sex in Education* (1873) maintained that females lacked the physical or emotional stamina to profit from rigorous study.

See also: Bell, Alexander Graham; Colleges and Universities; Home Economics; Literacy.

Further Reading

Brandt, Deborah. *Literacy in American Lives.* Cambridge, UK: Cambridge University Press, 2001.

Jones-Wilson, Faustine C., et al., eds. *Encyclopedia of African-American Education.* Westport, CT: Greenwood, 1996.

Rose, Willie Lee. *Rehearsal for Reconstruction: The Port Royal Experiment.* Athens: University of Georgia Press, 1999.

Sowell, Thomas. *Ethnic America: A History.* New York: Basic Books, 2000.

Williams, Heather Andrea. *Self-Taught: African American Education in Slavery and Freedom.* Chapel Hill: University of North Carolina Press, 2005.

Education, Higher

See Colleges and Universities

Election of 1860

The election of Abraham Lincoln to the U.S. presidency in 1860 signaled a triumph for the pro-North, antislavery Republican Party. Party loyalty firmed up in 1856 at its first convention, held at Lafayette Hall in Allegheny County, Pennsylvania, where Lincoln's oratory won him a two-year term in the U.S. House of Representatives. His denunciation of the Mexican-American War and of the U.S. Supreme Court's *Dred Scott* (1857) decision established his championship of human rights and national sovereignty.

During an unsuccessful run for the U.S. Senate in 1858, Lincoln warned that the unresolved issue of slavery threatened the Union. In debates with his Democratic opponent that year, U.S. Senator Stephen A. Douglas, Lincoln

Election of 1860: The Vote

Party/Candidates	Popular Vote	Electoral Vote	States (Electoral Votes)
Republican Abraham Lincoln (Illinois) Hannibal Hamlin (Maine)	1,855,993 (40%)	180 (59%)	California (4), Connecticut (6), Illinois (11), Indiana (13), Iowa (4), Maine (8), Massachusetts (13), Michigan (6), Minnesota (4), New Hampshire (5), New Jersey (4*), New York (35), Ohio (23), Oregon (3), Pennsylvania (27), Rhode Island (4), Vermont (5), Wisconsin (5)
Southern Democratic John C. Breckinridge (Kentucky) Joseph Lane (North Carolina)	851,844 (18%)	72 (24%)	Alabama (9), Arkansas (4), Delaware (3), Florida (3), Georgia (10), Louisiana (6), Maryland (8), Mississippi (7), North Carolina (10), South Carolina (8), Texas (4)
Constitutional Union John Bell (Tennessee) Edward Everett (Massachusetts)	590,946 (13%)	39 (13%)	Kentucky (12), Tennessee (12), Virginia (15)
Northern Democratic Stephen A. Douglas (Vermont) Herschel Johnson (Georgia)	1,381,940 (29%)	12 (4%)	Missouri (9), New Jersey (3*)
Total:	**4,680,723**	**303**	**33 states**

**Note:* New Jersey split its seven electoral votes 4–3 for Lincoln and Douglas, respectively.

asserted a compelling personal and professional integrity and respect for law. Douglas denounced secessionism and promoted the concept of popular sovereignty, which failed to sway Southern slave owners seeking assurance of their rights of property.

Before an audience of 1,500 at the Cooper Union for the Advancement of Science and Art in New York City on February 27, 1860, Lincoln impressed the Young Men's Republican Union, led by two abolitionists—author William Cullen Bryant and editor Horace Greeley. Lincoln voiced his intent to halt the spread of slavery into the American West. His research into the beliefs of 39 signers of the U.S. Constitution attested that 21, or nearly 54 percent, favored blocking the advance of human bondage into the territories. His three-stage argument debased the legitimacy of states' rights and defused threats of Southern withdrawal from the Union. A standing ovation recognized the speaker's logic, respect for the Constitution, and power to stir listeners. The *New York Tribune* printed the speech, which the Republican Party circulated in support of Lincoln's candidacy over challengers U.S. Senator William Henry Seward of New York; the former governor of Ohio, Salmon P. Chase; and attorney Edward Bates of Virginia. On a two-week tour of New England, Lincoln followed up with 11 speeches and earned the nicknames "Honest Abe" and "The Rail Splitter," a metaphor blending his frontier origins with his strike to the heart of false reasoning.

On the third ballot of the Republican National Convention in Chicago's Wigwam on May 18, 1860, to a deafening accolade, Lincoln seized the Republican nomination for U.S. president. His running mate, Hannibal Hamlin, a U.S. senator from Maine, became the front-runner for vice president after two votes. Lincoln allowed the abolitionist media and a flurry of campaign propaganda, including the earliest use of portrait campaign buttons, to win voters to the Republican ticket. A platform of protective tariffs, free farmland in the West, and completion of a transcontinental railroad sealed Lincoln's fate in the South. Illogically, the Charleston *Mercury* smeared him as a miscegenationist favoring biracial families.

On November 6, 1860, an 81 percent turnout of registered voters proved the people's concern for issues. Winning a plurality of sectional support in 16 Northern states plus California and Oregon, Lincoln and Hamlin carried 1,855,993, or 39.6 percent of the popular vote. According to a report in *Harper's Weekly,* they garnered only two of the South's 996 counties and received no support in nine Southern states. The duo claimed 180, or 59.4 percent, of 303 electoral votes, thus besting three contending pairs of opponents and making Lincoln the sixteenth president of the United States.

The victory dealt Democrats a smashing blow and forced Southern states' rights proponents to reexamine their tactics after dominating the presidency since 1789. As a result of the Republican sweep, South Carolina seceded from the Union on December 20, 1860, setting off a domino effect across the Deep South and into Florida and Texas. At a fearful pass in American history, the loss of 11 states tipped Congress toward Republican control, with 33 senators and 85 representatives in Lincoln's camp.

See also: Lincoln, Abraham.

Further Reading

Burlingame, Michael. *The Inner World of Abraham Lincoln.* Urbana: University of Illinois Press, 1997.

Holzer, Harold. *Lincoln at Cooper Union: The Speech That Made Abraham Lincoln President.* New York: Simon & Schuster, 2004.

Snodgrass, Mary Ellen. *The Underground Railroad: An Encyclopedia of People, Places, and Operations.* Armonk, NY: M.E. Sharpe, 2007.

Stephenson, Nathaniel W. *Abraham Lincoln and the Union.* New York: BiblioBazaar, 2008.

Election of 1864

A crucial wartime selection process, the presidential election of 1864 required a gesture of compromise toward inclusion and a change of name for the Republicans, to the National Union Party. Because of the uncertain outcome of the Civil War, U.S. Secretary of the Treasury Salmon P. Chase, newspaper editor Horace Greeley, and U.S. Senator Benjamin Franklin Wade questioned whether Lincoln could win a second term on the basis of his lenient Reconstruction plan. The National Union banner, led by a Western hero and radical abolitionist, General John Charles Frémont of Georgia, made

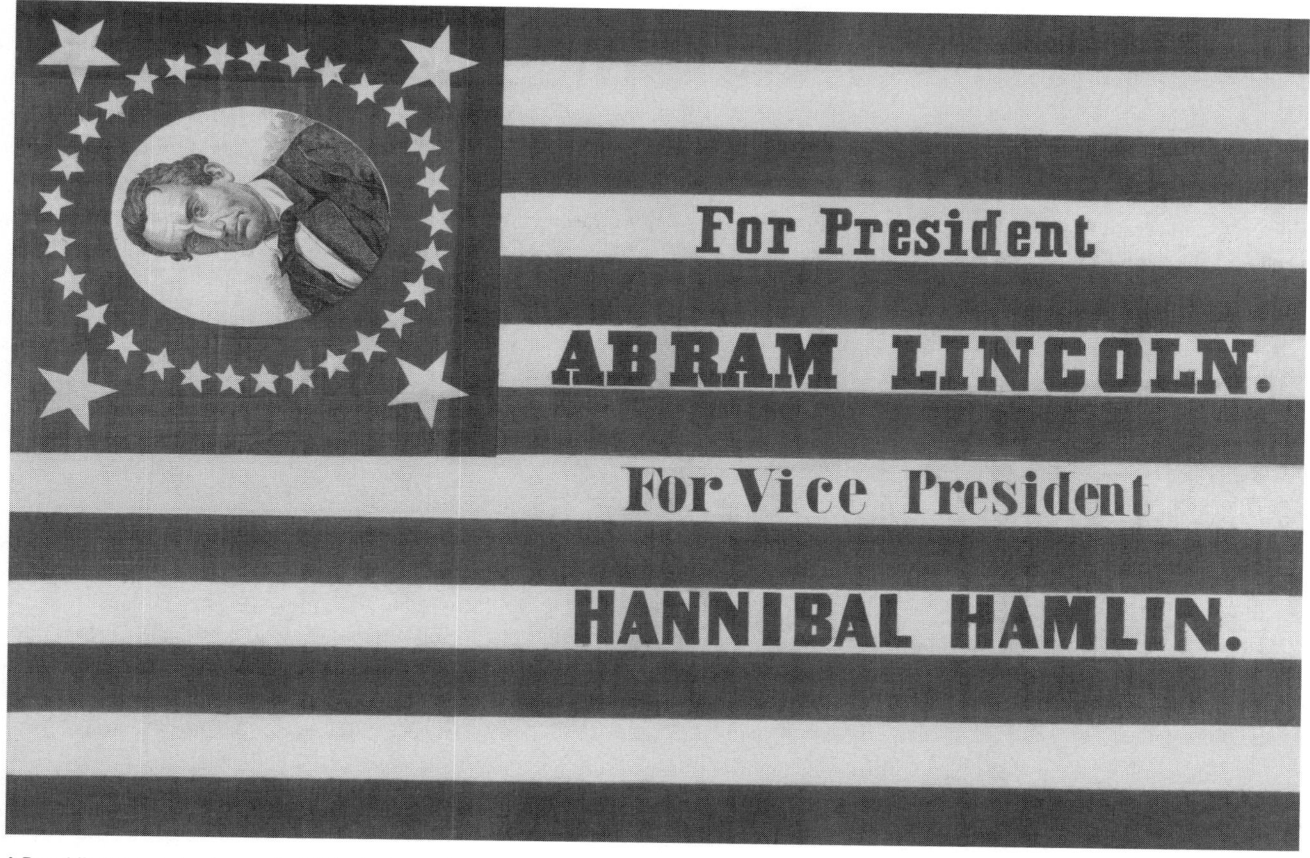

A Republican campaign banner in 1860 introduces the party's candidates, presidential nominee "Abram" Lincoln of Illinois and his running mate, Senator Hannibal Hamlin of Maine. *(Buyenlarge/Getty Images)*

room for War Democrats, who favored the nomination of General Ulysses S. Grant. Dedicated to winning the war and restoring the Union, Grant recoiled from the idea of running for public office and urged the party to remain loyal to the commander in chief.

The first presidential candidate to oppose slavery, Frémont earned the backing of editor Manton Marble of the New York *World* and the *New Nation* and the personal support of orator Frederick Douglass, abolitionist Wendell Phillips, and suffragist Elizabeth Cady Stanton. On August 29, General George McClellan easily beat former Congressman Thomas H. Seymour of Connecticut to become the standard-bearer of the badly splintered Democratic Party, which favored an immediate negotiation to end the war. McClellan stopped short of declaring the conflict a failure, but he lambasted Lincoln for issuing the Emancipation Proclamation and for mishandling the military. The Democrats called for a cease-fire. Republicans riposted by jeering at McClellan's wartime performance during the Peninsula Campaign of 1862 and at the Battle of Antietam later that year and by labeling all Democrats traitors to the Union.

Lincoln's Doubts

Even with a North Carolinian, Senator Andrew Johnson, a former slave owner, as his running mate, Lincoln doubted the strength of the Union cause among Northerners. Notably, support ebbed in Indiana, New York, and Pennsylvania. In 1862, Democrats had gained seats in Congress. The following year, Radical Republicans had chafed at Lincoln's failure to activate black regiments and at his lenient Reconstruction plan.

Patience with the war effort thinned after the Confederate victory at the Battle of Mansfield, Louisiana, on April 8, 1864, cost the army 2,235 soldiers killed, wounded, or captured. A serious loss at the Battle of Cold Harbor, Virginia, in early June depleted the superior strength of Generals Grant and Meade by 12,737 casualties. On July 30, the Battle of the Crater in Petersburg, Virginia, again sapped Union manpower with the loss of 3,798 combatants.

Meanwhile, citizens were suspicious of the paper money issued under the Legal Tender Act of 1862. Taxpayers resented the Revenue Act of 1862, which levied excise taxes on alcohol, jewelry, tobacco, and yachts. They despised the Office of Internal Revenue, which collected taxes on inheritance and corporations and a license tax on all professions except the clergy. In southern Illinois and in Missouri, factions resisted the draft and grumbled at inflation and the waste of the federal treasury on war debts.

At a turning point in the national outlook, unprecedented Union victories buoyed the Lincoln campaign. General William Tecumseh Sherman's capture of Atlanta on September 2 contributed to the president's reelection, as did Admiral David Farragut's seizure of Mobile Bay on August 5, General Philip Sheridan's victory in the Shenandoah Valley on September 19, and General Grant's September advance on Petersburg. A significant boost came from Horace Greeley, editor of the *New York Tribune,* who threw his support to Lincoln.

On September 17, 1864, Frémont, a potential Republican spoiler, favored winning the war over winning the

Election of 1864: The Vote

Party/Candidates	Popular Vote	Electoral Vote	States (Electoral Votes)
National Union Abraham Lincoln (Illinois) Andrew Johnson (North Carolina)	2,211,317 (55%)	212 (91%)	California (4), Connecticut (6), Illinois (16), Indiana (13), Iowa (8), Kansas (3), Maine (7), Maryland (7), Massachusetts (12), Michigan (8), Minnesota (4), Missouri (11), Nevada (2), New Hampshire (5), New York (33), Ohio (21), Oregon (3), Pennsylvania (26), Rhode Island (4), Vermont (5), West Virginia (5), Wisconsin (8)
Democratic George McClellan (New Jersey) George Pendleton (Ohio)	1,806,227 (45%)	21 (9%)	Delaware (3), Kentucky (11), New Jersey (7)
Total:	**4,017,544**	**233**	**25 states**

Note: The 11 Confederate states did not vote in the election.

White House. He made a private deal with Lincoln to withdraw from the campaign in exchange for Lincoln's removal from the cabinet of Postmaster General Montgomery Blair, a conservative malcontent.

Republican Victory

Against a Democratic plan to negotiate an end to the war and an honorable reconciliation of the Union, Lincoln's campaign forged ahead under a banner of unconditional surrender of the Confederacy. In late fall 1864, Secretary of War Edwin M. Stanton contributed to the Republican victory by arranging furloughs and distributing absentee ballots to Union sailors and soldiers, who were heavily pro-Lincoln, pro-Union, and antislavery. Helping to secure a win, working-class Americans—farmers, former military, and skilled laborers, especially in New England—and first-time voters championed the president. Democrats relied on turnout among Irish and German immigrants.

On election day, McClellan foresaw defeat and resigned his army commission. Cartoons pictured "Little Mac" as a disappointment to disillusioned Union soldiers, who favored "Uncle Abe's" stringent outlook on war and abolition. Deeply shaken, McClellan retreated into seclusion and remained mum on his reasons for ending his military and political career.

Nearly 74 percent of the electorate went to the polls on November 8, 1864. An easy victory and an electoral landslide returned Lincoln to the White House.

The election was the first for any nation embroiled in a major war. Lincoln interpreted the results as public support for the abolition of slavery and for his performance as commander in chief. Two days later, he congratulated the citizenry on conducting the nation's business, despite four years of civil turmoil. The victory put at Lincoln's disposal 149, or more than 78 percent, of Republican votes in the U.S. House of Representatives and 42, or 81 percent, in the Senate.

Six weeks later, Vice President Andrew Johnson found himself in the unenviable position of replacing Lincoln, who died of an assassin's bullet on April 15, 1865. No one succeeded Johnson as vice president.

See also: Lincoln, Abraham; Reconstruction.

Further Reading

Burlingame, Michael. *The Inner World of Abraham Lincoln.* Urbana: University of Illinois Press, 1997.

Holzer, Harold. *Lincoln at Cooper Union: The Speech That Made Abraham Lincoln President.* New York: Simon & Schuster, 2004.

Sears, Stephen W. *George B. McClellan: The Young Napoleon.* New York: Da Capo, 1999.

Stephenson, Nathaniel W. *Abraham Lincoln and the Union.* New York: BiblioBazaar, 2008.

Waugh, John C. *Reelecting Lincoln: The Battle for the 1864 Presidency.* New York: Da Capo, 2001.

Election of 1868

The first American presidential contest during Reconstruction, the election of 1868 attested to the popularity of a Union military hero, General Ulysses S. Grant, and to the firm hold that Republicans had on the nation's business. In contrast lay the political suicide of President Andrew Johnson, who destroyed his chances for reelection through petty tiffs with Congress, grudge holding toward the South, and enmity toward the wealthy.

At their assembly in Chicago on May 21, 1868, Republicans chose Grant as their candidate on the first ballot. The selection of Speaker of the House Schuyler Colfax as Grant's running mate required five ballots, as delegates pondered the chances of U.S. Senator Benjamin Franklin Wade and Reuben Fenton, governor of New York.

In a broad field that included General Winfield Scott Hancock and incumbent Andrew Johnson, the Democratic convention in New York City on July 9, 1868, chose a dark horse, attorney and businessman Horatio Seymour, two-time governor of New York, on the twenty-second ballot. In a headline, *The New York Times* reported the selection as "unanticipated." Seymour's running mate, former congressman Francis Preston Blair of Kentucky, who had abandoned the Republican Party over Reconstruction policies, won his candidacy on the first ballot.

The platforms of the Democrats and Republicans differed in tone. Seymour, a fiscal conservative, proposed limiting executive powers and repaying the war debt with greenbacks rather than gold. Democratic backers promised to speed up the Reconstruction process. The Democratic media reviled Grant as a drunkard; voters, however, identified the victorious general with patriotism and with grief for Abraham Lincoln's martyrdom. Although Grant chose not to campaign, he tapped into the national yearning for peace and an end to political character assassination in Washington.

Abetted by cartoons and editorials in the *New York Tribune,* the *New York Post,* and the *Hartford Post,* the Republican political machine libeled Seymour as a traitor, coward, and warmonger born of a mentally unstable father who had committed suicide. One cartoon pictured him in the guise

Election of 1868: The Vote

Party/Candidates	Popular Vote	Electoral Vote	States (Electoral Votes)
Republican Ulysses S. Grant (Ohio) Schuyler Colfax (New York)	3,013,790 (53%)	214 (73%)	Alabama (8), Arkansas (5), California (5), Connecticut (6), Florida (3), Illinois (16), Indiana (13), Iowa (8), Kansas (3), Maine (7), Massachusetts (12), Michigan (8), Minnesota (4), Missouri (11), Nebraska (3), Nevada (3), New Hampshire (5), North Carolina (9), Ohio (21), Pennsylvania (26), Rhode Island (4), South Carolina (6), Tennessee (10), Vermont (5), West Virginia (5), Wisconsin (8)
Democratic Horatio Seymour (New York) Francis Preston Blair (Kentucky)	2,708,980 (47%)	80 (27%)	Delaware (3), Georgia (9), Kentucky (6), Louisiana (7), Maryland (7), New York (33), New Jersey (7), Oregon (3)
Total:	5,722,770	294	34 states

Note: Mississippi, Texas, and Virginia did not vote, because they had not yet reentered the Union.

War hero Ulysses S. Grant and running mate Schuyler Colfax supported the Reconstruction plans of fellow Radical Republicans and easily defeated their Democratic opponents, Horatio Seymour and Francis P. Blair, in the 1868 election. *(MPI/Stringer/Getty Images)*

of Shakespeare's Lady Macbeth trying to expunge the stains of past sins from her hand. Rumors convinced voters that Seymour would raise inflation and allow a new outbreak of civil strife. Seymour chose not to engage in public name calling. Instead, he ignored the ad hominem abuse and limited his speeches in the North, charging Congress with weakening the fabric of government by restricting civil rights and by raising the national debt.

Black suffrage won the day for the Republicans. Grant, a swarthy media favorite, gained overwhelming support from 500,000 free black voters for his intent to punish Confederate rebels and to ensure full citizenship and constitutional rights for former slaves. To Grant's detriment, New York's William Magear "Boss" Tweed hustled thousands of Irish immigrants through corrupt naturalization procedures and into citizenship to bolster the Democratic vote. Nonetheless, with a voter turnout of 71.3 percent, the election named Grant the eighteenth president of the United States.

On December 25, 1868, Johnson departed the White House with a final act of clemency, granting unconditional amnesty for Confederates. Grant's inauguration valorized four years of war for the reaffirmation of constitutional values and civil rights. Contributing to the smooth transition was the Republican hold on 171, or nearly 71 percent, of the seats in the U.S. House of Representatives and 62 seats, or nearly 84 percent, in the Senate.

See also: Grant, Ulysses S.; Reconstruction.

Further Reading

Bunting, Josiah, III. *Ulysses S. Grant.* New York: Times Books, 2004.

Campbell, James E. *The American Campaign: U.S. Presidential Campaigns and the National Vote.* 2nd ed. College Station: Texas A&M University Press, 2008.

Heidler, David S., and Jeanne T. Heidler, eds. *Encyclopedia of the American Civil War: A Political, Social, and Military History.* New York: W.W. Norton, 2000.

Reichley, A. James, ed. *Elections American Style.* Washington, DC: Brookings Institution, 1987.

Stanley, George E. *The Era of Reconstruction and Expansion, 1865–1900.* Milwaukee, WI: World Almanac Library, 2005.

Election of 1872

Amid partisan wrangling, President Ulysses S. Grant easily won a second term in the White House on November 5, 1872. The liberal wing of the Republican Party, led by Senator Carl Schurz, had formed officially in Missouri in 1870 to agitate for more honest government, the removal of occupation forces from the South, and an end to Reconstruction. Liberal Republicans included prestigious politicians—among them Chief Justice Salmon P. Chase, Justice David Davis, U.S. senators Reuben Fenton and Charles Sumner, and Congressman George Washington Julian, an advocate of woman suffrage—and gained support from such major newspapers as the *Chicago Tribune,* the *Cincinnati Commercial,* the *Louisville Courier-Journal,* and the *New York Tribune.*

Victoria Claflin Woodhull's leadership of the Equal Rights Party, together with running mate Frederick Douglass, raised questions about women's absence from the governing process. Woodhull's age (34) disqualified her from legal consideration for the presidency, but that did not deter Susan B. Anthony and other females from attempting to vote. Anthony supported Grant because of the antifemale stance of his opponent, Horace Greeley, editor of the *New York Tribune.*

Called the Liberal Republican Party, the splinter group began plotting Grant's ousting at a convention in Cincinnati, Ohio, in April 1872. The media dubbed the anti-Grant faction the "Cincinnati soreheads." That spring, Greeley, a man of considerable influence, shifted his focus from journalism to a challenge against Grant for the White House. Greeley proposed a civil service overhaul and faulted the president with mismanagement. To prevent Grant from winning a second term, the editor abandoned the Radical Republicans and joined forces with the liberal members of the party, who were loath to anoint him as their candidate.

At Baltimore on May 5, on the sixth ballot, Greeley beat an aristocratic New Englander, Charles Francis Adams, Sr., the U.S. ambassador to Great Britain, for the presidential candidacy of the Liberal Republican Party. A political cartoon in *Harper's Weekly* depicted Greeley as a Lilliputian shouting complaints into the ear of "Gulliver Grant."

Conventions and Campaign

Although the messy election process found the parties in disarray, at the Republican convention held at Philadelphia's Academy of Music on June 5, 1872, a torchlight parade, bunting, chains of exotic flowers, and renditions of "Marching Through Georgia" and "John Brown's Body" celebrated the occasion. In lieu of the president, who was in Washington, an oversized portrait of General Grant in uniform on horseback dominated the stage.

In the background, intriguers colluded to dump Vice President Schuyler Colfax, whom the *New York Sun* later shamed for divergence of railroad funds for personal use during the Crédit Mobilier scandal. In Colfax's place, party regulars drafted four-term Massachusetts Senator Henry Wilson, a cobbler and former editor of the *Boston Republican.* For the first time in history, male and female reporters and telegraph operators kept Americans informed immediately of political proceedings.

The next day, Grant's backers claimed credit for a reduced national debt, pacification of Indians, extension of railroads to the West, suffrage for freedmen, the Civil Rights Act of 1871, and peace. Wilson won respect for his 11 years as chair of the Senate Committee on Military Affairs. Republican convention delegates swallowed their distaste for the incumbent's ineptitude and questionable appointments. On the first ballot, they chose Grant, with Wilson as his running mate; the announcement preceded accolades and rounds of "Hail to the Chief."

The candidates appeared on posters wearing carpentry aprons under "The Working Man's Banner." Postelection scrutiny found Wilson suspect of passing Union battle plans to rebel spy Rose O'Neal Greenhow and of bribing a congressman; however, a Senate inquiry found no basis for these charges.

Greeley exercised the journalistic side of his nature, alienating voters and reigniting old animosities with his impolitic opinions. During the campaign, he proposed lowering federal taxes, halting the land grab of railroads and corporations, and protecting free trade and public credit. His personal eccentricities—vegetarianism, spiritualism, and ever-present baggy overcoat and umbrella—and his unpredictable stance on tariffs and postwar amnesty served cartoonist Thomas Nast, who caricatured Greeley in *Harper's Weekly.* On August 10, Nast depicted Greeley as a babe in the woods asleep under a tree.

On September 2, Senator Charles Sumner supported Greeley's candidacy in a speech delivered in Boston at Faneuil Hall. Campaign literature proclaimed Greeley "The People's Choice." The opposition circulated a pamphlet, "One Hundred Reasons Why General Grant Should Not Be Re-Elected," which charged him with prejudice and resentment and compared his administration to the tyranny of Julius Caesar.

Incumbent Victory

Despite Grant's lax governance and his obligations to tycoons Cornelius Vanderbilt and John Jacob Astor III, his campaign discredited the gadfly Greeley. The popular vote of freedmen and veteran Union sailors and soldiers returned the president to the White House.

After losing the November 5 election to Grant and suffering the death of his wife, Greeley died in a sanitarium on November 29, 1872; it was the first death of a national candidate during the electoral process. Greeley's six electoral votes passed to four candidates—Benjamin Gratz Brown, governor of Missouri and Greeley's former running mate; U.S. Supreme Court Justice David Davis of Illinois; Thomas A. Hendricks, governor of Indiana; and Charles Jones Jenkins, governor of Georgia. Congress invalidated three posthumous votes for Greeley from Georgia voters.

Within 12 weeks, Grant and a Republican Congress flourished by passing the General Mining Act and the Amnesty Act. Vice President Henry Wilson suffered a paralytic stroke in 1873 yet continued presiding over the Senate.

Election of 1872: The Vote

Party/Candidates	Popular Vote	Electoral Vote	States (Electoral Votes)
Republican	3,597,439	286	Alabama (10), Arkansas (6), California (5), Connecticut (6), Delaware (3), Florida (4), Illinois (21), Indiana (15), Iowa (11), Kansas (5), Louisiana (8), Maine (7), Massachusetts (13), Michigan (11), Minnesota (5), Mississippi (8), Nebraska (3), Nevada (3), New Hampshire (5), New York (35), New Jersey (9), North Carolina (10), Ohio (22), Oregon (3), Pennsylvania (29), Rhode Island (4), South Carolina (7), Vermont (5), Virginia (11), West Virginia (5), Wisconsin (10)
Ulysses S. Grant (Ohio)	(56%)	(81%)	
Henry Wilson (New Hampshire)			
Liberal Republican	2,833,710	3	Georgia (3*)
Horace Greeley (New York)	(44%)	(0.9%)	
Benjamin Gratz Brown (Kentucky)			
Democratic	0	42	Kentucky (8*), Maryland (8), Missouri (6*), Tennessee (12), Texas (8)
Thomas A. Hendricks (Ohio)		(12%)	
National Union Party	0	18	Georgia (6*), Kentucky (4*), Missouri (8*)
Benjamin Gratz Brown (Kentucky)		(5%)	
Democratic	0	2	Georgia (2*)
Charles J. Jenkins (Georgia)		(0.6%)	
Liberal Republican	0	1	Missouri (1*)
David Davis (Maryland)		(0.3%)	
Total:	6,431,149	**352**	**37 states**

**Note:* The states of Georgia, Kentucky, and Missouri split their electoral votes.

On November 22, 1875, a lethal stroke felled him in the Capitol, leaving Grant without a vice president.

See also: Grant, Ulysses S.; Greeley, Horace.

Further Reading

Bunting, Josiah, III. *Ulysses S. Grant.* New York: Times Books, 2004.

Campbell, James E. *The American Campaign: U.S. Presidential Campaigns and the National Vote.* 2nd ed. College Station: Texas A&M University Press, 2008.

Reichley, A. James, ed. *Elections American Style.* Washington, DC: Brookings Institution, 1987.

Stanley, George E. *The Era of Reconstruction and Expansion, 1865–1900.* Milwaukee, WI: World Almanac Library, 2005.

Williams, Robert C. *Horace Greeley: Champion of American Freedom.* New York: New York University Press, 2006.

Election of 1876

Following the nation's centennial in July, the presidential election of 1876 put to the test the strictures of the U.S. Constitution on the authority of the Electoral College. When Republicans convened at Exposition Hall in Cincinnati on June 14, 1876, Harvard University intellectual James Russell Lowell spoke for Governor Rutherford B. Hayes of Ohio, a dark horse who faced respected contenders for the nomination. Among them were two senators—Oliver Hazard Perry Morton of Indiana and Roscoe Conkling of New York—and Secretary of the Treasury Benjamin Bristow of Kentucky. On the seventh ballot on June 18, Hayes won against his chief competitor, Senator James G. Blaine of Pennsylvania, a two-term secretary of state and former Speaker of the House. The first vice presidential ballot named civil libertarian William A. Wheeler, a veteran U.S. congressman from New York, as Hayes's running mate.

Democrats moved their assembly to Missouri for the first political convention held west of the Mississippi River. Amid fireworks at the St. Louis Merchants Exchange on June 27, Democrats, hungry for a win, pondered the chances of three governors—William Allen of North Carolina, Thomas A. Hendricks of Ohio, and Samuel J. Tilden of New York—and a Union hero of the Civil War, Winfield Scott Hancock of Pennsylvania. An outcry for reform arose because of the mishandling of executive powers during Ulysses S. Grant's eight years in the White House. On the second ballot on June 29, the assembly nominated Tilden, who in 1871 had prosecuted corrupt New York politicians and convicted William Magear "Boss" Tweed of graft, conspiracy, and embezzlement of $6 million from the New York City treasury. Hendricks, Tilden's closest challenger, won the vice presidential nomination on the first ballot.

The Democratic platform called for the ousting of carpetbaggers from the South, tariff reform, limited immigration from Asia, and an end to government land deals with railroad moguls. During the campaign, additional concerns arose from the Greenback Party in Indianapolis, which lobbied for the flooding of the economy with paper currency and for the enfranchisement of women, and from the Prohibition Party, which demanded the outlawing of the production and sale of whiskey, wine, and beer.

Both parties fought Washington corruption by nominating men of unimpeachable character. Because Democrats and Republicans agreed on the issues of civil service reform and the need to end Reconstruction, the campaign descended into name-calling and innuendo. Republicans

In the most contested U.S. election to that time, Republicans Rutherford B. Hayes and William Wheeler lost the popular vote in 1876, but a congressional commission declared them the winners of the Electoral College vote. *(Library of Congress)*

Election of 1876: The Vote

Party/Candidates	Popular Vote	Electoral Vote	States (Electoral Votes)
Republican Rutherford B. Hayes (Ohio) William A. Wheeler (New York)	4,034,142 (48.5%)	185 (50.1%)	California (6), Colorado (3), Florida (4), Illinois (21), Iowa (11), Kansas (5), Louisiana (8), Maine (7), Massachusetts (13), Michigan (11), Minnesota (5), Nebraska (3), Nevada (3), New Hampshire (5), Ohio (22), Oregon (3), Pennsylvania (29), South Carolina (7), Vermont (5), Wisconsin (10)
Democrat Samuel Tilden (New York) Thomas A. Hendricks (Ohio)	4,286,808 (51.5%)	184 (49.9%)	Alabama (10), Arkansas (6), Connecticut (6), Delaware (3), Georgia (11), Indiana (15), Kentucky (12), Maryland (8), Mississippi (8), Missouri (15), New York (35), New Jersey (9), North Carolina (10), Rhode Island (4), Tennessee (12), Texas (8), Virginia (11), West Virginia (5)
Total:	**8,320,950**	369	**38 states**

reminded voters that the Democratic Party welcomed former slaveholders and secessionists. Democratic militants sent racist paramilitary units to intimidate voters and to disrupt political rallies and strategy sessions.

Contributing to the uncertainty of the outcome was the admission of Colorado to the Union three months before the election. Because there was no time to organize voting districts, the legislature cast ballots on behalf of the state's citizens. On November 7, the election day muddle left both parties in an uproar.

Disputes over the electoral count in Florida, Louisiana, Oregon, and South Carolina resulted from eligibility squabbles in Oregon and from charges of election fraud and Democratic intimidation of Republican voters by the Ku Klux Klan, Red Shirts, and White Leaguers in the three Southern states. Raising the public drama, an unknown assailant fired a shot into the dining room of President-Elect Hayes. Additional quandaries over the symbols used on ballots marked by illiterate citizens forced electoral commissions to decide state outcomes.

To validate a winner, on January 29, 1877, a new federal law enacted by the lame-duck Congress authorized five congressmen, five senators, and five U.S. Supreme Court justices to form a new supervisory board, the Electoral Commission. To maintain order in Washington, President Grant ordered General William Tecumseh Sherman to post four artillery companies in the capital. At 3:38 A.M. on March 2, the 15 commissioners voted 8–7 to give the 20 disputed votes to Hayes, making Tilden the first winner of the popular vote to lose the electoral vote. Thomas Nast, a cartoonist for *Harper's Weekly,* pictured booted feet kicking the ballot box and implied that the Democrats were guilty of election fraud, which he symbolized with a pigsty.

On March 5, Hayes and Wheeler took the oath of office on a day marked by marching bands, a torchlight procession of white and black celebrants, fireworks, Chinese lanterns, and cannon fire. Disgruntled voters mocked Hayes as "His Accidency" and "His Fraudulency." Nonetheless, Hayes proved his competency by selecting valuable cabinet advisors and by withdrawing federal troops from the South. At his term's end, he chose not to stand for reelection. A recent widower, Vice President Wheeler performed his job as president of the Senate unenthusiastically and left politics at the end of his four-year term.

See also: Hayes, Rutherford B.; Reconstruction.

Further Reading

Holt, Michael F. *By One Vote: The Disputed Presidential Election of 1876.* Lawrence: University Press of Kansas, 2008.

Morris, Roy, Jr. *Fraud of the Century: Rutherford B. Hayes, Samuel Tilden, and the Stolen Election of 1876.* New York: Simon & Schuster, 2003.

Rehnquist, William H. *Centennial Crisis: The Disputed Election of 1876.* New York: Alfred A. Knopf, 2005.

Richardson, Darcy G. *Others: Third-Party Politics from the Nation's Founding to the Rise and Fall of the Greenback-Labor Party.* New York: iUniverse, 2004.

Trefousse, Hans L. *Rutherford B. Hayes.* New York: Times Books, 2002.

ELECTRICITY

After English physicist Michael Faraday invented the electric motor in 1837, labor-saving devices made inroads against human drudgery. Over the next three decades, the perfection of Thomas Davenport's direct current (DC) appliance motor and Samuel F.B. Morse's telegraph made practical everyday applications of electricity.

The genius who turned theory into common applications was Thomas Alva Edison, a self-educated electrical engineer from Milan, Ohio, who registered 1,093 patents over the course of his career. Beginning in the basement of a friend's house in Elizabeth, New Jersey, he experimented on an electric pen, telephone, electrical storage battery, fire alarm, galvanometer to measure electric current, microphone, electronic clocks and toys, railway signals, hearing aid, electromedical devices, arc lights, dynamo, radio, gas lighting machine, and tasimeter for measuring infrared radiation.

On June 1, 1869, Edison obtained his first U.S. patent, for an electric vote recorder, an in-house method of recording legislative votes with the flick of a switch. His stock ticker made order out of chaos in 25 Boston investment firms by tapping out paper messages from the New York Stock Exchange. In October, he joined businessman James Ashley and electrician Franklin Leonard Pope in the firm Pope, Edison, and Company, telegraph contractors and builders of electrical devices, but there was not enough demand for the stock ticker to turn a profit.

Edison overcame the problem of pragmatic uses for his tinkerings. At Newark in mid-February 1870, he partnered with machinist William Unger, the shop superintendent, and established the Newark Telegraph Works, which offered private line telegraphy. Edison created adjunct devices for his popular machines, including ink recorders, perforators, and typewriters.

At Ward Street in Newark, the firm of Edison and Unger completed a quadruplex telegraph, which sent four separate signals over the same wire—two incoming and two outgoing. The system provided general and commercial news, which Edison dispatched in mid-January 1872 through the American District Telegraph Company, an affiliation of 57 district telegraph systems. By autumn, his automatic telegraph system dispatched news from New York City to Washington, D.C., and Charleston, South Carolina.

Unlike the rest of the country, which was mired in the Panic of 1873, Edison profited. He traveled to London from May 23 to 27, 1873, and promoted his telegraphic advancement to the British post office. William Orton, president of Western Union, paid Edison $10,000 for the quadruplex system, which he announced on July 10, 1873, in *The New York Times.* On October 3, the four-message system went into commercial operation between New York and Boston. In December, the system sped messages between New York and Chicago with additional switching capabilities in Buffalo.

Orton advanced Edison the capital to build, staff, and operate a test laboratory at Menlo Park, New Jersey. With a partner, financier Joseph T. Murray, and a chief experimenter, London-born mechanic Charles Batchelor, in late December 1875, Edison set up the world's first research and development laboratory, equipped with an air pump, chemical lab, microscope, and spectroscope. For the financial security of all of Edison's staff, the famed "invention factory" allied its electronic concepts with a manufacturer and marketer.

Harnessing Talent

On December 30, 1874, to prevent Edison from signing a contract with Orton, Jay Gould, president of the Atlantic and Pacific Telegraph Company, paid $30,000 for all rights to the quadruplex. To make his company more competitive with Western Union, Gould offered Edison the post of company electrician, which Edison accepted.

In March 1875, Edison negotiated with a German firm for the sale of an automatic telegraphy system using a spectroscope. By summer, Edison had begun marketing his electronic pen with the aid of an agent, his nephew Charles Edison. In October, the inventor proposed an in-house telephone circuit for the New York Stock Exchange, a facsimile telegraph system, and "etheric force," the underlying technology of radio.

Despite claims of contract infringement raised by Orton, the collaboration between Edison and Gould paid off for both parties. After investing the cash he earned in a street railway system and in a new laboratory and more staff, Edison experimented with a sextuplex and an octruplex telegraphy system, small electric motors, a high-speed stenciling press, duplicating ink, and a sewing machine motor run by electromagnets. He devised a system of embossing a spiral disc with telegraphic dots and dashes. An operator used the sheet of raised lettering to relay messages automatically from one telegraph station to another. Once the world press learned of the inventor's genius, news stories informed readers of such innovative electronic projects in the making.

As a result of experiments begun in mid-February 1877, on November 29 of that year, Edison refined the phonograph, an amazing sound recorder that won him fame and wealth. He passed to his Zurich-born clockmaker and machinist, John Kruesi, the plans for a "stereoscopic view of the voice." By pressing tinfoil around a grooved brass cylinder and cranking the cylinder by hand, Edison achieved scratchy sound echoing from a stylus. On December 7, he carried his phonograph to New York City to demonstrate it for Alfred Beach, editor of *Scientific American.* Edison composed an essay, "The Phonograph and Its Future," for the May/June 1878 issue of the *North American Review* that predicted the use of the basic phonograph for office dictation, recorded books for the blind, speech teaching, preserving great verbal moments, and enhancing music boxes and talking dolls. As he worked to improve the phonograph, Edison sketched a design for a telephone recording device and laid it aside for future consideration.

Problem Solving

Simultaneous with Edison's varied lab creations, Alexander Graham Bell, a Scots teacher of the deaf living in Boston, studied electrical devices that replicated or transmitted sound. In 1874, he used the phonautograph to capture the two-dimensional shapes of sound waves with a moving pen that scratched lines on smoked glass. While experimenting with acoustic telegraphy in collaboration with his assistant, Thomas Augustus Watson, on June 2, 1875, Bell simplified the transmission of speech vibrations over a single reed.

A year later, Bell improved a water transmitter invented by Elisha Gray that carried vibration through a needle. Competition between Bell and Gray generated more than 600 lawsuits over which inventor deserved the rights to the new technology. After a successful transmission of sound from Cambridge to Boston, Massachusetts, on October 9, 1876, Bell patented his device and advanced to designing an electromagnetic telephone circuit. Orton rejected Bell's offer to sell Western Union the patent for $100,000.

Bell's "speaking telegraph" amazed visitors to the 1876 Centennial Exposition in Philadelphia. He predicted that the system would spread from house to house by interconnecting wires and become as indispensable to domestic life as water or gas pipes. In 1877, he formed the Bell Telephone Company, which made millions for its investors.

Bell augmented the system with a carbon button microphone, one of Edison's inventions that eliminated the mess of a liquid transmitter and the need to shout into the receiver. Edison had made his breakthrough after 188 days of testing 2,000 chemical compounds for conduction properties. The improved device contained a hammered metal diaphragm that amplified the sound of platinum needles moving across a graphite film. To produce the right consistency of graphite, Edison surrounded his back fence with kerosene lamps, which the night watchman scraped of soot and sliced into segments 11 inches (300 millimeters) thick. Meanwhile, Edison obtained a contract with Western Union to develop a separate prototype telephone unrelated in technology to Bell's patent.

The research and development at Menlo Park gained for Edison's team the respect of American and European scientists, who anticipated future breakthroughs in electrical engineering. On December 29, 1877, Edison joined other scientific consultants for the 1878 Paris Universal Exposition. A month later, viewers at the Royal Institution in London marveled at Edison's phonograph. On April 10, 1878, the *New York Daily Graphic* proclaimed Edison the "Wizard of Menlo Park."

In 1879, Edison hired an electrical engineer, William Joseph Hammer, who assisted in the refinement of the electric tramcar, ore separator, phonograph, and telephone. With Hammer's aid, Edison perfected the incandescent electric light at his workshop. A long-lived carbon filament extended a glow into the partial vacuum of a glass globe and burned for 40 hours. That same year, citizens of Cleveland, Ohio, enjoyed the first public street lighting by arc lamp, a boon to business and to law enforcement.

These beginnings prefaced widespread electrical illumination, as well as electrical mass transit. Electric streetcars introduced overhead wiring in Richmond, Virginia, in 1887, to operate a cost-effective street railway.

See also: Gas Lighting; Gould, Jay.

Further Reading

Baldwin, Neil. *Edison: Inventing the Century.* Chicago: University of Chicago Press, 2001.

Cropper, William H. *Great Physicists: The Life and Times of Leading Physicists from Galileo to Hawking.* Oxford, UK: Oxford University Press, 2001.

Pretzer, William S., ed. *Working at Inventing: Thomas A. Edison and the Menlo Park Experience.* Baltimore: Johns Hopkins University Press, 2002.

Stanley, George E. *The Era of Reconstruction and Expansion, 1865–1900.* Milwaukee, WI: World Almanac Library, 2005.

Emancipation Proclamation

A complicated two-stage executive order from President Abraham Lincoln, the Emancipation Proclamation began the freeing of slaves across America. The measure, composed in summer 1862, ultimately liberated about 4 million slaves, one-seventh of the nation's population. Congressman Thaddeus Stevens of Pennsylvania foresaw emancipation as a blow against the Confederacy and predicted that the loss of a coerced labor force would destroy the South's plantation economy. Preparing the way was a series of legal and martial assaults on the flesh trade:

May 4, 1861: Four weeks after the onset of the Civil War, Union soldiers stopped enforcing the Fugitive Slave Law of 1850 and allowed runaways to proceed through military lines to free states in the North.

May 24: General Benjamin Franklin Butler received fugitive slaves and set them to work on Fort Monroe, Virginia.

August 6: The First Confiscation Act freed blacks whom Union troops seized from rebel forces.

August 30: General John Charles Frémont liberated the slaves of Missouri secessionists.

March 13, 1862: Congress passed the Act Prohibiting the Return of Slaves, which required Union officers to stop owners from reclaiming runaways.

April 10: Congress offered compensation for slave owners who manumitted their chattel.

April 16: Congress forced the residents of the District of Columbia to free their 3,200 slaves.

June 19: Federal law overturned the U.S. Supreme Court ruling in *Dred Scott v. Sandford* (1857) by prohibiting human bondage in the Western territories.

July 17: The Second Confiscation Act liberated the slaves of insurrectionists.

The loosening of enslavers' hold on their property offered a number of possibilities. Journalist and politician Edward Thurlow Weed of Cairo in Greene County, New York, opposed emancipation out of fear that a sudden end to slavery would endanger the economy and victimize the poor. Gideon Welles, the secretary of the navy, doubted the long-term wisdom of the plan and feared a revolution and a lengthening of the war, as slave owners grew desperate to defend their lifestyle and economy. However, Attorney General Edward Bates, a proponent of black colonization in Africa, riposted that the president's instincts about human rights were true and honorable.

Lincoln moved cautiously among his advisers. On July 22, 1862, he discussed with his cabinet the need for a Union military triumph to add force to the radical law, which he feared would divide the North and weaken support for the Union army. Speaking privately with Vice President Hannibal Hamlin, he debated possible changes to the first draft, co-authored by Secretary of State William Henry Seward.

On August 19, 1862, Horace Greeley, the influential editor of the *New York Tribune,* lobbed a one-to-one editorial at the president demanding that the federal government outlaw the flesh trade. Three days later, Lincoln clarified that, as president, he owed his allegiance to the whole nation. He stated that he would liberate slaves if their freeing were in the best interest of national unity, but he would not jeopardize the Union by liberating the property of slave owners.

Spirit of the Times

Following the Union victory at the Battle of Antietam, Maryland, on September 17, 1862, conditions were right for Lincoln's drastic move. The preliminary stage of formal emancipation, issued on September 22, ended enslavement in all Confederate states that remained outside the Union as of January 1, 1863.

At the War Governors' Conference in Altoona, Pennsylvania, on September 24 and 25, the governors of Connecticut, Illinois, Indiana, Iowa, Kansas, Maine, Massachusetts, Michigan, Minnesota, New Hampshire, Ohio, Oregon, Pennsylvania, Rhode Island, Vermont, and Wisconsin backed Lincoln's proclamation. The governors of New Jersey and New York joined those of border states—Delaware, Kentucky, Maryland, and Missouri—in opposing the measure.

The second and most dramatic portion of the proclamation, dated January 1, 1863, took the form of a war measure mandated by Lincoln as commander in chief. It specified the emancipation of slaves in the rogue states of Alabama, Arkansas, Florida, Georgia, Louisiana, Mississippi, North Carolina, South Carolina, and Virginia. In addition, blacks obtained freedom in Union-controlled

Corinth, Mississippi; Hilton Head and Port Royal, South Carolina; Key West, Florida; North Carolina's Outer Banks; northern Alabama; Sea Island, Georgia; and the Upper Shenandoah Valley, Virginia. The order omitted the border states of Delaware, Kentucky, and Maryland, as well as Tennessee and parts of Louisiana, then under Union control, and the newly created state of West Virginia. Missouri remained exempt because of a late repeal of slavery by the state legislature. Texas became a slave paradise, as enslavers herded a quarter million chattel out of the plantation South and into a Southwestern Confederate stronghold. Owners withheld news of emancipation until June 19, 1865, a jubilant day that former slaves called Juneteenth.

The Emancipation Proclamation thus freed a relatively small number of slaves, as it applied primarily to Southern states over which the Union had no control at the time. But it did declare—to the nation and to the rest of the world—a fundamental shift in federal purpose: The Union was fighting the war to end slavery.

The Nation Responds

Without generating riot or violence, the proclamation had an explosive emotional impact on citizens of the nation and world. Lincoln's directive launched a crusade for freedom and the dismantling of a system of purchase, breeding, and sale of slaves that had evolved from the seventeenth century. The document established a federal policy of scorn to immorality and to profiteering from human misery. Vice President Hamlin described the edict as the era's greatest act. Grateful citizens failed to consider the political ramifications of Lincoln's act and honored him as the "Great Emancipator" for his uncompromising humanity and compassion. Reformer and presidential adviser Frederick Douglass assured libertarians that Lincoln would never reconsider or retract the revolutionary document.

At Fayetteville, New York, libertarians Henry Hill and Matilda Joslyn Gage posted bunting and flags to celebrate. Attorney and politician John Mercer Langston read the text aloud to the student body at Oberlin College, Ohio. Teacher Charlotte Forten assembled her classes at Camp Saxton, headquarters of the all-black First South Carolina Volunteers, for the reading; at the conclusion, she led her students in a chorus of "My Country 'Tis of Thee." At Port Royal, South Carolina, the Reverend Thomas Wentworth Higginson, an agent of the Underground Railroad, chose Dr. William Henry Brisbane, a rescuer on the secret network, to read the document. The text appeared in the evening edition of the Washington, D.C., *Star.* Emancipation preceded enlistment of 200,000 former bondsmen into the U.S. Army and U.S. Navy, thus increasing the manpower needed to end the war.

In Canada, England, France, and Italy, Lincoln's embrace of human rights trounced any sympathy or monetary support for the Confederacy. Although bondage was still legal in some Southern states, slaves who learned about the law fled by the thousands to the aid of Union regiments. They left behind jobs in Confederate military factories and mines, shipyards, forts, commissaries, hospitals, and prisons. The advance of federal forces met with jubilation as blacks claimed their civil rights and grasped the hands of their benefactors. On September 18, 1863, Lincoln concurred with Sarah Josepha Hale, editor of *Godey's Lady's Book,* that the nation needed a fixed annual thanksgiving to channel praise and gratitude for freedom and national unity.

Countering abolitionist joy, on December 23, 1862, Confederate President Jefferson Davis issued his own proclamation, declaring that captured black federal troops would be forced into slavery. The following day, in Pulaski, Tennessee, white supremacists formed the Ku Klux Klan, a clandestine paramilitary of Confederate veterans. In response, Lincoln pledged retaliation against Confederate prisoners of war if Confederate jailers failed to respect black or white Union captives. In gearing up his reelection campaign, the president used universal freedom as his key platform. The editor of the *Richmond Enquirer* foresaw a bloody slave insurrection, a clash also envisioned by Union General George Brinton McClellan.

On June 19, 1865, General Gordon Granger read to blacks in Galveston, Texas, their guarantee of civil and personal equality. Former slaves celebrated the day as Juneteenth, the nation's oldest folk celebration of emancipation. As secessionist states reentered the Union, within 18 months, 4 million former slaves embraced citizenship with ratification of the Thirteenth Amendment to the U.S. Constitution on December 18, 1865, which freed slaves in all states and territories.

When Clara Barton arrived at Andersonville Prison in Georgia on July 25, 1865, to mark the graves of unidentified dead, hundreds of black men, women, and children from the Americus area mobbed her seeking news of their freeing. According to Barton's later testimony before Congress on February 21, 1866, some blacks doubted her report that President Lincoln was dead; some feared that without him, they would be forced once more into bondage. They disclosed that their former masters allowed them to remain on plantations and work without pay. She read them the rules of sharecropping published daily in the Macon newspapers. On her advice, the ex-slaves returned to their jobs to earn wages until Christmas 1865. With cash earnings, they could look for farming jobs before the 1866 spring planting.

Religious pacifists felt their views vindicated and turned their efforts toward obtaining confiscated lands from Southern plantations for former slaves and toward securing black suffrage. Abolitionist Martin Robinson Delany advised President Lincoln on the needs of ex-slaves and promoted the humanitarian work of the Freedmen's Bureau, which Congress instituted on March 3, 1865.

In the aftermath of Lincoln's assassination the following month, abolitionist Henry Highland Garnet spearheaded a drive for a national monument to honor the author of the Emancipation Proclamation. On the seventh anniversary of the edict, in Columbia, South Carolina, Governor Robert Kingston Scott presided over a black celebration of freedom that began with a brass band leading marchers in a parade to the capitol. In Washington, D.C., Frederick Douglass made memorable comments on April 14, 1876, at the unveiling of the Freedmen's Monument. He delivered a tribute to the martyred President Lincoln and recognized that his name would forever be dear to blacks.

See also: Hamlin, Hannibal; Ku Klux Klan; Lincoln, Abraham; Thirteenth Amendment (1865).

Further Reading

Goodwin, Doris Kearns. *Team of Rivals: The Political Genius of Abraham Lincoln.* New York: Simon & Schuster, 2005.

Guelzo, Allen C. *Lincoln's Emancipation Proclamation: The End of Slavery in America.* New York: Simon & Schuster, 2004.

Snodgrass, Mary Ellen. *The Underground Railroad: An Encyclopedia of People, Places, and Operations.* Armonk, NY: M.E. Sharpe, 2007.

Stephenson, Nathaniel W. *Abraham Lincoln and the Union.* New York: BiblioBazaar, 2008.

Striner, Richard. *Father Abraham: Lincoln's Relentless Struggle to End Slavery.* Oxford, UK: Oxford University Press, 2006.

Everett, Edward (1794–1865)

Boston-born patriot and Whig statesman Edward Everett served his country as a U.S. congressman (1825–1835), governor of Massachusetts (1836–1840), ambassador to Great Britain (1840–1845), secretary of state (1852–1853), and U.S. senator (1853–1854). Born on April 11, 1794, he attended Boston Latin School before continuing his education at age 13 at Harvard University. After completing a degree in theology and ancient languages, he graduated as valedictorian with a master's degree in liberal arts and, at age 20, received ordination as a Congregationalist and Unitarian minister at the Brattle Street Church. At the University of Göttingen in Germany, he studied ancient and modern languages and, in 1818, became the first American to earn a doctoral degree.

During his four years as governor of Massachusetts, Everett fought for public education reform, revived pride in the Battles of Lexington and Concord and Bunker Hill, and wrestled with the social and economic problems of Irish Catholic immigrants arriving in Boston, sick and malnourished from the Irish potato famine. Despite humanitarian leanings, he resisted the pressure to support abolitionism, which he believed was premature.

Following four years as the U.S. envoy to Great Britain in the early 1840s, Everett taught Greek at Harvard for five years and served as university president until 1849. Under his administration, educator Louis Agassiz established graduate and research programs in science. Everett rankled at the disrepair of buildings and laboratories and punished students for setting bonfires, importing prostitutes, and carousing. For his conservatism, the student body named him "Old Granny," adorned his home with crude graffiti, and hanged him in effigy in Harvard Yard.

Everett's letter of 1850 defending U.S. Secretary of State Daniel Webster for scrutinizing the revolution in Hungary established a precedent of American involvement in foreign affairs. In 1852, President Millard Fillmore named Everett as U.S. secretary of state. The next year, he won a seat in the U.S. Senate, where he battled the Missouri Compromise. During the debate over the admission of Kansas and Nebraska as slave states, however, Everett's ill health impeded vigorous defense of his Unionist beliefs. He took up fund-raising to preserve Mount Vernon, which had been the home of George and Martha Washington during the nation's first presidency, and he continued supporting lyceums and serving as a director of the Boston Public Library.

In 1860, Everett's attentions turned to upholding the Union during threats of Southern secession. At the onset of the Civil War in April 1861, he displayed his talents as an orator by exhorting Northerners to abandon states' rights arguments and to support unity. To preserve the fragile nation, he agreed to Secretary of State William Henry Seward's request that Everett urge France to back the North against the Confederacy.

Rather than further political ends, Everett refused to engage in divisive partisanship or electioneering until peace was restored. The boost to the Lincoln administration earned him the president's regard, but, in 1862, after the failure of the Peninsula Campaign, Everett ventured to criticize the choice of General George Brinton McClellan as leader of the Army of the Potomac.

Everett ran unsuccessfully for U.S. vice president in 1860, on the Constitutional Union Party ticket headed by John Bell. He suffered defeat, deepened on November 19, 1863, by humiliation after President Lincoln delivered the Gettysburg Address. Following music performed by the U.S. Marine Band, Everett, a noted Greek revivalist, preceded Lincoln at the podium with a two-hour oration on the Athenian statesman Pericles, on classical commentary at military funerals, and on the events of the Civil War. Lincoln's elegant two-minute, 272-word eulogy at first appalled some journalists before becoming one the nation's most profound encomiums to patriotism and self-sacrifice. In a letter to Lincoln on November 20, Everett asked for the handwritten copy of the speech that the president used at the podium. Everett described the Gettysburg Address as "appropriate" and chastised himself for taking 120 minutes to say what the president had said in two minutes.

Severe illness in 1864 prevented the orator from touring the country to boost morale and to urge citizen respect for Lincoln's difficult decisions. At the president's reelection, Everett championed voters for keeping Republicans in power, rather than shifting parties to a new commander in chief. At age 70, three months before his death, Everett made a final address at Boston's Faneuil Hall anticipating Lincoln's second term of office. Following it, Everett proposed shipping free beef, flour, and pork to Savannah, Georgia, to save citizens from starvation.

At Everett's death from pneumonia on January 15, 1865, he was known as one of the nation's prime Ivy League politicians. President Lincoln ordered cannon salutes and federal buildings draped in mourning to honor his trusted supporter.

See also: Abolitionism; Agassiz, Louis; Gettysburg Address; Lincoln, Abraham.

Further Reading

Blight, David W. *Race and Reunion: The Civil War in American Memory.* Cambridge, MA: Belknap Press, 2001.

Boritt, Gabor. *The Gettysburg Gospel: The Lincoln Speech That Nobody Knows.* New York: Simon & Schuster, 2006.

Stephenson, Nathaniel W. *Abraham Lincoln and the Union.* New York: BiblioBazaar, 2008.

Varg, Paul A. *Edward Everett: The Intellectual in the Turmoil of Politics.* Cranbury, NJ: Susquehanna University Press, 1992.

Wills, Garry. *Lincoln at Gettysburg: The Words That Remade America.* New York: Simon & Schuster, 1992.

Ex Parte Milligan (1866)

According to *Ex parte Milligan,* a heroic and self-confident U.S. Supreme Court decision of April 3, 1866, civil courts have jurisdiction over military tribunals. On an individual basis, civilians have a constitutional right to demand a civil court trial rather than a military tribunal.

The case involved a wartime conspiracy against the U.S. government. The following subversives faced charges of involvement in terrorism:

- William A. Bowles, leader of the radical Democratic Knights of the Golden Circle (later called the Order of the Sons of Liberty).
- Harrison Horton Dodd, antiwar physician and founder and grand commander of the Order of the Sons of Liberty.
- Horace Heffren, attorney, teacher, editor of the Indiana *Washington Democrat,* and deputy grand commander of the Sons of Liberty.
- Stephen Horsey, farmer, wartime profiteer, and deputy chief of the Sons of Liberty.
- Andrew Humphreys, politician and Utah Indian agent.
- Lambdin Purdy Milligan farmer and attorney of Belmont County, Ohio.

Spies in the secret Knights of the Golden Circle, emboldened by the support of Indiana Governor Oliver Hazard Perry Morton, leaked the traitors' intent that liberated Confederate prisoners overpower the state governments of Indiana, Ohio, and Michigan. On July 30, 1864, the Indianapolis *Daily Journal* exposed the secret rites and constitution of the Sons of Liberty.

On August 20, Union soldiers foiled the insurrection by confiscating 400 revolvers and thousands of bullets from Dodd's print shop, along with texts of his pro-South speeches. On October 5, 1864, Union General Alvin Peterson Hovey ordered the six men arrested for plotting a coup in Indianapolis. Some 400 lesser members of the Sons of Liberty gained immediate release.

After a midnight raid, Milligan, incapacitated by leg surgery at Huntington, traveled by rail to an inhumane cell at the Soldier's Home Prison in Indianapolis. Bowles entered a lockup at the Federal Building. Dodd, facing a separate trial on September 22, escaped incarceration in the post office, fled north, and hid in Canada.

A civil court charged the defendants with planning to seize Union weapons and liberate rebel prisoners from Camp Morton, the former fairgrounds of the Indiana State Board of Agriculture, to create a Northwest Confederacy. Informers claimed that the militants, under orders from Confederate headquarters in Richmond, Virginia, had mustered a force in Canada for the purpose of invading Ohio.

The prosecution dropped the charges against Heffren and manipulated his testimony against the conspirators. On December 10, 1864, the four other subversives and Dodd, who remained at large, faced execution on the gallows the following May 19.

Shortly before his assassination, President Abraham Lincoln reviewed the Milligan case favorably, but stopped short of recommending clemency. On May 10, 1865, within four weeks of the Confederate surrender at Appomattox, Virginia, at a circuit court at Indianapolis, the traitors appealed the decision of a military court against civilians. On May 17, under suasion by Governor Morton, President Andrew Johnson commuted their sentences to life in prison.

On behalf of the five accused, on March 5, 1866, former U.S. Attorney General Jeremiah Sullivan Black, attorney David Dudley Field, and U.S. Representative (and future president) James A. Garfield argued the case against attorneys for the state, Benjamin Franklin Butler, Henry Stanbery, and Attorney General James Speed. The media and legal journals followed the debate for its impact on Reconstruction-era punishment of traitors.

For judges, legal scholars, historians, and political scientists, *Ex parte Milligan* took on a new significance. The Supreme Court ruled that the suspension of habeas corpus was lawful, but that the military deprived five citizens of a hearing in the civilian courts, which were still operating during wartime. All nine justices denied martial rule the right to try and execute the five cabal leaders. On April 3, 1866, Chief Justice Salmon P. Chase struck down the execution order and freed the four men from prison. Historians lauded the action as a triumph for constitutional liberty over extreme executive powers by the War Department, which made 13,535 political arrests during the Civil War.

Dodd returned from Canada and won a series of elections to mayor of Fond du Lac, Wisconsin. Milligan sued Hovey for libel, conspiracy, and false imprisonment and demanded $500,000 in damages. Milligan won the case, but received a settlement of only $5.

See also: Chase, Salmon P.

Further Reading

Hall, Kermit L., ed. *The Oxford Guide to United States Supreme Court Decisions.* New York: Oxford University Press, 2001.

Ivins, Molly, and Lou Dubose. *Bill of Wrongs: The Executive Branch's Assault on America's Fundamental Rights.* New York: Random House, 2008.

Kaczorowski, Robert J. *The Politics of Judicial Interpretation: The Federal Courts, Department of Justice, and Civil Rights, 1866–1876.* New York: Fordham University Press, 2005.

Patrick, John J., Richard M. Pious, and Donald A. Ritchie. *The Oxford Guide to the United States Government.* Oxford, UK: Oxford University Press, 2001.

Powe, Lucas A., Jr. *The Supreme Court and the American Elite, 1789–2008.* Cambridge, MA: Harvard University Press, 2009.

Exploration

As the United States approached its centennial in 1876, exploration lagged behind the challenge of surveying land still untapped by European Americans for hunting, touring, photographing, settling, and exploiting for plants, animals, minerals, and water.

In central California, a systematic yearlong perusal of Yosemite began in 1855 under the leadership of Allexey W. Von Schmidt, a Latvian astronomer and surveyor from Riga who served as civil engineer of San Francisco and U.S. deputy surveyor of public lands. Amid beautiful scenery, Von Schmidt wrote the earliest documentation of Mount Diablo and the Owens Valley, where he examined the ecosystem of Mono and Owens lakes, both saltwater. He continued through Tuolumne Meadows and the eastern slope of the Sierra Nevada in Mariposa and Tulare counties. Among the facts that he incorporated into his official report, his summary of native lifestyles described 1,000 Yosemite-Mono Lake Paiute, a poorly fed nation living primarily on fish, rabbits, and pine nuts.

In his travelogue *In the Heart of the Sierras: The Yo Semite Valley* (1886), British artist James Mason Hutchings documented his impressions of an isolated wilderness in 1855. His writings in *Hutchings' California Magazine* fostered tourism after Yosemite became a state park in 1864. Von Schmidt continued his work in 1861 in the Panamint Valley west of Death Valley in Inyo County, California. He described 200 Koso Panamint Indians of the Mojave Desert and reconnoitered 11,000 acres (4,450 hectares), telling potential settlers about tracts of arable land for agriculture and ranching near the Amargosa peak.

The 14-year exploration of California's Sierra Nevada mountain range made considerable advancement,

In 1871, geologist Ferdinand Vandeveer Hayden led a federal expedition to survey features in northwestern Wyoming that would be incorporated into Yellowstone National Park. The team included photographer William Henry Jackson, who took this shot. *(George Eastman House/Getty Images)*

beginning in 1860 under Yale-educated geologist Josiah Dwight Whitney, the first California Geological Survey chief and the compiler of *The Yosemite Book* (1868). His team consisted of experienced, scholarly men:

- Henry Nicholas Bolander, a German-born educator and California's state botanist and superintendent of schools.
- William Henry Brewer, chief botanist and author of *Up and Down California in 1860–1864* (1930) and cocompiler of *Botany of California* (1876).
- James Graham Cooper, zoologist and surgeon and author of *Ornithology* (1870).
- Richard D. "Dick" Cotter, an Irish mountain climber and cartographer.
- William More Gabb, a paleontologist and conchologist who studied fossils in gold-bearing slate and cowrote *Paleontology* (1864).
- James Terry Gardiner, Yale-graduated engineer and surveyor.
- Charles Frederick Hoffmann, a German topographer, landscape artist, and mining engineer and author of "Notes on Hetch-Hetchy Valley" (1868) and producer of a map of the central Sierra Nevada.
- Clarence Rivers King, a Yale-trained geologist and author of *Systematic Geology* (1878) and *Mountaineering in the Sierra Nevada* (1872).
- Lorenzo Gordin Yates, an English dentist and paleontologist and author of *Catalogue of the Ferns of North America* (1886).

King determined the age of the Sierras by identifying fossils in slaty bedrock. From the explorers' surnames came Mount Brewer, Mount Cotter, Mount Gabb, Mount Gardiner, Mount Hoffman, Mount King, and Mount Whitney, the last of which Cotter and King discovered in July 1864 and named for the chief surveyor. In late 1864, after Cotter mapped Yosemite, the expeditioners moved on toward the granite profile of the upper Sierra Nevada range, which Whitney compared to the Alps chain. As an outcome of fieldwork, Brewer credited Hoffman with introducing Americans to the systematic study of field topography.

The Fortieth Parallel

At the suggestion of James Terry Gardiner and Clarence King, the field expedition intensified in 1867 after Congress approved the Geological Exploration of the Fortieth Parallel, a six-year trek from Virginia City's Comstock

Lode in western Nevada to eastern Wyoming. King used as a selling point the appalling lack of U.S. geographic studies, in contrast to those of France, Germany, and Great Britain.

In 1868, scholars concentrated on the topography from California through the Great Basin and the Rocky Mountains and particularized the path of the Whitney glacier and the volcanic activities of Mount Hood, Mount Rainier, and Mount Shasta. Geologist James Duncan Hague, a graduate of Harvard and Göttingen universities and the compiler of *Mineral Industry* (1871), promoted prospecting in the West; ornithologist Robert Ridgeway contributed bird studies, which reached print in 1901 in the eight-volume treatise *The Birds of North and Middle America.*

Scholarly details of the Fortieth Parallel survey appeared in an eight-volume report that covered Shoshone Canyon and Falls in Idaho Territory and identified the Pliocene origins of Lake Bonneville and Lake Lahonton, Utah. Award-winning geologist Grove Karl Gilbert contributed meticulous information about the underwater shaping of Lake Bonneville, an Ice Age pluvial lake in the Great Salt Lake Desert that formed around 16,000 B.C.E.

Irish photographer Timothy H. O'Sullivan collected illustrations of austere vistas intended to lure adventurers to the exotic West. Among shots taken from 1868 to 1874 were hot springs and fissure vents and evidence of native life—pueblo communities, Navajo weaving, petroglyphs, the Mojave of Arizona and Colorado, and the prehistoric White House Ruins in Canyon de Chelly, Arizona.

Until the project's end, the intense scrutiny of California high country yielded data on numerous geographic features, including Mount Whitney, the highest peak in the continental United States, as well as the nation's first identified glacier, which King and his guide, John Hinckley Sisson, located on Mount Shasta in the state's Cascades Range in summer 1870. King returned to scale Mount Whitney in 1873, reaching its full elevation of 14,505 feet (4,421 meters).

Researching Alaska

Under the control of czarist Russia, the Alaskan Panhandle consisted of uncharted lands, waters, and island clusters inhabited by Athabascan, Haida, Tlingit, and Tsimshian tribes. The country remained largely uninvestigated by whites until Alexandre "Buck" Choquette, a French Canadian hunter and prospector from Quebec, tramped north from Victoria, British Columbia, in May 1861. Choquette chartered ten Tlingit guides to take him from the Nass River to Wrangell Island, Alaska, a waterbird habitat rich in forests, peatlands, and muskegs or bogs.

Along with his wife, Georgiana "Georgie" Shakes, daughter of Tlingit Chief Kadashan Shakes, Choquette canoed 800 miles (1,300 kilometers) through the panhandle and traded with tribes near Wrangell, where he arrived in June. He became fluent in Chinook and Tlingit dialects and located valuable deposits of blue and white marble. On September 12, north of Ketchikan in the Cassiar District, Choquette panned placer gold nuggets and dust at "Buck's Bar," a gravel bar southwest of Telegraph Creek along the upper Stikine River bed.

Six years before Alaska's purchase by the United States, Choquette settled on the Alaska–Canada border among the Tlingit at the Choquette River near the Stikine Hot Springs, where he became the first white man to explore the Great Glacier. Both the glacier and a nearby mountain now bear the name Choquette.

On January 10, 1862, Choquette returned to Victoria to glory in his gold strike. In spring 1862, reporters for the *Victoria Colonist* spread the word, luring thousands of prospectors and fortune hunters to the Pacific Northwest to Stikine Village, British Columbia. Choquette made his fortune in the fevered digging, called the Cariboo Gold Rush, and on March 13, 1866, opened the Ice Mountain Station, where he sold goods supplied by the Hudson's Bay Company. According to *Travels in Alaska* (1915), naturalist John Muir obtained supplies from Choquette before exploring the Great Glacier.

Miners leaving by water from Fort Highfield raced prospectors sledding up frozen rivers and streams to Glenora and to Telegraph Creek, British Columbia. With outsiders came smallpox, which swept the Tahltan Indian population on Dease Lake. Shortly before Choquette's death in Dawson City on June 17, 1898, novelist Jack London interviewed him for the details of his Alaskan exploration.

Government Survey

In early March 1865, on a grant from President Abraham Lincoln, a three-year engineering survey, the Western Union Telegraph Expedition, departed for Alaska under the direction of Smithsonian Institution naturalist Major Robert Kennicott, an expert on the Arctic tundra and subarctic forests. The party traveled in an armed flotilla led by the steamers USS *Saginaw* and *George S. Wright* and the flagship *Nightingale,* which previously had been used as a slave ship. Reconnoitering hundreds of miles by snowshoe, sledge, and bateaux, Kennicott began mapping the coastline from California, Oregon, and Washington Territory north and west along British Columbia.

During a first-time expedition over the Yukon watershed, Kennicott sought an undiscovered route to the polar sea over territory decimated of human nomads by epidemic scarlet fever. He sent 1,700 biological specimens to the Smithsonian, including new species of crustaceans, frogs, insects, lizards, owls, salamanders, skinks, snakes, sponges, toads, and turtles. At Russian Alaska, he portaged from Norton Sound 100 miles (160 kilometers) inland to the trading post at Fort Nulato.

A team member, Captain Frank Ketchum, accompanied by French Canadian mountain man Michael "Mike" Lebarge and Russian Spanish fur trader Ivan Lukeen, manned a sledge 500 miles (800 kilometers) up the Yukon River over ice several feet thick. The survey quashed a myth that Fort Yukon lay inside British territory. In March 1866, Ketchum and Lebarge traveled by dogsled and birch canoe to Fort Selkirk at the mouth of the Pelly River, the headstream of the Yukon River. A river, valley, and glacier now bear Ketchum's name; Lake Lebarge honors his teammate.

After Kennicott's sudden death on May 13, 1866, on the Lower Yukon at age 31 of congestive heart failure or possibly of self-administered strychnine poisoning, the Western Union expedition became the charge of William Healey Dall, an expert on mollusks and fish and the party's acting surgeon. Dall insisted that the team complete Kennicott's ambitious project.

From September 24, 1866, to fall 1868, Dall, accompanied by London-born sketch artist Frederick Whymper, trekked and mapped 1,600 miles (2,600 kilometers) to the sea, sampling the shallows and bottoms of the Bering Sea to Plover Bay as far west as Kamchatka, Siberia. Weathering temperatures as low as -68 degrees Fahrenheit (-55.5 degrees Celsius) at St. Michael, Alaska, the party encountered some 3,000 Eskimo and Tananá who thrived in the frigid arctic and had never seen a white man or been exposed to the technology of the Industrial Revolution.

A prolific writer and classifier, Dall identified 40 unsurveyed harbors and passages, located the northwestward curve of the Rocky Mountains, and surmised that the Yukon River was one of America's largest known waterways. He defied the myth of a warm Japanese current through the Bering Sea and discovered ground ice formations containing remains of mammoth and other Pliocene and Pleistocene species. He provided scientific data on the region and its resources, including Eskimo racial stock, the Nisqually language, mummies and fossils of prehistoric native Alaskans, details on the latent volcanoes Mount St. Elias and Mount Fairweather, mollusks, plankton, the titmouse, sheep, and gray and spiked whales.

The first white man to navigate the Yukon River to the Bering Sea, expeditioner William Healey Dall marveled, "Never again will it be possible for an ethnologist to see upon the Yukon such a body of absolutely primitive Indians untarnished by the least breath of civilization." While reconnoitering the tundra, his party introduced the Inuit to vegetables, flour, tea, butter, wool cloth, soap, candles, whiskey, and rifles.

Upon returning to the Smithsonian Institution in Washington, D.C., Dall began identifying and cataloguing specimens of plants and animals. In addition to lecturing, he issued *Alaska and Its Resources* (1870), which featured line drawings of dogsleds, kayaks, and forts, along with eyewitness accounts of Inuit homes, survivalism, and disease, deer and bear hunting, Yukon fishing, and commercially valuable furs and healing plants found in the region. Similar features fill Whymper's *Travel and Adventure in the Territory of Alaska* (1868), which included his sketches of a Chukchi house and skin canoe, Malamute and Tananá dress, Yukon River fish traps, a Co-Yukon deer corral, and the 30 active volcanoes of the Kamchatka Peninsula.

Dall accepted assignment to the U.S. Coast Survey and continued his geological missions on the schooner *Yukon* to the Aleutian Islands until 1874. While reconnoitering the Barren Islands, Kadiak group, Semidi Islands, and Shumagin Islands, he investigated the remains of prehistoric settlements, middens, and shell heaps and catalogued funeral masks and cave burial wrappings. He compiled the rituals of the Aleut, Eskimo, Inuit, and Kaniagmut for a scholarly treatise, *On the Remains of Later Prehistoric Man Obtained from Caves in the Catharina Archipelago, Alaska Territory* (1878). His collection of echinoderms and fossil mollusks passed to Louis Agassiz at the Museum of Comparative Zoology at Harvard University. Dall also reported on other exploration and mountaineering, including the scaling of the Makushin volcano on Unalaska Island in September 1867 by astronomer and explorer George Davidson.

See also: Agassiz, Louis; Alaska; Midway Islands; Mississippi River; Muir, John; Yellowstone National Park; Yosemite Valley.

Further Reading

Berton, Pierre. *The Klondike Fever: The Life and Death of the Last Great Gold Rush.* New York: Carroll & Graf, 2004.

Farquhar, Francis P. *History of the Sierra Nevada.* Berkeley: University of California Press, 2007.

Gifford, Terry, ed. *John Muir: His Life and Letters and Other Writings.* London: Baton Wicks, 1996.

Lingenfelter, Richard E. *Death Valley and the Amargosa: A Land of Illusion.* Berkeley: University of California Press, 1986.

Moore, James G. *Exploring the Highest Sierra.* Stanford, CA: Stanford University Press, 2000.

———. *King of the 40th Parallel: Discovery in the American West.* Stanford, CA: Stanford University Press, 2006.

F

Fessenden, William (1806–1869)

William Pitt Fessenden attended to the financing of the Union army during the Civil War. He displayed leadership during the Civil War and Reconstruction and served as a U.S. senator (1854–1864; 1865–1869) and secretary of the treasury (1864–1865) under President Abraham Lincoln.

Born to Ruth Greene and Samuel Fessenden in Boscawen, New Hampshire, on October 16, 1806, he grew up in a puritanical family that was abolitionist, Episcopalian, and Whig. Fastidious and well mannered, Fessenden spent early childhood with his grandmother in Fryeburg, Maine, and later taught school at Lewiston. He studied law at Bowdoin College before gravitating toward the temperance movement and the Republican Party.

He served in city offices, in the Maine legislature, and in the U.S. House of Representatives before moving on to the Senate in 1854. He suffered from recurrent malaria and fatigue following the death of his wife, Ellen Maria Deering Fessenden, on July 23, 1857. In 1861, he promoted an increase in tariffs and the Internal Revenue Bill.

Fessenden maintained a working relationship with the executive office and helped President Lincoln achieve reelection in 1864. He advised Lincoln to accept fugitive blacks into the military, rather than return them to their owners; he also recommended paying black soldiers the same wages as white soldiers. To Lincoln's suspension of habeas corpus, Fessenden defended arbitrary arrests, but, at a nadir of confidence in January 1863, he mourned the high army desertion rate resulting from the lack of cash to pay Union soldiers. Concerning the dispossession of Native Americans, he regretted that either blacks or Indians suffered discriminatory treatment.

On issues of fairness, he denounced the recruitment of Irish and German immigrants while rich white males paid as much as $800 to escape the draft. The war years brought honor to Fessenden's sons, General James Deering Fessenden and General Francis "Frank" Fessenden, who lost an arm in combat at the Battle of Shiloh, Tennessee, and to a war casualty, 21-year-old Lieutenant Samuel Fessenden, who ran away to join the Kansas army at age 15 and died following the Second Battle of Bull Run on September 1, 1862.

Fessenden despised time-servers and sycophants and favored unity among cabinet members. He came to admire President Lincoln for his honesty, patriotism, and political acumen. At first declining nomination to the cabinet, he accepted appointment as secretary of the treasury on July 5, 1864. He immediately faced a period beset by military defeats, departmental corruption, the collapse of the gold standard, and fiscal indebtedness of $161 million. *Harper's Weekly* featured him on its cover on July 30, 1864, and depicted him as intelligent, competent, and energetic. At the breaking point in national fiscal health, the treasury secretary battled the quandary by issuing inflationary greenbacks and by negotiating short-term loans from financier Jay Cooke. Fessenden chose a pay-as-you-go method of financing the war and introduced the 7.3 percent treasury note.

After Fessenden's eight months' service and subsequent resignation from the cabinet on March 3, 1865, he gladly yielded the treasury to banker Hugh McCulloch. Fessenden observed exhaustion in Lincoln and hoped that the president would live to see the Union restored.

Upon his return to the U.S. Senate following a mild bout of smallpox, Fessenden advanced to majority leader. From December 13, 1865, to March 2, 1867, he chaired the Joint Committee on Reconstruction, which took testimony from General Robert E. Lee and Confederate Vice President Alexander Hamilton Stephens on Southern tractability and oversaw the readmission to the Union of all of the rebel states except Tennessee. That same year, the Treasury Department honored Fessenden with the commissioning of the *William P. Fessenden,* a 180-foot (55-meter) revenue cutter on the Great Lakes.

In late March 1867, Fessenden rejected Secretary of State William Henry Seward's proposal to buy Alaska from Russia. During the second presidential impeachment hearings on March 5–6, 1868, Fessenden angered Radical Republicans by voting his conscience to acquit Andrew Johnson. In the last months of office as a senator, Fessenden died of an intestinal rupture on September 8, 1869, in Portland, Maine.

Further Reading

Hernon, Joseph Martin. *Profiles in Character: Hubris and Heroism in the U.S. Senate, 1789–1990.* Armonk, NY: M.E. Sharpe, 1997.

Rable, George C. *But There Was No Peace: The Role of Violence in the Politics of Reconstruction.* Athens: University of Georgia Press, 2007.

Vorenberg, Michael. *Final Freedom: The Civil War, the Abolition of Slavery, and the Thirteenth Amendment.* Cambridge, UK: Cambridge University Press, 2001.

Weigley, Russell F. *A Great Civil War: A Military and Political History, 1861–1865.* Bloomington: Indiana University Press, 2000.

Fetterman Massacre

In Wyoming's Powder River country during Red Cloud's War (1866–1868), the Fetterman Massacre gave the U.S. Cavalry a stunning defeat. While opening a passage from the Dakotas into Montana on the Bozeman Trail in May 1866, the Eighteenth Infantry, commanded by Colonel Henry Beebee Carrington at Fort Phil Kearny, Wyoming, constructed a bridge on the Montana border to ease passage of wagon trains.

A newcomer to Sioux territory in November 1866, Captain William Judd Fetterman was a Civil War hero with little experience fighting Indians. He incurred attacks in November and December by Oglala Lakota Chief Red Cloud, Miniconjou Chief Hump, and Hunkpapa chiefs Gall and Rain-in-the-face, leaders of Arapaho, Cheyenne, and Sioux braves, who targeted unguarded woodcutting details of 24 to 40 mule-drawn wagons. The Indians intended to discourage the desecration of the sacred Black Hills on the South Dakota border and to halt prospecting on traditional lands. In disagreement with Carrington's tactics, Fetterman boasted that he could defeat the Sioux with only 80 soldiers.

An hour after the woodcutters left on December 21, 1866, some 2,000 Indians ambushed them under the command of chiefs Red Cloud and Crazy Horse, Northern Cheyenne Chief Little Wolf, and Cheyenne war society leader Roman Nose. Fetterman, the senior officer, intervened with 78 soldiers, along with civilian scouts Isaac Fisher and James S. Wheatley, both armed with state-of-the-art Henry repeater rifles. The Indian decoys fled one by one, luring the military detail up Lodge Trail Ridge along Peno Creek, out of sight of the fort.

Against orders from Colonel Carrington not to pursue the enemy, Fetterman ascended the ridge and, surrounded by the enemy, engaged in a 20-minute battle. Against a rain of arrows, his men fired seven-shot Spencer carbines. After they ran through their ammunition, the soldiers fought for their lives with bayonets, knives, and gunstocks. In the final foray, Lieutenant George W. Grummond was nearly beheaded. Fetterman and Captain Frederick H. Brown, an avowed Indian hater, shot each other through the temples with pistols rather than undergo Sioux torture.

Through field glasses, Carrington observed the evolving ambush from his watchtower at the fort. When he arrived with a rescue party, he found 79 of the 80 victims naked and mutilated, a fact that the media sensationalized. One body, that of a bugler, Corporal Adolph Metzger, lay fully clothed and undesecrated beneath a buffalo robe. Historians interpreted the gesture as Sioux respect for a man who had fought with his bugle to the last. That night and the next morning, in subzero temperatures, Carrington's men recovered the bodies for burial. Five days after the massacre, the high command dismissed Carrington, ruining his career.

Carrington's first wife, Margaret Irvin Sullivant Carrington, recounted the details in *Absaraka, Home of the Crows: Being the Experience of an Officer's Wife on the Plains* (1868). His second wife, Frances Courtney Carrington, who was married to Lieutenant Grummond at the time of the Fetterman Massacre, recounted the details in *My Army Life* (1910). The women's texts vindicated the commander for his conservative policies. Another memoirist, Elizabeth Reynolds Burt, commented on events in "An Army Wife's Forty Years in the Service, 1862–1902" (unpublished).

In 1867, the naming of Fort Fetterman, Wyoming, honored the martyr of the massacre. Red Cloud's triumph elevated him to the only Indian war chief to claim a major victory against the U.S. military.

See also: Bozeman Trail; Crazy Horse; Red Cloud.

Further Reading

Dary, David. *The Oregon Trail: An American Saga.* New York: Alfred A. Knopf, 2004.

Johansen, Bruce E., and Donald A. Grinde, Jr. *The Encyclopedia of Native American Biography.* New York: Da Capo, 1998.

Lamar, Howard R., ed. *The New Encyclopedia of the American West.* New Haven, CT: Yale University Press, 1998.

Larson, Robert W. *Gall: Lakota War Chief.* Norman: University of Oklahoma Press, 2007.

Waldman, Carl. *Who Was Who in Native American History: Indians and Non-Indians from Early Contacts Through 1900.* New York: Facts on File, 1990.

Field, Cyrus W. (1819–1892)

Capitalist Cyrus West Field connected North America to Ireland via the transatlantic telegraph. The son of the Reverend David Dudley Field and Submit Dickinson Field, he was born in Stockbridge, Massachusetts, on November 30, 1819, and grew up in a pious household.

After completing Stockbridge Academy, he chose experience in merchandising over college. He clerked at A.T. Stewart & Company, a dry goods business in New York, and, from age 18 to 20, kept accounts at the newsprint paper mill of his brother, Matthew Dickinson Field, in Lee, Massachusetts. He also maintained a sales route to Boston, New York, Philadelphia, and Washington, D.C.

By 1840, Field owned his own paper mill, which failed. Two years later, he established Cyrus W. Field & Company at Westfield, Massachusetts, and married Mary Bryan Stone, the mother of their seven children. The paper industry made him independently wealthy at age 33, when he retired.

After consulting with Samuel F.B. Morse, in 1856, Field formed the Atlantic Telegraph Company with a grant from the British government and funds raised in England and Scotland. In a race to defeat Western Union's hopes of transoceanic communication, Field laid a preliminary cable across Cabot Strait from St. John's, Newfoundland, to Aspy Bay, Nova Scotia. The consortium of 30 members from Canada, Great Britain, and the United States chose Sir Charles Tilston Bright as chief engineer for the Atlantic crossing. They hired English surgeon Edward Orange Wildman Whitehouse as chief electrician and William Thomson as mathematician and scientific adviser. Whitehouse and Thomson disagreed over the speed of message transfer and the ultimate profitability of the venture.

In August 1857, Field's enterprise, with the support of President Franklin Pierce, began extending the first telegraph cable over the Atlantic Ocean aboard the HMS *Agamemnon.* The cable, a flexible bundle of seven copper wires that were triple-coated in gutta-percha (latex) and covered in tarred hemp, split 380 miles (610 kilometers) from Ballycarbery Castle, Ireland. A storm in June 1858 ended the second attempt, which involved a test of Thomson's mirror galvanometer and the splicing of two cable ends in the middle of the Atlantic.

On August 5, 1858, a third attempt extended the cable from continent to continent. Eleven days later, Queen Victoria congratulated Field and his associates with a telegraph to President James Buchanan. A 100-gun salute in New York City celebrated Field's success. A procession of dignitaries welcomed the favorite son of Massachusetts home to Stockbridge. Field declared that he hoped the telegraph would communicate messages of peace "from the Old World to the New." The cable remained in service for three weeks and then, after Whitehouse shocked the wire with 2,000 volts to achieve faster transmissions, broke. The jolt had destroyed the insulation. Because of the loss of $2.5 million, the consortium fired Whitehouse.

Although public confidence in the feasibility of Field's venture declined, innovation in telegraphy during the Civil War buoyed his hopes of an undersea link. On July 15, 1865, another cable placement from the SS *Great Eastern* failed when the cable snapped.

On July 28, 1866, a new Atlantic cable laid by the Anglo-American Telegraph Company proved more efficient, transmitting at a rate of eight words per minute. Within 24 hours, the company earned £1,000. On the homeward journey from the contact point at Valentia Island, Ireland, on September 7, Field—by this time, the renowned father of the Atlantic telegraph cable—repaired the first cable at Heart's Content, Newfoundland. By splicing the earlier effort, he established an alternate, but slower, route of telegraphy to London, which he had made the telecommunications capital of the world. The U.S. Congress awarded him a Gold Medal.

In 1877, Field controlled the New York Elevated Railroad Company. The overhead rail service introduced rapid transit to the city by passing from the South Ferry over Wall Street up the Bowery to the Grand Central Depot. He collaborated with investor Jay Gould on the building of the Wabash Railroad and, in April 1880, plotted a Pacific cable route from San Francisco to Hawaii and a double route from Hawaii to Japan and from Hawaii to Australia, with connections at Fiji and New Caledonia. Out of admiration for publisher Horace Greeley, Field purchased the *New York Evening Express* and, on December 5, 1881, merged it with the *Mail* to form the *New York Evening Mail and Express.*

In his seventies, Field experienced serious setbacks, beginning in 1882, when he was the intended recipient of a mail bomb that exploded in the carrier's bag before reaching him. Police arrested socialist George H. Hendrix for the assault. Field lost heavily on wheat futures and elevated rail stock in 1887, when he sold his shares of the New York Elevated Railroad to Gould. In March 1888, Field sold his newspaper.

His fortune gone, he relied on the benevolence of J. Pierpont Morgan. Field died from old age and exhaustion on July 12, 1892.

Further Reading

Chandler, Alfred D., Jr., and James W. Cortada, eds. *A Nation Transformed by Information: How Information Has Shaped the United States from Colonial Times to the Present.* Oxford, UK: Oxford University Press, 2000.

Fang, Irving. *A History of Mass Communication: Six Information Revolutions.* Boston: Focal Press, 1997.

Klein, Maury. *The Genesis of Industrial America, 1870–1920.* Oxford, UK: Oxford University Press, 2007.

Nickles, David Paull. *Under the Wire: How the Telegraph Changed Diplomacy.* Cambridge, MA: Harvard University Press, 2003.

Restivo, Sal P., ed. *Science, Technology, and Society: An Encyclopedia.* Oxford, UK: Oxford University Press, 2005.

Fifteenth Amendment

The last of three changes to the U.S. Constitution following the Civil War—collectively known as the Reconstruction Amendments—the Fifteenth Amendment became law on February 3, 1870. The measure forbade individual states from denying voting rights to citizens "on account of race, color, or previous condition of servitude."

Blacks had enjoyed citizenship since passage of the Fourteenth Amendment in 1868, but Jim Crow prohibitions and the terrorist night-riding of the Ku Klux Klan kept former slaves from exercising their full rights. In January 1869, members of the National Convention of the Colored Men of America, led by President William Nesbit from Altoona, Pennsylvania, head of the Pennsylvania State Equal Rights League, pressured President-Elect Ulysses S. Grant to extend suffrage as a cornerstone of equal rights. Despite opposition from Western states to giving voting rights to Chinese and Irish immigrants, the House bill passed on January 30 with a vote of 150–42.

Approved by the Senate on February 26, 1869, the Fifteenth Amendment advanced to the states for ratification. It passed in 28 states in 11 months, but lost in Delaware on March 18; in Kentucky on March 12; and in Ohio on April 30. A later rejection came from Tennessee on November 16. Oregon legislators chose to ignore the bill entirely.

Iowa's vote on February 3, 1870, secured the required three-fourths majority of states. Black voters in New York City led a celebratory parade. More votes followed ratification, including a rescission in New York on January 5, and rejection in California on January 28, to avoid giving Chinese Americans the vote. More rejections came from New Jersey on February 7 and Maryland on February 26. Goaded by *Harper's Weekly* illustrator Alfred Rudolph Waud and editor George William Curtis, New York overturned its rescission on March 30.

A poster from 1870 depicts celebratory events in Baltimore, Maryland, to mark ratification of the Fifteenth Amendment, which guaranteed the voting rights of African American males. *(Library of Congress)*

The amendment received the support of black orators Frederick Douglass and Frances Ellen Watkins Harper, *Harper's Weekly* editor George William Curtis and illustrators Thomas Nast and Alfred Rudolph Waud, and white suffragists Julia Ward Howe and Lucy Stone. At the May 1869 National Woman's Rights Convention in New York City, Douglass declared that post–Civil War violence against black males made their enfranchisement more urgent than that of women, who already possessed more social and economic rights than blacks of either gender. Out of regard for ex-slaves as equals, Republican Rutherford B. Hayes, then the governor of Ohio, crusaded for ratification of the amendment enfranchising black males.

Despite Douglass's comments and the support of some woman suffragists, overall the push for voting rights for black men antagonized the women's rights movement, including orator Sojourner Truth, Underground Railroad agent Harriet Tubman, and influential editor Lydia Maria Child, head of the Massachusetts Woman Suffrage Association. Women felt betrayed and shoved aside as less important in the making of national civil rights.

The campaign for black male suffrage forced leaders Elizabeth Cady Stanton and Susan B. Anthony to lobby against any constitutional alteration that perpetuated male dominance of the legal and legislative sphere. Attorneys Henry Rogers Selden and John Van Voorhis advised Susan B. Anthony to claim women's voting rights personally under the "New Departure Strategy," an argument framed by New York City feminist Victoria Claflin Woodhull, publisher of *Woodhull & Claflin's Weekly.*

For Thanksgiving 1869, cartoonist Thomas Nast drew for *Harper's Weekly* "Uncle Sam's Thanksgiving Dinner," an allegorical feast expressing his Reconstruction-era ideals. The drawing endorses the Fifteenth Amendment with the inclusion of African, Arab, Chinese, French, German, Irish, Italian, Native American, and Spanish celebrants at the table for the carving of the turkey. Women and children have equal representation at the meal. "Columbia" sits at the foot of the table as a symbol of American leadership in the world. All diners face a centerpiece honoring self-government and universal suffrage. Portraits of presidents George Washington, Abraham Lincoln, and Ulysses S. Grant look down from the wall.

However, the reality of enfranchisement was grimmer than Nast's idyllic feast. In the South, Jim Crow laws forced black voters to pass literacy tests and pay poll taxes in order to vote. The reading tests required blacks to analyze constitutional regulations to the satisfaction of registrars, many of them racist white males. On January 17, 1877, President Ulysses S. Grant confided to Secretary of State Hamilton Fish that the constitutional change had not, in fact, benefited blacks. The Fifteenth Amendment remained jeopardized by bias for another century, until the civil rights movement of the 1960s.

See also: Jim Crow; Ku Klux Klan; Nast, Thomas; Stanton, Elizabeth Cady; Thanksgiving.

Further Reading

Dailey, Jane, Glenda Elizabeth Gilmore, and Bryant Simon, eds. *Jumpin' Jim Crow: Southern Politics from Civil War to Civil Rights.* Princeton, NJ: Princeton University Press, 2000.

Keyssar, Alexander. *The Right to Vote: The Contested History of Democracy in the United States.* New York: Basic Books, 2000.

Olson, Lynne. *Freedom's Daughters: The Unsung Heroines of the Civil Rights Movement from 1830 to 1970.* New York: Simon & Schuster, 2001.

Rothenberg, Paula S., ed. *Race, Class, and Gender in the United States: An Integrated Study.* 7th ed. New York: Worth, 2007.

Sneider, Allison L. *Suffragists in an Imperial Age: U.S. Expansion and the Woman Question, 1870–1929.* New York: Oxford University Press, 2008.

Fish, Hamilton (1808–1893)

Hamilton Fish, who served as governor of New York (1849–1850), U.S. senator (1851–1857), and U.S. secretary of state (1869–1877) under President Ulysses S. Grant, gained respect for his meticulous and restrained statesmanship. A wealthy and prominent New Yorker, he was born on August 3, 1808, at 21 Stuyvesant Street in Greenwich Village to Revolutionary War veteran Nicholas Fish and Elizabeth Stuyvesant Fish, the scion of Peter Stuyvesant, a seventeenth-century settler of Dutch New York. Nicholas homeschooled his son and hired a French tutor to increase Hamilton's fluency in French.

A Phi Beta Kappa graduate and valedictorian from Columbia College, Fish studied under attorney Peter Augustus Jay and set up a practice in property law with William Beach Lawrence. He involved himself in Episcopalian charities and married Julia Ursin Neimcewicz Kean, a socialite and intellectual. As a Whig, Fish advanced in politics from a member of the U.S. House of Representatives (1843–1844) to lieutenant governor of New York (1848), before being elected to the governorship in the latter year.

At the onset of the Civil War, Fish campaigned for Abraham Lincoln's presidency and, as chairman of the Union Defense Committee, enlisted volunteers, bought military equipment, and distributed $1 million in aid to Union soldiers and their families. As an appointee of

Secretary of War Edwin M. Stanton, Fish requested an investigation of conditions in Libby Prison at Richmond, Virginia, and other rebel lockups, which Confederates refused. Fish then negotiated the principles of exchange of Union and Confederate prisoners of war that remained in use for four years.

In his eight years as secretary of state in the Grant administrations, Fish's refined manners and fluency in French proved useful. Upon taking office on March 17, 1869, he set standards of probity and judgment for U.S. consuls and his staff. During an era of expansionism in the Caribbean, beginning late in 1869, he failed to win Grant's purchase bid for the Dominican Republic and the leasing of Samaná Bay. Fish dissuaded Grant from involving the United States in the Ten Years' War in Cuba, which began in 1868, and composed a nonintervention message on June 13, 1870. In the settlement of U.S. claims against Great Britain in January 1871 for backing the Confederate raiders *Alabama, Florida,* and *Shenandoah,* Fish collected $15.5 million for the treasury. From March to July 1872, he engaged in talks with Japan's Meiji government concerning extradition treaties and tariffs. The discussion sent amateurish Japanese envoys on a hasty return trip to clarify protocols that Fish had outlined.

After the seizure of the gunrunner *Virginius,* which Cubans sailed under an American flag on October 31, 1873, Fish declined to rush into armed aggression to retaliate against the execution at Santiago of 53 American passengers and crew charged with piracy. Spain agreed to American demands for reparations in November 1873 and returned the *Virginius* along with a cash indemnity of $80,000. Fish attempted to replace European influence on Latin America with U.S. policies and trade, and he supported Grant in studying the possibilities for a canal across Nicaragua to gain access to the Pacific Ocean.

Fish concurred with the U.S. need for a military presence in the Pacific. In 1874, he aimed to establish a naval base at Pearl Harbor by negotiating with American sugar planters and King David Kalakaua to colonize the Hawaiian Islands. The agreement secured the island chain for American investment and ensured markets and trade far into the future. Fish brokered peace between Spain and its tributaries in 1875, proposing a six-nation settlement of Spanish claims to the republics of Bolivia, Chile, Ecuador, and Peru. Before Grant's departure from Washington, Fish began negotiations with Samoa for a U.S. base at Pago Pago, lest Britain or Germany seize the island first.

In the years after he left office, Fish remained a trustee of his alma mater and of the predecessors of the New York Public Library. He died suddenly from natural causes on September 7, 1893.

Further Reading

Beckert, Sven. *The Monied Metropolis: New York City and the Consolidation of the American Bourgeoisie, 1850–1896.* Cambridge, UK: Cambridge University Press, 2001.

Goodrich, Thomas. *The Darkest Dawn: Lincoln, Booth, and the Great American Tragedy.* Bloomington: Indiana University Press, 2005.

Herring, George C. *From Colony to Superpower: U.S. Foreign Relations Since 1776.* New York: Oxford University Press, 2008.

Silva, Noenoe K. *Aloha Betrayed: Native Hawaiian Resistance to American Colonialism.* Durham, NC: Duke University Press, 2004.

Fish Commission, U.S.

An independent federal agency established by congressional resolution, the U.S. Commission of Fish and Fisheries analyzed populations of aquatic mammals and fish in the nation's rivers and lakes and along the seacoasts. Empaneled by Congress on February 9, 1871, at the direction of President Ulysses S. Grant, the commission became the nation's first conservation agency overseeing renewable natural resources and investigating the problems of overfishing.

Field experts from Harvard, Wesleyan, and Yale universities reported to Spencer F. Baird, a volunteer and specialist in the birds and fish of Pennsylvania and secretary of the Smithsonian Institution. Without pay, Baird established the U.S. Fish Commission at Woods Hole on Cape Cod, Massachusetts. With an annual budget of $5,000, he applied scientific methods to the improvement and regulation of national renewable food sources. Operating out of the Smithsonian, the agency investigated decreasing fish populations, compiled catch and trade statistics on line and net fishing, and devised methods of enhancing commercial harvesting technology for fish, shellfish, and marine and fresh water mammals. The operation required the building of hatcheries and the inspection of the fur sealing industry in the Aleutian Islands and off the coast of Alaska. From the commission's data, Congress reviewed international treaties and tariffs, compiled marketing guides for the fish industry, and educated consumers on the consumption of sport fish and seafood.

The first year's studies concentrated on commentary, maps, and illustrations of explosives, grapples, nets, poisons, projectiles, and stationary pounds, traps, and weirs off the coasts of Noank, Connecticut; Portland, Maine; Newport, Rhode Island; and Edgartown, Hyannis, Lambert's Cove, Martha's Vineyard, Nantucket, Vineyard Haven, and Woods Hole, Massachusetts. For advice on increasing yields of alewives, bluefish, dogfish, flatfish, mackerel, menhaden, scup, and sea bass, Baird's team consulted with ichthyologists in London and Naples. Field surveys required the charting of spawning grounds and the monitoring of surface and bottom temperatures.

Additional research into insects, marine algae, parasites, sponges, and invertebrates and inspection of bridges, buoys, floating timbers, vessels, and wharves summarized the health of habitats off New England. Naturalist Theodore Gill, a librarian at the Smithsonian and the Library of Congress, catalogued East Coast fish and mollusks by genus, species, and order. With the statistics, the commission educated cod fishers on the use of the Norwegian gillnet and built the first fishery at Woods Hole for artificial fish propagation.

From 1872 to 1875, the commission moved inland to study the alewife, capelin, salmon smolt, shad, trout, and whitefish in the Great Lakes, the Alabama, Potomac, and Sacramento rivers, and the Gulf of Mexico, and along the coasts of Maine and New Brunswick. Consultation with German and Swedish salmon specialists on reproduction, migration, and disease preceded the building of the first site of the National Fish Hatchery System to propagate chinook salmon on the pristine McCloud River in north-central California. Necessary to spawning and upriver migration was the establishment of fish ladders over dams and locks. Agents led by ichthyologist Tarleton Hoffman Bean, the curator of fish for the U.S. National Museum, proposed extending salmon hatcheries to New Hampshire, New Jersey, Ohio, Pennsylvania, and Wisconsin and shipping salmon roe to New Zealand. Scrutiny of habitats intensified along the Atlantic Coast from Maine to North Carolina, with data gleaned from studies of pisciculture (the cultivation of fish) in Austria, France, Italy, Russia, and Switzerland.

Baird concentrated on the commercial breeding of fish as an industry and a cheap source of nourishing food for rural citizens. Throughout the Midwest and the South, he stocked rearing ponds, including one on the grounds of the Washington Monument. In 1873, trout culturist Livingston Stone, a founder of the American Fisheries Society, experimented with transporting 35,000 shad fry west by rail from northern lakes in New York for planting at Clear Lake Experimental Hatchery in California as food and sport fish. In baggage cars, agents aerated and agitated water in the holding barrels and milk cans and added ice to slow fingerling metabolism to reduce their oxygen needs. Ninety percent of the fry survived the trip. From 1875 to 1876, Stone furnished 1.5 million whitefish eggs to the project. Less successful was the commission program to stock the Mississippi River with salmon and shad.

The U.S. Fish Commission shifted its focus in 1877 to cod, herring, mackerel, and menhaden, a source of bait, food, guano, oil, and roe. Researchers identified bacterial sources of discoloration on salt cod. Data from Norwegian and Swedish fisheries branched out from oily fish to include clams, lobsters, oysters, seals, and whales. English ichthyologists shared advice on transporting sole and turbot to North America. Using chartered ships from the U.S. Coast Survey, the agency set up research stations and plotted higher spawning yields in ponds and hatcheries along the Clackamas River in Oregon, the Susquehanna River in Maryland, and the Connecticut River in Massachusetts. Pragmatic advice on deep-sea temperatures and artificial refrigeration with salts, ice machines, crystalloids, condensers, and glaciaria included peripheral commentary on desalinization.

The commission remained active for more than 30 years and enforced laws against harvesting with explosives or poisons. Experts trained marine biologists to document port and hatchery activity, sanitary seafood processing, petroleum pollution of oceans and waterways, and such naturally occurring phenomena as red tides.

The commission was renamed the Bureau of Fisheries in 1903 and transferred to the new Department of Commerce and Labor. In 1940, it merged with the Bureau of Biological Survey to form the Fish and Wildlife Service, part of the Department of the Interior.

Further Reading

Brunner, Ronald D., et al. *Adaptive Governance: Integrating Science, Policy, and Decision Making.* New York: Columbia University Press, 2005.

Pauly, Philip J. *Biologists and the Promise of American Life from Meriwether Lewis to Alfred Kinsey.* Princeton, NJ: Princeton University Press, 2000.

Reiger, John F. *American Sportsmen and the Origins of Conservation.* 3rd ed. Corvallis: Oregon State University Press, 2001.

Food and Food Preservation

After the onset of the Civil War, food availability and hoarding vaulted to primary importance as communities pondered the likelihood of child malnutrition and starvation. Without mentioning wartime privations, editorials and recipes in *Godey's Lady's Book,* a popular magazine published in Philadelphia, featured extensive information on making spruce beer and cheap soap, preventing rust in kitchen implements, and preserving fruit and flowers to add zing to humdrum meals.

In the South, Confederate soldiers ate from truck gardens, apiaries, dairies, hen yards, smokehouses, and orchards in season. However, Union sabotage of harbors and rail lines and the robbing of freight ships and cars produced shortages of rations for the military and civilians alike.

At Richmond, Virginia, the Confederate capital, profiteering pushed the price of bacon to 75 cents per pound, green tea to $7 per pound, and a bushel of salt to $30. In Columbia, South Carolina, the Columbia Mutual Supply Association formed on November 14, 1863, and offered purchase rights based on $100 shares in the association store. At the "Bee" Store, owned by William C. Bee, blacks shopped only on appointed days. These and other ploys failed to halt the rise of cornmeal prices to $5 per bushel, brown sugar to $6 per pound, and bacon to $2.50 per pound. Cattle on the hoof sold for $225 and whiskey for $60 per gallon.

Authorities forced farmers to tithe their produce at collection sites, which police guarded against enemy raids. For moneyed whites, James G. Gibbes auctioned kitchen staples, sardines, saltpeter, gin, and opium, goods delivered by the blockade runners *Alice* and *Fannie.* Following General William Tecumseh Sherman's four-day torching of Columbia and ripping up of rail lines, by March 1865, provisioners relied on wagon lines to feed the city on meager cabbages and beets.

For the elderly, infirm, and unemployed, the snaring of blackbirds, chickadees, and robins produced meat for songbird pies to relieve standard meals of cornbread. Cats and dogs disappeared from the streets. Roasted chinquapins, dandelion and melon seeds, okra, peanuts, and rye substituted for coffee, which drinkers sweetened with honey, jelly, or molasses. Vinegar pie replaced fruit pies. A black market arose in coffee, sugar, and meat from blockade runners and speculators, who sold to panicked homemakers and kitchen managers at orphanages, schools, restaurants, and hotels. Feisty females overran food warehouses and emporiums to plunder flour barrels, saltboxes, and sacks of wheat, rice, and corn that profiteers stored to drive up prices. Deserters confessed to their superiors the need to return home to plow and sow fields and to shoot deer and turkeys for their hungry families.

The control of rivers became crucial to food suppliers. According to the *Cincinnati Daily Gazette,* on June 12, 1861, a federal embargo on Mississippi River traffic from Paducah to Smithland, Kentucky, deprived families of corn, flour, hay, livestock, oats, pork, and wheat, an imposition that forced businesses to close. Individuals relied on a covert barter system in contraband items with suppliers in southern Illinois and Missouri. A parallel flow of coal, corn, flour, and wheat through the Chesapeake and Ohio Canal kept local families supplied.

An act of Congress required an official U.S. Treasury stamp to certify licit importation from licensed dealers of packages and barrels transported by water, rail, and wagon. The embargo remained in partial effect until August 29, 1865.

The Hungry South

To the south, distribution foundered. In Georgia, females, many of them soldiers' wives, rioted in Columbus in 1863 and in Atlanta and Savannah in April 1864 as a show of frustration with the long war. Smaller outbreaks wracked Blackshear, Cartersville, Colquitt, Forsyth, Hartwell, Stockton, Thomasville, and Valdosta. At Marietta, 28 women brandishing firearms and knives ambushed a supply train.

At 2 P.M. on March 18, 1863, in Salisbury, North Carolina, Mary Moore led 50–75 female householders on a food rampage. The women armed themselves with axes and hatchets for a raid on food hoarders and profiteers Michael Brown, John Ennis, Thomas Foster, and David Weil. The men negotiated on the spot and reduced the inflated price on ten barrels of flour. Merchants donated a bag of salt, a barrel of molasses, and $20 in Confederate currency. Another dealer gave three of his seven barrels of flour to soldiers' wives. According to the Salisbury daily *Carolina Watchman,* the women snagged ten more barrels of flour and rolled them out to a waiting wagon. Governor Zebulon B. Vance chose to admonish Moore's raiders rather than the speculators who flouted government price controls.

Two weeks later, on April 2, 1863, Mary Jackson, Minerva Meredith, and 46 mothers of starving children in Richmond, Virginia, engineered the largest wartime food riot. Armed with clubs, hammers, kitchen knives, and pistols, they plundered a grocery commissary and smashed windows in 12 stores along Cary and Main streets. The women skirmished for two hours over bread, bacon, and sides of beef, as well as leather shoes, candles, jewelry, and yard goods to use in trade for staples. The rampage arose at a time when army privates earned $11 per month and food prices were as much as 50 times what they had been in 1860 before stabilizing in the 1870s.

By the time the mob grew to 1,000 looters, Mayor Joseph Mayo, Virginia Governor John Letcher, and Confederate President Jefferson Davis, who lived two blocks away, intervened, mustered the urban guard, and placed cannon

Southern Food Prices, 1860–1877

Commodity	1860	1863	1870	1877
Bacon/pound	$1.25	$1.50	$0.16	$0.09
Beef/pound	0.10	4.00	0.07	0.08
Butter/pound	0.23	8.00	0.15	0.15
Coffee/pound	0.07	5.00	0.12	0.12
Flour/barrel	4.00	200.00	3.00	8.00
Potatoes/barrel	1.20	12.00	65.00	43.70
Sugar/pound	0.04	1.50	0.07	0.07
Wheat/bushel	1.50	4.00	1.29	1.34

at strategic locations. Court punishment ranged from fines to five-year jail terms. The Richmond *Examiner* dismissed the outcry for food as the work of Irish and Yankee sluts and criminals; the wealthy accused rioters of exaggerating their need. After food distribution worsened, in September 1863, aproned women in Mobile, Alabama, launched a food riot in grocery stores along Dauphine Street and demanded "Food or Death."

Georgia suffered a total trade collapse and a loss of $275 million in commerce. On General Sherman's march through Cobb County in June 1864, his provisioners looted corncribs, barns, root cellars, and spring houses, leaving households devastated. By war's end, a grim landscape revealed collapsed fences, smashed wagons, weedy fields, and roads clogged with stragglers returning home. When Robert E. Lee surrendered to Ulysses S. Grant in April 1865, the Union general sent food wagons to the Confederate troops, who raised a cheer after going hungry for two days.

Because seed and implement sellers demanded inflated prices, cash-strapped farmers raised mostly vegetables and small grains and traded in kind or labor. In 1867, an agent of the Freedmen's Bureau in Carroll County reported "the extreme destitute of this poor poverty stricken and God forsaken country . . . Nothing plentiful here except pine trees, flint rocks, and reconstructionists." A drought and resultant corn crop failure in 1866 and again in 1869 worsened the situation, forcing individuals to manage day by day on oats and sweet potatoes or to migrate west.

Frontier Food Distribution

Transportation across the frontier was the lifeline linking suppliers with soldiers, farmers, herders, miners, freighters, mailmen, missionaries, Pony Express riders, railroad crews, and homesteaders. Women who chose to relocate to the West gave up the convenience of fresh fish and shellfish from New England trawlers and the country store, where buyers could select by hand eggs, apples, and root vegetables from convenient baskets, candies and spices from glass jars, and dried peas and beans, brined pickles, and wheat wafers from kegs and barrels.

At the border of western Iowa, wharfmen hustled corn, oats, and wheat onto flatboats for transfer to the Nebraska shores. Across the Platte Valley in Nebraska, a natural highway to the Pacific Coast, deliveries from Missouri steamboats passed to ox-drawn wagon trains and across the Central Plains to trading posts in Denver, Colorado, and Salt Lake City, Utah. People depended on bulk shipments of salt, grains, flour, dried beef, fruit, delicacies, and whiskey and medicines to ease the hardships of frontier life. In lieu of regular deliveries, families relied on hardtack, salt pork, jerky, and dried beans.

Price was proportional to distance, degree of delicacy and perishability, and difficulty of packing and transport. Unusual overland loads brought frozen eggs and frozen oysters at $2.50 per quart from Omaha, Nebraska, to Denver. Apples fetched $15 per bushel. To rid stores of vermin, one wagoneer carried cats to Denver for sale to mining camps. At Leadville, Colorado's fastest growing boomtown, groceries sold for four times the price in Denver, with whiskey leading inflation at $1,500 per barrel because of the difficulty of transporting it over wagon trails into the Rocky Mountains. The success of freight and stage lines made famous the names William H. Russell, Alexander Majors, William Waddell, Benjamin "Ben" Holladay, Henry Wells, and William George Fargo, all of whom moved cargo rapidly and safely to its destination.

The distribution of staples to remote farms and ranches was crucial to family survival in the winter of 1874–1875, after a plague of grasshoppers mowed down crops along the Central Plains. Some survived by bartering with Indians for fish and game or by moving closer to civilization. A young mother, Emily McCorkle FitzGerald, recorded an army wife's grocery shopping in Sitka, Alaska, from 1874 to 1876 in *An Army Doctor's Wife on the Frontier* (1962). Daily, white women relied on door-to-door Tlingit vendors, who sold berries, birds, fish, and venison to replace beef, which arrived weekly by steamer.

Food Innovation

Rapid industrialization and improvements in coast-to-coast transportation transformed table fare. In 1859, Rumford baking powder bolstered the nutritional value of bread and baked goods by replacing the calcium and phosphates that flour lost in milling. Baron Justus Von Liebig marketed infant food that mimicked the texture, flavor, and nutrition of breast milk, a lifesaver to orphaned infants or those allergic to cow's milk.

Northern canning factories supplied kitchens with new technology—cherries, corn, peas, and tomatoes in tins. The *American Agriculturist* promoted recycling by describing the reshaping of used tins into feed cups, scoops, saucepans, fruit pickers, graters, and muffin rings. The narrow-neck canning jar served home canners in the late 1860s, as did John B. Bartlett's improved metal cap secured by elastic bands and, in 1874, the refinement of pressure canning.

At the Centennial Exposition in Philadelphia in 1876, brothers Charles and Maximilian Fleischmann introduced yeast cakes, a boon to bread makers. In New York City, the U.S. Dairy Company manufactured imitation butter, which preceded by one year the packaging of cream cheese in Chester, New York. A boost to sanitation, Premium soda crackers (saltines) and Hires Root Beer were available in 1876 in individual servings, rather than easily contaminated loose crackers in barrels and root beer kegs; Charles Hires, a pharmacist from Philadelphia, sold his blend of carbonated water and 25 berries, herbs, and roots at the Centennial Exposition. Chase & Sanborn added to the list of individually packaged foods by selling ground-roast coffee in metal cans.

Convenience foods improved the merchandising of table goods. By serendipity, a dry growing season in California vineyards produced raisins, a shelf-stable dried fruit that grocers sold on the stem. In 1861, Van Camp sold canned beans in tomato sauce. The first Campbell's soup appeared in grocery stores in 1869. The H.J. Heinz Company brought variety to the table with bottled flavorings and condiments—evaporated horseradish, mustard, pickles, tomato and walnut ketchup, fruit preserves, baked beans, bottled onions, chutney, fish sauce, jelly, sauerkraut, vinegar, and Worcestershire sauce.

In 1870, the Underwood Company, Henry Heinz's competitor, added to canned meats by introducing deviled (seasoned) ground ham, chicken, turkey, tongue, and lobster. The creation of a tear strip and key wind simplified the use of commercial tins. In 1875, the marketing of canned milk offered new possibilities for travel and trail food and infant feeding.

Ferdinand Schumacher, owner of the German American Cereal Company in Akron, Ohio, began advertising rolled oats in 1870 in the Akron *Beacon Journal,* source of the first cereal advertising campaign. On September 4, 1877, the trademark picture of a man in Quaker suit, vest, and hat became the logo of William Heston and Henry D. Seymour's Quaker Mill Company of Ravenna, Ohio. Their energetic advertising made oats a staple of the American breakfast menu.

See also: Heinz, H.J.; Home Economics; Stagecoach Travel.

Further Reading

Ball, Raymond F. *Marcy.* Charleston, SC: Arcadia, 2007.

Bynum, Victoria E. *Unruly Women: The Politics of Social and Sexual Control in the Old South.* Chapel Hill: University of North Carolina Press, 1992.

Hahn, Steven. *The Roots of Southern Populism: Yeoman Farmers and the Transformation of the Georgia Upcountry, 1850–1890.* New York: Oxford University Press, 2006.

Robertson, John. *Paducah, KY: Frontier to the Atomic Age.* Charleston, SC: Arcadia, 2002.

Rubin, Mary H. *The Chesapeake and Ohio Canal.* Charleston, SC: Arcadia, 2003.

Snodgrass, Mary Ellen. *Encyclopedia of Kitchen History.* New York: Fitzroy Dearborn, 2004.

Fort System

The U.S. federal fort system, which dates to 1794, adapted to suit the terrain, threats, and innovations in ordnance of the Civil War. After the rebel attack on Fort Sumter, South Carolina, on April 12, 1861, the Union army bolstered the Atlantic Coast network of masonry forts to protect ports and to defend Washington, D.C. Under the engineering specifications of the nation's third fort system, builders used brick-and-granite wall construction.

In 1862, Secretary of War Edwin M. Stanton reviewed the capital fort system, which relied primarily on Fort Washington on the Potomac River in Maryland. Stanton located and corrected weaknesses on the northwestern rim from Fort Massachusetts to the banks of the Potomac. A key installation at Fort Monroe in Hampton, Virginia, halted the Confederate advance during the Peninsula Campaign. Beginning in spring 1861, General Benjamin Franklin Butler provided safe harbor for fleeing slaves at Fort Monroe by listing them as contraband of war. A Union spy, Elizabeth Van Lew, offered volunteer assistance to runaways by supplying them with necessities that the fort lacked.

The exigencies of the Civil War forced Congress to rebuild Fort Wayne, Indiana, from a wooden outpost to a red brick training center for 1,000 recruits. Builders stabilized the structure with a cedar and oak log scarp or ditch below the rampart. The large number of enlistees required the mooring of the steamer *Mississippi* as a temporary barracks for four companies.

A U.S. Cavalry patrol departs Fort Bowie near the strategically important Apache Pass in the Chiricahua Mountains of Arizona. The fort, built in 1862, was a key Southwestern outpost during the Indian Wars. *(Time & Life Pictures/Getty Images)*

In the late 1800s, the U.S. military re-armed its forts with earthworks to support 10-, 15-, and 20-inch (25-, 38-, and 50-centimeter) Rodman guns, durable, 80-ton (73-metric-ton) cannon firing a half-ton shot. The largest cannon in the world at the time, Rodman guns cast in Pittsburgh and Reading, Pennsylvania, and at Cold Spring, New York, guarded harbors in Maine, Maryland, Massachusetts, New Jersey, Virginia, and Washington, D.C., as well as in New York at Fort Hamilton and the U.S. Military Academy at West Point. A model of American technology, the Rodman drew viewers to the U.S. Government Building at the 1876 Centennial Exposition in Philadelphia.

Indian wars in the West required constant land-based military readiness and forts equipped with mountain howitzers, bronze cannon, and Gatling guns. In 1862, General James Henry Carleton established Fort Bowie in southeastern Arizona on the New Mexico border, a central outpost during the U.S. Army's defeat of the Chiricahua Apache. Upgraded with adobe housing, a trading post, a hospital, and corrals, the fort remained essential to the subduing of the renegade Apache Chief Geronimo in 1886. Another government stronghold, Fort Douglas east of Salt Lake City, Utah, established in 1862 by Colonel Patrick Edward Connor, kept the peace in Mormon territory and protected mail carriers and telegraph lines along the Overland Mail route. In 1864, hostilities between the U.S. Army and the Lakota Sioux required the construction of Fort Rice on the upper Missouri River in North Dakota.

In 1866, the erection of Fort Kearney in south-central Nebraska shielded travelers from Indian raids along the Oregon and Bozeman trails as far west as Banner, Wyoming. Adobe and sod structures housed the First Nebraska Cavalry and the Seventh Iowa Cavalry. The supply staff outfitted and provisioned soldiers and pioneers, coordinated mail service, and, after 1867, guarded workers on the Union Pacific Railroad. With the arrival of train service on May 22, 1871, the army dismantled the fort and moved it 70 miles (110 kilometers) west to Fort McPherson.

Fort Leavenworth, Kansas, which once guarded the Santa Fe Trail, became a national cemetery authorized by President Abraham Lincoln in 1862 and the training ground for Buffalo Soldiers in 1866. The fort offered new service in 1875 as a maximum-security military prison and, in 1881, as a cavalry and infantry college.

Farther south, to protect the Anglo settlement of north Texas, in 1867, the army situated Fort Richardson on 300 acres (120 hectares) along Lost Creek in Jacksboro, Texas. The army backed the location with garrisons farther west at Fort Concho and Fort Griffin. The nation's largest outpost, Fort Richardson housed 666 men of the Sixth Cavalry under the command of General Philip Henry Sheridan, the first line of defense against Comanche and Kiowa raids. Other duties kept soldiers in the field escorting pioneers and cattle herds, tracking deserters and outlaws, protecting freed slaves, and superintending Reconstruction-era elections.

Subsequent occupancy of Fort Richardson brought the Fourth Cavalry in 1871. In July of that year, the fort was the location of the trial of Kiowa chiefs Big Tree and Satanta, the first Indians tried in a Texas court. The Fourth Cavalry, led by Colonel Ranald Slidell Mackenzie, ranged west from Fort Richardson to put down Comanche and Kiowa attacks led by Comanche Chief Quanah Parker and Kiowa Chief Red Warbonnet. The Eleventh Infantry occupied the fort in 1873 along with regiments of Buffalo Soldiers from the all-black Tenth Cavalry and the Twenty-fourth Infantry.

With peace assured in north Texas, the army abandoned Fort Richardson in May 1878. By the 1890s, the Western fort system was obsolete.

See also: Bozeman Trail; Oregon Trail.

Further Reading

Brown, Dee. *The American West.* New York: Simon & Schuster, 1995.

———. *Bury My Heart at Wounded Knee: An Indian History of the American West.* New York: Holt, Rinehart and Winston, 1970.

Buecker, Thomas R. *Fort Robinson and the American West, 1874–1899.* Lincoln: Nebraska State Historical Society, 1999.

Conway, James, and David F. Jamroz. *Detroit's Historic Fort Wayne.* Charleston, SC: Arcadia, 2007.

Lamar, Howard R., ed. *The New Encyclopedia of the American West.* New Haven, CT: Yale University Press, 1998.

Weaver, John R. *A Legacy in Brick and Stone: American Coastal Defense Forts of the Third System, 1816–1867.* McLean, VA: Redoubt, 2001.

Forten, Charlotte (1837–1914)

The first Northern black woman to teach in Southern freedmen's schools, Charlotte Louise Bridges "Lottie" Forten observed the transition of slaves to liberation. Born into a wealthy dynasty in Philadelphia on August 17, 1837, she grew up introspective and idealistic among liberal intellectuals dedicated to the Underground Railroad and abolitionism.

After the death of her mother, Mary Virginia Woods Forten, Charlotte, at age three, passed from the hands of her father, sail manufacturer Robert Bridges Forten, to the care of her grandmother, Charlotte Louise Forten, who homeschooled her and provided piano lessons. Her father retreated to Canada and England during threats of enslavement under the Fugitive Slave Law of 1850 and left Charlotte to board at the Salem, Massachusetts, home of orator Charles Lenox Remond, his sister, Sarah Parker Remond, and Charles's daughter.

Forten desegregrated her class of 200 at Higginson Grammar School for Girls, where she mastered art, cartography, geography, and history. After completing training in literature and educational method at the Salem Normal School, she graduated with honors for poetry. By joining the staff of Epes Grammar School, she became the system's first black teacher of white children.

At age 17, Forten began a decade-long chronicle of the antebellum North and the onset of the Civil War. She recorded her voracious readings in the Romantic poets and covered her early classroom experiences and involvement in the Salem Female Anti-Slavery Society and abolitionist fairs. Among her entries were the arrest of runaway slave Anthony Burns, which she described on May 25, 1854, and episodes of classism, racism, and sexism that lamented her displacement among white peers and among the less sophisticated of her own race.

In 1858, she required treatment for headaches and tuberculosis. She used her convalescence at the home of beautician Caroline Remond Putnam to read the social novels of Charles Dickens and to compose poems for *The Liberator* and the *National Anti-Slavery Standard.* In fall 1859, Forten began teaching at the Higginson School while taking advanced professional courses at the Salem Normal School. In spring 1860, she took sick leave to seek a water cure in Boston.

Mission to the South

On October 26, 1862, Forten, in company with missionary Ellen Murray and social worker Nelly Winsor, integrated an expedition of Quaker educators to recently captured Confederate territory. They sailed to the Sea Islands south of Charleston off the coast of South Carolina, then under control of 10,000 Union forces. At St. Helena Island, accessed from Beaufort by rowboat or ferry, Forten and Laura Matilda Towne, a teacher and homeopath, held classes for two years at The Oaks, a confiscated cotton plantation of 500 acres (200 hectares). They encountered Underground Railroad hero Harriet Tubman and enjoyed the singing of black boatmen, who serenaded them with "Ring Shout" and "Roll, Jordan, Roll." Towne's diary describes a smallpox epidemic and the two women's Christmas decorations of holly, mistletoe, pine boughs, magnolia leaves, and Spanish moss, an effort to supplant Congo-style spiritualism with Protestant religion.

Forten considered the relief effort a prime outlet for women seeking social volunteerism. It was an opportunity to hear firsthand the anecdotes and testimonials of former slaves, particularly women and children newly freed from coercion, concubinage, and the despair of babies sold from their mother's arms. Beginning in early November 1862, among 2,000 illiterate blacks, she and Towne opened classes first in a back room of the plantation, then at a one-room, two-story brick Baptist church a mile from Frogmore Plantation, a 2,139-acre (866-hectare) estate.

They taught 140 primary students to count, read, and sing the "John Brown" hymn and other patriotic songs in their native Gullah, an amalgam of West African dialects from Sierra Leone by which captives of various Gold Coast tribes communicated. One of the songs, "Christmas Hymn," poet John Greenleaf Whittier wrote especially for the curriculum. At night, while Towne treated the sick in their dirt-floored cabins, Forten taught literacy classes for liberated adults, one of whom nursed an infant while learning the alphabet. Forten exulted, "One cannot believe that the haughty Anglo Saxon race, after centuries of such an experience as these people have had, would be very much superior to them."

Because of the barbaric background, the nearly unintelligible language of plantation children, and the rudeness of racist Union soldiers, Forten found the experience challenging. She distributed gifts of clothing and picture books donated by Philadelphia matrons and introduced her pupils to the story of black hero Toussaint L'Ouverture, the Haitian liberator. After an attempted break-in at her bedroom, she armed herself with a pistol.

At a height of enthusiasm for liberty, on January 1, 1863, she assembled her classes at Camp Saxton, headquarters of the all-black First South Carolina Volunteers, for the reading of President Abraham Lincoln's Emancipation Proclamation. At the conclusion, she led her students in a chorus of "My Country 'Tis of Thee." As casualties from the Battle of Fort Wagner arrived in mid-July 1863, she nursed the wounded of the Fifty-fourth Massachusetts Volunteer Infantry, the nation's first black regiment, and mourned the death of its leader, Colonel Robert Gould Shaw, who had saluted her as a "daughter of the regiment."

Forten the Writer

At the Penn School, Forten taxed her lungs shouting over boisterous learners. Her respiratory sickness and the death of her father forced her to return home, where she began a career as a children's author and freelance translator of French and German novels. In May and June 1864, her memoir "Life on the Sea Islands" appeared in the *Atlantic Monthly* and introduced readers to the Port Royal Experiment, a program in which former slaves worked on land in South Carolina's Sea Islands that had been abandoned by plantation owners. At Boston, she found homes, health care, and jobs for former slaves by distributing government funds through the Freedmen's Relief Association.

At age 41, Forten wed Francis James "Frank" Grimké, a minister at the Fifteenth Street Presbyterian Church and co-founder of the National Association for the Advancement of Colored People. The couple settled in Washington, D.C., where she enlisted educators, taught school, and clerked for the U.S. Treasury.

In 1885, Forten returned to journal keeping and, for seven years, recorded the lifestyle of a refined, educated reformer dedicated to social justice. She extolled long-term friendships with civil rights heroes Frederick Douglass and William Lloyd Garrison. Her reflections presented readers a full evaluation of abolitionist lives and Reconstruction-era activism.

Forten lapsed into invalidism and died of cerebral hemorrhage on July 23, 1914. Historians value her diaries for summarizing the attitudes, observations, and evaluations of a free black female intellectual before, during, and after the Civil War.

See also: Child, Lydia Maria; Douglass, Frederick; Emancipation Proclamation; Lincoln, Abraham; Music; Underground Railroad.

Further Reading

Benstock, Shari, ed. *The Private Self: Theory and Practice of Women's Autobiographical Writings.* Chapel Hill: University of North Carolina Press, 1988.

Bunkers, Suzanne L., and Cynthia A. Huff, eds. *Inscribing the Daily: Critical Essays on Women's Diaries.* Amherst: University of Massachusetts Press, 1996.

Edgar, Walter B., ed. *The South Carolina Encyclopedia.* Columbia: University of South Carolina Press, 2006.

Epstein, Dena J. *Sinful Tunes and Spirituals: Black Folk Music to the Civil War.* Urbana: University of Illinois Press, 2003.

Hine, Darlene Clark, William C. Hine, and Stanley Harrold. *The African-American Odyssey.* 2nd ed. Upper Saddle River, NJ: Prentice Hall, 2005.

Holland, Rupert Sargent, ed. *Letters and Diary of Laura M. Towne: Written from the Sea Islands of South Carolina, 1862–1884.* New York: Negro Universities Press, 1969.

Nelson, Emmanuel S., ed. *African American Authors, 1745–1945: Bio-Bibliographical Critical Sourcebook.* Westport, CT: Greenwood, 2000.

Four Corners Region

The juncture of Arizona, Colorado, New Mexico, and Utah, Four Corners is the only union of four U.S. states at one geographic location. Three of the corners lie within the Navajo Nation and the fourth, Colorado, is located in the Ute Indian Reservation. Four Corners was a battleground of Mexicans, Navajo, and Pueblo in 1862, when the recall of Confederate troops to fight the Civil War left forts untended.

General James Henry Carleton intervened in the ongoing Indian wars by dispatching Colonel Christopher "Kit" Carson to uproot the Navajo. Aided by Ute enlistees, from January 6 to 22, 1864, Carson torched hogans and crops, seized herds, filled water holes with dirt, and destroyed 1,200 peach trees. On the 20-day Long Walk, he marched 9,000 Navajos 300 miles (480 kilometers) through Four Corners and Canyon de Chelly, Arizona, east to Bosque Redondo, New Mexico. Along the route, 2,000 died of exhaustion, malnutrition, and epidemic disease or from soldiers' bullets when the weary Navajo fell behind.

Hostilities worsened in 1865 as the prophet Antonga Black Hawk and his lieutenant, Jake Arapeen, sparred with the Mormon militia. The insurgents burned Ute dwellings and murdered women and children; Utes effectively halted white expansion into Utah. The state of war ended with Black Hawk's surrender in 1867 at the Uintah Reservation. He died in 1870 of tuberculosis, one of the white plagues that the Mormons introduced to the area.

Pacification of Four Corners tribes hastened in 1868, when the area received its first federal survey during the statehood inquiry for Colorado. After the surviving Navajo returned to the Four Corners area, the Kit Carson Treaty of 1868 settled Chief Ouray and the Southern Ute on 1.5 million acres (600,000 hectares) in southwestern Colorado.

Unscrupulous Indian agents reneged on promised blankets and food; squatters encroached on Ute territory. To survive, the Indians reverted to ancient styles of hunting and gathering. An inexperienced Indian agent, Nathanial Cook Meeker, exacerbated the racial situation in 1878 by forcing the Ute to plow their horse pasture and race track for a vegetable garden. On September 29, 1879, the Ute ambushed soldiers, clubbed Meeker, and staked his skull to the ground. The government subsequently forced Chief Ouray and his nation west into Utah, ending their traditional dominance of the Colorado Plateau.

Under the leadership of geologist and explorer John Wesley Powell in the late 1860s and early 1870s, the arid Colorado Plateau became a focus of botanic study of juniper pine, pinyon, and scrub brush and of geologic research into plate tectonics, Paleozoic fault lines, red rock stratification, erosion, and deposits of coal and iron. In 1874, the Hayden Geological and Geographical Survey of the Territories explored the remote sandstone cliff dwelling at Mesa Verde, Colorado, once home to an ancient Anasazi society related to the Hopi of Arizona and to residents of the Acoma Pueblo in New Mexico.

Painter and photographer William Henry Jackson took groundbreaking photos of artifacts of vanished Indian cultures and, under orders from leader Ferdinand Vandeveer Hayden, returned in 1875 to Canyon de Chelly to capture more detail in transparent images on glass. Jackson shaped scale model clay-and-plaster casts of petroglyphs, watchtowers, and worship kivas at the ruined Canyon of the Ancients for display at the 1876 Centennial Exposition in Philadelphia. Hayden reverenced the images of an "old, old people, whom even the imagination can hardly clothe with reality." Subsequent works by scientists and engineers produced accurate maps of 104,100 square miles (269,600 square kilometers) of lands in the Four Corners region.

See also: Long Walk of the Navajo; Utah Territory.

Further Reading

Brown, Kenneth A. *Four Corners: History, Land, and People of the Desert Southwest.* New York: HarperCollins, 1995.

Lamar, Howard R., ed. *The New Encyclopedia of the American West.* New Haven, CT: Yale University Press, 1998.

Sandweiss, Martha A. *Print the Legend: Photography and the American West.* New Haven, CT: Yale University Press, 2002.

Sundberg, Lawrence D. *Dinétah: An Early History of the Navajo People.* Santa Fe, NM: Sunstone, 1995.

Fourteenth Amendment

The second of three changes to the U.S. Constitution following the Civil War—collectively referred to as the Reconstruction Amendments—the Fourteenth Amendment became law on July 9, 1868. Overturning the U.S. Supreme Court's 1857 decision in *Dred Scott v. Sandford,* the amendment gave "equal protection of the laws" to former slaves, who had gained their freedom via the Civil Rights Act of 1866.

During state consideration of the amendment, it moved rapidly to ratification in New England and the North. Beginning with Connecticut in June 1866, the amendment passed in 28 states over a period of 24 months and two weeks. A total of eight states voted against the measure—Texas, Georgia, North Carolina, South Carolina, Kentucky, Virginia, Louisiana, and Delaware—between October 1866 and February 1867.

Most offensive to the South was the third section of the amendment, which deprived former rebels of appointment or election to state and federal offices. Rejection in the Confederate states sent a message to the Northern-controlled Congress that secessionist states would not tolerate a federalized central government supported by the votes of black illiterates at the local level with no background in civics. Governor Benjamin Humphreys of Mississippi declared the constitutional measure a violation of states' rights.

President Andrew Johnson chose to leave the matter in Southern hands. After Congress passed the Reconstruction Act on March 2, 1867, declaring martial law in the rebel states of Alabama, Arkansas, Florida, Georgia, Louisiana, North Carolina, Mississippi, South Carolina, Texas, and Virginia, the ten compromised governments had little choice but to agree to the Fourteenth Amendment or remain outlaw states. The South took a rapid retabulation of opinion.

Ohio rescinded its approval on January 15, 1868, claiming that the amendment violated the best interests of white people. A similar rescission occurred on February 20, 1868, in New Jersey, where legislators declared the punishment of the South an example of ex post facto law; Oregon withdrew its approval on October 15, 1868. More votes followed ratification, with rebels in Virginia, Mississippi, and Texas holding out to the last.

In 1870, enactment of the Fifteenth Amendment nullified Black Codes restricting the movement of blacks and preventing them from testifying against whites in court. Designers of the law intended it to entitle blacks to contracts and service on juries and to counter racist violence by such white supremacist groups as the Ku Klux Klan and the White Camellia. Subsequent Supreme Court tests of the definition of "citizenship" gave rights to Chinese Americans, Hispanics, and the offspring of illegal aliens before acknowledging the citizenship of American Indians.

See also: Ku Klux Klan.

Further Reading

Brown, Thomas J., ed. *Reconstructions: New Perspectives on the Postbellum United States.* Oxford, UK: Oxford University Press, 2006.

Epps, Garrett. *Democracy Reborn: The Fourteenth Amendment and the Fight for Equal Rights in Post–Civil War America.* New York: Henry Holt, 2006.

Keyssar, Alexander. *The Right to Vote: The Contested History of Democracy in the United States.* New York: Basic Books, 2000.

Nelson, William E. *The Fourteenth Amendment: From Political Principle to Judicial Doctrine.* Cambridge, MA: Harvard University Press, 1988.

Rothenberg, Paula S., ed. *Race, Class, and Gender in the United States: An Integrated Study.* 7th ed. New York: Worth, 2007.

Fraternal Organizations

The rise of fraternal organizations in America during the 1860s reflects a backlash against sectional hatred during the Civil War. Settlers belonging to the Odd Fellows, Templars, and Turnvereins took their brotherhoods west. In 1866, men in Denver, Colorado, organized the Pioneer's Association, a casual lodge composed of sport hunters.

In Washington, D.C., a secret brotherhood known as the Knights of Pythias formed on February 19, 1864, under the influence of Justus Henry "Harry" Rathbone, a 25-year-old clerk at the U.S. Treasury and a Royal Arch Mason and member of the Improved Order of Red Men. Rathbone read a proposed ritual to four friends—David L. Burnett, William H. Burnett, Robert A. Champion, and Edward S. Kimball—who instituted Washington Lodge No. 1. Basing the society's theme on the mythic friendship of Damon and Pythias, 52 members pledged themselves to benevolence, charity, friendship, and world peace. Although Rathbone would later withdraw in a squabble over control and form parallel knighthoods, the original lodge spread to California, Delaware, Kansas, Maryland, Missouri, New Jersey, and Pennsylvania. In 1871, members elected Samuel Read to the position of supreme chancellor. Two years later, lodge secretary-treasurer Clarence W. Barton absconded with $7,962.31 and left the lodge in debt for $17,000. The brothers decided to sell knight jewelry in 1874, a merchandising ploy that retired the debt and kept the

Knights solvent. Rathbone allied with the group again in 1876. At his death on December 9, 1889, lodge brothers performed Pythian honors over his grave and venerated him as founder of the order. By 1894, there were 500,000 members.

In New York City, a social brotherhood of actors known as the Jolly Corks proclaimed themselves a club to avoid public tavern blue laws requiring closure on Sundays. After the death of a member left his family destitute, on February 16, 1868, the founder and "imperial cork," 26-year-old Charles Algernon Sidney Vivian, an actor and singer at the American Theatre on Broadway, renamed the brotherhood the Benevolent and Protective Order of Elks. The metaphor suggested the noble elk in a distinctively American setting. The Elks required god-fearing qualities in members and redirected their activities toward service and charity. An hour before midnight, lodge proceedings halted for an ancient British custom—a salute to absent and deceased members. In 1890, the Elks held their first convention in Cleveland, Ohio.

The Shriners, a subsociety of Masons, formed at the Knickerbocker Cottage in Manhattan, New York, on August 13, 1870. Under the leadership of Irish American actor and composer William J. Florence and surgeon Walter Millard Fleming, the group took the name of the Ancient Arabic Order of the Nobles of the Mystic Shrine and modeled their emblem, costumes, and ritual after a staged musical held in Marseilles, France, by an Arab ambassador. Upon interviewing 11 men and determining their belief in God, the Shriners inducted them on June 16, 1871. The group held meetings in temples at Shrine mosques. On June 6, 1876, the brotherhood elected Fleming its first "imperial potentate." By 1878, there were 425 members in eight states. They typically formed mumming units in parades and dressed in Middle Eastern costumes to march to band music.

See also: Grange Movement.

Further Reading

Beito, David T. *From Mutual Aid to the Welfare State: Fraternal Societies and Social Services, 1890–1967.* Chapel Hill: University of North Carolina Press, 2000.

Kaufman, Jason. *For the Common Good? American Civic Life and the Golden Age of Fraternity.* New York: Oxford University Press, 2002.

Skocpol, Theda, Marshall Ganz, and Ziad Munson. "A Nation of Organizers: The Institutional Origins of Civic Voluntarism in the United States." *American Political Science Review* 94:3 (September 2000): 527–546.

Freedmen's Bureau

An idealistic effort at mass social reform, the Bureau of Refugees, Freedmen, and Abandoned Lands, commonly known as the Freedmen's Bureau, eased the transition from bondage to citizenship for 4 million blacks and assisted in the reunion of slave families.

After the Emancipation Proclamation began liberating blacks on January 1, 1863, abolitionist Martin Robinson Delany, the grandson of African captives and the nation's first black field commander, advised President Abraham Lincoln on the needs of ex-slaves and promoted humanitarianism. In autumn 1864, Delany's foresight proved a lifesaver to the ragged, malnourished camp followers who trailed behind General William Tecumseh Sherman on his march from Atlanta to the sea at Savannah, Georgia. A field order awarded the islands south of Charleston, South Carolina, to the newly liberated, who settled on abandoned rice plantations on the islands and along the St. Johns River in Florida.

A month before the war's end, Congress established a federal agency on March 3, 1865, as part of the Freedmen's Bureau Bill and empowered its officers to appropriate Confederate estates in Arkansas, Georgia, Louisiana, South Carolina, and Tennessee for use by 30,000 black farmers. All aspects of the resettlement came under the purview of the War Department.

For seven years, the Freedmen's Bureau chief, General Oliver O. Howard, a former officer of Sherman's staff, and Howard's assistant commissioner, General Clinton B. Fisk, made available homes and food banks, 100 hospitals and orphanages, and jobs for former slaves in the urban and rural South. Extensive paperwork recorded rescue operations and the distribution of 21 million meals, as well as the nuptials of cohabitating black couples, a stipulation imposed by Christian conservatives. For the agency's 4,000 schools, the government spent $5 million and printed an agency textbook stressing industry, ambition, and optimism among 100,000 pupils. At black centers in Arlington and Fort Monroe, Virginia; Washington, D.C.; Beaufort and Port Royal, South Carolina; New Orleans, Louisiana; Corinth and Vicksburg, Mississippi; Columbus, Kentucky; and Cairo, Illinois, Howard's staff delivered books and furnishings confiscated during the war and arranged free board and transportation for teachers.

The bureau profited from loyal staff. At Quindaro, Kansas, Charles Henry Langston, superintendent of the state Freedmen's Bureau, approved curricula and spearheaded

According to critic W.E.B. Du Bois, the Freedmen's Bureau developed into an ill-conceived labor board: "The two great obstacles which confronted the officers at every turn were the tyrant and the idler . . . the Devil and the Deep Sea." Amid thousands of men eager to earn wages lolled liberated field hands expecting "perpetual rest" under the hand of the former slaveholder, who intended to turn sharecropping into slavery in a new guise. Du Bois predicted that the clash would define national social issues into the twentieth century.

the state suffrage drive. Merchant Austin Franklin Williams used his Hartford, Connecticut, home office as an employment center for the bureau's New England and New York operations. In a community of 30,000 blacks in Richmond, Virginia, Rebecca Lee Crumpler, the nation's first black female physician, opened a medical clinic to provide free treatment for agency clients. In Washington, D.C., Dr. Alexander Augusta became the nation's first black hospital administrator at Freedmen's Hospital and Asylum, a 278-bed receiving and rehabilitation center for the aged, disabled, sick, and injured.

The Reverend John Watson Alvord, a roving education director, and journalist George Thompson Ruby of Galveston, Texas, inspected schools and evaluated administrators. In 1870, Alvord issued *Letters from the South, Relating to the Condition of Freedmen,* in which he noted the declining postwar death rate of blacks in Atlanta, Macon, and Savannah, Georgia. He tempered high hopes for amenable contract labor with warnings of fraud and betrayal by white employers.

From Washington to Texas, the bureau embroiled its 900 agents in the negotiation of employment contracts and in legal issues raised by amnesty for slaveholders. Agents opposed wage fraud, injustice in Southern courts, and the increase in vagrancy, theft, and burglaries. Of immediate concern, the Ku Klux Klan in Alabama, Arkansas, the Carolinas, Georgia, Kentucky, Louisiana, Maryland, Tennessee, Texas, and West Virginia practiced terrorism through intimidation of teachers, hate mail, school burnings, death threats, pistol-whipping, and lynching. At Pittsburgh, abolitionist George Vashon counseled freedmen on civil rights. On September 1, 1865, the Freedmen's Bureau protested the imprisonment of 21-year-old Caleb Day, an Underground Railroad conductor in Charles County, Maryland, for abetting the flight of blacks from former owners, a crime that no longer existed. To further the Port Royal experiment in settlement, bureau officials in Columbia, South Carolina, provided rail tickets to the coast for 250 black adults per week.

Because of a drought in winter 1865–1866, Freedmen's Aid societies issued 4,500 food parcels per month to the indigent. At 35 literacy centers in the Sea Islands, 2,000 students learned to read and write. In October 1866, when 10,304 citizens—8,243 former slaves and 2,061 whites, most aged and crippled—neared starvation, former slave owners in Georgia and South Carolina donated to community funds. By 1869, the bureau had reduced its emphasis on feeding, clothing, and housing the poor and concentrated on education and vocational training.

On the campaign trail for a second term in Cleveland, Ohio, on September 3, 1866, President Andrew Johnson opposed an outlay of $12 million for former slaves. He reasoned that the Union already had invested $3 billion in fighting a war to emancipate bondsmen. Taking a negative stance against blacks, he condoned the election of secessionist legislators from the South and warred with Congress over the style and severity of Reconstruction, the powers of the Civil Rights Bill of 1865, and passage of the Fourteenth Amendment ensuring the civil rights of blacks. On February 19, 1866, Johnson vetoed Senator Lyman Trumbull's bill increasing the bureau's power on the grounds of the illicit use of the military to punish racists and confiscate secessionists' property. On July 16, 1867, Congress settled on a second bill, extending the life of the bureau for a year and offering forfeited lands for sale to freedmen.

Opinions about the Freedmen's Bureau varied to extremes. In July 1867, Frederick Douglass rejected an appointment to chair the agency, which he viewed as a short-term means of placating newly freed blacks. General Howard used his influence to establish Howard University, a respected black institution begun in November 1866 in Washington, D.C. By the middle of Reconstruction, in June 1872, Congress had lost enthusiasm for the agency, which had spent a total of $20 million.

As altruists turned their attention from relief of blacks to establishment of vocational schools and colleges, crisis loomed for the poor. Some 50 benevolent and relief organizations, including the African Methodist Episcopal, African Methodist Episcopal Zion, and American Missionary Association outreaches, continued to aid the needy. Despite gaps and financial malfeasance, the cobbled-together efforts of officials and volunteers made inroads against more than two centuries of slavery by founding free public education institutions in the South, securing legal rights for blacks, establishing a free labor system, and creating a class of black landowners.

See also: Howard, Oliver Otis; Johnson, Andrew.

Further Reading

Cimbala, Paul A. *The Freedmen's Bureau: Reconstructing the American South after the Civil War.* Malabar, FL: Krieger, 2005.

Jenkins, Wilbert L. *Seizing the New Day: African Americans in Post–Civil War Charleston.* Bloomington: Indiana University Press, 2003.

Laurie, Bruce. *Beyond Garrison: Antislavery and Social Reform.* New York: Cambridge University Press, 2005.

Nolen, Claude H. *African American Southerners in Slavery, Civil War, and Reconstruction.* Jefferson, NC: McFarland, 2001.

Rose, Willie Lee. *Rehearsal for Reconstruction: The Port Royal Experiment.* Athens: University of Georgia Press, 1999.

Frontier Life

The lives of settlers in the American West focused on survival, personal welfare, and productivity in the outdoors. Details of dangers and challenges derive from diarist Harriet Bunyard's trek through Texas to California in 1869, *Mollie: The Journal of Mollie Dorsey Sanford in Nebraska and Colorado Territories, 1857–1866* (1959), and H.H. McConnell's *Five Years a Cavalryman or, Sketches of Regular Army Life on the Texas Frontier, 1866–1871* (1889).

Whether in the Florida and Louisiana swamps or the bay fronts of Washington Territory, introduction to a new race caused white settlers to reflect on the sources of ethnocentrism. In *The Life and Adventures of a Quaker Among the Indians* (1875), Thomas Chester Battey, a missionary from Starksboro, Vermont, recorded a candid confrontation with Comanche family life. A study of an Indian village was cause for ethnic contrast: "When a person becomes old and feeble, so as to become in their estimation burdensome, they are neglected; and when sickness and death come upon them, they are sometimes abandoned to die alone."

In 1873, journalist Isabella Bird, author of *A Lady's Life in the Rocky Mountains* (1897), observed Texas Indians during their frenzy over willful slaughter of the buffalo. She concurred with Battey on the disorder and squalor of Ute camps outside Denver, Colorado, and agreed with racists that settlement would never succeed until all Indians were extinct. In another incident, surgeon Thomas McGee treated a wounded soldier during a foray on an Arapaho settlement when a brave aimed his gun in their direction. McGee shot the Indian and went on with his life-saving ministrations.

For women and girls, crossing open territory in wagons demanded gender egalitarianism and an acceptance of reduced standards of living, such as tent living or acclimating to a sod hut. Cooking required skill at open fires and preparing meals in Dutch ovens, on johnnycake boards, or directly in hot ashes, the best place to cook salmon, elk ribs, buffalo hump, and beaver tail. From attorney Lewis Henry Morgan's *The Indian Journals, 1859–1862,* homesteaders learned to make pemmican, a blend of buffalo meat and suet, flavored with berries and pinyon nuts, carried as trail food. Crates of poultry and a fresh cow or goat added nourishment for children, nursing mothers, and the elderly and convalescents recovering from the inevitable rounds of dysentery and fever. Free-flowing water eased the dishevelment of Eastern families by offering places to bathe and to wash dishes and clothes.

The arrival of women to the male-dominated frontier civilized and refined lawless hamlets. Whether cooking for the Butterfield Stage Line, farming on the Pecos River, teaching at an Indian school in Oregon, or entertaining and tending bar in the goldfield dance halls of the Dakotas, females introduced sanitation, gentility, and education to communities. Upon arrival, housewives and young children performed the indoor labor on cabins, which consisted of mixing mud, clay, dung, and animal hair into a dough for paving a hearth with stones or sealing the chinks in log walls from draft.

The interior of the home as well as the corncrib, lean-to, poled chicken coop, and kitchen garden commanded daily attention and constant restocking. Lacking fresh produce and dry goods stores, frontier women excelled at plowing, sewing buckskin, cleaning game, making vinegar and cheese, and foraging for nuts and berries, wild grapes and greens, onions, mushrooms, and herbs. When fresh fruit was in season, thrifty cooks hydrated pulp into fruit

During his days as a Pony Express rider in Wyoming, William Frederick "Buffalo Bill" Cody spent his free time riding the Horseshoe Valley near Laramie Peak in the snow to track bear. His joy in solitude in the Far West enhanced a sense of liberty: "The perfect freedom which he enjoys is in itself a refreshing stimulant to the mind as well as the body," Cody wrote. He found ample wildlife—jackrabbit, antelope, and deer—and savored sage hen broiled over a grass fire for three meals. The idyllic overnight hunt concluded with an unforeseen encounter with criminals at a dugout and Cody's flight for his life on foot; he trekked 25 miles (40 kilometers) back to Horseshoe Station.

A family stands outside their ramshackle cabin on the Oklahoma prairie. Women and children joined in building and repairing homes, harvesting and preparing food, and the myriad other tasks of nineteenth-century frontier life. *(Hulton Archive/Getty Images)*

leather, a paste of wild apple, berry, or plum, a sweet and nutritious treat for housebound children.

The needs of other women and families brought females together to attend childbirth, barter for supplies, stitch scraps into quilts, mourn a prairie fire or a sudden death, comfort the sick, or celebrate a family event with a barn raising, hymn sing, or shared meal. To maintain family in a time of migration to the West, Sarah Josepha Hale, editor of *Godey's Lady's Book,* urged letter writing as a means of sharing new adventures and past memories.

An historic literary series, the "Little House" memoirs of Laura Elizabeth Ingalls Wilder captured a child's joy in Great Plains folk life at Pepin, Wisconsin, which ranged from a spelling bee to a family reunion with grandparents and dancing to her pa's fiddle music. Wilder outlined a frontier Christmas at their home in Independence, Kansas. Through her family's peripatetic history, she balanced the delights and tragedies, including a locust plague at their home in a dugout in Walnut Grove, Minnesota, and the blinding of sister Mary from scarlet fever in De Smet, South Dakota.

In 1871, Alice Kirk Grierson, author of *The Colonel's Lady on the Western Frontier* (1989), composed a letter on the difficulties of mental depression following the death of Edie, the fourth of her six children. Grierson admitted that constant childbearing and the demands of child care, cooking and sewing, and homeschooling sapped her strength, leaving her exhausted and bitter. Corroborating her jaundiced view are the lyrics of plains songs, "Bury Me Not on the Lone Prairie," "The Cowboy's Lament," "The Dreary Black Hills," and "Starving to Death on a Government Claim." In contrast, those durable frontierswomen with a gift for sketching, poetry, dried flower arranging, or crafts found outlets that extolled the beauties of the wilderness. Men provided their own crafts by whittling images of birds and mammals and turning pelts into bedspreads and throw rugs.

On viewing the plains of Moorhead, Minnesota, in July 1871, novelist and newspaperman Bayard Taylor, a writer for the *New York Tribune,* penned a reverie to the uncluttered vista:

> We went over long undulations of soil past the glimmer of virgin lakes, through the unshorn gardens of the wilderness. Prairie-grass and western winds, blue sky and bluer waters, vast horizons and flying clouds, and wanton interchange of belted light with shadow—they all filled us, if not with a new delight, yet with one which never grows stale from experience.

Homesteaders, Taylor noted, rapidly claimed acreage in Kansas, Minnesota, and Nebraska for the beauty of the land.

See also: Oregon Trail.

Further Reading

Bentley, Anna Briggs. *American Grit: A Woman's Letters from the Ohio Frontier.* Ed. Emily Foster. Lexington: University Press of Kentucky, 2002.

Brown, Dee. *The American West.* New York: Simon & Schuster, 1995.

———. *Bury My Heart at Wounded Knee: An Indian History of the American West.* New York: Holt, Rinehart and Winston, 1970.

Etulain, Richard W. *Beyond the Missouri: The Story of the American West.* Albuquerque: University of New Mexico Press, 2006.

Hagan, William T. *Charles Goodnight: Father of the Texas Panhandle.* Norman: University of Oklahoma Press, 2007.

Rose, Alexander. *American Rifle: A Biography.* New York: Bantam Dell, 2008.

G

Gage, Matilda Joslyn (1826–1898)

Writer, lecturer, and historian Matilda Electa Joslyn Gage compiled the suffragist archives into scholarly works and orations justifying women's enfranchisement. Born with a heart malfunction on March 24, 1826, in Cicero, New York, she was the only child of Helen Leslie Joslyn. She became a reformer like her father, Dr. Hezekiah Joslyn, an abolitionist and rescuer for the Underground Railroad at their home on Sophia Street. In girlhood, she met and admired orators Frederick Douglass, Abby Kelley Foster, and other antislavery agitators. She distributed abolitionist pamphlets and sang antislavery tunes on the street.

Her father trained her in anatomy, languages, and physiology to prepare her for entry to Geneva Medical College. After graduating from the Clinton Liberal Institute in 1845, she disappointed him by wedding a dry goods merchant, Henry Hill Gage, and settling in Fayetteville, New York. Despite threats of arrest, a $2,000 fine, and imprisonment, the couple and their five children openly operated an Underground Railroad depot at 220 East Genesee Street, where a trapdoor at the parlor hearth led to the cellar. Upon the execution of anarchist John Brown for leading a raid on the federal arsenal at Harpers Ferry, Virginia, in 1859, the Gages draped their front door in mourning.

An activist for women's rights, Gage became an officer of the New York Woman Suffrage Association and, in 1852, a speaker at the National Woman's Rights Convention. At the outbreak of the Civil War, she addressed the Women's Volunteer Aid Societies of the North, held teas and socials to buy equipment for the 122nd New York Volunteers, and collected supplies for Union military hospitals. The Gages posted bunting and flags on January 1, 1863, to celebrate the Emancipation Proclamation.

Her speech "On the Progress of Education and Industrial Avocations for Women" (1871) lauded Antioch and Oberlin colleges, Women's Medical College of Pennsylvania, and Cornell, Iowa State, Regent's, and Washington universities for admitting women and praised Presbyterians for ordaining female deacons. After co-founding the National Woman Suffrage Association (NWSA), she served as president from 1875 to 1876 and quashed a police charge that the 1876 NWSA convention in Philadelphia was an illegal assembly.

In support of divorce and women's sexual and reproductive rights, Gage wrote for the organization's newspaper, *The Revolution,* and, in 1878, edited her own paper, the *National Citizen and Ballot Box.* Her tracts include *Woman as Inventor* (1870), *Woman's Rights Catechism* (1871), and *Who Planned the Tennessee Campaign of 1862?* (1880), a postwar salute to strategist Anna Ella Carroll. After Susan B. Anthony's trial for illegal voting on June 17, 1873, Gage defended her own right to the ballot in an editorial for the Kansas *Leavenworth Times* and in an analysis for the *Albany Law Journal.*

Into the decade, Gage propagandized on suffrage and wrote for the *New York Evening Post* an editorial on the plight of the Iroquois and Mohawk and of Plains Indians tricked by false government treaties and denial of independent governments. The Mohawk adopted her into their number and named her "Sky Carrier."

When New York's women received the right to participate in school commissioner elections in 1880, she led 102 registered women voters to the polls in her town and became the first female citizen to mark a ballot. The bloc vote assured the election of all female officers.

Gage collaborated well with other radicals in decrying child sexual abuse, wife battery, unequal pay, and the double standard in legal matters that exonerated rapists. With Anthony and Elizabeth Cady Stanton, she wrote the "Declaration of Rights for Women" (1876), which demanded the right of self-government. The text impeached male government officials for making gender a crime and for taxation of women without representation. Central to the trio's concerns were possession of their own wages and property and the right to act as free agents in legal documents, contracts, and wills.

On July 4, 1876, Gage and Anthony interrupted Philadelphia officials during a reenactment of the signing of the Declaration of Independence to press their demands for women's civil rights. Gage accompanied Anthony on a tour through California, Colorado, the Dakotas, Michigan, and Wyoming. In 16 towns, Gage supported Anthony's harangues and tramped house to house to pressure voters to support full citizenship for women.

In league with Anthony and Stanton at the latter's home office in Tenafly, New Jersey, Gage sorted media clippings, letters, notes, and speeches before international assemblies as source material for the first three volumes of the six-volume *History of Woman Suffrage* (1881–1922). By forming the Woman's National Liberal Union with feminists, anarchists, prison reformers, and labor leaders, Gage brought federal attention to her actions and incurred the interception of her mail by the U.S. Post Office. She inflamed conservative Christian Frances Willard, leader of the Women's Christian Temperance Union, by publishing *Woman, Church, and State* (1893), a denunciation of church patriarchy, bigotry, and misogyny as expressed by concubinage, prostitution, the Inquisition, polygamy, and witch trials.

In orations, she lauded goddess cults of Ishtar, Isis, and Vestal Virgins and the clairvoyant Pythia of Delphi in early Mediterranean history for raising the prestige of female spirituality. Gage's argument equating women's subjugation with slavery and her demands for human rights for women outraged the male clergy. In 1895, she worked with a committee of 24 contributors—including Lillie Devereux Blake, Harriot Eaton Stanton Blatch, Frances Ellen Burr, Clara Bewick Colby, Ellen Batelle Dietrick, Ursula N. Gestefeld, the Reverend Phoebe Ann Coffin Hanaford, Frances Lord, and Louisa Southworth—in the composition of *The Woman's Bible* (1895–1898). After dissecting two copies of the Bible for verses mentioning women, they pasted each passage into a scrapbook and left space for signed analysis and commentary.

After her death from stroke on March 18, 1898, at the home of her daughter, Maud Gage Baum, in Chicago, Gage's papers and suffrage manuscripts passed to Radcliffe College.

See also: Anthony, Susan B.; Stanton, Elizabeth Cady.

Further Reading

Brammer, Leila R. *Excluded from Suffrage History: Matilda Joslyn Gage, Nineteenth-Century American Feminist.* Westport, CT: Greenwood, 2000.

Frisken, Amanda. *Victoria Woodhull's Sexual Revolution: Political Theater and the Popular Press in Nineteenth-Century America.* Philadelphia: University of Pennsylvania Press, 2004.

McMillen, Sally. *Seneca Falls and the Origins of the Women's Rights Movement.* New York: Oxford University Press, 2008.

Sneider, Allison L. *Suffragists in an Imperial Age: U.S. Expansion and the Woman Question, 1870–1929.* New York: Oxford University Press, 2008.

Snodgrass, Mary Ellen. *Encyclopedia of Feminist Literature.* New York: Facts on File, 2006.

Gas Lighting

The commercial sale of butane, carbon monoxide, ethylene, hydrogen, methane, and propane gas for lighting American cities aroused interest in the early nineteenth century. Gas lamps flamed 12 times brighter than natural light and extended the workday. By replacing oil lamps with "inflammable air," consumers saved themselves the tedium of filling wells, trimming and lighting wicks, and washing soot from fragile glass globes.

In 1816, Baltimore became the first U.S. city to begin lighting its streets with gas lamps; by the 1830s, Peale's Gas Light Company supplied fuel for lighting 3,000 homes and 100 streetlights in the city. In 1825, New York City invested in a similar commercial gas utility, which brought mellow gas flames into everyday use. For easy cleaning, users raised and lowered parlor and foyer chandeliers by counterweights or a water-slide rise-and-fall system. Lacking bulky fuel tanks, ornate fixtures attached to a gas pipe protruding from a circular ceiling medallion. After William A. Smith drilled an oil well in Titusville, Pennsylvania, on August 27, 1859, marketers began replacing animal and vegetable oils with invisible fossil fuels and monopolized the gas utility in each company's region.

Manufacturers of gas who used cannel coal and oil shale as sources switched to steam-generated gas and petroleum gas in the 1860s. The dependability of coal gas produced measurable results, supporting combustion up to or more than twice as long as equal quantities of spermaceti candles, wax candles, stearic acid, sperm oil, tallow, olive oil, or rapeseed oil.

Contributing to the economy of manufactured gas were the facts that it cost a fraction of the price of other fuels and that it rid dwellings of the smell from dirtier fuels, the mess of dripping wax and coal or wood ash, and the sooty smoke that coated draperies, windows, and furnishings. Entrepreneurs George F. Gilman and George Huntington Hartford, founders of the Great Atlantic & Pacific Tea Company, drew customers to their Manhattan store at 31 Vesey Street by highlighting the interior with red and gold leaf and illuminating it with gas jets in chandeliers and curted arches.

In *The American Woman's Home, or Principles of Domestic Science* (1869), home economists Catharine Esther Beecher and her sister, Harriet Beecher Stowe, advised that reliance on insufficient light was poor economy compared to the danger of the shadowy gloom in halls, porches, alcoves, closets, and stairwells. The authors maintained that gas cost less than kerosene for lamp fuel and made a stronger flame than candles, but a gas flame was not so bright as an Argand lamp burning costly sperm oil. The text advocated a variety of lighting sources for reading, for carrying about the house and yard, and for setting in the sickroom or kitchen on safe metal bases. For testing the flammability of oil for a soft, steady glow, the authors suggested heating an iron spoonful of fuel over a lamp. If the vapor combusted rapidly, it was too volatile for safe household use. Another issue, pipe fitting, required careful specifications for aligning conduits and jets to prevent leaks.

From natural gas seeps in Charleston, West Virginia, active in the 1860s, entrepreneurs began experimenting with illuminating urban streets and homes, beginning with the residence of metalsmith William Henry at 200 Lombard Street in Philadelphia, Pennsylvania. Homeowners liked gas light for its convenience, safety, cleanliness, decoration, and easily controlled heat and brilliance. By 1876, the processing of carbureted water gas from coal tar or petroleum increased the availability of low-price lighting for homes and facilitated longer workdays for factories and shops. Proponents advocated gas illumination in churches and schools and the lighting of amusements, parks, intersections, alleys, and squares to protect citizens from criminals.

As electric lighting gained popularity for its smokeless, flameless illumination of rooms in the late 1870s, the gas industry sought profits from supplying stoves, cookers, water heaters, and furnaces with a fuel that was less explosive and messy than liquid oil or gasoline. In 1877, inventor Thomas Alva Edison marketed an electronic gas lighter. Within a decade, resilient mantles made from rare earth metals improved the radiance of white light. By 1885, Massachusetts had organized a state gas commission to supervise gas service and pricing. The extension of pipelines from natural gas fields in Oklahoma and Texas to Chicago in the 1890s replaced reliance on manufactured gas.

See also: Home Economics.

Further Reading

Cropper, William H. *Great Physicists: The Life and Times of Leading Physicists from Galileo to Hawking.* Oxford, UK: Oxford University Press, 2001.

Klein, Maury. *The Genesis of Industrial America, 1870–1920.* Oxford, UK: Oxford University Press, 2007.

Snodgrass, Mary Ellen. *Encyclopedia of Kitchen History.* New York: Fitzroy Dearborn, 2004.

Whitten, David O., and Bessie E. Whitten. *The Birth of Big Business in the United States, 1860–1914: Commercial, Extractive, and Industrial Enterprise.* Westport, CT: Greenwood, 2006.

Geronimo (1829–1909)

Reputedly America's greatest guerrilla strategist, Geronimo, a shaman and seer, defended the Chiricahua Apache against incursions by Spanish and white settlers from the late 1850s to the 1880s. The grandson of Chief Mahko near Turkey Creek in southwestern New Mexico, he received the name Goyothlay (Yawner) at his birth in 1829. After he returned from a trading expedition to discover that Mexican raids had taken the lives of his mother Juana, his wife Alope, and their three sons, he chose the name Geronimo, for Saint Jerome.

From 1858 to 1886, the wily combat tactician eluded some 8,500 Mexican and U.S. forces and scouts by disappearing among the boulders of the Dragoon Mountains or the caves of the Chiricahua Mountains in southeastern Arizona. In 1861, he married Cochise's niece, She-gha, the fourth of his nine wives. Cochise supported Geronimo's retaliation against Mexicans and whites. In Geronimo's absence from camp, Mexican troops slew women and children, including Geronimo's third wife, Nana-tha-thtith, and their child.

After Lieutenant George Nicholas Bascom tricked Cochise and members of his family on February 4, 1861, for allegedly rustling 20 head of cattle at Sonoita Creek and kidnapping the 12-year-old stepson of rancher John Ward, the false arrest resulted in the hanging of three Apaches, including Cochise's brother, Coyuntura. Geronimo retreated to Apache Pass to counsel Indians on methods of retaliation. He spent summer 1862 with eight braves attacking mule trains traveling through the Sierra de Sahuaripa mountain range east of Hermosillo, Mexico. During one raid, he fell unconscious to the ground from a gash to the head from a rifle butt.

At Apache Pass on July 15, 1862, Geronimo's band joined Cochise and his father-in-law, Mangas Coloradas, and their 200 guerrilla warriors to ambush the only source of water in the area. The small band intended to ward off the 2,000 troops of General James Henry Carleton, whom John Downey, governor of California, had sent east with two howitzers to annihilate the Apache. When artillery proved too destructive, the Apache withdrew.

The U.S. military built Fort Bowie on the Overland Mail route as a headquarters of anti-Apache patrols and a shield for wagon trains crossing west through Apache Pass. After General Joseph Rodman West's betrayal and murder of Mangas Coloradas on January 17, 1863, under a white truce flag at Fort McLane in southwestern New Mexico, Geronimo accepted the leadership of Victorio, until his death in 1880, and of Nana, Geronimo's brother-in-law, who replaced Victorio.

A Long Pursuit

The military pursued Geronimo into Mexico, expecting to outmaneuver or exhaust his small band and waste their resources. In 1868, however, General Edward O.C. Ord was so frazzled by the search for renegade Apaches and the protection of Arizona settlers that he telegraphed Washington for additional forces. The situation remained difficult and policies unclear in 1869 at the inauguration of President Ulysses S. Grant. In August 1870, Chiricahua murdered 12 settlers, wounded another, and caused $10,000 worth of property damage. According to an article in *Outing* magazine published in 1906, Geronimo's band partially depopulated Arizona by killing 176 people and driving off hundreds more from 1869 to 1870.

In response to the guerrilla band, General William Tecumseh Sherman feared that whites had attempted settlement too soon along the Mexican border. Still resentful toward intruders on Apache land, Geronimo continued marauding by raiding cattle herds in Mexico and stealing supplies from townspeople. He took time out in 1870 to officiate at the birth of his nephew Daklugie, the son of Juh, and to pray for the recovery of Geronimo's sister, Ishton, who labored near death for four days. Upon his return to family life from years of living on the run, a vision revealed to Geronimo that he would live a long life and die peacefully.

On and Off the Reservation

Geronimo spent the remainder of his years moving on and off government reservations, especially when game was scarce and winters were hard on his band. In fall 1872, he settled with other Indians on the Chiricahua Apache Reservation in southern Arizona. Restless and dissatisfied, he and Juh left in 1873 and warned the Apache that whites could not be trusted to obey treaties and keep promises.

In 1874, Geronimo feared for the health of Cochise, who died on June 8, leaving his eldest son, 39-year-old Taza, a weak replacement leader. Geronimo spent part of the year in Mexico among the Nedni Apache and Chief Juh, whom he counted as friends. The band enjoyed relative peace and more plentiful game.

In June 1876, after a government order the previous year to remove the Chiricahua to the San Carlos Reservation in eastern Arizona, Geronimo led a band of braves to Mexico to avoid being forcibly settled with some 325 Apache captives in a total Indian population of 4,200. During subsequent raids, media legends declared him brutal and savage and endowed him with the powers of invisibility and of walking without leaving footprints.

In December 1877, John Philip Clum, the San Carlos Indian agent, and his Apache police force lured Geronimo and his wives and children from Ojo Caliente in northern New Mexico to a peace parley. After a three-week march, Clum forced Geronimo onto the reservation in irons on charges of robbery, rustling, and murder. As starvation and smallpox decimated his band, on April 4, 1878, Geronimo fled with his son Chappo to join Juh at their famous secret stronghold in the Sierra Madre Mountains of Mexico.

At the final capture of Geronimo, 16 braves, 12 women, and six children in January 1886, his illicit activities had cost the federal law enforcers more than $1 million. Authorities sent some of his family to Fort Marion and incarcerated Geronimo, two of his wives, and 450 of his followers at Fort Pickens in St. Augustine, Florida, where She-gha died on September 8, 1887. A prisoner of war at Fort Sill, Oklahoma, into the twentieth century, Geronimo succumbed to pneumonia on February 17, 1909.

See also: Cochise; Mangas Coloradas; New Mexico Territory.

Further Reading

Brown, Dee. *The American West.* New York: Simon & Schuster, 1995.

———. *Bury My Heart at Wounded Knee: An Indian History of the American West.* New York: Holt, Rinehart and Winston 1970.

Johansen, Bruce E., and Donald A. Grinde, Jr. *The Encyclopedia of Native American Biography.* New York: Da Capo, 1998.

Lamar, Howard R., ed. *The New Encyclopedia of the American West.* New Haven, CT: Yale University Press, 1998.

Roberts, David. *Once They Moved Like the Wind: Cochise, Geronimo, and the Apache Wars.* New York: Simon & Schuster, 1993.

Waldman, Carl. *Who Was Who in Native American History: Indians and Non-Indians from Early Contacts Through 1900.* New York: Facts on File, 1990.

Gettysburg Address

A revered speech delivered by President Abraham Lincoln on November 19, 1863, the Gettysburg Address remains one the nation's most profound encomiums to patriotism and self-sacrifice. At the dedication of the Soldiers National Cemetery on 17 acres (6.9 hectares) in Gettysburg, Pennsylvania, four and a half months after the decisive Battle of Gettysburg, Pennsylvania, the two-minute eulogy provided a brief but enduring comment on martyrdom and the principles of American democracy.

The invitation had arrived only 17 days before the event. At 10 A.M. on the day of the dedication, President Lincoln, dressed in a black suit, white gauntlets, and top hat and accompanied by Secretary of State William Henry Seward and Secretary of the Treasury Salmon P. Chase, rode in a three-quarter-mile (1.2-kilometer) procession with 15,000 mourners, local citizens and dignitaries, four military bands, and the governors of Indiana, Maryland, New Jersey, New York, Ohio, and Pennsylvania. Along Baltimore Street, the president was somber, as he viewed the bullet holes, rifle pits, and general destruction left by the Battle of Gettysburg. He brooded over the ongoing war.

For the lengthy ceremony, President Lincoln sat on the dais in a rocking chair. Following music by Birgfeld's Band and the U.S. Marine Band and a prayer by the Reverend Thomas Hewlings Stockton, chaplain of the U.S. Senate, came the speech of statesman Edward Everett, a respected Greek revivalist at Harvard University and pastor of the Brattle Street Church in Boston, Massachusetts. At noon, Everett delivered a two-hour oration on the Athenian statesman Pericles and on classical commentary at military funerals.

At about 2 P.M., Lincoln stood before the crowd, bowed his head, then, in a high tenor voice recognizable for its twangy Kentucky dialect, delivered from memory his ten-sentence, 272-word eulogy, which he had written on White House stationery. Viewers recalled that his lips quivered as he swept his hand toward the concentric semicircles formed of raw graves. Applause was sparse, but an Associated Press stenographer, Charles Hale, telegraphed the speech to newspapers.

On November 24, the Harrisburg *Patriot and Union* dismissed the speech as a "silly" attempt to impress voters before the 1864 presidential election. The Eaton, Ohio, *Register* of November 30 noted the quieting effect of the address on the audience, which had been standing for hours. George William Curtis, in a commentary for *Harper's Weekly,* admired the speech for being "felicitous" and "earnest."

In a letter to Lincoln, Everett admitted that he had been bested by a two-minute speech that summarized what Everett had taken 120 minutes to say. He asked Lincoln for a handwritten copy of the address, which the president mailed to him.

Lincoln's concise rhetoric set a standard for definitions of liberty. It captured the precarious state of a nation warring over essential issues of slavery and states' rights. The sonorous opening—"Four score and seven years ago"—introduced a scriptural tone on a sacred occasion, burial honors to casualties of war. In simple, gracious terms, the address praised the 7,500 deceased Union soldiers

The second draft of Lincoln's Gettysburg Address is believed to have been penned in Gettysburg on the morning he delivered it and held in the president's hand during the historic ceremonies at Soldiers National Cemetery on November 19, 1863. *(MPI/Stringer/Getty Images)*

killed in a horrendous destruction of human life, which Lincoln esteemed as "the last full measure of devotion." To establish unity, a pervasive imagery of life cycles contrasted the soldiers' martyrdom with a "new birth of freedom."

The president's skill at parallelism—"of the people, by the people, for the people"—stressed the essence of a governing system empowered by the will of common citizens rather than aristocracy or royalty. In closing with a prophecy that the republic "shall not perish from the earth," the text lifted the day's events to global significance by picturing the United States as both a work in progress and a beacon of freedom to other nations. In 1917, historian Orton Hoffman Carmichael reverenced the Gettysburg Address as "America's only Psalm."

See also: Everett, Edward; Lincoln, Abraham.

Further Reading

Blight, David W. *Race and Reunion: The Civil War in American Memory.* Cambridge, MA: Belknap Press, 2001.

Boritt, Gabor. *The Gettysburg Gospel: The Lincoln Speech That Nobody Knows.* New York: Simon & Schuster, 2006.

Stephenson, Nathaniel W. *Abraham Lincoln and the Union.* New York: BiblioBazaar, 2008.

Varg, Paul A. *Edward Everett: The Intellectual in the Turmoil of Politics.* Cranbury, NJ: Susquehanna University Press, 1992.

Wills, Garry. *Lincoln at Gettysburg: The Words That Remade America.* New York: Simon & Schuster, 1992.

Gibbs, Josiah Willard (1839–1903)

The recipient of America's first doctorate in engineering, Joseph Willard Gibbs, the scientific forefather of the revolution in twentieth-century physics, introduced American universities to the theoretical sciences. The most influential physical chemist since Antoine Lavoisier, Gibbs advanced theoretical (nonlaboratory) chemistry, mathematics, and physics with concepts of entropy, algorithms, elasticity, surface phenomena, and equilibrium.

A native of New Haven, Connecticut, and scion of scholars, he was born on February 11, 1839, to Mary Anna Van Cleve Gibbs and philologist Josiah Willard Gibbs, Sr., a Hebrew scholar and member of a learned English family that had settled in the Massachusetts Bay Colony in 1658. Surrounded by four sisters—Anna Louisa, Emily Philips, Julia, and Eliza—Gibbs anchored his life and career to Yale University, where his father taught sacred literature and involved translators in the trial of the black mutineers of the slave ship *Amistad.*

In early childhood, Gibbs suffered physical impairment from a bout of scarlet fever that limited his physical stamina for the rest of his life. Educated at the Hopkins Grammar School and Yale, he was shy and withdrawn from social gatherings and close to his older sister Anna Louisa, who shared his reticence. He graduated Phi Beta Kappa at age 19 with prizes in Latin oratory and composition and mathematics before completing a doctorate at Yale's new Sheffield Scientific School with a dissertation on gear design in 1863.

On April 17, 1866, he patented an automatic brake for railcars that operated without the intervention of a brakeman. For three years, he tutored a few students in Latin and physics before departing for Europe with his sisters, Anna Louisa and Julia, the only other surviving members of his family of seven. On an inheritance from his deceased parents, he spent his late twenties studying chemistry and thermodynamics at the universities of Berlin and Heidelberg and at the Sorbonne and Collège de France in Paris, where he achieved greater fame than in his native land. During a winter on the Mediterranean, he recuperated from tuberculosis.

At age 30, Gibbs joined Yale's graduate department of mathematics and physics, and labored in private over concepts that he substantiated with rigorous logic. He lectured on water waves, diffraction, polarization, reflection, and refraction and began publishing innovative treatises on graphical analysis of chemical systems, beginning in 1873 with "Graphical Methods in the Thermodynamics of Fluids" and "Method of Geometrical Representation of the Thermodynamic Properties of Substances by Means of Surfaces."

He established his mastery of physical chemistry with a work titled *On the Equilibrium of Heterogeneous Substances* (1875–1878), a comprehensive textbook on electrical and electromagnetic phenomena in chemical and physical reactions. Issued serially in *Transactions of the Connecticut Academy,* it covered concepts of free energy and the geometric and mathematical calculation of particles in motion and achieved prestige in translations into French and German for use in rigorous European science courses.

A solitary man, Gibbs lived in his childhood home with his sister and brother-in-law, Julia Gibbs Van Name and Addison Van Name, the librarian at Yale and a teacher of Hebrew. To maintain his health, Gibbs rode horseback, took his nephews and nieces for sleigh rides, and ventured alone on walks about New Haven. He influenced the scholarship of his nephew and namesake, conservationist Willard Gibbs Van Name. Gibbs held memberships in intellectual societies in Boston; London and Manchester, England; Berlin, Munich, and Erlangen, Germany; Christiana, Denmark; and Haarlem, Holland. He maintained correspondence with the discoverers of his day, notably Austrian physicist Ludwig Eduard Boltzmann, German mathematician David Hilbert, Austrian physicist Ernst Mach, and French mathematician and physicist Jules Henry Poincaré.

By age 41, when Gibbs was earning $2,000 per year at Yale, he rejected an offer from Bowdoin College in Maine and a 50 percent raise to teach in Baltimore, Maryland, at Johns Hopkins University, the nation's first research university. In 1880, he won the Rumford Prize from the American Academy of Arts and Sciences for new theories about heat. In his mid-forties, he wrote on optics, osmosis, elliptical orbits, color dispersion, and semipermeable films and formulated the concept of vector analysis, the basis of description of magnetism, gravity, and fluid flow. In 1889, he shifted his field of endeavor to theories of light velocity and contributed to studies of crystals and the orbits of comets and planets.

Awards late in Gibbs's life acknowledged his greatness by associating him with the genius of Galileo and Isaac Newton. A modest scholar, he received honorary degrees from Williams College and from Christiana, Erlangen, and Princeton universities. In 1901, he accepted the Copley Medal from the Royal Society of London.

After his sudden death on April 28, 1903, the American Chemical Society established the prestigious Willard Gibbs Medal in his honor. His theories attained global recognition with the publication of Gilbert Newton Lewis and Merle Randall's *Thermodynamics and the Free Energy of Chemical Substances* (1923). Professorships at Rutgers and Yale bearing his name encouraged theoretical studies in statistical mechanics. The American Mathematical Society declared Gibbs America's greatest scientist and an influence on economist Irving Fisher and on Nobel laureates Lars Onsager and Max Planck, theorist of quantum mechanics.

Further Reading

Alter, Stephen G. *William Dwight Whitney and the Science of Language.* Baltimore: Johns Hopkins University Press, 2005.

Caldi, D.G., and George D. Mostow, eds. *Proceedings of the Gibbs Symposium: Yale University, May 15–17, 1989.* Providence, RI: American Mathematical Society, 1990.

Cropper, William H. *Great Physicists: The Life and Times of Leading Physicists from Galileo to Hawking.* Oxford, UK: Oxford University Press, 2001.

Mehra, Jagdish. "Josiah Willard Gibbs and the Foundation of Statistical Mechanics." *Foundations of Physics* 28:12 (December 1998): 1785–1815.

Godey's Lady's Book

Godey's Lady's Book, a media standard of women's tastes, interests, and opinions nationwide, influenced American lives and perceptions of manners and values. In June 1830, from his office at Chestnut and Sixth streets in Philadelphia, 25-year-old journalist Louis Antoine Godey launched America's first women's fashion magazine featuring material from French women's magazines. *Godey's* success made Philadelphia America's publishing mecca. It rose in popularity from a circulation of 10,000 to 40,000 in 1839 to become the "queen of household magazines," with a readership of 1 million.

Godey extended the range of interest with letters and writings from California, Hawaii, Texas, Washington Territory, and Wisconsin and copyrighted the text to prevent pilfering by other publishers. His own column, "Godey's Arm Chair," lauded advancements in telegraphy, gas fixtures, and railroads and the use of ice for medical treatment. In 1836, he merged *Godey's* with the *American Ladies' Magazine,* issued in Boston.

Readers admired the fashion plates of *Godey's Ladies Book,* groupings of subdued women and children in chic costumes hand-tinted by 150 watercolorists working from home offices. Garments for specific occasions ranged from the morning negligee and lady's drawers and nightgowns to the matinee skirt, Josephine shawl, ball gown, fichu, wedding gown and mantilla, opera hood, hairpiece, and Zoave jacket. Instructions for crochet, embroidery, knitting, and ornate monogramming featured chemises, frocks, and caps for infants and toddlers, as well as bedspreads, mittens, socks, ruffs, and gaiters.

Twelve issues of *Godey's Lady's Book* sold for $2.00 per year and could be "clubbed" with additional subscriptions to *Arthur's, Atlantic Monthly, Galaxy, Harper's Bazaar, Peterson's, St. Nicholas, Waverley,* and *Youth's Companion.* The magazine offered a lending library of recommended works on the "common culture" and posted addresses for mail order of hair ornaments, pins, bracelets, necklaces, earrings, yarn, envelopes, bonnets, layettes, yard goods, scarves, and even pianos. During the Civil War, the staff turned the magazine into an oasis from abolitionist and combat news, with only brief mention of the Union army, General George Brinton McClellan, and President Abraham Lincoln.

Sarah Hale's Domain

In 1837, Sarah Josepha Hale, a widow and mother of five in need of a job, began editing *Godey's Lady's Book.* She held the position for four decades. In addition to offering flower arrangements, piano and vocal solos and polkas, gossip about Queen Victoria and the Empress Eugenie, and paper dolls, the magazine published suggestions for fair crafts and house plans—for example, for a two-story Italian cottage featuring two chimneys and corbeled roof and a two-story English cottage with double porch and ornate wood trim. Biographies introduced American readers to the past heroics of Isabella of Spain, Dolley Madison, Abigail Adams, and Mary Queen of Scots and to contemporary sculptor Harriet Hosmer and hospital administrator Florence Nightingale, hero of the Crimean War. Medical advice extended from posture improvement and brushing the teeth with a pinch of borax to reducing fever with wet sheets, dosing children with opiates, and identifying cholera infantum and hereditary diseases.

Although opposed to suffrage and women's rights conventions, Hale spoke reassuringly about female equality and women's roles in business, design, and industry. She endorsed women's influence on curtailing math and Latin as the core of school curricula and on upgrading children's physical education, behavior, and spirituality. She encouraged the formulation of opinions in diaries and journals. For maintaining extended family ties in a time of migration to the West, she urged letter writing as a means of sharing new adventures and past memories. Practical answers to everyday problems included rainy-day puzzles, acrostics, and riddles for children. She introduced the sewing machine, china mending, and chemistry lessons on sulfur and carbon, and recipes for chlorinated cleaning solutions and metal polish. She extolled women for religious missions and for volunteering during the Civil War and predicted the need for female workers to replace men killed in combat.

Godey's in a Time of Change

By 1860, in contrast to *Harper's Magazine*'s outreach of 110,000, *Godey's Lady's Book* circulated to 150,000 homes, in part because Hale convinced males to buy subscriptions for their wives' and daughters' edification. In addition to assisting women on making comfortable homes and cooking nutritious and attractive meals, she supported Mount Holyoke and Vassar College, the Ladies' National Association for the Diffusion of Sanitary Knowledge, the Women's Hospital of Pennsylvania, the Seamen's Aid Society, the Fatherless and Widows' Society of Boston, and the Jewish Foster Home Society in Philadelphia as well as jobs for women in the U.S. Post Office and public schools and traditional names for baby girls.

In 1870, Hale praised the work of home economist Catharine Esther Beecher and coined the term "domestic science" to legitimize the professional nature of innkeeping, home design, invalid cookery, and housekeeping in mansions, hotels, restaurants, schools, and hospitals. Her recipe collections featured multi-ethnic cuisine contributed by English, French, German, Irish, Italian, Scandic, and Scots readers, including an 1865 recipe for potato chips. She endorsed the equal wage drive for women and crusaded for wives to receive rights to their own homes, furnishings, savings, and children. Godey issued his own observation that the magazine was not a luxury, but a necessity to domestic economy.

Godey's Lady's Book suffered a decline in readership during the Southern port blockade. Black-market copies heartened Confederate women with news of European fashions and foodstuffs they could no longer buy. Factory girls in Massachusetts wore copies of *Godey's* to tatters; Irish servant girls in Boston bought cheap ginghams and calico and copied the ornate fashions intended for brocade and velvet. Hale's essays on the evils of the tight corset and once-a-week bathing appeared next to cheerful advice on horseback riding, croquet, and swimming for girls and picnicking and games of charades as family enjoyments.

Following the sale of the magazine to journalist Frank Andrew Munsey in 1877, the title changed to *Godey's Magazine.* A shift from conventional beliefs and sugary refinement was apparent in the first installment by the new editor in January 1878, the serialization of Bret Harte's realistic novel *The Hoodlum Band.* The magazine lost ground to more aggressive, pro-woman media, particularly the *Atlantic Monthly* and *Harper's Magazine,* but it remained in publication until 1898.

See also: Hale, Sarah Josepha.

Further Reading

Clark, Gregory, and S. Michael Halloran, eds. *Oratorical Culture in Nineteenth-Century America: Transformations in the Theory and Practice of Rhetoric.* Carbondale: Southern Illinois University Press, 1993.

Collins, Gail. *America's Women: Four Hundred Years of Dolls, Drudges, Helpmates, and Heroines.* New York: William Morrow, 2003.

Levander, Caroline Field. *Voices of the Nation: Women and Public Speech in Nineteenth-Century American Literature and Culture.* Cambridge, UK: Cambridge University Press, 1998.

Sachsman, David B., S. Kittrell Rushing, and Roy Morris, Jr., eds. *Seeking a Voice: Images of Race and Gender in the 19th Century Press.* West Lafayette, IN: Purdue University Press, 2009.

Snodgrass, Mary Ellen. *Encyclopedia of Feminist Literature.* New York: Facts on File, 2006.

Gold Rushes

The frenzy following gold strikes marked periods of optimism and growth on the American frontier. Following the Pikes Peak Gold Rush in Colorado in 1858–1859, the discovery of placer (surface) gold in river gravel at Pierce, Idaho, ground sluicing (hydraulic mining) of nuggets from the Mother Lode in California's Sierra Nevada, and Ferdinand Boulanger's strike at Fort Colville, Washington, in 1860, miners rushed to the areas to pan manually or to set up rocker boxes for screening ore or sluice boxes for trapping heavy gold particles from streams.

U.S. politicians began to view settlement and transportation problems in the Far West as national issues. Crucial to the independence of the Confederacy were Southwestern gold veins in former Spanish lands, particularly the Patagonia Mine at Mowry, Arizona. On February 28, 1861, the U.S. Congress created the Territory of Colorado, where gold mining prospered in the San Juan Mountains at La Plata, Red Mountain, Rico, and Telluride. Interest shifted to Hahn's Peak in late summer 1862, when the Union sought precious metals to finance the Civil War.

The press spiced the news with directions to gold discoveries. Alexandre "Buck" Choquette's strike on the Alaska–Canada border in 1862 piqued U.S. interest in Alaska, which then belonged to Russia. In Oregon, fortune hunters sought William C. Aldred's gold discovery in Canyon City in June 1862, when the population burgeoned to 10,000. More favored the gold strikes at Auburn in October 1861, at Griffin Gulch south of Baker City in 1862, and, the next year, at Sparta. To the northwest, some 10,000 new arrivals overran gold-mining territory in Boise County, Idaho. The era produced the richest strikes in American history.

On July 28, 1862, John White's discovery of gold north of the Cache Valley in Montana invigorated migration to mining sites from California, Oregon, and Washington. With the publication of Montana gold strikes, majority whites prevailed in ousting minority Chinese prospectors from the rush. By 1865, Montana's population reached 30,000; many of this number were short-term residents dependent on trades linked to profitable mining. The most lucrative strike, the Drumlummon gold operation on Silver Creek at Marysville in April 1876, boosted territorial prosperity and lured newcomers.

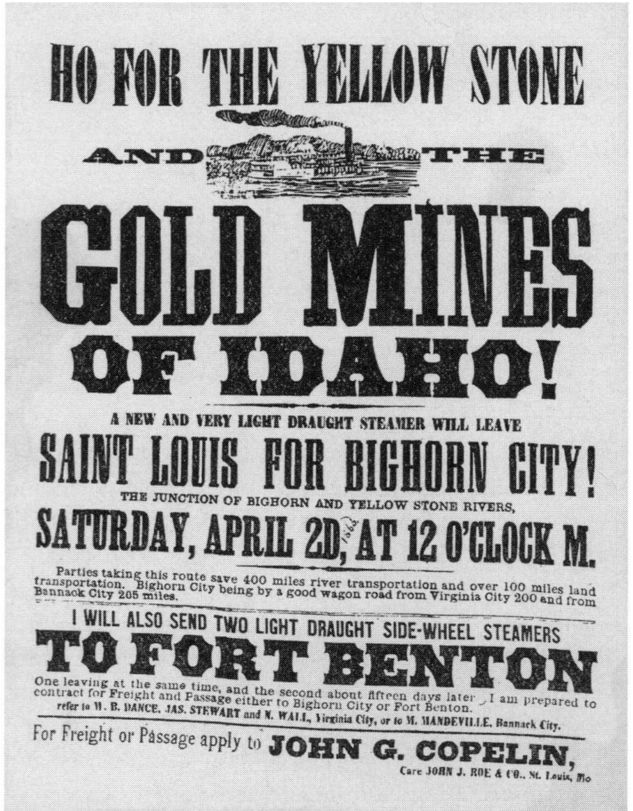

A poster advertises steamboat transportation to gold mining regions in Idaho Territory in 1863. Major strikes in Arizona, the Dakotas, Idaho, Montana, and other Western territories attracted tens of thousands of prospectors in the 1860s and 1870s. *(Stock Montage/Getty Images)*

After General George Armstrong Custer led prospectors into the Black Hills between South Dakota and Wyoming in 1874 and located gold along French Creek in the Badlands, 1,000 prospectors stampeded onto Indian lands. Crazy Horse, chief of the Oglala Lakota Sioux, led warriors from the Great Sioux Reservation to defend his people's territory against get-rich-quick prospectors. In mid-November 1875, federal orders directed the entire Sioux Nation to settle on the Great Sioux Reservation and live off federal bounty. In addition to promises of food and blankets, the Sioux received guarantees that the military would ban unauthorized whites.

Major Gold Strikes, 1862–1876

Date Discovered	Location	Discoverer(s)
1862	Hahn's Peak, Colo.	Joseph Hahn
1862	La Paz, Ariz.	Pauline Weaver
6/1862	Canyon City, Ore.	William C. Aldred
7/28/1862	Bannack, Mont.	John White
8/2/1862	Boise Basin, Idaho	George W. Grimes and Moses Splawn
1863	Rich Hill, Ariz.	Pauline Weaver
1863	Wickenburg, Ariz.	Henry Wickenburg
5/16/1863	Alder Gulch, Mont.	Henry Edgar and William Fairweather
1864	Helena, Mont.	John Cowan, John Crab, D.J. Miller, and Reginald Stanley
6/1867	South Pass City, Wyo.	Tom Ryan
1876	Bodie, Calif.	Standard Mine & Mill
4/1876	Marysville, Mont.	Thomas Cruse
4/9/1876	Lead, S.Dak.	Alex Engh, Hank Harney, Fred Manuel, and Moses Manuel

The rush peaked on April 9, 1876, at the Homestake Mine near Lead, South Dakota, America's richest underground deposit. More profitable discoveries enticed miners to Deadwood. With the bankrolling of mine speculators, the town acquired notoriety for brothels, cardsharps, gunfighters, claim jumping, and robberies of stagecoach deliveries to Cheyenne, Wyoming.

See also: Colorado; Mining; Montana Territory.

Further Reading

Berton, Pierre. *The Klondike Fever: The Life and Death of the Last Great Gold Rush.* New York: Carroll & Graf, 2004.

Castor, Stephen B., and Gregory C. Ferdock. *Minerals of Nevada.* Reno: Nevada Bureau of Mines and Geology and University of Nevada Press, 2004.

Dumett, Raymond E., ed. *Mining Tycoons in the Age of Empire, 1870–1945: Entrepreneurship, High Finance, Politics, and Territorial Expansion.* Burlington, VT: Ashgate, 2009.

Isenberg, Andrew C. *Mining California: An Ecological History.* New York: Hill and Wang, 2005.

Lamar, Howard R., ed. *The New Encyclopedia of the American West.* New Haven, CT: Yale University Press, 1998.

Gold Standard

Pro and con, the gold standard became the political rallying cry of the 1870s. From August 1861 to April 1862, President Abraham Lincoln's economic policy protected "hard money" (federal reserves of gold and silver) by uncoupling the value of paper bills—"soft money"—from precious metals. His administration circulated $5, $10, and $20 demand notes and suspended redemption in gold coins. Thus, American currency relied solely on citizen trust.

Declared legal tender for the payment of debt by the Legal Tender Act of February 12, 1862, paper money increased the flow of cash to cover Civil War expenses and the seasonal debts of farmers and rural people. Because the Civil War extended longer than expected into 1864, Secretary of the Treasury William Pitt Fessenden faced the collapse of the gold standard and $161 million in war debt, which the government retired with inflationary greenbacks. At the breaking point in national fiscal stability, he chose a pay-as-you-go method of financing the last year of the war and introduced the 7.3 percent treasury note. Citizens expressed their distaste for the loss of purchasing power of wartime paper currency by hoarding coins and selling them to jewelers and silverware makers.

The U.S. Treasury, reeling from wartime exigencies, had to realign monetary values with British Canadian, Dutch, German, and Scandinavian traders, who began adopting the gold standard in 1871. To restore American credit with other world economies, President Ulysses S. Grant on February 12, 1873, signed the fourth Coinage Act, which dropped silver from federal currency standards and replaced a bimetal system with a gold standard.

The choice of gold specie as a basis maintained a fixed relationship to a single metallic standard. However, the shift reduced mining profits in Colorado, Idaho, Montana, Nevada, and Utah, the primary silver-producing states. Because nations dumped their silver to keep abreast of the U.S. economy, the sudden change depressed the value of silver in Carson City, Nevada, the ore center of the Western boom. In Terre Haute, Indiana, Orlando J. Smith, editor of the *Daily Express,* urged Congress to reconsider the gold standard and reinstate paper money.

The Rise of Plutocracy

While industrialization brought new wealth to the South, the depressed money supply jeopardized farms, mining operations, private schools, and small factories and businesses, including the shop of Civil War photographer Mathew Brady. Owners of small factories responded to mechanized overproduction by cutting wages and workers' hours. Farmers lacked cash to pay rising fertilizer prices and freight rates. In North Carolina, private universities—Davidson, Wake Forest, and Trinity (later Duke)—competed with public institutions for students and shrinking endowments. Tight money destabilized Jay Cooke & Company, a financial firm that had overtaxed its credit to extend the Northern Pacific Railway through Duluth, Minnesota, to the Great Lakes.

A U.S. stock market crash on September 18, 1873, triggered the Panic of 1873 and marked the beginning of the Long Depression, a price decline caused by the ruin of the Cooke's firm and other banks. The collapse bankrupted 18,000 businesses and 89 railroads and deflated prices, worker buying power, and real estate values. The economy lagged until the return of the U.S. gold standard in January 1879.

During the five-year slowdown, creditors benefited from the deflation caused by complete reliance on one precious metal as a medium of exchange. Rail owners transporting gold and silver ores to processing centers plunged the territory into rail control wars. Shrewd financiers enriched themselves. Capitalists Andrew Carnegie, Thomas Edison, Henry J. Heinz, Rowland Hussey Macy, Cyrus McCormick, John D. Rockefeller, and Cornelius Vanderbilt financed projects at the expense of their cash-poor competitors. Mark Twain and Charles Dudley Warner satirized the selfishness of railroad owners, industrialists, financiers, and capitalists in their novel *The Gilded Age* (1874), a slap at shallow money grubbers and exploiters of workers. The public demonized greed and reasoned that the availability of ore after discovery of the Comstock Lode made silver the wise choice for backing legal tender.

Gold and Politics

While the economy tilted dangerously toward wealth in the hands of a few, white and black populists pressured Congress to combat unemployment and poverty by reining in big business. Debtors, mainly factory workers and Southern and Western farmers, struggled with inflation. They opposed a tight money supply controlled by banks and smeared the demonetization of silver as the "Crime of 1873." Farmers favored higher prices to increase their cash flow to pay debts.

Worried debtors supported the national Greenback Party, an antimonopolist revolt that produced the largest unsuccessful third-party movement in American history. To save paper money, on June 10, 1874, Midwesterners coordinated state conventions in Illinois and Indiana. When Democrats ignored the issue of usury, a small consortium met on November 25 at Indianapolis to fight the debt-based economy. The meeting brought together rural insurgents from Connecticut, Illinois, New York, Ohio, Pennsylvania, and West Virginia, whom the press named the Greenback Party. Led by industrialist Peter Cooper and former Democratic Congressman Samuel Fenton Cary of Ohio, the coalition promoted the circulation of paper currency and resolved to break the private bank monopoly over the cash supply.

The monetary issue provoked harsh retorts. During Grant's presidency, Thomas Nast, illustrator for *Harper's Weekly,* used his cartoons and lectures to endorse a revival of citizen solvency by a return to the gold standard. Republican Congressman John Sherman of Ohio led the crusade to guarantee the nation's economy with gold. Passage of the Specie Resumption Act in January 1875 backed circulating currency with gold as of January 1, 1879, the date the U.S. Treasury resumed specie payments to underwrite paper notes. The Treasury sold bonds to create a gold reserve that nearly equalized the market value of gold and the government's legal tender notes. At the 1876 Republican convention, orator Robert Green Ingersoll defended the gold standard. His opponent, James Baird Weaver, an Ohio attorney and politician, denounced the gold standard and advocated a liberal currency circulation policy.

Simultaneously, labor organizations allied with Cooper's supporters to form the Greenback-Labor Party, which sent 14 congressmen to Washington in 1877. The party platform challenged a government that boosted a handful of plutocrats to an economic and political stranglehold over the nation's productivity. To democratize government and spread wealth, Greenbackers crusaded for woman suffrage, federal regulation of interstate commerce, a graduated income tax, and a return to silver money, which would elevate purchasing power and promote economic recovery.

Representative Richard P. Bland, a Democrat from Missouri and the leader of the "silverites," gave ringing speeches demanding restitution of the "dollar of our daddies." In 1878, the U.S. House of Representatives agreed to the Bland-Allison Act, which allowed unlimited coinage of silver. To secure passage in the Senate, Republican Senator William Boyd Allison of Iowa proposed that the U.S. Treasury purchase between $2 million and $3 million in silver per month at market prices and mint the bullion into silver dollars. President Rutherford B. Hayes rejected the bill, but Congress overrode his veto. U.S. money equated the value of all moneys—gold, silver, and paper currency. Nonetheless, the national economy remained unstable into the 1890s.

See also: Banking and Finance.

Further Reading

Allen, Larry. *The Encyclopedia of Money.* 2nd ed. Santa Barbara, CA: ABC-CLIO, 2009.

Eichengreen, Barry J. *Globalizing Capital: A History of the International Monetary System.* 2nd ed. Princeton, NJ: Princeton University Press, 2008.

Lewis, Nathan K. *Gold: The Once and Future Money.* Hoboken, NJ: Wiley, 2007.

Goodnight-Loving Trail

On August 26, 1866, Colonel Charles "Chuck" Goodnight, a Texas Ranger and the "Father of the Texas Panhandle," established the Goodnight-Loving Trail (also known as the Pecos Trail) in collaboration with stockman and freighter Oliver Loving, the first drover to herd longhorns to Chicago cattle pens. After 1865, they scouted the Southwest for markets for the feral cattle that were left unherded in south-central Texas while stockmen fought the Civil War. The partners signed a $12,000 contract with beef dealer James Patterson to provide 2,000 cattle—a difficult mix of steers, cows, and calves—for soldiers and 8,000 Mescalero Apache and Navajo settled at Fort Sumner, New Mexico. Following the Butterfield Overland Mail Route, on June 6, 1866, Goodnight led the way for Loving and 16 cowboys, including Bose Ikard, a famed black cowboy who carried Goodnight's cash.

Goodnight established a 700-mile (1,100-kilometer) swing from Fort Belknap, Texas, on the Brazos River west over deserts and Indian territory. The trail began at Young County, Texas, and veered southwest at Horsehead Crossing to the Middle Concho River at San Angelo. From there, the drovers passed 80 miles (130 kilometers) over grassless, waterless country to the Pecos River south of Carlsbad, New Mexico, and, at Loving's Bend, turned north to Fort Sumner. Along the way, they lost 300 animals to thirst and alkaline pools. To keep the cows moving, cowboys killed calves born on the trail and crossed and recrossed the Pecos to find the safest routes.

Goodnight and Loving profited at a rate of 8 cents per pound for beef on the hoof. At an average of 800 pounds (360 kilograms) per animal, the total per head came to $64, or a $54 profit over the selling price of $10 in central Texas. Because Patterson documented the first drive, the Goodnight-Loving route entered official military records.

The Second Drive

The partners separated, with Loving driving a herd of 750 to Denver cattle pens over a route he had traversed in 1860. On the South Platte River, he sold cows and calves to self-made Colorado millionaire John Wesley Iliff.

Meanwhile, Goodnight, in partnership with John Simpson "Cow John" Chisum, a Concho River stockbreeder, hired four cowboys to drive them. Before setting out, the boss forced his crew to sign contracts that promised no cursing, drinking, gambling, or fighting and that agreed to hang any drover who violated the pledge. The boss kept his word at the hanging of a cowboy from a wagon tongue for committing murder. Over the trail, the men directed a second herd of 1,200 steers, which Goodnight bought with profits from the first drive.

In terms of tractability and speed, steers were easier to manage than cows with calves. When a pack mule ran away, Goodnight lost all of the party's food, except for a side of bacon. He bargained with a produce seller for a cartload of watermelons to tide them over until they reached a trading post. The boss encountered threats from Mexican bandits and a wild merger of steers with a buffalo herd that ended peacefully.

At Bosque Redondo south of Fort Sumner, he penned the steers and sold beeves at the Santa Fe market, while filling the U.S. Army's monthly order. The profits—$10,000 in gold—survived an Indian ambush. At Bosque Grande in southern New Mexico, Goodnight and Loving purchased a supply ranch to extend the monthly provisioning of Fort Sumner into spring 1867.

The Third Drive

As Indian predations worsened with two murders and the rustling of 6,000 cattle, Goodnight and Loving parted for a third drive. Traveling with a top cowhand, "One-Armed Bill" Wilson, Loving scouted the trail and planned to complete contract negotiations before competitors arrived at the fort. Comanche warriors surrounded the men and delivered a lethal blow to Loving's wrist and side.

After Loving died of gangrene at Fort Sumner on September 25, 1867, Goodnight kept a deathbed promise to his partner to split the profits of $72,000. Goodnight transported Loving's remains 600 miles (960 kilometers) in a crude coffin made from flattened oilcans. On February 8, 1868, Loving's survivors received the remains for burial in Weatherford, Texas, and accepted $36,000 in profits. At Rock Creek Bridge Ranch, Goodnight continued his stock breeding of cattalo (cattle and buffalo), invested in Durham bulls, and restored a herd of buffalo to the plains.

Goodnight extended the Goodnight-Loving Trail from New Mexico up the Santa Fe Trail through Pueblo, Colorado, to Denver and established another feeder ranch and relay station at Trinidad. In autumn 1867, he moved northwest to the Union Pacific railhead at Cheyenne, Wyoming, to deliver cattle to John Wesley Iliff.

To simplify the herding of Texas longhorns, Goodnight adapted an army surplus supply vehicle into the first chuck wagon, a portable cowboy mess hall named for the inventor. Cooks also carried simple first aid kits and treated contusions, cuts, diarrhea, broken bones, and snakebite.

On the return trip south, Goodnight avoided Richens Lacy "Uncle Dick" Wooton's toll station at Raton Pass on the New Mexico–Colorado border, which charged a dime per head of cattle. Goodnight straightened the trail by shifting east to Alamogordo Creek and to the Canadian River Valley west of Fort Bascom and through Tinchera Pass, Colorado, into New Mexico, the final alteration of the original Goodnight-Loving Trail. In 1875, at the end of hostilities with the Comanche and Kiowa, another swing east from Fort Sumner provided an alternate trail to Granada, Colorado.

By striking a deal with bandit "Dutch" Henry Boren to avoid rustling his cattle, Goodnight in 1877 stocked acreage at Palo Duro Canyon, Texas, where buffalo grass offered plentiful pasturage. At Old Home Ranch, the first in the Panhandle, he settled his wife, Mary Ann Dyer Goodnight, and went into banking. On 1 million acres (400,000 hectares), he raised 100,000 cattle, bred new strains, promoted irrigation, and, in 1878, blazed another route, the Palo Duro–Dodge City Trail, extending from his ranch in the Texas Panhandle north to Dodge City, Kansas.

The Goodnight-Loving Trail remained in use in drives to Arizona, New Mexico, Colorado, and Wyoming by Chisum and his competitors—cattlemen A.D. Cantrell, Ed Gregory, William J. "Bill" Hayes, John Larn, J.K. Millwee, and brothers Ben and George Reynolds. A famous black cowboy, Nat Love, used the trail in spring 1874 to drive longhorns from New Mexico to Ogallala, Nebraska. Partners John Wesley Iliff and brothers Colonel Dudley Hiram Snyder and Captain John W. Snyder used the trail in 1877 to drive 28,000 head of two- and three-year-old steers to Denver. At the height of traffic, some 100,000 cattle per year followed the trail, until the laying of railroads in the 1880s and the fencing of the open range with barbed wire.

See also: Cattle and Livestock.

Further Reading

Brown, Dee. *The American West.* New York: Simon & Schuster, 1995.

———. *Bury My Heart at Wounded Knee: An Indian History of the American West.* New York: Holt, Rinehart and Winston, 1970.

Hagan, William T. *Charles Goodnight: Father of the Texas Panhandle.* Norman: University of Oklahoma Press, 2007.

Lamar, Howard R., ed. *The New Encyclopedia of the American West.* New Haven, CT: Yale University Press, 1998.

Massey, Sara R., ed. *Texas Women on the Cattle Trails.* College Station: Texas A&M University Press, 2006.

Nolan, Frederick W. *Tascosa: Its Life and Gaudy Times.* Lubbock: Texas Tech University Press, 2007.

Gould, Jay (1836–1892)

Jason "Jay" Gould, America's notorious financier and railroad magnate, won the loathing of citizens for enriching himself off gold, land, railroad, and telegraph speculation. He became the richest man in the world.

The ill-famed robber baron was born on May 27, 1836, in Roxbury, New York, to storekeeper and hardware dealer John Burr Gould and Mary Ann Moore Gould. The family sufficed on homegrown food and homemade clothing and furniture. At his mother's death in 1841, Gould came under the control of the first of two stepmothers. He left Hobart Academy at age 16 to clerk and, lacking funds for a college education, kept accounts in Edward Burhans's store and blacksmith shop in Roxbury.

Gould bought his first property and learned mathematics from his sister. By age 15, he co-owned an unprofitable tin shop on Main Street, making buckets, cups, and pans, while grooming himself for wealth. He taught himself civil engineering and made and sold plat maps of Albany, Delaware, Greene, and Ulster counties and of Oakland County, Michigan, and Geauga and Lake counties in Ohio. At age 20, he completed the compilation of *History of Delaware County, and Border Wars of New York* (1856).

From investments in timber, banking, and tanning, Gould built Gouldsborough, a company town in northeastern Pennsylvania comprised of worker lodgings, a post office, a dry goods store, and a mule-powered device to crush oak bark into an acid solution to fill tanning vats. With the proceeds from rapid expansion, he bought out his partner and dominated the local leather industry, earning profits totaling $80,000. Canny and elusive, he extricated himself from legal entanglements at Gouldsborough and settled into a bank and brokerage house in Stroudsburg, Pennsylvania.

Gould moved to New York City in 1859 and revived the Rensselaer & Saratoga Railroad by close management of operational details. When overwork sapped his vigor, he returned home to the care of his sisters, Anna, Elizabeth, Nancy, and Sarah Gould. In 1863, he wed Helen Day "Ellie" Miller, the mother of their two daughters and four sons.

Speculation in gold and the Rutland & Washington Railroad made him a millionaire before 1865. His collection of rail stock and proxies involved him in the Missouri, Kansas & Texas, St. Louis & Northern, St. Louis & San Francisco, and Atchison, Topeka, & Santa Fe railroads. Under his leadership, the Wabash Railroad gained an Atlantic port at Baltimore. He profited from the Rensselaer and Saratoga lines by consolidating them, earning a profit of $100,000.

Railroads and Gold

To ensure the success of his investments in the Erie Railroad, in October 1867, Gould joined broker James "Diamond Jim" Fisk, Jr., in a bitter rivalry with "Commodore" Cornelius Vanderbilt over control of Erie Railroad stock. The "Erie Wars" involved the partners with embezzler William Magear "Boss" Tweed, a seedy opportunist who bribed judges and legislators through the Democrat political machine of Tammany Hall.

By "bulling" (forcing up) the rail stock and issuing $5 million in watered-down stock certificates, Fisk and Gould reaped $10 million in a single day. When Vanderbilt sent gangs of toughs to seize Gould's records, Gould retreated over the Hudson River and armed Jersey City, New Jersey, with cannon and a shore patrol of gunmen. His graft and civil malfeasance earned the scorn of cartoonist Thomas Nast, who, in 1869, pilloried Tammany criminal acts and bribery of state legislators in *Harper's Weekly*. In March 1872, a month after Fisk's murder, a court forced Gould to pay $7.5 million in restitution for their stock manipulation.

During a financial lull following the inauguration of President Ulysses S. Grant in March 1869, Fisk and Gould defamed themselves by trying to corner the gold market to enhance freight transport over the Erie Railroad. Gould initiated the market rise in March by purchasing $7 million in precious metals and continued the cornering effort through the summer. During the course of the scandal, he exploited his contacts with President Grant, First Lady Julia Dent Grant, Secretary General Horace Porter, and a government insider, General Daniel Butterfield, then assistant U.S. treasurer. On September 24, stock market speculation provoked the panic of Black Friday, when gold prices fell by 27 percent, ruining half of Wall Street and precipitating breakdowns and suicides. Fisk and Gould fled to Gould's office at the Opera House and remained out of sight behind a security force.

The hoarding of precious metals threatened U.S. greenbacks, bonds, agricultural exports, and credit and initiated a two-week market frenzy that stymied foreign trade. Insider information ensured Gould's proceeds, which he lost in lawsuits. The media vilified him for his power over the economy and for his willingness to ruin competitors for the sake of personal gain. The scandal sullied the reputation of President Grant and forced Butterfield to resign his cabinet office.

Stratagems

At the height of the post–Civil War speculation boom, an intricate caper involved Gould in the bribery of a jewel thief, Herbert Hamilton, who posed under the title Lord Gordon-Gordon of Scotland. Gordon-Gordon offered to help Gould gain control of the Erie Railroad by resigning his directorship on March 9, 1872. When the Erie Railroad board reorganized, Gould lost his last chance of controlling it. Gordon-Gordon's default precipitated the arrest of the swindler and a trial on May 17, at which he fabricated a genealogy of European relatives. After the court ascertained that the kinship was a lie, Gordon-Gordon jumped bail of $37,000.

Because he had bilked Gould of $1 million, in October, Gordon-Gordon crossed the Great Lakes to Munro House in Winnipeg. On July 2, 1873, Gould and five kidnappers trailed him. The pursuers seized Gordon-Gordon, but the Northwest Mounted Police intervened and jailed Gould's gang. Governor Horace Austin of Minnesota retaliated by putting the state militia on alert and threatening to invade Canada. After Canadian officials ordered Gordon-Gordon's deportation, he held a lavish party at his hotel, then shot himself.

Following Gould's involvement in the Gordon-Gordon fiasco, he turned his financial interests to investment in mergers of the Atlantic and Pacific Telegraph and Western Union Telegraph companies and to the building of the Manhattan Elevated Railway and the Atlantic & Great Western, Kansas Pacific, Lackawanna, Missouri Pacific, Pacific Mail, and Union Pacific railroads. In 1874, he stole from William Orton, president of Western Union, the work of Thomas Alva Edison, creator of the quadruplex telegraph, which sent four separate signals over the same wire—two incoming and two outgoing.

To wrench the Union Pacific out of financial danger, he reduced the wages of Chinese coolie laborers to less than a dollar a day. As a result of suppressing costs, in 1875, he declared the first stock dividend for the Union Pacific. By age 54, when he merged the Rio Grande Railroad with the South Park, he controlled 11 percent of the nation's rolling stock. In January 1881, he netted $3.1 million by selling his shares in the South Park Railroad to the Union Pacific and invested in the St. Louis, Fort Scott, & Wichita, a small line that he wielded into profit. His daredevil risk taking stripped his cash supply in 1883, forcing him to consider retirement. To the surprise of his enemies, he weathered the market downturn and began clawing his way back to being the king of railroads.

Gould's moneymaking stratagems played poorly in the press. Reporters mocked his philanthropy toward slum children as face-saving gestures. During rail strikes in 1886, he dispatched strikebreakers to batter disgruntled laborers. Ever secretive, he concealed from the media his grief for his dead wife and the consumption that was killing him. For his Fifth Avenue home, he built a collection of French paintings by Eugène Delacroix, Jean-François Millet, and other artists of the Belle Epoque.

At his death from pulmonary consumption and hemorrhage on December 2, 1892, Gould's estate of $77 million and the 67-acre (27-hectare) Gothic revival country house at Lyndhurst, New York, passed to his children under management by his son, George Jay Gould. Following his burial in a grand Ionic mausoleum at Woodlawn Cemetery in the Bronx, Pinkerton agents faced off against anarchists to prevent grave robbing. Trustees took charge of his investments in Western Union Telegraph, Manhattan Elevated, American Cable, and the Missouri Pacific, Texas & Pacific, Union Pacific, and Wabash railroads.

The *New York Tribune* published the only unprejudiced obituary. Gould's legend grew with revelations of his contractual and legal conniving against rivals to dominate America's infrastructure.

See also: Nast, Thomas; Vanderbilt, Cornelius.

Further Reading

Beckert, Sven. *The Monied Metropolis: New York City and the Consolidation of the American Bourgeoisie, 1850–1896.* Cambridge, UK: Cambridge University Press, 2001.

Lane, Charles. *The Day Freedom Died: The Colfax Massacre, the Supreme Court, and the Betrayal of Reconstruction.* New York: Henry Holt, 2008.

Morris, Charles R. *The Tycoons: How Andrew Carnegie, John D. Rockefeller, Jay Gould, and J.P. Morgan Invented the American Supereconomy.* New York: Henry Holt, 2005.

Renehan, Edward J., Jr. *The Dark Genius of Wall Street: The Misunderstood Life of Jay Gould, King of the Robber Barons.* New York: Basic Books, 2005.

Grange Movement

The National Grange of the Order of Patrons of Husbandry bonded white farm families into a hierarchical society bent on common economic and political self-betterment. America's oldest agrarian organization, it began on December 4, 1867, as a class-action lobby against grain warehousing fees, high interest rates, and parasitic middlemen. During the rise of industrial urbanism, reformer Oliver Hudson Kelley, a staff member of the U.S. Department of Agriculture, became the father of the Grange Movement, which endorsed self-sustaining farms as a source of dignity and mutual understanding.

At the urging of President Andrew Johnson, on January 13, 1866, Kelley made a postwar fact-finding mission to the South, where cotton gins, sugarhouses, and barns lay in ruins and weeds choked the grain and rice fields of a demoralized people. Paralleling the ritual of Freemasonry, he founded the cooperative in Washington, D.C., as an antidote to Southern agricultural loss during the Civil War, especially in Alabama and Mississippi.

For organizational concepts, Kelley turned to seven advisers: Universalist minister Aaron Burt Grosh; farmer Caroline Arabella Hall; William Morton Ireland, chief clerk of the U.S. Post Office; banker Francis Marion McDowell; William Saunders, a botanist; U.S. Treasury agent John Richardson Thompson; and U.S. Treasury agent John Trimble. By 1869, secure in its moral and pragmatic foundation, the Grange Movement spread to the Dakotas, Iowa, and Minnesota.

By accessing lines of communication with other farmers, agrarian families fought for a greater share of national prosperity and social respect. Returning Confederate soldiers and former prisoners of war jockeyed for better lives and greater creature comforts on devastated acreage plundered in their absence. The Mississippi Grange, founded in May 1871, built a membership of 30,000, with "knights of the plow" in every county. From 1873 to 1875, national membership by men, women, and teens—called "brothers" and "sisters"—grew from 200,000 to 858,050, turning the Grange into a formidable voting bloc.

In the Midwest in 1870, farmers welcomed the concept of group action through cooperative planting, irrigation, and harvesting as a means of reducing implement costs, which ranged upward to $125 for a mower and $225 for a reaper. Briefly, Iowa and Nebraska volunteers experimented with cooperative Grange implement factories, which failed in 1875.

Issues favored by Grangers ranged from temperance and community service to free rural mail delivery and parcel post, farm credit, education by federal extension agencies, family health services, and woman suffrage. In Maine, the popularity of the Grange alarmed merchants, who launched rumor wars against farmers for promulgating a "secret society" dedicated to spending less cash at local stores.

Orator Mary Anne Bryant Mayo of Battle Creek, Michigan, advanced in Grange authority and traveled the state to promote grassroots accomplishments by women and children. Among her humanitarian efforts was the thriving Fresh Air Outing Program—the rescue of slum children and their mothers from polluted cities for two-week summer vacations in the country. Into the late 1870s, Grangers fought a deadlier plague—unscrupulous railroad barons such as James "Diamond Jim" Fisk, Jr., and Jason "Jay" Gould, who used court and legislative privileges to control huge financial empires at the expense of the working class.

An Era of Change

Along with the building of rail and telegraph networks, John Deere's invention of the steel plow, and fencing with barbed wire, the Grange increased efficiency and conveniences to homesteaders in remote areas. Farmers strengthened market demand for food products and invested profits in land, hired labor, and machinery. Nebraska farmers, led by John Weir, banded under the Grange Movement on February 22, 1872, organizing 20,000 members into 50 chapters. Grangers founded cooperative stores and lobbied for state regulation of railroad freight charges.

Shopping by Montgomery Ward catalogs, the only illustrated publication on farms, encouraged illiterate and immigrant children and adults to learn to read. Orders were slow until the Illinois and Iowa Grange chose Montgomery Ward as its purchasing agent and general supply house. Dealings with owner Aaron Montgomery Ward saved rural families one-third to one-half the cost of dealing with local dry goods vendors. In exchange for Grange patronage, Ward allowed members a ten-day grace period on cash purchases. From Grange mailing lists, he extended his catalog coverage of rural areas under the slogan "Grangers Supplied by the Cheapest Cash House in America."

Kelley's innovative thinking boosted pragmatism to the forefront of national philosophy. His influence turned the New Hampshire Grange into a force for local fellowship and good deeds, notably, the formation of a choir, the mentorship of young and inexperienced landowners, and the support of farm widows. At Plymouth, Connecticut, Grange meetings developed into a Chautauqua-style institute by including musicales, recitations, essays, and agrarian debate. In Brattleboro, Vermont, physician and Grange overseer Willard H. Pierce edited New England's oldest agrarian journals, *Grange Horse* and the *New England Farmer*; in Little Rock, Arkansas, in 1874, farmers issued the *Weekly Grange,* which denounced political partisanship in favor of populist movements.

Kelley added to members' goals the balancing of classical and mathematical curriculum in public schools with the addition of agricultural and industrial studies as preparations for the real world. In place of rote lessons in Latin, he proposed hands-on training in practical life skills, including seed planting on sunny windowsills for kindergartners and home economics classes in cooking and sewing for female students. Tennessee farmers bolstered his efforts by requesting curriculum changes by the state legislature. In Rhode Island, Grangers promoted prizes at corn shows, market gardening, better roads, and a farmers' credit bureau. Maryland farmers profited from experimental stations, which tested hybrid seed; in Indiana, planters attended free weeklong seminars at Farmers' Institutes.

Legislation and Local Action

Grangers fostered independence from federal solutions to farm problems. To protect the rural family from sweeping legislative action favoring cattlemen, lumbermen, and miners, smallholders organized an Oregon chapter in 1873. That same year, Minnesota farmers cooperated with the St. Paul & Sioux City Railroad to supply free shrubs and trees to prairie settlements. In Florida, cotton growers outside Jacksonville in the St. Johns River basin operated their own steamboat, thereby cutting delivery costs by $1.50 per bale. In 1874, California Grangers invested in a rail spur to carry wheat from Monterey 20 miles (32 kilometers) east into the Salinas Valley. The following year, to uplift family farms from the stigma of ignorance and backwardness, Grangers in Alabama, California, Louisiana, Michigan, Mississippi, North Carolina, and South Carolina pressed for free agricultural academies to teach technologically advanced farming and livestock breeding methods. In Colorado in 1876, nesters resorted to Grange lobbying to protect smallholders from the domination of beef barons and rail and storage companies.

The Grange in Illinois, Iowa, Minnesota, and Wisconsin became more politically sophisticated during litigation against rail monopolies before the U.S. Supreme Court. The high court's ruling in *Munn v. Illinois* (1877) sided with farmers against price fixing at grain elevators, which the justices deemed a public rather than an entrepreneurial interest. By electing Grangers to state legislatures, farmers crusaded for regulation of rail and handling charges. Politicians managed a delicate balance of regulatory laws with the enticement of Eastern investors to state projects.

During periods of hostility between beef barons and nesters, the Grange spoke for farmers. Against Grangers' political clout, the Colorado Stock Growers' Association promoted branding as proof of ownership and lobbied Congress to set aside the open range from homestead laws that allowed smallholders to fence their acreage. Agricultural interests won the struggle for domination in the 1880s, when greed and arrogance destroyed corporate ranching by promoting overstocking and overgrazing. In Texas, 2,000 Grangers gave up on the cooperative society in 1877 and formed the Texas Farmers' Alliance, a political action group and a precursor of the Populist Party.

Further Reading

Barron, Hal S. *Mixed Harvest: The Second Great Transformation in the Rural North, 1870–1930.* Chapel Hill: University of North Carolina Press, 1997.

McGrath, Robert C., Jr. *American Populism: A Social History, 1877–1898.* New York: Hill and Wang, 1993.

Schmidt, Alvin J., ed. *The Greenwood Encyclopedia of American Institutions: Fraternal Organizations.* Westport, CT: Greenwood, 1980.

Woods, Thomas A. *Knights of the Plow: Oliver H. Kelley and the Origins of the Grange in Republican Ideology.* Ames: Iowa State University Press, 1991.

Grant, Ulysses S. (1822–1885)

From Union military tactician to two-term U.S. president (1869–1877), Ulysses Simpson Grant dominated nineteenth-century American history for more than a quarter century. The son of a tanner, Jesse Root Grant, he was born on April 27, 1822, in Point Pleasant, Ohio, to Hannah Simpson Grant, who named him Hiram Ulysses. He grew up on a farm in Brown County, one of the heavily traveled routes of the Underground Railroad from Kentucky over the Ohio River.

Under the nickname "Sam," Grant attended the U.S. Military Academy at West Point, New York, until 1843, serving as quartermaster. In 1846, he soldiered under General Winfield Scott in the Mexican-American War, earning respect for his horsemanship and for two acts of bravery under fire, including the rescue of a fallen comrade.

He married Julia Boggs Dent, the mother of their daughter and three sons, on August 22, 1848. In 1853, he received a commission to Washington Territory and to Fort Humboldt, California, as an army pay officer. At age 32, Grant resigned his commission to farm and returned to civilian life in St. Louis, Missouri, without political ambitions or a party affiliation. He sold real estate, collected customs, worked as county engineer, and sold harnesses and saddles with his younger brothers, Orvil and Simpson Grant, in a leather shop in Galena, Illinois.

Joining the Northern military effort after the outbreak of the Civil War, Grant took command of an Illinois regiment under appointment by the governor in

May 1861. Three months later, President Abraham Lincoln named him brigadier general in the Union army, for which he trained the Twenty-first Illinois Infantry. In late winter 1862, Grant's troops captured Fort Henry and Fort Donelson, Tennessee, where victory opened the state to Union forces and Northern hopes for a quick end to the war. Doggedly, from April 6 to 7, 1862, Grant commanded Union forces at the Battle of Shiloh, which produced 24,000 casualties. That fall, he laid the Union siege at Vicksburg, Mississippi, which precipitated a Confederate surrender on July 4, 1863, effectively cutting off the trans-Mississippi states from the rest of the Confederacy. The fall of Vicksburg coincided with the Battle of Gettysburg in Pennsylvania, giving Union forces the momentum and strategic advantage to win the war.

In another string of victories, at Chattanooga from June 7 to November 25, 1863, Grant seized the initiative against General Robert E. Lee's forces and wore down the enemy's spirit, manpower, and infrastructure with the invasion of Atlanta, Georgia, in summer 1864. On March 12, 1865, Grant advanced to general in chief of U.S. armies and masterminded a total war on five fronts, concluding with the evacuation of the Confederate capital at Richmond, Virginia, on April 2. A week later, he accepted Lee's surrender at Appomattox Court House, Virginia. Exultation proved short-lived, however. Days later, Grant served as a pallbearer at the funeral of President Abraham Lincoln.

From General to President

Postwar popularity swept Grant into military prominence and to appointment by President Andrew Johnson as secretary of war, which Grant refused. The creation of standing regiments of blacks was the work of Grant, who directed a Peace Plan through Congress on July 28, 1866, against Democratic opposition. By 1868, Johnson and Grant had stanched congressional enthusiasm for genocide and restrained the U.S. Cavalry from intensifying hostilities against Native Americans, which was costing the government $1 million for every Indian killed.

On a platform of national peace and amnesty for secessionists, Grant, at age 46, ran for the presidency against Horatio Seymour, the former governor of New York. With positive publicity from political cartoonist Thomas Nast of *Harper's Weekly,* Grant entered the White House on March 4, 1869, as the eighteenth and youngest president of the United States. He immediately backed greenbacks with gold, modernized the national treasury, and secured monetary plates at the Bureau of Printing and Engraving to halt counterfeiting. By improving tax collection and boosting foreign trade, he lowered the national debt by $50 million.

He began repairing the ravages of war in Washington, D.C., with upgraded water and sewer service and paved streets. To improve drainage and suppress outbreaks of malaria, civil engineers smoothed hills and filled ravines. A railway to Point Lookout encouraged tourism; streetcars carried newcomers from the suburbs to the Capitol, White House, and center market, where parks and street crews improved plantings.

Republican dominance of Reconstruction forced civil rights on the disgruntled South and placed state violence under the control of local government. In January 1869, members of the National Convention of the Colored Men of America, led by President William Nesbit of Altoona, Pennsylvania, head of the Pennsylvania State Equal Rights League, pressured President-Elect Grant to extend suffrage as a cornerstone of equal rights. Despite opposition from Western states to giving voting rights to Chinese and Irish immigrants, the House bill passed on January 30, 1869, by a vote of 150–42. The Civil Rights Act of April 1871, written by Union General Benjamin Franklin Butler, outlawed the Ku Klux Klan and gave the president the power to suspend habeas corpus and to wield martial law against racist conspiracies.

A cleanup of guerrilla hit squads began in October 1871 with federal control over paramilitary activities in the Carolinas, Louisiana, and Mississippi by the Klan, Red Shirts, and White League. The newly created Department of Justice issued 4,000 indictments and convicted 1,150 Klan terrorists. Modifying the get-tough tone of his third year in office, Grant composed a Thanksgiving proclamation on October 28, thanking God for peace and an end to bloodshed. On May 22, 1872, he signed the Amnesty Act, which restored citizenship to all but 500 secessionists, including former Confederate President Jefferson Davis.

The frontier posed problems of distance and control, particularly the domain of Hawaiian King David Kalakaua and the traditional homelands of Plains and Pacific Coast Indians. To end genocide and to save money and military effort, President Grant stipulated the terms of his Peace Policy during his State of the Union address on December 4, 1871. His solution called for a reorganization of the Office of Indian Affairs and the hiring of religious leaders to supervise agencies and Christian schools to ready Native Americans for citizenship. He appointed his old friend General Ely Samuel Parker, a native Seneca, as commissioner of Indian affairs. Grant ordered Parker to round up roving bands of renegades and place them on reservations to protect them from white vengeance and to prevent them from violating the peace.

In Dakota Territory, appointment of scandal-ridden Governor John A. Burbank in 1869 led to party patronage and speculation in real estate on native land. Grant replaced Burbank with John L. Pennington, an ineffectual authority figure during the face-off between the Sioux and gold miners. A similar shuffling of appointments removed an anti-Indian administrator, Alvan Flanders, from governing Washington Territory. When Oglala Sioux Chief Red Cloud and Brulé Sioux chiefs Big Bear, Little Swan, and Red Dog and an entourage of 14 Indians arrived in Washington, D.C., on June 2, 1870, President Grant hosted them at a lavish banquet in the state dining room.

In fall 1872, the president furthered his Peace Policy by dispatching General Oliver Otis Howard to Arizona and New Mexico to pacify the Apache, Maricopa, Navajo, Papago, Pima, and Yuma. With scout Thomas Jefferson Jeffords, Howard brokered an accord with Cochise and the Chiricahua Apache and earned as a reward command of the Department of the Columbia.

Second Term

In November 1872, Grant handily won reelection against liberal candidate Horace Greeley, a political novice and gadfly editor of the *New York Tribune.* Grant's second term plunged the president into late Reconstruction strife, including the ravages of the James Gang in the Midwest and an unstable economy that triggered the Panic of 1873.

In 1874, the toll of rioting in New Orleans, Louisiana, reached 13 dead and 53 wounded before Grant countermanded racist city police by stationing federal troops throughout the Mississippi Delta. Satirists in subsequent Mardi Gras processions mocked the president by depicting him as a grub worm.

Also during his second term, Grant initiated sweeping civil service reform, creating the first Civil Service Commission to prevent insider appointments from clogging officialdom with inept clerks. Because Plains Indians relied on the buffalo for food and shelter, Grant refused to sign a congressional bill in 1874 to shield herds from stalkers. In Nevada on March 23, 1875, he established the Pyramid Lake Indian Reservation, a landmass of 477,000 acres (193,000 hectares). He later visited the Paiute and proclaimed them slovenly, lazy, and dirty, but not wild or threatening.

For the remainder of his presidency, Grant fought accusations of favoring old friends for government positions and for allowing extortion and profiteering to proliferate in the military, the court system, and the governance of Indians. In 1874, the theft of federal taxes by Treasury Secretary William Adams Richardson and his assistant, John D. Sanborn, preceded evidence of graft closer to home. On October 19, 1875, Secretary of the Interior Columbus Delano resigned after discovering that his son, John Delano, had conspired with President Grant's brother, Orvil Grant, to enrich themselves on government contracts. Virtually paralyzed by Democratic control of Congress, Grant accepted the resignation of Secretary

The commander of all Union forces during the Civil War and the eighteenth president of the United States, Ulysses S. Grant is regarded by historians as a master military commander but an unsuccessful chief executive. His two terms were marred by scandal. *(Spencer Arnold/Stringer/Getty Images)*

of War William Worth Belknap, whom the Senate tried on March 2, 1876, for selling appointments of Indian post traders for $20,000. While the citizenry suffered economic depression, the rebuilding of the cabinet preoccupied Grant.

After his second term, Grant suffered regrets, including the knowledge that Secretary of the Navy George Maxwell Robeson had used $320,000 in bribes from military contractors to purchase personal vacation property. In 1877, Grant confided to Secretary of State Hamilton Fish that the Fifteenth Amendment had not benefited blacks as he had hoped. After a decade of bloody Indian wars, politicians scrapped Grant's Peace Policy as unworkable and closed Indian agencies as corrupt and cruel. The former president began negotiations with Samoa for a U.S. military base at Pago Pago, but left unfinished the study of a canal across Nicaragua to gain more convenient access to the Pacific Ocean.

In retirement, Grant traveled, moved to New York City, and wrote his two-volume *Personal Memoirs of U.S. Grant* (1885), in which he reviled the Mexican-American War as an excuse to extend slavery into the Southwest. He worried about the survival of his family. Poverty following a swindle by the banking firm of Grant & Ward and of the Marine Bank forced him to seek reinstatement in the army to obtain a pension of $13,500 per year. Friends pressed monetary gifts on Grant. With a deal arranged by friend Mark Twain, Grant wrote professionally for *The Century Magazine,* which paid him $500 each for three articles on the Battles of Shiloh and Vicksburg. The eyewitness accounts boosted magazine circulation by 100,000 and served Stephen Crane as the source of the fictional *The Red Badge of Courage* (1895).

The former president's health declined from pleural pneumonia, inflamed throat glands, and a hip injury caused by a fall on ice. After 19 months of suffering from sleeplessness and the inability to swallow or speak, he died on July 23, 1885, of tonsillar cancer, leaving his family secure with $450,000 in royalties from his autobiography.

His reputation suffered posthumously in 1910 with the serialization by the *Atlantic Monthly* of the three-volume *Diary of Gideon Welles,* a covert vilification by the former naval secretary that dismissed Grant as an unprincipled alcoholic. Historians debate Grant's inability to demand probity from his friends, but laud him for upholding civil rights for blacks and Indians and for relying on arbitration to keep the United States out of war.

See also: Fish, Hamilton; Gould, Jay.

Further Reading

Bunting, Josiah, III. *Ulysses S. Grant.* New York: Times Books, 2004.

Campbell, James E. *The American Campaign: U.S. Presidential Campaigns and the National Vote.* 2nd ed. College Station: Texas A&M University Press, 2008.

Reichley, A. James, ed. *Elections American Style.* Washington, DC: Brookings Institution, 1987.

Stephenson, Nathaniel W. *Abraham Lincoln and the Union.* New York: BiblioBazaar, 2008.

Striner, Richard. *Father Abraham: Lincoln's Relentless Struggle to End Slavery.* Oxford, UK: Oxford University Press, 2006.

Great Atlantic and Pacific Tea Company

The Great Atlantic and Pacific Tea Company, the nation's prototype of the cross-country supermarket chain, introduced store brands, economy, and self-service shopping coast to coast. Founded in 1859 in Elmira, New York, it was first known as the Great American Tea Company, a consignment seller of wholesale teas.

The original partners—leather merchant George Francis Gilman and dry goods clerk George Huntington Hartford—marketed bargain-priced coffee and tea arriving from Asia by clipper ship. Gilman's father, shipbuilder Nathaniel Gilman, imported the first bulk commodities in his own ships from China and Japan. Alongside the docks of New York Harbor, they sold goods at 2 cents above cost from a cart that Hartford had inherited from his brother. To hot beverages, the vendors added a spice line, including allspice, cinnamon, cloves, ginger, mustard, and pepper.

As their business prospered, Gilman and Hartford sold staples and luxury items by mail order. Local consumers could buy on credit at cargo prices and have goods delivered in glossy red wagons drawn by teams of eight dapple gray horses harnessed with gold bells and spangled leather. In Lower Manhattan, the vendors drew commerce to a red-awninged warehouse at 31–33 Vesey Street—the subsequent location of the World Trade Center—by selling directly to the consumer; their space expanded with the addition of 35–37 Vesey Street. Along with groceries, customers received free calendars, paper fans, seasonal trading cards, china mugs, and glass cruets and serving pieces. For lithographs of baseball, ice skating, and badminton, the company produced primitive art reflecting American community values.

Competitors predicted that undercutting by such wholesalers would destroy the nation's small businesses. Independents fought back with frivolous lawsuits charging Gilman and Hartford with being anticompetitive. Rumor campaigns charged the entrepreneurs with selling spoiled and used tea leaves.

Advertising in the 1860s

Early in their partnership, Gilman and Hartford used eye appeal and advertising to advantage. Their full-color circulars contained price lists and special interest news and features, as well as ads for Bomosa, Golden Rio, Java, and Mocha coffees, names rich in exotic appeal. A full-page ad in the 1865 *Horticulturist* exploited the romance of importing by announcing the arrival of 22,000 half chests of tea aboard the clipper ship *Golden State,* owned by Jacob Aaron Westervelt, the mayor of New York City. In 1867, a full-page ad explained to bargain hunters the cost cycle inflicted by bankers, importers, speculators, and wholesalers on imported goods. By removing the middleman, Gilman and Hartford reduced the price of tea from $1 per pound to 30 cents.

The vendors made bold claims about quality—for example, that its condensed milk was made in porcelain rather than copper pans. They boasted that they specialized in supplying goods to boardinghouses, country clubs, hotels, institutions and schools, restaurants, and steamboats. Drawing shoppers to the company's tea emporium were crystal chandeliers with red, white, and blue globes reflected on a tin ceiling. The owners touched up the decor with arching gas jets, vermilion paint, and gold leaf panels featuring Chinese motifs. Cashiers rang up purchases at a pseudo-Asian pagoda. Out front, the Hartford brothers suspended the letter "T," a 6-foot (1.8-meter) sign highlighted by gas jets.

In 1869, Hartford extended the range of products with Thea Nectar, his own brand of tea mixed from damaged loads and stale leaves with black tea. After patenting his trademark, he packaged it in 1-pound (0.45-kilogram) tin caddies and marketed it as an exclusive brand, "The Tea of All Teas," a pure, nutritious beverage made from delicate leaves cured on porcelain.

A National Chain

In their third year of business, the partners opened a store at Broadway and Bleecker streets in Lower Manhattan, billed as the world's largest tea store. In 1863, the food retail business spread through New York and to ten Atlantic seaboard cities, including Boston and Philadelphia. Gilman and Hartford added olive oil and castile soaps, vanilla extract, dried fruit, condensed milk, Worcestershire sauce by the half pint or quart, and baking powder to the beverage line; the company also offered sugar in confectioners, granulated, and loaf form. Coffee roasters operated round the clock and spread an appealing aroma down Broadway. A chemist mixed the baking powder on site to prove that it was unadulterated.

For advertising, Gilman favored the *American Horticultural Annual, American Phrenological Journal, Appleton's, Harper's Weekly, Musical Record, Our Boys and Girls, Southern Farm and Home, School Journal, Sun's Guide to New York, Gem of the West, Water Cure Journal,* and the *Herald of Health.* Ad copy targeted tea drinkers with the choice of Assam, Bey-Jop, Celinrus, Congo, foo chow, Formosa, green gunpowder, young Hyson, imperial, moyune, oolong, orange pekoe, silver leaf, souchong, and sun-dried varieties grown on the company's private tea plantations. In 1869, a club plan rewarded teachers and buyer cooperatives with incentives and a savings of one-third for bulk orders. All goods came with a money-back guarantee.

Over 5,000 routes, salesmen extended high-volume business to 30 states in New England, the South, and the Midwest. With the completion of the Transcontinental Railroad on May 10, 1869, the owners changed the firm's name to the Great Atlantic and Pacific Tea Company (A&P), to reflect sales on the West Coast and to gain sales momentum from the historic event. The transport of goods by refrigerated cars allowed A&P to supply the Midwest with fresh fruits, vegetables, and seafood, as well as butter, cocoa, flour, and canned pears and tomatoes.

To assist Chicago after the Great Fire of October 8–10, 1871, A&P donated a trainload of relief supplies and dispatched employees to distribute it. Promoting the city's rebuilding, Gilman and Hartford established an anchor store in Chicago. By 1878, the chain had 75 stores, including major locations in Baltimore, Buffalo, Cleveland, Milwaukee, Newark, and Washington, D.C.

Gilman retired from the partnership and lived lavishly at his home in Bridgeport, Connecticut, on earnings of $40 million. He died intestate on March 3, 1901, and left the Gilmans in legal limbo, requiring four years of litigation to purchase control of the company.

An American Institution

While Hartford served Orange, New Jersey, as mayor, his sons, merchandiser George Ludlum Hartford and operations manager John Augustine Hartford, began assuming more company responsibilities in their mid-teens. At the suggestion of George Ludlum Hartford, in 1880, the labeling of house-brand baking powder with the logo A&P prefaced an era of merchandise produced by company bakeries, factories, and meat packers, the beginnings of one-stop shopping. The company showcased its more successful product, Eight O'Clock Coffee, a light roast that had remained unbranded since its introduction in 1859. (It survives today as one of America's oldest brand names.) The Hartford brothers added more house logos to their array—America's Choice, Ann Page, Health Pride, and Master Choice. Attention to quality foods and cash-and-carry economy won customer loyalty.

In 1881, the company became the nation's first chain of 100 stores and, at its height, grew by three new store openings per day. A company manual listed the essentials of sales courtesy—a friendly smile and erect posture above a clean smock, straight tie, and creased trousers. A&P rewarded shoppers with gifts and premiums, such as scalloped napkins, egg beaters, majolica creamers, china pickle dishes and tea sets, spoon holders, glass sugar bowls, and syrup cups.

Spreading to Montreal, Canada, the chain grew to 4,544 stores in 1920 and easily weathered the 1929 stock market crash while operating 15,418 stores. By the 1930s, the company operated at 16,000 locations with total annual sales reaching $1 billion.

Further Reading

Anderson, Avis H. *A&P: The Story of the Great Atlantic & Pacific Tea Company.* Charleston, SC: Arcadia, 2002.

Hallett, Anthony, and Diane Hallett. *Entrepreneur Magazine: Encyclopedia of Entrepreneurs.* New York: Wiley, 1997.

Lurie, Maxine N., and Marc Mappen, eds. *Encyclopedia of New Jersey.* New Brunswick, NJ: Rutgers University Press, 2004.

Smith, Andrew F., ed. *The Oxford Companion to American Food and Drink.* New York: Oxford University Press, 2007.

Great Lakes

A cluster of five fresh water bodies comprising 95,000 square miles (246,000 square kilometers) of surface on the U.S. border with Ontario, Canada, the five Great Lakes—Erie, Huron, Michigan, Ontario, and Superior—provide North America today with a source of recreation, water transportation, fishing, and scenic travel. In pre-Columbian history, the environs hosted approximately 120 native hunter-gatherer tribes.

Lake Indian culture depended on watershed flora and fauna, which fed indigenous peoples, supplied them with medicines and hides, and populated their oral beast fables and mimetic dances. In the 1830s, the federal government began claiming the valuable borderland by forcing tribes onto reservations. By the 1870s, the last of the Winnebago departed the Great Lakes Basin for Camp Winnebago, Nebraska, clearing the way for European profiteering and settlement.

Industry and freight replaced native dominion. Shipbuilding aimed for larger and faster lakers. Barges, steamers, and coasters carried wheat to grain elevators in Chicago, Illinois; Duluth, Minnesota; Erie, Pennsylvania; and Milwaukee, Wisconsin. Freighters sped coal, iron ore, and limestone to steel mills and to railheads in Erie and Ashtabula, Ohio. Coal traffic centered on docks in Erie and Cleveland, Ohio. Oil shipments from Detroit, Michigan, to Liverpool, England, flourished in 1862 but came to a temporary mid-winter halt because of ice obstruction at Quebec on the St. Lawrence Seaway. Other foreign vessels from England, Ireland, and Norway turned U.S. lake ports into global trading centers.

Guarding the Lakes

In 1861, the posting of six revenue cutters out of New York Harbor increased federal patrols of the Revenue Cutter Service, an armed maritime law enforcement agency and forerunner of the Coast Guard. The U.S. Treasury Department enlisted members to halt smuggling and slave importation along the Canadian border and to provide rescue for foundering or burning watercraft. The small fleet of cutters collected duties and monitored some 1,500 vessels, varying in tonnage and value.

The patrols faced an increasing challenge. The largest tow set out from the Detroit River to Lake Erie on July 14, 1862, with the tug *Kate Williams* pulling ten loaded vessels, a Great Lakes record. That same month, the first propeller ship with an iron hull, the 200-foot (60-meter) *Merchant,* built at a Buffalo, New York, shipyard, introduced freight and passenger service to Chicago at a speed of 14 miles (22 kilometers) per hour. Twelve more iron steamers entered competition in 1868. Contributing to the expansion of lake trade was "Commodore" Cornelius Vanderbilt's control of the Michigan Southern Railroad from Chicago to Detroit and connection with the Canada Southern and the Great Western of Canada, which carried passengers from Buffalo.

With prosperity and speed of transport came ecological damage and regulation. Dams in Canada and the United

Major Native Tribes in the Great Lakes Region

Area	Tribes
Lake Erie	Erie, Iroquois, Kickapoo, Neutral, Shawnee
Lake Huron	Fox, Huron, Neutral, Nipissing, Ojibwa, Ottawa, Petun, Potawatomi, Sac
Lake Michigan	Illini, Iowa, Mascouten, Menominee, Miami, Oneida, Potawatomi, Santee Dakota, Winnebago
Lake Ontario	Algonquin, Cayuga, Huron, Iroquois, Mohawk, Neutral, Oneida, Onondaga, Seneca
Lake Superior	Fox, Gros Ventre, Menominee, Ojibwa, Santee Dakota

States severely limited the annual salmon and sturgeon runs to spawning grounds in the 1860s. Passage of the British North America Act by the British Parliament on July 1, 1867, fostered binational cooperation to enhance banking, commerce, and trade on both sides of the border. Shipyards commissioned more bulk freighters, beginning in 1869 with the launching of the 1,000-ton (900-metric-ton) *Robert J. Hackett.*

The flurry of business from the early 1800s rapidly denuded forests of timber, which shipbuilders such as German immigrant Henry B. Burger of Rand & Burger in Manitowoc, Wisconsin, favored for the crafting of full-rigged schooners, a common sight on the Great Lakes until 1880. Lake Superior traders transported pine and hemlock for homes and businesses over the Dakotas to settlers of the Great Plains. Rapidly, lumber camps in Wisconsin's Black, Chippewa, and Wolf river districts declined.

By 1875, fishing along Wisconsin's shores had fallen to 75 percent of its usual harvest, in part because of the overfishing of trout, salmon, and graylings and the infestation of the invasive alewife and mollusks.

Gateway to Liberty

The separation of Northern U.S. states from Canada made the Great Lakes a steady conduit for escaped slaves, especially after passage of the Fugitive Slave Law of 1850. Volunteers such as Grace Whitlock Stoneman and Joseph Stoneman on Lake Erie in Cleveland opened their homes as waystations of the Underground Railroad. Two ministers, Amos S. Tryon and Josiah Tryon, operated a milling and boatworks at Niagara Falls, New York, and concealed runaways among goods bound over Lake Erie and Lake Ontario. At Pittsburgh, Pennsylvania, Martin Robinson Delany and the Reverend Lewis Woodson transported slaves out of state and over Lake Erie. On a flight through Detroit, Michigan, Jane King Walls and John Freeman Walls escaped pursuers by crossing a short distance to Amherstburg, Ontario, via the steamer *Pearl.* Captain John N. Stewart of Buffalo, New York, began navigating Lake Huron from Saginaw, Michigan, in 1862, and hid runaways in his stateroom aboard the sidewheeler packet *Bay City.* Quaker Josiah Osborn managed risky relays of Kentucky slaves through his home in Calvin, Michigan, past border lookouts to the west and across Lake Michigan. On Lake Ontario in 1861, Captain Horatio Nelson Throop used his schooner *Rival* as a source of rescue, while he ferried wheat to Kingston, Ontario. A family member and co-conspirator, James T. Holling, captain of the *Charger,* provided a similar water transport for runaways. On a fourth try, the escape route of slave William A. Hall took him from Nashville, Tennessee, to Ottawa, Illinois, and through Chicago to Wisconsin, where he crossed Lake Superior.

In the 1860s, Confederate spying and insurgency flourished along the Great Lakes, where slave catchers profited from the rapid sale of runaways. To deflect the Civil War from Pennsylvania and Virginia, rebel raiders intended to launch marine forays from Canada into Northern U.S. industrial centers, a source of Union maritime wealth. In 1864, Confederates captured the steamer *Philo Parsons* and the *Island Queen* at Put-in-Bay, Ohio, but they scuttled both in Lake Erie because a traitor disclosed their plans. Union troops executed the plotter, John Yates Beall, on February 24, 1865, at Governors Island, New York.

According to Secretary of the Navy Gideon Welles, the *Georgian,* a Confederate laker built on Georgian Bay, Ontario, failed to disrupt Union shipping lanes because of technical problems with the propeller. Rebel forces planned to use the *Georgian* as a base of operations for the release of 3,200 rebel officers imprisoned on Johnson's Island on Lake Erie north of Sandusky, Ohio.

Another plot intended the use the *Georgian* to seize a paddle frigate, the dilapidated USS *Michigan,* the Union's only warship on the lakes. The Confederates proposed to send a visitor aboard to drug the table wine of Captain John C. Carter and the crew. The frigate, a major source of enlistment for the U.S. Navy, recruited 4,000 sailors during the war, most assigned to the Mississippi squadron and the rest to patrol Atlantic port blockades. To increase enthusiasm for service, the Treasury Department offered enlistees a salary of $3 per day and a $100 bounty. The frigate landed squads of marines at Buffalo and Milwaukee in August 1863 to quell 7,000 draft rioters, who attempted to torch grain elevators.

When intrigue on the lakes ceased with the armistice of April 9, 1865, lake freighters resumed a remunerative business with the United States, Canada, and foreign traders. At war's end, revenue cutters searched vessels for assassins who may have conspired with shooter John Wilkes Booth to kill President Abraham Lincoln. The Treasury Department honored Secretary of the Treasury William Pitt Fessenden with the commissioning of the *William P. Fessenden,* a 180-foot (55-meter) revenue cutter anchored at Detroit.

Reconstruction

Postwar lake traffic incurred peacetime obstacles. As early as colonial days, night traffic required the outfitting of lighthouses and reef lights, the staffing of lifeboat stations, and the dredging of shoals, wrecks, and snags from harbors.

A freak storm on November 16, 1869, added wreckage to the usual list of sinkings and burned vessels. The gale struck most lake ports and cost a majority of ship owners crew, goods, and floating stock, including the steamer *City of Sandusky,* which collided with the steamer *Susan Ward* at St. Clair Flats, Michigan. The total loss of 56 schooners, 18 scows, eight barks, six propeller boats, four brigs, three barges, and one tug preceded a decline in sidewheelers and the commissioning of 67 lakers, the beginning of recovery for regional businesses.

Lake traffic remained subdued in 1871, when the Great Chicago Fire of October 8–10 caused more loss of shipments, grain-filled elevators, and dock property. Flames consumed the *Navarino,* a new $50,000 propeller steamer of the Goodrich Transportation Company, owned by Captain Albert Edgar Goodrich. The steamer had moored at the Goodrich wharf at the North Pier since its commissioning on April 8. Captain Joseph Gilson attempted to maneuver the *Navarino* into deep water with the tug *Magnolia,* but the steamer grounded on the riverbank. Gilson rescued the company records and wharf personnel aboard the *Skylark,* which he towed away from danger. Burning buildings and ships generated smoke and ash that imperiled navigation for weeks.

Larger replacement vessels lowered freight rates and increased competition among investors, who demasted tall ships and revamped propeller lakers and schooners to produce more lumber and steam barges, package freighters, and screw tugs. Renewing hopes of a business resurgence was the passage of the steamer *Wisconsin* from Oshkosh, Wisconsin, south over the Fox and Wisconsin rivers to Prairie du Chien on the Iowa border. Entrepreneurs proposed extending the southern route by connecting Lake Michigan to the Mississippi River by canal.

See also: Fessenden, William; Indian Reservations; Law Enforcement.

Further Reading

Dear, I.C.B., and Peter Kemp, eds. *The Oxford Companion to Ships and the Sea.* 2nd ed. Oxford, UK: Oxford University Press, 2005.

O'Brien, T. Michael. *Guardians of the Eighth Sea: A History of the U.S. Coast Guard on the Great Lakes.* Honolulu, HI: University Press of the Pacific, 2001.

Rodgers, Bradley A. *Guardian of the Great Lakes: The U.S. Paddle Frigate* Michigan. Ann Arbor: University of Michigan Press, 1996.

Roland, Alex, W. Jeffrey Bolster, and Alexander Keyssar. *The Way of the Ship: America's Maritime History Reenvisioned, 1600–2000.* Hoboken, NJ: Wiley, 2008.

Winks, Robin W. *The Blacks in Canada: A History.* Montreal, Canada: McGill-Queen's University Press, 2005.

Greeley, Horace (1811–1872)

A philanthropist, reformer, and proponent of abolitionism and homesteading, newspaper publisher Horace Greeley did much to mold the issues and opinions of his day. He was born on February 3, 1811, to weaver Mary Woodburn Greeley and an alcoholic day laborer, Zaccheus Greeley, on a farm 5 miles (8 kilometers) from Amherst, New Hampshire. His slow rousing at birth caused historians to surmise that he suffered from Asperger's syndrome, a form of autism marked by monomania, frustration, and social isolation.

Young "Hod" Greeley received substandard homeschooling from age two and read the Bible and *The Columbian Orator* as his chief forms of self-education. Rather than accept a scholarship to Phillips Exeter Academy from a Bedford minister, he joined his parents in fleeing bankruptcy and settled on the Minot estate in western Vermont at age ten to clear land with his father and eight-year-old brother, Barnes. In the evening, Horace read Shakespeare, history, British fiction, and the Bible from the landlord's library.

Greeley quit school at age 14 and apprenticed in the printing trade in April 1826 at East Poultney, Vermont, under Amos Bliss, editor of the *Northern Spectator.* To develop an affordable newspaper, Greeley became a journeyman printer in Pennsylvania for the *Erie Gazette.* After the failure of his first publication, the *Morning Post,* in New York City, at age 23, he established the *New Yorker,* a weekly journal featuring current events, the arts, and book reviews.

In 1836, he married suffragist Mary Young "Molly" Cheney, a schoolteacher and mother of their seven children whose health failed after the birth and death of their first child in fall 1838. Because of his wife's depression and household neglect, Greeley established late-night habits of office work and slept at a boardinghouse.

He edited a Whig political paper, the *Jeffersonian,* and a campaign paper, the *Log Cabin,* which supported Whig presidential candidate William Henry Harrison by influencing the vote of 90,000 readers. Although an object of ridicule for his eccentric dress in a long white Irish linen overcoat, loose black pantaloons, and oversized boots paired with a bright umbrella and yellow carry-all, Greeley became a popular platform speaker on reform issues in the United States and Canada.

The *Tribune*

In 1841, Greeley found his métier in the *New York Tribune,* America's first national newspaper. Circulated by rail and steamer, the spirited penny daily advanced in readership from 500 to 112,000 by 1854. Despite his lack of formal training, Greeley stocked his staff with such quality reporters as Charles Anderson Dana, Margaret Fuller, Jane Grey Swisshelm, and Karl Marx, a foreign correspondent in London. The editorial page blazed Greeley's reformist opinions about utopian communities, pacifism, vegetarianism, and temperance, which he favored, and about capital punishment, land speculation, monopolies, railroad barons, and slavery, which he denounced.

In a show of support for workers' rights, he fostered labor unions and offered his staff a share of the paper's profits. He condemned the Mexican-American War of 1846–1848 and crusaded for the training of females in trades to free them from the financial tyranny of men. In 1850, he endorsed the first National Woman's Rights Convention, but he did not support the right of women to the ballot.

His abolitionist paper summarized fugitive slave rescues as a means of informing the nation about the inhumane and unconstitutional strictures of the Fugitive Slave Law of 1850, which required citizens to assist U.S. marshals in returning blacks to bondage. After passage of the controversial Kansas-Nebraska Act of 1854, he hired correspondent Samuel Forster Tappan to survey the transport of slaves from Missouri. He praised the civil disobedience of Underground Railroad conductors, endorsed the establishment of free black communities in the Midwest, and made discreet donations to acts of antislavery protest and sabotage.

Greeley was one of the founders of the Republican Party, which took shape at the first convention in 1856 at Lafayette Hall in Allegheny County, Pennsylvania. Joining him in forming the party platform were Underground Railroad agents Joshua Reed Giddings, George W. Jackson, and Owen Glendower Lovejoy and attorney Abraham Lincoln, whom Greeley characterized as an able statesman and sustainer of democracy. The editor derided President James Buchanan as a rich man's advocate and hailed the presidency of Lincoln and the selection of Edwin M. Stanton as an obdurate secretary of war.

Greeley's editorials favored the conservation of Yosemite, California, which he visited in summer 1859 via the newly formed Leavenworth & Pikes Peak Express. As he passed through Kansas, he regretted the mistreatment of Native Americans, whom he compared to degraded and squalid children. Along the 700-mile (1,100-kilometer) route, he mourned the waste of buffalo herds by foolhardy hunters; he suffered bruising in an overturned coach during an Indian ambush outside Denver, Colorado, during the Pikes Peak Gold Rush. In Utah, he heard a sermon by Mormon elder Orson Pratt and judged Mormonism to be dogmatic and brutal, and its scripture, the Book of Mormon, to be worthless.

Upon returning to New York in October, Greeley crusaded for the completion of a Transcontinental Railroad as a boost to the U.S. mail service and to safe and speedy transportation to the Pacific Coast. He admitted that rail building was expensive and doubted the government's favoritism toward railroad barons, but he envisioned a rail network as a cornerstone of the military, food distribution, and the national economy.

The War Years and Reconstruction

As civil war presaged a grim fight by the "Cotton states" for autonomy from federal control, Greeley became a confrontational hawk given to invective, petulance, and self-righteousness. Upon Lincoln's inauguration on March 4, 1861, Greeley took aim at the appointment of cabinet members and earned the spite of Secretary of the Navy Gideon Welles, who called Greeley a shallow, wishy-washy, and imprudent meddler and self-promoter. Greeley's anti-slavery lecture at the Smithsonian Institution on January 3, 1862, won the admiration of President Lincoln, who intended to study a copy of the text in more detail. Despite Lincoln's goodwill, Greeley lost sleep and struggled to control his impulse to second-guess the president.

Democrats attacked the *Tribune* for the editor's zigzag logic. Greeley's insistent editorials demanding an immediate assault on the Confederate capitol at Richmond, Virginia, reached a quarter million readers, most in the rural North. On another subject, he extolled agrarian reform in the Homestead Act, which Lincoln signed on May 20, 1862, and took a stern tone in regard to Southern secession. The editor declared that the distribution of free land in the West encouraged higher wages in the East and enticed former slaves to build homes and businesses without rewarding Southern rebels.

A strident voice for abolition, newspaper editor Horace Greeley pushed President Lincoln to emancipate the slaves in 1862. Running for president on the Liberal Republican and Democratic tickets in 1872, Greeley won 2.8 million votes—and died soon thereafter. *(Apic/Getty Images)*

On August 19, 1862, Greeley lobbed a one-to-one editorial at Lincoln, demanding that the federal government outlaw the flesh trade. Three days later, Lincoln clarified that, as president, he owed his allegiance to the whole nation. He stated that he would free blacks if their emancipation were in the best interest of national unity, but he would not jeopardize the country by liberating slaves. Unknown to Greeley was Lincoln's draft of the Emancipation Proclamation, issued on September 22, 1862, and enacted on January 1, 1863.

In the mid-1860s, Greeley produced a succession of opinions that some readers found inconsistent. He lobbied for a Union armistice with the Confederacy, advocated equality for former slaves but not for women, and expressed wavering support for Lincoln's reelection as well as tentative backing of Treasury Secretary Salmon P. Chase for president. He warned the nation of Confederate agents, saboteurs, and potential kidnappers and murderers of the president.

After Lincoln's assassination on April 15, 1865, Greeley mourned the death of a great-hearted leader and vilified Stanton for judging shooter John Wilkes Booth and his accomplices at a secret military tribunal rather than an open civil trial. Stanton riposted with the threat of a lawsuit against the *Tribune* for siding with assassins. During this stressful period, fraught with national exhaustion and grief, Greeley composed a meticulous, two-volume Civil War history, *The American Conflict: A History of the Great Rebellion in the United States of America, 1860–65,* which he issued in 1864 and 1866.

Losing Touch

In a foreshadowing of Greeley's gradual decline, he sided with Radical Republicans against President Andrew Johnson and maintained that the South deserved severe punishment, yet he endorsed amnesty for rebel officials. To assist the work of nurse Clara Barton in identifying the remains of prisoners of war buried at Andersonville Prison in Georgia, he published her compilation of names, which extended more than five pages. On April 25, 1866, he honored the Ladies' Memorial Society in Columbus, Mississippi, for tending the graves of the 1,000 dead, Union and Confederate, at Friendship Cemetery following the Battle of Shiloh.

On March 30, 1867, Greeley led the media in directing snide lampoons at Secretary of State William Henry Seward for the purchase of Alaska from the Russians. Half the *Tribune*'s readers canceled their subscriptions after Greeley helped fund $100,000 in bail for defeated Confederate President Jefferson Davis. In 1872, Greeley favored investigation of civil service corruption under President Ulysses S. Grant. To prevent Grant's reelection, the editor abandoned the Radical Republicans and defeated Charles Francis Adams, the U.S. ambassador to Great Britain, for the presidential candidacy of the Liberal Republican Party.

The celebrated editor lost his following as he veered from journalism to political ambitions. In 1871, his experimental agrarian colony in Greeley, Colorado, failed. During his run for the White House, Greeley's absent-mindedness and erratic departure from previous opinions served Thomas Nast as source material for cartoons in *Harper's Weekly.* As Greeley's mind slipped further from reason, his partner, Whitelaw Reid, took control of the *New York Tribune* and brought to a halt Greeley's use of the editorial page as a personal rant.

About the time of the death of Greeley's wife, Grant trounced his vulnerable opponent at the polls. In the midst of the election, Greeley suffered a breakdown, lapsed into mania, and died on November 29, 1872, at Dr. George C.S. Choate's private sanitarium in Westchester County, New York.

In New York City, day and night, streams of mourners filed by Greeley's remains at City Hall and spread camellias over his family pew at the Universalist Church of the Divine Paternity on Fifth Avenue in Manhattan. In an era of sensationalism and inaccuracy in the media, his admirers, including Chief Justice Salmon P. Chase and trial attorney Clarence Darrow, championed Greeley's lifelong dedication to straightforward news and the uplift of the dispossessed.

See also: Chase, Salmon P.; Lincoln, Abraham; Seward, William Henry; Stanton, Edwin M.

Further Reading

Blight, David W. *Race and Reunion: The Civil War in American Memory.* Cambridge, MA: Belknap Press, 2001.

McMillen, Sally. *Seneca Falls and the Origins of the Women's Rights Movement.* New York: Oxford University Press, 2008.

Snodgrass, Mary Ellen. *The Underground Railroad: An Encyclopedia of People, Places, and Operations.* Armonk, NY: M.E. Sharpe, 2007.

Striner, Richard. *Father Abraham: Lincoln's Relentless Struggle to End Slavery.* Oxford, UK: Oxford University Press, 2006.

Williams, Robert C. *Horace Greeley: Champion of American Freedom.* New York: New York University Press, 2006.

H

Habeas Corpus, Suspension of

The bedrock of individual civil liberty dating to the Magna Carta of 1215, habeas corpus, a judicially enforceable order or petition, protects citizens from unlawful custody and arbitrary jailing. Known throughout legal history as the "great writ" and the foundation of English common law, the full Latin term *habeas corpus ad subjiciendum* translates as "let you have the body [of the detained person] for examination." It obligates law enforcers to prove their authority and to legitimate grounds for seizing and detaining a citizen for the purpose of questioning and prosecution.

Until President Abraham Lincoln issued the Emancipation Proclamation on January 1, 1863, the Fugitive Slave Law of 1850 denied the civil rights of bondsmen. Free black abolitionists Frederick Douglass, Martin Robinson Delany, Sojourner Truth, and Harriet Tubman denounced the law for violating a fundamental principle of democracy, the right to challenge unlawful imprisonment and to demand just cause for apprehension. The situation for blacks worsened in 1857. Until national abolition, the U.S. Supreme Court's decision in *Dred Scott v. Sandford* set a precedent that negated the personhood of black chattel, thus denying them the right to demand freedom from illegal confinement.

During four years of combat, Lincoln, the nation's commander in chief, combated individual threats to the citizenry and government as a means of preserving the Union. On April 27, 1861, following the outbreak of Civil War 15 days earlier, the president followed the advice of Attorney General Edward Bates and suspended the right of habeas corpus. The U.S. Constitution allowed for the suspension in Article I, Section 9, clause 2 to ensure public safety in cases of rebellion or invasion. Lincoln's act constituted the first contravention of civil rights and court orders in the nation's history.

Opinions divided on legalities. William Pitt Fessenden, financier of the Union army, defended arbitrary federal arrests of terrorists and hostile agents. Secretary of the Navy Gideon Welles disputed the power of naval officers to search and seize enemy ships as a violation of habeas corpus. Nonetheless, Welles backed the president and devoted himself to winning the war.

Sedition in the South

As secessionism swept the South and threatened the statehood of Maryland, Lincoln faced a possible encirclement of the nation's capital by the enemy. Rather than bombard Baltimore, as proposed by General Winfield Scott, the president secretly chose to round up Copperheads (Southern sympathizers) in the Midwest and along a military line from Philadelphia through Annapolis, Maryland, to Washington, D.C.

In January 1862, Jefferson Davis, president of the Confederate States of America, plotted a similar course of action by suspending habeas corpus. Despite the commitment of Southerners to the fundamental rights of whites, the rebel congress empowered Davis to impose martial law in the Confederate capital of Richmond and 10 miles (16 kilometers) beyond for no longer than six months. To secure the area from federal invasion, Davis formed a military police and counterespionage corps. In one year, 1,800 Southern men used the writ as a means of eluding the draft.

By mid-war, out of fairness to antisecessionists, Georgia governor Joseph Emerson Brown and North Carolina governor Zebulon Baird Vance defied Davis's denial of civil rights as evidence of despotism. In 1864, Davis legitimized his suspension of habeas corpus as a means of collaring draft dodgers, deserters, freebooters, and military turncoats.

After Union General Benjamin Franklin Butler placed Baltimore under martial law on May 13, 1861, federal agents arrested editor Beale H. Richardson and the staff of the Baltimore *Republican,* as well as editors E.F. Carter and W.H. Neilson of the *Daily Gazette* and the *Evening Transcript,* and suppressed further pro-South issues of the *Evening Post* and *Evening Loyalist.* Detective Allan Pinkerton, head of security, incarcerated secessionist legislators and the Baltimore mayor, city councilmen, police commissioner, and police chief at Fort McHenry, a federal prison for political dissidents and prisoners of war. Enemy blockade runners, contraband mail carriers, spies, and traitors faced prison at hard labor or the gallows. Animosities in Maryland launched a four-year grudge against the Union.

In the first-ever revolt of states against the Union, more infringements on civil rights affected American shores. The Union navy halted harbor traffic in the South and began blockading Confederate ports. The arrest of secessionist John Merryman, a lieutenant in the Maryland state militia, for burning bridges and cutting telegraph lines, precipitated Merryman's lawsuit against the federal government for unjust incarceration. In the U.S. Supreme Court case *Ex parte Merryman* (1861), Chief Justice Roger B. Taney agreed with Merryman that the president had violated the Constitution by denying a citizen the protection of habeas corpus. Taney declared the suspension of civil liberties the province of Congress alone. Because of Taney's bold confrontation of the executive branch, Radical Republican congressmen considered impeaching him.

Public opinion pressed President Lincoln to renew his pledge to respect citizen rights. On February 14, 1862, he eased off his initial militancy by conferring amnesty on political prisoners who posed no threat of terrorizing the Union or of spying on or deterring the Union military.

Second Suspension

Following the Confederate victory at the Second Battle of Bull Run, Virginia, on August 28–30, 1862, the heightened threat to Washington, D.C., and the Union forced the president to toughen his stance on civil liberties. To suppress protesters, rebels, insurgents, and prisoners of war, he issued a proclamation on September 24, 1862, silencing antiwar newspapers and suspending habeas corpus nationwide. The proclamation justified the military seizure of those abetting revolt, resisting the draft, or interfering with volunteer enlistment.

Conservative factions accused President Lincoln of wielding unconstitutional executive powers that overrode the checks and balances provided by the judicial and legislative branches. His military tribunals altered standard civil court procedure by acting quickly, relying on prison interrogation, and concealing confidential events from the public.

On March 3, 1863, under the Habeas Corpus Act, Congress legitimated Lincoln's arbitrary arrests, by which the military apprehended suspects to be judged by civil courts. Controversy arose because the law left undelineated the president's power to suspend citizen rights during war. Against the opinion of Secretary of War Edwin M. Stanton, the majority of Supreme Court justices allowed the executive branch legal leeway to conduct arbitrary arrests so long as the nation battled an internal rebellion. By the resumption of constitutional protections in 1866, the number of arbitrary wartime jailings had reached 13,535.

On April 3, 1866, the Supreme Court ruled in *Ex parte Milligan* that civil courts had jurisdiction over military tribunals. The justices ruled that the suspension of habeas corpus during an insurrection was lawful, but that the military had deprived five citizens of a hearing in the civilian courts, which were still in operation. A unanimous vote denied martial rule the right to try and execute five conspirators against the Union. The same day, Chief Justice Salmon P. Chase struck down the execution order and freed four of the traitors from prison. Historians lauded the action as a triumph for constitutional liberty over extreme executive powers by the War Department. Ironically, on May 13, 1867, a writ of habeas corpus freed Jefferson Davis from federal prison at Fort Monroe under bail of $100,000, paid by editor Horace Greeley.

Protecting Freedmen

During congressional debate on the Fourteenth Amendment to the Constitution in 1867, Congress allowed federal courts to nullify unlawful state court convictions and sentences by imposing federal writs of habeas corpus, particularly for freedmen victimized by Black Codes. To ensure enforcement, Congress passed the Reconstruction Act of July 19, 1867, which placed military leaders over five districts encompassing ten of the former Confederate states. The due process clause of the Fourteenth Amendment ensured citizen rights to a fair hearing. A state prisoner could not petition a federal judge for habeas corpus until first exhausting all remedies available under state law. Similarly, a soldier or sailor could not demand the writ in federal court until exhausting the remedies provided for in the military court system.

President Ulysses S. Grant bolstered the justice system with the Civil Rights Act of April 20, 1871, written by Republican Congressman Benjamin Franklin Butler of Massachusetts. The law granted the commander in chief unlimited power over racist conspirators. The president exercised executive authority in October in South Carolina by outlawing the Ku Klux Klan and suspending habeas corpus. Grant's defiance of nightriders won citizen approval and contributed to his reelection.

On May 22, Grant restored full citizenship to all but 500 Confederates still aggrieved at the failure of "the cause." A cleanup of Klan, Red Shirts, and White League raiders began in October 1871 with federal surveillance of white paramilitary activities in the Carolinas, Louisiana, and Mississippi. The newly created Department of Justice issued 4,000 indictments and convicted 1,150 Klansmen of terrorism.

See also: Baltimore, Maryland; Copperheads; *Ex Parte Milligan* (1866); Law and Courts; Lincoln, Abraham.

Further Reading

Kaczorowski, Robert J. *The Politics of Judicial Interpretation: The Federal Courts, Department of Justice, and Civil Rights, 1866–1876.* New York: Fordham University Press, 2005.

McPherson, James M. *Battle Cry of Freedom: The Civil War Era.* New York: Oxford University Press, 1988.

Nelson, William E. *The Fourteenth Amendment: From Political Principle to Judicial Doctrine.* Cambridge, MA: Harvard University Press, 1988.

Striner, Richard. *Father Abraham: Lincoln's Relentless Struggle to End Slavery.* Oxford, UK: Oxford University Press, 2006.

Weigley, Russell F. *A Great Civil War: A Military and Political History, 1861–1865.* Bloomington: Indiana University Press, 2000.

Hale, Sarah Josepha (1788–1879)

A pioneering magazine editor and philosopher, Sarah Josepha Buell Hale championed the establishment of Thanksgiving as a national holiday and respect for women as the shapers of American moral standards. A prominent intellectual, she was born on October 24, 1788, in Newport, New Hampshire, to enlightened parents who encouraged education for girls.

After the death of her husband, attorney David Hale, in 1812, she supported their five children on proceeds from her writings on patriotism, humanitarianism, the arts, and pacifism. She raised cash to build the Bunker Hill Monument in Boston and to purchase and refurbish Mount Vernon, the Virginia home of George and Martha Washington. Hale's first novel, *Northwood, a Tale of New England* (1827), initiated the slave genre in U.S. fiction. In Boston, she edited *Ladies' Magazine,* her vehicle for introducing the concept of a national day of thanks.

No friend to woman suffrage, Hale preferred unobtrusive female advocacy for the Christian home. She stressed economic independence and nudged women into the task of keeping household budgets and records as a hedge against penury from widowhood and single parenthood. She directed thinking away from gendered politics, war, and religious sectarianism toward acceptance of women's behind-the-scenes posts as shapers of social standards. At her suggestion, the Massachusetts legislature considered, but rejected, rent control on small apartments as a boon to women living alone.

In Philadelphia in 1837, she began a 40-year job editing *Godey's Lady's Book,* a touchstone of women's tastes and opinions in both the North and the South. In addition to offering house plans, sheet music, and dress patterns, she wrote knowledgeably about female roles in business, design, and industry and their influence on classrooms and children's physical education, morals, and spirituality. She encouraged submissions by women under their own names rather than male or gender-neutral pseudonyms, thus fostering the female literary renaissance preceding the Civil War. By 1860, *Godey's* circulated to 150,000 homes, in part because Hale convinced males to buy subscriptions for their daughters' edification.

Hale's influence spread her vision of responsible womanhood into the professional realm. She denounced the bundling of girls in multiple petticoats to protect their virtue. For nonwhite females, she championed resettlement of former slaves in Liberia and awareness of women's issues in China, Japan, and the Ottoman Empire. For the sake of benevolence, she lauded female journalists, missionaries, and medical workers. Hale promoted the writings of Harriet Beecher Stowe and her sister, Catharine Esther Beecher, a teacher and reformer who advanced homemaking from household drudgery to a domestic science that educated innkeepers, chefs, nutritionists, sanitarians, and managers of retirement homes, orphanages, kindergartens, hospitals, and tourist cottages.

Hale fostered Philadelphia's first female medical college, and, on January 18, 1861, she co-founded Vassar College in Poughkeepsie, New York, a flagship of women's colleges taught by a female faculty. She opposed obligatory uniforms for students and sold dubious parents on the idea that their daughters should receive the same training that their brothers did at Harvard and Yale.

Hale recognized women's ability to organize projects and attain goals. She supported the antislavery craft fair, a source of fund-raising from the sale of baked goods, basketry, calligraphy, infant clothes, jams and jellies, jewelry, pressed flowers, and quilts and other needlework. She recognized in the New England concept of Thanksgiving a fount of ideals beneficial to the nation as a whole, particularly the strengthening of the family.

In vain, she petitioned four presidents—Zachary Taylor, Millard Fillmore, Franklin Pierce, and James Buchanan—to support a national day of thanks. In the middle of the Civil War in 1863, President Abraham Lincoln agreed with Hale that the United States needed an annual holiday of thanksgiving as a source of union. In 1872, she published a five-stanza thanksgiving hymn honoring pilgrims and liberty and thanking the "Great All-Giver" that North and South were again members of one "home."

Hale compiled *Woman's Record, or Sketches of Distinguished Women, from the Creation to A.D. 1868* (1853, 1855, 1872), a panoramic history of women's role in civilization, and a guidebook to courtesy and right thinking, *Manners; or, Happy Homes and Good Society All the Year Round* (1868). In the latter, she declared, "The real progress of humanity must have its root in moral goodness." Still productive at the age of 90, she died on April 30, 1879.

See also: Lincoln, Abraham; Macy's; Thanksgiving.

Further Reading

Collins, Gail. *America's Women: Four Hundred Years of Dolls, Drudges, Helpmates, and Heroines.* New York: William Morrow, 2003.

Kaplan, Amy. "Manifest Domesticity." *American Literature* 70:3 (September 1998): 581–606.

Levander, Caroline Field. *Voices of the Nation: Women and Public Speech in Nineteenth-Century American Literature and Culture.* Cambridge, UK: Cambridge University Press, 1998.

Sachsman, David B., S. Kittrell Rushing, and Roy Morris, Jr., eds. *Seeking a Voice: Images of Race and Gender in the 19th Century Press.* West Lafayette, IN: Purdue University Press, 2009.

Snodgrass, Mary Ellen. *Encyclopedia of Feminist Literature.* New York: Facts on File, 2006.

Hamlin, Hannibal (1809–1891)

The nation's fifteenth vice president (1861–1865), serving under President Abraham Lincoln, Hannibal Hamlin held a prestigious political record as an abolitionist and champion of civil rights. Born on August 27, 1809, to Anna Nancy Livermore Hamlin and physician Cyrus Hamlin, he was a native of Paris, Maine. On both sides of his lineage, he was a scion of pilgrims of the Massachusetts Bay Colony and of distinguished professionals. After study at Hebron Academy in Maine, he ran the family farm following his father's death.

Hamlin taught at Paris Hill School and worked in surveying on the Dead River and in journalism and printing for the *Jeffersonian,* a Whig political paper. He set his course on reading law with Samuel Clement Fessenden and serving Hampden, Maine, as city attorney. During the second year of his practice with Fessenden and Harvard-educated lawyer Thomas Amory Deblois, Hamlin campaigned for the statehouse, where he crusaded against the death penalty.

Hamlin's ambitions turned from his home state to Washington, D.C. After a failed campaign for the U.S. House of Representatives in 1840, he won terms in the House (1843–1847) and Senate (1848–1857; 1857–1861; 1869–1881). In his first terms as a legislator, he influenced the House Rules Committee and angered President James K. Polk by taking an independent stand on slavery, at odds with Democrat legislator Jefferson Davis of Mississippi. Hamlin earned respect for his quiet efficiency, for completing difficult political maneuvers, and for voting on principle rather than partisan loyalty. He respected the manual laborer and favored suffrage for residents of the District of Columbia. An opponent of human bondage, he challenged Kentucky Senator Henry Clay on the spread of slavery to the West.

After the Democratic Party endorsed the Kansas-Nebraska Act, Hamlin quit the party ranks in June 1856 and became a member of the newly established Republican Party. Later that year, Republicans in Maine nominated him for the governorship, and he won the election handily that fall. In the meantime, earlier in 1856, his wife, Sarah Jane Emery Hamlin, had died of consumption. Five months later, he wed her sister, Ellen Vesta Emery.

In late February 1857, six weeks after becoming governor of Maine, Hannibal resigned from office and returned to the U.S. Senate. A Radical Republican, he was a strong supporter of President Lincoln. As the presidential ticket of 1860 took shape, Hamlin correctly predicted civil war and was startled to find himself the Republican candidate for vice president. Known for probity, he countered a bizarre accusation from South Carolina's *Charleston Mercury* that he bore black ancestry.

In 1861, Hamlin served the Lincoln White House as a distant and often absent vice president who missed the power and prestige of being a senior senator. Although the position limited his direct influence on governmental affairs, he consulted with President Lincoln on cabinet appointments; he favored naming William Henry Seward as secretary of state and Gideon Welles as secretary of the navy. After the Confederacy fired on Fort Sumter on April 12, 1861, Hamlin mustered a Maine regiment for the

Union army. He banned liquor from the Senate chamber and committee rooms, endorsed the enlistment of slaves in summer 1861, and, in 1862, advocated immediate emancipation of slaves.

Quiet mutterings about nominating Hamlin to replace Lincoln on the Republican ticket in 1864 caused the vice president to state his loyalty to the nation's troubled leader. Despite Hamlin's skill at platform oratory and his unity with the president, in June of that year, the National Union Party humiliated him by dropping him from the nomination in favor of a "War Democrat" from Tennessee, Andrew Johnson, who was less eager to punish Southern secessionists than Hamlin.

Hamlin continued taking various roles in government, earning a reputation as a do-nothing because of his discreet, courteous style. After service as a corporal in the Coast Guard in Maine, he spent a year collecting port duties in Boston. With other civil appointees, in 1869, he resigned in protest of President Andrew Johnson's onerous Reconstruction policies and abasing of freedmen. Hamlin gladly returned to the Senate in 1869 and chaired committees on manufacturing, mining, postal service, foreign relations, and the governance of Washington, D.C.

Weakened by heart disease, he ended his legislative career in 1881, after which President James A. Garfield posted him as U.S. ambassador to Spain. He retired the following year to his mansion in Bangor, but continued to volunteer as a regent of the Smithsonian Institution. While playing cards at the Tarratine Club in Bangor on July 4, 1891, Hamlin collapsed and died of heart failure.

Further Reading

Goodwin, Doris Kearns. *Team of Rivals: The Political Genius of Abraham Lincoln.* New York: Simon & Schuster, 2005.

Rable, George C. *But There Was No Peace: The Role of Violence in the Politics of Reconstruction.* Athens: University of Georgia Press, 2007.

Smith, Adam I.P. *No Party Now: Politics in the Civil War North.* Oxford, UK: Oxford University Press, 2006.

Stephenson, Nathaniel W. *Abraham Lincoln and the Union.* New York: BiblioBazaar, 2008.

Hardin, John Wesley (1853–1895)

Career gunman and gambler John Wesley "Wes" Hardin set a record for vicious shootings, many of them lawmen and members of posses. A native of Bonham, Texas, he was born on May 26, 1853, to a refined mother, Mary Elizabeth Dixon Hardin, and a Methodist circuit rider, the Reverend James Gibson Hardin.

While attending his father's parochial school, Hardin knifed a fellow student in the chest and throat for taunting him. At age 15, he shot a freedman named Mage for seeking vengeance after losing to Hardin in a wrestling match. Pursued by three Union soldiers, Hardin killed all three with a shotgun and six-shooter, suffering only a minor wound in his arm. Within two months, the boy raised his number of kills to six by shooting a fellow card player and a mugger.

For the next year, Hardin boarded with relatives and herded cattle to Kansas. Upon his arrest at age 17 for the murder of Marshal Laban John Hoffman in Waco, Texas, on January 6, 1871, he planned a break from custody. As three lawmen transported him to trial, Hardin pulled a pistol from his overcoat and shot Texas State policeman Jim Smalley. In an effort to curb state crime, Governor Edmund J. Davis offered a $1,100 reward for Hardin's capture. Within days, the teenager engaged in a shootout with a rival trail boss as the two jockeyed for precedence up the Chisholm Trail toward Abilene, Kansas. Of the seven Mexican drovers killed, Hard in shot six.

In Abilene, Hardin made friends with Marshal James Butler "Wild Bill" Hickok but had to flee a room at the American House Hotel after shooting through the wall in an attempt to stop roomer Charles Couger from snoring. Hardin fled over the roof and rode off on a stolen horse.

Pursued by two Texas State policemen in Gonzales County, Texas, on October 6, 1871, Hardin shot officer Green Paramore and wounded John Lackey. In Trinity City, Texas, on August 7, 1872, Hardin incurred a shotgun injury to the kidney by a farmer, Philip A. Sublett. From prison, Hardin tried to square himself with the law, but faced too many murder charges to end his criminal career. On November 19, 1872, he sawed his way out of the Cherokee County jail and fled with a price on his head.

Hardin's felonies grew more brazen on May 17, 1873, when he shot Sheriff John Marshall "Jack" Helm in Albuquerque, Texas, for threatening Hardin with a knife. Hardin survived a second shotgun blast in August.

The following year on May 26, Hardin ended his twenty-first birthday celebration by joining accomplice James Taylor, an anti-Reconstructionist, on a main street of Comanche, Texas, in shooting Deputy Sheriff Charles M. Webb in the abdomen, hand, and head. After the Hardin family's placement in protective custody, a mob lynched his brother, 24-year-old Joseph Gibson "Joe" Hardin, and two cousins, Bud and Tom Dixon, killing them by slow asphyxiation.

In August, Hardin married Jane Bowen—who became the mother of their two daughters, Mary Elizabeth "Mollie" Hardin and Jane "Jennie" Hardin, and one son, John Wesley Hardin, Jr.—and avoided arrest by traveling through New Orleans to elude Pinkerton agents. The Hardin family resettled first in Jacksonville, Florida, then in Eufaula, Alabama, under the alias J.H. Swain.

In Pensacola, Florida, on July 23, 1877, Texas Ranger John Barclay Armstrong seized Hardin from a train, killed Hardin's companion, Jim Man, and bound Hardin to a seat in the smoking car. A chronicle of the Texas Court of Appeals described Hardin as "achieving a remarkable and wide-spread reputation for sanguinary deeds." Immured in ball and chain at Huntsville Prison on October 5, 1878, on a 25-year sentence for killing Deputy Webb, Hardin struggled for five years with plans to make keys to the cells and tunnel beyond the wall. Jailers beat him 39 strokes with a lash and locked him in a dark cell for three days without food or water. Regular lashings and limited rations ensued for real and imagined infractions of prison rules.

Hardin attempted to abandon crime, working in the prison's boot, quilt, and wood shops, settling into law and religious studies, and managing the Sunday school. A wound inflicted by Sublett became abscessed and required two years' recuperation before he could walk again. During this period, Hardin's wife died at age 38.

Upon his pardon by Governor James Stephen "Jim" Hogg on February 17, 1894, after 16 years in prison, Hardin lived with his children in Gonzales. He obtained a law license and moved to El Paso to open a law office. He courted a widow, Beulah M'Rose, whom Constable John Selman, Sr., arrested for carrying a concealed pistol.

On August 19, 1895, Selman shot Hardin in the back of the head during a dice game at the Acme Saloon in San Antonio. At age 42, the gunman died instantly. Hardin's legend, including anywhere from 30 to 44 kills, grew with the publication of dime novels and his autobiography, *The Life of John Wesley Hardin* (1896).

Further Reading

Lamar, Howard R., ed. *The New Encyclopedia of the American West.* New Haven, CT: Yale University Press, 1998.

Metz, Leon Claire. *John Wesley Hardin: Dark Angel of Texas.* Norman: University of Oklahoma Press, 1998.

Smallwood, James M. *The Feud That Wasn't: The Taylor Ring, Bill Sutton, John Wesley Hardin, and Violence in Texas.* College Station: Texas A&M University Press, 2008.

Utley, Robert M. *Lone Star Justice: The First Century of the Texas Rangers.* Oxford, UK: Oxford University Press, 2002.

Harper, Frances Ellen Watkins (1825–1911)

Progressive abolitionist and suffragist Frances Ellen Watkins Harper became America's first successful black female journalist and the nation's most popular black poet of her day. Born to free blacks in Baltimore on September 24, 1825, she passed to her uncle and aunt, educator and Underground Railroad agent William Watkins and his wife Henrietta at 113 South Eutaw Street, after Harper's parents' deaths in 1828. She studied rhetoric, elocution, composition, and the Bible at Watkins's school, the Academy for Negro Youth, founded in 1847 by the African Methodist Episcopal Church.

She worked as a domestic and nanny for a Quaker family who operated the Armstrong & Berry bookshop on Baltimore Street, and as a teacher of needlework at Union Seminary in Wilberforce, Ohio, where she was the first female faculty member. While teaching 53 children in Little York, Pennsylvania, in 1853, she found the schedule of daily lessons in arithmetic, geography, grammar, reading, spelling, and writing too debilitating to continue.

She became politicized by protesters of the sexual subjugation of women and, in 1853, by the sale into bondage of free black Northern visitors to Maryland. After joining William Still in the Underground Railroad movement in Philadelphia, she maintained a safehouse at 27 Bainbridge Street, submitted abolitionist verse to William Lloyd Garrison's weekly, *The Liberator,* and lectured on abolitionism for the Maine Anti-Slavery Society.

At age 29, while writing for Mary Ann Shadd Cary's Toronto newspaper the *Provincial Freeman,* she anthologized her *Poems on Miscellaneous Subjects* (1854), a brisk seller that raised funds at abolitionist fairs. One poem in the collection, "The Slave Mother," dramatizes the merchandising of a woman at a slave market, where the mother is sold away from her son. In the *Anti-Slavery Bugle,* she issued the poem "Bury Me in a Free Land" (1858), a soulful motto of her platform oratory for the American Anti-Slavery Society.

Despite chronic ill health, she promoted the rights of black bondswomen. At venues in New England, the Midwest, and Canada, she crusaded for nonviolence, education for freedmen, and female equality. With "The Two Offers," issued in the 1859 issue of *Anglo-African Magazine,* she became the first published black American short fiction writer. In a letter to the *Weekly Anglo-African* on June 23, 1860, she appealed to Philadelphians to rescue runaways. In the July 17, 1860, issue of the *National*

Poet and novelist Frances Harper advocated for abolition, the rights of freed slaves and women, and temperance. On the lecture circuit, she roused audiences with impassioned readings of her verse. *(The Granger Collection, New York)*

Anti-Slavery Standard, she published a hopeful paean to abolitionism, "Thank God That Thou Hast Spoken."

Her three-year marriage to Fenton Harper, a widower with three children, ended with his death in May 1864. After the confiscation of her household goods to pay debts, Harper sold their farm in Grove City, southwest of Columbus, Ohio, and moved the children back East. There she joined other abolitionist females in comforting Mary Ann Day Brown, the widow of anarchist John Brown.

Harper feared that activists lost their interest in former slaves after the Emancipation Proclamation. She combined her concerns for freedmen and her activism on behalf of black women. On May 10, 1866, she shared a platform with Susan B. Anthony and Elizabeth Cady Stanton at the Eleventh National Woman's Rights Convention. Harper delivered a panegyric, "We Are All Bound Up Together," in which she declared, "Justice is not fulfilled so long as woman is unequal before the law." As examples of insults to black females, she cited an attempt by a train conductor in Washington, D.C., to make her move to the smoking car and Philadelphia streetcar rules that forced black women to ride on the driver's platform.

Harper and her two-year-old, Mary E. Harper, moved to Philadelphia and adopted Unitarianism. In 1867, Harper supported her household by traveling the lecture circuit to Demopolis, Eufaula, Mobile, and Montgomery, Alabama; Darlington and Sumter, South Carolina; and Athens, Columbiana, and Greenville, Georgia, to deliver speeches on education, challenges to black voters, and white male aggression against black women. She shamed the federal government for refusing to intercede. During the tour, she faced challengers who proclaimed her a white male.

For the *Christian Recorder,* the journal of the African Methodist Episcopal Church, Harper serialized three novels, *Minnie's Sacrifice* (1869), *Sowing and Reaping* (1876–1877), and *Trial and Triumph* (1888–1889), long-neglected works on marriage and temperance that feminists reissued in the 1990s. She wrote essays exposing lynching, arranged marriage, abusive husbands and fathers, alcoholism, and racism. In 1869, at a meeting of the American Equal Rights Association, she stated that racial bias was much more demoralizing than sexism. One of her longest works, *Moses, a Story of the Nile* (1869), honors the liberator of the Hebrew people for courage and leadership. Admirers called Harper the "Bronze Muse" and the "mother of black journalism."

Into advanced age and feebleness, Harper's dedication to equality and literacy remained unwavering. On the theme of Reconstruction, she dramatized a female survivor in *Sketches of Southern Life* (1872) and pictured mixed-race people in a novel, *Iola Leroy; or, Shadows Uplifted* (1892), a postbellum vision of an assertive female, a free-born mulatta. The novel subverts plantation stereotypes by presenting the tragedy of fractured slave families.

At the 1875 convention of the American Woman Suffrage Association, Harper gave priority to black female suffrage over white. To the 1893 World's Congress of Representative Women, she lauded the New Woman, a female who channeled her talents and intelligence toward achieving social progress. Two years later, in *The Martyr of Alabama and Other Poems* (1895), she decried the victimization of blacks by vicious whites.

At her death on February 20, 1911, she received encomiums from critic W.E.B. Du Bois and author Henry James.

See also: Underground Railroad.

Further Reading

Crow, Charles L., ed. *A Companion to the Regional Literatures of America.* Malden, MA: Blackwell, 2003.

Dunbar, Erica Armstrong. *A Fragile Freedom: African American Women and Emancipation in the Antebellum City.* New Haven, CT: Yale University Press, 2008.

Foster, Frances Smith, ed. *A Brighter Coming Day: A Frances Watkins Harper Reader.* New York: Feminist Press, 1990.

Harper, Frances Ellen Watkins. "We Are All Bound Up Together." In *Ripples of Hope: Great American Civil Rights Speeches,* ed. Josh Gottheimer. New York: Basic Civitas Books, 2004.

Snodgrass, Mary Ellen. *Encyclopedia of Feminist Literature.* New York: Facts on File, 2006.

———. *The Underground Railroad: An Encyclopedia of People, Places, and Operations.* Armonk, NY: M.E. Sharpe, 2007.

Harper's Weekly

A national illustrated journal published in New York City from 1857 to 1916, *Harper's Weekly* followed the tenets of its subtitle, "A Journal of Civilization," to become a phenomenon of American news publication. Originally titled *Harper's Monthly,* the magazine was the creation of four brothers, Fletcher, James, John, and Wesley Harper. It evolved into *Harper's Weekly,* a 16-page tabloid that Fletcher Harper inaugurated on January 3, 1857, to suit middle-class family interests. The newspaper quickly displaced the more conservative women's magazine *Godey's Lady's Book,* edited by Sarah Josepha Hale, who focused on domesticity over political consciousness for women.

The *Harper's* staff specialized in national and global news, editorials, and essays. The magazine featured illustrations by Winslow Homer and Frederic Remington, Mathew Brady's photos of the Battle of Antietam and the White House welcome of Oglala Lakota Sioux Chief Red Cloud, John Dare "Jack" Howland's coverage of the Medicine Lodge Council of 1867, a droll caricature of the mythic Texas Ranger, and political cartoons by William Allen Rogers and Thomas Nast. Serialized works by English authors ranged from Wilkie Collins's Gothic novel *The Moonstone* (1868) and George Eliot's *The Mill on the Floss* (1860) to Charles Dickens's coming-of-age classic *Great Expectations* (1860) and Thomas Hardy's *Far from the Madding Crowd* (1874). American works included short fiction by Frances Hodgson Burnett, George Washington Cable, William Dean Howells, and Henry James and William H. Prescott's history *Conquest of Mexico* (1843). Among features from the plantation South, David Hunter Strother of Martinsburg, West Virginia, working under the pseudonym "Porte Crayon," provided a pen-and-ink sketch of runaway slaves called maroons. Strother pictured their lives on the run in the Dismal Swamp and taking temporary shelter in a ramada cobbled together out of scrap lumber, cypress knees, and pine boughs. Circulation began with 7,500 copies the first day and grew to 50,000 by December 1850; within a decade, *Harper's* sold 200,000 copies.

The Civil War turned *Harper's Weekly* into a definitive source of information. At the beginning of the conflict in 1861, the editors dispatched reporters and artists to combat sites and supported patriotism, abolitionism, President Abraham Lincoln, and the Union. Fletcher Harper extended a free subscription to any Union officer who sent in an address and promised in return to publish eyewitness accounts of the war. On September 6, 1862, *Harper's* saluted volunteer nurses with a pen-and-ink collage of sedate women in neat flowing skirts, mending men's socks and shirts, laundering nightshirts, taking dictation from men sending messages home, and attending the suffering. When Confederate mails stopped receiving the *Atlantic Monthly, Frank Leslie's Illustrated,* and *Harper's Weekly,* and when the port blockade halted delivery from England of *Blackwood's* and *Cornhill,* the South launched its own publications in Richmond, beginning with the *Magnolia Weekly* and the *Southern Illustrated News.*

Key to *Harper's* reader appeal was quality illustration of news, such as famed posse member Steve Venard shooting a stage robber on May 15, 1866, at the South Yuba River, California, and the laying of an undersea cable by the International Ocean Telegraph Company on May 29, 1867, from Key West, Florida, to Havana, Cuba. Art reproductions required teams to carve on wood the photos of war leaders, battle plans, and detailed pen-and-ink sketches of civilian privations for stamping the outlines onto newsprint. Weekly coverage and maps of major events—the Battle of Bull Run in July 1861, Union captives at Libby Prison in Richmond in 1862, the New York City draft riots and the Gettysburg Address in 1863, New York women's antislavery fairs in 1864, and the fall of Charleston, South Carolina, in 1865—increased circulation to 300,000 and boosted public respect for the paper's integrity and fair coverage.

In September 1863, *Harper's* featured a panorama of General Henry Hastings Sibley's advance with the Seventh Minnesota Volunteers against the Sioux in Dakota Territory; in December, Republican editor George William Curtis advocated black civil rights and Radical Reconstruction. Artist Alfred Rudolph Waud moved on assignment with the Army of the Potomac and illustrated the dangers to slaves in cotton and rice fields; his brother, William Waud, gave inside details of the inauguration of Confederate President Jefferson Davis, General William Tecumseh Sherman's scorched-earth policy through Georgia, and Lincoln's funeral cortege from Washington, D.C., to Springfield, Illinois. Artist Theodore Russell Davis earned a following for his sketches of combat in Georgia; for coverage of stagecoach travel and boomtowns in Colorado in 1865; for Lieutenant Colonel George Armstrong Custer's Plains command in 1867, collaboration with scout William Averill "Medicine Bill" Comstock with other guides, and attack on a Cheyenne village the next year; and for a view of the U.S. Senate during the 1868 impeachment trial of President Andrew Johnson. Battlefield coverage placed in the American language unforgettable place-names—Gettysburg, Shiloh, Vicksburg, Antietam, Chickamauga.

At war's end, the *North American Review* lauded *Harper's Weekly* for its variety, consistency, and excellence in journalism and illustration. The staff retained its reputation for revealing the workings of politics, such as George William Curtis's editorial of February 13, 1869, supporting passage of the Fifteenth Amendment and a cartoon depicting Secretary of War Edwin M. Stanton manipulating the Tenure of Office Bill to prevent President Andrew Johnson from replacing him. By 1870, the paper cost $4 for 52 issues. Ad fees ranged from $1.50 per line in one of the 22 inside pages to $2 per line for a spot on the back cover.

In its fourteenth year of publication, circulation reached a height during coverage of the first black voters at the polls and of exposés of bribery and corruption in New York City by William Magear "Boss" Tweed's ring. Subsequent issues—covering the election of Ulysses S. Grant, immigration, Chinese and Indian rights, woman suffrage, vaccinations for children, conservation, civil service reform, and homesteading over the Oregon Trail—required top-notch research and collaborative writing. *Harper's Weekly* was absorbed by *The Independent* in 1916.

See also: Brady, Mathew; Hale, Sarah Josepha; Ku Klux Klan; Nast, Thomas; Red Cloud; Weapons.

Further Reading

Adler, John, with Draper Hill. *Doomed by Cartoon: How Cartoonist Thomas Nast and* The New-York Times *Brought Down Boss Tweed and His Ring of Thieves.* Garden City, NY: Morgan James, 2008.

Brown, Joshua. *Beyond the Lines: Pictorial Reporting, Everyday Life and the Crisis of Gilded Age America.* Berkeley: University of California Press, 2002.

Sachsman, David B., S. Kittrell Rushing, and Roy Morris, Jr., eds. *Seeking a Voice: Images of Race and Gender in the 19th Century Press.* West Lafayette, IN: Purdue University Press, 2009.

Shirley, David. *Thomas Nast: Cartoonist and Illustrator.* New York: Franklin Watts, 1998.

Trager, James. *The New York Chronology: The Ultimate Compendium of Events, People and Anecdotes from the Dutch to the Present.* New York: HarperResource, 2003.

Harte, Bret (1836–1902)

Journalist and author Francis Brett Harte diversified American literature by avoiding European models to champion the local color of the frontier West. Born in Albany, New York, on August 25, 1836, and reared in Brooklyn, he was fatherless from age eight and largely unschooled except by his private readings. Ten years later, he set out for the Pacific Coast to mine, guard Wells Fargo deliveries, and write for the *Northern Californian,* a Uniontown weekly. His exposé of the massacre of 100 Miyot Indians at Humboldt Bay on February 26, 1860, by the Humboldt militia enraged a lynch mob, who plundered the newspaper office. Harte escaped upriver by steamer.

At 24, Harte settled in San Francisco, married Anna Griswold, and issued a gossip column, novels, poems, and 74 prose works in a local journal, the *Golden Era.* He began with "My Metamorphosis" (1860), a satiric tale of a European tourist swimming nude who poses as a statue to conceal his embarrassment. Harte's humorous works ranged to sly racial commentary in "Plain Language from Truthful James" (1860), a 60-line ballad about Ah Sin, an ostensibly naive Chinese card player who outwits two white cardsharps at euchre.

Maturation

Harte matured as a writer under the guidance of a San Francisco intellectual, Jessie Benton Frémont, who introduced him to her abolitionist salon. Among the literati, Harte met novelist Herman Melville and landscape designer Frederick Law Olmsted. For extra cash, Harte worked at surveying and as a clerk and secretary to the superintendent at the U.S. Mint on Commercial Street.

In 1860, he turned accounts from the goldfields into fiction and dialect humor, including the stories "The Man of No Account," "M'liss," "The Work on Red Mountain," and "A Night at Wingdam." In a heraldic ode, "The Pony Express," published in the *Golden Era* on July 1, 1860, he honored "the bold Knife of the Pony Express" and wished "God Speed the Express," which journeyed six days a week both ways from St. Joseph, Missouri, to San Francisco.

Perhaps because of the demands of a wife and son, Griswold Harte, the author picked up his pace in 1864 with the "Bohemian Papers," a series covering such local topics as encroaching urbanism in "Mission Dolores" and imported coolie labor in "John Chinaman." In May, he partnered with humorist Mark Twain, a reporter for the *Morning Call* who shared Harte's disdain for European styles and topics, and engaged in a congenial writers' rivalry. At age 30, Harte co-founded the *Californian,* a literary weekly that published his reviews, topical articles, serialized novels, and a collection of Civil War verses, as well as Twain's "The Celebrated Jumping Frog of Calaveras County" (1865).

Harte mourned the loss of Abraham Lincoln as an icon of the West and "the representative American." He wrote of the slain president, "His eloquence and humor partook of the local and material influences, mixed with that familiar knowledge of men and character which the easy intercourse of the pioneer had fostered." In "A Second Review of the Grand Army," published May 24, 1865, Harte composed a moving salute to a two-day parade down Pennsylvania Avenue past the Capitol, featuring the assembled 150,000 men of the Army of Georgia, Army of the Potomac, and Army of the Tennessee. The reverie pictured phantoms dead of bullet wounds, fever, and starvation in prison and concluded with a blue cap waved at the poet.

In 1867, Harte assisted Twain in refining the final copy of the latter's novel *The Innocents Abroad* (1869). Twain praised his friend for quality editing and for a steady friendship that survived their fractious collaboration. With *Muck-a-Muck* (1867), Harte parodied James Fenimore Cooper; with *The Haunted Man* (1867), he turned keen burlesque against Charles Dickens's *A Christmas Carol.*

Despite its triumphs, the era strapped Harte financially, requiring him to review plays for the *Morning Call* and freelance Western commentary for the *Christian Register,* a Unitarian weekly issued from Boston, and for the Springfield, Massachusetts, *Republican.* To the latter, he contributed a poem ridiculing an anthropological hoax in "To the Pliocene Skull" (1866), a satiric "geological address" mocking scientific analysis of a reputed prehistoric fossil, the "Calaveras Skull," that miners located on February 25, 1866. He derided Hispanic terms in a letter chortling, "we have *ranchos* instead of farms and *vaqueros* for milk-maids."

Critics charged Harte with developing a snide insider's voice for his Eastern readers that condescended to the antics and pretensions of less genteel residents of the West Coast. The publication of *The Lost Galleon and Other Tales* (1867), an anthology of ballads and comic rhymes, earned Hart a comeuppance from the San Francisco *Dramatic Chronicle,* which accused him of stealing his motif, style, and tone from Robert Browning, Oliver Wendell Holmes, and John Greenleaf Whittier.

Mid-Career and Late Works

Work from Harte's mid-career far surpassed his early and late writings in quality and originality. In 1868, he succeeded at editing the *Overland Monthly,* one of the West's prize contributions to American literature, which promoted the first fiction of Jack London, the satire of Ambrose Bierce, and the egalitarian verse of Walt Whitman.

Harte published two of his classic stories, "The Outcasts of Poker Flat" (1869), a sentimental gesture to California's multicultural mix, and "The Luck of Roaring Camp" (1868), a parody of the welcome from magi and shepherds to the Christ Child. "The Luck" bears a fleeting implication of farewell to the third of the author's five children, a son who died unnamed a week after birth in 1867. Despite the outrage of religious reviewers who considered it sacrilege, "The Luck" earned a steady editorial accolade from the East.

Within the first six months of publication for the *Overland Monthly,* Harte's skillful writing boosted circulation to 3,000 and extended its popularity to Nevada, Oregon, and the Atlantic seaboard. Reprints of his fiction appeared in the *Albany Evening Journal, Godey's Lady's Book,* the *Hartford Courant,* the *Newport Mercury,* the *New York Evening Post,* the *Providence Journal,* and the *Springfield Republican* and in England in *Fun* and the *Piccadilly Annual.*

To the chagrin of Anton Roman, publisher of the *Overland Monthly,* Harte insisted on truth in print. He refused to gloss over the San Francisco earthquake of October 21, 1868, which Roman suppressed lest the news stymie investment. Harte's detractors considered him frivolous and aloof from the business world, but he refused to retreat from presenting the real Pacific Coast experience to the outside world. With "Don Diego of the South" (1869), written in the style of Robert Browning's dramatic monologues mixed with the lilt of dance hall ditties, Harte mocked the womanizing of Hispanic grandees. He collected these early works into his first noteworthy anthology, *The Luck of Roaring Camp and Other Sketches* (1870).

In 1871, Harte returned East to write for the *Atlantic Monthly* in Boston, through which he befriended poets Henry Wadsworth Longfellow and James Russell Lowell. The publisher offered him $10,000 for 12 stories per year, the highest retainer for any American author; nevertheless, Harte's work declined in quality. His collaboration with Twain produced a racist play, *Ah Sin, the Heathen Chinee* (1876). The suspense tale "At the Mission of San Carmel" (1877) recycled biracial romance from his frontier writings. A meditation on nature, "The Old Camp-Fire" (1893), expressed his regard for camaraderie among the redwoods and his dread that the telegraph and railroad endangered Western beauty.

At the end of Harte's career, he took a mistress and abandoned his family, accepted consulships in Germany and Scotland, and retired to London to write for hack publishers. At Camberley, England, he died of throat cancer on May 5, 1902. Subsequent surveys of his work credit him with creating Western caricatures—the foul-mouthed stage driver, coarse miner, chivalrous rascal, noble Indian, pathetic tramp, humble Chinaman, and the "soiled dove" with the heart of gold.

See also: Olmsted, Frederick Law, Sr.; Post Office and Postal Service; Twain, Mark; Whitman, Walt.

Further Reading

Hicks, Jack, James D. Houston, Maxine Hong Kingston, and Al Young, eds. *The Literature of California: Native Beginnings to 1945.* Berkeley: University of California Press, 2000.

Lamar, Howard R., ed. *The New Encyclopedia of the American West.* New Haven, CT: Yale University Press, 1998.

Rubery, Matthew. *The Novelty of Newspapers: Victorian Fiction After the Invention of the News.* New York: Oxford University Press, 2009.

Scharnhorst, Gary. *Bret Harte: Opening the American Literary West.* Norman: University of Oklahoma Press, 2000.

Scofield, Martin. *The Cambridge Introduction to the American Short Story.* Cambridge, UK: Cambridge University Press, 2006.

Hawaiian Islands

World greed threatened the independence of the Hawaiian Islands during the reign of the charismatic King Alexander Liholiho Iolani Kamehameha IV (1855–1863) and his British Hawaiian consort, Queen Emma Naea Rooke. To avoid war with the U.S. Navy, the king chose to remain neutral during the American Civil War, a conflict that raised the demand for sugar on the mainland as well as the intent of missionaries to civilize Hawaii from its heathen ways.

Because of the rise in antiblack and anti-Indian attitudes among whites and because of episodes of bigotry in his dealings with foreigners, Kamehameha IV retreated from close association with the United States. To escape American Protestant meddling in plantation capitalism, public school language instruction, and domestication of women, he cultivated ties with Great Britain and with Anglican churchmen, welcoming Thomas Nettleship Staley as the bishop of Honolulu.

The religious maneuvering for power heightened in 1861, including the mission work of conservative Quakers Hannah Elliot Shipley Bean and Joel Bean of West Branch, Iowa. The Hawaiian-language newspaper *Ka Hoku o ka Pakipika* (Star of the Pacific), co-edited by future king David Kalakaua and supported by Kamehameha IV, issued anticolonial propaganda and praised indigenous cultural events and the 266 island schools where students learned lessons in the native tongue. As commercial exploiters continued to arrive from the United States and imported laborers from Asia, outsiders spawned outbreaks of influenza, measles, and leprosy, a scourge to native Hawaiians.

For the sake of his people, Kamehameha IV built up the waterfront, experimented with new hybrid rice seed, imported honeybees, and added a waterworks, an interisland steam line, and gas lines. To halt the rapid decline in the native Hawaiian population, he promoted health and sobriety and care for paupers and the elderly at the Queen's Medical Center, the nation's largest medical facility. Queen Emma contributed to the project by collecting money to combat epidemics of measles, smallpox, and whooping cough. The royal couple converted to Anglicanism, built St. Andrew's Cathedral in 1866, and opened Iolani College for boys and St. Andrew's Priory for girls. In 1874, the king translated into Hawaiian the Episcopal Book of Common Prayer.

Following the death of Kamehameha IV from depression, alcoholism, and asthma at age 29, the crowning of his older brother, King Lot Kapuaiwa Kamehameha V, on November 30, 1863, began a nine-year reign. In addition to promoting the island livestock industry, he rejected the old constitution and sought more executive power. He signed a new constitution on August 20, 1864, that defied democratic principles by limiting voters to literate, property-owning residents. In April 1865, he sent an emissary to China, India, and Malaya to procure laborers, exotic food plants and insect-eating birds, and medical information on leprosy. The next month, under the king's aegis, the dowager Queen Emma began a year's goodwill tour of England.

Kamehameha V initiated a vigorous construction campaign. Local building projects included a prison, Honolulu lighthouse, post office, royal mausoleum, girl's school, barracks for the security guard, a quarantine station for immigrants, and an insane asylum. He laid the cornerstone for St. Andrew's Cathedral, licensed native physicians, and opened a permanent quarantine of 140 lepers at Kalawao, a 4-square-mile (10-square-kilometer) compound on the Kalaupapa Peninsula on Molokai.

The king welcomed foreign embassies and supported the erection of government offices at the Ali'iolani Hale and the planning of the Royal Hawaiian Hotel in Honolulu, an invitation to island tourists. He suppressed hula dancing and banned alcohol in 1865 as a major cause of Hawaiian ill health and death, and he advocated sanitation measures and preventive medicine over the ancient practice of the *kahunas* (native priests).

A setback to the king's connection with the mainland, the Pacific Mail halted postal delivery to Hawaii because of the limited size of Honolulu Harbor and cultivated a safer, shorter, faster route via the northern arc to Hong Kong and Yokohama, Japan. Regular mail delivery via the steamers *Ajax, Commodore Preble, Commodore Stockton,* and *Fremont* began on January 13, 1866, but failed after a few round-trips. The impasse ended in 1868 with an island grant to the California, Oregon, and Mexican Company, which delivered mail every three weeks from Portland, Oregon.

In late October 1871, the loss of a whaling fleet in the Arctic Sea cost Honolulu shippers $200,000 per year in oil revenues. Improving trade and tourism in 1872, a regular steamship service from Australia through the islands to California increased the flow of visitors. At Kamehameha V's sudden death from heart failure at age 42 on December 11, 1872, he left no heirs.

At the end of 1872, the throne passed to Lot's cousin, King William Charles Lunalilo, composer of Hawaii's first national anthem, "E Ola Ke Ali'i Ke Akua" (God Save the King, 1860). He spent his 13 months as monarch trying to democratize the islands and relieve economic loss from the foundering whaling industry, which had declined to 47 ships from a height of 471 in 1844. For the sake of public health, he added 500 diagnosed lepers to the colony at Molokai. At Lunalilo's death from tuberculosis and alcoholism at age 39 on February 3, 1874, King David Kalakaua began a 16-year reign.

A scholar and diplomat, Kalakaua followed the mottos "Increase the Race" and "Hawaii for Hawaiians." Ironically, he increased the importation of foreign laborers by transporting 180 Portuguese workers from the Azores and Madeira. Reared in the study of law and politics, he depended on advice from his wife, Queen Esther Julia Kapiolani, a speaker of the native language whom he married in 1863. Kalakaua's conservative, anti-Calvinist principles called for a return to the hereditary monarchy, public coronation, and royal residence at Iolani Palace, the only royal dwelling in the United States. English opposition to his crowning required intervention from the British and American navies, which anchored warships in the harbor and dispatched marines.

Out of love for Hawaiian culture, Kalakaua traveled the entire island cluster and outraged missionaries by betting on horse races and drinking and gambling at all-night parties in the Royal Boat House in Honolulu Harbor. He advocated revival of the hula and Polynesian myth, more ukulele music and ritual chanting, reinstitution of surfing and martial arts, and the recognition of an original song, "Hawaii Ponoi" (Hawaii's True Sons, 1874) as the national anthem. The king supported a stronger presence of Hawaiian representatives in Washington, D.C., during the presidency of Ulysses S. Grant.

Kalakaua was the first Hawaiian monarch to travel to the United States and to sail around the world. In 1874, he negotiated with Secretary of State Hamilton Fish on the colonization of the Hawaiian Islands to provide a U.S. naval base at Pearl Harbor. On January 1, 1875, the islands signed the Reciprocity Treaty with the United States, granting exclusive rice and sugar trading rights, a move that promised relief of Hawaii's national debt of $355,000 and economic boom times as American investors descended on the islands to stake claims. At a time when the native population shrank to 48,000, Queen Kapiolani sought to lower infant and maternal death rates by establishing the Kapiolani Maternity Hospital, a birthing center for Hawaiian mothers.

See also: Damien, Father; Dentistry; Fish, Hamilton; Midway Islands.

Further Reading

Chambers, John H. *Hawaii.* Northampton, MA: Interlink, 2006.

Herring, George C. *From Colony to Superpower: U.S. Foreign Relations Since 1776.* New York: Oxford University Press, 2008.

Okihiro, Gary Y. *The Columbia Guide to Asian American History.* New York: Columbia University Press, 2001.

Pletcher, David M. *The Diplomacy of Involvement: American Economic Expansion Across the Pacific, 1784–1900.* Columbia: University of Missouri Press, 2001.

Silva, Noenoe K. *Aloha Betrayed: Native Hawaiian Resistance to American Colonialism.* Durham, NC: Duke University Press, 2004.

Hayes, Rutherford B. (1822–1893)

An abolitionist attorney and soldier, Rutherford Birchard Hayes—the nineteenth president of the United States (1877–1881)—ended Reconstruction and fostered national harmony. A native of Delaware, Ohio, he was born on October 4, 1822, ten weeks after the death of his father, merchant and distiller Rutherford Hayes, of epidemic malaria. The family claimed descent from seventeenth-century English and Scots colonists of Connecticut.

Reared and homeschooled by his mother, Sophia Birchard Hayes, and her brother, banker Sardis Birchard, Hayes studied at the Norwalk Seminary and at Isaac Webb's Maple Grove Academy in Middletown, Connecticut. He completed a bachelor's degree and graduated valedictorian from his class at Kenyon College in Gambier, Ohio. Upon completion of two years at Harvard Law School, he opened an office with partner Ralph Pomeroy Buckland in Lower Sandusky, Ohio. During Hayes's practice of law in Cincinnati, Ohio, he gained a reputation for patriotism and honesty.

In opposition to the Fugitive Slave Law of 1850 and to the caning of John Joliffe, the Cincinnati attorney for the Underground Railroad, Hayes offered Levi Coffin, coordinator of slave rescue, free court defense of black runaways. After marrying Lucy Ware Webb, a Methodist abolitionist from Chillicothe, Ohio, in 1852, Hayes crusaded for abolition of human bondage and denounced extradition of runaways from free territory. In 1855, Hayes partnered with abolitionist attorney Salmon P. Chase to stop the recapture of Rosetta Armstead, a Kentucky slave girl. At age 36, Hayes advanced to Cincinnati's city attorney.

General

During the Civil War, at age 40, Hayes resolved to fight for the Union and abolitionism. He served as a brigadier general in the Twenty-third Ohio Volunteers along with future president William McKinley and gained a positive view of slaves fleeing the plantation South. In battles in the Virginia and West Virginia mountains and at South Mountain and Antietam, Maryland, Hayes survived the deaths of four mounts shot from under him. He incurred a serious fall, five gunshots to his head, foot, and ankle, and a musket ball above the left elbow, becoming the only U.S. president wounded in the Civil War. While lying in no-man's-land beside a rebel casualty, Hayes made friends with his enemy in jolly conversation. He commented in his diary that, for the first time in his life, he lost count of the days of the week. A family at Middletown, Maryland, sheltered him while he slowly recovered.

Days before the Confederate surrender at Appomattox, Virginia, in April 1865, Hayes won election to Congress, even though he refused to resign his commission and campaign in person for office. After winning a second term, he resigned from Congress in July 1867 to pursue the governorship of Ohio, which he won in 1868 and again in 1876.

As governor, Hayes founded the Soldiers' and Sailors' Orphans' Home at Xenia and the Agricultural and Mechanical College, the beginning of the Ohio State University. He supported postwar charities, bolstered the Ohio State Library archives with historical documents and portraits, and built a memorial to Abraham Lincoln and Union soldiers in the statehouse rotunda. Out of regard for former slaves as equals, he crusaded for ratification of the Fifteenth Amendment enfranchising black males.

President

In opposition to Democrat Samuel J. Tilden, at the end of the first year of his second term as governor of Ohio, Hayes ran for U.S. president on the Republican ticket. In a contested election that awarded the popular vote to Tilden, Hayes won the electoral vote after Congress settled contested counts in Florida, Louisiana, Oregon, and South Carolina. He agreed to the Compromise of 1877, by which he would appoint one cabinet member from the South and would relieve the former Confederacy of occupation forces and end Reconstruction.

In his inaugural address on March 5, 1877, Hayes promised to serve "the social order and all the peaceful industries and the happiness that belongs to it"—a pledge he kept by furthering plans for the Panama Canal, halting the inflation of value in silver coinage, and banning electioneering by civil servants. For the sake of national growth, he promoted the Desert Land Act, encouraging settlement and irrigation of arid lands in the West.

After the withdrawal of Union troops from the South on April 24, his term required constant amelioration of party relations concerning the use of federal troops to supervise elections. In August 1877, he angered prolabor forces during the Baltimore & Ohio Railroad strike by dispatching federal troops to disperse rioters in northern rail centers. Quick action quelled rumors of communist insurgency, America's first "red scare." Violent clashes cost 70 civilian lives, $600,000 to unions, $2.1 million to the Burlington Railroad, and $5 million each to the cities of Baltimore, Chicago, and Pittsburgh.

Revered for his fairness and dignity, Hayes made strides toward national civil rights. He signed bills enforcing black rights and allowing Chinese immigration. In 1879, he granted female lawyers the privilege to press cases before the U.S. Supreme Court. He campaigned for a one-term, six-year limit on the executive office and refused to run for a second term. In 1878, he voiced his distaste for politics: "Nothing brings out the lower traits of human nature like office-seeking."

Retiring to his Spiegel Grove mansion in Fremont, Ohio, he served as a trustee of the Peabody Fund for the education of black children in the South and, in 1886, became the first president of the Civil War Library and Museum of Philadelphia. In his last months, he toured Southern schools for the Slater Fund, a charity underwriting education for freedmen.

Three years after his wife's death from stroke, Hayes suffered a heart attack on a train to Cleveland and died of heart disease on January 17, 1893. Fellow veterans bore his coffin to its burial on the family grounds. Among presidents, he retains honor as a strict constitutionalist and a champion of national unity and the rights of some 4 million former slaves.

See also: Chase, Salmon P.; Desert Land Act (1877); Jones, Mother; Panama Canal.

Further Reading

Campbell, James E. *The American Campaign: U.S. Presidential Campaigns and the National Vote.* 2nd ed. College Station: Texas A&M University Press, 2008.

Holt, Michael F. *By One Vote: The Disputed Presidential Election of 1876.* Lawrence: University Press of Kansas, 2008.

Morris, Roy, Jr. *Fraud of the Century: Rutherford B. Hayes, Samuel Tilden, and the Stolen Election of 1876.* New York: Simon & Schuster, 2003.

Rehnquist, William H. *Centennial Crisis: The Disputed Election of 1876.* New York: Alfred A. Knopf, 2005.

Reichley, A. James, ed. *Elections American Style.* Washington, DC: Brookings Institution, 1987.

Trefousse, Hans L. *Rutherford B. Hayes.* New York: Times Books, 2002.

Heinz, H.J. (1844–1919)

German American industrialist Henry John "Harry" Heinz, a leading condiment producer, introduced table-ready foods to grocery shelves worldwide. Born on October 11, 1844, to immigrants from Kallstadt, Bavaria, he grew up in Birmingham outside Pittsburgh, Pennsylvania. In boyhood, he learned thrift and waste reduction as well as Christian and pacifist values. By age six, he worked in the family vegetable beds and gathered produce to sell door to door and to process into horseradish sauce, a popular table flavoring with Pennsylvania's European ethnic groups. He also sold jelly made by his German Lutheran mother, Anna Margaretha Schmidt Heinz, at their home on Main Street.

By 1854, at age ten, he tended his own three-quarters of an acre (0.3 hectare). Two years later, he purchased a horse and cart to supply vegetables to grocers from his 3.5-acre (1.4-hectare) plot and hired two women to help with the food processing. In 1861, he made $2,400 from his food deliveries and from the horseradish sauce that he and his staff made. He extended sales by calling on bars, grocers, hotels, meat markets, the Monongahela House, and other men's clubs and saloons. He kept his wagons scrubbed and his horses groomed and impressed buyers with his first-in, first-out stock rotation method, which ensured quality and freshness.

Heinz earned a business degree in Etna and worked as a brick maker at Kier Brothers in Pittsburgh, while maintaining his agrarian sideline. At age 21, he surprised his father, John Henry Heinz, by collecting past-due company debts and building a two-story brick house for his wife, Sarah Sloan "Sallie" Young Heinz. Within a year, he stretched his acreage to capacity of planting and harvesting. In 1869, he and partner Lewis Clarence Noble sold evaporated horseradish from their bottling factory, Anchor Pickle & Vinegar Works, which Heinz set up in a 6-foot by 8-foot (1.8-meter by 2.4-meter) room in the family basement. The next year, he traveled as a company salesman while Noble controlled the financing.

The business grew to lengthening delivery routes, a two-story stable for its Percheron horses, and warehousing in Chicago and St. Louis of crated goods shipped from the Pittsburgh factory on Second Avenue between Grant and Smithfield. Heinz expanded plantings to 160 acres (65 hectares) of cabbage and cucumbers and 20 acres (8 hectares) of horseradish and, in 1872, numbered bottles as a means of quality control.

Heinz introduced imported European condiments, mustard, pickles sweetened with saccharine, and a wide-mouth packing jar with a horse head glass lid. In its sixth year, the company added a tomato and walnut ketchup, but the business foundered because of a crop surplus. The company overcame a stagnant economy after the Panic of 1873 as well as the Great American Railroad Strike of 1877, which caused riots in Pittsburgh.

The year 1875 marked a turning point for Heinz and his company. The family lived on credit. At the depth of financial despair at Christmas, he resolved to survive a financial downturn that left one-quarter of Pittsburgh laborers out of work. He imported premium malt vinegar, marketed crocks of fruit preserves, sold 15,000 barrels of pickles, and mass-produced home containers on equipment designed in his factory. Restaurants and hotels preferred his celery sauce, made by a time-consuming process.

In 1876, Heinz allied with his brother, John Heinz, and cousin, Frederick Heinz, at a two-story farmhouse in Sharpsburg, Pennsylvania, to form F&J Heinz, a manufacturer of baked beans, bottled onions, chutney, fish sauce, jelly, pickles, preserved fruit, sauerkraut, vinegar, and Worcestershire sauce. His ketchup contained salt and vinegar plus spices—allspice, black and white pepper, brown and cane sugar, cayenne, celery seed, cinnamon, cloves, garlic, ginger, horseradish, mace, mustard seed, and slippery elm. To guarantee customers a wholesome product of consistent quality, rather than tomatoes adulterated with turnips or wood fiber, he sold ketchup in glass bottles. By buying tomatoes at their peak to reduce waste and by offering consistent quality, he was able to charge less than the $3 per pint of competitors. In the first year, the company grossed $44,474 for its national brand.

Heinz was an idea man. He favored brand-name advertisement and the introduction of his children to the family business as an assurance of longevity. At the 1876 Centennial Exposition in Philadelphia, he examined other sauces, particularly William Underwood's mushroom, tomato, and walnut recipe for ketchup, and he targeted the maker of Tabasco sauce as a competitor. He pioneered such technological advancements as shipping in refrigerated railcars, automated vegetable sizing and sorting, cooking with pressurized steam, and vacuum canning. His factories featured assembly line corking and wrapping of jars.

In 1877, he began marketing seeds for hybrid cucumbers and tomatoes, added chow-chow to his product line, and introduced tin cans to his line of glass containers and wooden barrels. As the result of an 1866 visit to Fortnum & Mason, the London supplier of the royal family, Heinz became one of the initial American food packagers to sell internationally. For maximum distribution, he marketed various grades of ketchup under the Duquesne, Howard, Keystone, and Standard brands.

In 1888, Heinz bought out his partners and changed the firm's name to the H.J. Heinz Company, maker of "57 varieties" of nourishing condiments, sauces, and soups. He honored his home state by patenting a logo in the shape of a keystone—the symbol of Pennsylvania—and selected an octagonal bottle with a neckband and screw-on cap.

As a philanthropist, Heinz supported the Methodist Episcopal Church and the temperance movement, and founded Pittsburgh's Sarah Heinz settlement house. As a businessman, he insisted on a clean, safe work environment, free dental care for employees, and locker rooms with running water. He opened rooftop gardens for workers and issued *Pickles,* one of the first employee newsletters. The company advertised on horsecars and on the sides of his delivery wagons and gave public factory tours of the company complex on the north shore of the Allegheny River.

Heinz also pioneered the fair treatment of employees at his seed farms, container factories, and 20 food processing plants, including a pickle factory in Holland, Michigan, the largest of its kind in the world. Women who handled vegetables and packed pickles received weekly professional manicures. By the turn of the century, Heinz's name attached to businesses in Antwerp, Bermuda, Liverpool, London, Mexico City, Montreal, Sydney, and Toronto. In 1906, he lobbied for the Pure Food and Drug Act and advised grocers to rid their stock of foods containing preservatives.

Heinz died on May 14, 1919, at age 74. The family firm continued to grow by adding the Ore-Ida, Star-Kist, and Weight Watchers brands.

Further Reading

Foster, Debbie, and Jack Kennedy. *H.J. Heinz Company.* Charleston, SC: Arcadia, 2006.

Skrabec, Quentin R., Jr. *H.J. Heinz: A Biography.* Jefferson, NC: McFarland, 2009.

Smith, Andrew F., ed. *The Oxford Companion to American Food and Drink.* New York: Oxford University Press, 2007.

———. *Pure Ketchup: A History of America's National Condiment, with Recipes.* Columbia: University of South Carolina Press, 1996.

Snodgrass, Mary Ellen. *Encyclopedia of Kitchen History.* New York: Fitzroy Dearborn, 2004.

Hickok, James Butler "Wild Bill" (1837–1876)

A law enforcer and saloon gambler, James Butler "Wild Bill" Hickok established a reputation for riflery and gunfighting. A farm boy from Homer, Illinois, he was born on May 27, 1837, and grew up in an abolitionist household.

At age 19, with older brother Lorenzo, he took civil service jobs in Arkansas and southwest Missouri. Alone, he settled in Kansas in October 1861 as a $100-a-month ox team master out of Sedalia, Missouri, traveling over the Santa Fe and Oregon trails. While riding and tending stock for the Pony Express, he incurred an attack by a bear that required counterattack with a bowie knife and extensive recuperation for Hickok. He won election as constable of Monticello Township, Kansas, and served in General James H. Lane's Free State Army, a vigilante band warring against enslavers.

During a land dispute on July 12, 1861, over a late payment to the Rock Creek Pony Express Station, in Nebraska Territory, Hickok initiated his reputation as a gunfighter by shooting David Colbert McCanles and his employee, James Woods, to death at Rock Creek. Aiding him in the fight was Pony Express rider James W. "Dock" Brink. Six years later, George Ward Nichols popularized the name "Wild Bill" by embellishing the killings in a February 1867 issue of *Harper's Weekly.* The Welsh journalist and later African explorer Henry Morton Stanley increased the legend with an interview with Hickok for the *New York Herald.*

On July 21, 1865, Hickok hunted buffalo and initiated the "Western walk-down on Main Street" by shooting cowboy David Tutt, Jr., in a 50-yard (45-meter) face-off in Springfield, Missouri, over a stolen watch. Tutt died at the scene. Decked in shoulder-length hair and buckskins and armed with a .36-caliber Colt Navy revolver, Hickok scouted for the U.S. Seventh Cavalry, organized in July 1866 and led by Lieutenant Colonel George Armstrong Custer. In 1868, Hickok accepted a post as deputy U.S. marshal in Hays, Kansas, where he jailed horse thieves and timber rustlers. During the establishment of Fort Sill, Oklahoma, in winter 1869, Hickok joined William Frederick "Buffalo Bill" Cody in scouting for Major General Philip H. Sheridan and for the Buffalo Soldiers of the Ninth Cavalry.

Elected sheriff of Ellis County, Kansas, on August 23, 1869, Hickok quelled widespread crime and countered threats on his life by keeping his back to the wall. Because of his bloody encounters, he lost reelection the following November. For a salary of $150 per month and a portion of court fines, in 1871, as marshal of Abilene, Kansas, he performed the same cleansing of drunken, lawless wranglers driving cattle through town. One of the outlaws he subdued, John Wesley Hardin, performed his signature cross-hand draw to impress the marshal. The accidental shooting of a deputy soured the lawman's reputation and ended his career in law enforcement on December 13 with his firing.

Until 1874, he gave target shooting exhibitions in Buffalo Bill's Wild West Show that displayed his speed and accuracy at the cross-body draw, an underhanded pull on the revolvers turned butt forward and spun toward the target for double firing. Resettled in Cheyenne, Wyoming, Hickok gambled and, at age 39, wed Agnes Lake Thatcher, the widow of a circus entrepreneur, whom he abandoned to take up prospecting. While gambling and prospecting for gold in Deadwood, South Dakota, he faced decreasing eyesight from trachoma, a bacterial infection of the eye.

His reputation made him a celebrity, and he continued his gambling in saloons. Upon meeting memoirist Annie Donna Fraser Tallent in the streets of Deadwood, he countered her low opinion of his reputation: "I never allowed a man to get the drop on me. But perhaps I may yet die with my boots on."

On August 1, 1876, he angered Jack McCall by beating him in a poker game in Nuttal & Mann's Saloon No. 10. The next day, McCall shot Hickok in the back of the head, killing him instantly. Legend describes Hickok's poker hand at the moment of death as the "dead man's hand": two black aces and two black eights. His murderer went to the gallows the following March 1.

Dime novels elaborated on Hickok's reputation as a card player, pistoleer, and civilizer of the frontier. Martha Jane Canary, the legendary army scout known as "Calamity Jane," compiled an autobiography in 1877 claiming that she had once been Wild Bill's wife.

See also: Buffalo Soldiers; Dakota Territory; Hardin, John Wesley.

Further Reading

Carter, Gregg Lee, ed. *Guns in American Society: An Encyclopedia of History, Politics, Culture, and the Law.* Santa Barbara, CA: ABC-CLIO, 2002.

Lamar, Howard R., ed. *The New Encyclopedia of the American West.* New Haven, CT: Yale University Press, 1998.

Rosa, Joseph G. *The West of Wild Bill Hickok.* Norman: University of Oklahoma Press, 1994.

———. *Wild Bill Hickok: Gunfighter: An Account of Hickok's Gunfights.* Norman: University of Oklahoma Press, 2003.

Turner, Thadd. *Wild Bill Hickok: Deadwood City—End of Trail.* Baton Rouge, LA: Universal, 2001.

Home Economics

An endeavor for girls from prehistory, home economics advanced to a science of domestic management and skills in the mid-1800s. The profession of home care arose at a time when 30 percent of U.S. households had live-in servants, most employed through agencies.

Passage of the Morrill Land Grant Act on July 2, 1862, authorized federal distribution of public lands and construction of 59 agricultural and vocational colleges, called land-grant colleges. Women displayed their interest in housekeeping and family health and hygiene by reading up-to-date articles in *Godey's Lady's Book* on invalid cookery, toddler diet, food preservation, homemade cleaning solutions and polishes, and weights and measures.

As home fires gave way to efficient coal- and wood-fired kitchen stoves and gas lighting, reformer and educator Catharine Esther Beecher, a teacher of domestic arts at the Hartford Seminary in Connecticut, formulated the first comprehensive theory of home economics. She and her sister, novelist Harriet Beecher Stowe, demanded equal representation for girls in practical career classes and considered the job of cleaning the home and preparing meals a Christian duty. They called for coursework and laboratory preparation in the science-centered liberal arts in the groundbreaking *The American Woman's Home, or Principles of Domestic Science* (1869), *Miss Beecher's Housekeeper and Healthkeeper* (1873), and *The New Housekeeper's Manual* (1873), experienced-based works that differentiated between American and British domestic concepts. The latter, a reform guide for professional homemaking, pictured the American homemaker as the angel of the household, rather than the superintendent of minions. Beecher and Stowe projected an upgrading of everyday labor to a well-organized and executed career that deserved dignity and adequate pay.

Siding against their sister-in-law, Eunice Bullard Beecher, the sisters defended Irish immigrant maids and cooks from widespread denunciation as ignorant, dishonest, and dirty. The authors advised untrained readers on cooking infant and invalid diets, planting berries and orchards, sanitizing dishcloths, monitoring stove gases, and establishing an ice chest and root cellar. For the average kitchen, they required an aboveground room with an underground drain, good lighting, and whitewashed walls and ceiling. The minimum essentials ranged from linen dishcloths and tea towels to an ample sink and slop pail, both scalded daily with lye.

The washing of good crystal, china, and silver preceded the scouring of griddles, kettles, and roasters and the drying of tins and teapots to prevent rust. For a serviceable floor surface, they suggested either oilcloth or paint rather than brick or unfinished planking and described how to sweep the surface with used tea leaves.

They ranked foods in order of value to the body, beginning with bread and butter, meat, and vegetables, and concluding with tea and other beverages. For moral, religious, and health reasons, the list ruled out alcohol, opiates, and tobacco. Beecher and Stowe cited as an example of training Elizabeth Coane Goodfellow's Cooking School, a tutorial that debuted in Philadelphia in 1842 and impressed Quakers with an emphasis on purity and wholesomeness in cookery.

The Demonstration Kitchen

Practical home economics training got its start in Boston. During the influx to the city during Reconstruction, Unitarian philanthropist Mary Porter Tileston Hemenway taught public school students at a cooking and sewing institute, the Boston Normal School of Cooking, later named the Mary Hemenway Department of Household Arts of Framingham. She pioneered experimental kitchens in five Boston schools, where girls studied cooking and appliance layout and attended demonstrations. The success of the Hemenway method furthered the establishment of six more laboratory kitchens serving 1,600 students.

In 1877, on Boylston Street, Dr. Harriet Clisby, a homeopathic physician from London, founded the Women's Educational and Industrial Union. Advised by Louisa May Alcott and Julia Ward Howe, the institution enrolled immigrant and rural girls to learn skills in innkeeping, restaurant management, and hospital dietetics. To uplift poor women, the union taught hygiene and wellness, arranged consultations with female doctors, and served nutritious lunches. Training in vocational home economics, consumer skills, and placement in jobs was the work of activist Abby Morton Diaz and reformer Mary Morton Kimball Kehew.

For a family of means in the 1870s, the kitchen included plumbing and drainage, a coal- or wood-fired stove, ample storage space, and an assortment of utensils and appliances. Home economics had emerged as a science and formal field of study. *(MPI/Stringer/Getty Images)*

Contributing resources for professional schools, Juliet Corson, superintendent of the New York Cooking School and editor of *Household Monthly,* established a Free Training School for women at Roxbury, a Boston suburb, in 1873 to teach secretarial skills, proofreading, cooking, and sewing. In November 1876, she opened the New York Cooking School at St. Mark's Place, a forerunner of formal domestic scholarship. She lectured at the Training School for Nurses in Washington, D.C., and compiled seminal texts, *Fifteen Cent Dinners for Workingmen's Families* (1877) and *Cooking School Text Book and Housekeeper's Guide to Cookery and Kitchen Management* (1879). Her handbooks classified food groups by nutritional value and suggested the inclusion of broth, cheap meats, lentils, pasta, and rice pudding to menus for the cash-strapped cook. Chapters illustrated methods of detecting spoilage and food adulterants, such as copper sulfate, salicylic acid, chalk, and sawdust. Corson insisted that home economics professionals understand utensil selection, stove maintenance, fire making, temperature control, weights and measures, and sanitation. For housewives, she published articles in *Harper's Bazaar* on basic housewifery, including making candles and soap and serving leftovers. She recommended that girls seeking a domestic profession get hands-on training in a professional kitchen, such as a boarding school or retirement home, the source of training for cooking doyenne Fannie Farmer.

The Professional Domestic

Another innovation in home economics was the broadening of options for female lives from wifedom and motherhood to teaching, dressmaking, millinery, and professional cooking and table service. At Iowa State Agricultural College (now Iowa State University) in Ames, after the introduction of coeducation in 1871, scholar and suffragist Mary Beaumont Welch, wife of college president Adonijah Strong Welch, taught botany, chemistry, geology, physics, and physiology in the nation's first home economics department. At the president's residence, South Hall, she gave demonstrations and designed extension work, the nation's first home outreach from a federal land-grant institution. Her students spent two hours each day in supervised instruction in a dining room, experimental kitchen, or pantry. Pedagogy included lectures on infant and invalid care, training of children, management of servants, food and butchery basics, test of good flour, use of baking powder as a leavening agent, water purity and drainage, hospitality and manners, and selecting home furnishings. Welch published the school's first text, *Mrs. Welch's Cookbook* (1884), based in part on her studies in New York City and Kensington, England.

The Iowa model influenced subsequent home economics curricula. In 1873, Kansas State Agricultural College opened a department of domestic economy, where department head Nellie Kedzie Jones focused on critical thinking skills for farm wives and rural women. Honored as the school's first female professor, she lectured on the chemical composition of baked goods and meat and the food value of vegetables as well as gardening, home bookkeeping, and residential architecture. Her lobbying to the state legislature secured for the college Domestic Science Hall, the nation's first home economics building.

Mounting support for women's rights increased respect for women's education. In 1874, Illinois Industrial University at Urbana offered a homemaking curriculum taught by Louisa Catherine Allen, later Louisa Gregory, wife of university president John Milton Gregory. At a separate boarding facility, women kept house and followed a course outline of chemistry, botany, food studies, cooking, domestic hygiene, physics, household esthetics, domestic economy, and landscape gardening. In Boston, Maria Parloa opened a cooking school and distributed meals to the poor. She proposed simplification of domestic drudgery through the kitchen range and other labor-saving inventions, the focus of her advice in *The Appledore Cookbook* (1872).

Among the era's domestic trends were the retirement of the fussy parlor, the purchase of functional, easily cleaned implements, and furnishings with a minimum of knickknacks. The father of the Grange Movement, Oliver Hudson Kelley, an employee of the U.S. Department of Agriculture, proposed the balancing of classical studies with the addition of agricultural and industrial studies in public schools. In place of rote lessons in Latin, he fostered hands-on training in practical life skills, including home economics for female students. By 1890, there were scholarly home economics departments in Manhattan, Kansas; Corvallis, Oregon; Brookings, South Dakota; and West Lafayette, Indiana, at Purdue University.

See also: Food and Food Preservation; Gas Lighting; *Godey's Lady's Book*; Grange Movement.

Further Reading

Collins, Gail. *America's Women: Four Hundred Years of Dolls, Drudges, Helpmates, and Heroines.* New York: William Morrow, 2003.

Forman-Brunell, Miriam, ed. *Girlhood in America: An Encyclopedia.* Santa Barbara, CA: ABC-CLIO, 2001.

Hayden, Dolores. *The Grand Domestic Revolution: A History of Feminist Designs for American Homes, Neighborhoods, and Cities.* Cambridge, MA: MIT Press, 1981.

Kaplan, Amy. "Manifest Domesticity." *American Literature* 70:3 (September 1998): 581–606.

Snodgrass, Mary Ellen. *Encyclopedia of Kitchen History.* New York: Fitzroy Dearborn, 2004.

Homestead Act (1862)

On May 20, 1862, President Abraham Lincoln signed a revolutionary concept into law—the Homestead Act, providing for the supervised distribution of free land. It was the fifth time that Congress studied the proposal, which had originated with Thomas Jefferson's concept of the yeoman farmer and required the activism of Speaker of the House Galusha Aaron Grow to pass.

The legislation initiated the nation's largest land reform by offering 60-acre (24-hectare) plots of federally surveyed land on January 1, 1863, to citizens and potential citizens, male or female, at least 21 years of age. The expanse in public domain totaled 270 million acres (110 million hectares), or 10 percent of the nation's area, which included land in the West as well as in Alabama, Florida, Illinois, Indiana, Michigan, Mississippi, Ohio, and Wisconsin. According to reformers George Henry Evans and Horace Greeley, editor of the *New York Tribune,* the bill encouraged higher wages in the East and enticed former slaves to build homes and businesses, but excluded Southern rebels. (The later Indian Homestead Act of 1875 extended the offer of free land to Native Americans.)

Filers paid a $10 fee and signed a commitment to live on the property for five years and to "prove up" or enhance the property—build a dwelling measuring at least 12 feet by 14 feet (3.7 meters by 4.2 meters), sink a well, fence a pasture, and plow 10 acres (4 hectares) or plant 10 acres of trees. Union soldiers could deduct combat time from the residency requirement. By an alternate option, six months after a down payment of $1.25 per acre, each homesteader received a deed.

The concept drew 2 million settlers to 370,000 parcels. The first was Daniel Freeman, a Union scout who chose land near Beatrice, Nebraska, for himself and his wife, Elizabeth Agnes Suiter Freeman. Their one-room cabin sat amid Otoe Indians, who called on the Freemans for medical assistance. Opposition to the distribution of cheap land came from pro-Indian forces in Oklahoma

On the way to their new homestead, a pioneering family poses with their wagon in Nebraska's Loup River Valley. To certify their claim, they agreed to occupy the land for five years and improve it. *(MPI/Stringer/Getty Images)*

and Nebraska, formerly occupied by the Ponca. One example from young adult literature of homesteading near Amerindians is the land occupied by the family of Laura Ingalls Wilder in Indian Territory outside Independence, Kansas.

Obstacles beset the pioneers. Pioneers could survive in Colorado, Montana, Nevada, New Mexico, Utah, and Wyoming only by homesteading land around a water source and grazing stock on nearby public lands. In Washington State, farmers had to cut timber and contend with flooding rivers, poor soil drainage, and limited markets for crops. Because of adequate water and pasturage, plots in the southern Dakotas and northeastern Nebraska retained higher value. Speculators in Nebraska profited from homestead land purchased illegally. They offered free travel and rooms in Burlington and Lincoln to westerers claiming land offered by the Burlington & Missouri River Railroad Company in Iowa and Nebraska at 6 percent interest.

In 1870, the population of Nebraska began increasing tenfold as 20,000 buyers moved onto government land. The shortage of forestation for lumber forced some settlers to construct sod huts. Arid locations could not sustain the same boom as that in Nebraska because parcels were too small and too dry to support agriculture and ranching. The building of rail lines, John Deere's invention of the steel plow, the formation of the Grange, fencing with barbed wire, and shopping by Montgomery Ward catalogs increased efficiency and conveniences to settlers homesteading in remote areas.

See also: Grange Movement; Oklahoma Territory.

Further Reading

Conlin, Joseph R. *The American Past: A Survey of American History.* 9th ed. Boston: Wadsworth/Cengage Learning, 2009.

Etulain, Richard W. *Beyond the Missouri: The Story of the American West.* Albuquerque: University of New Mexico Press, 2006.

Griffin, Lee. *Kalamazoo and Southwest Michigan: Golden Memories.* Charleston, SC: Arcadia, 2001.

Lamar, Howard R., ed. *The New Encyclopedia of the American West.* New Haven, CT: Yale University Press, 1998.

Stanley, George E. *The Era of Reconstruction and Expansion, 1865–1900.* Milwaukee, WI: World Almanac Library, 2005.

Horse Breeding

Between the settlement of virgin land and the invention of the tractor and automobile, American horse breeding concentrated both on sturdy carriage and draft animals and horseflesh for riding and racing. The American Saddlebred, also called the Denmark or Kentucky Saddler, stood out from the broad-backed, thick-legged dray as a handsome gaited riding animal favored on Kentucky plantations for its height and style. The saddle horse carried its head high on a long, flexible neck and displayed alertness with wide eyes and pricked-up ears. Farther south, the Tennessee Walker, a scion of the Narragansett Pacer, suited riders in rocky and mountainous terrain. A broad-chested breed, the horse developed a unique running walk that was comfortable to long-distance riders.

Before the Civil War, breeders and planters focused on the qualities of the Kentucky thoroughbred. The conflict destroyed popular racing as a sport and a source of income for breeders.

In 1861, the military began buying from breeders of the Tennessee Walker and the Morgan, a compact American line raised for strength, intelligence, and a sensible disposition in Massachusetts and Vermont. Morgans pulled cannon and stood obediently within range of gunfire, a trait of General Philip H. Sheridan's horse, Rienzi. The Morgan was also a favorite of Pony Express riders, along with the Appaloosa, Kentucky thoroughbred, mustang, palomino, and pinto.

In the West, the mustang, called the bronco or cow pony, developed from the mounts of explorers, pioneers, and traders that mated with herds descended from the Iberian mounts of Hernán Cortés and other Spanish conquistadors. It won regard for its short muscular frame, wiriness, and serviceability. The most famous survivor of the Battle of the Little Bighorn on June 25, 1876, was Comanche, a wounded Morgan mustang, the 14-year-old buckskin hybrid of Captain Myles Walter Keogh.

Native Americans developed varied reputations as horse handlers. Unlike the horse-thieving Cheyenne and the horse-eating Apache, domesticators among the Comanche and Shoshone propagated hardy, controllable riding stock. Across the Southern Plains, the Comanche seized quality animals through raiding and war. They valued paint or pinto stallions for their courage, camouflaged coloring, and intelligence and trained one-year-olds for battle. To strengthen the line, the Comanche gelded weak males and swapped unsuitable animals, often to the Kiowa, the prime horse traders of the plains.

The most successful horse producers lived farther west. Using stock from the Shoshone, who preferred mountain-raised lines for stamina, the Nez Percé produced the "Palouse" or Appaloosa, a graceful, versatile breed with a spotted hide, striped hooves, high spirits, and fast gait. Nez Percé stockmen groomed hunting animals in eastern Oregon and Washington for tracking buffalo. The Nez Percé Nation lost much of its durable stock on October 5, 1877, after the capture of Chief Joseph and his followers at the Bear Paw Mountains, Montana, by Colonel Nelson A. Miles and the U.S. Cavalry. American settlers valued the remnants of the Nez Percé stock and crossed the slender Appaloosa with stouter, more muscular horses.

Through natural selection, Western ranchers promoted feral traits by letting their horses run loose in winter to forage on public land and mate with wild herds. By killing lead stallions and introducing pedigreed males, breeders augmented the feral gene pool with selected traits suited to the needs of the cowboy. Wranglers trained the Western riding horse to neck rein, a one-handed control that allowed the rider to aim and throw the lariat with the opposite hand.

In the mid-1800s, Captain Richard King of the King Ranch outside Brownsville, Texas, developed the American quarter horse, a calm, loyal, intelligent work animal and trail rider. After 1870, Samuel "Burk" Burnett, a stockman at the Four Sixes Ranch at Guthrie, Texas, continued refining the hybrid. A national favorite, the American quarter horse attained popularity at rodeos, where cowboys demonstrated roping, riding, barrel racing, and intricate herding techniques.

See also: Cattle and Livestock; Ranching.

Further Reading

Beisel, Perky, and Rob DeHart. *Middle Tennessee Horse Breeding.* Charleston, SC: Arcadia, 2007.

Cassidy, Rebecca. *Horse People: Thoroughbred Culture in Lexington and Newmarket.* Baltimore: Johns Hopkins University Press, 2007.

Greene, Ann Norton. *Horses at Work: Harnessing Power in Industrial America.* Cambridge, MA: Harvard University Press, 2008.

McShane, Clay, and Joel A. Tarr. *The Horse in the City: Living Machines in the Nineteenth Century.* Baltimore: Johns Hopkins University Press, 2007.

Horse Racing

Horse racing in America got its start over varied terrain in unofficial, stand-alone events, some open to all comers, regardless of breed, age, and size of entries. In Sonoma County, California, spring races begun in 1861 featured two-year-old American quarter horses, a hybrid refined on Texas cattle ranches for stamina and obedience.

Two years later, at a height of Civil War anguish, William Riggin Travers and John Hunter scheduled escape from sectionalism by building a flat track at an elegant retreat, Saratoga Springs, New York, the nation's oldest sports venue. From August 3 to 6, 1863, proprietor John Morrissey offered two races per day with purses ranging from $300 to $500. In a spirit of union, the field featured horses from Illinois, Kentucky, Missouri, Ohio, Wisconsin, and Canada. Black and white jockeys competed in America's first racially integrated sport. The

Travers Stakes, a juried run over 1.75 miles (2.8 kilometers) at Saratoga on August 2, 1864, featured three-year-old colts, fillies, and geldings, all thoroughbreds. The following August, *Harper's Weekly* published Winslow Homer's drawing of fashionable women in the viewing stands.

At the suggestion of Maryland governor Oden Bowie, a breeder of thoroughbreds, the city of Baltimore entered the racing circuit on October 25, 1870, with the building of the Pimlico track, a 1.2-mile (1.9-kilometer) dirt circuit that is the nation's second oldest sports locale. On May 23, 1873, the Preakness Stakes was named in honor of the first Pimlico champion, Preakness, a thoroughbred from Woodburn Farm, Kentucky, that won the first Dixie Stakes (or Dinner Party Stakes) on October 25, 1870. The first to take the Preakness Cup, Survivor, a bay stallion ridden by British jockey George Barbee, held the course record of a ten-length win for 132 years. On October 23, 1877, the track sponsored "The Great Race," a 2.5-mile (4-kilometer) match; the U.S. Congress closed for the day so legislators could join the 20,000 attendees. Lithographers Nathaniel Currier and James Merritt Ives created a print of the event.

In 1875, Colonel Meriwether Lewis "Lutie" Clark, Jr., founded the Kentucky Derby, a two-minute race that emulated English racing at Epsom Downs and at the Grand Prix de Paris. Run on 1.5 miles (2.4 kilometers) over a dirt track at Churchill Downs in Louisville, the event debuted on May 17, when 15 entries raced before a crowd of 10,000. The prize went to Aristides, a three-year-old chestnut stallion born at the McGrathiana Farm in Fayette County, Kentucky, and owned by Ansel Williamson, a former Virginia slave. On June 19, 1867, the black jockey, Oliver Lewis, rode Aristides to second place at the Belmont Stakes in Elmont, New York. Beating Aristides was a bay filly, Ruthless, the first winner of the Belmont Stakes with a lifetime take of $11,000.

See also: Horse Breeding.

Further Reading

Cassidy, Rebecca. *Horse People: Thoroughbred Culture in Lexington and Newmarket.* Baltimore: Johns Hopkins University Press, 2007.

Gems, Gerald R., Linda J. Borish, and Gertrud Pfister. *Sports in American History: From Colonization to Globalization.* Champaign, IL: Human Kinetics, 2008.

Hotaling, Edward. *They're Off: Horse Racing at Saratoga.* Syracuse, NY: Syracuse University Press, 1995.

Rader, Benjamin G. *American Sports: From the Age of Folk Games to the Age of Televised Sports.* 5th ed. Upper Saddle River, NJ: Prentice Hall, 2004.

Hospitals and Asylums

In the mid-1860s, American cities began building more hospitals to cope with the sick, injured, and handicapped poor and mentally incompetent, including alcoholics, drugs addicts, epileptics, and ineducable mental defectives. Whether financed by city and state funds, universities, private companies, legacies, or charities, these comprehensive care centers relieved patient neglect in workhouses and almshouses with dignified, science-based treatment and pharmacology.

Firsts from Boston City Hospital include a lazarette for smallpox victims in 1865, disinfection of a wound with phenol (carbolic acid) in September 1867, the issuance of an in-house clinical journal in 1869, and the addition of outpatient clinics by 1877 in dermatology, gynecology, laryngology, neurology, and otology. Nationwide, a hospital network founded in 1870 to tend to sick and injured merchant seamen developed into a service to control contagion. The Public Health and Marine Hospital Service shortened its name in 1912 to the Public Health Service.

America's oldest public hospital, Bellevue, a former almshouse overlooking the East River in New York City, first received patients in 1736. The Bellevue Hospital Medical College opened in March 1861, making Bellevue the first American hospital to be allied with a medical school. The 13-man faculty taught anatomy, chemistry, clinical medicine, obstetrics and gynecology, orthopedics, physiology and hygiene, surgery, therapeutics, and toxicology. By April 1861, the college hovered on collapse after surgeons, ward orderlies, and board members left to join the Union army and navy. During the Civil War, staff compiled monographs for the Union army, notably, Dr. Stephen Smith's essays in 1863 and 1864 on arteries and veins, gunshot wounds, and amputations, resections, and other surgical operations.

Further strapping the staff, invasive typhus killed six of the 21 members in a period of 36 months; by 1866, two more joined the list of deceased, one from typhus and another from cholera. Within the year, the hospital campaigned for the opening of the New York City Department of Health as a bulwark against outbreaks of plague, yellow fever, and other epidemic contagion. Faculty losses coincided with heavy patient loads, which reached 11,411 in 1860, requiring the hiring of fill-in helpers and attendants from the penitentiary. From 1863 to 1870, the hospital board remodeled the amphitheater and increased patient capacity to 1,200 beds. A staff

Hospitals and Asylums, 1861–1877

Institution	Founder	Location	Founded
Alabama Insane Hospital	State government	Tuscaloosa, Ala.	1861
Alexian Brothers Hospital for Men and Boys	State government	Chicago	1866
Athens Lunatic Asylum	State government	Athens, Ohio	1874
Baltimore Eye and Ear Dispensary	Charity	Baltimore	1874
Bay View Asylum and Hospital	City government	Baltimore	1866
Boston City Hospital	City government	Boston	1864
Broughton Hospital	State government	Morganton, N.C.	1875
Central Pacific Hospital	Central Pacific Railroad	Sacramento, Calif.	1871
Chicago Hospital	City government	Chicago	1876
Chicago Hospital for Women and Children	Mary Harris Thompson	Chicago	1865
Chicago Marine Hospital	Federal government	Chicago	1871
Columbia Hospital for Women	Federal government	Washington, D.C.	1866
Cook County Hospital	City government	Chicago	1866
Danville State Hospital	State government	Danville, Pa.	1872
Denver Hospital	City government	Denver	1862
Grace Hospital	Amos Chafee; James McMillan	Detroit, Mich.	1869
Greystone Park Psychiatric Hospital	State government	Hanover, N.J.	1876
Harper Hospital	Federal government	Detroit, Mich.	1861
Hudson River State Hospital	State government	Poughkeepsie, N.Y.	1866
Jews Hospital Pediatric Clinic	Abraham Jacobi	New York City	1874
Michigan Retreat for the Insane	Sisters of Charity	Detroit, Mich.	1870
New England Hospital for Women and Children	Maria Elizabeth Zakrzewska	Boston	1862
New York Medical College & Hospital for Women	Clemence Sophia Lozier	New York City	1863
New York Medical College Pediatric Clinic	Abraham Jacobi	New York City	1860
Northern Illinois Hospital and Asylum for the Insane	State government	Jacksonville, Ill.	1872
Providence Hospital	Sisters of Charity	Washington, D.C.	1861
Queen's Medical Center	Queen Emma Rooke	Honolulu, Hawaii	1860
Riverside Hospital	City government	New York City	1875
Savannah Hospital	City government	Savannah, Ga.	1872
Seattle Hospital	City government	Seattle	1877
Sisters of Providence Hospital	Sisters of Charity	Seattle	1878
St. Joseph's Hospital	Sisters of Charity	Lake View, Ill.	1868
St. Joseph's Retreat for the Insane	Mary DeSales	Dearborn, Mich.	1860
St. Luke's Free Hospital	Grace Episcopal Church	Chicago	1865
St. Luke's Hospital	St. Paul's Episcopal Church	Detroit, Mich.	1861
St. Mary's Hospital	Federal government	Detroit, Mich.	1863
Trans-Allegheny Lunatic Asylum	State government	Weston, W.V.	1864
University of Michigan Hospital	University of Michigan	Ann Arbor, Mich.	1869

(continued)

Hospitals and Asylums, 1861–1877 *(continued)*

Institution	Founder	Location	Founded
U.S. Marine Hospital	Federal government	Detroit, Mich.	1860
Warren State Hospital	State government	Warren, Pa.	1874
Washington Asylum	Federal government	Washington, D.C.	1865
Western Health Reform Institute	Ellen Gould White	Battle Creek, Mich.	1866
Western Pennsylvania Hospital for the Insane	State government	Pittsburgh	1862
Winnebago State Hospital	State government	Oshkosh, Wis.	1873
Woman's Hospital	Ladies' Christian Union	Detroit, Mich.	1868
Woman's Hospital	Ann Preston, Quakers	Philadelphia	1862
Worcester State Hospital	State government	Worcester, Mass.	1877

examiner directed transfer of the insane to an asylum. The busy intake resulted in a dismaying number of surgical patients dying of erysipelas (streptococcal infection), puerperal or childbed fever, and pyaemia, an invasive form of septicemia. A decade later, the medical board increased antiseptic conditions for open wounds, which dramatically reduced deaths from in-house septic infection to six per year.

Bellevue Hospital produced a number of firsts. In 1861, Lewis Albert Sayre adapted plaster of Paris bandaging to the treatment of scoliosis and spinal tuberculosis. A year later, cardiology researcher Austin Flint, a professor of medical practice, identified a mid-diastolic aortic rumble or regurgitation, designated the Austin Flint heart murmur, later corrected by mitral valve replacement. In 1867, the staff opened the nation's first outpatient department, the Bureau of Medical and Surgical Relief for the Out of Door Poor. The following year, Stephen Smith, New York City's first commissioner of public health, launched a national drive for vaccinations.

In June 1869, Bellevue's house physician, Dr. Edward Barry Dalton, a veteran surgeon of the Army of the Potomac medical corps, founded a city emergency ambulance service. He equipped each of the two horse-drawn vans with pull-out floors and snap-on horse harnesses, along with brandy, tourniquets, bandages, sponges, splints, oakum and padding, handcuffs and belts with buckles, antiseptics, and a tube of persulphate of iron to help curb bleeding. By 1879, aided by New York City police, emergency vehicles transported 1,812 patients and made all conveyances to and from prisons. Over the next decade, the van system inspired additional emergency corps at New York Hospital, Roosevelt Hospital, St. Vincent's, and Presbyterian Hospital.

Bellevue's staff looked beyond individual New York patients to large-scale solutions to illness. Dr. Stephen Smith presided over the first American Public Health Association in 1871 and promoted congressional interest in a National Board of Health. In May 1873, Bellevue's board of directors opened the New York Training School for Nurses, the nation's first nursing school, founded on the method that Florence Nightingale introduced at Scutari Hospital during the Crimean War. Contributing volunteer aid, a cadre of 60 women under the supervision of Louisa Lee Schuyler, a proponent of the U.S. Sanitary Commission, augmented the nurse staff. When the first class of nine finished training two years later under Helen Bowden, a London nurse-educator, one graduate was named superintendent of the newly opened Boston Training School for Nurses. Additional nursing schools followed the Bellevue plan at Connecticut State Hospital, Massachusetts General Hospital, and New York City's Charity Hospital.

More Bellevue innovations followed in 1874 with the creation of America's first children's clinic, a separate maternity ward, and, the next year, an orthopedics department. In 1876, the board opened the nation's first emergency department, which focused on concussions and compound fractures.

Further Reading

Brown, Thomas J. *Dorothea Dix: New England Reformer.* Cambridge, MA: Harvard University Press, 1998.

Dowling, Harry F. *City Hospitals: The Undercare of the Underprivileged.* Cambridge, MA: Harvard University Press, 1982.

Freemon, Frank R. *Gangrene and Glory: Medical Care During the American Civil War.* Urbana: University of Illinois Press, 2001.

Bellevue Hospital in New York City, the oldest public hospital in America, was also the first to be allied with a medical school (1861). Seen here is the surgery room in about 1880. *(Apic/Getty Images)*

Grob, Gerald N. *Mental Institutions in America: Social Policy to 1875.* New Brunswick, NJ: Transaction, 2009.

Schultz, Jane E. *Women at the Front: Hospital Workers in Civil War America.* Chapel Hill: University of North Carolina Press, 2004.

Howard, Oliver Otis (1830–1909)

A commanding military figure and humanitarian, General Oliver Otis Howard earned his reputation during the Civil War and the Indian Wars. Born on November 8, 1830, he was a native of Leeds, Maine, the scion of a colonial Massachusetts patriot and a Revolutionary War veteran, and the son of farmer Rowland Bailey Howard. After his father's death in 1839, his mother, Eliza Otis Howard, reared him and sent him to Monmouth Academy. He completed North Yarmouth Academy and Kents Hill School and finished his education with degrees from Bowdoin College and the U.S. Military Academy at West Point, with a specialty in ordnance.

During his posting in Tampa, Florida, during the Third Seminole War, he became a devout Christian and advocate of temperance and the Young Men's Christian Association (YMCA). After teaching math at West Point, he fought in the Civil War at Bull Run, Antietam, Chancellorsville, and Gettysburg and commanded the Army of the Tennessee. On June 1, 1862, command of a brigade at Fair Oaks, Virginia, resulted in two wounds to his right arm, which Union surgeons amputated.

Beginning in May 1865, Howard superintended the Bureau of Refugees, Freedmen, and Abandoned Lands—commonly known as the Freedmen's Bureau—which aroused opposition from the Ku Klux Klan in Alabama, Arkansas, the Carolinas, Georgia, Kentucky, Louisiana, Maryland, Tennessee, Texas, and West Virginia. The next year, he led a consortium in proposing the founding of Howard University in Washington, D.C., to train a black professional class of attorneys, dentists, doctors, ministers, and teachers. He served as president of the university from 1860 to 1874. Public and media ridicule of the uplift of former slaves forced Howard to defend his fiscal integrity, his budget of $100,000 per year and $50,000 for famine relief, and the work of his staff.

In fall 1872, President Ulysses S. Grant furthered his Peace Policy by dispatching Howard to Arizona and New Mexico to pacify the Apache, Maricopa, Navajo,

Papago, Pima, and Yuma. With scout Thomas Jefferson Jeffords, Howard brokered an accord with Cochise and the Chiricahua Apache. Howard approached Cochise unarmed and reached mutually agreeable terms in 11 days. The general selected Apache, Papago, and Pima ambassadors to take to New York City, Philadelphia, and Washington, D.C. He introduced them to the railroad and telegraph and to education for the deaf, which the visitors compared to Indian sign language.

In 1874, at the urging of President Grant, Howard accepted command of the Department of the Columbia in the Pacific Northwest. He moved his family to Portland, Oregon, where he governed affairs for 20 tribes as well as for the natives of Alaska. He set up a branch of the YMCA and, against federal law, hired former rebels from the South. According to his autobiography, *My Life and Experiences Among Our Hostile Indians* (1907), he was a strict moralist who alleviated racial tension in Alaska by participating with the Stickeen in a potlatch, where he distributed 100 blankets. He made friends with immigrant Chinese and countenanced marriages between soldiers and Indian wives. He produced a column for the *Portland Bee,* lectured on events of the Civil War, and published two children's books, *Donald's School Days* (1879) and *Henry in the War* (1899).

Howard fought in the Indian Wars from his post at Fort Vancouver in Washington Territory and completed the Modoc campaign in 1873 by sending prisoners to Indian Territory (Oklahoma). Out of fairness to the Nez Percé, he studied treaty law, which substantiated the tribe's claim to the Wallowa Valley in Oregon. The Indians honored Howard's bravery in battle by naming him "Cut-Arm."

Upon crossing the Yellowstone River in search of Chief Joseph, Howard rebuked his white scouts for killing and scalping an elderly Nez Percé brave and, in *Nez Percé Joseph* (1881), pondered the incompatibility of being a soldier and a Christian. Against personal principles, under military orders, on October 5, 1877, Howard forced the surrender of Chief Joseph and the Nez Percé, who had fled more than 1,700 miles (2,700 kilometers) from Oregon and Washington territories southeast through Montana and Idaho territories and northeast into Wyoming.

Howard served as superintendent of the U.S. Military Academy from 1881 to 1882, a period of racial undercurrent and rampant hazing at the institution. He retired from the army in 1894 with the rank of major general. He devoted much of his later life to writing, producing his *Life of William Tecumseh Sherman* (1891), *General Taylor* (1892), *Famous Indians I Have Known* (1907), and, two years before his death, an autobiography. He died suddenly of heart attack on October 26, 1909, following a speaking engagement in Burlington, Vermont.

See also: Alaska; Cochise; Diseases and Epidemics; Joseph, Chief; Ku Klux Klan; Montana Territory; Weapons.

Further Reading

Cimbala, Paul A. *The Freedmen's Bureau: Reconstructing the American South after the Civil War.* Malabar, FL: Krieger, 2005.

Johansen, Bruce E., and Donald A. Grinde, Jr. *The Encyclopedia of Native American Biography.* New York: Da Capo, 1998.

Lamar, Howard R., ed. *The New Encyclopedia of the American West.* New Haven, CT: Yale University Press, 1998.

Stanley, George E. *The Era of Reconstruction and Expansion, 1865–1900.* Milwaukee, WI: World Almanac Library, 2005.

Waldman, Carl. *Who Was Who in Native American History: Indians and Non-Indians from Early Contacts Through 1900.* New York: Facts on File, 1990.

Howe, Julia Ward (1819–1910)

Julia Ward Howe, an abolitionist lecturer, transcendentalist, and didactic poet, stirred the emotions of Unionists with her scriptural verse. A native of New York City, she was born on May 27, 1819, to poet Julia Rush Cutler and financier Samuel Ward, the prominent and wealthy son of a colonel in the Continental army. After her mother's death in 1824, she witnessed her father's prostration and took comfort in the love of her grandfather, Samuel Ward, and three bachelor uncles, John, Richard, and William Ward.

Reared by governesses, she spent her childhood learning Greek and Romance languages from tutors and attended a private school on Fifth Avenue. She resented the education of her brothers at boarding schools, where they studied math and science, both forbidden to female students. From age 16, she taught herself by reading from the home library and, in 1835, published her first poems in the *American.* After abandoning her father's grim Calvinism for Unitarianism, she submitted critiques to the *Literary and Theological Review* and the *New York Review.*

In 1843, she wed surgeon and reformer Samuel Gridley Howe, who was 18 years her senior. She called him "Chev" for his honorary title of chevalier for fighting in the Greek War of Independence. The couple lived in Boston, where Samuel Howe established the New England Institute for the Blind. In 1853, he joined his wife in editing *The Commonwealth,* an abolitionist journal. The couple grew apart in the 1850s, because Samuel poured his energies into work. He tyrannized his wife, squandered her inheritance, and prohibited her from participating in social activism. She proposed divorce, but relented after he threatened to exile her from their six children.

Beginning in her late twenties, Julia Ward Howe composed spiritual and patriotic verse and issued a collection, *Passion-Flowers* (1854), anonymously out of obedience to her husband's demands. One poem, "The Heart's Astronomy," acknowledges her ambivalence toward motherhood and her yearning for intellectual liberation. In 1856, her five-act play *Leonora, or the World's Own* pondered questions of sexuality and self-assertion on stages in New York and Boston. In 1860, she became an admirer of radical abolitionist William Lloyd Garrison and the Underground Railroad.

During a humanitarian visit with the wounded in Washington, D.C., in November 1861, she felt ill prepared to aid the U.S. Sanitary Commission. She urged mothers, wives, and sisters of the fallen to tend military cemeteries and to promote humanity and the family.

To channel patriotic sentiments, in predawn light on November 19, 1861, at the Willard Hotel in Washington, D.C., Howe scribbled "The Battle Hymn of the Republic" on a scrap of Sanitary Commission stationery. With the fervor of the peace effort, she fit the six verses and chorus to the tune of "John Brown's Body," a popular Union marching ditty. Howe's lyrics, published in February 1862 in the *Atlantic Monthly,* looked to God for triumph rather than to weaponry or combat heroics.

At a low point in the war, Union prisoners in Libby Prison in Richmond, Virginia, sang the anthem to celebrate the victory at Gettysburg on July 3, 1863. Later in the year, Howe returned to Washington to visit the wounded and to rally the Army of the Potomac. Admirers thrust copies of the anthem at her for autographs; in June 1872, the Jubilee Singers of Fisk University performed the anthem in Boston at the World's Peace Jubilee.

Howe delighted in the admission of women to Oberlin College (1837) and in the founding of Vassar (1861), Wellesley (1870), and Smith (1871) colleges for women. With some prompting from the Reverend Thomas Wentworth Higginson, she began reading her scholarly papers in public and preaching at Protestant churches. In 1868, she joined the Reverend Olympia Brown and Lucy Stone in founding the New England Woman Suffrage Association, the nation's first suffrage organization.

Within months, however, a schism with Susan B. Anthony and Elizabeth Cady Stanton allied Howe with the moderate wing of women's rights groups. In 1869, with the Reverend Henry Ward Beecher, Antoinette Brown Blackwell, Henry Brown "Harry" Blackwell, and Lucy Stone, Howe co-founded the American Woman Suffrage Association, which sought enfranchisement for women at the state level and promoted passage of the Fifteenth Amendment to the U.S. Constitution, granting the vote to black males. She lived to see suffrage granted in four states.

Julia Ward Howe escaped the limited vision of woman as homemaker to embrace the concept of woman as inspiration. To honor female heads of families, she joined a campaign to establish Mother's Day.

Her experiences convinced her of the futility of war and of women's ethical initiative for peace. She declared, "Woman must be the moral and spiritual equivalent of man. How, otherwise, could she be entrusted with the awful and inevitable responsibilities of maternity?" It bemused her that "the roughest, most vicious and most careless men" expect ethical behavior from women, particularly in regard to the rearing of children.

In 1870, Elizabeth Stuart Phelps published Howe's "Mother's Day Proclamation" in *The Women's Journal* and, in 1877, featured Howe's call to support full citizenship for women. Howe attended the Woman's Peace Congress, held in London in 1872, and convened the Woman's Ministerial Conference on May 29, 1873, which featured speakers Mary Graves, Lorenza Haynes, and Eliza Tupper Wilkes. To support herself in widowhood, in company with her 22-year-old daughter Maud, Howe lectured on peace during a three-year tour of the Prairie states, Europe, and the Middle East. In 1893 at the World Parliament of Religions in Chicago, she presented a sermon, "What Is Religion?"

At Howe's death from pneumonia at age 91 on October 17, 1910, more than 4,000 mourners gathered at her memorial service. Posthumously, in 1908, she became the first female elected to the American Academy of Arts and Letters.

See also: Brown, Olympia; Stone, Lucy; Washington, D.C.

Further Reading

Heidler, David S., and Jeanne T. Heidler, eds. *Encyclopedia of the American Civil War: A Political, Social, and Military History.* New York: W.W. Norton, 2000.

Laderman, Gary, and Luis D. León, eds. *Religion and American Cultures: An Encyclopedia of Traditions, Diversity, and Popular Expressions.* Santa Barbara, CA: ABC-CLIO, 2003.

Rappaport, Helen. *Encyclopedia of Women Social Reformers.* Santa Barbara, CA: ABC-CLIO, 2001.

Snodgrass, Mary Ellen. *Encyclopedia of Feminist Literature.* New York: Facts on File, 2006.

———. *The Underground Railroad: An Encyclopedia of People, Places, and Operations.* Armonk, NY: M.E. Sharpe, 2007.

Ziegler, Valarie H. *Diva Julia: The Public Romance and Private Agony of Julia Ward Howe.* Harrisburg, PA: Trinity Press International, 2003.

Hutterites

A pacifist sect of Anabaptists, Hutterites promote communal living and peace. Founded by hatmaker Jakob Hutter in the Tyrol of Austria in 1536, the body of Christians known as "plain people" reflects the tenets of the Amish and Mennonites. Because of ongoing Catholic persecution, Hutterite refugees migrated their *Bruderhofs* (communes) across Eastern Europe and settled in Romania, the Crimea, and the Ukraine until forced conscription and compulsory Russian language education once again drove them out of their homes.

On April 14, 1873, two leaders, Paul Tschetter and Lorenz Tschetter, began scouting Dakota Territory, Nebraska, and Manitoba, Canada. They requested from President Ulysses S. Grant conscientious objector status for 40 Hutterite families, which Grant denied. The president backed the "Mennonite Bill" in December 1873, which failed the following year because of the corruption of Secretary of the Interior Columbus Delano.

Despite the absence of congressional support, some 1,200 Hutterites began emigrating from Radichev, Russia, on June 7, 1874, leaving behind only two dissenting families. The newcomers, traveling in eight ships from Bremen and Hamburg, Germany, to New York City, sought New World farms and ranches that looked like the agrarian landscape of the Steppes. On a four-week stopover in Lincoln, Nebraska, one party lost 37 members to dysentery.

German-speaking colonies formed under strict collectivist principles. The original 450 communal immigrants tended toward marriage within the group, singing of martyr hymns from their *Gesangbuch* (hymnal), and behaviors imitating the first assembly of Christ's disciples at Jerusalem.

Blacksmith and preacher Michael Waldner, formerly of the Ukraine, governed the 113 members of Bon Homme Colony, which was built on 2,500 acres (1,000 hectares) at Tabor along the Missouri River near Yankton, South Dakota; the colonists became known as the Schmiedeleut (blacksmith's people). The area was rough pioneer territory awash in crime, gambling, and prostitution. The Dakota Territory Bureau of Immigration welcomed the pious Hutterites as stabilizers of families and agriculture.

Preachers Peter Hofer and Darius Walter of Molotschna, Ukraine, supervised the 40 families in the group known as the Dariusleut (Darius's people). They arrived on 5,400 acres (2,185 hectares) north of Yankton at Wolf Creek near Silver Lake, South Dakota, on August 8 and later spread to Alberta, Canada.

On 5,440 acres (2,200 hectares) outside Ethan, South Dakota, in 1877, teacher Jacob Wipf coordinated the Lehrerleut (teacher's people) at Elm Spring, a colony of 13 ultraconservative families. They, too, spread over the Dakotas and into Montana, Alberta, and Saskatchewan, Canada. Between 1874 and 1879, an unincorporated group, the 830 Prairieleut (prairie people), purchased individual homesteads on South Dakota grasslands.

Hutterite leadership specified gender roles, with men heading families, labor, religion, and education and women supervising food, child care, needlework, and healing. The Yankton *Press and Dakotan* welcomed the Russians for their thrift and industry, which saw them through prairie fires, drought, floods and blizzards, and plagues of grasshoppers and locusts.

In September 1877, Waldner, Walter, and Wipf discussed the merger of the Dariusleut, Lehrerleut, and Schmiedeleut communes and the allocation of responsibilities and land titles. The trio wrestled with a longstanding feud over basic utopian concepts—labor versus relaxation and obedience versus individualism. One holdout, Joseph "Yos" Hofer, retained his money rather than deposit it in the communal treasury and defected to join the Prairieleut. Like other noncommunal Hutterites, Hofer initiated family squabbles between Prairieleut dissenters and those who "came to congregation."

Further Reading

Fogarty, Robert S. *All Things New: American Communes and Utopian Movements, 1860–1914.* Lanham, MD: Lexington, 2003.

Hostetler, John A. *Hutterite Society.* Baltimore: Johns Hopkins University Press, 1997.

Janzen, Rod. *The Prairie People: Forgotten Anabaptists.* Hanover, NH: University Press of New England, 1999.

Kirkby, Mary-Ann. *I Am Hutterite: The Fascinating True Story of a Young Woman's Journey to Reclaim Her Heritage.* Nashville, TN: Thomas Nelson, 2010.

Sreenivasan, Jyotsna. *Utopias in American History.* Santa Barbara, CA: ABC-CLIO, 2008.

I

Idaho Territory

On March 4, 1863, the U.S. Congress nationalized Idaho Territory, an intermountain domain of 326,000 square miles (844,000 square kilometers), by separating it from Washington Territory. The area, governed by attorney William Henson Wallace, included the present-day states of Idaho, Nebraska, Nevada, and Wyoming as well as eastern Oregon. From its beginning, Idaho earned a reputation for devaluing human rights. Laws passed from the 1840s to 1866 outsourced the mentally ill to other states, outlawed miscegenation, taxed Chinese Americans $4 per month for residency, prevented black pioneers from settling there, and banned black children from schools.

When Montana became part of Idaho Territory in 1863, highwaymen dominated the region with disorder, lawlessness, and terrorism. The following year, vigilantes ended one reign of outlawry by hanging road agents without trials. The reduction of Idaho Territory began in May 1864 with the establishment of Montana Territory. In 1865, Boise replaced the first capital at Lewiston. Idaho shrank further in July 1868 with the loss of more land to western Nevada.

Indian problems in southern Idaho proved more troubling than the naive Governor Caleb Dell Lyon, a New Yorker, expected during his 26 months in office. On October 10, 1864, he negotiated a treaty with Chief Tam Tomeco and 25 other Boise Shoshone dignitaries living along the Boise River. In exchange for the land inhabited by some 300 Indians, Lyon promised them equality, a reservation yet to be chosen, and fishing rights. The Indians agreed to collaborate with law officers in rounding up murderers and horse thieves, but native actions belied the accord. Indians on the Owyhee River south of Boise stole some 450 cattle, horses, oxen, and sheep. To the southeast, stage travel outside Salmon Falls required military escort to prevent Indian ambush. On July 12, 1865, Judge C.G. Stafford and 162 residents of Boonville, Ruby City, and Silver City complained of dangers to citizens and businesses from hostile Indians. To the detriment of the Owyhee mine, Indians attacked throughout the Pueblo Valley. They horrified whites with their extremes, including burning at the stake and dismembering.

Governor Lyon found himself in a no-win situation of trying to uphold treaties and laws while placating take-action frontiersmen. On December 10, 1865, he sent A.G. Turner to the Goose Creek Mountains to reassess Shoshone unrest and to sort out the causes of upheaval. Seeking more permanent measures, U.S. Senator James Willis Nesmith of Oregon proposed urging white people to kill all Indians. An overview of vigilantism in the *Owyhee Avalanche* listed citizen bounties on Indian scalps at $100 for a male, $50 for a female, and $25 for a child. Bloodshed continued in earnest throughout 1866, forcing Indians to hide rather than hunt and fish for their living. Before Governor Lyon returned to his home in Staten Island, New York, an audit found him guilty of stealing $46,418.40 in federal funds allocated for Indian relief.

The shift in Idaho demographics from some 1,500 indigenous Nez Percé, Shoshone, and Snake to dominant white settlers at Wellsville and north into the Cache Valley worsened racial tensions. Led by Nez Percé guide Jane Silcott, Wilbur F. Bassett and Elias D. Pierce struck gold on Indian land along Orofino Creek, a tributary of the Clearwater River 1 mile (1.6 kilometers) outside Pierce, Idaho, in autumn 1860. Another gold strike in 1861 on the Salmon River lured 10,000 speculators, miners, wagoneers, and merchants to the Boise Basin from Puget Sound, Washington, and San Francisco, California.

Crime escalated in spring 1862 into rustling, mail and stage robbery, and revenge killings that forced the territory to begin construction of a territorial prison, which opened in 1870. Because the stampede to Idaho inhibited the lifestyle of native peoples, James Duane Doty, superintendent of Indian affairs for the territory, pressed for relief of destitute natives through federal gifts of livestock.

Further threatening native survival, the discovery of gold north of Cache Valley in Montana on July 28, 1862, and a strike of gold and silver on the Owyhee River in 1863 invigorated migration from California, Oregon, and Washington. Ore shipments required overland freight, assay, and mail deliveries to Salt Lake City, Utah. General Benjamin Alvord complained about the opening of grog shops and the intrusion of prospectors on Nez Percé land as sources of violence. Despite his inspections and alerts, the Pioneer Mining Company gained permission in 1866 to prospect on Indian reservations. The Gilmer and Salisbury Stage Company and freight lines further angered Indians by grazing herds on rich bottomlands without paying for the privilege. Settlers compounded the insult by cutting timber and firewood from native woodlands.

Federal intervention became a necessity. Colonel Patrick Edward Connor positioned the Third California Volunteer Infantry Regiment to protect delivery routes and to ensure peace along Idaho's borders with Montana and Utah. In 1863, he struggled to recruit soldiers from wagon trains to guard the Beaverhead Mines in southeastern Montana. Heightening tensions, the organization of proslavery sympathizers into racist mobs increased before President Abraham Lincoln's reelection in 1864. General Alvord observed, "Through Oregon and Idaho Territory there are secret clubs whose members are armed and more or less organized, and I doubt not their purposes are of a treasonable character."

In November, Allen Francis, the U.S. consul to British Columbia, reported that a rebel faction met in a saloon to stir secessionism and to seize a vessel from Vancouver Island to aid the Southern cause. Alvord applauded federally funded inducements of $150 to army volunteers and credited Union detectives with routing out sedition among secessionists east of the Cascade Mountains.

The late 1860s saw the emergence of law and order. Congress withheld $200,000 in Indian reparations, because reports from Secretary of the Interior James Harlan about Governor Lyon described him as a swindler. In 1865, workers organized the state's first labor union, the Owyhee Miners' League. By 1868, the state population approached 50,000, an uptick fueled by short-term speculators and profiteers.

Idaho took its present shape and developed a reputation among farmers for dry, cold weather suited to stock raising, orchards of pome and stone fruit, and the harvesting of grains, wild grasses, and wild rye. It acquired prominence in pioneer history for gold, lead, and silver strikes at Florence, Idaho City, Pierce, and Silver City and for the advance of transcontinental rail service in 1869. It earned the name "Gem State" for its deposits of agate, amethyst, jasper, onyx, opal, quartz crystal, sapphire, and star garnet and for unfounded rumors of diamond deposits. The settlement of Chinese laborers complicated the demographic picture, as did the arrival of black barbers, launderers, nurses, and wranglers to serve the mining camps.

By 1870, Idaho's population had reached 15,000. Despite political maneuvering in 1887 to obliterate the territory by dividing it between Nevada and Washington, President Grover Cleveland preserved the boundaries. Idaho entered the Union as the forty-third state on July 3, 1890.

See also: Joseph, Chief; Montana Territory; Washington Territory.

Further Reading

Blair, Karen J., ed. *Women in Pacific Northwest History.* Rev. ed. Seattle: University of Washington Press, 1988.

Gerassi, John. *The Boys of Boise: Furor, Vice and Folly in an American City.* Seattle: University of Washington Press, 2001.

Lamar, Howard R., ed. *The New Encyclopedia of the American West.* New Haven, CT: Yale University Press, 1998.

Morehouse, Stephen C., and Beaverhead County Museum. *Beaverhead County.* Charleston, SC: Arcadia, 2008.

Pomeroy, Earl S. *The Pacific Slope: A History of California, Oregon, Washington, Idaho, Utah, and Nevada.* Lincoln: University of Nebraska Press, 1991.

Immigration

Surges of immigration fueled America's rise to global dominance of agriculture, finance, industry, mining, and transportation. The 1860s saw the arrival of 2,081,261 immigrants; in the 1870s, the nation incurred a 7.6 percent rise in foreign-born citizens, to 2,742,287. A haven to those escaping the Irish potato famine, urban centers received newcomers who introduced artistic, cultural, and entrepreneurial diversity.

As a result of the immigrant influx of 1860, one-quarter of New Yorkers—204,000—were native-born Irish; in 1870, 1.8 million Americans claimed Irish birth. In Massachusetts, between 1860 and the 1870s, Boston's population ballooned 41 percent. East Boston, which comprised Armenians, Austrians, British, Canadians, Germans, Irish, Italians, Polish, Russians, and Scandinavians, developed into a waterfront metropolis. Incoming woodworkers and shipwrights constructed banks, churches, homes, hotels, schools, and shops, as well as schooners, factories, mills, warehouses, and yachts. Admitted under the Burlingame Treaty of 1868, Chinese laborers joined Jewish and Syrian workers at South Cove enclaves, where merchant Oong Arshowe opened Boston's first tea and coffee shop.

In New Jersey and New York throughout the 1870s, Hasids (ultra-orthodox Jews) from Belarus, Galicia,

A Thomas Nast cartoon in 1871 shows Columbia (the symbol of American ideals) protecting a Chinese immigrant and warning an Irish mob that "America means fair play for all men." Asian immigrants in particular aroused fears of ethnic "otherness." *(The Granger Collection, New York)*

Germany, Lithuania, Moldova, Poland, and Ukraine introduced Yiddish culture. Because of outsider clannishness, New York City's Lower East Side had the highest population density on the globe, the majority of them Jews born in Poland or Russia.

In the Pacific, among native-born sugar plantation laborers in Hawaii, Japanese workers dwelled apart and sent home for picture brides. Multilingual German-born Bishop Herman Koeckemann ministered to native Hawaiians and foreigners from the Philippines, Poland, Portugal, and Spain by conducting masses in their native languages.

Along the Atlantic Coast and Great Lakes, refugees arrived from the Old World with the intent of fleeing ethnic and religious persecution and mandatory military service, such as that ordered by Ottoman Sultan Abdul Hamid II. Because of a universal call-up of males to the military in the Austro-Hungarian Empire, the city of Cleveland, Ohio, became home to 13 Czech neighborhoods comprising 696 families.

Skilled workers answered the call of industrial recruiters. Youths such as the Japanese *Issei* (first generation) of San Francisco were labeled "birds of passage," because they intended to return home as soon as economic and political oppression ended in Japan. Seamstresses empowered the growing sweatshop industry by cutting and stitching cheap garments and housewares. Kinship provided a safety zone for the orphaned, elderly, homeless, sick, injured, and unemployed.

Cultural Mix

As settlers assimilated, community life flourished along with schools, churches and synagogues, and newspapers, including the *American Israelite, Arbeiter, Irish American, Jewish Messenger, L'Eco d'Italia, Messager Franco-Américain, Scandinavisk Post, Soziale Republic,* and *Volksblatt.* In Memphis, Tennessee, Germans and Italians had an impact on music societies, the forerunners of the Memphis Brass Band and the Memphis Symphony Orchestra.

In Baltimore, the nation's first Catholic archdiocese, Father James Gibbons assisted non-English speakers with housing and language problems and helped to Americanize and unify native and immigrant Catholics and to combat racism in labor unions. To ease urban crowding, he promoted colonization and land ownership in the Dakotas, Illinois, Iowa, Minnesota, Nebraska, and Wisconsin. Meanwhile, the South spurned European laborers and relied instead on agrarian profits from cotton, rice, sugar, and tobacco raised by black field hands, some of them newcomers from the Caribbean and China filling jobs left vacant by departing freedmen.

Overall, the nation had reason to be grateful for the toil and innovations of foreigners. Historians single out Bavarian immigrants Aaron Meier and Jeanette Hirsch Meier, founders of Meier & Frank in Portland, Oregon; Swedish rancher and sugar planter Svante Magnus Swenson; Chinese brewer Ho Ah Kow, who sued the city of San Francisco for the civil rights of jail inmates; and another city resident, herbalist Fong Dun Shung, who treated problem pregnancies, syphilis, and tuberculosis with indigenous plants.

In the Midwest, the Dakota Territory Bureau of Immigration and the Wisconsin Commission of Immigration welcomed alien colonists as stabilizers of towns and agriculture. To provide new arrivals with cash, commissioners set up bank exchanges to facilitate the transfer of funds and organized farmers' market days, a place to trade and barter produce and exchange news from home. In September 1874 near Topeka, some 1,500 Volga Russian

Mennonites introduced "Turkey Red" wheat, the hardy winter variety that made Kansas the nation's breadbasket.

Floridians owed the founding of the sport fishing and vacation haven of Fort Myers to Spanish mail boat captain Manuel A. Gonzalez and his Bahamian wife, Evalina J. Weatherford Gonzalez. German shipman Henry Burger of Manitowoc, Wisconsin, built full-rigged schooners for service on the Great Lakes. Portuguese sailor Bernardo Fernandez and Carlotta Cuadra Fernandez founded the waterfront economy of Pinole, California. More familiar to readers of American history are British actor and reformer Fanny Kemble; Canadian landscape artist Edward Bannister; Danish journalist Jacob Riis; German cartoonist Thomas Nast, lumber baron Frederick Weyerhäuser, and U.S. Secretary of the Interior Carl Schurz; Hungarian publisher Joseph Pulitzer; and three Scots—inventor Alexander Graham Bell, conservationist John Muir, and iron and steel magnate and philanthropist Andrew Carnegie.

Immigrants and Violence

The Civil War precipitated the exploitation of aliens. The Union army profited from volunteers Michael Corcoran and Thomas Francis Meagher, who recruited and led the Irish Brigade at the Battles of Bull Run and Antietam. President Abraham Lincoln saw incoming residents as replacements for casualties of the Civil War, which killed 620,000 and left some 55,000 disabled as amputees. His National Conscription Act (or Enrollment Act) of February 16, 1863, called up white males aged 20–45 and permitted a commutation fee of $300, by which draftees could hire substitute soldiers, usually poor immigrants. Speaking in ethnic terms, pacifists interpreted the call-up as a class-, faith-, and race-based quid pro quo—the sacrifice of German and Irish males to free black slaves.

At an emotional peak two days after the New York draft lottery, mobs erupted in tenements, where two-thirds of the populace was foreign born. From July 13 to 16, rioters from foundries, machine shops, railroads, shipyards, and street gangs plotted an ethnic uprising. In a show of class hatred toward the privileged, gangs of barbers, bootblacks, brick makers, coachmen, cooks, hod carriers, launderers, longshoremen, porters, stablemen, waiters, and whitewashers aimed to shake the municipal power structure. Because of the domination of Irish scrappers, Americans stigmatized them as unprincipled hoodlums. Encouraged by President Lincoln and Secretary of State William Henry Seward, Congress passed the Emigrant Aid Act of 1864, but stopped short of paying transatlantic passage for Danish, French, German, Icelandic, Norwegian, and Swedish men willing to fill vacancies in Union regiments.

By smearing aliens as spies, troublemakers, and promoters of atheism, drugs, and prostitution, white American bigots stirred nativism, anti-Catholicism, and anti-immigration antagonisms. Smallpox outbreaks in New York City and Philadelphia among uninoculated children from France and Germany raised suspicions of slum dwellers as perpetrators of infection. In Hawaii, a leprosy epidemic spurred nativist charges that Chinese immigrants carried the disease. In 1862, Congress restricted the transport of outsiders from China, the first racial group to arouse fear of ethnic "otherness." Federal agents discouraged smugglers by seizing the vessels that carried contract laborers to the West Coast. The Bureau of Immigration, a division of the U.S. Treasury, monitored the recruitment of Asian coolie labor. Although the Naturalization Act of 1870 barred Asians from citizenship, the inpouring of foreigners doubled.

The ongoing shift in demographics provoked social and labor clashes. Xenophobes boosted the Bowery Boys, Ku Klux Klan, Wide Awakes, and other pseudo-patriotic hate groups. Rumors alleged that aliens would overrun factory crews, forcing Americans into joblessness. To maintain national integrity and protect citizens from foreign undesirables and imported contagion, Congress on March 3, 1875, passed the Page Act, which barred the recruitment of Asian slave laborers, convicts, and prostitutes. The ban on Chinese women condemned America's Chinatowns to a bachelor society—male enclaves without wives and children. Temperance leaders stereotyped German and Irish Catholics as drunks, malcontents, and tools of the pope.

Nevertheless, outstanding peacemakers made inroads against prejudice. In Portland, Oregon, General Oliver Otis Howard befriended immigrant Chinese and countenanced mixed-race marriages. The New York City Mission Society ministered to urban have-nots by distributing 1.2 million evangelistic tracts in Armenian, Chinese, English, German, Italian, Polish, Russian, Spanish, and Yiddish. The society formed a visiting nurse corps and opened multilingual libraries and bathhouses for tenement families lacking bathing facilities. Home economics mavens Catharine Beecher and Harriet Beecher Stowe defended Irish immigrant maids and cooks from unsubstantiated charges of ignorance, filth, and larceny.

Deception of Aliens

The exploitation of strangers relied on language differences and unfamiliarity with patent law and labor standards. At Hartford, Connecticut, Samuel Colt acquired

European gunsmithy techniques from German machinists. Asian immigrants to Stockton, California, undertook menial jobs peddling produce, laundering, gardening, cooking, waiting tables, housekeeping, and tending children. In California, Nevada, Oregon, and Washington, Chinese and Japanese outsiders toiled on railroads and in mines and quarries at two-thirds the pay rates offered to white workers. In Pennsylvania coal mining camps, illiterate aliens from Czechoslovakia, Italy, Lithuania, and Poland incurred accidents because they were unable to read safety instructions written in English.

Plutocrats enriched themselves by firing and blacklisting disgruntled natives and replacing them with non-English-speaking aliens desperate for regular work. To lessen overhead costs in Chicago meatpacking houses, Philip Danforth Armour forced newcomers and ex-slaves to process animal carcasses at the rate of 13 per minute. Bethlehem Steel in Pennsylvania hired German or Irish immigrants to work 12-hour days shaping 20,000 tons (18,000 metric tons) of rails annually.

Immigrants became the dupes and victims of politicians and industrialists. Conservative Democrats relied on the bloc votes of Irish and German immigrants to defeat liberal candidates. East of the Mississippi River, the influx of Chinese, Germans, Irish, and Italians filled inner cities with slum dwellers left jobless after the postwar boom. Crime rates increased; prisons filled with corrupt guards and ungovernable inmates who brutalized each other. In Baltimore, the crowding of newcomers into docks, factories, ironworks, shipyards, and urban housing provoked the secretive American or "Know-Nothing" Party, notorious for its anti-immigrant rowdyism, street thuggery, and corrupt law enforcers and court judges.

In the West, the Union Pacific Railroad established the Wyoming Coal and Mining Company and hired Scandinavian immigrants to break a strike by working for $2 a day. A second strike at the Union Pacific Coal Department in Sweetwater and Washakie, Wyoming, in 1875 resulted in the hiring of 150 Chinese scabs, who proved dependable and hardworking.

During labor clashes in western Pennsylvania mines, Irish labor reformer Mary Harris "Mother" Jones coached uneducated immigrants to combat profiteers. To fight starvation and unfair labor practices in Reading, she educated laborers on capitalistic ploys that slashed wages by 80 percent and crushed collective bargaining. As a result, the U.S. Senate investigated complaints about working conditions and mine safety.

See also: Catholicism; Education; Hutterites.

Further Reading

Anbinder, Tyler. *Five Points: The 19th-Century New York City Neighborhood That Invented Tap Dance, Stole Elections, and Became the World's Most Notorious Slum.* New York: Simon & Schuster, 2001.

Bergquist, James M. *Daily Life in Immigrant America, 1820–1870.* Westport, CT: Greenwood, 2008.

Burlingame, Dwight F., ed. *Philanthropy in America: A Comprehensive Historical Encyclopedia.* Santa Barbara, CA: ABC-CLIO, 2004.

Jung, Moon-Ho. *Coolies and Cane: Race, Labor, and Sugar in the Age of Emancipation.* Baltimore: Johns Hopkins University Press, 2006.

Schaefer, Richard T., ed. *Encyclopedia of Race, Ethnicity, and Society.* Los Angeles: Sage, 2008.

Indian Appropriation Act of 1871

In 1871, the federal government altered its statutes and executive orders on Native Americans by recognizing them as a single ethnic entity rather than as members of separate tribes. As a means of ending the Indian Wars, the arbitrary shift in policy under President Ulysses S. Grant foreclosed a century of 372 treaties. Under international law, previous negotiators had honored sovereign indigenous nations with individual treaties, 140 of which provided for education through sectarian "contract" schools.

The abrupt legislation in 1871 resulted from a squabble between the U.S. House of Representatives and Senate over the appropriation of funds to the Yankton Sioux, who depended on federal food supplies after the virtual extermination of the buffalo. To save money, confusion, and time, at the direction of the House, the Indian Appropriation Act simplified the process of modifying white–Indian relations by issuing single messages to the native peoples as a whole rather than having to send federal ambassadors to each of 550 nations.

On March 3, Congress placed Indian negotiations in the hands of a guardian, Columbus Delano, head of the U.S. Department of the Interior. In an era of fraudulent land claims, racial segregation, and nepotism, Delano had the power to invalidate past treaties, establish nonsectarian "government" schools, and levy revenue tax on liquor and tobacco in native lands. By phasing out past treaties and dismantling the tribal structure, the law reclassified Indians as federal wards under the U.S. Constitution and demoted hereditary chiefs from positions of influence and authority. The legislation implied that

Indians were incapable of solving ethnic educational, medical, and relational dilemmas, particularly the problematic legal status of Native Americans in the United States.

The act recognized the nation's need to ensure the well-being of individual Indians and prefaced the instatement of natives as U.S. citizens. Felix Reville Brunot, an experienced observer of Indians in California, Colorado, Montana, Oregon, Washington, and Wyoming, provided worthy advice. As chair of the ten-man Board of Indian Commissioners, Brunot supported Grant's peacemaking policy toward an unfortunate race deserving of justice and mercy. In addition to fostering Christian missions and literacy training, Brunot proclaimed it his duty to help assimilate and transform Native Americans into responsible, self-supporting U.S. citizens. He undertook the task of supervising accounts and vouchers, investigating contracts and cash outlays, inspecting goods purchased for reservations, and auditing the records of Indian Bureaus. Supporting Brunot's theories of native settlement, Quaker artist Vincent Colyer, who served as secretary of the Board of Indian Commissioners, surveyed Alaska, Kansas, Oklahoma, Oregon, and Washington and recommended more emphasis on schooling and health care.

In a less benign treatise, *The Indian Question* (1874), Francis Amasa Walker, a skeptical superintendent of Indian affairs, concurred with the act but for different reasons. He agreed with the guardian–ward relationship as a means of keeping "beggar-like," "cowardly," "cunning," "false," "heathen," "lazy," "mean," and "thieving" Indians permanently on lands that lacked agrarian and mineral value.

Subsequent lawsuits challenged the wording of the Indian Appropriation Act of 1871 concerning the acquisition of Indian lands and the enforcement of civil and criminal law on reservations. Despite the unwillingness of legislators to respect individual power structures, by 1911, Congress had ratified 73 additional "agreements" with tribes, mostly concerning the cession of land to whites.

Further Reading

Brown, Dee. *The American West.* New York: Simon & Schuster, 1995.

———. *Bury My Heart at Wounded Knee: An Indian History of the American West.* New York: Holt, Rhinehart and Winston, 1970.

Johansen, Bruce E., and Donald A. Grinde, Jr. *The Encyclopedia of Native American Biography.* New York: Da Capo, 1998.

Lamar, Howard R., ed. *The New Encyclopedia of the American West.* New Haven, CT: Yale University Press, 1998.

Schaefer, Richard T., ed. *Encyclopedia of Race, Ethnicity, and Society.* Los Angeles: Sage, 2008.

Waldman, Carl. *Who Was Who in Native American History: Indians and Non-Indians from Early Contacts Through 1900.* New York: Facts on File, 1990.

Wilson, James. *The Earth Shall Weep: A History of Native America.* New York: Atlantic Monthly Press, 1999.

Indian Reservations

The Indian Removal Act, passed by the U.S. Congress in 1830, called for the relocation of all Indians living east of the Mississippi River to lands to the west. Most of the approximately 100,000 natives who survived the removal settled in Indian Territory in present-day Oklahoma. The extensive areas acquired by the United States in the Mexican-American War of 1846–1848 were home to another 150,000 indigenous people, whom U.S. armed forces would fight for decades to subjugate. The Indian Appropriations Act, passed by Congress in 1851, marked the beginning of a new effort by federal military enforcers to herd native tribes onto reservations.

In a diary entry on December 4, 1862, Secretary of the Navy Gideon Welles recoiled from counterproposals by U.S. congressmen from Minnesota to execute 300 native captives, an idea too horrible to contemplate. He wrote, "To take the lives of these ignorant barbarians by whole, after they have surrendered themselves prisoners, it would see the sentiments of the representatives were but slightly removed from the barbarians whom they would execute."

The pace of settling Indians on reservations picked up after General William Tecumseh Sherman, demobilized from the Civil War, took command of the Military Division of the Missouri, with jurisdiction from the Mississippi Valley to the Rocky Mountains. To shield railroads from Indian forays and to otherwise suppress native peoples, he assigned tribes to identifiable territories and judged all Indians off reservations to be hostile and worthy of death. As a means of quelling Indian revolts, he ordered General Philip Henry Sheridan to destroy the buffalo and thereby starve Plains nations. Sheridan attacked native camps during the winter when cold weather weakened tribes due to limited food supplies and mobility.

Some 8,000 Mescalero Apache and Navajo were settled at Fort Sumner, New Mexico, between 1863 and 1868. In this same period, the Cheyenne remained virtually homeless. Along the Powder River in Wyoming, General Patrick Edward Connor attempted to end forays on Western settlers traveling the Bozeman Trail and the Powder River Road. The creation of reserves led to the systematic incarceration of Western tribes in compounds resembling prisons or concentration camps.

American Indian Reservations

Reservation	Location	Founded	Tribes
Abiquin	Abiquin, N.Mex.	1874	Jicarilla Apache, Capote Ute, Wiminuche Ute
Alsea	Waldport, Ore.	August 11, 1855	Alsea, Coosa, Sinselaus Sioux, Umpqua
Blackfeet	Browning, Mont.	1851	Blackfeet, Blood
Bois Forte	Nett Lake, Minn.	1866	Bois Forte Chippewa
Bosque Redondo	Pecos Valley, N.Mex.	January 6, 1864	Mescalero Apache, Navajo
Brazos	Young County, Tex.	summer 1854	Anadarko, Caddo, Tonkawa, Waco
Cahuilla	Palm Springs, Calif.	1877	Cahuilla
Camp Apache	Payson, Ariz.	July 1869	Chilion, Coyotero Apache
Camp Grant	Tucson, Ariz.	1863	Aravaipa Apache
Camp Verde	Camp Verde, Ariz.	April 23, 1875	Mojave Apache
Canada Alamosa	Horse Springs, Ariz.	1877	Mogollan Apache
Capitan Grande	Lakeside, Calif.	1875	Kumeyaay, Viejas
Carlin Farms	Elko, Nev.	May 10, 1877	Western Shoshone
Chehalis	Grays Harbor, Wash.	July 8, 1864	Cahokiam, Chehalis, Chinock, Clatsop, Cowlitz, Hamptolop
Cherokee Nation	Tahlequah, Okla.	1839	Cherokee
Cheyenne-Arapaho	Concho, Okla.	February 18, 1861	Kiowa-Apache, Northern Cheyenne, Sans Arc Apache, Southern Arapaho, Staked Plain Apache
Cheyenne River	Eagle Butte, S.Dak.	1868	Blackfeet Sioux, Cuthead Sioux, Minneconjou, Sans Arc, Two Kettle Sioux
Chiricahua	Apache Pass, Ariz.	fall 1872	Chimehueva, Chiricahua Apache
Choctaw Nation	Idabel, Okla.	1820	Choctaw
Cimarron	Cimarron, N.Mex.	1850	Muache Ute
Coeur d'Alene	Coeur d'Alene, Idaho	November 8, 1873	Coeur d'Alene
Colorado River	Julesburg, Colo.	March 3, 1865	Chimehuevi, Chilion, Coahuilla, Cocopa, Hualpai, Mojave, Walapai, Yuma
Courte Oreille	Hayward, Wis.	1872	Lac Courte Oreille Chippewa
Creek Nation	Ocmulgee, Okla.	1867	Creek, Seminole
Crow Creek	Crow Creek, S.Dak.	1862	Crow Creek Sioux, Dakota, Nakota
Denver	Denver	1868	Ute
Devil's Lake	Devil's Lake, N.Dak.	1871	Santee Dakota, Wahpeton Sioux
Flathead	Ronan, Mont.	July 9, 1855	Flathead, Kootenay, Pend d'Oreilles
Fort Berthold	Fort Berthold, N.Dak.	April 12, 1870	Arikara, Gros Ventre, Mandan
Fort Colville	Colville, Wash.	April 9, 1872	Calispell, Chelan, Colville, Entiat, Lake, Metho, Moses Columbia, Nespectum, Nespelem, Okanaga, Palu, San Poel, Southern Columbia, Spokane, Wenatchi
Fort Hall	Fort Hall, Idaho	1863	Bannock, Bruneau, Fort Hall Shoshone
Fort Lemhi	Salmon, Idaho	1875	Lemhi Shoshone
Fort Peck	Poplar, S.Dak.	1871	Assiniboine, Sioux
Fort Sill	Comanche County, Okla.	June 2, 1875	Comanche
Fort Stanton	Fort Stanton, N.Mex.	1871	Jicarilla Apache, Mescalero Apache
Gila River	Phoenix, Ariz.	1859	Gila Apache

(continued)

American Indian Reservations *(continued)*

Reservation	Location	Founded	Tribes
Grande Ronde	Eugene, Ore.	June 30, 1857	Calapooia, Clackama, Cow Creek, Kalapuya, Luckamute, Mollalu, Mollel, Nehalim, Nestucalip, Nextucca, Oregon, Route River, Salmon River Santaim, Shasta, Tillamook, Upper Chinook, Wappato, Yamhill
Grand River	Gren River, S.Dak	1868	Blackfeet Sioux, Hunkpapa, Sans Arc, Yankton Sioux
Great Nemaha	Falls City, Neb.	July 15, 1830	Fox, Iowa, Sac
Great Sioux	Black Hills, S.Dak., and Boyd County, Neb.	1868	Teton Sioux
Green Bay	Green Bay, Wis.	February 3, 1838	Menominee, Oneida
Hoopa Valley	Hoopa, Calif.	1864	Humboldt, Hunsatung, Hupa, Klamath, Miskeet, Redwood, Saiaz, Sermolton, Sia, Tishlanaton
Jicarilla Apache	Dulce, N.Mex.	1875	Jicarilla Apache
Jocko	Arlee, Mont.	1872	Flathead
Kansas	Topeka, Kans.	1846	Kansa
Kiowa-Comanche	Hobart, Lawton, and Anadarko, Okla.	July 20, 1867	Comanche, Delaware, Kiowa, Staked Plain Apache
Klamath	Chiloquin, Ore.	1864	Coahuila, Klamath, Modoc, Snake
Lac du Flambeau	Vilas County, Wis.	1854	Lac De Flambeau Chippewa
Lake Superior	Fond du Lac, Minn.	1854	Fond du Lac Chippewa, Ottawa, Potawatomi
Lake Traverse	Roberts County, S.Dak.	1869	Sisseton Sioux, Wahpeton Sioux
La Pointe	La Pointe, Wis.	1836	Bad River Chippewa, Boise Forte Chippewa, Lake Superior Chippewa, Mississippi Chippewa
Leech Lake	Cass County, Minn.	1855	Pillager Chippewa, Winnebagoshish Chippewa
Los Coyotes	Los Coyotes, Calif.	January 31, 1870	Cahuilla, Diegueño, San Luis Rey, Serrano, Temecula
Madison	Kitsap County, Wash.	January 22, 1855	S'Klallam, Skokomish, Twana
Makah	Flattery, Wash.	January 31, 1855	Makah
Malheur	Lake Malheur, Ore.	September 12, 1872	Bannock, Chasta, Northern Paiute
Maricopa	Gila River, Ariz.	February 28, 1859	Maricopa, Pima
Mescalero	Otero County, N.Mex.	1849	Lipan and Mescalero Apache
Milk River	Fort Assiniboine, Mont.	October 1868	Assiniboine, Hunkpatina Sioux, River Crow, Santee Dakota, Teton Sioux, Yankton Sioux
Moapa River	Moapa River, Nev.	March 1875	Chemehuevi, Kaibab, Pawipit, Paiute, Shivwit
Modoc	Miami, Okla.	1873	Modoc
Mountain Crow	Billings, Mont.	July 15, 1868	Mountain Crow
Muckleshoot	Muckleshoot Prairie, Wash.	1874	Muckleshoot
Muddy Lake	Muddy Lake, Nev.	1860	Shoshone, Timapanago
Navajo	Chuska Mountains, Ariz.	June 1, 1868	Navajo
Nez Percé	Lapwai, Idaho	June 9, 1863	Nez Percé
Nisqually	Thurston County, Wash.	December 26, 1854	Nisqually
Northern Cheyenne	Lame Deer, Mont.	1877	Northern Cheyenne

(continued)

American Indian Reservations *(continued)*

Reservation	Location	Founded	Tribes
Oakland	Oakland County, Okla.	1858	Nez Percé, Ponca, Tonkawa
Ojo Caliente	Grant County, N.Mex.	1868	Chiricahua Apache
Omaha	Thurston County, Neb.	1856	Omaha
Oneida	Hobart and Oneida, Wis.	1838	Oneida
Osage	Osage County, Okla.	1872	Osage
Oto	Otoe, Neb.	1854	Missouri, Oto
Pembina	Great Falls, Minn.	1868	Pembina Chippewa
Piegan	Browning, Mont.	1858	Piegan Blackfeet
Pine Ridge	Pine Ridge, S.Dak.	1868	Oglala Sioux
Ponca	Niobrara, Neb.	1858	Ponca
Port Isabel	Yuma, Ariz.	1853	Cocopah
Potawatomi	Topeka, Kans.	1846	Potawatomi
Puyallup	Tacoma, Wash.	December 22, 1854	Puyallup
Pyramid Lake	Pyramid Lake, Nev.	1875	Paiute, Ute
Quapaw	Quapaw, Okla.	1877	Fox, Kaskaskia, Kansa, Meeto, Miami, Modoc, Nez Percé, Omaha, Osage, Ottawa, Peoria, Piankeshaw, Ponca, Quapaw, Seneca, Shawnee, Wea, Wyandotte
Quinaielt	Grays Harbor, Wash.	1854	Hoh, Quilehute, Quinaielt, Quit
Red Cliff	Sandy Lake, Wis.	1854	Red Cliff Chippewa
Red Cloud	Fort Robinson, Neb.	August 1873	Brulé Sioux, Northern Arapaho, Northern Cheyenne, Oglala Sioux
Rio Verde	Wickenburg, Ariz.	October 1871	Tonto Apache, Yavapai, Yuma Apache
River Crow	Bighorn, Mont.	1868	River Crow
Rosebud	Rosebud, S.Dak.	1868	Rosebud Sioux
Round Valley	Round Valley, Calif.	April 18, 1864	Clear Lake, Concon, Little Lake, Nomelaki, Pitt River, Potter Valley, Redwood, Wailaki, Wylacki, Yuki
Sac and Fox	Stroud, Okla.	1869	Fox, Kickapoo, Sac, Shawnee
Salt Lake	Salt Lake, Utah	1861	Weber Ute, Zuni
San Carlos	San Carlos, Ariz.	1872	Aravaipa Apache, Chiricahua Apache, Pinal Apache, Tonto Apache, Yavapai
Sand Creek	Sand Creek, Colo.	1864	Southern Cheyenne
San Sebastian	San Sebastian, Calif.	July 22, 1863	Tejon
Santee Dakota	Niobrara, Neb.	1862	Santee Dakota
San Xavier	Sells, Ariz.	1874	Papago
Shoalwater Bay	Willapa Bay, Wash.	1866	Shoalwater Bay
Shoshone	Fort Washakie, Wyo.	1869	Bannock, Shoshone, Ute
Siletz	Siletz, Ore.	1856	Naltunnetunne
Skokomish	Skokomish, Wash.	1855	Chimakum
Spanish Fork	Spanish Fork, Utah	1859	Ute
Squaxin	Squaxin Island, Wash.	December 26, 1854	Squaxin

(continued)

American Indian Reservations *(continued)*

Reservation	Location	Founded	Tribes
Standing Rock	Standing Rock, S.Dak.	February 28, 1877	Blackfeet, Hunkpapa, Yankton Sioux
Stockbridge	Ashland, Wis.	1871	Mohican, Stockbridge
Tongue River	Tongue River, Mont.	1877	Northern Cheyenne
Tulalip	Mukilteo, Wash.	January 22, 1855	Tulalip
Tule River	Tulare County, Calif.	1864	Keawah, Manache, Owen River, Tejon, Tule, Wichumni
Turtle Mountain	Belcourt, N.Dak.	December 21, 1882	Minnesota Chippewa
Uintah	Uintah Valley, Utah	October 3, 1861	Cumumba, Pahvant, Sanpitch, Sheberetch, Tumpanuwac, and Uinta-at Ute
Umatilla	Pendleton, Ore.	June 9, 1855	Cayuse, Umatilla, Walla Walla
Upper Milk River	Milk River, Mont.	1868	Assiniboin, Gros Ventre, River Crow
Upper Missouri	Helena, Mont.	1869	Brulé Sioux, Yankton Sioux
Ute	Ignacio, Colo.	1868	Ute
Walker River	Schurz, Nev.	1859	Northern Paiute
Warm Springs	Wasco County, Ore.	June 25, 1855	Terrino, Warm Spring, Wasco
Washoe	Washoe County, Nev.	July 10, 1865	Washoe
Whetstone Creek	Lower Brulé, S.Dak.	1866	Lower Brulé Sioux
White Earth	White Earth, Minn.	1867	Grand Portage Chippewa, White Earth Chippewa
Wichita	Wichita, Kans.	1867	Delaware, Ionie, Keechie, Pawnee, Penetethka Comanche, Tawacanie, Towaccaro, Waco, Wichita
Wind River	Wind River, Wyo.	1868	Northern Arapaho, Eastern Shoshone
Winnebago	Camp Winnebago, Neb.	1865	Winnebago
Yainax	Klamath Lake, Ore.	1864	Klamath, Modoc, Yahuskin
Yakama	Yakima County, Wash.	1855	Kahmiltpa, Klikatat, Kowassay, Ochechole, Palouse, Pisquose, Seapeat, Shyick, Siaywa, Skinpa, Tlingit, Winatchepum, Wisham, Yakama
Yankton	Charles Mix County, S.Dak.	April 19, 1858	Yankton Sioux
Zuñi	McKinley County, N.Mex.	March 16, 1877	Zuñi

Source: Klaus Frantz, *Indian Reservations in the United States: Territory, Sovereignty, and Socioeconomic Change,* Chicago: University of Chicago Press, 1999.

To save money and military effort, President Ulysses S. Grant in his State of the Union address on December 4, 1871, proposed a "Peace Policy" as a solution to the Indian problem. His plan called for the reorganization of the Office of Indian Affairs and the hiring of religious leaders to supervise agencies and Christian schools with the goal of preparing Native Americans for citizenship.

In June 1872, the secretary of the interior assigned legislator James A. Garfield to ease an impasse in Montana Territory by parlaying with Chief Charlot and forcing the Flathead off Bitterroot lands and onto the Jocko Indian Reservation. Charlot refused, and Garfield insulted him by dealing with lesser authority, chiefs Adolph and Arlee. Afterwards, the Office of Indian Affairs published a false report that Charlot had agreed to the removal.

In Colorado, on September 13, 1873, U.S. Commissioner of Indian Affairs Felix Brunot completed the Brunot Treaty (also known as the San Juan Cession), removing 4 million acres (1.6 million hectares) from the area of the Ute Reservation in San Juan County. Another blow to Indian autonomy, the treaty, negotiated with railroad promoter Otto Mears and Indian agent Charles Adams, opened traditional Indian territory to silver miners and settlers. The settlement of the Ute on the San Juan County reservation proved short-lived, however, as increased white insurgency required another removal in summer 1875, this time, to the Uncompahgre River Valley. The establishment of cattle ranches in the region drove wild game farther from the Ute, leaving them dependent on government issues of dried beef.

Meanwhile, among the Ponca, Chief Standing Bear earned respect for defying U.S. government orders to settle on reservations. A peace lover born in Nebraska on the Omaha Reservation, he grew up at the mouth of the Niobrara River on the northeastern boundary of the Dakotas, where his nomadic people hunted buffalo and ample wild game and raised vegetables and corn. Belligerent Sioux forced the Ponca off their traditional hunting grounds south and east of Butte. In 1858, Standing Bear's people moved south to 96,000 acres (39,000 hectares) in Boyd and Knox counties in Nebraska. By the terms of the Treaty of Fort Laramie of 1868, which ended the Powder River War, government agents inadvertently assigned Ponca land to the Great Sioux Reservation farther east and south. As a result, the Ponca lost traditional burial grounds between the Niobrara and Ponca Creek. To halt Sioux raids on Ponca goods and livestock and to circumvent an Indian war, Secretary of the Interior Carl Schurz stripped the Ponca of their property in 1876.

With the cooperation of Standing Bear, the Ponca and Indian agents surveyed the promised permanent homeland on the Osage Reserve in Osage County, Oklahoma. Standing Bear rejected it, because the land was not arable. On February 21, 1877, he and seven chiefs began a winter march north over the prairie to their former land and reached home on April 2, 1877. In May, soldiers marched 681 members south to the Quapaw Reserve in the northeastern corner of Oklahoma Territory. Both Black Elk and Standing Bear lost daughters to the dangerous journey.

In 1879, after one-third of the population died of starvation and malaria during the first year in Oklahoma, Standing Bear led his people north to their former lands on the Omaha Reservation. After a decade of bloody Indian wars, politicians scrapped Grant's Peace Policy as unworkable and Indian agencies as corrupt and cruel.

See also: Buffalo Soldiers; Bureau of Indian Affairs; Child, Lydia Maria; Cochise; Crazy Horse; Geronimo; Sitting Bull.

Further Reading

Brown, Dee. *The American West.* New York: Simon & Schuster, 1995.

———. *Bury My Heart at Wounded Knee: An Indian History of the American West.* New York: Holt, Rinehart and Winston, 1970.

Gibson, Arrell Morgan. *The History of Oklahoma.* Norman: University of Oklahoma Press, 1984.

Johansen, Bruce E., and Donald A. Grinde, Jr. *The Encyclopedia of Native American Biography.* New York: Da Capo, 1998.

Marks, Paula Mitchell. *In a Barren Land: American Indian Dispossession and Survival.* New York: William Morrow, 1998.

Mathes, Valerie Sherer, and Richard Lowitt. *The Standing Bear Controversy: Prelude to Indian Reform.* Urbana: University of Illinois Press, 2003.

Michno, Gregory. *The Deadliest Indian War in the West: The Snake Conflict, 1864–1868.* Caldwell, ID: Caxton, 2007.

Wilson, James. *The Earth Shall Weep: A History of Native America.* New York: Atlantic Monthly Press, 1999.

Industry and Manufacturing

In the third quarter of the nineteenth century, the United States began its rise from an agrarian economy to an industrialized superpower. By 1860, manufacturing netted a return of $800 million from the production of $1.9 billion in goods. During four years of the Civil War, small operators set aside ideas ready for domestic merchandising, such as the ironworks and carriage and harness factory at Baton Rouge, Louisiana, which closed in 1861 when employees left for military service. Instead, the war spurred the rapid output of uniforms, boots, blankets, Colt revolvers, Christian Spencer's lever-action seven-shot carbine, and Richard Jordan Gatling's machine gun.

Individual contributions to the Industrial Revolution were initially modest, including the production of barbed wire, canned fruit, celluloid, electric lightbulbs, Elgin watches, and grain threshers. In the Adirondack Mountains of New York, the town of Malone processed 21,000 pounds (9,525 kilograms) of wool from 9,000 sheep to make Franklin County a top milling operation. At Chicopee, Massachusetts, the manufacture of agricultural tools derived from the invention of the Yankee Blade, a self-sharpening edge requiring emery and oil abraded in a reverse motion. At Redding, Connecticut, the weaving of wire cloth at the Gilbert and Bennett factory in 1861 stimulated a demand for door and window screening against insects, an innovation that enhanced home hygiene and community sanitation.

Revolutionary shifts in postwar energy sources produced dramatic change. The demise of water and wood as fuels was predictable. At Fayette, Michigan, colliers hewed forests for charcoal and sold denuded land to farmers. Within 24 years, the cost of hauling logs to blast furnaces ruined the business, a collapse that also struck New Jersey ironworks. The application of the Bessemer steel process to railroads and steam boilers replaced animal, human, and water power for transportation and industry. By 1870, steam engines generated more thrust than waterwheels, as at the silk mills in Paterson, New Jersey, and for turbines at the Lowell, Massachusetts, textile factories.

Destruction of the nation's infrastructure—bridges, highways, and trestles, such as the dams and raceways destroyed by Confederate forces at Harpers Ferry, Virginia—required replacement, which engineers crafted out of steel, a new material that was stronger than iron. Discoveries of coal and oil in Pennsylvania and iron ore along Lake Michigan and Lake Superior nourished the factory system with raw materials. Simultaneously, steel improved farm yields with stronger, lighter plows, harrows, and reapers. At the Springfield Armory in 1870, artisans profited from fine-honed steel tools that attained a precision of two-thousandths of an inch.

The Industrial Economy

Economist David Ames Wells, a proponent of global free trade, foresaw a viable economy based on the expansion of industrial wealth and the collection of taxes to retire the national debt. As a means of attracting venture capital for daring enterprise, the corporation replaced individual and partnered ownership of such patented innovations as machines that canned food in tins, knitted and serged clothing, and separated kerosene from petroleum. The sale of stock drew a variety of investors looking for limited liability for their capital.

With the advent of print advertising in black and white and in color, name-brand products dotted the commercial landscape—Alexander Graham Bell's telephone, George M. Pullman's railcars, Eliphalet Remington's typewriter, Richard Joshua Reynolds's cigarettes, Isaac Merritt Singer's domestic sewing machine, John Batterson Stetson's hats, Levi Strauss's blue jeans, George Westinghouse's train engines, and Linus Yale's padlocks.

Images popularized luxury items and a more cosmopolitan attitude toward the home and personal costume. Other products contributed magazine images of food and wellness—Philip Danforth Armour's processed meats, Gail Borden's condensed milk, Charles and Maximilian Fleischmann's yeast cakes, Henry J. Heinz's ketchup, Hires Root Beer, John Harvey Kellogg's and Will Keith Kellogg's breakfast cereals, Eli Lilly's pharmaceuticals, Charles Pillsbury's flour, Lydia Pinkham's tonics, Quaker Mills's oatmeal, Baron Justus Von Liebig's infant food, and Thomas Bramwell Welch's pasteurized grape juice. The explosion of industrial wealth dropped prices and credit rates and raised real income by 60 percent. For machinists, welders, and seamstresses, regular employment improved

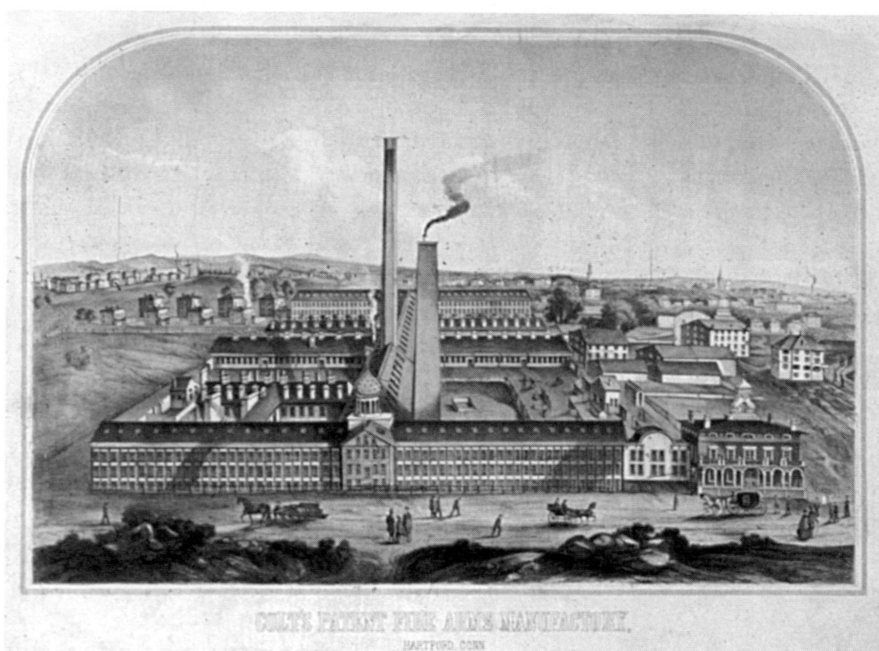

The Colt firearms factory in Hartford, Connecticut, pictured here in 1865, pioneered mass-produced weapons with interchangeable metal parts. The Civil War and the movement west spurred production of Colt revolvers. *(MPI/Stringer/Getty Images)*

family cash flow to pay for improved nutrition for their families.

West of the Mississippi River, factory work improved the nation's trade and transportation. Anheuser-Busch Brewery delivery vans distributed German beer to the environs of St. Louis, Missouri. Whitewater, Wisconsin, thrived from the manufacture of transport wagons, a favorite of frontier families. In 1862, George Black Russell's Detroit Car Works employed 75 men to build $60,000 worth of freight cars for the Michigan Southern & Cincinnati Air Line Railroad and a similar order for the Detroit & Milwaukee and Grand Trunk railways. On August 20, 1870, the Kimball Manufacturing Company of San Francisco completed two of the first two horsecars for Sacramento and prospered from the production of cable cars, omnibuses, and steam rolling stock.

From 1870 to 1880, manufacturing increased from 60 percent to 74 percent of the gross national product and boosted consumerism. As the United States became industrialized, the rise of the robber barons—Jay Cooke, Andrew Carnegie, J. Pierpont Morgan, John D. Rockefeller, Leland Stanford, and Cornelius Vanderbilt—attested to the control of finance, oil and coal, railroads, telegraph, and steel mills by monopolies. The unfair competition overwhelmed small businesses, which could not afford cutthroat price cutting and advanced technology, such as belt-driven McKay sole stitchers and Goodyear welt machines for the shoemaking and saddlery industry. Despite the cost to the underdog, the Centennial Exhibition of 1876 in Philadelphia glorified a model of industrial horsepower, the Corliss Centennial Engine, the world's largest steam engine.

The Factory Worker

The removal of laborers from the outdoors to factories and mills introduced environmental hazards. The most vulnerable, underage workers, toiled for $1 per day amid complex, high-speed and dangerous pulleys and gears. In 1870, French Canadians migrating to Lowell, Massachusetts, to work in textile factories incurred a higher death rate from respiratory failure. Historians blamed untenable living conditions in Little Canada (Pawtucketville) for worker debility from brown lung, pneumonia, and tuberculosis. Contributing to vision and respiratory illness among weavers, the whirling of cotton fibers from spinning wheels and drums jeopardized eyes, mouth, nose, and lungs.

Sweatshops profited from the labors of immigrants and women, who produced cheap garments and housewares at low piece rates. In crowded facilities, they tolerated steamy environments that spread consumption and endangered workers with factory fires. Following the Great Chicago Fire of 1871, insurance firms influenced the style and materials that companies chose to build factories. More significant to socioeconomics, the control of prosperity by a few generated the nation's first permanent working class. Its members suffered cyclical depressions and irregular employment, such as the 3 million jobs lost during the Panic of 1873.

The drive for efficiency and speed beset workers with noise and hazard from fatigue and accidents, as well as the dehumanization of people trying to keep up with machines, such as the multispool Furbush loom, which wove three-color patterns and plaids. Labor leaders began to see the wisdom of limiting the workday to ten hours, a concession that 20,000 striking shoemakers in Lynn, Massachusetts, demanded in 1860. To the detriment of the laboring class, the country lacked trade unions until 1868, when the Knights of Labor geared up for 21 successful labor candidacies for the Massachusetts legislature. The women's movement and the Women's Christian Temperance Union harnessed the outrage of wives and mothers against the virtual enslavement of factory workers and against the appeal of saloons and taverns as a solace to demoralized wage earners.

Until the intervention of the U.S. government in fair labor practices, the only recourse for the individual factory employee was unionizing, strikes, and collective bargaining, tactics that imperiled the bold. By 1890, federal authorities involved themselves more intimately with the work of individuals and corporations and the inequalities of urban industrialism.

See also: Bicycles; Labor and Labor Unions; Pillsbury, Charles Alfred; Railroads; Technology and Invention; Weapons.

Further Reading

Baldwin, Neil. *Edison: Inventing the Century.* Chicago: University of Chicago Press, 2001.

Gordon, Robert B., and Patrick M. Malone. *The Texture of Industry: An Archaeological View of the Industrialization of North America.* New York: Oxford University Press, 1994.

Hapke, Laura. *Sweatshop: The History of an American Idea.* New Brunswick, NJ: Rutgers University Press, 2004.

Klein, Maury. *The Genesis of Industrial America, 1870–1920.* Oxford, UK: Oxford University Press, 2007.

Whitten, David O., and Bessie E. Whitten. *The Birth of Big Business in the United States, 1860–1914: Commercial, Extractive, and Industrial Enterprise.* Westport, CT: Greenwood, 2006.
Wolff, David A. *Industrializing the Rockies: Growth, Competition, and Turmoil in the Coalfields of Colorado and Wyoming, 1868–1914.* Boulder: University Press of Colorado, 2003.

Internal Revenue Act of 1864

From 1861 to 1865, the need for funding for the Civil War required a series of federal taxes on citizen wealth. Secretary of the Treasury Salmon P. Chase attempted to finance the Army of the Potomac by borrowing funds and by collecting customs duties and tariffs. The latter method fluctuated, depending on the success of the Confederate navy at interfering with Northern shipping. Surprisingly, at a total of $3 billion, the conflict proved more costly than predicted.

President Abraham Lincoln rejected the imposition of a property tax at the suggestion of Chase and Thaddeus Stevens, chairman of the House Ways and Means Committee. Such a tax would overburden Western landowners, Lincoln believed, and would not consider intangible income from bonds, cash, mortgages, and stocks. Instead, the president signed the Revenue Act of 1861, which levied a flat-rate tax, a temporary emergency impost collected by individual states. The rates were 3 percent on income over $800 and 5 percent on the income of expatriates. Meanwhile, national indebtedness rose at the rate of $2 million per day.

Within a year, tax collection became more complicated and bureaucratic. On July 1, 1862, a second Revenue Act created the Office of Internal Revenue and replaced the initial flat rate with a progressive 3 percent tax on incomes over $600 and a 5 percent tax on incomes over $10,000. The levy extended for only 12 months and empowered the commissioner of internal revenue, George S. Boutwell, to require paymasters to withhold the impost from soldiers, civil servants, and U.S. congressmen.

On June 30, 1864, Lincoln increased tax rates based on citizens' ability to pay—5 percent on incomes from $600 to $5,000, 7.5 percent on earnings from $5,000 to $10,000, and 10 percent on incomes of $10,000 or more. The returns were due on the first Monday in May. Additional taxes applied to inheritance, manufactured goods, and warehouse inventories and required federal adhesive stamps for the sale of billiard tables, carriages, cosmetics, documents, furs, gas, horses, jewelry, liquor, magazines, matches, medicine, newspaper advertising, paint, perfume, photographs, playing cards, processed food, soap, sweets, tobacco, and yachts. The extent of excise taxes and the calculation of fines for nonpayment and fraud caused Boutwell to describe the bureau as the largest federal department ever organized. The law tripled the annual collection to $61 million, 75 percent of which derived from the Northeast.

A lawsuit challenged the Internal Revenue Act of 1864 for its application to salaries as well as to gains from realty, rent, interest, and dividends. Attorney and tariff reformer William McKendree Springer of Springfield, Illinois, challenged the law in 1865 by refusing to pay $4,799 exacted on $50,798 in income, which derived from his professional practice and from interest on U.S. bonds. Springer protested in writing a law that he declared unconstitutional and void. On March 15, 1867, tax collector David Littler sold Springer's house and adjacent barn to retire the tax debt and a penalty of $480.78. The U.S. Supreme Court, in an opinion by Justice Noah Haynes Swayne, upheld the law and rejected Springer's suit, which claimed that federal agents cited the wrong date on which Congress amended the law.

Expiration of the Internal Revenue Act in 1873 ended a levy that, over nine years, netted $340 million.

See also: Chase, Salmon P.; Cooke, Jay.

Further Reading

Blankson, Samuel. *A Brief History of Taxation.* Hammersmith, UK: Lulu, 2007.
Conlin, Joseph R. *The American Past: A Survey of American History.* 9th ed. Boston: Wadsworth/Cengage Learning, 2009.
Hall, Kermit L., ed. *The Oxford Guide to United States Supreme Court Decisions.* New York: Oxford University Press, 1999.
Horwitz, Morton J. *The Transformation of American Law, 1870–1960: The Crisis of Legal Orthodoxy.* New York: Oxford University Press, 1992.
Kersch, Ken I. *Constructing Civil Liberties: Discontinuities in the Development of American Constitutional Law.* Cambridge, UK: Cambridge University Press, 2004.

Jacobs, Harriet (1813–1897)

An eyewitness contributor of the female perspective on human bondage, activist and teacher Harriet Ann Jacobs escaped sexual enslavement and published a memoir of a mother's life on the run. The mulatto granddaughter of a white planter at Edenton, North Carolina, she was born on February 11, 1813. She and her younger brother John were the slaves of Margaret Horniblow, who taught Harriet needlework, reading, and spelling. At the death of their parents, carpenter Daniel Jacobs and breeder Delilah Horniblow, Harriet worked from age six into her preteens as a house servant before becoming caregiver to Mary Matilda Norcom, the two-year-old daughter of Dr. James and Mary Matilda Norcom.

At age 15, Harriet evaded the sexual advances of James Norcom, who refused to let her wed a freedman carpenter. In self-defense, she became the mistress of North Carolina legislator Samuel Tredwell Sawyer. From their secret affair, she bore two children, Joseph S. Jacobs in 1829 and Louisa Matilda Jacobs in 1833. Norcom used the children as bargaining tools to entrap Jacobs. Harriet concealed their father's name and hid them in the cottonmouth-infested Carolina swamps to prevent their sale as chattel.

Advised by Bishop Daniel Payne, a black Underground Railroad transporter, Jacobs fled slavery in June 1835. She provided the details of her escape in *Incidents in the Life of a Slave Girl* (1861), which she began writing in 1853 and published under the pseudonym "Linda Brent." She hid on a ship and sought refuge on the Albemarle Sound. According to a newspaper ad, Norcom offered $100 for her seizure.

At the residence of her grandmother, freedwoman Molly Horniblow, a former plantation cook and seamstress, Jacobs cowered for seven years in a cubbyhole under an eave that was too low for her to stand or even sit erect. Through a peephole, she viewed her children, who believed her to be dead. In 1842, she took passage to the Chesapeake Bay and New York and traveled by steamer to New Haven, Connecticut, and by train to Boston, Massachusetts. At age 31, Jacobs reunited with her children, whose father had bought their freedom. In 1845, she escaped racism and perpetual pursuit for the first time when she accompanied poet Nathaniel Parker Willis to England, serving as a nurse to his daughter Imogen. Four years later, Jacobs settled in Rochester, New York, where she made friends with libertarian William Cooper Nell and Quaker anti-slavery agents Amy Kirby Post and Isaac Post, a pharmacist. Jacobs lived with Amy's parents for a year and educated her children at local schools.

After passage of the Fugitive Slave Law of 1850, Quaker abolitionists Cornelia Grinnell Willis and Nathaniel Willis paid $300 in 1852 to free Jacobs from Norcom's persecution. Publisher Lydia Maria Child, editor of the *National Anti-Slavery Standard,* and Amy Post assisted Jacobs in composing her autobiography. Jacobs excerpted some of the episodes in Horace Greeley's *New York Tribune,* but publication in the *Tribune* ceased because the sexual stalking scenes offended public taste. The work thrived in 1862 in a British edition, which Jacobs's brother John popularized among bookshop owners. Long mistaken for a novel by a white author, the autobiography proved to be the most intense slave narrative composed by a woman.

During the Civil War, Jacobs served as a nurse and teacher to black soldiers and refugees and as a placement worker for orphans in Alexandria, Virginia, and Savannah, Georgia. She refuted allegations that blacks were lazy by exposing the low wages that whites offered.

After operating a boardinghouse near the Harvard University campus, Jacobs retired to her daughter Louisa's home in Washington, D.C., where she died on March 7, 1897. In the 1980s, literary historian Jean Fagan Yellin uncovered the real identity of Linda Brent's pseudonymous memoir.

See also: Child, Lydia Maria.

Further Reading

Blackford, Holly. "Figures of Orality: The Master, the Mistress, the Slave Mother in Harriet Jacobs's *Incidents in the Life of a Slave Girl: Written by Herself.*" *Papers on Language and Literature* 37:3 (Summer 2001): 314–336.

Jacobs, Harriet A. *Incidents in the Life of a Slave Girl: Written by Herself.* Ed. Janet Fagan Yellin. New York: Harvest, 1983.

Levander, Caroline Field. *Voices of the Nation: Women and Public Speech in Nineteenth-Century American Literature and Culture.* Cambridge, UK: Cambridge University Press, 1998.

Snodgrass, Mary Ellen. *Encyclopedia of Feminist Literature.* New York: Facts on File, 2006.

———. *The Underground Railroad: An Encyclopedia of People, Places, and Operations.* Armonk, NY: M.E. Sharpe, 2007.

James Gang

The James Gang, known for lawless sprees and daylight robberies, established a model of frontier crime in Alabama, Arkansas, Iowa, Kansas, Kentucky, Louisiana, Minnesota, Missouri, Texas, and West Virginia. The makeup of the group varied, but members tended to share a youthful distaste for Northern aggression against Southerners during the Civil War. Brothers Frank and Jesse James and Thomas Coleman "Cole" Younger all came from Confederate households—those of the Reverend Robert and Zerelda Elizabeth Cole James of Kearney, Missouri, and of Bersheba Leighton Fristoe and Henry Washington Younger of Jackson County, Missouri—that owned slaves and sided with rebels during the Kansas–Missouri border clashes. The rancor of pro-Union and rebel kin and neighbors turned the James and Younger youths to crime.

The gang got its start in semimilitary arson and murder when members rode with Captain William Clarke Quantrill, who led guerrilla bushwhackers against abolitionist communities. On August 21, 1863, 20-year-old Frank James and 19-year-old Cole Younger joined Quantrill's 450 pillagers at their hideout at Mount Oread, Kansas. Before dawn, the band rode south and overran Lawrence, Kansas, a stronghold of 41 U.S. soldiers and a company of abolitionist Jayhawkers (antislavery vigilantes). The gang robbed a bank, ransacked a clothing store, burned the Lawrence *Journal,* and slaughtered 183 males, some as young as 14.

On September 27, 1864, Frank James and Jesse James joined some 80 outlaws in the looting and burning of a northern Missouri train and depot. The raiders separated civilians from military personnel and executed 22 Union soldiers by smashing skulls, bayoneting entrails, and slitting throats.

In the nation's first daytime bank heist, the gang, under the direction of Arch Clement, rode independently on February 13, 1866, when Jesse James, Cole Younger, and others robbed the Clay County Savings Association at Liberty, Missouri, of $62,000 in cash, bonds, and tax stamps. Jesse James regretted the death of a 17-year-old bystander. The spree continued in Lexington, Missouri, on October 30, 1866, when the gang seized $2,011 from the Alexander Mitchell Bank.

The James Gang became more methodical in midcareer. On May 22, 1867, they robbed the Hughes & Wasson Bank in Richmond, Missouri, of $4,000 and shot two law officers. On March 20, 1868, the gang asked a clerk to cash a bond at the Southern Deposit Bank in Russellville, Kentucky, which they robbed of $15,000. Buoyed by success, the gang struck in Gallatin, Missouri, at the Daviess County Savings Association on December 7, 1869.

At Corydon, Iowa, they robbed the Ocobock Brothers Bank of $40,000 on June 3, 1871. The bank's board of trustees summoned the Pinkerton National Detective Agency from Chicago to give chase. Agent Robert Pinkerton and the Daviess County sheriff trailed the robbers to Civil Bend, Missouri, and launched a shootout from which the gang escaped.

The pistoleers continued their recklessness on April 29, 1872, in Columbia, Kentucky, where they shot a Bank of Columbia clerk. After the reward for his capture rose to $25,000, Jesse James argued with the editor of the *Kansas City Times,* rationalizing the crime as less heinous than the reign of carpetbaggers in the South. On July 21, 1873, the gang derailed a train engine of the Rock Island Railroad outside Adair, Iowa, and seized from the safe $2,337 in Federal Reserve notes. On January 31, 1874, on the Iron Mountain Railway outside Gads Hill, Missouri, the robbers emptied the train's safe of $10,000 and pillaged $2,000 more from the wealthier passengers, but not from Confederate veterans.

In a face-off, officers shot John Younger dead and wounded Jim Younger. Governor Silas Woodson posted a $2,000 reward; the Missouri legislature allocated $10,000 for a manhunt. However, trackers failed to halt the next robbery near Lexington, Missouri, on August 30, 1874, or the stunning robbery of the Kansas Pacific Railway outside Muncie, Kansas, on December 8, 1874, which netted the gang $55,000. The spree continued at the Huntington Bank in West Virginia on September 5, 1875, when the gang seized $10,000.

The danger of bodily harm heightened the vengeance of Frank and Jesse James. On September 7, 1876, in Northfield, Minnesota, the gang targeted the First National Bank for its ties to pro-Union investors; Jim Younger and his youngest brother Bob survived gunshots. On September 21, a posse pursued part of the gang to the Hanska Slough and injured the Younger brothers, who surrendered. Cole, Jim, and Bob Younger pled guilty and received life sentences in prison at Stillwater, Minnesota.

The notorious Western outlaw and gang leader Jesse James *(right)* poses with his older brother Frank and his mother Zerelda in the late 1870s. The James brothers, native Missourians, began their life of crime as teenagers. *(The Granger Collection, New York)*

The James brothers made their way to Tennessee and spent three years farming at Whites Creek. A final train robbery of $15,000 on September 7, 1881, on the Chicago & Alton Railroad at Glendale, Missouri, forced Governor Thomas Theodore Crittenden to raise the reward for their capture to $10,000.

With the aid of turncoats Bob Ford and Dick Liddil, the governor arrested Clarence Hite. On April 3, 1882, in St. Joseph, Missouri, during the planning of a robbery of the Platte City Bank in Platte City, Missouri, Ford earned a pardon from Governor Crittenden by shooting Jesse James, the most wanted criminal in America. Jesse died unarmed at age 34 from a bullet behind the left ear. Frank James surrendered to the governor's agents on October 4, 1882. Two trials found him innocent of robbery and murder.

See also: Quantrill, William.

Further Reading

Dellinger, Harold, ed. *Jesse James: The Best Writings on the Notorious Outlaw and His Gang.* Guilford, CT: TwoDot, 2007.

Hamm, Mark S. *In Bad Company: America's Terrorist Underground.* Boston: Northeastern University Press, 2002.

Seal, Graham. *Encyclopedia of Folk Heroes.* Santa Barbara, CA: ABC-CLIO, 2001.

Yeatman, Ted P. *Frank and Jesse James: The Story Behind the Legend.* Nashville, TN: Cumberland House, 2000.

Jehovah's Witnesses

Members of a millennialist Christian sect, Jehovah's Witnesses comprise an American faith grounded in Bible reading, correction of erroneous Christian creeds, and anticipation of the end-time.

Growing up in Pittsburgh, founder Charles Taze Russell shifted among faiths. In 1870, at age 18, he accepted the belief of zealot Adventist preacher Jonas Wendell of Edinboro, Pennsylvania, that Jesus Christ would return to Earth in 1874. At Allegheny, Russell and his family began a five-year analysis of the Bible with Millerite Adventist preachers George Stetson and George Storrs, publisher of the religious journal *The Herald of Life and the Coming Kingdom.* During the group's lengthy clarification of beliefs, the Russells were rebaptized.

Under the influence of Nelson Horatio Barbour, a Second Adventist and the author of *Evidences for the Coming of the Lord in 1873, or The Midnight Cry* (1871), Russell professed in 1876 that Christ had returned to Earth invisibly in autumn 1874 and that the Christian dead would arise in April 1878. He spurned the celebration of Christmas and Easter as pagan and embraced pacifism and an abhorrence of government, elections, and wars. He liquidated his five clothing stores to fund Barbour's publication of *Three Worlds, or Plan of Redemption* (1877) and his own pamphlet, *The Object and Manner of Our Lord's Return* (1877). Russell and Barbour anticipated a 40-year harvest, to be followed in 1914 by the apocalypse.

The failure of his initial religious predictions dismayed Russell, and in 1878, he severed connections with Barbour and prophecy. In July 1879, Russell began dictating his own biblical interpretations through a Christian tract, *Zion's Watch Tower and Herald of Christ's Presence,* which he distributed to 6,000 readers. By 1880, there were 30 Watch Tower congregations in seven states.

Russell established an outreach to nonbelievers through the Zion's Watch Towers Tract Society and the compilation of *Food for Thinking Christians* (1881). After his Bible study groups swelled in Ohio, Virginia, West Virginia, and New England, 4,000 newspapers began issuing his sermons, which challenged the concept of hell, of the revelation of God through unguided Bible reading, and of the membership of the Holy Spirit in the Trinity.

He promoted God's favoritism toward Jews and the power of pyramidology, based on the Great Pyramid of Giza in Egypt, which he insisted was a monument to God's prophecy. Russell died in 1916. A pyramid marks his gravesite in Pittsburgh. In 1931, under Russell's successor, Joseph Franklin Rutherford, the Watch Tower Society took the name Jehovah's Witnesses.

Further Reading

Ankerberg, John, John Weldon, and Dillon Burroughs. *The Facts on Jehovah's Witnesses.* Eugene, OR: Harvest House, 2008.

Chryssides, George D. *Historical Dictionary of Jehovah's Witnesses.* Lanham, MD: Scarecrow, 2008.

Gallagher, Eugene V., and W. Michael Ashcraft, eds. *Introduction to New and Alternative Religions in America.* Westport, CT: Greenwood, 2006.

Gruss, Edmond C. *Jehovah's Witnesses: Their Claims, Doctrinal Changes, and Prophetic Speculation: What Does the Record Show?* Fairfax, VA: Xulon, 2001.

Jim Crow

The Reconstruction era reached a social nadir with the emergence of a racial caste system, a deterrent to civil rights for blacks. The extremes of post–Civil War segregation found support among racist ministers, eugenicists, and politicians who manipulated voters by warning of the mongrelization of the white race through miscegenation, either by casual intimacy, cohabitation, or marriage. Newspapers, cartoons, posters, and other publications fostered racism by describing blacks as inferior and animalistic and by abasing individuals as "buck," "coon," "darky," "mammy," "nigger," "picaninny," and "sambo." In 1828, black minstrel Thomas Dartmouth "Daddy" Rice entertained white audiences by playing the self-deprecating slave who sings "Jump, Jim Crow."

The Civil Rights Act of March 1, 1875, formulated by U.S. Congressman Benjamin Franklin Butler and Senator Charles Sumner, both radical Republicans from Massachusetts, guaranteed all citizens access to public transportation, recreation and amusement, and hotels and inns, but not to schools and cemeteries. In reality, the law, like the Fourteenth and Fifteenth amendments to the U.S. Constitution, had little impact on social behaviors grounded in slavery and white supremacy.

For example, during the initial tours of the Fisk Jubilee Singers from Fisk University in Nashville, Tennessee, the white director, missionary George L. White, had to beg for rooms and takeout food for the nine black performers in Northern cities, where hotels and restaurants refused to accommodate blacks. The hardships of touring forced a disbandment of the singers, who worked themselves into sickness and exhaustion while raising $170,000 to keep the university solvent. Ironically, they gained the respect of the crowned heads of Europe, including Queen Victoria of Great Britain, King Willem I of the Netherlands, and Emperor Wilhelm I of Germany.

Derived from Black Codes dating to 1800 and restyled by Democrats to suppress freedmen, Jim Crow restrictions on blacks banned them from juries, polling places, and militias. Taken from minstrel performances in blackface, the term "Jim Crow" caricatured institutionalized racism, which denied blacks legal recourse against whites, even those guilty of beatings, emasculation, and lynching. Blacks and whites lived, ate, traveled, and worshipped separately. State statutes segregated parks, transportation, public schools, barbershops, fountains, and toilets. Racists remanded blacks to the "coloreds only" section of prisons, hospital wards, trains, libraries, and theaters and to beverage and food service at the back entrance of cafés, saloons, and diners.

In public, black men did not shake hands with whites and refrained from touching white women. Rules of etiquette denied blacks the courtesy titles of Mr., Miss, and Mrs., as well as Doctor or Reverend for black professionals.

The election of President Rutherford B. Hayes in 1876 and his curtailment of Reconstruction effectively disenfranchised black Republicans and, with the withdrawal of federal troops, heightened the menace of Jim Crow laws to black citizens in the South. Out of fear of black retaliation, Southern law enforcers increased arrests of blacks by holding them to a higher standard of public behavior and by automatically accepting the word of a white against a black in questionable circumstances.

From 1865 to 1867, the state prison in Nashville, Tennessee, saw a rise in the number of black inmates, from 33 percent to 58 percent. Similar increases in black prisoners occurred in Alabama, Florida, Georgia, Mississippi, and North and South Carolina. On May 11, 1868, Governor Thomas Rugor of Georgia leased 100 black inmates to work on the Georgia & Alabama Railroad. John William Henry, released from a Virginia prison to labor on Big Bend Tunnel for the Chesapeake & Ohio Railroad in 1870, was the basis of the folk song "John Henry, the Steel-Drivin' Man."

Mississippi re-created a microcosm of slavery by leasing black criminals as a source of cheap labor. A brutal system of punishment, forced labor mimicked the plantation system by coercing shackled chain gangs to cultivate cotton, harvest turpentine, build railways, drain bogs, and dig ditches and irrigation lines to improve a state that had incurred severe loss of infrastructure during the Civil War. Punishment for runaways ranged from reduced rations to lashings and solitary confinement to an airless "hot box." In Texas, inmates worked without pay in coal mines, farms, railways, and sawmills, where they incurred high incidences of injury and death.

In 1893, abolitionist Frederick Douglass condemned the convict lease system and lynch laws as double infamies of class legislation. From blacks persecuted under Jim Crow imprisonment and chain gangs came a segment of American musical heritage, the work song and call-and-response chant, such as "I Workin' on the Chain Gang" and "Paul and Silas Bound in Jail," which bemoaned unjust courts, unfair toil, squalor, and death threats from armed guards.

See also: Fifteenth Amendment; Fourteenth Amendment; Hayes, Rutherford B.; Knights of the White Camellia; Ku Klux Klan; Music.

Further Reading

Brown, Gary. *Texas Gulag: The Chain Gang Years, 1875–1925.* Austin: Republic of Texas, 2002.

Dailey, Jane, Glenda Elizabeth Gilmore, and Bryant Simon, eds. *Jumpin' Jim Crow: Southern Politics from Civil War to Civil Rights.* Princeton, NJ: Princeton University Press, 2000.

Hine, Darlene Clark, and Earnestine Jenkins, eds. *A Question of Manhood: A Reader in U.S. Black Men's History and Masculinity.* 2 vols. Bloomington: Indiana University Press, 1999–2001.

Klarman, Michael J. *From Jim Crow to Civil Rights: The Supreme Court and the Struggle for Racial Equality.* New York: Oxford University Press, 2004.

Nolen, Claude H. *African American Southerners in Slavery, Civil War, and Reconstruction.* Jefferson, NC: McFarland, 2001.

Woodward, C. Vann. *The Strange Career of Jim Crow.* 3rd ed. New York: Oxford University Press, 2002.

Johnson, Andrew (1808–1875)

The seventeenth president of the United States (1865–1869), Andrew Johnson served a lengthy political career tarnished by his obstinacy and imprudence. Born in Raleigh, North Carolina, on December 29, 1808, he was reared by his mother, weaver Mary McDonough "Polly" Johnson, after the drowning of his father, constable and bank porter Jacob Johnson, in 1812.

Illiterate in boyhood, Johnson learned tailoring from his mother at age nine and, in his early teens, worked in Laurens, South Carolina. His employer, James J. Selby, aroused an interest in oratory by reading his apprentices famous English and American speeches. Johnson learned reading, writing, and math from his wife, 16-year-old Eliza McCardle Johnson, whom he wed in 1827 in Greeneville, Tennessee.

By championing farmers and tradesmen, Johnson worked his way up in Democratic politics from debater to alderman to mayor and, in 1835, to representative in the Tennessee House. After two years supporting yeoman farmers in the state senate, in 1843, he stirred interest in free farmland for the poor during his first term in the U.S. Congress. To extend citizenship into the frontier, he advocated the annexation of Texas. At age 45, he was elected governor of Tennessee, pledging to benefit the commoner rather than kowtow to party politics. He served from 1853 to 1857.

As a Democrat in the U.S. Senate from 1857 to 1862, Johnson endorsed passage of the Homestead Act, which President Abraham Lincoln signed on May 20, 1862, to encourage settlement of the West. Johnson, himself a slave owner, made difficult choices in December 1860, including a denunciation of anarchist John Brown's raid on the federal arsenal at Harpers Ferry, Virginia. Upon the senator's return to Tennessee in April 1861, he encountered threats of lynching. According to Frederick William Seward, son and biographer of Secretary of State William Henry Seward, "Andrew Johnson, whose outspoken 'Unionism' was in marked contrast to the course of his fellow senators from the South, was denounced with bitterness, and burned in effigy."

Johnson maintained Democratic beliefs that the U.S. Constitution guaranteed the right to own slaves and that Kansas should be admitted to the Union as a slave state. He teetered toward Republicanism by supporting states' rights but by declaring secession unconstitutional. Appointed by Lincoln as military governor of Union-occupied Tennessee, Johnson quelled Confederate influences and backed full citizenship for black males. He jailed secessionist clergy, turned anti-Unionists out of office, and taxed aristocrats to support laboring-class families whose men had been drafted into the Confederate army, leaving women and children defenseless. By 1863, the Tennessee legislature considered requesting readmission to the Union.

The ideal campaign partner for Lincoln, Johnson was elected U.S. vice president in November 1864. While recovering from a bout of typhoid fever, he disgraced himself at the inauguration on March 5, 1865, by making a drunken, rambling speech and by insulting black orator Frederick Douglass and his wife. Johnson's social gaffes worsened after he failed to make a condolence call on Lincoln's widow and sons Robert and Thomas "Tad" Lincoln in April 1865. The *New York World* castigated the vice president as an alcoholic boor; the *New York Herald* labeled his appearance a disgrace. Various parties called for his resignation.

Former Tennessee governor, U.S. congressman, and senator Andrew Johnson acceded to the presidency upon the assassination of Abraham Lincoln in April 1865. Three years later, Johnson became the first president to be impeached—but he served out his term. *(Library of Congress)*

In part because of the combat death of his 33-year-old son Charles, who served as an assistant surgeon outside Nashville during the Civil War, Johnson supported vengeful Northerners who wanted to execute Confederate President Jefferson Davis for treason. The vice president posted a $100,000 reward for Davis's arrest and for the seizure of the Confederate treasury.

After 40 days in office as vice president, Johnson took the oath of office as the new president following Lincoln's assassination. Under the equivocal status as National Union Party spokesman, Johnson was an obstinate white supremacist who wavered between Democratic and Republican philosophies on the punishment of Southern rebels and the protection of freedmen. He professed a class hatred of wealthy plantation owners and a sympathy for the laboring-class Southern men who had fought for the Confederacy to maintain their aristocratic lifestyle. He condoned the election of legislators from the South and warred with Congress over the style and severity of Reconstruction, the expenditures of the Freedmen's Bureau, the powers of the Civil Rights Bill of 1865, and passage of the Fourteenth Amendment to the U.S. Constitution.

During his reelection campaign in 1866, Johnson faced jeering crowds, called Congress "this common gang of cormorants and bloodsuckers," and accused legislators of maligning him. On October 26, 1866, a cartoon in *Harper's Weekly* urged him to take his medicine, which bore the label "Fourteenth Amendment." Because of his undignified campaign style and anticongressional stance, he lost handily to Republicans.

Johnson's acts as president included forcing the French out of Mexico, signing a bill (albeit reluctantly) admitting Nebraska to the Union on March 1, 1867, and backing Secretary of State William Henry Seward on the purchase of Alaska from Russia on March 30. Johnson and Seward anticipated profits from Eskimo dogs and possible deposits of coal, gold, graphite, and iron. Nonetheless, hostile congressmen, led by Thaddeus Stevens and Benjamin Franklin Butler, objected to what they perceived as Johnson's contempt for Congress and his exceeding of executive authority. They listed their grievances in a single bill of impeachment on November 21, 1867, which won only 53 percent of the vote. A second impeachment trial on March 5, 1868, charged Johnson with firing Secretary of War Edwin M. Stanton in violation of the Tenure of Office Act. The vote count in the Senate—35 to 19—lacked one "yea" to reach the two-thirds vote required to force Johnson from the presidency. He departed the White House after a final act of clemency—unconditional amnesty for Confederates—on Christmas Day 1868.

After failed campaigns for the U.S. Senate in 1868 and for the House of Representatives in 1874, Johnson finally returned to the former body in March 1875. He served barely five months before dying on July 31, 1875, from the effects of two strokes. By his wishes, he was buried with his head resting on a copy of the U.S. Constitution and his corpse wrapped in an American flag.

See also: Homestead Act (1862); Lincoln, Abraham; Reconstruction; Seward, William Henry.

Further Reading

Brinkley, Alan, and Davis Dyer. *The American Presidency.* Boston: Houghton Mifflin, 2004.

Conlin, Joseph R. *The American Past: A Survey of American History.* 9th ed. Boston: Wadsworth/Cengage Learning, 2009.

Foner, Eric. *Reconstruction: America's Unfinished Revolution, 1863–1877.* New York: HarperCollins, 2002.

Schroeder-Lein, Glenna R., and Richard Zuczek. *Andrew Johnson: A Biographical Companion.* Santa Barbara, CA: ABC-CLIO, 2001.

Winik, Jay. *April 1865: The Month That Saved America.* New York: HarperCollins, 2002.

Jones, Mother (1837–1930)

A crusader for civil rights and a debater of workplace issues for nearly six decades, Mother Jones reverenced the worker uprising as a citizen protest against economic oppression. Born Mary Harris on a farm in Cork, Ireland, on August 1, 1837, she came of age amid ongoing class struggle between British occupation forces and the landless Irish peasantry. Her grandfather went to the gallows for defending Irish freedom from British insurgents. The family survived the potato famine of 1845. They fled death threats in Ireland and settled in Canada, where her father found jobs constructing canals and railroads.

North America introduced her to quality education. With a teaching certificate, she taught in Toronto, Ontario. In 1860, she moved south to assume classroom duties at St. Mary Academy, an all-girls convent school operated from 1846 by the Sisters of the Immaculate Heart of Mary in Monroe, Michigan. In Memphis, Tennessee, at age 24, she married a union man, iron molder George E. Jones. In October 1867, when yellow fever took her husband and their four children, she treated other victims of the scourge.

Jones's career in populist labor organization and social reform began in Chicago, where she sewed for rich families on Lake Shore Drive. Outside the mansions of the rich, she observed the unemployed and hungry, with whom she commiserated. She lost her home and dressmaking business on October 8, 1871, to the Great Chicago Fire, after which workers in her husband's union became her surrogate family. Among the survivors of destruction, she resided temporarily with refugees in the cellar of Old St. Mary's Church on South Michigan Avenue.

A self-proclaimed "hell-raiser," Jones rallied the Noble and Holy Order of the Knights of Labor to denounce wage slavery and to oppose child and convict labor, monopolies, and conspicuous wealth. The Knights developed a collective mentality that excluded capitalists, doctors, financiers, investors, lawyers, and liquor manufacturers, whom Jones rejected as social parasites. With radical oratory, she advocated equal wages for male, female, white, and nonwhite workers and rallied the underclass to fight against factory, rail, and mine owners. To exaggerate her grandmotherly pose, she dressed in black matronly garb and added seven years to her age by claiming to have been born in 1830.

Labor activists introduced Mother Jones to the Order of the Knights of St. Crispin, a shoemaker's organization founded in 1867, which became the nation's largest union by 1870. She educated herself on the plight of people injured in the workplace, on the powerlessness of their families, and on prison conditions for protesters of unfair employment. In 1873, she witnessed appalling conditions in Pennsylvania's coal mines, where malnourished children, most of them Irish, worked for pennies. Rather than ally with suffragists, she championed the return of women to the home.

From 1877 to the end of her life, Jones had no permanent address. For humanitarian reasons, she traveled to every major strike and industrial hot spot and lived in tents and lean-tos while organizing labor stoppages and educating the poor about class warfare and the hereditary nature of "involuntary poverty." Among unorganized laborers, she boosted the morale of bottle washers, brewers, cigar makers, knitters, lumberers, machinists, miners, rail men, sewers, silk weavers, streetcar conductors, and telegraphers. Her charismatic rallies mustered workers to demand their rights from management. She gained followers by incorporating women and children among the ranks of the disgruntled and leading them in public processions. Loyalists declared her a mythic icon, the "Miner's Angel."

During the Long Strike of 1874–1875, Jones educated the coal diggers of western Pennsylvania on the tyranny of capitalism, which crushed unions and slashed wages by 80 percent. In Reading in 1876, she encouraged illiterate immigrant laborers against the cruelties of anti-union mogul Franklin Benjamin Gowen and a gang of managers of canals, coal mines, docks, and shipping. He retaliated by calling her a socialist agitator and labor manipulator. She retorted that the soldiers of class warfare must fight starvation, exploitation, and a pro-management court system. In mid-July 1877 in Pittsburgh, she heartened Baltimore & Ohio rail strikers by organizing women's auxiliaries, arming them with pot lids and mops, and teaching them methods of hoisting banners and chanting in support of an eight-hour workday. Her reasoning was logical—more rest for workers reduced errors and accidents caused by exhaustion and loss of concentration.

Mother Jones remained a radical force into her nineties. In her later triumphs, she co-formed the United Mine Workers in 1901 and, in articles for the *International Socialist Review,* denounced child labor and open machines that maimed and crippled young workers. In 1902, attorney Reese Blizzard called Jones "the most dangerous woman in America." She survived police persecution and house arrest in Pratt, West Virginia, after organizing children into a crusade for fair treatment of workers. At her release from confinement, the U.S. Senate launched an investigation of coal miners' complaints about working conditions and mine safety. A similar demand for reform in Colorado brought her to New York City to the Broadway office of plutocrat John D. Rockefeller, Jr., whom she convinced to examine mines belonging to Standard Oil. In 1905, she was the only female present at the founding of the Industrial Workers of the World. In 1914, she protested the massacre of miners and their families after goons burned a tent colony in Ludlow, Colorado.

At age 93, she defended strikers at a West Virginia coal mine against intimidation. Five years later, she published the *Autobiography of Mother Jones* (1925). After decades of leading worker revolt among textile workers, seamstresses, steelworkers, and streetcar conductors, she died in Hyattsville, Maryland, on November 30, 1930.

See also: Labor and Labor Unions.

Further Reading

Gorn, Elliott J. *Mother Jones: The Most Dangerous Woman in America.* New York: Hill and Wang, 2002.

Murrin, John M., et al. *Liberty, Equality, Power: A History of the American People.* 4th ed. Belmont, CA: Thomson/Wadsworth, 2009.

Palladino, Grace. *Another Civil War: Labor, Capital, and the State in the Anthracite Regions of Pennsylvania, 1840–1868.* New York: Fordham University Press, 2006.

Steel, Edward M., Jr., ed. *The Court-Martial of Mother Jones.* Lexington: University Press of Kentucky, 1995.

———, ed. *The Speeches and Writings of Mother Jones.* Pittsburgh: University of Pittsburgh Press, 1988.

Joseph, Chief (1840–1904)

Chief of the Wallowa band of Nez Percé, Chief Joseph kept his nomadic band out of reach of the U.S. Army until he had no other choice but to surrender. Born in 1840 in Wallowa in northeastern Oregon, he learned from his father, Joseph the Elder, of insurgent whites and their greed for Indian territory for farming and pasturing stock.

On June 9, 1863, gold prospectors at Pierce, Idaho, convinced the government to seize 6 million acres (2.4 million hectares) of Nez Percé land, leaving the natives only 780,000 acres (316,000 hectares) around Fort Lapwai, Idaho. Old Chief Joseph remained firm in claiming the tribe's traditional territory and refused to sign a treaty that seized 700,000 acres (283,000 hectares) for white settlers of Idaho, Oregon, and Washington territories. Before his death in summer 1871 at a camp at the confluence of the Lostine and Wallowa rivers, he advised Young Joseph to refuse treaties and to halt confiscation of Nez Percé burying grounds and the desecration of ancestors' bones. Two years later, young Chief Joseph successfully negotiated a federal guarantee of his people's rights with President Ulysses S. Grant, who assured half the Wallowa Valley to the Nez Percé.

An executive reversal in 1877 pitted Chief Joseph against General Oliver Otis Howard, a one-armed Civil War hero who forced a resettlement of the Nez Percé from the Wallowa Valley east into Idaho. On May 15, Howard gave Chief Joseph 30 days in which to comply. With Howard's 90 troops of the First Cavalry in pursuit, Chief Joseph led 250 of his people across the Snake River toward Canada. They rode their prize Appaloosas and hunted buffalo in Yellowstone for the last time. For three months, his followers, joined by the bands of Looking Glass, Toohoolhoolzote, and White Bird, journeyed 1,700 miles (2,700 kilometers) from Oregon and Washington

Chief Joseph of the Nez Percé in northwest Oregon commanded a series of remarkable victories over superior U.S. forces in summer 1877, then led a long retreat toward Canada. He surrendered to spare his starving people, uttering the famous words, "I will fight no more forever." *(Library of Congress)*

territories southeast across Montana and Idaho territories and northeast into Wyoming.

The rapid deployment cost the tribe hundreds of cattle and horses lost along the way as well as an alliance with the Flathead, who gave them no help. For drinking water on the move, Joseph's followers suspended buffalo horns by thongs into streams. On July 8, some 75 volunteers departed Mount Idaho to assist General Howard, but they turned back after two days' ride. At Kamiah, Idaho, the army arrested the 35-member band of Chief Red Heart, who was not involved in the flight to Canada. On August 9, a pitched battle at Big Hole, Idaho, reduced Chief Joseph's followers by 90 casualties, many of them women and children. The army suffered 39 casualties. Because they traveled without a doctor, soldiers received only first aid.

Conditions worsened for the Nez Percé after a 5-inch (13-centimeter) snowfall on October 1 and after Howard summoned assistance from Colonel Nelson Appleton Miles from Fort Keogh, Montana. Some warriors wore only breechcloths and moccasins. Children and the elderly had no blankets. The next day, a U.S. sharpshooter killed Chief Looking Glass with a single bullet to the head.

At noon on October 5, 1877, at the Bear Paw Mountains, Montana, 40 miles (64 kilometers) from the Canadian border, Joseph surrendered 380 Nez Percé to Colonel Miles as a means of sparing his people exposure and starvation or death from the Hotchkiss gun, a mounted machine gun that sprayed bullets by crank from a cartridge belt. After the presentation of Nez Percé to Colonel Miles at Chinook, Montana, Chief Joseph made a heartfelt speech declaring himself weary of running: "Hear me, my chiefs! I am tired; my heart is sick and sad. From where the sun now stands, I will fight no more forever."

Chief Joseph ended his life a captive. His captors transported him to the Dakotas and Fort Leavenworth, Kansas, then south to Oklahoma. At the Oakland Reservation near Tonkawa, epidemic disease assailed the Nez Percé survivors. On a state visit to Washington, D.C., in January 1879, Chief Joseph begged President Rutherford B. Hayes to allow his people to return to the Pacific Northwest. Instead, government officials incarcerated some of the Nez Percé in Idaho. Joseph entered confinement at the Fort Colville Indian Reservation in central Washington Territory, where he died on September 21, 1904.

See also: Buffalo; Horse Breeding; Idaho Territory; Montana Territory; Oregon; Washington Territory; Weapons.

Further Reading

Calloway, Colin G., ed. *Our Hearts Fell to the Ground: Plains Indian Views of How the West Was Lost.* Boston: Bedford/St. Martin's, 1996.

Cozzens, Peter, ed. *Eyewitnesses to the Indian Wars, 1865–1890.* 5 vols. Mechanicsburg, PA: Stackpole, 2001–2005.

Johansen, Bruce E., and Donald A. Grinde, Jr. *The Encyclopedia of Native American Biography.* New York: Da Capo, 1998.

Moulton, Candy. *Chief Joseph: Guardian of the People.* New York: Macmillan, 2006.

Waldman, Carl. *Who Was Who in Native American History: Indians and Non-Indians from Early Contacts Through 1900.* New York: Facts on File, 1990.

Judaism

Throughout the Civil War and Reconstruction eras, American Jews influenced life in the North, South, and West through altruism, commerce, and social and political activism.

In San Francisco in 1856, Levi Strauss, the inventor of denim jeans, settled his mercantile business near the waterfront and, into the 1860s, promoted the city's first synagogue, Temple Emanu-El. Under Rabbi Elkan Cohn, the temple became a religious and educational haven for the families of elite financiers, merchants, and politicians.

As war divided the nation, Jews took sides like the rest of the populace. Rabbi David Einhorn faced ouster from Baltimore, Maryland, after he called slavery a national cancer. In the first weeks of the war, Rabbi Samuel May Isaacs, a New York editor of the *Jewish Messenger,* published "Stand by the Flag!," an essay on patriotism lauding the U.S. Constitution for guaranteeing Jews the right of worship. In outrage, a congregation in Shreveport, Louisiana, censured Isaacs and resolved to honor the Southern Confederacy. Rabbi Morris Jacob Raphall of New York City condoned slavery, as did the nation's most prestigious Jewish intellectual, Rabbi Isaac Mayer Wise of the Lodge Street Synagogue in Cincinnati, Ohio.

Patriotism in the South flourished alongside spirituality among Jews. Joseph Goldsmith served as an unofficial chaplain to the wounded in Richmond, Virginia, and observed the Sabbath, Rosh Hashanah, and Yom Kippur with Jewish soldiers. Nurse and spy Rosanna Dyer Osterman of Galveston, Texas, died a martyr to the cause in a steamboat explosion on January 1, 1863, leaving bequests to a widows' and orphans' home, a sailors' home, and Houston's first Jewish benevolent society. Attorney and statesman Judah P. Benjamin, a Yale University graduate and former U.S. senator, supported Southern independence and secession, but favored abolition of slavery. From 1861 to 1865 at the Confederate capital in Richmond, he served President Jefferson Davis first as attorney general, then as secretary of war and secretary of state. After the Emancipation Proclamation of January 1, 1863, Benjamin promoted the enlistment of freedmen into the Confederate army and navy. In 1866, Southern Jews in Richmond buried 30 combat casualties in the Cemetery for Hebrew Confederate Soldiers, the world's only Jewish military burial ground outside Israel.

On the Union side, Jews lobbied for federal recognition of their loyalty and for the overturn of the chaplaincy law of 1861, which banned rabbis from combat field service. On July 17, 1862, Congress altered the law to legitimize the ministry of rabbis.

Insults to Jews worsened on December 17, 1862, when General Ulysses S. Grant blamed "Israelites" for feeling "privileged" to indulge in cotton speculation and smuggling in Mississippi. Grant called Jews vagrants, traitors, and nuisances, and ordered the deportation of Jewish families from military zones in Kentucky, Mississippi, and Tennessee. Jews protested the outrage at rallies in Cincinnati, Louisville, and St. Louis and telegraphed their fury to the White House from Chicago, New York, and Philadelphia.

On January 3, 1863, Prussian brothers from Paducah, Kentucky—sutler Cesar J. Kaskel and clothier Julius W. Kaskel—joined Adolphus Simeon Solomons, a co-founder of the American Red Cross, and U.S. Congressman John Addison Gurley in persuading President Abraham Lincoln to rescind Grant's orders. On January 5, Rabbi Isaac Mayer Wise complained to Secretary of War Edwin M. Stanton about the insult and visited the capital to thank President Lincoln for his rejection of ethnic stereotyping. In 1874, Grant, then president of the United States, redeemed himself with American Jews by leading his cabinet to Rabbi Jacob Voorsanger's dedication of Adas Israel at G and Sixth streets, the oldest synagogue in Washington, D.C.

Jewish Activism

The Underground Railroad received Jewish support in the form of donations, transportation, and volunteers. Immigrants Jacob Benjamin, August Bondi, and Theodore Wiener of Ossawatomie, Kansas, supported anarchist John Brown's plot to foment a black revolt.

For eight years at Temple Beth El in Detroit, Michigan, Rabbi and Cantor Leibman Adler advocated slave rescue. His sermons compared the plight of runaway blacks to that of the Hebrew children in Exodus. He urged his reformed congregation to help refugees escape bounty hunters and kidnappers during their crossing of the Detroit River to Windsor, Ontario. Under his influence, Underground Railroad conductors Emil S. Heineman, Fanny Butzel Heineman, and Mark Sloman provided clothing and disguised fleeing slaves on the way to Canada to help them elude lookouts.

The Confederate surrender at Appomattox, Virginia, preceded Passover, when abolitionist Jews augmented their thanks with blessings on the nation. At Lincoln's assassination, rabbis compared him to Moses, who led Israelites to the Promised Land, but died without entering. In the aftermath of General William Tecumseh Sherman's scorched-earth policy in the South, theologian Isaac Leeser of Philadelphia, publisher of the *Occident and American Jewish Advocate,* mourned the destruction of South Carolina's synagogues. The Reconstruction period saw growth in Jewish houses of worship, particularly reformed or liberalized congregations. In 1866, the opening of the Plum Street Temple across from Cincinnati's City Hall made Rabbi Isaac Mayer Wise's reformed congregation the nation's second largest. By 1868, 30 synagogues, including Temple Israel in Boston and Rodeph Shalom in Philadelphia, attracted younger membership and Gentile visitors by adopting choirs and pipe organs, integrating men and women in pews, conducting services in English rather than Hebrew or German, and easing ritual requirements for prayer shawls and covered heads during worship. On March 22, 1874, the Young Men's Hebrew Association opened in Manhattan, offering youth lectures, Bible and Hebrew classes, a library, and coursework in bookkeeping, drafting, physical education, and shorthand.

Opposing Visions

Rabbi Wise provided intellectual leadership, through published tracts, the newspaper *The American Israelite,* and the prayer book *Minhag America* (1847), as well as organizational skills. In 1873, he founded the Union of American Hebrew Congregations, an attempt at allying Jews professing disparate beliefs. President Moritz Loth energized plans for opening Jewish publishing houses and preparatory schools, and outlined Torah curricula and standardized rituals that preserved Jewish identity. In October 1875 in Cincinnati, the Union opened the Hebrew Union College, the nation's first Jewish seminary, with funding provided by industrialist Henry Adler of Lawrenceburg, Indiana. Rabbi Wise presided over the teaching of Torah and classical texts and the ordination of rabbis entering the ministry. Upon his visit to San Francisco in 1877, Wise discovered a dismaying relaxation of ritual, violation of the Sabbath, and synagogues in debt from poor congregational support.

Throughout the 1870s, Hasidism, an ultra-orthodox form of Jewish fundamentalism, increased its influence on American religious life with waves of Yiddish-speaking immigrants from Belarus, Galicia, Germany, Lithuania, Moldova, Poland, and the Ukraine. They settled primarily in New Jersey and New York, one of the world's densest concentrations of practicing Ashkenazic (Central European) Jews. To shield their culture and beliefs from Americanization, they avoided intermarriage with Gentiles and built neighborhood synagogues, yeshivas, and day schools where the Hebrew language dominated. Politically, they favored social progressivism and supported labor unions and liberal civil rights movements.

Reformed Jewish Congregations Founded in 1861–1877

Congregation	Location	Founded	Head Rabbi
Adas Israel	Washington, D.C.	1876	Jacob Voorsanger
Adath Israel	Owensboro, Ky.	1877	David Feuerlicht
Ahawath Chesed	New York City	1872	Adolph Huebsch
B'er Chayim	Cumberland, Md.	1865	Isaac Baum
Berith Sholom	Troy, N.Y.	1870	A.S. Braudle
Beth Israel	West Hartford, Conn.	1876	Isaac Mayer
Bikur Cholim	Donaldsonville, La.	1872	Henry S. Jacobs
B'nai Israel	Galveston, Tex.	1870	Alexander Rosenspitz
B'nai Israel	Baltimore	1876	Henry Schneeberger
B'nai Sholom	Quincy, Ill.	1870	Adolph Ollendorf
Chicago Sinai	Chicago	1861	Bernhard Felsenthal
Mickve Israel	Savannah, Ga.	1874	Isaac P. Mendes
Mikveh Israel	Philadelphia	1860	Isaac Leeser
Plum Street	Cincinnati, Ohio	1866	Isaac Mayer Wise
Shaarei Shamayim	Madison, Wis.	1863	—
Talmud Torah Adereth El	New York City	1863	—
Temple Israel	West Lafayette, Ind.	1867	Del Banco (reader)
Temple of Israel	Wilmington, N.C.	1876	Samuel Mendelsohn
Union Temple	Brooklyn, N.Y.	1876	—

Countering Rabbi Wise's reform movement, orthodox fellowships in Chicago and St. Louis retained traditional Torah study. In the 1880s, a compromise faith, Conservative Judaism, chose a middle path by honoring orthodox ritual while acknowledging nineteenth-century values.

See also: Strauss, Levi; Thanksgiving.

Further Reading

Cutler, Irving. *Jewish Chicago: A Pictorial History.* Charleston, SC: Arcadia, 2000.

Goldman, Karla *Beyond the Synagogue Gallery: Finding a Place for Women in American Judaism.* Cambridge, MA: Harvard University Press, 2000.

Moore, Deborah Dash, ed. *American Jewish Identity Politics.* Ann Arbor: University of Michigan Press, 2008.

Rosenbaum, Fred. *Cosmopolitans: A Social and Cultural History of the Jews of the San Francisco Bay Area.* Berkeley: University of California Press, 2009.

Sarna, Jonathan D. *American Judaism: A History.* New Haven, CT: Yale University Press, 2004.

Shevitz, Amy Hill. *Jewish Communities on the Ohio River: A History.* Lexington: University Press of Kentucky, 2007.

K

Kansas

A gateway to the West, Kansas figures prominently in nineteenth-century American history. Contributing to interstate transportation from the 1850s to 1866, Benjamin "Ben" Holladay operated the Holladay Overland Mail & Express out of Atchison, Kansas, serving cities as far west as Boise, Idaho; Virginia City, Montana; Placerville, California; and Walla Walla, Washington. Freighter Ashbel Holmes Barney delivered passengers and parcels by the United States Express and the Wells Fargo mail service to bankers, miners, and the military in the Far West. Partners Alexander Majors, William H. Russell, and William Waddell ran the Pony Express from April 6, 1860, to October 26, 1861; riders left St. Joseph, Missouri, and crossed Kansas on a 1,966-mile (3,163-kilometer) gallop to San Francisco. The trio also operated a livestock market at Kansas City, selling oxen from their herd of 50,000 to farmers and travelers.

The east–west Santa Fe Trail and north–south Chisholm Trail turned Kansas into a thoroughfare for settlers, drovers, and traders. In 1861, pioneers in Salina, Kansas, thrived from the sale of travel supplies and whiskey to buffalo hunters, prospectors, and cavalry on their way to the Rocky Mountains. Citizens enjoyed a peaceful coexistence with the Kansa, who traveled from Indian lands to buy from white traders.

At the onset of the Civil War, the Osage and Shawnee of Oklahoma clustered on the southern border of Kansas. Because of the introduction of European diseases in virgin populations, outbreaks of cholera, measles, and smallpox threatened Wichita. Ralph Waldo Emerson and his wife, Lydia Jackson Emerson, of Concord, Massachusetts, were among the supporters of the Underground Railroad who enlisted slave conductors to extend the rescue network through slave-free Kansas.

Statehood

On January 29, 1861, the territory entered the Union as a free state and the thirty-fourth star on the American flag, ending years of bloody conflict between Free Soilers and proslavery forces. Kansans chose as their state motto *Ad astra per aspera,* Latin for "to the stars through hard times."

Interrupting the peace and prosperity of frontier folk was an impromptu raid in September 1862 by outriders and rustlers, who left citizens vulnerable, without horses, mules, guns, and ammunition for self-protection and hunting. The violence of "Bleeding Kansas" worsened on August 21, 1863, when William Clarke Quantrill's paramilitary raiders went on a murder and arson spree in Lawrence.

Buffalo Soldiers trained at Fort Leavenworth after September 21, 1866, and rode from Fort Riley, Kansas, to Fort Gibson in eastern Oklahoma and over the Southwestern Great Plains. The cavalry shielded builders of corduroy roads and workers on the Kansas Pacific Railway, where the laying of track incited Arapaho, Cheyenne, and Kiowa against border towns and engineering parties. The military, vigilantes, and local law officers combated heightened postwar violence by the Cheyenne against Kansas homesteaders in April 1867 and among cattle drovers in the state's notorious cow towns—Abilene, Wichita, and Dodge City.

Demographic Changes

Kansas underwent significant change in the postwar years. Within weeks of the Confederate surrender at Appomattox, Virginia, on April 9, 1865, a state census identified 127,270 Kansans as white, 12,527 as black, and 382 as American Indian. The founding of the Kansas State Normal School at Emporia, Lincoln College at Topeka, and a state university at Lawrence coincided in 1866 with the survey and sale of 500,000 acres (200,000 hectares) of state land for railway construction.

In summer 1867, the opening of the Chisholm Trail through Abilene boosted the number of transient drovers and their herds, as well as seasonal uproar. Simultaneously, Susan B. Anthony and the Reverend Olympia Brown accompanied Lucy Stone and Henry Brown "Harry" Blackwell to Kansas to rally suffrage supporters. Brown described the atmosphere of the state as "just emerging from the effect of the border ruffian raids and the war in which many of her men had been killed." The situation for farmers proved difficult because of bouts of malaria and plagues of grasshoppers.

In October 1867, Comanche Chief Ten Bears, Southern Cheyenne Chief Black Kettle, Arapaho Chief Raven, and Kiowa Chief Satanta signed the Treaty of Medicine Lodge. Negotiated at Medicine Lodge Creek, Kansas, the agreement sent individual nations to reservations in Indian Territory (Oklahoma) as a two-way protection of the peace. In exchange for native lands, the government promised to feed and clothe the Indians and to teach them trades and subsistence farming techniques.

Lawlessness increased during the transition of Kansas from raw frontier. One of the most famous of peacekeepers during rough times was James Butler "Wild Bill" Hickok, who served Ellis County as sheriff on August 23, 1869, after the disappearance of the former officeholder, Thomas Gannon, the previous April; Hickok advanced to marshal of Abilene in 1871. On September 11, 1874, Cheyenne Chief Medicine Water kidnapped the Germaine sisters—18-year-old Katherine Elizabeth, 12-year-old Sophia Louise, seven-year-old Julia Amanda, and five-year-old Nancy Adeline—from a migrant camp on the Smoky Hill River in western Kansas. The abduction followed the shooting of their father, John Germaine, and murder of his other daughter Rebecca Jane Germaine, siblings Stephen and Johanna Germaine, and their mother, Lydia Germaine. In the hands of renegade dog soldiers, Katherine Elizabeth Germaine reported beatings, starvation, forced labor, and frostbite in deep snows on the Llano Estacado (Staked Plains) of the Texas Panhandle before her rescue at McClellan Creek on November 8, 1874, by Lieutenant Frank Baldwin. The upgrading of law enforcement proved even more necessary on December 8, 1874, when the James Gang flagged the Kansas Pacific Railway outside Muncie and seized $55,000, one of the most daring train robberies in American history.

As a business nexus, Kansas dominated much of Plains travel and trade. In May 1871, merchant W.C. Lobenstein of Leavenworth, Kansas, the first dealer to profit from buffalo kills, supplied 500 hides to an English tanner who manufactured leather goods for the British army. British investor and philanthropist William Henry Blackmore, co-author of *The Hunting Grounds of the Great West* (1878), reported on the plight of Kansans who depended on buffalo meat for food in 1873 after grasshoppers devoured their crops:

> Troops were considerately sent by the Government to the Republicans to kill meat for the starving families. When the soldiers arrived, however, at their hunting-grounds, there was but little meat for them to kill, as the "buffalo skinners" had anticipated them and had slaughtered nearly every buffalo in the district.

In place of a sea of wild migratory herds came the graded cattle of William Carl, introduced north of Medicine Lodge in spring 1873, and Jacob Buller, leader of Russian Mennonites, who arrived at Topeka on September 23, 1874, under the auspices of the Santa Fe Railroad. The following year, hamlets, coal yards, switching stations, and depots of the railroad stretched track more than 2,100 miles (3,400 kilometers).

By May 1877, some 8,000 Mennonites occupied 88,000 acres (36,000 hectares) of railroad land in one of the state's most prosperous colonies. At Goessel, Kansas, the Mennonites experimented with winter-hardy, high-yield "Turkey Red" wheat, the crop responsible for turning Kansas into the Midwestern breadbasket it remains today.

See also: Anthony, Susan B.; Black Communities; Blackmore, William Henry; Brown, Olympia; Dodge City, Kansas; James Gang; Quantrill, William; Stone, Lucy.

Further Reading

Glasrud, Bruce A., and Michael N. Searles, eds. *Buffalo Soldiers in the West: A Black Soldiers Anthology.* College Station: Texas A&M University Press, 2007.

Londré, Felicia Hardison. *The Enchanted Years of the Stage: Kansas City at the Crossroads of American Theater, 1870–1930.* Columbia: University of Missouri Press, 2007.

Miner, Craig. *Kansas: The History of the Sunflower State, 1854–2000.* Lawrence: University Press of Kansas, 2002.

Napier, Rita. *Kansas and the West: New Perspectives.* Lawrence: University Press of Kansas, 2003.

Salina History Book Committee. *Salina: 1858–2008.* Charleston, SC: Arcadia, 2008.

Shortridge, James R. *Cities on the Plains: The Evolution of Urban Kansas.* Lawrence: University Press of Kansas, 2004.

Vestal, Stanley. *Dodge City, Queen of Cowtowns: "The Wickedest Little City in America," 1872–1886.* Lincoln: University of Nebraska Press, 1998.

Kemble, Fanny (1809–1893)

British actor and diarist Frances Anne "Fanny" Kemble Butler surveyed the Southern plantation system and published accounts of white brutality and war's destruction. A member of the Kemble-Siddons stage dynasty, she was born in London on November 27, 1809. She was the niece of tragedienne Sarah Kemble Siddons, whom a statue honors in Westminster Abbey.

In childhood, Kemble rode horseback, studied in France, and, at age 18, composed *Francis I* (1827), a lyric melodrama. By age 20, at Covent Garden, she advanced to the lead role in *Romeo and Juliet* opposite her parents, Charles and Maria Theresa Kemble, as Mercutio and Lady Capulet.

Beginning in 1832, she captured the American imagination during a 13-year residency in the United States. She made headlines for her chic outfits and hairstyles and won the attention of poet Walt Whitman. Her diary, *Journal of a Residence in America* (1835), ridiculed American social climbers and denounced the idle rich who led lavish lifestyles on the proceeds of the flesh trade.

Following her marriage in 1834 to Philadelphia attorney Pierce Butler, son of the formulator of the Fugitive Slave Law of 1793, Kemble was unaware of his prominence among enslavers. She realized that she had wed the heir to a 1,500-acre (600-hectare) plantation at Butler Island and 1,700 acres (690 hectares) at St. Simons Island, Georgia, operated by 638 slaves. She investigated the unsanitary state of slave quarters and observed the whipping of naked black women with rawhide. Older females described their use as breeders, which kept them in a state of pregnancy or breastfeeding of children for field labor or sale.

Kemble set up a slave infirmary and intervened against overseers who forced pregnant and ailing women to plant and harvest cotton, rice, and tobacco. Her introduction of literacy and vocational training put her at risk for violating laws forbidding the education of slaves. In her writings, she described slave flight and the workings of the Underground Railroad.

After Kemble separated from Butler in 1846, she resided with daughters Sarah and Frances in Rome, Italy, a sojourn she chronicled in *A Year of Consolation* (1847). After the separation, Butler gambled away his fortune and, in 1859, sold 436 slaves at the largest slave auction in the nation's history. The family split over slavery, with Kemble and older daughter Sarah favoring the emancipation of slaves and Butler and Frances defending bondage. During winter 1862–1863, Frances Butler superintended the plantations to force the remaining slaves to work harder. In her *Journal of a Residence on a Georgian Plantation, 1838–1839* (1863), the most detailed antebellum denunciation of bondage, Kemble exposed Butler's greed, as well as his spousal abuse for her involvement with the Underground Railroad. To the dismay of the Butler family, the diary stirred the public in America and Europe and increased the demand for emancipation.

In letters published as *Further Records, 1848–1883* (1891), Kemble expressed the economic and social turmoil of the Civil War and Reconstruction eras. In divorce proceedings, she lost child custody and property, to which women had no rights. Her daughters, formerly two of America's richest girls, moved to a Philadelphia boardinghouse. Kemble settled in Lenox, Massachusetts, supported suffrage, and adopted the harem trousers introduced by Amelia Jenks Bloomer.

After Butler's death in 1867, Kemble returned to Philadelphia. In 1877, she repatriated to England, where she supported herself by delivering Shakespearean recitations, translating the works of Friedrich Schiller and Alexandre Dumas, and publishing an autobiography, *Records of a Girlhood* (1878), as well as poems, essays, travelogues, drama, and a novel, *Far Away and Long Ago* (1889). After extensive tours of Europe and the United States, she died in London on January 15, 1893. Historians credit her with promoting abolitionism and dissuading some undecided British authorities from supporting the Confederacy during the Civil War.

See also: Diseases and Epidemics.

Further Reading

Clinton, Catherine. *Fanny Kemble's Civil Wars.* New York: Simon & Schuster, 2000.

———, ed. *Fanny Kemble's Journals.* Cambridge, MA: Harvard University Press, 2000.

David, Deirdre. *Fanny Kemble: A Performed Life.* Philadelphia: University of Pennsylvania Press, 2007.

Sizer, Lyde Cullen. *The Political Work of Northern Women Writers and the Civil War, 1850–1872.* Chapel Hill: University of North Carolina Press, 2000.

Snodgrass, Mary Ellen. *Encyclopedia of Feminist Literature.* New York: Facts on File, 2006.

King, Richard (1824–1885)

The founder of a Texas cattle empire, Captain Richard King built the King Ranch, called the "cradle of American cattle ranching," outside Brownsville in south Texas. The first stockman to selectively breed for specific traits, he produced the nation's first unique cattle, the Santa Gertrudis, from Texas shorthorns and Brahmas.

An Irish American born in New York City on July 10, 1824, he fled indenture to a jeweler at age nine by hiding aboard a steamer headed to Mobile, Alabama. With only a few months of formal education, he advanced from steamboat pilot to boat magnate and profited on troop transport and freight during the Seminole, Mexican-American, and Civil wars. On tough, arid range, King diversified his investments in 1860 by launching the Santa Gertrudis Ranch, later known as the King Ranch.

In late 1863, Union troops seized Brownsville and destroyed King's ranch. He hid out at Matamoros until President Andrew Johnson granted him amnesty for illegal freighting during the Civil War blockade. During Reconstruction, King and his partner Mifflin Kenedy monopolized cotton and mercantile shipping along the Rio Grande.

Upon King's return to the Nueces Strip between Brownsville and Corpus Christi, his acumen at building cattle, horse, sheep, and mule herds earned him respect. In addition to developing the American quarter horse for working cattle, he was one of the pioneer drovers, pushing more than 100,000 head north 1,000 miles (1,600 kilometers) over the Chisholm Trail to market at Abilene, Kansas. Stockmen recognized King's Running W brand and his insistence on strict legality in buying animals and property.

In feudal hacienda style, his staff of Kineños (King's people) were born, reared, educated, and hired on the ranch. As members of the extended household, they remained employed at full pay through retirement. In March 1875, he financed the Corpus Christi, San Diego, & Rio Grande Railroad as well as abattoirs (slaughterhouses), icehouses, riverboat design, and ocean shipping out of Corpus Christi, all of which offered opportunities to his workers.

To protect his investment, King hired Leander Harvey McNelly, a captain of the Texas State Police, as a privately funded security guard. McNelly halted the thievery of Juan Nepomuceno Cortina, a pro-Union bandit who crossed the Rio Grande with his 2,000 hired guns to raid Brownsville ranches and to funnel stolen cattle to Cuba. In June 1875, McNelly succeeded in a shooting war that wiped out Mexican bandits. In a bold daylight raid the next November, McNelly and a special force of agents recovered 400 stolen cattle in Mexico and drove them back to Brownsville.

At King's death from stomach cancer in San Antonio on April 14, 1885, he left his 600,000 acres (240,000 hectares) of prime ranchland for his wife, Henrietta M. Chamberlain King, and heirs. They expanded King Ranch to 860,000 acres (348,000 hectares), the size of Rhode Island, representing the world's largest ranch.

See also: Cattle and Livestock; Chisholm Trail; Ranching; Range Wars; Stagecoach Travel.

Further Reading

Colley, Betty Bailey, and Jane Clements Monday, with Beto Meldonado. *The Master Showmen of King Ranch: The Story of Beto and Librado Maldonado.* Austin: University of Texas Press, 2009.

Cypher, John. *Bob Kleberg and the King Ranch: A Worldwide Sea of Grass.* Austin: University of Texas Press, 1995.

Lea, Tom. *The King Ranch.* Boston: Little, Brown, 1974.

Monday, Jane Clements, and Frances Brannen Vick. *Petra's Legacy: The South Texas Ranching Empire of Petra Vela and Mifflin Kenedy.* College Station: Texas A&M University Press, 2007.

Thompson, Jerry. *Cortina: Defending the Mexican Name in Texas.* College Station: Texas A&M University Press, 2007.

Knights of the White Camellia

A secret, white supremacist vigilante group in the postbellum South, the Knights of the White Camellia (or Camelia) expressed the anguish and vengeance of Dixie patriots during Reconstruction. Founded on May 23, 1867, by Colonel Alcibiades DeBlanc, a Confederate hero and attorney, at Franklin in St. Mary's Parish, Louisiana, the brotherhood opposed the indignities foisted on defeated Southerners by Union occupation troops and carpetbaggers. DeBlanc mustered a militia of 600 and demanded a state tax boycott in protest of Reconstruction. Members swore that they would never wed a black woman or vote for a black official. They identified themselves to others by passing the left index finger over the left eye.

Before a local election in April 1868, Knights beat and intimidated candidate William B. Phillips at Alexandria, Louisiana, for being a radical Yankee. U.S. marshals arrested four brothers for the act, but the courts did nothing to suppress their terrorism at the polls. In June, the Knights held a convention in New Orleans and set up an internal organization of some 500 members.

Seeking the return of white supremacy to the plantation South, the members enlisted newspaper publishers, military officers, physicians, attorneys, sheriffs, and judges from the Carolinas to Texas. The Knights promoted antebellum society, discouraged racial mixing, and pledged to oppose black candidates for office and to restore white purity and genteel customs to demoralized institutions.

The *New Orleans Daily Picayune* commiserated with racists, who retaliated against black voters with violence. The group survived until 1869, when militants gravitated to the more secretive Ku Klux Klan, White Brotherhood, and White League, a Louisiana militia armed with rifles and revolvers.

See also: Ku Klux Klan.

Further Reading

Borsella, Cristogianni. *On Persecution, Identity and Activism.* Wellesley, MA: Dante University Press, 2005.

Gray, Michael. *Hand Me My Travelin' Shoes: In Search of Blind Willie McTell.* New York: Bloomsbury, 2009.

Lane, Charles. *The Day Freedom Died: The Colfax Massacre, the Supreme Court, and the Betrayal of Reconstruction.* New York: Henry Holt, 2008.

Martinez, J. Michael. *Carpetbaggers, Cavalry, and the Ku Klux Klan: Exposing the Invisible Empire.* Lanham, MD: Rowman & Littlefield, 2007.

Rable, George C. *But There Was No Peace: The Role of Violence in the Politics of Reconstruction.* Athens: University of Georgia Press, 2007.

Ku Klux Klan

The formation of the Ku Klux Klan (KKK) in Pulaski, Tennessee, on December 24, 1864, advanced the cause of white supremacists. Triggering their anger was President Abraham Lincoln's issuance of the Emancipation Proclamation two years before on January 1, 1863. A pseudo-Christian, pseudo-military terrorist brotherhood, the Klan emerged in part because of President Andrew Johnson's hostility to the congressional plan for Reconstruction.

General Oliver Otis Howard, head of the Freedmen's Bureau, called the Klan "a monster terrible beyond question." In his autobiography, Otis cited incidents of intimidation of teachers, hate mail, school burnings, death threats, pistol-whipping, hangings, and other forms of terrorism. Even though President Ulysses S. Grant put a stop to Klan outrages, Otis noted, "Negro voting, negro office holding, and negro domination were put under an effectual ban."

Klansmen fostered racist uprisings and domestic marauding of their targets. Established at a law office of Thomas McKissick Jones, the clandestine paramilitary was the concept of six white supremacists—law student James Rankin Crowe of Sheffield, Alabama; musician J. Calvin Jones of Pulaski; attorney John B. Kennedy of Lawrenceburg, Tennessee; attorneys John Calhoun Lester and Richard Robert Reed of Giles, Tennessee; and Frank Owen McCord, editor of the Pulaski *Citizen.* All Confederate veterans of Scots-Irish descent in their mid-twenties, they followed Grand Dragon General Nathan Bedford Forrest of Chapel Hill, Tennessee, the Confederate leader responsible for the massacre of black Union soldiers captured on April 12, 1864, at Fort Pillow, Tennessee. Members, calling themselves an "invisible empire," chose a title imitating *kyklos,* the Greek word for "circle," and the Scottish "clan" and celebrated a name that sounded like the rattling of bones.

Throughout Reconstruction, the Klan recruited Confederate veterans and grudge-holding white smallholders. As a safety valve for outrage against the loss of the Civil War, members pestered and menaced carpetbaggers from the North and former slaves with chain rattling, ghost pranks, rowdyism, and vandalism directed at freedmen's schools and black voters. In 1866, Klan mayhem in Memphis, Tennessee, resulted in the burning of 12 black churches and schools and the murder of 46 black citizens.

As KKK fanaticism advanced from vigilantism to felonies during the granting of civil rights for former slaves,

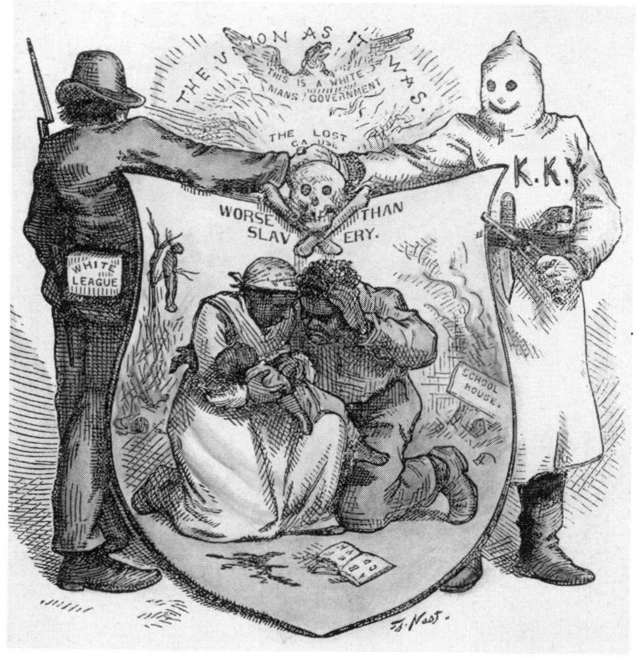

An 1874 political cartoon by Thomas Nast characterizes the harassment of blacks by the Ku Klux Klan and the White League as "Worse than Slavery." Anti-Klan legislation had outlawed the hate group in 1871, but racial violence continued. *(The Granger Collection, New York)*

by 1869, members ranged beyond central control. Goading their anger were the adoption of the Fourteenth Amendment to the U.S. Constitution in July 1868, granting black citizenship, and congressional passage of the Fifteenth Amendment early the following year, proposing to give black males the vote. In Alexandria, Louisiana, terrorists demolished the *Rapides Tribune,* a Republican paper. They committed serious crimes featured in headlines of the Memphis *Avalanche* and Nashville *Union and Dispatch.* Edward Pollard, editor of the Richmond *Examiner,* proclaimed the perpetrators noble heroes against black insolence and white treachery.

Forays involved some 550,000 male nightriders garbed in belted white robes and conical hoods adding up to 2 feet (1.2 meters) to their height. The disguise cloaked raids across the former Confederate states and as far south as Florida. Vandals targeted women and children, knocked over grave markers, seized weapons, and set crosses on fire. They ousted families from their homes, stampeded livestock, lashed adults, kidnapped children, and, in October 1868, assassinated Republican Congressman James M. Hinds of Arkansas. Focusing on male heads of households, members chased with hounds, pistol-whipped, emasculated, bludgeoned, drowned, and hanged blacks who competed economically with poor whites.

In response, black regiments in Alabama and South Carolina patrolled neighborhoods. In 1870, William Woods Holden, the governor of North Carolina, mustered the state militia against the nightriders.

Detailed coverage in *Harper's Weekly* of KKK activity from May to December 1871 enlightened the public about an insidious racist paramilitary that tortured and murdered black voters, burned a black orphanage, and requested amnesty for their terrorist violence. Under President Ulysses S. Grant, the Civil Rights Act of 1871, written by Union General Benjamin Franklin Butler, outlawed the hate group. Nonetheless, in 1873, Klan members slew 50 blacks and two whites in Colfax, Louisiana.

See also: Law and Courts; Fifteenth Amendment; Fourteenth Amendment; Knights of the White Camellia.

Further Reading

Borsella, Cristogianni. *On Persecution, Identity and Activism.* Wellesley, MA: Dante University Press, 2005.

Lane, Charles. *The Day Freedom Died: The Colfax Massacre, the Supreme Court, and the Betrayal of Reconstruction.* New York: Henry Holt, 2008.

Martinez, J. Michael. *Carpetbaggers, Cavalry, and the Ku Klux Klan: Exposing the Invisible Empire.* Lanham, MD: Rowman & Littlefield, 2007.

Snodgrass, Mary Ellen. *Civil Disobedience: An Encyclopedic History of Dissidence in the United States.* Armonk, NY: M.E. Sharpe, 2009.

Wade, Wyn Craig. *The Fiery Cross: The Ku Klux Klan in America.* New York: Oxford University Press, 1998.

L

Labor and Labor Unions

Demands of the Civil War years and Reconstruction spotlighted weaknesses in investing, labor policies, national industry, and product distribution. As the United States became industrialized, the rise of a plutocracy attested to the control of banking, oil and coal, railroads, telegraph, and steel mills by monopolies and the unfair competition against small businesses, which could not afford advanced technology, such as shoemaking machinery.

As mechanization threatened employment, worker safety, and wages, especially for women and children, management paid as little as $3 per day to women and a third that amount to children. Capitalists maintained a stranglehold on jobs by firing and blacklisting disgruntled workers, replacing laborers with non-English-speaking immigrants, reducing wages while increasing production rates, and breaking unions and strikes.

Grassroots efforts to equalize opportunities for men and women of varied ethnicities and cultures initiated unionism. Three prewar English journals—*American Banker and Workingmen's Leader, Mechanic's Own,* and *New England Mechanic*—and the German-language *Arbeiter* and *Soziale Republic* advocated arbitration and eschewed extreme labor stoppage and strikes as methods for improving the lot of workers.

Against the growing power of corporations, the Iron Molders' International Union in Albany, New York, in 1860, followed the advice of foundry man William H. Sylvis of Armagh, Pennsylvania, a writer for the *Workingman's Advocate,* the voice of the Chicago Trades Assembly. Sylvis chose political pressure as a means of upgrading workers' lives. He denounced the call for civil war because of the detrimental effect combat would have on unionizing and on workers' pay, especially in the prairie states and the West. He warned laborers against infighting and promoted the selfish maxim "Get all you can, and keep all you get."

As labor conditions worsened, workers began to unite. In 1861, blacksmiths and machinists held a convention in Pittsburgh to report on the shrinkage of their numbers as a result of the paralysis of the economy and growing joblessness. Business remained stagnant into mid-1862, when the Legal Tender Act of July 11 increased the national cash flow by $300 million and boosted trade.

In December 1864, a lockout of printers in Boston, Massachusetts, initiated interunion cooperation and issuance of a general labor newspaper, the *Daily Evening Voice,* which fostered solidarity among female members of the Sewing Machine Operators' Union of New York City. A similar situation among striking printers in St. Louis, Missouri, resulted in another organ of discontent, the *Daily Press,* the only one of 130 prolabor papers that urged the hiring of freed slaves. Contributing to the one-sided wartime boom, wholesale prices rose by 107 percent by 1865, increasing the wealth of capitalists but not of farmers and unskilled laborers.

From 1863 to 1873, while the United States advanced from an agrarian to an industrial nation, reformers put into publication 120 more journals to vocalize worker discontent. Newcomers to organization in 1864 included bookbinders, bricklayers, brush makers, cabinetmakers, carpenters, carvers, coach painters and trimmers, coopers, jewelers, painters, piano makers, plumbers, shipwrights, slate and metal roofers, stevedores, stonecutters and flaggers, tailors, and wheelwrights. More skilled workers began to consider organizing. Their fervor reached 61 trades represented by nearly 350 unions by 1865.

By late 1865, the list of organized trades expanded with axe makers, boiler makers, brass foundry men, cobblers, collar makers, curriers, engineers, garment cutters, gas and steam fitters, glassblowers, hat makers, horseshoers, joiners, leather finishers, marble cutters, plasterers, rail engineers, saddlers, seamen, spar makers, tinplate and sheet ironworkers, tinsmiths, upholsterers, and varnishers. The most aggressive growth occurred among blacksmiths and machinists, with 29 unions, and among iron molders, with 24. The industrial states of Massachusetts, New York, and Pennsylvania led the movement with 60 percent of the new unions. Strikes increased from 38 in 30 trades in 1863 to 108 in 48 trades in 1864 and to 85 in 46 trades in 1865.

Unions and the Family

To raise workers' standards of living, the National Labor and Reform Party and the National Labor Union proposed a system of mutual aid. Unions sought to improve workplace conditions, particularly the shortening of 18-hour workdays, which demanded 108-hour weeks with only one day of rest. In Denver, Colorado, both carpenters and typesetters organized to demand a standard salary of $4 per day. In Boston, Ira Steward, a machinist laboring 12-hour shifts, led the 1863 convention of the International Union of Machinists and Blacksmiths (IUMB) in demanding a law limiting workdays to eight hours.

To maintain worker communication and enhance solidarity, unions needed more national assemblies and their own media. On June 6, 1863, the IUMB began issuing *Fincher's Trades' Review,* a weekly advisory that Jonathan C. Fincher published for the Philadelphia Trades Assembly. The review kept workers in 36 states, Washington, D.C., Canada, and Great Britain informed of the rise of inflation over wages, and it urged members to pressure major political parties to acknowledge the plight of the working class.

Iron molder Robert Gilchrist, president of the Louisville Trades Assembly, took a different approach by proposing reform through a national federation of workers, an idealistic concept for its day. Fellow unionists supported individual trades by boycotting companies that refused to pay union scale. Instead, the unions listed cooperative stores and groceries that supported the workers' initiative. Additional benefits from free libraries and lobbyists upgraded the living standards of working-class families.

As president of the Boston Eight Hour League and the National Ten Hour League and, in 1864, founder of the Labor Reform Association, Ira Steward vocalized worker frustration with schedules that undermined health and family life. Collaborating with Boston abolitionist orator Wendell Phillips, Steward and George McNeill, a textile worker from age ten, in 1866 organized the Grand Eight Hour League of Massachusetts; however, the organization foundered because of white worker clashes with imported Chinese labor. A similar impasse within the Cigar Makers International Union, formed in 1864, pitted skilled male cigar rollers against female workers, who endangered male dominance in the industry by accepting lower wages.

To counter worker solidarity, management began forming employer unions, such as the Employers' General Association of Michigan, the Master Mechanics of Boston, and the New York Master Builders' Association, and used gender and race conflicts as a wedge by hiring nonwhite males, immigrants, and women to break strikes led by white male citizens.

Spreading the Wealth

The depression of 1866 energized labor leaders to pursue a strategy of greater prosperity by giving more people jobs and a greater share of company earnings to boost the economy and enhance the buying power of the laboring class. At a consortium of trade unions in Baltimore on August 20, 1866, labor leaders established the National Labor Union, a federation led by William Sylvis that represented 60,000 members of 50 local trade unions. The attempt to solve numerous complex issues—inflation, monetary and land reform, contract prison labor, public works, racism against blacks and Asians, and women's rights—sapped the efforts of reformers.

By the end of the 1860s, the demand for the eight-hour workday had spread to legislatures in Connecticut, Illinois, Missouri, and New York. The New York State Assembly passed weak laws that favored employer demands. In Wisconsin, a time-limit law benefited only women and children. In 1868, the U.S. Congress enacted an eight-hour law covering only hirelings and mechanics working for the federal government. In 1872, Republicans made the unsettled issue of shorter workdays a party objective.

A nationwide union called the Order of the Knights of St. Crispin, organized in Massachusetts by skilled shoemakers in 1867, grew into the country's largest labor group and a vocal outlet for workers by 1870. Shoemaker Newell Daniels organized the worker collective, a powerful merger of 50,000 workers with global ties. Using unannounced strikes, arbitration, and negotiation as leverage against management, the Knights sought to stabilize earnings, halt the importation of immigrant laborers, and counter gender discrimination against the women's auxiliary, the Daughters of St. Crispin. Again, racism weakened worker organization by turning local workers against Chinese newcomers.

Among the Knights of Labor, which tailor Uriah Smith Stephens organized in Philadelphia in 1869, members demonized wage slavery and opposed child labor, monopolies, conspicuous wealth, and convict labor, the force that built a new penitentiary in Columbia, South Carolina. Under the leadership of radical orator Mary Harris Jones, better known as Mother Jones, the Knights favored equal wages for male and female and white and nonwhite workers. The Knights excluded capitalists, doctors, financiers, investors, lawyers, and liquor manufacturers, whom Jones rejected as social parasites. The association alerted workers to the aggregation of wealth, the connivance of land speculators, and the network of technicalities, delays, and bias that created a class of beggars. In Leadville, Colorado, the demand for tunnelers and smelters lured Austrian, Croat, Italian, Serb, and Slovenian workers to the area. In the late 1870s, low-paid miners, united by the Knights of Labor, forced issues of safety and compensation through unionization, walkouts, and strikes.

The concept of a national organization for trades built momentum. By 1869, the total number of national union members reached 171,571. According to William Sylvis, "Cooperation is taking hold upon the minds of our members." A year before his death in 1869, he was confident of a new era in labor–management relations.

Sylvis's rosy outlook for workers failed to factor in shifts in the economy. Increasing market instability in 1873 and lower demand for farm and manufactured goods caused the bankruptcy of financier Jay Cooke and his scandal-ridden company, the first loss resulting from a nationwide bank panic and stock market collapse. Some 5,000 business failures slashed incomes, especially among unemployed workers. The panic crushed unions by 73 percent, a setback that lasted for five years. Among them were the Sons of Vulcan, puddlers who turned pig iron into steel. In 1876, iron and steel laborers in the Chicago area formed the Amalgamated Association of Iron and Steel Workers, builders of railroads, bridges, and skyscrapers and forerunner of the United Steelworkers.

American Trade Union Membership, 1869

Union/Trade	Membership
Knights of St. Crispin	50,000
Miners	30,000
Iron molders	17,000
Typographers	17,000
Bricklayers	15,000
Machinists and blacksmiths	10,000
Carpenters and joiners	6,000
Cigar makers	5,000
Coopers	5,000
Locomotive firemen	3,000
Cigar packers	2,500
Plasterers	2,500
Masons	2,000
Tailors	2,000
Grand Forge of the U.S.	1,600
Painters	1,500
Metalworkers	850
Engineers	621
Total:	171,571

On July 16, 1877, a wildcat strike erupted in the rail industry over the lowering of wages by the Baltimore & Ohio Railroad and fueled a national work stoppage. Mother Jones and a coterie of female agitators supported militant Baltimore and Ohio rail strikers in Pittsburgh. Violence and arson in Baltimore, Chicago, Pittsburgh, and St. Louis required President Rutherford B. Hayes to dispatch the military, but the return of peace cost 53 lives and nearly $10 million in property loss. State legislatures retaliated by funding National Guard units and criminalizing collective worker action. In private, former president Ulysses S. Grant criticized Hayes for being too lenient.

Labor and Racism

Vast changes in the Midwest, especially the formation of the National Grange of the Order of Patrons of Husbandry, accompanied the arrival of the railroad and attendant greed and corruption by railroad barons such as James "Diamond Jim" Fisk, Jr., and Jay Gould.

In 1868, the Union Pacific opened a coal mine at Rock Springs, Wyoming, establishing the Wyoming Coal and Mining Company as operators. When the labor movement encouraged a strike for better pay, management chose to hire Scandinavian immigrants at the rate of $2 per day. Because citizen laborers threatened their replacements, the U.S. Army positioned troops at the mine.

A second strike in 1875 resulted in the Union Pacific Coal Department hiring 150 Chinese strikebreakers from the Far West to settle at Sweetwater and Washakie, Wyoming. The editor of the *Rock Springs Independent* published an anti-Asian accusation that the Chinese carried leprosy and demanded that the immigrants must go. Against Republican rabble-rousing, the railroad kept the Chinese miners, who proved productive and dependable.

After completion of the Transcontinental Railroad across the American Southwest on May 10, 1869, the loss of jobs aroused outrage and xenophobia among white West Coast laborers. Scapegoaters of the Chinese coolie labor pool blamed them for lower wages and for unfair job competition because of their lower standard of living, which Gould reduced further by cutting their wages to less than a dollar a day.

The Railroad Strike of 1877—the first nationwide industrial job action in U.S. history—led to rioting in cities across the country. Before federal troops restored order, the property damage in Pittsburgh *(above)* and elsewhere reached $10 million. *(Kean Collection/Getty Images)*

On October 29, 1877, former sailor Dennis Kearney, a 30-year-old drayman and rabble-rouser from Oakmount, Ireland, rallied thousands of protesters to the Crocker Mansion on Nob Hill in San Francisco. As head of the Workingman's Trade and Labor Union of San Francisco, he denounced the wealth of rail and realty moguls and charged the Central Pacific Railroad with unfair employment of cheap Asian laborers. In a speech at Faneuil Hall in Boston, Kearney stereotyped Asian workers as "leprous Chinese pirates" and slum dwellers who "cut the throats of honest laboring men." His specious arguments ranged from claims of racial favoritism toward the Chinese to criticism of the mayor, police department, district attorney, and entrepreneur Leland Stanford for impeding the progress of the white working class.

Kearney's populist agitation plagued Chicago and Anaheim, California, and advanced on the state capitol at Sacramento. In March 1877, Kearney roused a backlash against the "Yellow Peril" by dispatching goon squads to attack hop field stoop laborers, set fire to their quarters, lynch employers of the Chinese, and burn pro-Asian businesses. In July, a three-day rampage resulted in five Chinese murders, ransacking of Chinese laundries, burning of hayricks and lumber stacks, and a raid on the Pacific Mail Steamship docks.

At Kearney's arrest on November 3, 1877, for disturbing the peace and inciting a riot, the mayhem stopped temporarily. Later in the month, some 10,000 California laborers of the Workingmen's Party revived the racial hooliganism by celebrating Kearney's leadership in a Thanksgiving parade. Followers processed through Asian neighborhoods, brandishing clubs and pick handles and shouting hate messages, a justification for the Chinese Exclusion Act of 1882.

See also: Gould, Jay; Grange Movement; Hayes, Rutherford B.; Jones, Mother; Music.

Further Reading

Borsella, Cristogianni. *On Persecution, Identity and Activism.* Wellesley, MA: Dante University Press, 2005.

Hapke, Laura. *Sweatshop: The History of an American Idea.* New Brunswick, NJ: Rutgers University Press, 2004.

Knight, Peter, ed. *Conspiracy Theories in American History: An Encyclopedia.* Santa Barbara, CA: ABC-CLIO, 2003.

Murrin, John M., et al. *Liberty, Equality, Power: A History of the American People.* 4th ed. Belmont, CA: Thomson/Wadsworth, 2009.

Palladino, Grace. *Another Civil War: Labor, Capital, and the State in the Anthracite Regions of Pennsylvania, 1840–1868.* New York: Fordham University Press, 2006.

Steel, Edward M., Jr., ed. *The Court-Martial of Mother Jones.* Lexington: University Press of Kentucky, 1995.

Land-Grant Colleges

Congress met the demands of the Industrial Revolution in 1862 by passing a visionary bill—the Morrill Land-Grant Act—that revolutionized the nonsectarian college curriculum and broadened student demographics from the elite to the working class. Signed into law by President Abraham Lincoln on July 2, 1862, the bill authorized federal distribution of public lands and the construction of agricultural and vocational colleges, called land-grant colleges.

Republican Congressman Justin Smith Morrill of Vermont, chairman of the House Committee on Ways and Means, authored the law in 1857; Congress passed the bill two years later, but President James Buchanan vetoed it. Adding an amendment that provided for instruction in military tactics, Morrill resubmitted the legislation five years later. The act proposed funding at least one college per state offering modern agrarian, military, and technical skills accessible to all, especially farmers.

The states received 17.4 million acres (7 million hectares) of public plots, parceled out at 30,000 acres (12,200 hectares) for each legislator. Thus, the smallest states anticipated a minimum of 90,000 acres (36,500 hectares). New York received the largest share of 980,000 acres (397,000 hectares); Pennsylvania got 780,000 acres (316,000 hectares), the second-largest allotment. Congress distributed portions west of the Mississippi River to those states lacking public property; thus, Illinois, for example, received 25,000 acres (10,100 acres) in Minnesota and Nebraska. The total acreage sold for $7.55 million.

Under the provisions of the Morrill Land-Grant Act, states had to apply within two years and open their schools within five. Proceeds from land sales built institutions featuring coursework in agriculture, engineering, and military science, but some schools lacked sufficient endowments to sustain their offerings. For a model, legislators looked to the nation's original agrarian institution, the Agricultural College of the State of Michigan, one of the first to offer architecture. Chartered in 1855, the college favored the inductive method of teaching, practical application of theory, and three hours per day of manual labor, a necessary element of President Theophilus C. Abbot's "whole student" philosophy. President Abraham Lincoln was so impressed with the school's four-year setup and master's degree program that he selected the Michigan "ag" school as a model for the nation.

The State University Movement

With the support of the Grange Movement (National Grange of the Order of Patrons of Husbandry) and three state legislatures—those of Iowa, Michigan, and Pennsylvania—the land-grant college movement gained momentum. The first land-grant institution, Iowa State Agricultural College, opened on September 11, 1862, and admitted male and female students. The curriculum prepared civil, electrical, mechanical, and mining engineers and trained agronomists at the Iowa Experiment Station and in the animal husbandry laboratory.

Kansas State Agricultural College at Manhattan and Massachusetts Agricultural College at Amherst went into construction in 1863. "K-State" opened with equal male and female numbers and broadened the choices of careers for women with the creation of a home economics department in 1873, the beginning of county extension programs. "Mass Aggie" offered its first 50 enrollees hands-on expertise in the chemistry lab and Durfee Plant House, the first research greenhouse on the campus.

Also in 1863, gentlemen farmers revamped the Farmers' High School of Pennsylvania into the state's first land-grant college, which formed the nucleus of Pennsylvania State University. The underlying strategy was to distract boys from industrial urbanism and its vices and to inculcate the traditional values of steady labor and worker dignity.

Research and laboratory experimentation introduced Americans to thinking skills based on problem solving rather than rote memorization of theory, such as the Forest Experiment Station established at the University of Maine. By 1868, land-grant colleges operated as far west as California, Minnesota, Texas, and Wisconsin. For black students, Alcorn State University at Lorman, Mississippi, offered its initial student body of 179 males experience with farming and mechanics. In Texas, segregationists founded two land-grant institutions—Prairie View State Normal and Industrial College for blacks and the Agricultural and Mechanical College of Texas for whites.

Some months before the completion of the Transcontinental Railroad, educators merged the College of California, a liberal arts school teaching classical Greek and Latin, with the Agricultural, Mining and Mechanical Arts College. The union formed the University of California, Berkeley, a leader in higher education in the Far West. In San Francisco in 1873, the University of California added its first medical school, the impetus for land-grant curricula in medicine, nursing, and nutrition. In the Midwest the same year, Ohio Governor Rutherford B. Hayes oversaw the sale of 630,000 acres (255,200 hectares) at 50 cents per acre, which endowed the Ohio Agricultural and Mechanical College at Columbus, the beginning of Ohio State University. In the Pacific Northwest, enrollment at the University of Oregon lured talented students and researchers away from Eastern universities.

National Precedent

Land grants invigorated in-state dissension and college rivalries. Illinois agriculturists and industrialists fought over the land-grant money, delaying any choice of a campus location for a year. In 1864, in defiance of claims by Princeton University, educators reclassified Rutgers Scientific School as New Jersey's first land-grant college. Trustees, led by President George Hammell Cook, fortified scientific offerings with courses in agriculture, chemistry, and engineering and built the Agricultural Experiment Station at College Farm.

In New York in 1865, Quaker philanthropist Ezra Cornell funded the first semiprivate land-grant school, one of the eight Ivy League campuses. He co-founded Cornell University, a practical professional institution chartered through the lobbying of its first president, Andrew Dickson White, a Yale University–educated teacher of English and history. To satisfy federal requirements for land-grant colleges, Cornell staff offered separate courses for state and out-of-state students.

In a period of antithetical views on educational philosophy, the independence of the new state institution gained the support of Penn State President Evan Pugh, an agricultural chemist; Yale academician Daniel Coit Gilman; and George W. Atherton, one of the chief campaigners for the Morrill Land-Grant Act and a lobbyist for a library endowment at Penn State by Scots industrialist Andrew Carnegie. Sarah Josepha Hale's editorials for *Godey's Lady's Book* endorsed the land-grant universities and crusaded for girls' schools and medical colleges for women in order to raise women's personal aims to include public and private education and a broader choice of professions. Criticism of the land-grant movement from three prestigious university presidents—Charles William Elliot of Harvard, James McCosh of Princeton, and Noah Porter of Yale—alleged that "cow colleges" cheapened and diluted higher education.

Amid differences of opinion about the nation's educational direction, the enrollment of land-grant universities in 1876—117 at the universities of Minnesota and Missouri, 80 at the University of Kentucky, 75 at the University of Nebraska, and three at Louisiana State University—suggested that white parents and students were not sold on technical education or on nonsectarian schools. Compared to a national enrollment in non–land grant universities of 19,263, the institutions funded by the Morrill Land-Grant Act drew only 2,674 or 13.9 percent of the nation's students. Because the chief beneficiaries continued to be blacks and minorities, poor students, and women, both Congress and the Grange requested an investigation of the lack of interest.

By 1879, the vision of the land-grant college admitted students to five different educational models:

Number and Type	Examples
19 State facilities	Arkansas, California, Delaware, Florida, Georgia, Illinois, Kentucky, Louisiana, Maine, Massachusetts, Minnesota, Missouri, Nebraska, Nevada, New Hampshire, Ohio, Tennessee, West Virginia, Wisconsin
8 Agricultural and mechanical colleges	Alabama, Colorado, Kansas, Mississippi, Oregon, Purdue (Ind.), Texas, Virginia
6 Black institutions	Alabama, Alcorn (Miss.), Arkansas, Kentucky, Lincoln (Mo.), Prairie View (Tex.)
6 Private institutions	Brown (R.I.), Cornell (N.Y.), Massachusetts Institute of Technology, Rutgers (N.J.), Sheffield (Conn.), Vermont
4 Agricultural colleges	Iowa, Maryland, Michigan, Pennsylvania

See also: Colleges and Universities; Cornell, Ezra; Home Economics.

Further Reading

Alter, Stephen G. *William Dwight Whitney and the Science of Language.* Baltimore: Johns Hopkins University Press, 2005.

Cross, Coy F., II. *Justin Smith Morrill: Father of the Land-Grant Colleges.* East Lansing: Michigan State University Press, 1999.

Geiger, Roger L., ed. *Perspectives on the History of Higher Education, 2007.* New Brunswick, NJ: Transaction, 2007.

Jones-Wilson, Faustine C., et al., eds. *Encyclopedia of African-American Education.* Westport, CT: Greenwood, 1996.

Williams, Roger L. *The Origins of Federal Support for Higher Education: George W. Atherton and the Land-Grant College Movement.* University Park: Pennsylvania State University Press, 1991.

Law and Courts

From the Civil War through Reconstruction, the U.S. court system created precedents for a revolutionary shift in national law governing citizenship and civil rights, immigration, and interstate commerce. The case of John "Jackey" Anderson, the son of a black runaway, made him a cause célèbre in the United States, Canada, and England. A slave in Howard County, Missouri, Anderson escaped bondage in late September 1853 and stabbed to death a pursuer, Seneca T.P. Diggs. After Anderson reached Windsor, Ontario, in spring 1860, a Detroit slave owner named Brown obtained a court judgment under the 1842 Webster-Ashburton Treaty legitimating the fugitive's extradition. Slave transporters predicted that the precedent would spell the end of the Underground Railroad. Intervention by the British and Foreign Anti-Slavery Society saved the secret network. On February 9, 1861, a new judgment by a Toronto court found in Anderson's favor.

The outbreak of Civil War on April 12, 1861, motivated President Abraham Lincoln to suspend the writ of habeas corpus, the first infringement on constitutional rights and due process in the nation's history. After Union General Benjamin Franklin Butler placed Baltimore, Maryland, under martial law on May 13, detective Allan Pinkerton, head of security, incarcerated secessionist legislators and the city's mayor, councilmen, police commissioner, and police chief at Fort McHenry, a federal prison for political dissidents and prisoners of war.

The arrest of secessionist John Merryman, a lieutenant in the state militia, for burning bridges and cutting telegraph lines precipitated a suit against the federal government for unjust imprisonment. In the case of *Ex parte Merryman,* U.S. Supreme Court Chief Justice Roger B. Taney concurred with Merryman that the president had abused executive powers by denying a citizen due process of law. Taney scolded President Lincoln for transgressing a cornerstone of civil liberty that dated to the Magna Carta of 1215.

On February 14, 1862, Lincoln eased off his initial militancy by granting amnesty to political prisoners who posed no public or political threat. On March 3, 1863, Congress indemnified Lincoln's arbitrary arrests under the Habeas Corpus Act. The law left undelineated the president's power to suspend citizen rights during war.

In a subsequent wartime case, *Ex parte Milligan,* the Supreme Court decided on April 3, 1866, that civil courts had jurisdiction over military tribunals. In that decision, the high court determined that the suspension of habeas corpus during an insurrection was lawful, but that the military had deprived five citizens of a hearing in the civilian courts, which were still in operation. All nine justices denied martial rule the right to try and execute five conspirators against the Union. The same day, Chief Justice Salmon P. Chase struck down the execution order and freed four of the traitors from prison. The judgment validated constitutional liberty over extreme executive powers by the War Department, which had made 13,535 political arrests during the Civil War.

Slaves Become Citizens

The most controversial alteration in constitutional law, the Thirteenth Amendment to the U.S. Constitution, recognized the rights of black chattel to freedom from bondage. President Lincoln introduced the preliminary stage of formal liberation on January 1, 1863, by issuing the Emancipation Proclamation. On December 6, 1865, six months after Lincoln's assassination, ratification of the Thirteenth Amendment prohibited slavery as a denial of personhood. To ensure obedience to federal law and to suppress the Ku Klux Klan and the passage of racist Black Codes, Congress instituted a federal enforcement agency, the Freedmen's Bureau. Passage of the Civil Rights Act of 1866 ensured unimpeded citizenship for ex-slaves in the North and South. In an extension of human rights, legislators in 1868 banned the sale of female and child slaves among the Navajo.

The Fourteenth Amendment (ratified July 9, 1868) and Fifteenth Amendment (ratified February 3, 1870) conferred on black males civil rights and the vote, but stopped short of granting Asians, Native Americans, and women full citizenship. Most offensive to the South was the third section of the Fourteenth Amendment, which excluded former rebels from appointment or election to state and federal offices. The enactment nullified Black Codes that restricted the movement of blacks and forbade them from testifying against whites in court. These landmark amendments quashed states' rights to regulate the human condition of U.S. residents. Delayed ratification in the Confederate states sent a message to the Republican-controlled Congress that secessionist Democrats would not tolerate a federalized central government elected by black illiterates with no background in civics.

During the settlement of the contested presidential election of 1876, the Compromise of 1877 reduced federal powers by removing Union occupation forces from the South. The U.S. government abandoned efforts to ensure racial equality and allowed former Confederate states to dispossess freedmen of many aspects of their newly won liberty. Subsequent Supreme Court tests of the definition of "citizenship" acknowledged the civil rights of Chinese Americans, Hispanics, women, and the offspring of illegal aliens, but not of Indians. The Fifteenth Amendment remained jeopardized by bias for another century until the civil rights movement of the 1960s.

To ensure white supremacy, the South enacted Jim Crow laws that intimidated black voters with literacy tests and poll taxes. Racist authorities condoned the terrorist night-riding of the Ku Klux Klan that kept ex-slaves in quasi-bondage.

In 1877 in Columbia, South Carolina, the arrest of 220 Klansmen preceded the prosecution of five members for conspiracy to hinder black citizens from voting. Dr. Edward T. Avery and Robert Mitchell faced federal charges of intimidating and threatening a black male for participating in the 1870 and 1872 elections. In U.S. circuit court, prosecutor David T. Corbin and South Carolina Attorney General Daniel Henry Chamberlain raised a defense before judges Hugh Bond and George Bryan and pled the case before juries dominated by freedmen. The court convicted the five defendants of two of the four counts of impeding civil liberties. In all, 53 Klansmen pled guilty and served cell time at the federal penitentiary in Albany, New York. As a result of judicial severity, South Carolina's Ku Klux Klan lowered its public profile but continued to persecute ex-slaves, immigrants, Catholics, and Jews.

Law in the West

The frontier introduced legal questions unprecedented in antebellum courts. In Utah Territory in 1861, third Mormon president John Taylor claimed the rights of the holy priesthood, which placed the laws of the Latter Day Saints above the dictates of the U.S. Constitution. To halt Mormon hegemony in Utah Territory, President Lincoln on July 8, 1862, signed the Morrill Anti-Bigamy Act criminalizing polygamy, the wedlock of one man with multiple wives. Violators risked a $500 fine and five years' imprisonment for each illicit union. In defiance of federal law, church elders continued to add brides to their households.

On January 2, 1872, judicial authorities made a test case by charging Apostle Daniel H. Wells, the mayor of Salt Lake City, with cohabiting with seven women and by citing Brigham Young for 54 felonious marriages. To simplify prosecution of polygamists, the Poland Act of 1874 extended federal judicial power over civil and criminal courts in Utah Territory. High-profile polygamists responded by going into exile with their contraband households in other territories and Canada.

On the Pacific Coast, racism conflicted with the profit motive. The importation of laborers from China, Japan, and the Philippines in the mid-1800s filled a need for unskilled workers on Hawaiian sugar plantations and during the construction of the Transcontinental Railroad in the West. Rail capitalists lobbied for the Burlingame-Seward Treaty, which on July 28, 1868, lowered trade barriers by conferring most-favored-nation status on China. A diplomatic triumph for Secretary of State William Henry Seward, the agreement validated free migration, permanent residency, and freedom of thought and religion among Chinese workers in the United States.

Upon the completion of railway building on May 10, 1869, California laws halted the hiring of Asian laborers for city projects and industry. Federal justices intervened against the California caste system that banned Asians from assimilating into white communities. On May 31, 1870, Congress nullified state taxes on aliens and banned "onerous conditions" that violated civil rights. A subsequent law, the Page Act of 1875, barred the recruitment of Asian slave laborers, convicts, and prostitutes. The ban on female Chinese immigrants condemned America's Chinatowns to a bachelor society—male enclaves without wives and children.

In the 1870s, legislatures in Illinois, Iowa, Minnesota, and Wisconsin enacted so-called Granger Laws, the first attempts to suppress grain and rail monopolies by regulating rates for transportation, grain elevators, and warehousing for small farmers and bulk shippers. Senator William B. Allison of Iowa had gained prominence in the 1863 case *Gelpke v. City of Dubuque,* in which the U.S. Supreme

Court held cities responsible for bond redemption. Lobbyists from the National Grange of the Order of Patrons of Husbandry championed farmers and ranchers held hostage by Northeastern wealth and industrial power.

To ease the plight of smallholders from uncertain profits and debt, the Supreme Court ruled in favor of railroad storage fees in the case of *Munn v. Illinois* (1877). In the opinion of Chief Justice Morrison Remick Waite, the state had the authority to regulate property in the public's interest where a private company served public needs. Justice Stephen Johnson Field cast the lone dissenting vote against federal regulation on the grounds that the state subverted the right to private property.

Women's Rights

In 1868, women's rights advocates and the radical feminist press denounced the capital sentence of Hester Vaughan for infanticide. At her trial in New York City on June 30, 1868, a doctor surmised that Vaughan, who was unattended during labor, bludgeoned her newborn's cranium with a blunt instrument. Because laws prohibited females from testifying, an all-male jury found her guilty. Judge James R. Ludlow decided to make an example of Vaughan by ordering her hanging. After Dr. Susan A. Smith learned that the mother had been unconscious after extended travail and may have unintentionally harmed the infant's head in delivery, the physician demanded a retrial. Feminists declared Vaughan a victim of poverty and male supremacy and charged the legal system with denying her a trial by her peers. Smith and Dr. Clemence Sophia Lozier produced enough data, petitions, and letters of protest to persuade Governor John W. Geary to pardon Vaughan.

As further evidence of gender oppression, women's rights leaders revived the colonial protest of taxation without representation. In 1874, two elderly intellectuals attacked the state tax structure of Connecticut. Scholar Julia Evelina Smith and her younger sister, orator Abby Hadassah Smith, challenged a tax increase on their Glastonbury acreage, Kimberley Farm, where they supported themselves through the sale of butter and cheese. They highlighted the plight of disenfranchised women by refusing to pay a levy that targeted widows and unmarried females. On November 5, 1873, town officials refused to place the Smiths on the agenda or to exempt disenfranchised women from property tax. Municipal authorities claimed the proceeds from the sale of the sisters' seven Alderney cattle and pasture. With the backing of orator Abby Kelley Foster and suffragists Susan B. Anthony, Elizabeth Cady Stanton, and Lucy Stone, the sisters sued the tax collector and won a small but significant victory for women.

See also: Ex Parte Milligan (1866); Jim Crow; Law Enforcement; Polygamy.

Further Reading

Beatty, Jack. *Age of Betrayal: The Triumph of Money in America, 1865–1900.* New York: Alfred A. Knopf, 2008.

Kaczorowski, Robert J. *The Politics of Judicial Interpretation: The Federal Courts, Department of Justice, and Civil Rights, 1866–1876.* New York: Fordham University Press, 2005.

Keyssar, Alexander. *The Right to Vote: The Contested History of Democracy in the United States.* New York: Basic Books, 2000.

Lane, Charles. *The Day Freedom Died: The Colfax Massacre, the Supreme Court, and the Betrayal of Reconstruction.* New York: Henry Holt, 2008.

Nelson, William E. *The Fourteenth Amendment: From Political Principle to Judicial Doctrine.* Cambridge, MA: Harvard University Press, 1988.

Odo, Franklin, ed. *The Columbia Documentary History of the Asian American Experience.* New York: Columbia University Press, 2002.

Paludan, Phillip S. *Covenant with Death: The Constitution, Law, and Equality in the Civil War Era.* Urbana: University of Illinois Press, 1975.

Snodgrass, Mary Ellen. *The Underground Railroad: An Encyclopedia of People, Places, and Operations.* Armonk, NY: M.E. Sharpe, 2007.

Law Enforcement

In the 1860s and 1870s, the United States maintained order through a loosely interlinking system of city and federal marshals, U.S. Cavalry, state rangers, Wells Fargo detectives, Pinkerton agents, and bounty hunters. For most settled areas, citizens relied on sheriffs, constables, night watches, and justices of the peace, who served as both arresting officers and magistrates.

Early in the nineteenth century, cities created models of civil control based on a military chain of command. Richmond, Virginia, formed a police department in 1807. By 1860, the city employed 35 roundsmen (or watchmen) superintended by eight officers. The burgeoning of the city as the capital of the Confederate States of America required a night patrol of one captain, three lieutenants, and 40 privates to protect a population of 100,000.

When Virginia returned to the Union in 1870, Richmond's officers, uniformed in blue and armed with revolvers, mounted horse patrols and reported crime from telegraph call boxes. Police in San Francisco broke the standard dress code by wearing gray uniforms and equipping themselves with revolvers, billy clubs, and concealed bowie knives, a necessary armament against unemployed railroad workers, radical labor agitators, and racist city gangs, who rioted in July 1877 against Chinese immigrants.

In New Orleans, Louisiana, an integrated police force dressed in blue frock coats marked by a crescent-and-star badge. Members conspired with the White League, a racist paramilitary group, to direct riots against blacks. The illegal militia, led by Sheriff Christopher Columbus Nash, armed members with Colt revolvers, Winchester rifles, and Prussian needle guns, short-range bolt-action rifles. In 1874, the death toll in New Orleans reached 13, with 53 wounded before President Ulysses S. Grant suppressed racist police by stationing federal troops throughout the Mississippi Delta. In October, Thomas Nast, a cartoonist for *Harper's Weekly,* lampooned white supremacist police as partners with the Ku Klux Klan in a tyranny "worse than slavery."

Standards in the Making

Lacking standardization, the professionalism of police departments varied as widely as the demands of the job. The 21 men patrolling the waterfront town of Alexandria, Virginia, combated crime as well as the drunken antics of U.S. sailors. In Springfield, Ohio, Marshal John E. Donovan earned only $25 a year and transported drunks to jail by wheelbarrow; city officials in Los Angeles, California, made do in 1869 with only six officers to patrol a cluster of brothels, opium dens, and saloons. At San Diego, California, citizens had no marshal and used an iron cage as a jail. To keep the peace, the first marshal barred Indians and Mexicans from the city's environs. In contrast, Detroit, Michigan, established a detective bureau, a harbor and river patrol, and a sanitary survey to aid the Board of Health in preventing epidemics.

The police of Charleston, South Carolina, signed on to serve at $1 per day, a salary commensurate with that of teachers. By 1873, Charleston policemen wore uniforms and followed law enforcement regulations. In Missouri after 1869, St. Louis police received instruction at the city's police academy.

In Savannah, Georgia, the danger of Union invasion proved so great that the city armed its policemen with muskets and drilled them like soldiers in the town squares. The force retained its military aura in 1865, when General Robert M. Anderson returned from duty in the Confederate army to serve as police chief of Savannah's 116 officers. After two policemen died in a riot in 1868, Officer R.E. Read was buried in plot number 911, the future designation of emergency services.

Urban police adapted to the times and to technological advances. In 1853, New York City disbanded a constabulary dating to the colonial era and formed the nation's first professional force, commanded by a captain. Authorities modeled the organization on British "bobbies," named for founder Sir Robert Peel. Within months, Boston organized a similar force and armed men with clubs. Pittsburgh, Pennsylvania, established a law enforcement department in 1857 with one chief and nine constables. In Philadelphia in 1860, the formation of a special harbor patrol extended police jurisdiction over ports. In this same period, Baltimore officials began an ongoing modernization program to expand citizen protection from peacekeeping to crime prevention and investigation.

At New Haven, Connecticut, in 1861, police received annual salaries of $550 and standard dress that included blue coats and trousers, a shield, and an imposing bell-crowned helmet. In 1873, the city centralized its management by building a city complex at 165 Court Street comprising a police department, city court, fire department, and court of health. To speed felons to jail, officers mounted the "Black Maria," a horse-drawn patrol wagon.

Trenton, New Jersey, made similar upgrades in a unified city system of government. To focus police on law enforcement, in 1875, the city council relieved men of the job of cleaning, lighting, and extinguishing street lamps.

Police and Violence

Instances of police brutality in the 1860s demanded a closer look at the broad powers of officers. In Lower Manhattan, on July 13–16, 1863, police and fire departments struggled to suppress unruly laborers during the four-day draft riots, the nation's largest civil insurrection to that time. Arson and threats against the *New York Tribune,* Armory, and residences of prominent Republicans required the mounting of Gatling guns on wagons. Four regiments of federal troops and three of state militia battled the final foray on the evening of July 16, when the riot converged on Gramercy Park, where 120 insurgents died. Police could not halt the burning of 50 buildings and the loss of $5 million in private property.

A decade later, on January 13, 1874, the Tompkins Square Riot in the East Village involved 7,000 unemployed immigrant workers in hand-to-hand skirmishes with mounted police. Labor leader Samuel Gompers and reporters for the *New York Sun* and *The New York Times* charged officers with swinging clubs indiscriminately at men, women, and children.

To prevent similar instances of police brutality, the Chicago Police Department in 1861 placed three commissioners in charge of controlling violence and corruption and established detective divisions to investigate complex crimes and conspiracies. To increase efficiency in ethnic neighborhoods, the department hired blacks and Irish immigrants. In 1875, a study of Chicago's policing disclosed continued graft perpetrated by precinct captains and politicians.

In Columbia, South Carolina, law enforcement struggled with the doubling of the population from 8,000 to 16,000 following the transfer of the Confederate treasury from Richmond, Virginia, and the posting of troops. Off-duty officers could earn extra pay for capturing runaways and whipping slaves. In addition to grog shops, gambling dens, and brothels, the creation of Castle Sorghum in November 1861 and the confinement of 150 Union prisoners of war placed extra stress on the city police force, which increased to 17 in February 1864. To maintain order, the following February, the State Executive Council posted cadets from Arsenal Academy to patrol the "deadline," a boundary of boards outlining the 5-acre (2-hectare) open ground. The teenage guards were unable to stop Union captives from exchanging greenbacks with slaves for Confederate currency and from mocking and insulting the city's women, who complained of the outrage. More duties sapped the police force after authorities forced farmers to tithe their produce at collection sites, which officers guarded against enemy raids.

During Reconstruction, an increase in vagrancy, theft, and burglaries attested to widespread hunger, as the Freedmen's Bureau struggled to dispense welfare to the poor and unemployed. Southern police attempted to ease the fears of white citizens that former slaves intended to wreak havoc in vindication of centuries of bondage. Columbia's Fourth Ward organized an official city guard, a vigilante-style militia that patrolled streets alongside federal officers.

Guarding the President

Washington, D.C., posed unique policing challenges. For President-Elect Abraham Lincoln, detective and spymaster Allan Pinkerton of Glasgow, Scotland, headed the Union Intelligence Service. Pinkerton thwarted an assassination plot by a pro-Confederacy faction led by a Corsican barber, Cypriano Ferrandini, in Baltimore, Maryland, on February 22, 1861, ten days before Lincoln's first inauguration. Pinkerton's method was to bypass part of the 70-stop train ride through Eastern cities and to cut telegraph wires to and from Baltimore.

Simultaneously, U.S. Marshal Ward Hill Lamon, an attorney and a general in the Union army, served as Lincoln's bodyguard. Armed with two derringers, two pistols, and two knives, he offered the president-elect a pistol and bowie knife, both of which Lincoln refused. Lamon escorted Lincoln on a special night train from Harrisburg, Pennsylvania, to Washington, D.C., thus avoiding conflict in Baltimore. Lamon remained in the president's entourage, posted officers around the presidential mansion, and insisted on escorting him to the polls and on shadowing him on November 19, 1863, during delivery of the Gettysburg Address.

Lamon was as tall as Abraham Lincoln and stout in defense of the president. Because Lincoln chose Senator Charles Sumner and 67-year-old Baron Friedrich von Gerolt, the Prussian ambassador and a Union sympathizer, to accompany him to the theater in December 1864, Lamon smirked, "Neither . . . could defend himself against an assault from any able-bodied woman in this city." In retrospect of Lamon's fearlessness and audacity, attorney Leonard Swett, in a memoir for the *North American Review*, asserted, "Mr. Lincoln knew the shedding of the last drop of blood in his defense would be the most delightful act of Lamon's life, and that in him he had a regiment armed and drilled for the most efficient service."

Even though Lincoln felt safe and preferred less shielding, Lamon guarded the president until the officer's retirement on April 13, 1865, the night before Lincoln's assassination. The stalwart bodyguard regretted Lincoln's decision to attend the play at Ford's Theatre without proper protection. In one final act of devotion, Lamon accompanied the presidential coffin to Springfield, Illinois, for interment.

On July 5, 1865, Hugh McCulloch, head of the U.S. Department of the Treasury, commissioned a permanent Secret Service under the direction of William P. Wood to counter gambling, robbery, counterfeiting, and crimes against government officials.

Law and the West

On the American frontier, appointments spread a few lawmen over wide areas traversable only by canoe, on horseback, or by foot or snowshoe. For the entire area of Washington Territory, law enforcement was the duty of one man, Marshal James Patton Anderson, who operated out of an office in Olympia. The sheriff of San Diego County, California, James McCoy, held his elected position from 1862 to 1872 and, with Deputy Tom Fox, patrolled 15,000 square miles (39,000 square kilometers) while collecting unpaid taxes, selling federal property, and settling run-ins between citizens and Indians.

In southern Idaho, criminality escalated with street shootouts, which caused the death of Marshal Sumner Pinkham on July 23, 1865, in Idaho City. After Deputy Sheriff Orlando "Rube" Robbins collared the shooter, he left office to work professionally riding shotgun for the John Hailey stage line. One of the West's mythic lawmen, Robbins achieved a reputation for an admirable string of arrests.

Law enforcement involved settlers in quasi-legal activities and suspension of civil rights to quell rampant stock thievery, fraud, claim jumping, stage and train robbery, assault, arson, and murder. Sworn officers confronted a folk vigilante system that fostered outback order, such as the actions of Cheyenne, Wyoming, hangmen who pistol-whipped and executed killer Charles Martin and mule thief Charles J. Morgan on March 21, 1868, on a tripod gallows behind the Elephant Corral. At Dodge City, Kansas, where authorities reputedly hired peacekeepers by the day, 50 men got into a shootout among 35 wagons on September 8, 1868, resulting in two deaths.

The Bannack Vigilante Committee, led by Paris Pfouts, Wilbur Fisk Sanders, and James Williams, lynched Sheriff Amos Henry Plummer of Bannack, Montana, on January 10, 1864, because he had challenged the committee for hanging bandits. Vigilantes contended that Plummer had masterminded stagecoach robberies. The hanging occurred during a brutal few months in which 100 citizens either disappeared or died violently. After the sheriff's burial at Hangman's Gully under a pile of rocks, grave robbers twice vandalized the site, pilfering the right arm and cranium of the deceased.

Another victim of anarchy, William Ayers, a U.S. deputy marshal in Indian Territory (Oklahoma), survived a bullet wound while taking prisoners to Fort Smith, Arkansas. At Muskogee, Oklahoma, prisoner John Billy shot Ayers and killed his deputy Perry DuVal with a bullet to the head, but the villain did not elude his fate—the gallows on April 3, 1874. Other peacekeepers from the Great Plains to California incurred harassment, suffering, disgrace, or death for their efforts.

Frontier justice produced episodes clouded by perjury and inept investigation. At Virginia City, Montana, in spring 1865, a tense situation arose in the Alder Gulch mining town over a flour shortage. Sheriff Neil Howie required 23 deputies to break up rioters threatening merchants for hoarding food staples. The boundaries of right and wrong blurred in 1865 in Laramie, Wyoming Territory, where Nathaniel Kimball Boswell, the first sheriff of Albany County, fought Marshal "Big Steve" Long's extortion plots and intimidation of settlers. Boswell and a lynch mob seized Long on October 18, 1868, and hanged him with his half brothers, Ace Moyer and Con Moyer, barkeeps at the Bucket of Blood saloon. Settlers respected Boswell, made him warden of the Wyoming Territorial Prison, and elected him to the U.S. Congress.

In 1869 in Denver, Marshal David J. Cook rid the region of the murderous Musgrove-Franklin Gang. In Cook's memoir, *Hands Up; or, Thirty-Five Years of Detective Life in the Mountains and on the Plains* (1897), he captured the tension between formal law and folk vigilantism: "The lynchings [the law officers] would gladly have prevented, but it was useless for them to fly in the face of an entire community, which had been outraged and which was aroused, not so much to vengeance as to the necessity of protecting itself against the rough element of the plains."

The situation did not improve in 1872, when the U.S. Supreme Court set a precedent in the case of *Taylor v. Taintor* by naming bounty hunters as agents of bail bondsmen. Bounty hunters received the right to cross state lines and enter private residences without a warrant to apprehend fugitives.

Guns and Order

Because of the fragility of investments in livestock, the lifestyle of cowboys and outlaws in cattle country encouraged particularly unscrupulous and reckless behavior. By 1871, the emergence of Abilene, Kansas, as a shipping point for Texas longhorns via the Union Pacific Railroad generated cowboy celebrations, fueled by on-site payoffs to some 5,000 drovers. Policing challenged Marshal Thomas James "Tom Bear River" Smith, who banned guns in the Abilene city limits. Armed mainly with his two fists, he survived two murder attempts before he died of a bullet to the chest and decapitation by farmer Andrew McConnell on November 2, 1870. Smith's replacement, James Butler "Wild Bill" Hickok, arrived the next spring and encountered a serious threat, outlaw John Wesley Hardin.

In 1874, lawman Leander Harvey McNelly, a captain of the Texas State Police, led a special force funded by stockmen to combat Mexican rustler Juan Nepomuceno Cortina, a former supporter of the Union army. Until his arrest by Mexican officials in 1875, Cortina, known as the

"Red Robber of the Rio Grande," outraged carpetbaggers by rustling their cattle, driving them over the Tex-Mex border, and transporting them to Cuba. He threatened the King Ranch at Corpus Christi, the growing empire of Captain Richard King, whom Cortina's gang sprayed with some 30 bullets while King was being conveyed by ambulance from Santa Gertrudis Creek.

In 1876, Marshal Timothy Isaiah "Big Jim" Courtright, the first lawman elected in Fort Worth, Texas, took on an unsavory town and brought it to order with the aid of his guns. In Dodge City, Kansas, Marshal William L. "Buffalo Bill" Brooks performed a similar service by cleaning up shooters and killers. Like Cook and Courtright, Brooks gunned down the lawless, but he ended his career on July 29, 1874, in a noose for stealing horses and mules from the Southwestern Stage Company.

In Helena, Montana, Seth Bullock, the sheriff of Lewis and Clark County, faced down a lynch mob in 1873 before moving on to the position of sheriff of Deadwood, a lawless mining town founded in 1875 in South Dakota. In August 1877, with the help of stage guard Daniel Boone May, Bullock rounded up three robbers of the famed Deadwood Stage, a frequent target of road agents. After more than a decade of law enforcement, in 1875, Sheriff John Hicks Adams of Santa Clara, California, earned citizen praise by hanging Tiburcio Vasquez, a notorious gangster and robber.

In Muskogee, Oklahoma, former slave Bass Reeves, an appointee of "hanging judge" Isaac Charles Parker, made a name for himself in 1875 as the first black U.S. deputy marshal. Because of his knowledge of the Creek and Seminole and their languages, he served in Indian Territory as a federal peace officer at a time when the herding of cattle over the state drew horse thieves, outlaws, and rustlers.

Buffalo hunter and teamster Wyatt Earp of Monmouth, Illinois, contributed to the mythos of the Western lawman after becoming the constable of Lamar, Missouri, in 1869. He fled the state under charges of horse thievery and returned to law enforcement in 1875 as marshal of Wichita, Kansas, where he kept the peace during outbursts of cowboys on end-of-trail revelry. In 1876, he performed the same job in Dodge City, Kansas, before his famous post in Tombstone, Arizona, site of the shootout at the OK Corral. While in Dodge City, he partnered with William Barclay "Bat" Masterson, his deputy and a respected detective and pursuer of criminals. Wyatt Earp's brothers held similar posts—Deputy Sheriff Morgan Earp and James C. Earp in Dodge City in 1875 and 1876 and, in 1877, Sheriff Virgil Earp in Yavapai County, Arizona, where his brother, Warren Earp, served as deputy.

In 1877, the law enforcement career of Matthew Nunan, an immigrant from Limerick, Ireland, came to an end in San Francisco County, California, where he administered the House of Corrections. During his one-year tenure as sheriff, according to an article in *The New York Times,* Nunan enforced the Queue Ordinance of 1876, which required the cutting of hair of Chinese prisoners to a length of 1 inch (2.54 centimeters)—an insult to their dignity.

The lopping of a braided pigtail from a Chinese prisoner, Ho Ah Kow, who was serving time for living in a boardinghouse crowded beyond legal limits, resulted in a $10,000 lawsuit against the sheriff. In a landmark decision backing the civil rights of aliens, the court entailed Nunan's property to pay retribution. Nunan returned to the beer business at Hibernia Brewery and kept a journal, *Diary of an Old Bohemian* (1927).

See also: Anthony, Susan B.; Buffalo Soldiers; Crime and Punishment; Hardin, John Wesley; Hickok, James Butler "Wild Bill"; Jim Crow; King, Richard; Knights of the White Camellia; Ku Klux Klan; Parker, Isaac; Range Wars; Stagecoach Travel; Stanton, Edwin M.

Further Reading

Allen, Fredrick. "Montana Vigilantes and the Origins of the 3-7-77." *Montana* 54 (Spring 2001): 3–19.

Dellinger, Harold, ed. *Jesse James: The Best Writings on the Notorious Outlaw and His Gang.* Guilford, CT: TwoDot, 2007.

Jarvis, Donna, Stephen W. White, Charles Wilson, and Michael Woody. *Detroit Police Department.* Charleston, SC: Arcadia, 2008.

Metz, Leon Claire. *John Wesley Hardin: Dark Angel of Texas.* Norman: University of Oklahoma Press, 1998.

Rosa, Joseph G. *The West of Wild Bill Hickok.* Norman: University of Oklahoma Press, 1994.

Thompson, Jerry. *Cortina: Defending the Mexican Name in Texas.* College Station: Texas A&M University Press, 2007.

Wilson, R. Michael. *Outlaw Tales of Wyoming: True Stories of the Cowboy State's Most Infamous Crooks, Culprits, and Cutthroats.* Guilford, CT: TwoDot, 2008.

Lilly, Eli (1838–1898)

Pharmaceutical researcher and philanthropist Eli Lilly created one of the world's most respected drug laboratories and the first prescription drug manufacturing firm. Born of Swedish ancestry on July 8, 1838, on a plantation in Baltimore County, Maryland, he came from an activist household that supported abolitionism and temperance.

At age 16, he apprenticed with mortar and pestle at the Good Samaritan Pharmacy in Lafayette, Indiana. Under a British apothecary, Henry Lawrence, Lilly experimented with gel coatings to make medicines easier to swallow. He stuck a pill on the end of a needle in a cork and dipped the pill in melted gelatin. He increased productivity by replacing the cork with a bar holding a row of needles.

After studying pharmacology at Asbury College (now DePauw University), Lilly opened his first pharmacy in 1861 in Greencastle, Indiana, but halted his business plans that May to recruit men for the Union army. On September 19, 1863, he served as a cavalry and artillery officer at the Battle of Chickamauga, Georgia. Following his capture at Sulphur Trestle, Tennessee, by Confederate General Nathan Bedford Forrest in December 1864, Lilly spent four months in a prisoner of war camp in Enterprise, Mississippi.

Dubbed "Colonel" Lilly, the industrialist returned to Indianapolis after the war to work for Pattison, Moore & Talbott, wholesale grocers and druggists. He ventured into the cotton market on 1,200 acres (485 hectares) at Port Gibson south of Vicksburg, Mississippi. A drought bankrupted him in 1868.

While in partnership with James William Binford at the Binford & Lilly Red Front Drugstore in Paris, Illinois, in 1869, Lilly pursued his intent to formulate and mass-produce wholesale drugs that he based on the latest science and ethically advertised and distributed. He planned to market treatments and curatives that were higher in quality and more standardized than patent medicines and to dispense them at doctors' requests rather than through hucksterism. For a location, in 1873, he chose Indianapolis, a city blessed with railroad connections and abundant water. For partners, he engaged a dentist, John F. Johnson, and a chemist, John Newell Hurty, whom Lilly had trained in the drug business. The trio's firm, Johnson & Lilly, Manufacturing Chemists, remained in business for three years.

On May 10, 1876, Lilly negotiated with Augustus Kiefer, the owner of A. Kiefer Drug Company, to buy the medicines that Lilly planned to manufacture. The industrialist and other family members went into medicinal manufacturing in a two-story building at 15 West Pearl Street in an alley of the warehouse district. His son, 14-year-old Josiah Kirby "J.K." Lilly, washed bottles and ran errands.

Their first product, a diuretic called fluid extract of buchu, sold for $2 per pound. Lilly solved the problem of perforated gel-coated pills and began selling the first self-locking coated medicines. Among the company's stock were carminatives and laxatives for infants and parturient women, antispasmotics for asthma and whooping cough, slippery elm tablets for bronchitis, coconut oil soaps and mentholated creams for skin irritation, and cod liver oil for tuberculosis and rickets. In 1876, Lilly made $3,477 in profits in eight months; in 1877, he earned $11,318.73. The business expanded so rapidly that he had to relocate his research lab twice in four years, first to 36 South Meridian, then to the corner of Alabama and McCarthy streets.

Lilly's firm profited most from gel-coated lozenges and capsules, cough syrups and elixirs, medicinal plant extracts, and the founder's own invention, fruit-flavored pills. The company motto stressed professionalism: "If It Bears a Red Lilly, It's Right." The initial price list identified "312 fluid extracts, 189 sugar-coated pills, 199 gelatin-coated, 50 elixirs, 15 syrups, five wines," as well as soap, face cream, and shampoo. To protect contents from light damage, Lilly sold liquids and solids in amber bottles. He profited at producing coco-quinine, a treatment for malaria, the disease that, in 1866, killed his first wife, Emily Lemon Lilly, and their unborn son.

Lilly devoted his retirement to charitable work, to heading the forerunner of the chamber of commerce, and to establishing the Indianapolis water department. His company aided medical advancement by producing antidepressants, insulin, methadone, penicillin, pneumococcus antigen, polio vaccine, and treatments for venereal disease.

Lilly died of cancer at age 59 on June 6, 1898, leaving his firm to his son and a grandson and namesake, Eli Lilly, Jr. The staff continued Colonel Lilly's promotion of federal regulation of pharmaceuticals, which began in 1906 with the creation of the Food and Drug Administration.

Further Reading

Bodenheimer, David J., and Robert G. Barrows, eds. *The Encyclopedia of Indianapolis.* Bloomington: University of Indiana Press, 1994.

Finkelman, Paul, ed. *Encyclopedia of the United States in the Nineteenth Century.* New York: Scribner's, 2001.

Grimm, Robert T., Jr., ed. *Notable American Philanthropists: Biographies of Giving and Volunteering.* Westport, CT: Greenwood, 2002.

McTavish, Jan R. *Pain and Profits: The History of the Headache and Its Remedies in America.* New Brunswick, NJ: Rutgers University Press, 2004.

Lincoln, Abraham (1809–1865)

As the sixteenth president of the United States from March 1861 until his assassination in April 1865, Abraham Lincoln balanced the plight of slaves against the danger of a sundered Union by ending human bondage while winning the Civil War.

The son of Nancy Hanks Lincoln and farmer Thomas Lincoln, he was born on February 12, 1809, in Hardin County, Kentucky. In 1815, he enrolled in a school taught by Zachariah Riney and Caleb Hazel. At age seven, he lived in Perry County, Indiana, where his father established a farm. Following his mother's death in 1818, Abraham, his brother Thomas, and their older sister Sarah grew up under the care of a beloved stepmother, Sarah Bush Johnston Lincoln. The elder Thomas Lincoln moved the family to new acreage in Macon County and Coles County, Illinois, before Abraham's departure from home.

The young Lincoln worked on a flatboat bound for New Orleans, clerked in a store at New Salem, served as a captain in the Illinois militia, and managed the New Salem post office. At age 25, he began work as Sangamon County surveyor. While dodging the label of abolitionist, he won election as a Whig to the first of four terms in the Illinois legislature on a platform advocating expanded river trade and the construction of a Beardstown and Sangamon Canal.

After he wed Mary Todd, future mother of their four sons, in 1842, the family settled in Springfield, Illinois. Without formal legal training, Lincoln practiced law with William Herndon.

The slavery issue dominated politics, the press, and public discourse, leading Lincoln to conclude that enmity among citizens would lead to war. In 1849, he and attorney Salmon P. Chase joined U.S. Congressman Joshua Reed Giddings in outlining the abolition of slavery in the District of Columbia. With his speech "Against the Extension of Slavery," delivered on October 16, 1854, Lincoln grew bolder in declaring bondage a hateful institution based solely on greed.

After the Republican Party took shape in 1856 at its first convention at Lafayette Hall in Allegheny County, Pennsylvania, Lincoln advanced to a two-year term in the U.S. House of Representatives. His speeches clarified his position on issues of human rights and national sovereignty. He denounced the U.S. Supreme Court's decision in *Dred Scott v. Sandford* (1857), which denied the humanity of slaves, and he vilified President James K. Polk for falsifying the cause of the Mexican-American War of 1846–1848.

During an unsuccessful run for the U.S. Senate in 1858, Lincoln warned that the nation would founder under the unresolved issue of slavery. In debates with his Democratic opponent, U.S. Senator Stephen A. Douglas, Lincoln asserted a compelling humanism that established his moral integrity. At Cooper Union in New York City on February 27, 1860, he impressed Republicans and abolitionists with his intent to halt the spread of slavery into the American West.

First Presidential Campaign

By May 1860, Lincoln had outpaced former Ohio governor Salmon P. Chase and U.S. Senator William Henry Seward to seize the Republican candidacy for U.S. president. Lincoln was the first chief executive to seek advice from a black counselor, orator Frederick Douglass, who spoke from experience about the misery of enslavement. Lincoln allowed the abolitionist press and a flurry of campaign propaganda to win voters to the Republican ticket, which he shared with vice presidential candidate Hannibal Hamlin, a U.S. senator from Maine.

Winning a plurality of the popular vote in 17 Northern states plus California and Oregon, on November 6, Lincoln claimed 180 of 303 electoral votes, defeating Southern Democrat John C. Breckinridge (72 electoral votes), Constitutional Unionist John Bell (39 votes), and Democrat Stephen A. Douglas (12 votes). The victory dealt the Democrats a significant defeat and forced states' rights proponents to reexamine their tactics.

As a result of the Republican sweep, South Carolina seceded from the Union on December 20, 1860, setting off a domino effect across the Deep South and into Florida and Texas. In New Orleans, Louisiana, during Mardi Gras, satiric mumming mocked Lincoln, whom men in blackface rode through town on a rail, while boys frolicked about tossing flour.

On the way to Washington, D.C., the president-elect made appearances at Indianapolis, Columbus, Pittsburgh, Philadelphia, and New York. Upon his arrival in Cincinnati, Ohio, he faced a daunting schism of public opinion—the vigorous support of Midwesterners and the defection of seven states from the Union. Ten days before the inauguration, the journey of more than 70 whistle-stops ended at the Willard Hotel in Washington, D.C., raising the spirits of Unionists and abolitionists. Along the way, on February 22, 1861, detective and spymaster Allan Pinkerton and Lincoln's bodyguard, U.S. Marshal Ward Hill

Lamon, altered the itinerary from Baltimore to foil an assassination plot by Confederate agitator Cypriano Ferrandini, a Corsican barber.

On March 4, Lincoln took the oath of office, replacing James Buchanan, a Southern apologist for slavery. In the months preceding the completion of the transcontinental telegraph, Lincoln's inaugural address sped west by Pony Express courier William J. "Billy" Cates, who bore the mail pouch out of St. Joseph, Missouri, on the way to California.

Governing During Wartime

Lincoln's first 100 days in office demanded skilled coordination. For secretary of state, he chose party rival William Henry Seward. Challenging the new president's thinking on slave rescue were members of the American Anti-Slavery Society and attorney Salmon P. Chase, who urged Lincoln to defy enslavers and to end the Civil War by enlisting blacks in the Union army. To shore up national unity and to thwart further defections to the Confederate States of America, the president chose to maintain an antislavery yet anti-abolition stance.

When Lincoln refused to grant an audience to Southern emissaries, Confederate President Jefferson Davis ordered the bombardment of Fort Sumter in the harbor of Charleston, South Carolina, on April 12, 1861, the first engagement of the Civil War. A triumph for the Confederacy, the support of Southwesterners in July 1861 centered pro-South efforts at the capital of Mesilla. Running counter to the Southwest, residents of the newly created Dakota Territory declared the new president a trustworthy wielder of statecraft. To pay for the war, on August 5, Lincoln signed the Revenue Act of 1861, the nation's first income tax law, which collected 3 percent of income above $800.

To isolate seditious, polygamous Utah Mormons from mainstream Christian pioneers, Lincoln on March 2, 1861, agreed to the incorporation of Nevada Territory, reducing Utah's land by 10,740 square miles (27,817 square kilometers). The act terminated Mormon hopes of establishing a religious state called Deseret. Brigham Young sneered at President Lincoln for declining to denounce anti-Mormon persecution and declared him "Abel" Lincoln, a reference to the Bible's first murder victim. To settle racial problems on the frontier, on October 3, Lincoln selected the Uintah Valley Reservation, more than 2 million acres (810,000 hectares) in the Uintah Basin of northeastern Utah, as a Ute homeland. In a study of the white utopists in Utah, he read the Book of Mormon (1830), a scripture unique to the Latter Day Saints.

On May 20, 1862, Lincoln signed a revolutionary piece of legislation—the Homestead Act, a supervised distribution of free land that offered property ownership to all except those who abetted the Confederate cause. On July 8, 1862, to curtail Mormon domination of Utah Territory, Lincoln signed the Morrill Anti-Bigamy Act outlawing polygamy, which critics equated with female brainwashing, house arrest, bondage, and child rape.

In December 1862, Lincoln encouraged the settlement of mining districts in the Western territories, a source of profit to underwrite the costs of war. At his direction, Congress passed the Organic Act of May 26, 1864, which separated Montana Territory from Idaho Territory and the Dakotas.

On a grant from the executive office, in early March 1865, a three-year engineering survey, the Western Union Telegraph Expedition, led by Smithsonian Institution naturalist Major Robert Kennicott, began mapping the coastline from California, Oregon, and Washington Territory north and west along British Columbia. The project indicated Lincoln's intent to add more states to the salvaged Union.

Lincoln and Civil Rights

During four years of combat, Lincoln actuated his powers as commander in chief and challenged threats to the Union in the hope of a rapid end to the rebellion. During his sixth week in office, he suspended the right of habeas corpus, blockaded Southern ports, and drafted men for the Union army and navy. He dispatched 75,000 troops under the command of General George Brinton McClellan to surround the capital, arrest the mayor of Baltimore and other agitators, and halt rebel insurgencies in Maryland.

On August 22, 1862, a month after the failure of the Peninsula Campaign to seize the rebel capital of Richmond, Virginia, the president sent a letter to the *New York Tribune* concerning the frenzied abolitionist editorials of Horace Greeley, who once had called Lincoln an able statesman and sustainer of democracy. To Greeley's "The Prayer of Twenty Millions," a demand for immediate emancipation of blacks, Lincoln replied that, as head of state, he owed allegiance to the whole nation. He indicated that he would emancipate slaves if their liberty were in the best interest of national unity, but he would not jeopardize the country by freeing slaves.

Unknown to Greeley was Lincoln's draft of the Emancipation Proclamation, which was issued on September 22, 1862. The document, which became official on January 1, 1863, began dismantling the Southern plantation system and sanctioned the use of black recruits in the Union army. Martin Robinson Delany, a grandson of African captives and the nation's first black field commander, advised the president on the needs of free blacks and aided the work of the Freedmen's Bureau in transitioning former chattel to citizenship.

During the worst of combat, Lincoln often sat beside Ely Samuel Parker, General Ulysses S. Grant's personal aide, and discussed telegrams revealing the war's progress and the achievements of black regiments. In confidence, the two men exchanged ideas on federal policies toward Indians that influenced the conduct of the Indian Wars and, later, the decisions of the Office of Indian Affairs. In March 1863, Southern Cheyenne Chief Black Kettle journeyed to Washington, D.C., to discuss conditions for Plains Indians, whose sufferings demanded federal amelioration.

Lincoln made necessary visits to the army and navy and strove to select apolitical leaders of the Army of the Potomac who would fight the Confederacy to a standstill. He went through a series of military commanders, each of whom met defeat—Winfield Scott, McClellan, Henry Halleck, Ambrose Burnside, Joseph Hooker, and George Meade.

On July 30, 1863, the president, out of anguish at the casualty rate, called for retaliation against Confederate soldiers for every Union soldier killed and every black enslaved by the enemy. Gloom infested the White House on September 20 after the rebel victory at Chickamauga, Georgia, and in November, when Lincoln contracted a mild case of smallpox.

At an upturn, the appointment of General Grant as commander of the Union army on March 10, 1864, gave the president the fighting strategist he had been seeking. To reward the Union military, Lincoln drafted 200,000 more men, reorganized the pension program, and launched a series of national cemeteries for the interment of fallen soldiers. Under the General Law System, the government remunerated soldiers who suffered disability or disease and allotted payments to their widows, children under 16 years of age, and other dependent relatives.

Presidential Compassion

Perhaps because of his own grief following the death of his 12-year-old son William Wallace "Willie" Lincoln from typhoid fever on February 20, 1862, the president sympathized with other citizens trapped by ineluctable circumstances. On July 29, 1863, he pondered the rebuke of Massachusetts Senator Charles Sumner for forcing Quakers to obey conscription laws and to pay war taxes. In August 1863, a similar censure from Shaker elders Bishop Harvey L. Eads and John N. Rankin protested militarism and conscription, which forced their pacifist congregation to shed blood. They begged for exemption for Shaker males, who threatened to flee to Tennessee in order to escape coercive enlistment.

On December 30, 1863, Lincoln communicated through Secretary of War Edwin M. Stanton the reclassification of Shakers as conscientious objectors. On February 24, 1864, an amended Conscription Act declared conscientious objectors official noncombatants and released them from the army. President Lincoln expressed his sympathy for pacifists and allowed them to keep their military mounts.

Lincoln looked beyond war to citizen concerns. On September 28, 1863, he saw an institutionalized harvest festival as a source of national order, propriety, and unity. He agreed with Sarah Josepha Hale, editor of *Godey's Lady's Book,* that an annual Thanksgiving holiday would give Americans an opportunity to express praise and gratitude to the Almighty.

At the dedication of the Soldiers National Cemetery on 17 acres (7 hectares) in Gettysburg, Pennsylvania, on November 19, 1863, four and a half months after the decisive Battle of Gettysburg, Lincoln delivered the Gettysburg Address, one the nation's most profound encomiums to patriotism and self-sacrifice. His brief comment on martyrdom alluded to the freeing of slaves and honored all who had died defending the principles of liberty and democracy.

Reuniting the Nation

At the height of war, the president foresaw the possibility of guerrilla warfare in the coming decade. On December 8, 1863, he initiated Reconstruction by offering amnesty to Southerners who reclaimed their U.S. citizenship and liberated their slaves. In summer 1864, he pocketed a bill proposed by Congressman Thaddeus Stevens and senators Charles Sumner and Benjamin Wade that called for a majority of citizens in each rebel state to swear an oath that they never promoted secession. With more generosity toward the rebels, Lincoln crafted the "Ten Percent Plan," which restored Southern states in which 10 percent of the citizens declared themselves loyal.

Lincoln's landslide victory at the polls in 1864 proved his assumption correct—that most Americans favored forgiveness and peace over rancor. General William Tecumseh Sherman's capture of Atlanta on September 1,

1864, increased popular trust in the president and raised hopes of an end to the war. Lincoln's second inaugural address, delivered on March 4, 1865, contained some of his most conciliatory words. To vengeful factions, he proposed healing: "With malice toward none; with charity for all; with firmness in the right, as God gives us to see the right, let us strive on to finish the work we are in; to bind up the nation's wounds."

To hasten the return of peace, Lincoln conferred for two weeks with General Grant and General Sherman at City Point, Virginia, on the best way to end the war. The president made a call on the abandoned Confederate capitol in Richmond and received accolades from ex-slaves, who dubbed him "Father Abraham."

After the signing of the truce between Grant and Confederate General Robert E. Lee at Appomattox Courthouse on April 9, 1865, federal activism focused on indigent widows and youth left homeless and vulnerable. Lincoln received the praise of James Russell Lowell, a respected intellectual and diplomat, who delivered his "Commemoration Ode" at Harvard University to honor the war dead and to celebrate Lincoln's leadership during a perilous upheaval. Lowell honored the president's foresight in mustering the nation's first black brigade. Under Lincoln, Reconstruction reasserted the tenets of the republic, which proclaimed freedom and equality as human rights.

An Unfinished Presidency

The shooting of President Abraham Lincoln at Ford's Theatre at 9 P.M. on April 14, 1865, stifled the celebration of peace and jolted citizens into mourning. Actor John Wilkes Booth plotted to shoot the president and to dispatch co-conspirators George Andreas Atzerodt and Lewis Thornton Powell (alias Lewis Paine) to murder Vice President Andrew Johnson and Secretary of State Seward. The attack occurred the day after the retirement of Lincoln's executive bodyguard, Marshal Lamon.

At a high point in the humor of Tom Taylor's domestic farce *Our American Cousin* (1858), Booth entered the president's box and waited for audience laughter to cover the sound of his derringer. Major Henry Reed Rathbone leaped at the assassin, but he fell seriously injured from knife wounds to the head and arm. While Rathbone's fiancée, Clara Hamilton Harris, comforted the first lady, Dr. Charles Leale, an army surgeon and the author of *Lincoln's Last Hours* (1909), attended the president and assessed his cranial wound as mortal.

The funeral procession of slain President Abraham Lincoln arrives at New York's City Hall on April 25, 1865. Millions came out to pay their respects as a special train transported his casket from Washington, D.C., to Springfield, Illinois, over 13 days. *(George Eastman House/Getty Images)*

In his autobiography, presidential advisor Frederick Douglass extolled Lincoln's egalitarianism:

> His personal traits and public acts are better known to the American people than are those of any other man of his age. He was a mystery to no man who saw him and heard him. Though high in position, the humblest could approach him and feel at home in his presence. Though deep, he was transparent; though strong, he was gentle; though decided and pronounced in his convictions, he was tolerant toward those who differed from him, and patient under reproaches.

Rescuers transported the dying president across the street to the residence of William Petersen, where Robert Todd Lincoln, a captain on the staff of General Grant, hurried to his father's side. Dr. Leale eased pressure on the president's brain by pushing aside a bone fragment to allow free bleeding. Lincoln expired the next morning at 7:22 A.M. After 40 days in the office of vice president, Andrew Johnson took the oath of office on April 15, 1865.

Martial law, superintended by Secretary of War Stanton, limited access to businesses, schools, and amusements as military police searched for the assassins. Federal agents pursued Booth to Virginia, where he died of gunshot wounds on April 26 in a barn south of the Rappahannock River. Thousands viewed Lincoln's coffin in the U.S. Capitol Rotunda, mourned at the White House funeral on April 19, and watched the funeral train transport the president's remains to Oak Ridge Cemetery in Springfield, Illinois, for burial on May 4.

Pundits enumerated Lincoln's triumphs—the admission of West Virginia to the Union; the Morrill Land-Grant Act, which established agricultural schools in each state; the repeal of the Fugitive Slave Law; federal support for the Transcontinental Railroad and a national banking system; the issuance of paper currency; the appointment of five U.S. Supreme Court justices; and the creation of the U.S. Department of Agriculture. Overall, during a four-year war that sundered the Union, Lincoln commanded an army and navy, managed the nation's business, and freed 4 million blacks from bondage.

See also: Booth, John Wilkes; Bureau of Indian Affairs; Douglass, Frederick; Draft and Draft Riots; Election of 1860; Election of 1864; Emancipation Proclamation; Gettysburg Address; Hamlin, Hannibal; Law Enforcement; Lowe, Thaddeus; Nebraska; Seward, William Henry; Stanton, Edwin M.; Taxes and Tax Law; Welles, Gideon.

Further Reading

Burlingame, Michael. *The Inner World of Abraham Lincoln.* Urbana: University of Illinois Press, 1997.

Donald, David Herbert. *Lincoln.* New York: Simon & Schuster, 1995.

Goodwin, Doris Kearns. *Team of Rivals: The Political Genius of Abraham Lincoln.* New York: Simon & Schuster, 2005.

Holzer, Harold. *Lincoln at Cooper Union: The Speech That Made Abraham Lincoln President.* New York: Simon & Schuster, 2004.

Paludan, Phillip Shaw. *The Presidency of Abraham Lincoln.* Lawrence: University Press of Kansas, 1994.

Stephenson, Nathaniel W. *Abraham Lincoln and the Union.* New York: BiblioBazaar, 2008.

Waugh, John C. *Reelecting Lincoln: The Battle for the 1864 Presidency.* New York: Da Capo, 2001.

Wills, Garry. *Lincoln at Gettysburg: The Words That Remade America.* New York: Simon & Schuster, 1992.

Wilson, Douglas S. *Lincoln's Sword: The Presidency and the Power of Words.* New York: Alfred A. Knopf, 2006.

Literacy

Learning first reached the American colonies in the hands of pious Europeans and remained a province of religion and altruism. In New England, illiteracy hampered few people, as seventeenth-century English Puritans and Quakers sought to teach all Christians to read scripture. The connection between Bible reading and piety produced a high level of education among Christian utopists in New Harmony, Indiana; Armenian Christians in Worcester, Massachusetts; and Jews of Staten Island, New York, and New Orleans, where Judah Touro built a public literacy center. Among Shakers and their converts in Georgia, Indiana, Kentucky, and Ohio, religious schools gained prominence for academic excellence. In Guilford County, North Carolina, Quakers typically homeschooled their children, producing a respectable reading comprehension rate among the devout. Conversely, among freedmen, by 1865, perhaps as few as 5 percent could decipher the written word. Within five years, the literacy rate rose to 20 percent.

Among Amerindians, children acquired basic skills, symbol recognition, and culture through family storytelling and one-on-one training. Formal education from missionaries at the Klamath, Umatilla, and Warm Springs agencies in Oregon; the Arikara day schools at Fort

Berthold, North Dakota; the Presbyterian mission school on the Omaha Reservation in Nebraska; and the Seneca Indian School in Wyandotte, Oklahoma, focused on Christian principles, scripture, and European values. Day schools allowed children to remain with the tribe while receiving the education that native leaders demanded in treaties with the U.S. government. Although humanitarians and philanthropists favored assimilating pupils into white society, Indian parents vigorously opposed the erasure of nativism. By the late 1870s, missionaries proposed a stringent separation of children from tribes and native customs, language, and religion through English-only classes at some 25 Eastern boarding schools.

Immigrants outside the Judeo-Christian majority gained little by coming to the land of promise. While their children received a high rate of literacy and training in handwriting, spelling, and reading at one-room schoolhouses, illiterate Euro-American miners in the Pennsylvania coalfields risked their lives because of the inability to read safety instructions. The exception to low levels of literacy, Icelanders arrived in Michigan and Utah with a keen appreciation of books and learning as well as collections of Icelandic poems and sagas. Asian children in Hawaii received thorough training at the Royal School after 1839, but Chinese, Filipino, and Japanese immigrants to California in the decades following the 1849 Gold Rush remained mired in menial work as peddlers, launderers, gardeners, cooks, waiters, nannies, and houseboys. In 1859, a segregated facility, the Oriental School for Chinese children in San Francisco, functioned only in the evenings and closed by state mandate in 1871. Private Chinese language schools served youth from families who shared the cost of hiring teachers. Demands in 1885 forced the California Supreme Court to open a new Oriental School system in Chinatown.

Into the mid-nineteenth century, Xs or hand-printed surnames on wills, deeds, and petitions attested to individual learning levels, especially among plowmen enlisting in the Confederate infantry and Native Americans signing treaties with the U.S. Army. Reflecting the opposite pole of education standards in New England and the North Atlantic coast, 80 percent of whites in Georgia in 1850 were illiterate. Those self-willed enough to learn by trial and error chose newspaper headlines, primers, and posters as means of identifying the shapes of letters and numbers and the sounds and meanings of words, monetary denotation, and symbols.

Though verbally multilingual, Roman Catholic immigrants passing through Baltimore or Boston harbor or Ellis Island, New York, clung to the parish priest or to German or Irish immigrant societies for aid in deciphering written English. Illiterate parents kept children home from public classrooms to prevent influence by Protestant teachers and tended to promote pidgin conversation and splintered understanding. Irish Catholics in Sacramento, California, revered schools taught by Irish nuns and Christian Brothers, who offered instruction through lessons on Irish history and poetry, a curriculum that isolated rather than democratized.

Progressive Education

Other conduits of learning assistance uplifted the poor. As a part of child care services, the New York City Mission Society provided instruction in reading and writing as well as in courtesy and table manners. In Cincinnati, Ohio, and other major cities, transportation companies coded horsecars and street maps with primary colors to enlighten those who could not read. In Tubac, Arizona, Charles Debrille Poston aided illiterate Mexican residents by marking monetary notes with symbols—a lion for $10, a chicken for 25 cents.

At Portsmouth Plaza in San Francisco's Chinatown and among Poles and Russians in Milwaukee, Wisconsin, and Toledo, Ohio, public scribes conducted a vital service by writing letters and interpreting legal documents for immigrants. A similar system benefited newcomers at the Italian bank in Manhattan's Little Italy, which became an employment office, travel service, and business center.

Librarians, such as the staff at Medford, Massachusetts; Dunbar, Pennsylvania; Hopkinsville, Kentucky; Parsons, Kansas; and Salem, Ohio, and at Maria Cary's book collection in Lexington, Massachusetts, in 1868, made the push for community education, especially among women and youth. A more varied library in King of Prussia, Pennsylvania, offered intergenerational training through a homework center, Grange hall, church, and literary society. Meanwhile, staff at the Atlanta, Georgia, public library served only white patrons, a common form of discrimination throughout the postwar South.

Migrant laborers from the Appalachian Mountains to Baltimore often learned from their children, who brought lessons home from classrooms. At Maine State Prison, tutors from Portland aided both the underschooled and the blind; a similar system at Sing Sing Prison in Ossining, New York, relied on a trustee, who received supervision from a civilian teacher. To empower the visually handicapped, educator Samuel Gridley Howe insisted on Braille mastery for the blind at the Perkins Institute in Watertown, Massachusetts.

In New York State, businessman Lewis Miller and the Reverend John Heyl Vincent, founders of the Chautauqua adult education movement, plotted a method of extending basic skills to rural farms, herding camps, and ranches. They outlined a uniform two-week study course and published gardening and song books and children's stories for use in summer camps, traveling tent assemblies, and regular Sunday school education equivalent to that of normal schools. The duo set up the first Chautauqua Assembly on August 4, 1874, on Lake Chautauqua near Jamestown in western New York, and extended service to Plainfield, New Jersey.

Home study and the nation's first correspondence courses encouraged mothers to refine their learning and to assist in their children's home schooling. The more enthusiastic women continued their education through independent town study groups, library membership, missionary societies, reading clubs, and literary circles, avenues for the literate to enter the American intellectual and social mainstream.

Literacy and Freedmen

Abolitionism preceded literacy as a libertarian goal for human chattel. Opponents of education for slaves took issue with assembling blacks in a classroom, distracting them from their duties, and introducing them to world geography and the possibility of running away or repatriating to Africa. To suppress insurrections, whites kept Northern and abolitionist newspapers out of the hands of literate blacks.

Wherever African Methodist Episcopal (AME) churches served black communities, sanctuaries did double duty as worship centers and as waystations, social welfare centers, and literacy training centers for adults and children. Openmindedness about alternative beliefs and ethics spurred Quakers to open slave schools and to support AME churches in teaching refugees to fend for themselves.

On a 1,500-acre (600-hectare) plantation at Butler Island and 1,700 acres (700 hectares) at St. Simons Island, Georgia, English actor Fanny Kemble pitied the lot of her husband's 638 slaves. She involved herself in slave flight and the workings of the Underground Railroad. For those unable to flee, she promoted health clinics, literacy, and vocational training, which violated laws forbidding the education of slaves.

Americans paralleled Kemble's outreach with additional gifts to the ignorant. Editor Lydia Maria Child heightened her activism in 1860 as an antislavery tractarian. She issued a radical leaflet, "The Duty of Disobedience to the Fugitive Slave Act" (1860), a directive on aiding black escapees in defiance of federal marshals. She gathered supplies for the rescue of contraband slaves during the Civil War and donated to teacher Charlotte Forten's academy, a keystone of the Port Royal Experiment in the settlement of freedmen.

Child gathered anecdotes and verse by black authors in *The Freedmen's Book* (1865), a common primer in literacy classes containing writings by Frederick Douglass, Charlotte Forten, William Lloyd Garrison, Frances Harper, and Phillis Wheatley, America's first black author. At Quindaro, Kansas, education for black children was available from Eben Blachley, a Presbyterian teacher. In an abandoned brewery in September 1862, he founded the Quindaro Freedman's School, the first black academy west of the Mississippi and the nucleus of Western University.

At war's end, ignorance condemned ex-slaves to a lowly existence. The Fourteenth Amendment to the U.S. Constitution (1868) gave "equal protection of the laws" to former slaves, but excluded Asians and Native Americans, polygamists, anarchists, and the illiterate. During Reconstruction, rising literacy rates threatened the status quo in areas where white unskilled laborers vied with freedmen for jobs. The possession of reading skills provoked violence and vandalism directed at freedmen's schools and black voters from terrorists in the Ku Klux Klan.

Despite the danger, General Alfred S. Hartwell published a letter in the *Daily Phoenix* urging freedmen to become literate and to uphold the family rather than wander the countryside in idleness. In 1865, Fanny Jackson Coppin, a black college graduate, established the Institute for Colored Youth in Philadelphia; Sarah Babcock, an activist educator from Plymouth, Massachusetts, chose to live in Camden, South Carolina, to found a freedmen's academy.

Controversy raged amid postwar altruism over the value of literacy as opposed to the acquisition of skills and common knowledge, such as an understanding of currency and weights and measures. Presbyterian philanthropists at Norfolk Mission College for Negroes advocated a liberal arts curriculum based on classical learning. In 1867, educator Samuel Chapman Armstrong, president of Hampton Normal and Agricultural Institute in Norfolk, Virginia, aimed at providing rudimentary skills in graduates within a two-year program. Norfolk blacks seized the opportunity to become literate as a means of rising socially and economically. Through concerted effort, teachers elevated blacks to a 70 percent literacy rate by 1910. Major demographic divergences occurred in white/nonwhite, native/immigrant, and North/South figures.

More Opportunities

Paralleling the rising literacy of American audiences, magazines, story papers, juveniles, miscellanies, travelogues, gossip sheets, literary reviews, and women's journals offered illustrated fiction and nonfiction to suit individual tastes. In the South, Jim Crow laws forced black voters to pay poll taxes and to pass literacy tests in order to register to vote. The reading tests involved analysis of constitutional regulations to the satisfaction of registrars, many of them racist white males.

On the frontier, Arizona Territory's third governor, Anson P.K. Safford, established a reputation for opening a public school system in Tucson in March 1872. Within four years, the census noted that 1,450 of the city's children were literate. The opening of the territorial penitentiary at Yuma on July 1, 1876, provided rehabilitation for convicts through crafts, schooling, and a library.

To the end of the nineteenth century, one-on-one efforts at church schools, Carnegie learning centers, freedmen's societies, and public libraries elevated people from ignorance to self-sufficiency. The national illiteracy rate shrank from 20 percent in 1870 to less than 3 percent in 1940.

See also: Child, Lydia Maria; Forten, Charlotte; Harper, Frances Ellen Watkins; Kemble, Fanny.

Further Reading

Benstock, Shari, ed. *The Private Self: Theory and Practice of Women's Autobiographical Writings.* Chapel Hill: University of North Carolina Press, 1988.

Brandt, Deborah. *Literacy in American Lives.* Cambridge, UK: Cambridge University Press, 2001.

Bunkers, Suzanne L., and Cynthia A. Huff, eds. *Inscribing the Daily: Critical Essays on Women's Diaries.* Amherst: University of Massachusetts Press, 1996.

Nelson, Emmanuel S., ed. *African American Authors, 1745–1945: Bio-Bibliographical Critical Sourcebook.* Westport, CT: Greenwood, 2000.

Towne, Laura M. *Letters and Diary of Laura M. Towne: Written from the Sea Islands of South Carolina, 1862–1884.* Ed. Rupert Sargent Holland. New York: Negro Universities Press, 1969.

Williams, Heather Andrea. *Self-Taught: African American Education in Slavery and Freedom.* Chapel Hill: University of North Carolina Press, 2005.

Literature

Creative writing in America during the 1860s and 1870s examined the hopes, regrets, and dilemmas of the period. A former U.S. congressman, pacifist Clement Laird Vallandigham of Ohio, went to prison in May 1863 on the order of Union General Ambrose Burnside for denouncing the military draft and for inciting resistance to the Civil War. Intrigued by Vallandigham's renunciation of his U.S. citizenship, author Edward Everett Hale composed an allegory, "The Man Without a Country," published anonymously in the *Atlantic Monthly* in December 1863.

To dramatize self-absorption and statelessness, a framework narrator characterizes protagonist Philip Nolan, a minor accomplice of traitor Aaron Burr during the presidency of Thomas Jefferson. Nolan escapes execution and lives in soul-shriveling exile on a series of warships. Hale enhances the banishment during Nolan's encounter with black slaves, who clamor to return to Portuguese West Africa. Over 55 years at sea, he hears no mention of home and yearns for family, friends, and country.

At a climactic moment, Nolan reads to illiterate sailors Sir Walter Scott's ballad *The Lay of the Last Minstrel* (1805). Overcome by nostalgia for "my own, my native land," he hurls the book into the waves and retreats to his cabin for two months. In penance for his reckless dismissal of his homeland, he builds a shrine to George Washington and makes an out-of-date U.S. map and flag. Readers popularized Hale's realistic cautionary tale for extolling patriotism during the Union's trial by secessionism. In the darkest months of the Civil War, the story sold a half million copies.

Humor and honor served the writing style of James Russell Lowell, a respected Fireside Poet and editor of the *Atlantic Monthly.* For a recitation at Harvard University, he composed the "Commemoration Ode" (1865), a serious meditation on the triumph of Unionism and the wisdom of Abraham Lincoln, "one of Plutarch's men [who] talked with us face to face." Two years later, Lowell anthologized volume 2 of the *Biglow Papers* (1867), 11 letters that explore the opinions of the American commoner. Through a fictional persona, Yankee farmer Hosea Biglow, the folksy satire muses in dialect on Confederate President Jefferson Davis, patriotism, the Emancipation Proclamation, and Reconstruction ignominy.

Beginning in October 1861 and continuing for six years, Lowell imparted the pathos and valor of the North–South conflict. Speaking through his court jester and a vain pedant, Birdofredum Sawin and the Reverend Mr. Wilbur, the poet used burlesque to condemn national recklessness. The series paid tribute to the author's three nephews killed in the war and gave thanks for "a nation saved, a race delivered." Lowell exposed the mounting corruption of President Andrew Johnson and Northern politicians, whom he derided as sources of "half-baked schemes . . . by all sorts o' never-heard-on fellers." The writer delighted in seeing his contemporary witticisms posted in shops and lauded by British readers.

The postwar era gave voice to the selfless who staffed military medical corps, including Louisa May Alcott and Walt Whitman, both hospital assistants in Washington, D.C., and authors of first-person reflections on battlefield suffering. In *Nurse and Spy in the Union Army* (1865), Sarah Emma Evelyn Edmonds of Michigan recorded seeing the shelling that blasted soldiers "as if smitten by thunderbolts." Scots nurse Kate Cumming of Mobile, Alabama, published *A Journal of Hospital Life in the Confederate Army in Tennessee* (1866), a memoir of her humble chores in laundry and kitchen and her travail in September 1863 as a battlefield nurse at Chickamauga. Cornelia Philips accounted for the soldiers' diminished condition in *The Last Ninety Days of the War in North Carolina* (1866), a bitter memoir of thousands of deaths accelerated by shortfalls of food and medicine. Mary Livermore, a patriot from Boston, detailed sacrifice and endurance in *My Story of the War* (1887). Fannie A. Beers, author of *Memories: A Record of Personal Experiences and Adventures During Four Years of War* (1888), recalled daily portions of mule meat at army messes in Alabama, Georgia, and Virginia. These and other pieces of history honed the era's taste for realism and offered female authors opportunities to publish in a male-dominated market.

One of the weakened prisoners of war pitied in combat narratives, Georgia-born blockade runner Sidney Lanier, a survivor of Camp Point Lookout in Maryland, spent the remaining 16 years of his life writing regional verse while fighting "prison lung" (consumption). Immersed in the cadence, dialect, and immediacy of the American South, he contributed to *Harper's Monthly, Lippincott's Magazine, Round Table,* and *Scribner's Monthly* personal verse and lyric retreats into the outdoors composed in the genial style of nature lover Henry David Thoreau.

Still possessed by war flashbacks, Lanier wrote "Corn" (1875), an imagistic glimpse of sturdy stalks overlaid by subconscious memories of marching soldiers. In maturity, he found a luxuriance and grandeur in the outdoors in his most published works, "The Symphony" (1875), "The Song of the Chattahoochee" (1877), and "The Marshes of Glynn" (1878), set in Brunswick, Georgia. In "The Symphony," an early conservation paean, he regrets that factories pollute the sky and the spirit with industrial "swinehood." Lanier derides consumerism and chides capitalists for ignoring the fact that "the time needs heart" and commands, "Change thy ways." Lanier's "The Marshes of Glynn," like John Keats's odes, cloaks in metaphor the tide that sweeps the poet out to the deep, where enigmatic seabed shapes fill him with awe. As tuberculosis saps his strength and lessens his days, a verse epiphany of mortality reminds him, "I know that I know."

As Lanier's haunted phrases suggest, the growth of urbanism and the Americanization of secessionists provided poignant themes. Postwar laments—Caroline Augusta Ball's "The Jacket of Gray" (1866) and Varina Howell Davis's "Christmas in the Confederate White House" (1896)—recount the losses and privations of the four-year insurrection. In 1875, George Washington Cable, a Louisiana Creole artist, mused over the loss of privacy in a classic New Orleans short story, "Jean-ah Poquelin." The setting pictures the title figure's waning grasp on dignity and discretion while he shields his ailing brother from local recoil from leprosy.

The permanent transformation of land and people weighed on Confederate General Robert E. Lee in his "Farewell Address to his Soldiers" (1865) and troubled Chief Joseph, who expressed his despair in a speech, "I Will Fight No More Forever" (1877). Joseph reveals a heart "sick and sad," a relentless grief he shares with the loser of the Civil War and with reformer Lydia Maria Child, author of *An Appeal for the Indians* (1868).

The growth of a new class of downtrodden, the exploited factory worker, compelled Rebecca Harding Davis to plead their humanity in the novella *Life in the Iron Mills* (1861), an instant best seller. Based on illiterate foundry laborers in Wheeling, West Virginia, the plot characterizes Deborah as a dispirited cotton mill picker who anticipates "no warmth, no brilliancy, no summer." The public's enthusiasm for Davis's woman-centered prose led to her publication of *Margret Howth: A Story of Today* (1861), "The Wife's Story" (1864), and *Earthen Pitchers* (1873–1874), all of which survey the torment inflicted on laboring females.

A mellow optimism dominated the canon of Davis's contemporaries. Balladeer and odist Henry Wadsworth Longfellow, creator of the American epic *Song of Hiawatha* (1855), achieved lasting fame for stanzas that readers memorized and treasured. In 1863, he mythologized the courage of the colonial post rider in "The Midnight Ride of Paul Revere," a stirring recitation piece. The thrust of the horseman on a mission impresses on readers that history is filled with real choices, the substance of heroism. The burden of grief for the poet's wife, Frances "Fanny" Longfellow, who died of burns after her

Poet Henry Wadsworth Longfellow, photographed here in his Cambridge, Massachusetts, study in 1870, established the literary legacy of the period with verse extolling the American character in crisis. *(Hulton Archive/Getty Images)*

dress caught fire, isolated him in acute melancholy and the terrors of madness.

In recovery, Longfellow anthologized *Household Poems* (1865), a collection of his most-cited short works. He embraced a postwar repose and acceptance of simple pleasures, the theme of "The Children's Hour," in which his three daughters clamor for time with father. A mature gratitude for the heart-lifting moment filled "A Psalm of Life," "Midnight Mass for the Dying Year," and "Hymn to the Night," an ode that engenders darkness with a mystic femininity. Longfellow honored stoic labor in "The Village Blacksmith," a tribute to the skilled worker who accepts "Toiling,—rejoicing,—sorrowing" as ineluctable human cycles. By extolling the American character in crisis, the poet established the period's literary legacy.

In contrast to Longfellow's stoic universalism, Horatio Alger, a New York journalist, championed American ideals that derived from the Protestant ethic and republican wholesomeness. A success at juvenile fiction, he introduced the mythic underdog in the "Ragged Dick" series, six episodic novels beginning with *Ragged Dick, or, Street Life in New York with the Bootblacks,* serialized in *Student and Schoolmate* from January to June 1867. Like Alcott's Jo March and Mark Twain's Huck Finn and Tom Sawyer, Alger's title figure establishes his instinctive pluck in the opening lines with his cry, "Shine yer boots, sir?"

Alger expanded his male cast in 1871 to another hard-bitten wanderer, "Tattered Tom," who invigorates didactic themes with street argot and the city cavalcade of horsecar rides, barrow vendors, and rooming house solitude. Alger's friendless teen males—subjects of the episodes *Ben the Luggage Boy, Dan the Newsboy, Julius: The Street Boy Out West,* and *Mark the Match Boy*—overcome orphaning and want by remaining true to hard work and clean living and by capitalizing on strokes of luck, the rewards to good boys. Alger's subsequent poem, "Grand'ther Baldwin's Thanksgiving" (1875), graced the American holiday with a table blessing rich in gratitude for family, bounty, and peace.

Homegrown stories of survivalism by Alcott, Alger, and Twain vied with haphazard events of immigrant literature. Such works include the coming to knowledge of slavery in English actor Fanny Kemble's *Journal of a Residence on a Georgian Plantation* (1863).

A cultured Jewish critic of the times, sonneteer Emma Lazarus, educated in German Romantic literature, encompassed more layered traditions than the colonialism of Longfellow or the immediacy of Ragged Dick. Writing in her teens to her death at age 38, she submitted verse to *The Century Magazine, Critic, Index, Lippincott's, The New York Times,* and *Scribner's Monthly* and translated classic Hebrew works for the *American Hebrew.* In anguish at imperial Russian anti-Semitism, Lazarus assisted illiterate Eastern European refugees. For two decades, she probed the tensions of North America's "virgin world" accommodating lofty ideals from ancient Judaism. For "In the Jewish Synagogue at Newport" (1867), she contrasts "this new world of life" and "this relic of the days of old" and imagines the visitor in the role of Moses confronted by the burning bush.

For the base of the Statue of Liberty to be built in New York Harbor, Lazarus produced a masterwork, "The New Colossus" (1883), an ode to nationhood invigorated by "huddled masses yearning to breathe free." The statue's lifted lamp raises a tribute to hope that democracy achieves the immigrants' aspirations.

See also: Alcott, Louisa May; Dickinson, Emily; Jacobs, Harriet; Twain, Mark; Whitman, Walt.

Further Reading

Benstock, Shari, ed. *The Private Self: Theory and Practice of Women's Autobiographical Writings.* Chapel Hill: University of North Carolina Press, 1988.

Bunkers, Suzanne L., and Cynthia A. Huff, eds. *Inscribing the Daily: Critical Essays on Women's Diaries.* Amherst: University of Massachusetts Press, 1996.

Crow, Charles L., ed. *A Companion to the Regional Literatures of America.* Malden, MA: Blackwell, 2003.

Nelson, Emmanuel S., ed. *African American Authors, 1745–1945: Bio-Bibliographical Critical Sourcebook.* Westport, CT: Greenwood, 2000.

Snodgrass, Mary Ellen. *Encyclopedia of Feminist Literature.* New York: Facts on File, 2006.

———. *Encyclopedia of Southern Literature.* Santa Barbara, CA: ABC-CLIO, 1997.

Little Bighorn, Battle of the

A significant U.S. military defeat by Plains Indians, the Battle of the Little Bighorn—informally known as Custer's Last Stand or the Battle of the Greasy Grass—coincided with preparations for the celebration of the nation's centennial.

In spring 1876, during the Great Sioux War, bands of Northern Cheyenne and Sioux deserted reservations and camped along the Little Bighorn and Rosebud rivers east of Billings in south-central Montana. By June, their number reached 15,000. On June 25, 1876, Lieutenant Colonel George Armstrong Custer force-marched 12 companies of the U.S. Seventh Cavalry, comprising 700 men, toward the Little Bighorn River. His intent was to pacify the area to protect settlers and miners who speculated on making a fortune in Indian territory.

Awaiting Custer were the assembled Arapaho, Northern Cheyenne, and Lakota forces headed by Oglala Lakota war strategist Crazy Horse and Hunkpapa chiefs Gall and Sitting Bull, who camped with their families in 949 lodges. Custer recognized a threat when he sighted a huge herd of horses and cook fires of a massive Indian village.

Against the advice of Arikara and Crow scouts, Custer disobeyed orders to wait until June 26 and mounted an attack at noon against 1,800 warriors led by Crazy Horse and Chief Gall. Too late, the general discovered that the Indians carried rapid-fire Henry and Spencer rifles. He had chosen not to include Gatling guns in his equipage, which would have evened out the threat, which rose from three-to-one to five-to-one during the progress of the conflict. Contributing to the one-sided battle was the delay of General George Crook's Third Cavalry following the Battle of Rosebud Creek on June 17.

Custer, who fell along with his 225 men, Colonel Myles Walter Keogh, and their mounts at Last Stand Hill, died of head and chest wounds. The surviving officers, Major Marcus Reno and Captain Frederick Benteen, held out for two days in rifle pits and behind supply boxes and returned to Custer's men to bury the dead. Chief Gall explained that Indians left Custer's corpse unmolested because they did not recognize him.

Official army casualty counts list 268 dead and 55 wounded—nearly half the Seventh Cavalry in all. Figures from the coalition of Plains Indians vary from 36 to 136 dead and around 160 wounded.

At Deadwood, South Dakota, memoirist Annie Donna Fraser Tallent, author of *The Black Hills, or, The Last Hunting Ground of the Dakotahs* (1899), described the construction of rude stretchers to convey the wounded 20 miles (32 kilometers) to the steamer *Far West* for conveyance to Fort Abraham Lincoln. She reported on the assembling of miners to hear the news: "The eager groups of men gathered at the doors of numerous business

The most famous survivor of Custer's Last Stand was a 14-year-old buckskin gelding named Comanche, a Morgan mustang. The mount of Captain Myles Walter Keogh, the horse was a seasoned, 900-pound (400-kilogram) veteran first wounded by an arrow at an engagement on the Cimarron River, southeast of Dodge City, Kansas. Both Comanche and Keogh suffered at the Little Bighorn, where Keogh died with his horse's reins in hand.

Weak from hunger and blood loss from two arrows to the hindquarters and seven gunshot wounds to the neck, right shoulder, left leg, and knee, Comanche wandered an arroyo with his bit dangling and his saddle slipped around his belly. He won the sympathy of Lieutenant Henry James Nowlan, who refused to shoot the suffering beast. Nowlan fed the horse a mash made of bran and Hennessy cognac and treated the wounds with a zinc wash. On a bed of prairie grass, Comanche traveled with wounded soldiers aboard the steamer *Far West* to Fort Abraham Lincoln south of Mandan, North Dakota, for recuperation.

After a year in a belly-band sling, Comanche had recovered sufficiently to tour parades, band concerts, and patriotic events honoring the Seventh Cavalry until his death from colic at age 29 on November 6, 1891, at Fort Riley, Kansas. His scarred, stuffed remains drew visitors at the 1893 World's Columbian Exposition in Chicago.

houses in excited discussion of the terrible disaster gave evidence of how deeply and universally the people of the Hills of all classes were touched by the unexpected calamity." The gambling houses closed out of respect; miners wept. Local people blamed the U.S. government for failing to back up its effort to bring law and order to the Dakotas.

The overwhelming victory for Plains Indians initiated a war to the death against the U.S. Army. By mid-July, the army dispatched replacement forces to the Yellowstone River. Some 4,000 soldiers, led by General Alfred Terry, continued pursuing the Lakota northeast until their eventual deaths or incarceration on Indian reservations. By 1877, Congress reassured the nation by funding a 1,000-man army at Fort Custer and Fort Keogh in southeastern Montana.

The mythic Custer became a hero to American children, who acted out the massacre in play. Memoirist Elizabeth Bacon "Libbie" Custer spent her widowhood defending her husband from ignominy with the books *Boots and Saddles* (1885), *Following the Guidon* (1890), and *Tenting on the Plains* (1893).

See also: Bureau of Indian Affairs; Crazy Horse; Custer, George Armstrong; Montana Territory; Sitting Bull; Weapons.

Further Reading

Calloway, Colin G., ed. *Our Hearts Fell to the Ground: Plains Indian Views of How the West Was Lost.* Boston: Bedford/St. Martin's, 1996.

Cozzens, Peter, ed. *Eyewitnesses to the Indian Wars, 1865–1890.* 5 vols. Mechanicsburg, PA: Stackpole, 2001–2005.

Donovan, James. *A Terrible Glory: Custer and the Little Bighorn, the Last Great Battle of the American West.* New York: Little, Brown, 2008.

Johansen, Bruce E., and Donald A. Grinde, Jr. *The Encyclopedia of Native American Biography.* New York: Da Capo, 1998.

Lamar, Howard R., ed. *The New Encyclopedia of the American West.* New Haven, CT: Yale University Press, 1998.

Utley, Robert M. *The Lance and the Shield: The Life and Times of Sitting Bull.* New York: Ballantine, 1994.

Wilson, James. *The Earth Shall Weep: A History of Native America.* New York: Atlantic Monthly Press, 1999.

Long Walk of the Navajo

Throughout 1860, peaceful Navajo living on the northern end of the Arizona–New Mexico border faced constant skirmishes with Mexican Americans, Ute, and Pueblo. One thousand Navajo militants initiated hostilities against the U.S. Army on April 30, 1860, when an attack on Fort Defiance criminalized as rebels Barboncito, a political leader and ritual chanter from Canyon de Chelly, Arizona, and Manuelito, a war chief from Utah.

On February 15, 1861, a federal treaty robbed the Navajo of four sacred mountains—Mount Blanca and Mount Hesperus in Colorado, Mount Taylor in New Mexico, and the San Francisco Peaks in Arizona—and one-third of their ancestral land. The onset of the Civil War a year later and the encroachment of Confederate troops along the Rio Grande delayed army strategies to subdue the Navajo and stop raids by and against them.

In 1863, Barboncito joined Manuelito in revolt against General James Henry Carleton over army control of grazing land and the government's failed delivery of promised grain and hay. During a three-year period, the Navajo fended off Mexican and Ute enslavers and complained to Indian agents about threats to their agrarian way of life.

Carleton decided to end the constant skirmishing. Aided by Ute enlistees, from January 6 to 22, 1864, Colonel Christopher "Kit" Carson applied a scorched-earth policy toward the Navajo by burning their hogans and crops, seizing their herds, filling water holes with dirt, and destroying their 1,200 peach trees.

Carleton initiated a 20-day forced march—known as the Long Walk of the Navajo—across central New Mexico toward Fort Sumner, the first reservation west of Indian Territory (Oklahoma). Nearly 9,000 Indians journeyed in three columns, each 10 miles (16 kilometers) long. Carleton routed the Indians south through Four Corners—the geographic union of Arizona, Colorado, New Mexico, and Utah—and Canyon de Chelly and east to Bosque Redondo, a trading post in the Pecos Valley of eastern New Mexico, where 400 Mescalero Apaches were encamped. Over 300 miles (480 kilometers) of rugged travel, moccasins and blankets turned to tatters; some 300 Navajo died of cold, exhaustion, and illness. Soldiers shot those too weak or sick to continue and buried them in shallow graves.

At a location designed to accommodate 5,000, the army crowded in twice that number, overrunning food and water supplies, sanitary facilities, and firewood. In a virtual concentration camp, the Indians drank impure water and sickened from chicken pox, dysentery, malaria, pneumonia, and smallpox. They rejected the treatment of military doctors and begged for native herbs. Soldiers infected hundreds of Navajo girls and women with gonorrhea and syphilis.

Outrage unified the nomadic Navajo into a fighting force; however, in September 1864, Carleton captured Barboncito and added him to the inmates at the 40-square-mile (100-square-kilometer) enclosure. Sharing the property with the Mescalero Apache for four years, the Navajo attempted to grow crops in poor soil and to defend their sheep from Mexican raiders and coyotes.

Less amenable to compromise than Barboncito, Chief Manuelito refused to surrender and go to Fort Sumner. "I will stay in my own country," he declared. "I've got nothing to lose but my life. The soldiers can come and take that whenever they please! But I will not go." He and his band remained at Dinetah southwest of the Little Colorado River. In June 1865, Barboncito succeeded in leading 500 escapees from their insufferable conditions and allied once more with Manuelito.

The two leaders oversaw the security of Navajo on the outside at Black Mesa, Shonto, and the Chuska Mountains. Through late summer 1866, Manuelito continued fighting off Ute and Zuni raiders at Dinetah until September, when he and his people surrendered at Fort Wingate. Barboncito remained free until November 1866, when he and 21 companions followed Manuelito to the fort. They found widespread despair from dying horses and sheep and low yields of corn and pumpkins because of drought and storms. In September 1867, Manuelito left the area to drive off Comanche and Ute attackers. More than 2,000 Navajo died of smallpox. In May 1868, Barboncito journeyed to Washington, D.C., to discuss the lethal conditions with President Andrew Johnson.

On June 1, 1868, through two interpreters—one Navajo to Spanish, the other Spanish to English—Barboncito negotiated with General William Tecumseh Sherman for release of the Navajo, who returned to traditional territory. Sherman's comments implied that the Navajo were not as industrious as whites. Barboncito detailed his people's need for familiar land, forest for firewood, and healing plants to rescue them from disease and despair at trying to subsist on unfamiliar meals of wheat flour, sugar, and coffee. His skill at dealing with whites saved his people from incarceration in Oklahoma and liberated more than half the tribe enslaved in New Mexico. Sherman agreed to supply clothing, corn, cattle, goats, horses, and sheep.

Superintended in peacekeeping by Barboncito, 7,304 Navajo left Bosque Redondo on June 18. As they herded 2,000 sheep and 1,500 horses and mules along the way, they could travel only 10–12 miles (16–19 kilometers) per day toward Fort Wingate to inhabit their allotted 3.5 million acres (1.4 million hectares).

The returnees settled Canyon de Chelly and land between the San Mateo Mountains, New Mexico, and the San Juan River in Utah to hunt and trade. Despite hostility from Apache, Ute, New Mexicans, and Mormons, the return helped make the Navajo one of the nation's most prosperous tribes.

The lengthy task of keeping the peace among quarrelsome young braves over the second "long walk" exhausted Barboncito, who died on March 16, 1871, at age 50. The following year, Manuelito assumed the post of Navajo police chief. In 1873, during the Chiricahua Apache wars, 50 of his braves found work as army scouts tracking the forces of Chief Victorio. Manuelito continued efforts to improve conditions in 1876 through conferences with President Ulysses S. Grant.

Further Reading

Iverson, Peter, and Monty Roessel. *Diné: A History of the Navajos.* Albuquerque: University of New Mexico Press, 2002.

Johansen, Bruce E., and Donald A. Grinde, Jr. *The Encyclopedia of Native American Biography.* New York: Da Capo, 1998.

Lamar, Howard R., ed. *The New Encyclopedia of the American West.* New Haven, CT: Yale University Press, 1998.

Sundberg, Lawrence D. *Dinétah: An Early History of the Navajo People.* Santa Fe, NM: Sunstone, 1995.

Waldman, Carl. *Who Was Who in Native American History: Indians and Non-Indians from Early Contacts Through 1900.* New York: Facts on File, 1990.

Lowe, Thaddeus (1832–1913)

An aeronaut, chemist, and meteorologist, Thaddeus Sobieski Constantine "Thad" Lowe masterminded the American military's first air corps during the early years of the Civil War. Born to settlers of Jefferson Mills, New Hampshire, on August 20, 1832, Lowe was a scion of veterans of the American Revolution and the War of 1812. Self-educated on loaned books, he prepared to be a shoemaker, until he became fascinated with the study of hydrogen gas.

At age 25, Lowe built a reputation as an India silk balloon maker and entertainer at fairs by giving balloon rides to paying passengers. At Hoboken, New Jersey, he mastered cutting, stitching, and seam-proofing balloons for tethered flights to fill orders from around the nation. In 1859, he plotted the construction of a balloon that could cross the Atlantic Ocean.

On November 1, 1859, he readied the *City of New York,* a balloon 200 feet (60 meters) high with an eight-man gondola, for a test flight on June 28, 1860, from Philadelphia to New Jersey. Renamed the *Great Western* at the suggestion of newspaper editor Horace Greeley, the balloon ripped and required a second test on September 29. On April 19, 1861, a subsequent test routed Lowe 900 miles (1,450 kilometers) from Cincinnati, Ohio, to the Chesapeake Bay in Maryland. The balloon actually landed nine hours later at Pea Ridge, 20 miles (32 kilometers) from Unionville, South Carolina. Because of the state's secession from the Union and the onset of the Civil War the previous week, Confederate soldiers arrested Lowe for spying, making him one of the South's first prisoners of war. His wife, Leontine Augustine Gaschon Lowe, rescued him in a buckboard.

At the command of Secretary of the Treasury Salmon P. Chase, Lowe met with President Abraham Lincoln and Secretary of War Simon Cameron on June 11, 1861, to discuss a demonstration of the balloon *Enterprise* over the White House South Lawn, the Columbian Armory, and the Smithsonian Institution. After building seven varnish-coated silk spy balloons, Lowe devised a flag and torch system for the U.S. Army Signal Corps that directed artillery crews by day or night.

Lowe flew over Arlington and Falls Church, Virginia, to observe the progress of the war. From his observation platform, on July 21, 1861, he and accompanying Union officers surveyed the First Battle of Bull Run at Manassas, Virginia. From aloft, he mapped Richmond, photographed combat, and delivered to President Lincoln the first air-to-ground telegraph message. Lowe required rescue by his wife after he landed in enemy territory and twisted an ankle.

General Winfield Scott ordered Lowe to create a balloon corps for the Army of the Potomac. Commission in the Union Army Balloon Corps left Lowe vulnerable to capture and execution for wartime spying. Using the coal barge *General Washington Park Custis* as the nation's first aircraft carrier, Lowe provided surveillance over Yorktown and Mechanicsville, Virginia, and at the Battle of Seven Pines, Virginia, on May 31–June 1, 1862. At the last engagement, he contracted malaria and required a month's recuperation. He returned to work for General Ambrose Burnside to spy on Fredericksburg, Virginia, on December 11, 1862, and again for General Joseph Hooker at Chancellorsville on April 30, 1863.

Army authorities lost confidence in the balloon corps in 1863, forcing Lowe's resignation on May 8 and abandonment of the corps to his assistants, Ezra Allen and James Allen. Lowe settled at Valley Forge, Pennsylvania, to farm and to advise balloonists in Brazil, England, and France. He gave balloon rides in New York City over Central Park. In the 1870s, he educated Count Ferdinand von Zeppelin on hydrogen gas ballooning, the predecessor to the dirigible.

Lowe's genius sparked a number of multipurpose concepts. He invented an altimeter and a steam-powered submarine; his monitoring of weather conditions preceded the establishment of the United States Weather Bureau. His principles of physics revolutionized the use of anthracite coal gas for home heating and lighting, for fueling lanterns, and for freezing water into ice. The icemaker served not only restaurants and hotels but also emergency clinics and surgeries. Lowe also launched a refrigerated steamer from Norristown, Pennsylvania, to Galveston, Texas, delivering fresh fruit and returning with beef.

After retiring to Los Angeles in 1887, he began a water-gas franchise to cool ice plants, built the Echo Mountain hotel and observatory, and incorporated the Mount Lowe Railway. At his death in Pasadena on January 16, 1913,

Mount Lowe carried his name. His granddaughter, Florence Lowe "Pancho" Barnes, pioneered women's aviation.

Further Reading

Evans, Charles M. *The War of the Aeronauts: A History of Ballooning During the Civil War.* Mechanicsburg, PA: Stackpole, 2002.

Heidler, David S., and Jeanne T. Heidler, eds. *Encyclopedia of the American Civil War: A Political, Social, and Military History.* New York: W.W. Norton, 2000.

Patris, Michael A., and Mount Lowe Preservation Society. *Mount Lowe Railway.* Charleston, SC: Arcadia, 2007.

Sterling, Christopher H., ed. *Military Communications: From Ancient Times to the 21st Century.* Santa Barbara, CA: ABC-CLIO, 2008.

Lumbering

From the discovery of the New World, the accessibility of timber contributed to North American bounty. Lumbering communities took pride in their work ethic. Hardy "buckers" sawed trunks into standard 10-foot (3-meter) lengths. In the 1860s, they applied steam power to "jacking" logs, raising timbers from riverbanks to sawmills for cutting to commercial dimensions.

In New England, loggers from the British Isles and French Canada supplied building materials for expanding communities, as well as crafters of buckets, ox yokes, cider kegs, vats and tubs, dough trays, paddles and spoons, and cutting boards. Specialists advertised maple for common wares and wool wheels, pine for sailboat masts and window blinds, and walnut for elegant tables and mantels. Oak suited dairiers for cheese baskets and butter presses. Chair makers and coopers prized ash for its elasticity; elm was the choice of cabinetmakers for its interlocking grain. Cedar offered fragrant veneer for lining chests, closets, and coffins.

For cutters, trimmers, and loaders, lumbering was onerous work. Timber cruisers scouted the thickest stands of white pine and built bunkhouses and cook shanties as well as animal barns and granaries for the crew and their oxen and horses. At the beginning of logging season in late fall, clear-cutting began with the readying of sleds in predawn gloom. After chopping with single-bit axes and felling with crosscut saws came the limbing and skidding of trunks, binding of sheared logs onto drays, and hauling of the day's load at sunset for decking into stacks. Throughout winter, 30-foot (9-meter) piles of logs froze into ramparts. During spring wood drives, loggers pushed the trunks apart with peavey hooks (iron-tipped poles) and shoved them from rollways into thawing waters. Crews stationed on the shores used pickaroons (hooked tools) to break up logjams.

Timber barons gripped workers in a financial stranglehold. In the early 1870s in Newport, Michigan, a lumberjack's pay was 15 cents per 100 board feet (0.24 cubic meters). Wages took the form of scrip redeemable only at company stores. Timber companies monopolized retail trade and produced debt peonage by lending cash at high interest. Owners created an agro-forest economy by buying up local produce, thus creating a symbiotic relationship with farmers.

In June 1872, to protect lumberjacks from maiming or death without compensation, a labor movement in Williamsport, Pennsylvania, led by Thomas H. Greevy, negotiated for ten-hour workdays at the region's 30 sawmills. A strike precipitated the "Sawdust War," which concluded with the arrest of leaders and the sentencing of union organizers to 12 months at hard labor. After timber barons stripped the forests in 1873 of 1,582,450 logs, they abandoned the Susquehanna River Valley, leaving lumberjacks unemployed. The state claimed the land for back taxes and began reforestation.

The Move Westward

Timber cutting in New Hampshire and Maine shifted from independent companies to lumbering associations that traded from Bangor directly with fir, pine, and spruce buyers in Boston. Before the boom in pulpwood for papermaking, the North Country cooperatives abandoned the White Mountains after leveling forest expanses for sawlogs and cordwood.

Under the Homestead Act of 1862, migrant laborers could claim 160-acre (65-hectare) plots on the frontier and clear-cut their property for a steady profit. Resettled on the Great Lakes among Central European, French Canadian, and Scandinavian loggers, New England immigrants profited during the boom years, which began in the mid-1860s. In 1864, timber magnate Henry W. Sage, a founder of Wenona, Michigan, began building a fortune from the sale of wood cut from Michigan, New York, and Wisconsin. In a cooperative venture with the Northern Railway of Canada, his business, the Rama Timber Transport Company, engineered a canal and portage tramway to carry logs from the Black River in eastern Michigan to Lake Couchiching, Ontario.

Along fast currents, the loggers built dams to hold back the stream. At portable mills, sawyers completed the processing by trimming and sawing logs into standard dimensions. After dismantling their sawmills, lumberjacks moved on, leaving behind slash (branches and treetops), which posed a danger of forest fire. On barges to Chicago, Bohemian, Irish, and Polish lumbermen hustled pine and hemlock boards from schooners arriving from the Upper Great Lakes to the Lumber Exchange at Wolf Point, north of the city center. Timber passed to the Midwest by wagon, canal boat, and rail. Traders transported finished lumber for homes and businesses over the Dakotas to settlers of the Great Plains.

Lumber companies faced the inevitable exhaustion of forests. The flurry of business on the Great Lakes rapidly denuded timberland of usable wood, which shipbuilders such as German immigrant Henry Burger of Rand & Burger in Manitowoc, Wisconsin, favored for the crafting of full-rigged schooners, a common sight on the Great Lakes until 1880. Employment at lumber camps in Wisconsin's Black, Chippewa, and Wolf river districts declined.

Like pioneers, lumbermen pressed farther west. At Saginaw, Michigan, Arthur Hill foresaw the depletion of local hardwoods and expanded his investments to Minnesota and to the abundant fir stands in Oregon, Washington, and Canada, which supplied shipbuilders as far south as San Francisco. At Muskegon, Michigan, Charles Hackley dominated the wood trade by progressing with the times from rough timber to small wood for domestic needs, such as dowels and curtain rollers.

In the South, almost immediately after the end of the Civil War, the abundance of woodlands supplied rebuilders of devastated homes and businesses. At the all-black community of Mound Bayou, Mississippi, freedmen financed their migration from plantations by supplying timbers to railroad builders.

In the absence of slave labor, Georgia and Mississippi initiated convict leasing to turpentine and lumber camps and sawmills. Outside the South, Nebraska, New Mexico, and Washington furthered the same system of cheap penal labor. The prisoners, mostly blacks, performed grueling chopping and loading while wearing leg shackles. After promoters advertised for hearty lumbermen and sturdy women and families to settle Washington Territory, the influx of outsiders decreased the need for convict loggers.

Investor John C. Ainsworth created the Oregon Steam Navigation Company, a network of steamer routes and portage railways that monopolized freight passage from lumber camps across the Pacific Northwest as far inland as the Columbia River ports at Astoria, The Dalles, and Portland. Ambitious lumbermen took advantage of the Desert Land Act, passed on March 3, 1877, to promote the irrigation and cultivation of 640-acre (259-hectare) plots of semi-arid public land. The legislation encouraged the sharing of resources for wood harvesting in less accessible parts of Oregon; nevertheless, lumber barons concealed the prime fir and pine on their claims on the Pacific slope.

Collateral Investment

To increase profits from mining and railroads, investors put cash into the lumber industry. In 1876, Nebraska's fortunes shifted with the coming of rail lines that linked Missouri River traffic with Burlington & Missouri River railcars at Plattsmouth. High employment from lumberyards and construction jobs brought newcomers to the region. Ironically, the shortage of trees on the Plains forced some settlers to construct sod huts.

In 1877, the Desert Land Act encouraged the sharing of resources and the growth of lumbering in less accessible parts of the frontier. Pioneering at treeless Virginia City, Nevada, required land clearing around Lake Tahoe and the building of skid roads, wood flumes, and narrow gauge railways to carry sugar pine logs to market. From 1876 to 1877, Alvinza Hayward and Norton P. Chipman's Sierra Flume and Lumber Company cut 93 million board feet (220,000 cubic meters) of wood for milling into telegraph poles, mine supports, doors and sashes, and blinds for sale across the United States and to Asia, Australia, and South America.

The most famous of the national lumber barons, German immigrant Frederick Weyerhäuser, earned the title of "Timber King." He harvested millions of board feet of timber in Arkansas, Louisiana, Washington, and Wisconsin and showed his respect for the land by protecting the undergrowth that replenished clear-cut stands. After establishing a mill and lumberyard at Rock Island, Illinois, Weyerhäuser expanded his holdings in 1860 with a sawmill on the Mississippi River. In response to increased demand for lumber during the Civil War, he and his partner Frederick Denkmann purchased struggling operations, secured large yellow pine tracts in Wisconsin, and invested in timber processing in Arkansas and Louisiana. A clever acquisitions strategist, Weyerhäuser excelled at introducing investors to opportunity. In 1872, with a confederation of wood middlemen, he established the Mississippi River Boom and Logging Company, which employed some 20,000 laborers. During the busy winter months, he lived among lumberjacks and shared their accommodations. In 1879 at Chippewa Falls, Wisconsin, Weyerhäuser built the largest lumber mill in the world.

Further Reading

Casler, Walter C., Thomas T. Taber III, and Benjamin F.G. Kline, Jr. *Logging Railroad Era of Lumbering in Pennsylvania.* Strawburg: Railroad Museum of Pennsylvania, 1999.

Hickman, Nollie W. *Mississippi Harvest: Lumbering in the Longleaf Pine Belt, 1840–1915.* Jackson: University Press of Mississippi, 2009.

Schweikart, Larry, and Lynne Pierson Doti. *American Entrepreneur: The Fascinating Stories of the People Who Defined Business in the United States.* New York: American Management Association, 2010.

Tindall, George Brown. *South Carolina Negroes, 1877–1900.* Columbia: University of South Carolina Press, 2003.

Wilson, Donald A. *Logging and Lumbering in Maine.* Charleston, SC: Arcadia, 2001.